Pro SharePoint Designer 2010

Steve Wright and David Petersen

Pro SharePoint Designer 2010

ISBN 978-1-4302-3617-7

ISBN 978-1-4302-3618-4 (eBook)

President and Publisher: Paul Manning
Lead Editors: Jonathan Hassell
Technical Reviewer: Corey Erkes
Editorial Board: Steve Anglin, Mark Beckner, Ewan Buckingham, Gary Cornell, Jonathan Gennick, Jonathan Hassell, Michelle Lowman, James Markham, Matthew Moodie, Jeffrey Pepper, Frank Pohlmann, Jeff Olson, Douglas Pundick, Ben Renow-Clarke, Dominic Shakeshaft, Matt Wade, Tom Welsh
Coordinating Editor: Jessica Belanger
Copy Editor: Sharon Wilkey
Compositor: Bytheway Publishing Services
Indexer: SPI Global
Artist: April Milne
Cover Designer: Anna Ishchenko

Distributed to the book trade worldwide by Springer Science+Business Media, LLC., 233 Spring Street, 6th Floor, New York, NY 10013. Phone 1-800-SPRINGER, fax (201) 348-4505, e-mail orders-ny@springer-sbm.com, or visit www.springeronline.com.

For information on translations, please e-mail rights@apress.com, or visit www.apress.com.

Apress and friends of ED books may be purchased in bulk for academic, corporate, or promotional use. eBook versions and licenses are also available for most titles. For more information, reference our Special Bulk Sales–eBook Licensing web page at www.apress.com/bulk-sales.

The source code for this book is available to readers at www.apress.com. You will need to answer questions pertaining to this book in order to successfully download the code.

To my wife, Janet, for all you do.
—Steve

To my high school business teacher, Mrs. Evelyn Alpers. Thank you for setting the course.
—David

Contents at a Glance

Contents

About the Authors

 **Steve Wright** is a senior manager and SharePoint solution lead for Sogeti USA in Omaha, Nebraska. Over the last 20+ years, Steve has worked on air traffic control, financial, insurance, and a multitude of other types of systems. He enjoys speaking at user group meetings and MSDN events, and holds 45 Microsoft certifications. Steve has contributed to and performed technical reviews for several previous titles covering Microsoft products, including SharePoint, Access, Windows, SQL Server, and BizTalk Server. For the past several years, he has focused on building highly customized SharePoint solutions.

 **David Petersen** is a senior SharePoint consultant in Omaha, Nebraska. A frequent speaker at SharePoint Saturday conferences and user group meetings, he has a passion for helping organizations maximize their investment in SharePoint. He started programming computers in 1979, and after an eight-year stint in the United States Marine Corps, has held positions in IT organizations from desktop support, to IT director, to starting his own consulting company. He wrote his first web part in 2001 for (Tahoe Server) SharePoint Portal Server and he has specialized in building custom SharePoint solutions for the last several years.

About the Technical Reviewer

 **Corey Erkes** is a senior consultant for Sogeti USA in Omaha, Nebraska. Corey has worked with a wide range of companies at different points in the life cycles of their SharePoint implementations. He is passionate about SharePoint and loves working with companies to maximize the out-of-the-box features to bring immediate return on investment to organizations. In addition to his work as a consultant, Corey is also one of the founding members of the Omaha SharePoint Users Group.

Acknowledgments

I would like to thank Jonathan for giving me the opportunity and encouragement to take on my first book project as a lead author. I knew I would never be able to complete all of the chapters needed to fill a book like this without help, so special thanks to David Petersen for agreeing to add his voice to this book. You can hear more of his voice at SharePoint Saturdays throughout the Midwest (www.sharepointsaturday.org). Thanks also to Corey (and his wife Laura) for sacrificing the time to do the technical review for me. Corey can also be found running the Omaha SharePoint Users Group (www.omahamtg.com). Finally, I would like to thank my wife, Janet, and our children, Jon, Evan, and Troy, for keeping me at least marginally sane and motivated. You are why I do the things I do.

Steve Wright

Steve, thank you for inviting me to participate with you in writing this book. I have enjoyed working with you over the years. You are a great mentor and friend. Thanks to Jonathan Hassell and Jessica Belanger at Apress for making this process run smoothly. Thank you, Corey, for your expert suggestions. My business teacher at Stover High School, Mrs. Evelyn Alpers, allowed me to unbox the school's first computer, a Radio Shack TRS-80. It was an experience that changed my life and began a love of programming that has endured over 30 years. Thank you! Finally, my wife Patti and our daughters, Sarah, Hannah, Rebekah, and Emily, have had to pick up the slack around the house while I locked myself in the basement for months. Thank you for your love, understanding, and support. This wouldn't have been possible without you.

David Petersen

Preface

First, a confession: I am not a professional web designer. I am a web developer, a code junkie, a rip-it-open-and-see-how-it-works kind of guy. When Jonathon Hassell approached me about doing a book on SharePoint Designer, my first response was "Why me?" After a series of conversations, I came to understand that my point of view could be useful for explaining SharePoint Designer's "sweet spot" in the SharePoint solution space.

When I first encountered FrontPage 2003, I was not impressed. It seemed to me to be an over-engineered HTML editor that required server extensions and an awkward security configuration to even function properly. Since I spent most of my working life in Visual Studio, it seemed natural to me that that would be the place to build SharePoint solutions. All I really knew of FrontPage was that every SharePoint site I knew of that had allowed its use became unmanageable. The lack of proper controls eventually led to inconsistencies and upgrade problems that were difficult or impossible to fix.

Over the last couple of releases, as FrontPage has become SharePoint Designer, Microsoft has made excellent progress in helping users avoid the problems caused in previous versions. With the 2010 release, SharePoint Designer has become far more than a mere web page editor. It is now a platform for creating powerful applications within SharePoint. Many of the solutions that would have required a developer to create in previous releases are now accessible to site designers and power users through SharePoint Designer.

What Software Will I Need?

The short answer to this question is, of course, none. This is a book. A better answer is that, in order to fully learn the concepts presented, you will want to have the following software available. Fortunately, all of these products can be downloaded as evaluation editions, and they can all run on a single 64-bit virtual machine.

- *SharePoint Designer 2010*: This available as a free, fully licensed download from Microsoft.
- *InfoPath Designer 2010*: This application is needed for the final two chapters only.
- *SharePoint Server 2010*: Standard Edition will be sufficient for the earlier chapters in the book, but you will want to have an Enterprise server available later on.

■ **Caution** If your server is running Windows SharePoint Services 3.0 or Microsoft Office SharePoint Server 2007, *stop!* You cannot use SharePoint Designer 2010 with any previous version of SharePoint. You will need to download and use SharePoint Designer 2007 for use in such an environment.

Finding What You Need in This Book

This book has been created to lead a first-time user from installation of SharePoint Designer through creating advanced web sites that provide a platform for complex business processes. The chapters are divided into three parts: the basics, advanced web sites, and enterprise business solutions.

■ **Note** This book is about a specific tool designed to work with the SharePoint platform. A certain familiarity with the SharePoint environment and web design in general is assumed. If terms such as HTML, CSS, lists, libraries, and pages are alien to you, you may want to review them before diving too deeply into SharePoint Designer.

Part I: Covering the Basics

Our first four chapters cover the product fundamentals. This introductory material is intended for web designers and developers who are new to SharePoint Designer. Readers with some familiarity with SharePoint Designer may wish to skim these chapters for topics that are new to them. For beginning users, these chapters are best read in order.

Chapter 1: A Quick Guide to SharePoint Designer

This chapter introduces SharePoint Designer and discusses some of the key concepts around the product. You will walk through the installation process and be taken on a quick tour around the user interface. The chapter concludes with a discussion of best practices to observe when using SharePoint Designer.

Chapter 2: Editing Pages

Chapter 2 introduces you to creating and editing pages in SharePoint Designer. The various views, task panes, and tools are described with step-by-step exercises.

Chapter 3: Using SharePoint to Storing Data

Chapter 3 covers using SharePoint designer to customize the data stored within SharePoint in lists and libraries. The interfaces for customizing site columns and content types will be explored as well.

Chapter 4: Managing Web Parts

Web parts are the "widgets" of SharePoint. This chapter covers creating, editing, and customizing web parts and their connections through SharePoint Designer. Using ASP.NET controls within SharePoint pages is also covered.

Part II: Advanced Site Customization

Chapters 5 through 9 cover various topics and can be read in whatever order they are needed. This is more-advanced material that will be most understandable to readers already familiar with the concepts covered in Part I.

Chapter 5: Displaying Data

Chapter 5 focuses on displaying data within SharePoint pages. This includes data stored within SharePoint lists and libraries as well as tabular data stored in a database such as Microsoft SQL Server.

Chapter 6: Styles and Themes

Chapter 6 covers the techniques needed to "brand" a SharePoint site. Branding refers to the fonts, colors, images, and layouts of the pages within a site.

Chapter 7: Managing Publishing Sites

This chapter covers the use of the web content management (WCM) process defined to manage the formal creation and delivery of site content in SharePoint. This is done using SharePoint "publishing" sites.

Chapter 8: Advanced Site Customizations

Chapter 8 covers deep customizations of a site's navigation and search features. This allows a site to be truly unique and not so "SharePoint-looking."

Chapter 9: Client-Side Programming

Client-side programming refers to code that executes outside of SharePoint, usually in a web browser. This code is typically written in JavaScript. SharePoint 2010 includes a new client-side object model that creates excellent opportunities to improve site performance and behavior.

■ **Note** The material in Chapter 9 will be of interest primarily to professional developers.

Part III: Integrating SharePoint

The final three chapters are intended for enterprise developers and power users to enable SharePoint to act as a platform for integrated business solutions.

Chapter 10: Consuming External Data

Chapter 10 examines the techniques available for accessing data that resides outside SharePoint. This data could be available in a database, a line-of-business application, or a web service.

Chapter 11: Using InfoPath Forms

While Microsoft InfoPath is a separate product from SharePoint Designer, InfoPath forms are often components in SharePoint solutions. This chapter provides an introduction to using InfoPath forms within SharePoint. You will explore using forms to customize data entry for SharePoint lists, to provide document information panels within Office client applications, and to create documents in SharePoint libraries that can be integrated with other data sources in SharePoint.

Chapter 12: Automating with Workflows

Chapter 12 describes the Windows Workflow Foundation (WF) engine, which is hosted within SharePoint. Using SharePoint Designer, the user can create complex business processes that execute in a managed environment.

In Conclusion

As a developer, I have come to appreciate the value that SharePoint Designer can bring to a SharePoint solution. It allows site designers a degree of autonomy that has been problematic in the past. With SharePoint Server 2010 and SharePoint Designer 2010, Microsoft has shifted the line between control and flexibility.

David and I have spent a great deal of time attempting to create a guide for power users, professional designers, and developers that will help you get the most out of your SharePoint environment. We hope you find this book a valuable resource.

— Steve Wright

PART I

■ ■ ■

Covering the Basics

C H A P T E R 1

A Quick Guide to SharePoint Designer

SharePoint Designer (SPD) is a Windows client application used to design rich, highly customized SharePoint solutions. SPD is intended for use primarily by web site designers to enable detailed customization of pages, lists, libraries, and many other SharePoint artifacts. Although SPD includes features that may be useful to developers and administrators, it is first and foremost a design tool. SPD is ideal for creating business process workflows, integrating with line-of-business databases, and creating custom presentations of business information on the SharePoint Server platform.

This chapter introduces SharePoint Designer 2010. You will learn about the history of the product and explore the new features of SPD's 2010 version. You will walk through the installation of the application and its user interface. The rest of this book is dedicated to examining each of the areas where SPD can simplify web site development and customization.

You will learn about the following topics in this chapter:

- History of SharePoint Designer
- New features in the 2010 version
- Installation of the application
- Setup of an existing SharePoint environment for designer access
- Overview of the user interface
- Best practices for using SharePoint Designer in the enterprise

From FrontPage to SharePoint Designer

SPD 2010 is the latest version of the product previously known as FrontPage. Let's consider how we got to where we are today. Back in the 1990s, there was a company called Vermeer Technologies Incorporated (VTI). VTI created a product for editing web pages called FrontPage. In January of 1996, Vermeer was purchased by Microsoft.

■ **Note** Have you ever wondered why SharePoint contains directories with names such as _vti? Well, now you know!

Microsoft rebranded the product and released MS FrontPage version 1.1. This product was originally included on the Windows NT 4.0 installation media as a separate installable component. FrontPage consisted of three major components: the FrontPage Explorer, the FrontPage Editor, and the Internet Information Server (IIS) Extensions.

The explorer was a file management utility similar to Windows Explorer. The editor was simply an HTML page editor that could attach to the web site for editing. The IIS Extensions were a set of components that had to be deployed on the target web server in order for FrontPage to connect to and manage a web site. The IIS Extensions (later renamed FrontPage Server Extensions) were a major headache for web site administrators and developers because they were often difficult to enable and secure properly.

FrontPage versions 97 and 98 were released rapidly as Microsoft improved the editing experience, but the overall design of the application did not change much.

With FrontPage 2000, Microsoft made several important changes to the product. The explorer and editor were combined into a single application. FrontPage was also made a part of the MS Office family of products and included in some editions of MS Office 2000. FrontPage 2002 was included with Office XP.

FrontPage 2003 became the first version of MS FrontPage to be sold as a separate retail product instead of as part of Office or an operating system. While still supporting FrontPage Server Extensions, Microsoft began moving away from using a proprietary server extension for site editing. FrontPage 2003 included support for standards-based interfaces such as Web-Based Distributed Authoring and Versioning (WebDAV) and FTP. FrontPage 2003 was also the first version to support the editing of Windows SharePoint Services 2.0 sites.

■ **Note** Starting with Microsoft Windows Vista and Server 2008, the FrontPage Server Extensions are no longer part of the Windows operating system. As of December 2010, they are no longer supported by Microsoft.

In December 2006, Microsoft announced that FrontPage was being split into two new products. Microsoft Expression Web would be designed for artistic designers who need to create stunning user interfaces for professional-looking web sites. Microsoft SharePoint Designer would be targeted to business and development professionals for creating and managing content in a SharePoint environment.

SharePoint Designer 2007 was the previous release, before the 2010 version covered in this book. SPD 2007 was still primarily a web page editor that used SharePoint to store its pages. SPD 2010 supports editing only SharePoint content, and many new features have been added to support creating most SharePoint artifacts by using graphical editors instead of XML or HTML.

■ **Note** Good news! As of March 31, 2009, Microsoft is no longer selling SharePoint Designer but giving it away. It is available for free from the Microsoft download site, as described later in this chapter.

What's New in SharePoint Designer 2010?

As we have mentioned, SharePoint Designer 2010 is not a massive redesign of the product, but several valuable additions have been made.

User Interface Enhancements

The SPD 2010 user interface will be familiar to users of the 2007 product, but there are several additions to note. The most obvious are the Ribbon menu and the Navigation pane. The Ribbon menu is the same type of context-sensitive menu that was introduced in Office 2007 and is now in use in all of the MS Office 2010 applications. The Navigation pane provides access to many new gallery, settings, and editor pages.

External Content Type Editor

In SharePoint 2007, the Business Data Catalog feature held great promise. However, it was virtually impossible to use without purchasing third-party tools to define the extensive XML declarations required. With the release of Business Connectivity Services (BCS)—no, that's not the Bowl Championship Series!—in SharePoint 2010, you can create external content types (ECTs) to define external data. SharePoint Designer 2010 has a built-in editor for ECTs, eliminating the need for third-party tools.

Workflow Design Enhancements

Workflow is an area of extensive improvement in SharePoint Designer 2010. SPD 2007 allowed the user to create workflow definitions that were connected to a single list or library, making them difficult to reuse without a developer's intervention. In 2010, SharePoint Designer can create reusable workflows that are independent of specific lists. SPD 2010 also supports improved security models with impersonation steps. SPD-designed workflows can now include custom activities created in Visual Studio and workflows designed in MS Visio 2010.

Installing and Using the Application

SharePoint Designer 2010 is available as both a 32-bit application and a 64-bit application. Remember that SPD is a client application, not a server application, so the "bit-ness" of the application depends on your desktop environment, not the SharePoint server you intend to use. This makes sense if you consider that SharePoint Server 2010 is available in only a 64-bit version.

Here are some rules to use in determining which version of SPD to use in your environment:

- If your server is running Windows SharePoint Services 3.0 or Microsoft Office SharePoint Server 2007, *stop*! You cannot use SPD 2010 with any previous version of SharePoint. You will need to download and use SharePoint Designer 2007.

- If you have both SharePoint 2010 and 2007 in your environment and need to load both versions of SharePoint Designer, use the 32-bit version and *be sure to install SharePoint Designer 2007 first*.

- If you are using a 32-bit operating system, you will use the 32-bit version of SPD.

- If you have MS Office loaded, you will use the same bit-ness as your office installation.

- You can run 64-bit SPD *only* if you are on a 64-bit OS, using 64-bit MS Office (or no Office), and are not going to use SharePoint Designer 2007.

Based on these restrictions, most installations of SharePoint Designer 2010 in mixed 32-bit/64-bit environments will probably be 32-bit installations. There are really no important differences between the two versions.

Next, you need to ensure that your operating system is compatible with SharePoint Designer 2010. Most of Microsoft's modern operating systems are supported as long as the most recent service packs have been applied. Specifically, the OSs supported are as follows

- Windows 7 (32- or 64-bit)

- Windows Server 2008 R2 (32- or 64-bit)

- Windows Server 2003 R2 (32- or 64-bit)

- Windows Vista Service Pack 1

- Windows XP Service Pack 3

Now that you have determined the OS and version of SharePoint Designer to install, you can download the free installation package from the Microsoft Download Center web site:

- 32-bit: www.microsoft.com/downloads/en/
  details.aspx?displaylang=en&FamilyID=d88a1505-849b-4587-b854-a7054ee28d66

- 64-bit: www.microsoft.com/downloads/en/details.aspx?FamilyID=566D3F55-77A5-
  4298-BB9C-F55F096B125D

The downloaded package will be a single executable file with a name such as en_sharepoint_designer_2010_x64_515562.exe. Run this executable on the computer where the application will be used. It will take a few seconds for the files to be extracted and the setup program to launch.

In most cases, you can simply perform a default installation at this point by clicking the Install Now button, as shown in Figure 1-1. If you wish to change the installation directory or optional components, you can click Customize to set those options as shown in Figure 1-2.

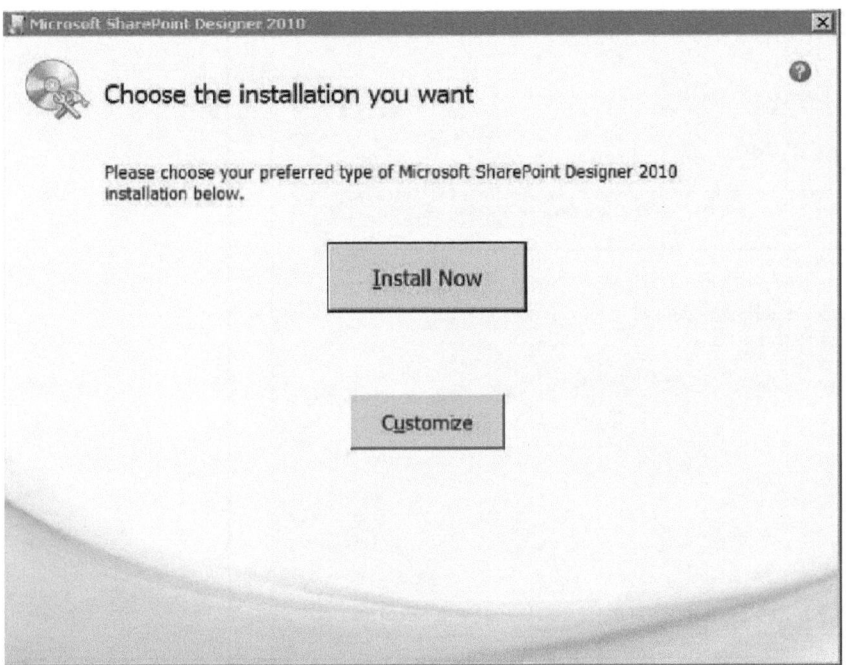

Figure 1-1. SharePoint Designer installation main menu

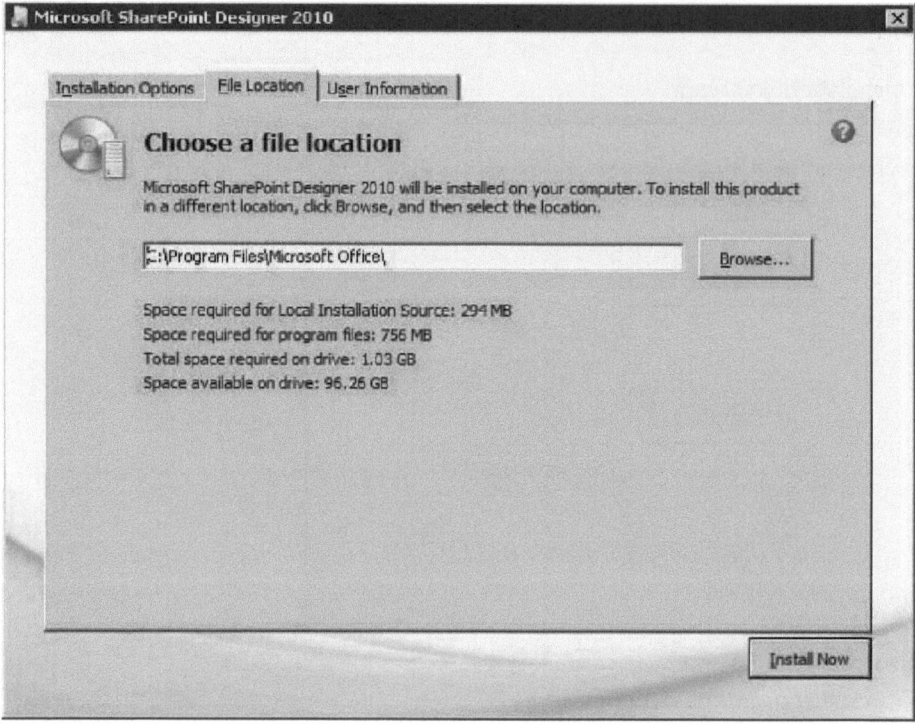

Figure 1-2. *SharePoint Designer installation customization screen*

After you click Install Now on either of these screens, the installer shows a progress bar while it installs the application. Once the installer completes, the application is ready to use.

Setting Up SharePoint Server for Designer Access

SharePoint Designer 2010 can be a very powerful tool for creating SharePoint solutions. Like any powerful tool, it can be dangerous in the wrong hands. From the point of view of a system administrator, SharePoint Designer is a development tool, so it may not be appropriate for use in a production environment. As such, there are multiple configuration options within SharePoint Server 2010 that control which actions can be performed by SharePoint Designer users.

The first set of options can disable SharePoint Designer access or limit the changes it can make. Before accessing SharePoint Server for the first time, ensure that your administrator has enabled this access. These settings are configured via the SharePoint Central Administration web site, under General Application Settings, shown in Figure 1-3.

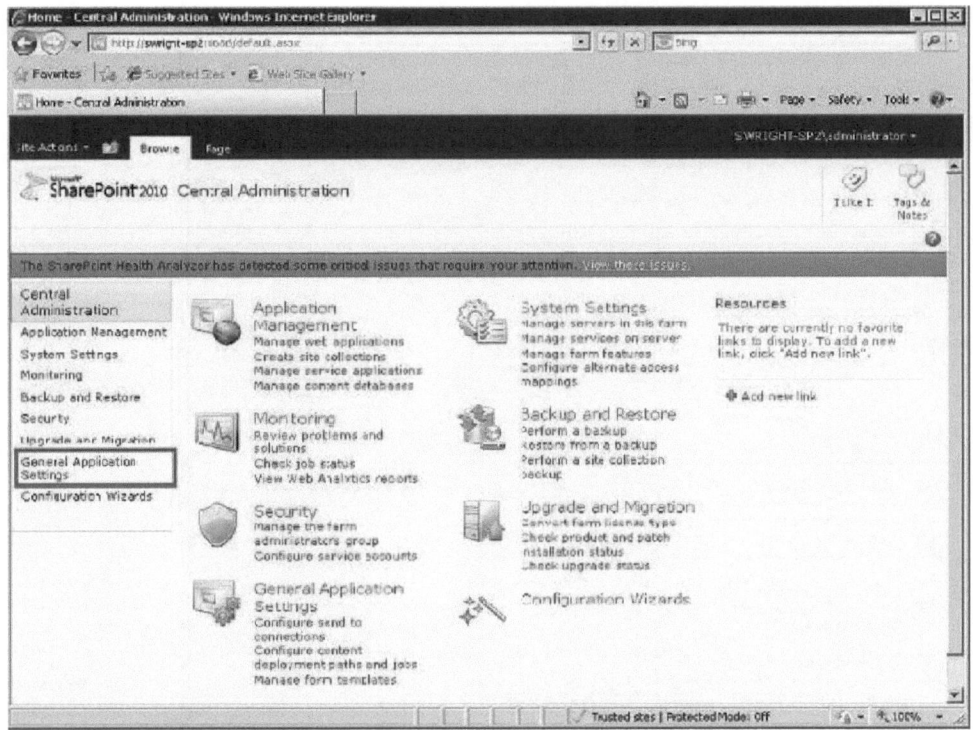

Figure 1-3. *SharePoint Central Administration*

From the General Application Settings page, select Configure SharePoint Designer Settings, as shown in Figure 1-4.

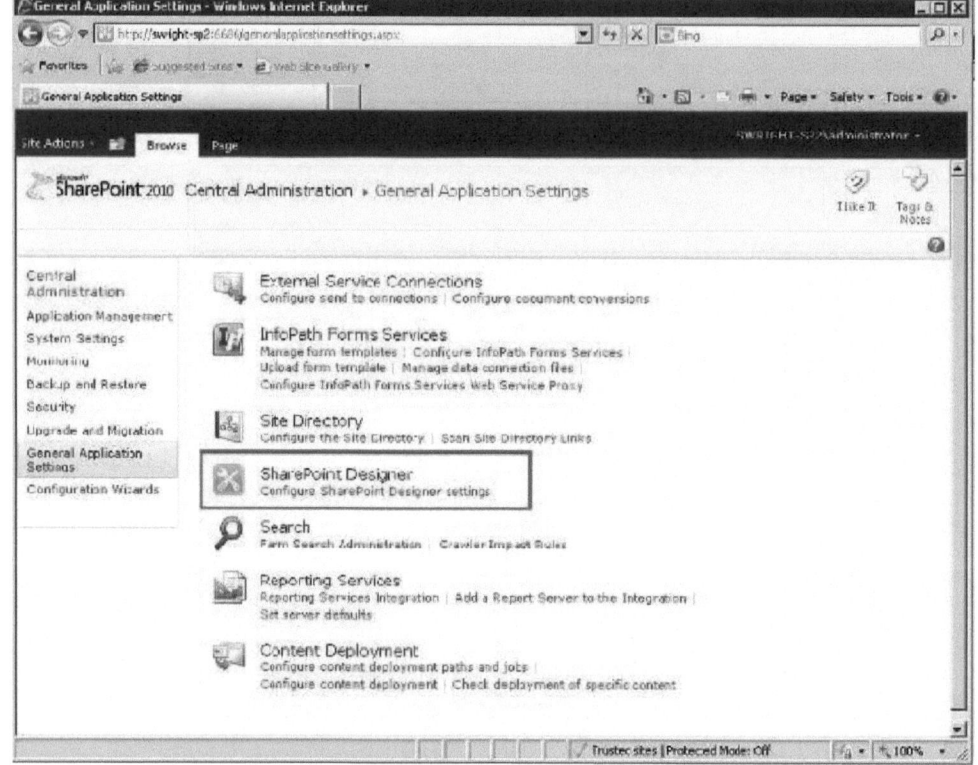

Figure 1-4. General Application Settings page

■ **Note** If SharePoint concepts such as web applications, site collections, and sites are new to you, take a moment to look at www.mssharepointtips.com/tip.asp?id=1014. Doing so will make this section much easier to understand.

The SharePoint Designer Settings page displays, as shown in Figure 1-5. This page presents the available options and their current settings. Note that you can set these options on a per web application basis. To see and set the options for a web application other than the default, select it by using the Web Application drop-down list near the top of the form.

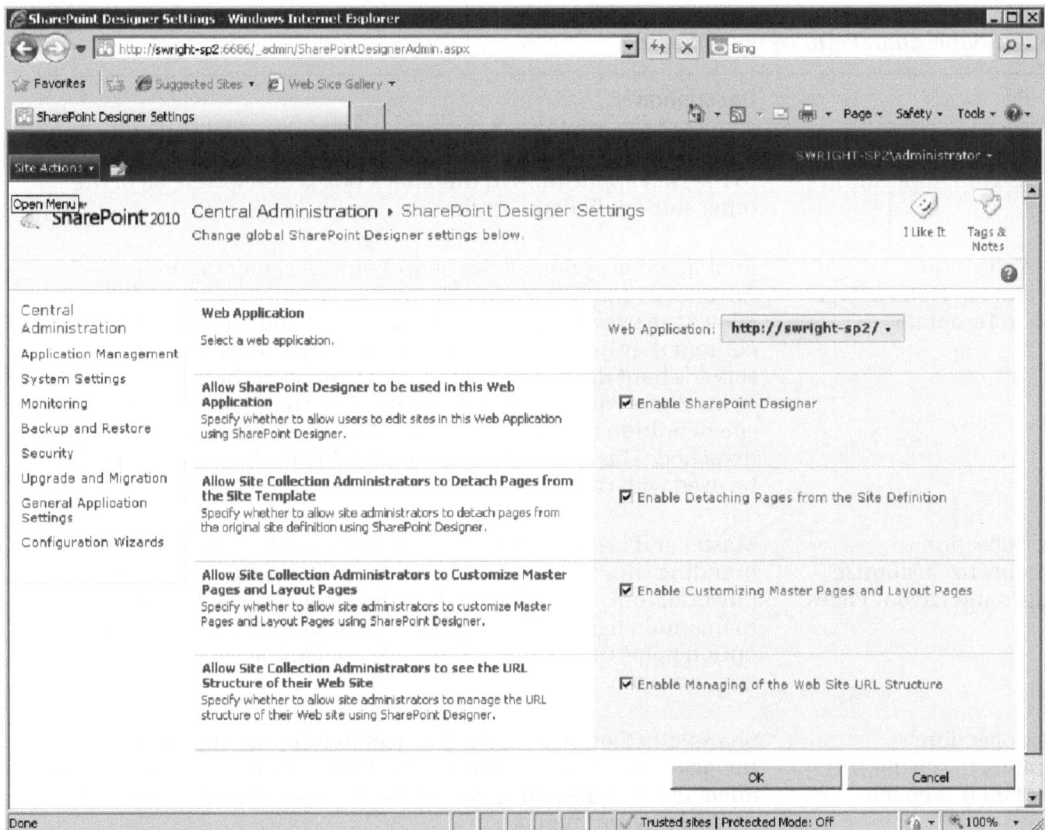

Figure 1-5. SharePoint Designer Settings page

■ **Tip** If you need to control SharePoint Designer's settings at the site collection level instead of the web application level, you can do this from the Site Settings page in the root site of the collection. Look for the SharePoint Designer Settings option under Site Collection Administration.

Table 1-1 lists the SharePoint Designer settings available for a web application.

Table 1-1. *Available SharePoint Designer Settings*

Setting	Description
Allow SharePoint Designer to Be Used in This Web Application	This setting controls the ability of SharePoint Designer to attach to the web application. If this check box is deselected, all of the other settings become irrelevant.
Allow Site Collection Administrators to Detach Pages from the Site Template	Enabling this option allows SharePoint Designer to run in Advanced mode instead of Normal mode. Advanced mode allows the user to "ghost" pages by modifying them from the content they originally had in the site definition stored on the server's hard drive. The customized version of the page is stored in the SharePoint content database. Any changes made to the site definition files are not reflected in pages that have been detached. This can create maintainability problems and should be used with care.
Allow Site Collection Administrators to Customize Master Pages and Layout Pages	Master and layout pages (along with themes) are the keys to branding sites within SharePoint. SharePoint Designer contains powerful tools for updating these files. Most organizations prefer to maintain tight control of their site branding. Disabling this option helps to lock down the site's appearance in a production environment.
Allow Site Collection Administrators to see the URL Structure of their Web Site	SharePoint Designer allows the user to examine and rearrange the pages and folders within a site. Because this can dramatically affect users of the site, this is a function that should be limited in a many environments.

Once SharePoint Server has been configured to allow SharePoint Designer access, the user connecting to the site must have the Use Remote Interfaces permission. This permission allows the user to use several types of remote interfaces, including web services and the WebDAV publishing interface, but SharePoint Designer is the one that interests us. The Use Remote Interfaces permission is part of all the default permission levels except Limited Access and Restricted Read. Any user who is assigned any of the other permission levels can connect to the web site with SharePoint Designer. However, SharePoint Designer still obeys all of the normal permissions enforced by SharePoint Server. If the user does not have permission to read or change an item in the SharePoint site, that user will not be able to do so using SharePoint Designer.

Connecting to Your Site with SharePoint Designer

Let's begin by verifying that you can open a site in SharePoint Designer. Start the SharePoint Designer 2010 application from the Start menu on your desktop, as shown in Figure 1-6. The icon is located in the SharePoint group. Note that this is different from the Microsoft SharePoint 2010 Products or Microsoft Office groups that may also be present on your system if you are running SharePoint Designer directly on the SharePoint server in a development or testing environment.

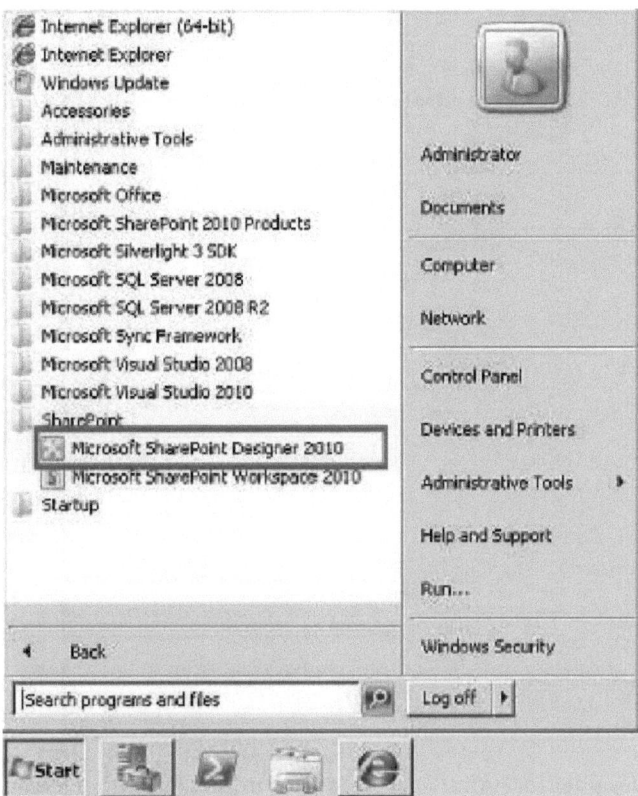

Figure 1-6. *SharePoint Designer on the Start menu*

When the application opens, you will see the Backstage area of the user interface, as shown in Figure 1-7. This is described more fully in the next section.

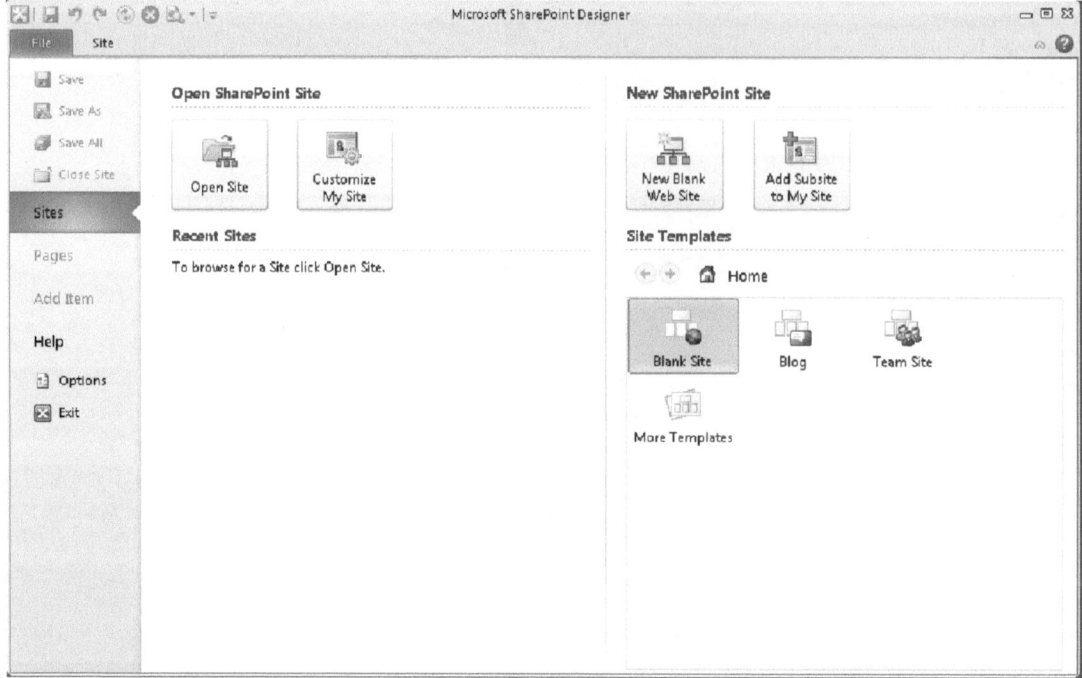

Figure 1-7. SharePoint Designer Backstage view

Users of previous versions of SharePoint Designer (or FrontPage) will notice immediately that SPD 2010 no longer opens an empty HTML page on startup. Unlike previous versions, SPD 2010 isn't a web page editor that happens to be able to connect to SharePoint. This version is fully committed to working with SharePoint sites. Note that there isn't even an option to open a file on this screen. The only options available are for opening SharePoint sites.

Click the Open Site button and type in the URL of your SharePoint site. After a few seconds of connecting, you should see the new Site Settings page, as shown in Figure 1-8.

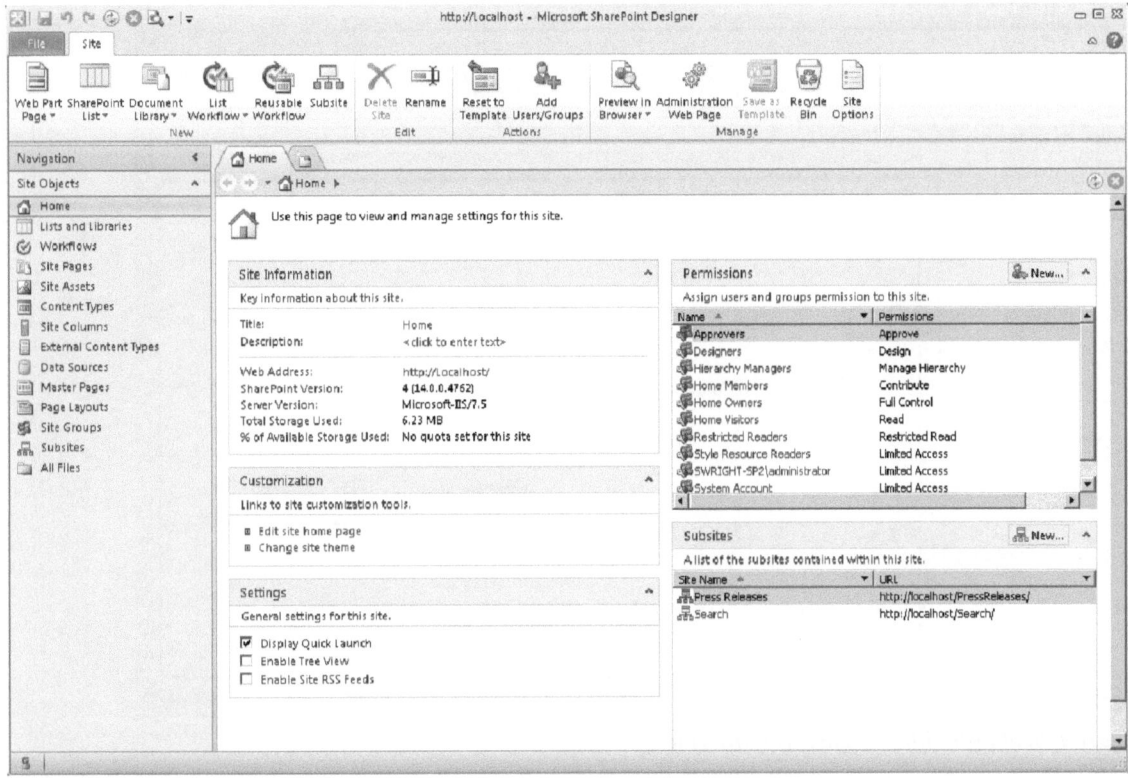

Figure 1-8. SharePoint Designer Site Settings page

A Tour of the SharePoint Designer User Interface

In this section, you will walk through SharePoint Designer's user interface. The 2010 version has many areas that were not previously present in the application. With all of the options and terminology involved, it is easy to get lost.

Application Layout

To get started, take a look at the arrangement of items in the SharePoint Designer user interface, shown in Figure 1-9.

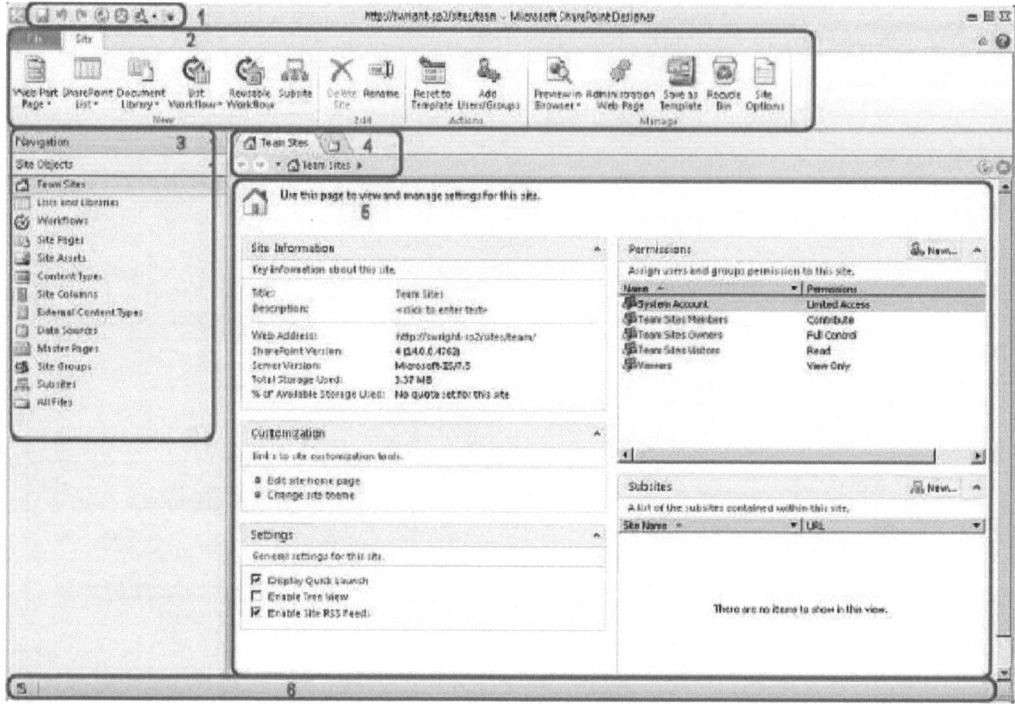

Figure 1-9. SharePoint Designer user interface

Starting from the top, the first item is the Quick Access Toolbar (1). This toolbar can be configured to expose an arbitrary set of buttons as defined by the user. Next is the Ribbon menu system (2) that has been inherited from the Microsoft Office application suite. To the left of the main area of the window is the Navigation pane (3). To the right is the main window (5) of the application. This window has a tabbed interface with its own navigation controls (4), which appear at the top of the window. At the bottom of the window is the Status Bar (6).

■ **Tip** The Status Bar in SharePoint Designer has an interesting feature found all the way in the lower left-hand corner of the window. The icon that appears here can be used to switch the connection from one set of user credentials to another. This allows the user to switch to more- or less-privileged credentials as needed without having to restart the application.

Each of these areas is described in more detail in the following sections. Later chapters of this book also describe many of the tools that appear in these sections. We do not attempt to list them exhaustively here.

Ribbon Menu

The menu system of the SharePoint Designer application is based on the Ribbon menu found in other Microsoft Office 2010 applications. As the user moves around the application, the menus and options appearing on the Ribbon will change accordingly. Figure 1-10 shows the options available on the Insert tab of the Ribbon when a page is being edited.

The File tab always appears on the far left. This tab is used to activate the Backstage area described in the following section.

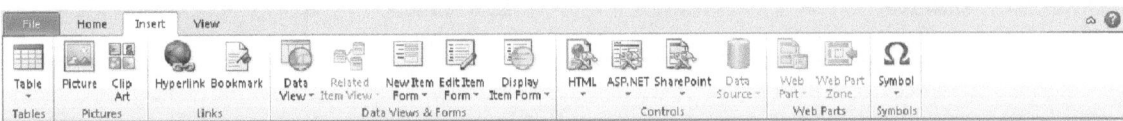

Figure 1-10. *The Ribbon menu (page editor options)*

Backstage

The Backstage area of the application can always be accessed by using the File tab on the Ribbon menu. The options available depend on the state of the application. On the left is a menu with the usual file-handling commands such as Save, Save As, and Close. Beneath those options is a set of pages that enable the user to create or open sites, pages, or other artifacts.

Because SharePoint Designer 2010 can be used to edit only SharePoint 2010 sites, if there is no site connected, the only options enabled are those used to open a site. In Figure 1-11, the Site page of the Backstage area shows options for opening ordinary sites, the user's My Site, or recently used sites. The options on the right can be used to create new sites via various templates. By selecting More Templates and connecting to an existing site, you can select any of the templates on that server.

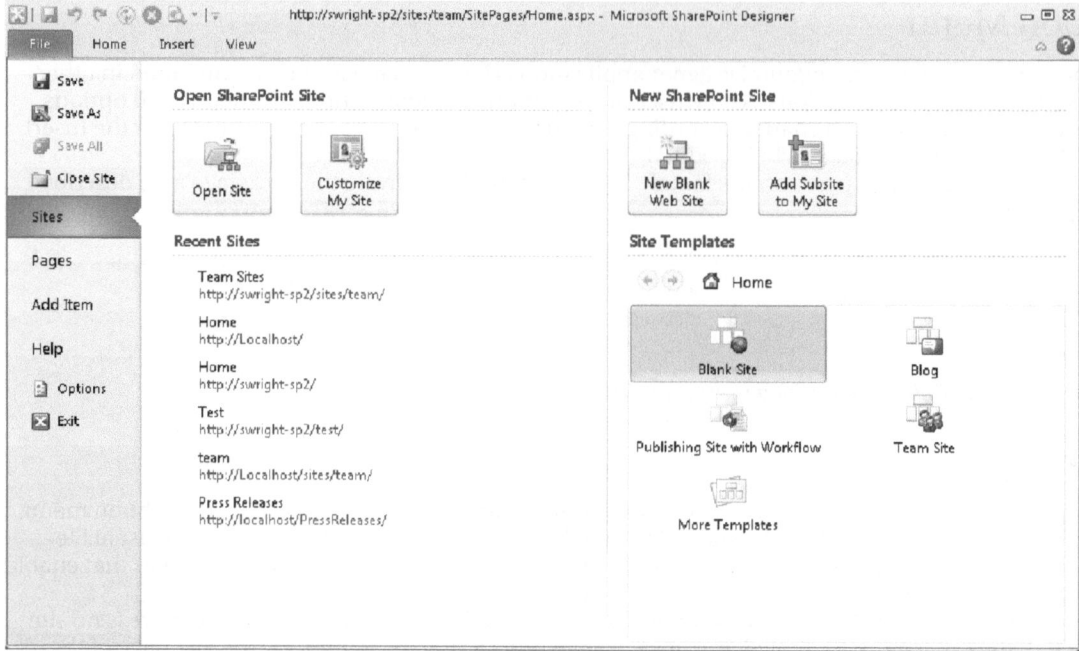

Figure 1-11. Backstage—Sites page

■ **Tip** You can add site templates to your favorites list by right-clicking the template and selecting Add to Favorites.

Similarly, the Pages page can be used to open or create pages within the currently connected site. The Add Item page is used to add pages, lists, libraries, or workflows to the site.

Near the bottom of the left-hand menu is the Options link. This link opens the SharePoint Designer Options dialog box, shown in Figure 1-12. Here you can customize many aspects of the application's default behavior.

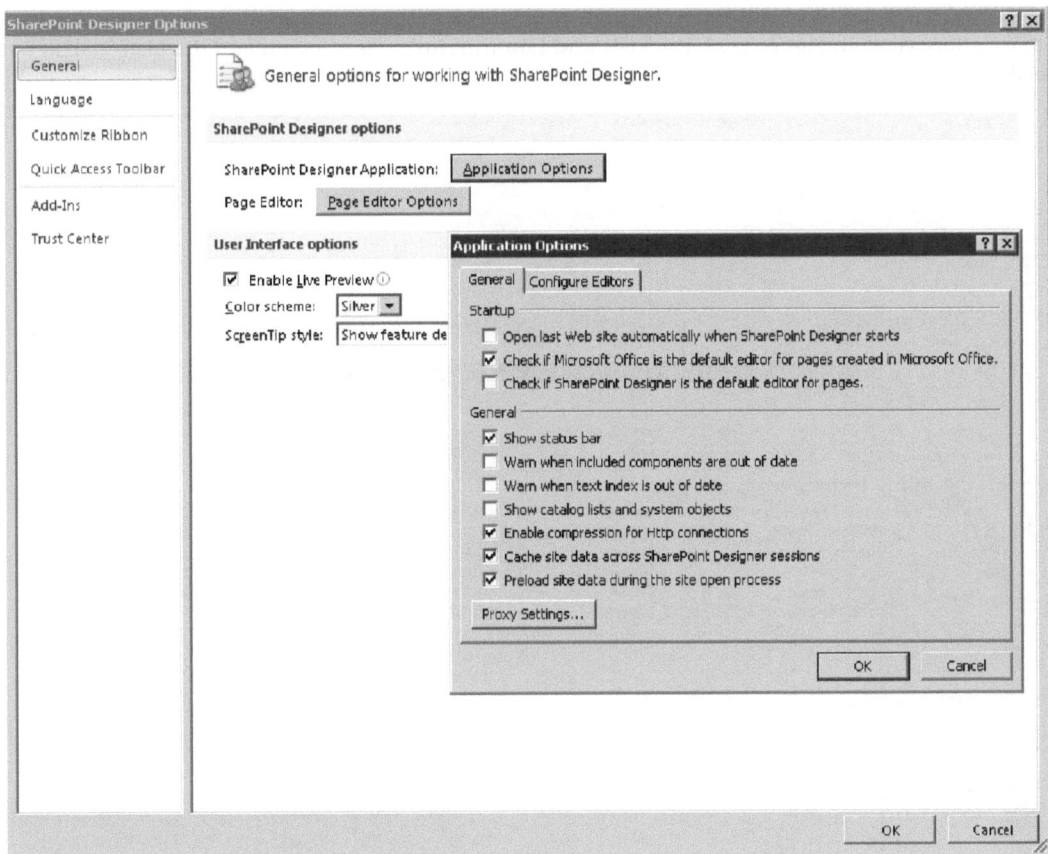

Figure 1-12. SharePoint Designer Options dialog box

Navigation Pane

The Navigation pane may be the most useful addition to the user interface in SPD 2010. This menu contains links to all of the artifacts that exist within the current site. Unlike the previous version of SharePoint Designer, this menu is organized by the type of artifact, not the folder structure of the web site. It is no longer necessary to memorize where each item in the site is kept in order to find it. However, because old habits die hard, the All Files link will display a file browser window.

■ **Note** In this context, *artifact* is used as a generic term for any of the components that make up a SharePoint site. This includes lists, libraries, site columns, content types, and so on. One of SharePoint Designer's strengths is that it tends to manage all artifacts in the same way whenever appropriate.

When the user clicks a link in the Navigation (or *Nav* for short) pane, the main window to the left switches to a Gallery view. In Figure 1-13, the Lists and Libraries link was selected and the Lists gallery page is displayed.

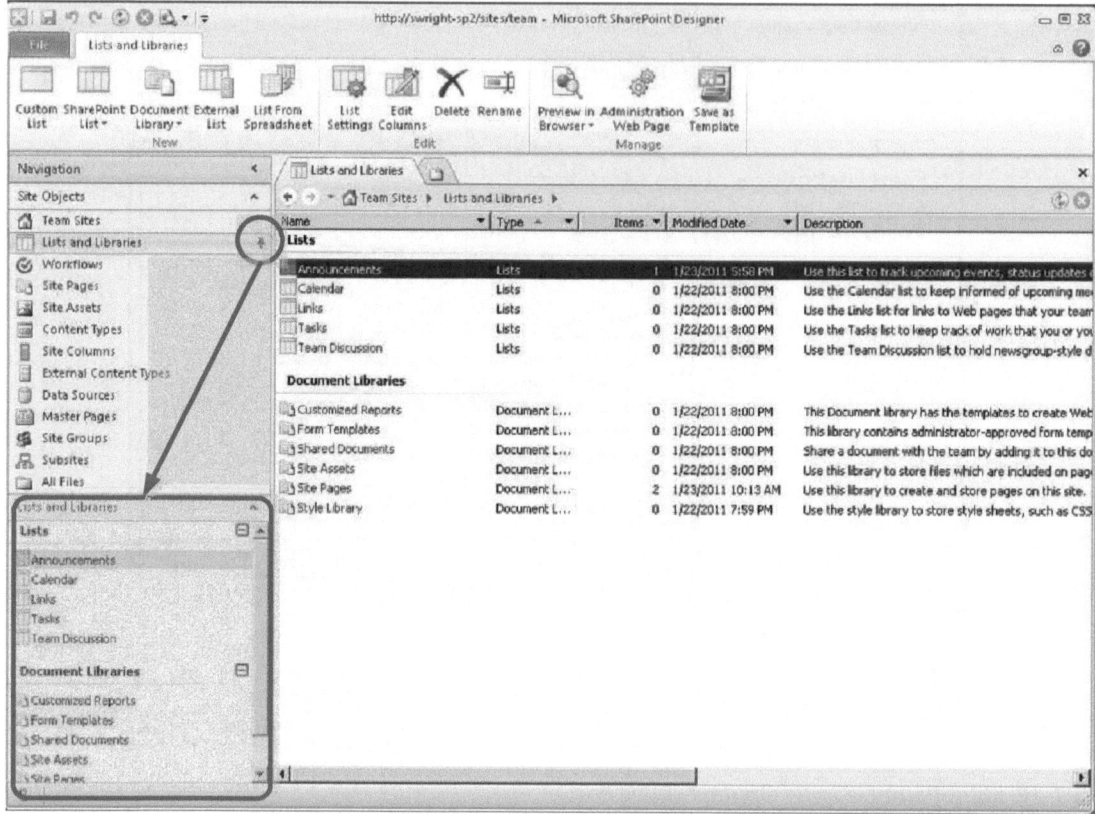

Figure 1-13. *SharePoint Designer Navigation pane*

Another feature of the Nav pane is the ability to pin one of the object types. This is done by clicking the pin that appears to the right of each link when you hover over it. Once pinned, a listing of that object type's gallery will appear below the links in the Nav pane. Only one object type can be pinned, so pinning a different type removes the "mini-gallery" for the previously selected type.

Main Window Navigation

The main window also contains a set of navigation controls for organizing your work space, as you can see in Figure 1-14.

The top line consists of a set of tabs that work the same way the tab bar works in Internet Explorer (IE). You can drag tabs into whatever order you wish, open new tabs, and close unneeded tabs. Each tab even has its own history list, just as in IE. The left and right arrows on the next line and the history drop-down next to them work in the manner you would expect. You can traverse back to previously viewed objects or galleries.

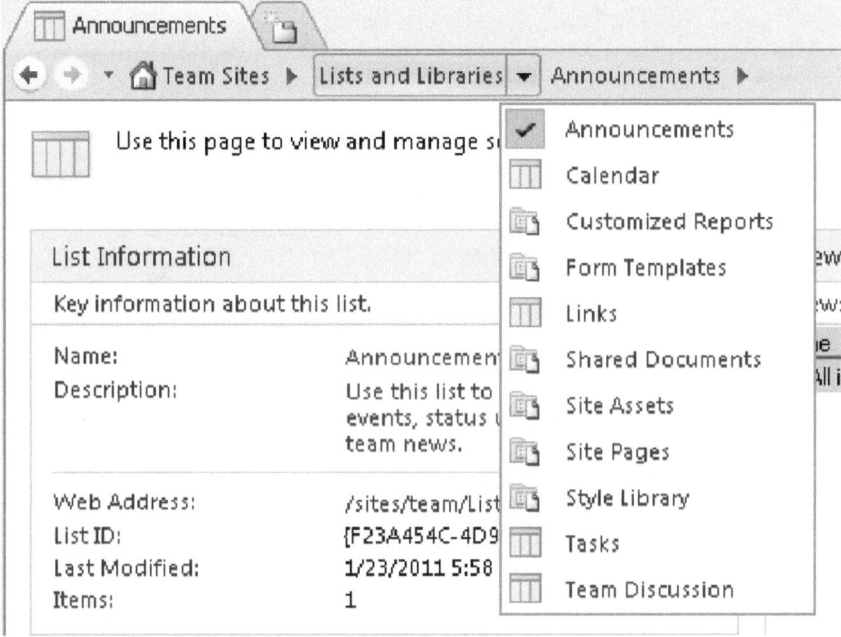

Figure 1-14. Main window navigation controls

The other item on this second line is a fully interactive breadcrumb control. Like any breadcrumb, it shows the path of the item currently displayed in the main window, and the user can navigate up the hierarchy by clicking one of the higher levels. Additionally, you can select the arrow next to any node to access a context-sensitive menu of navigation options from that node.

The Main Window

The main window is, of course, where most of the work is done. There are three types of pages that can appear in this area: gallery pages, settings pages, and object editors.

Gallery pages are used to display a list of artifacts in the site. The exact fields shown depend on the type of artifacts being displayed and the features enabled within the site.

Settings pages are also sometimes called *summary pages* because they summarize all the settings associated with a particular item. When you first open a site, the site's settings page is displayed. The site setting page is also the default page shown when new tab is opened. Settings pages, like the one shown in Figure 1-15, provide a plethora of information and possible actions in one place.

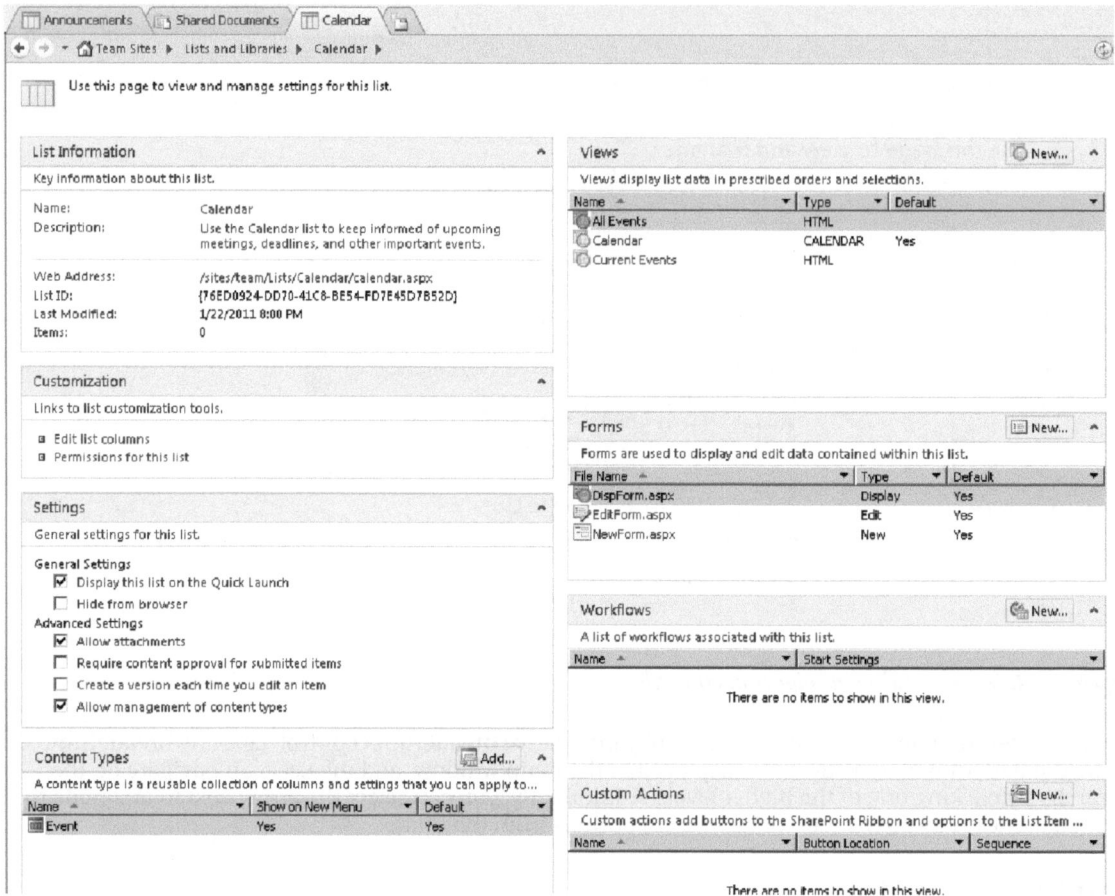

Figure 1-15. A list settings page

Of course, SharePoint Designer wouldn't be of much use if it didn't allow you to edit pages and other site content. Editor windows are available for many SharePoint artifacts and can often be reached quickly by double-clicking the item's name in a gallery page. Settings pages also generally contain Edit links that can be used to launch an editor for the item.

Figure 1-16 shows the Page Editor window. This window might remind you of previous versions of SharePoint Designer or FrontPage. In addition to page editing, many other editors have been added to SharePoint Designer to take it from being primarily a web page editor to a full-featured SharePoint solution editor. You will examine many of these editors in detail in later chapters.

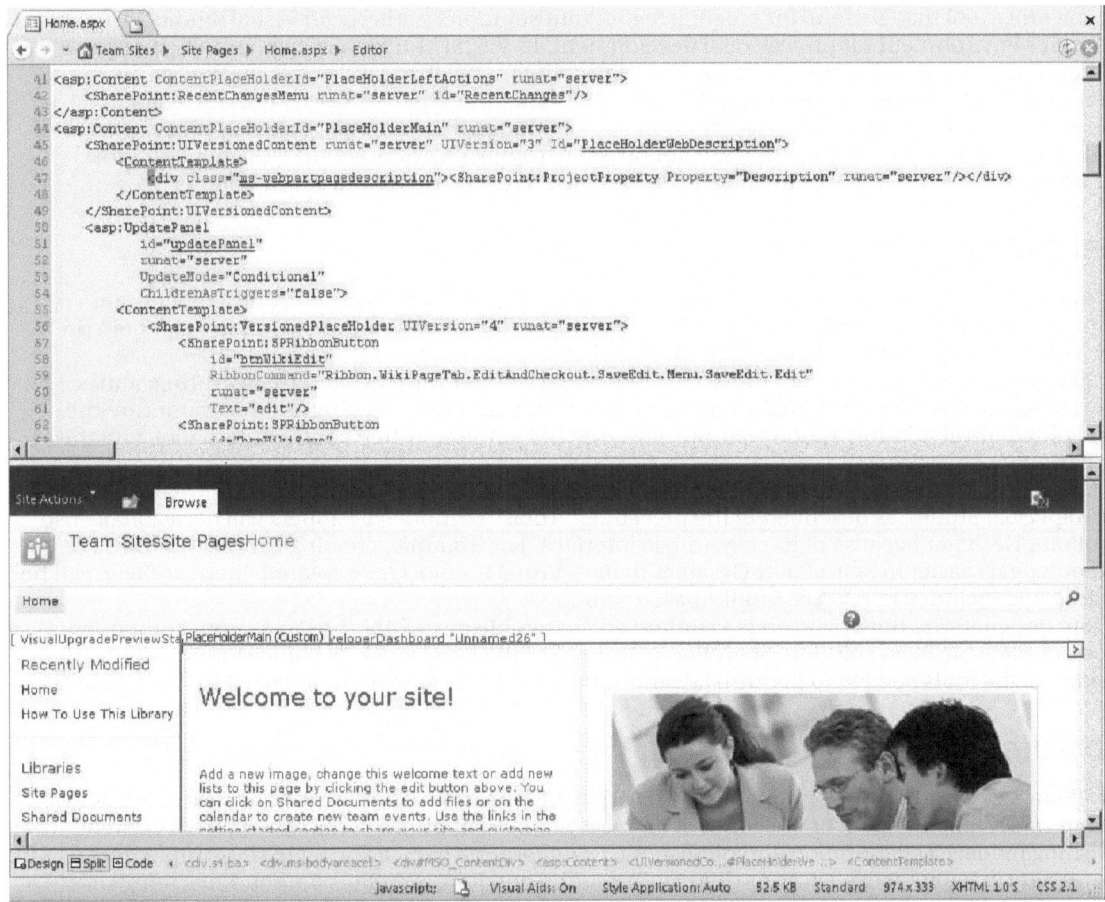

Figure 1-16. The Page Editor window

Best Practices

In this section, we discuss some best practices associated with building SharePoint solutions by using SharePoint Designer.

Tools

SharePoint Designer is not the only tool available for working with SharePoint. The most obvious tool, aside from SPD, is the web browser itself. Through the web browser, the user can do a great deal of customization to SharePoint sites and pages. The user can also create new sites, lists, libraries, pages, and more. The user can edit pages within the web browser including using an onscreen rich text editor. Users can add, remove, and configure web parts and publish changes to other users. SharePoint Designer is an extension of this capability that enables more-complex customizations to be made that include workflows, master and layout pages, and so on.

The other tool that is useful for creating SharePoint solutions is Microsoft Visual Studio 2010. This is Microsoft's environment for professional development. In Visual Studio, a developer can create new features, web parts, event receivers, and other code components that run "under the covers" in SharePoint. Visual Studio is a very powerful tool but it is not intended for use by non-developers. SharePoint Designer is designed to create "no-code" solutions. For example, Visual Studio can be used to create very complex workflows that are not possible from within SharePoint Designer, but most ordinary workflows are well within SharePoint Designer's reach, as you will see in Chapter 12.

User Roles

There are three major contributors to most SharePoint solutions: administrators, developers, and designers. Each of these types of users will find features within SharePoint Designer to help them do their work, but they often have other tools that are better suited to their needs.

SharePoint administrators are those IT professionals tasked with installing, configuring, and maintaining the SharePoint environment. The tools most commonly used by administrators are the SharePoint Central Administration web site, the STSADM command-line configuration tool, and the new PowerShell interface.

Developers create the code components that go into a SharePoint solution. These are typically built by using Visual Studio, as described in the preceding "Tools" section. Developers will occasionally use SharePoint Designer because of its easy-to-use interface. For example, creating simple workflows or content types is easier in SharePoint Designer than in Visual Studio. Once created, these artifacts can be exported and included in a Visual Studio-based solution.

Site designers are those who create content and assemble out-of-the-box or custom components into a complete business solution. SharePoint Designer is the application of choice for these users. It provides all the tools needed to perform advanced integration work without the need to write code.

Site Templates

SharePoint Server 2010 is designed for use in a variety of scenarios including intranet, extranet, and Internet sites. Depending on how a site is to be used, SharePoint implements two different content publishing models: collaboration and publishing. *Collaboration sites* (a.k.a. *team sites*) implement functionality that allows users to contribute information and jointly create content. *Publishing sites* (a.k.a. *web content management, or WCM, sites*) are used when a small set of contributors will be creating the content and making it available to a wide audience such as that on the Internet. Figure 1-17 shows the two publishing models.

■ **Note** Managing publishing sites is presented in detail in Chapter 7.

When planning a SharePoint site, it is important to start with the correct type of site template. A collaboration template, such as Team Site or Document Workspace, will support the collaboration content model by default. A publishing template is designed for the publishing model. Although collaboration features can be used on publishing sites and vice versa, it is always best to start with the site template that most closely matches the desired behavior of the final site.

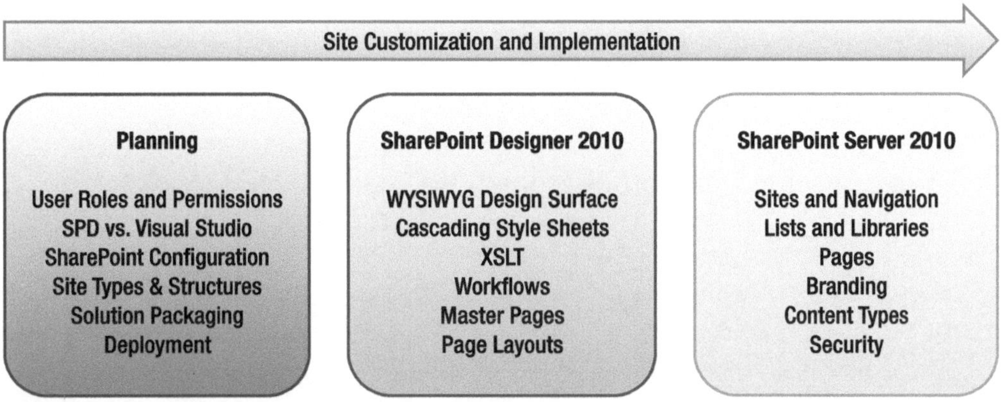

Figure 1-17. SharePoint content management models

Summary

In this chapter, you have explored the following:

- The history and features of SharePoint Designer 2010
- Installing the application
- Preparing a SharePoint environment for designer access
- The user interface of SharePoint Designer
- Some best practices for using SharePoint Designer

CHAPTER 2

Editing Pages

This chapter introduces you to creating and editing pages in SharePoint Designer 2010. As mentioned in Chapter 1, SharePoint Designer is the latest version of what was Microsoft FrontPage. But instead of an HTML editor that connects to SharePoint, SharePoint Designer 2010 is fully integrated with SharePoint. In this version, it is not even possible to create or edit a web page without being connected to a SharePoint site first. Because of this tight integration, SharePoint Designer makes customizing SharePoint 2010 sites easy, while still giving you the power to make changes previously available only through Visual Studio.

But, before you begin creating pages in SharePoint Designer, you'll take a tour of the editing tools the application provides. The main interface of SharePoint Designer is the Page Editor. The main components of the Page Editor are the task panes, the Ribbon, the editing surface, and the status bar. You will explore these components in detail as you work through this chapter's exercises.

You will learn about the following topics in this chapter:

- SharePoint Designer 2010's task panes

- The Ribbon and its menus

- The three editing views available

- Creation of code snippets

- Creation of a web part page

■ **Note** For all exercises in this chapter, you will use the default Team Site web template. For most page-editing exercises, you will use the Home.aspx page or create new pages in the site.

Task Panes

SharePoint Designer 2010 has several *task panes* available to you (see Figure 2-1). These task panes can be docked inside the application workspace or they can be floated. You can move a task pane around by dragging its title bar. If you want to dock the task pane, drag it to the edge of the application workspace where you want the task pane docked. Each task pane can be closed by clicking its X icon in the upper-right corner of the task pane title bar.

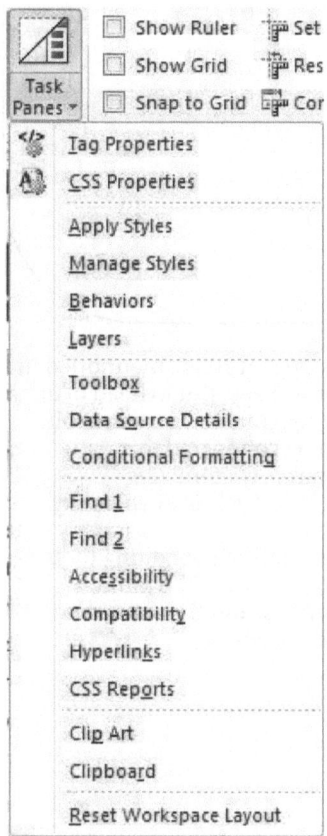

Figure 2-1. Available task panes

■ **Note** Some task panes open automatically, depending on the menu item you select. You can open any task pane by clicking the Task Panes menu item on the Ribbon's View tab.

The task panes are grouped according to function. The functional areas are Properties, Styles and Behaviors, Tools, Reports, and External Resources.

Properties Panes

SharePoint Designer has two Properties panes: Tag Properties and CSS Properties.

The *Tag Properties task pane* enables you to view and edit the properties of the current tag. This pane is displayed automatically when you right-click properties on any element on the page.

The *CSS Properties task pane* enables you to quickly view and edit the properties of all Cascading Style Sheets (CSS) elements on the page. You can see which rules apply to the current object on the editing surface and other CSS elements that you can modify.

Styles and Behaviors Panes

The four Styles and Behaviors panes enable you to easily change the style or behavior of elements on a web page—including internal, external, or inline styles. Behaviors fall into this category because they usually consist of CSS element changes based on certain behaviors.

The *Apply Styles task pane* lists all CSS styles loaded on the current page's style sheets. These include internal, external, and inline CSS. The view of the styles can be modified by using the Option menu.

The *Manage Styles task pane* lists all styles that are defined in the page's internal and external style sheets, but not the inline style sheets. By using the pane's Option menu, you can list all styles or only those used on the current page or the current element.

In the Apply Styles and Manage Styles task panes, each style is denoted by an icon depending on where it is derived from (see Table 2-1).

Table 2-1. Style Task Pane Symbols

Symbol	Description
Red dot	An ID-based style
Green dot	A class-based style
Blue dot	An element-based style
Yellow dot	An inline style
Circle around a colored dot	A style used in the current page
@ symbol	A style imported from external CSS elements

The *Behaviors task pane* enables you to assign one or more behaviors (small pieces of CSS or JavaScript) to the currently selected object. These behaviors aren't available for all objects but are related to events and are used to perform specific functionality based on those events. As one example, you might add a behavior to the page load event to redirect the user to a new page if that user is using an unsupported browser (see Figure 2-2).

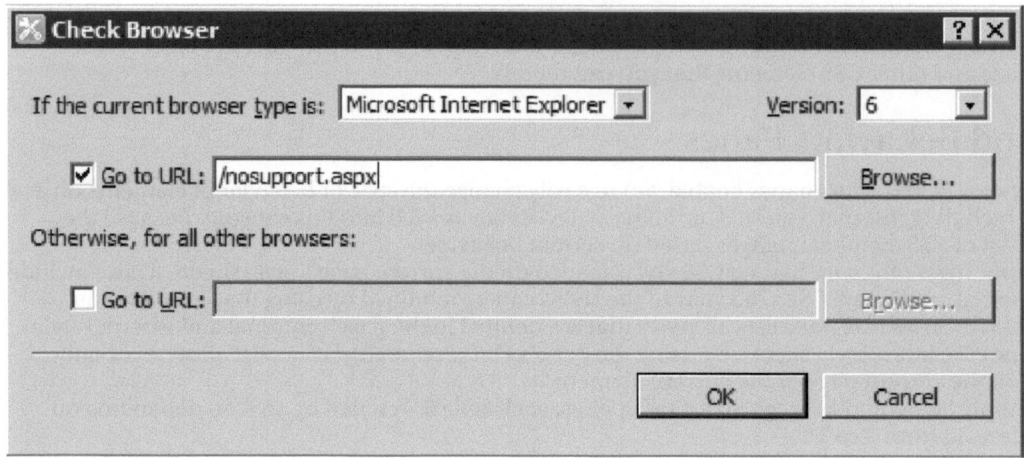

Figure 2-2. *Check Browser behavior*

The *Layers task pane* helps you manage the `<div>` tags in your page when the position type is something other than none.

EXERCISE 2-1. USE TAG PROPERTIES, CSS PROPERTIES, AND LAYERS TASK PANES

In this exercise, you will use the Tag Properties, CSS Properties, and Layers task panes to investigate the anatomy of a page. Follow these steps:

1. Open a basic page in SharePoint Designer 2010. For this example, create a basic SharePoint site based on the Team Site template. Open the Home.aspx page in the Site Pages document library (see Figure 2-3).

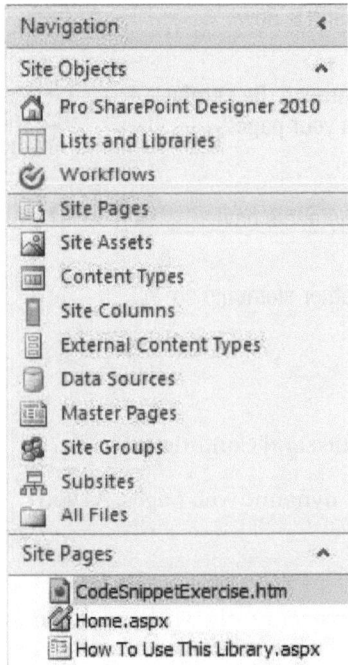

Figure 2-3. Site Pages menu item

2. Open the Tag Properties task pane and the CSS Properties task pane from the Task Panes menu on the Ribbon's View tab.

3. Click around the editing surface. Notice the different tag properties and CSS properties of each element that you click. Notice that the CSS Properties task pane will tell you which CSS rule is currently applied to the element that you clicked.

4. Add an inline style to an element: Click the paragraph on the page that begins with *Add a new image, change*. In the CSS properties, change the font family to Times New Roman and change the font size to medium. *Don't worry; you are not going to save the changes*.

5. Click the image element on the right-hand side of the page and view the CSS properties currently applied to it.

6. Find the Border CSS property. Click the plus (+) sign to display the three properties that make up a border designation. Change *border width* to *thick*. Change *border color* to *#00FF00* (a real bright green). Change *border style* to *solid*. Notice that you now have a thick, bright green border around your image.

7. Now click the Tag Properties task pane.

8. Click the image control and notice that the Tag Properties task pane is now displaying your border inline style properties for the image.

9. On the style line of your tag property, delete just the border declaration. Be careful not to delete the margin declaration. The border disappears from your page.

10. Now click back to the CSS Properties task pane.

11. Click the image element again and notice how the border style elements have been deleted.

12. Click around the page and notice the tag and CSS properties of other elements on the page.

Tools Panes

Three Tools panes are provided in Page Editor: Toolbox, Data Source Details, and Conditional Formatting.

The *Toolbox task pane* contains objects that enable you to create rich, dynamic web pages. As you can see in Figure 2-4, these objects are grouped into three panes:

- The *HTML Controls section* contains standard HTML elements.

- The *ASP.NET Controls section* contains standard ASP.NET server controls. These are client-side controls with server-side functionality. If you are an ASP.NET developer, you will recognize these controls as the same controls available to you in Visual Studio.

- The *SharePoint Controls section* contains controls that are specific to SharePoint functionality. They are also ASP.NET controls, so they can be controlled by server-side code.

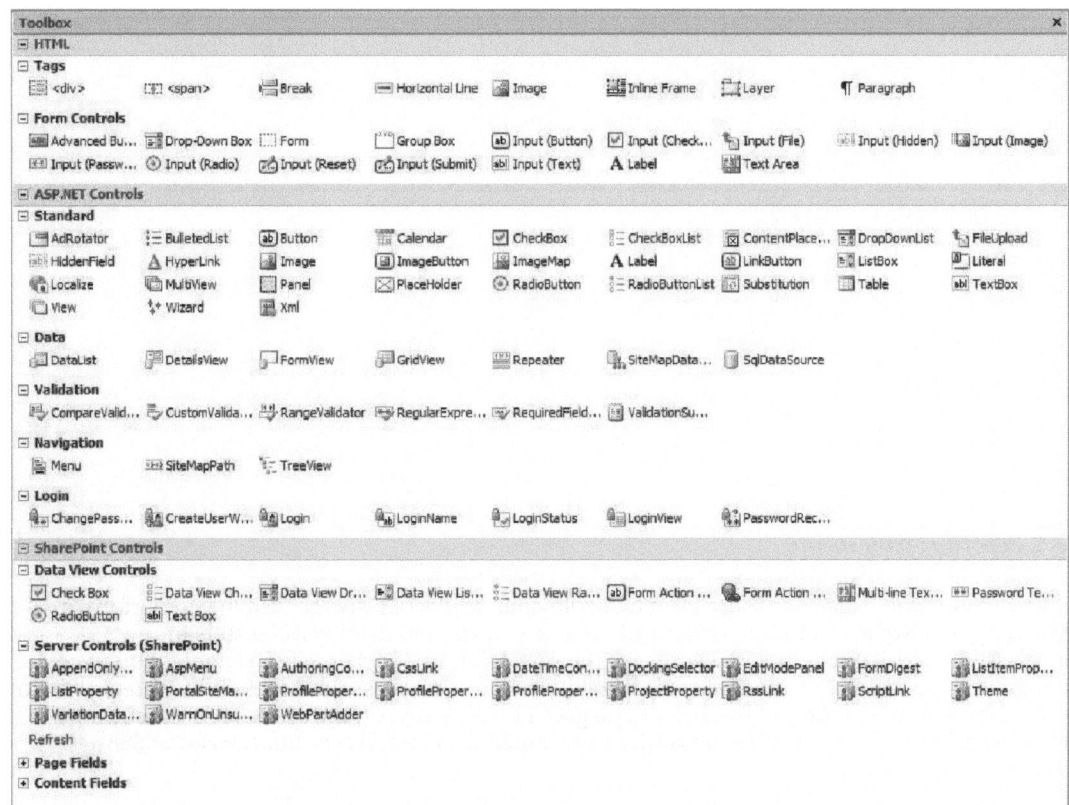

Figure 2-4. Toolbox task pane

The *Data Source Details task pane* enables you to see the current data source and to insert data fields into a page to create a view of the data on the page.

The *Conditional Formatting task pane* enables you to specify different formatting options for an HTML tag, data value, or range of text, depending on whether they meet the conditions you set. A common use of this is to alternate shading on table rows.

Reporting Panes

The Reporting panes are unique in that they are not limited to any one page. They are always docked at the bottom of the editing surface and present the results of an action, such as a searching or page analysis. When more than one pane is displayed, they are arranged in a tabbed format. SharePoint Designer has six Reporting panes: Find 1, Find 2, Accessibility, Compatibility, Hyperlinks, and CSS Reports. Figure 2-5 shows the menu displayed.

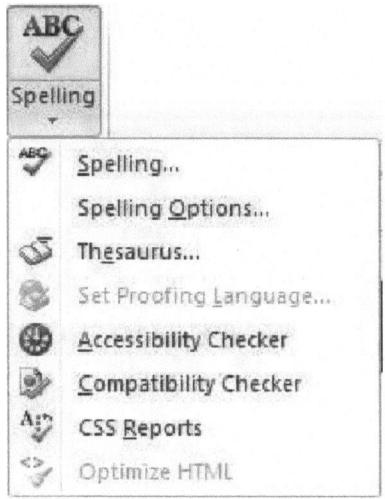

Figure 2-5. Reporting pane menu

The *Find 1* and *Find 2 task panes* are used to display the results of a search. When you perform a Find All search, you have the option to select which pane you want to display the results in.

The *Accessibility task pane* gives you access to the Accessibility Checker, which enables you to create content that is more accessible to people with disabilities. You can access the Accessibility Checker from the Proofing menu on the Ribbon or by clicking the green begin arrow on the Accessibility task pane. Your page can be checked against WCAG Priority 1 or 2 guidelines and Access Board Section 508 specifications.

■ **Note** The *WCAG Priority 1 or 2 guidelines* are the Web Content Accessibility Guidelines 1.0 or 2.0 published by the World Wide Web Consortium (W3C). These guidelines indicate how to make web content accessible to people with disabilities.

The *Access Board Section 508 specifications* detail electronic and information technology standards administered by the Access Board, the federal agency created in 1973 to ensure accessibility for people with disabilities.

The *Compatibility task pane* enables you to run the Compatibility Checker against your page to make sure it is compatible with HTML or CSS standards. You can access the Compatibility Checker through the Proofing menu on the Ribbon or the green begin arrow on the Compatibility task pane.

The *Hyperlinks task pane* enables you to list all of the hyperlinks on your page. You can also use it to verify your hyperlinks against the current web site.

The *CSS Reports task pane* displays the results of the CSS Checker. You can use the CSS Checker to check for CSS errors on your page or to get a usage report of class, ID, or element selectors on the current page, open pages, or all pages. The CSS Checker can also be accessed from the Proofing menu on the Ribbon.

External Resources Panes

Because SharePoint Designer is part of the Microsoft Office family, it shares some common elements (such as the Ribbon) that make using SharePoint Designer a familiar experience for Microsoft Office users. The Clip Art and Clipboard task panes, which are the External Resources panes, are two of the elements shared with other Microsoft Office applications. As such, these task panes behave differently than other task panes. First, they dock on only the right-hand edge of the application. They can't be grouped with other task panes docked on the right edge of the editing surface. They dock outside the editing surface, as they do in all other Microsoft Office applications. You can't view both the Clip Art and Clipboard task panes at the same time. You must toggle between the two with a special toolbar menu at the top of the task pane.

The *Clip Art task pane*, shown in Figure 2-6, is a view of the Microsoft Office Clip Art Manager. The clip art you can use in Microsoft Word, Excel, and PowerPoint is also directly available to you in SharePoint Designer. You can search for illustrations, photos, video, and audio stored in the Clip Art Manager or on Office.com. To insert a clip art item, you can drag it right to the editing surface, from the right-click menu of the art or by just double-clicking the clip art.

Figure 2-6. Clip Art task pane

The *Clipboard task pane* is like the Clip Art task pane in behavior. It contains items that have been saved to the Windows Clipboard from other applications.

The Ribbon

The *Ribbon* has become the toolbar/menu interface in the latest Microsoft Office product line. This is a rich, dynamic, and flexible menu system. Each SharePoint object will have one or more Ribbon menus, depending on the functionality required.

Figure 2-7 shows the Ribbon that is displayed for basic page-editing operations. It consists of Home, Insert, View, and Layout tabs, which are detailed further in the rest of this section.

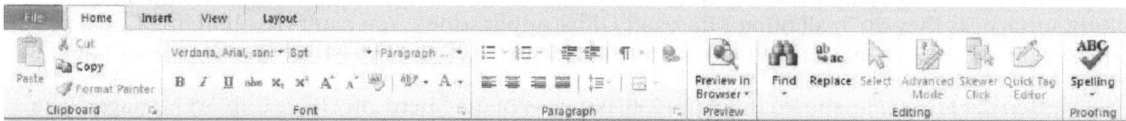

Figure 2-7. Ribbon menu

Home Tab

The Home tab, shown previously in Figure 2-7, consists of basic rich-text editing tools, very much like the tools available to you in any other Microsoft Office application. However, this tab has a few menu items that are specific to SharePoint Designer 2010, including Advanced Mode, Skewer Click, and Quick Tag Editor options.

Advanced Mode

Previous versions of SharePoint supported the concept of ghosted and unghosted pages. This referred to pages in which elements had been changed from the underlying site definition. In SharePoint 2010, Microsoft has changed the terminology of this same concept to *customized* and *uncustomized*. *Customized* refers to pages that have been modified from the site definition.

Site definitions contain page layouts that are predefined and provide a common base for the web site. In Basic editing mode, you are allowed to edit only those portions of the page that have been designated in the page layout as editable. If you want to edit elements outside these basic regions, you need to use Advanced mode.

Advanced mode decouples the page from its site definition. That means that any upgrades or modifications to the underlying site definition will not be picked up in the page. You always have the option to revert back to Basic mode, but all changes made outside the editable regions will be lost. Another disadvantage to customizing pages is that customized pages are stored in the database instead of on the file system, which slows down page rendering.

EXERCISE 2-2. USE BASIC AND ADVANCED MODES

In this exercise, you will work with a page in both Basic mode and Advanced mode to understand the differences between the two:

1. Open the Home.aspx page (Figure 2-8), located in the Site Pages of a basic Team site.

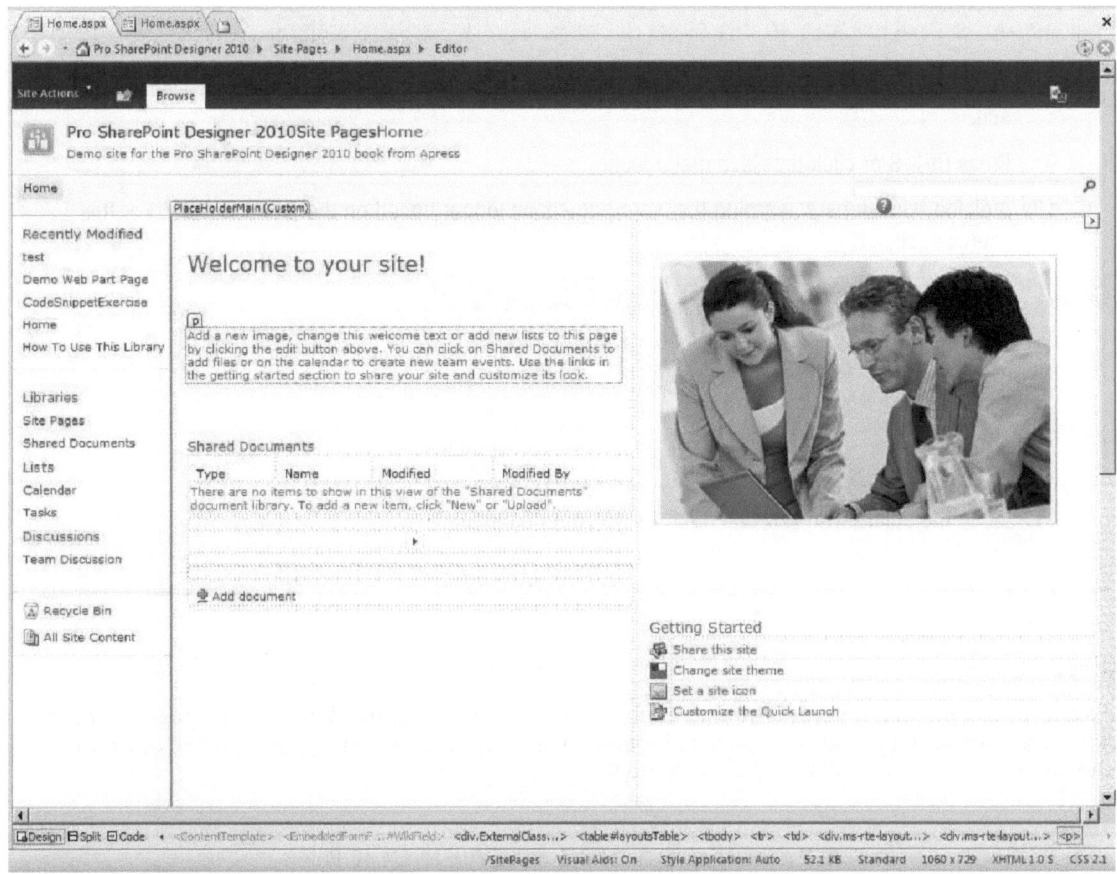

Figure 2-8. Team Site home page

2. Notice that the top navigation bar reads *Editor*.

🏠 Pro SharePoint Designer 2010 ▶ Site Pages ▶ Home.aspx ▶ Editor

3. Use your mouse to click the Welcome to Your Site heading.

4. Notice that you can edit the text on that heading.

5. Click the left navigational menu labeled Libraries. Your cursor becomes a circle with a line through it. Notice that you cannot change anything in that area of the page.

6. Click around other parts of the page. Notice the different areas that you can edit and the areas that you cannot edit.

7. Now click the Advanced Mode icon. The top navigation bar changes to *Advanced Editor*.

🏠 Pro SharePoint Designer 2010 ▶ Site Pages ▶ Home.aspx ▶ Advanced Editor

8. After the page refreshes, click the different areas of the page. More areas are now available to edit.

9. Press Ctrl+S or click the Save menu icon.

10. A dialog box appears, warning that your page is no longer based on the site definition. For this exercise, click No.

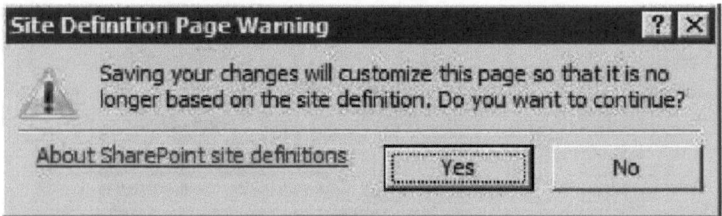

11. Close the editing window and do not save your changes.

Skewer Click

The *Skewer Click menu* is a new menu that enables you to drill down into elements of a page. Think of sticking a skewer through a stack of papers. When you click an element on a page, you will see a menu of all the different objects that make up that element.

EXERCISE 2-3. USE SKEWER CLICK

Try out the Skewer Click menu by following these steps:

1. Open the Home.aspx page, located in the Site Pages of a basic Team site.

2. Click the Skewer Click menu.

3. Click the main image on the page. A menu, shown in Figure 2-9, pops up.

Figure 2-9. *Skewer Click menu*

4. Run your cursor over the menu items. Notice that as you move the cursor over a particular menu item, the related element is highlighted on the page.

5. Move your cursor all the way back to the img menu item.

6. Click outside the image element to close the Skewer Click menu.

Quick Tag Editor

The *Quick Tag Editor* enables you to quickly edit the HTML tags on a page. This is a quick alternative to switching to Code mode.

EXERCISE 2-4. USE THE QUICK TAG EDITOR

Follow these steps to practice using the Quick Tag Editor:

1. Open the Home.aspx page in Design mode.

2. Click the main image.

3. Click the Quick Tag Editor button on the Ribbon.

4. Notice the HTML code for the `<img>` tag. Also notice that you have the options of wrapping the `<img>` tag in other HTML and of inserting other HTML via the drop-down list on the left side of the dialog box.

5. If you made any changes to the tag, you could click the green check mark at the top-right of the dialog box to save your changes. For this exercise, click the red X to close the dialog box without saving any changes.

■ **Note** As you clicked around the image element on the Home.aspx page in Exercise 2-4, two more special menus appeared on the Ribbon: the Table Tools and Picture Tools menus. You'll learn about using those menus in later sections of this chapter.

Insert Tab

The Insert tab provides access to almost all of the insertable objects available to you in SharePoint Designer. It is divided into seven sections:

- *Table* inserts an HTML table with the number of columns and rows specified.

- *Pictures* inserts images from your file system or from the Clip Art Manager.

- *Links* inserts a hyperlink to other locations or inserts a bookmark to another location on the same page.

- *Data Views & Forms* inserts custom views of data connections or custom New/Edit/Display forms for that data. This menu item is discussed in more detail in later chapters.

- *Controls* provides menu items that correspond to the Toolbox task pane covered previously.

- *Web Parts* inserts SharePoint web parts and web part zones into pages. Although you can insert web parts only into web part zones in the web interface, you can insert web parts anywhere on the page when using SharePoint Designer.

- *Symbol* easily inserts the special symbols that are sometimes difficult to do with the keyboard.

Some of these Insert sections have contextual menus that provide greater control over those elements.

Picture Tools

The Picture Tools menu, shown in Figure 2-10, gives you greater control over the picture elements inserted into a page.

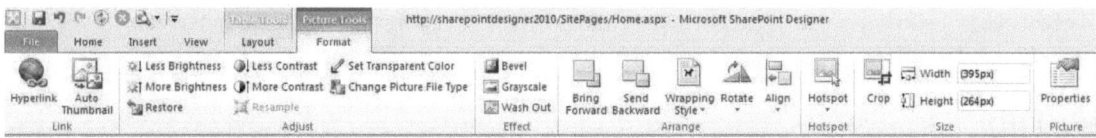

Figure 2-10. *Picture Tools menu*

Some of the things you can do with the menu are as follows:

- Automatically create a thumbnail link
- Perform simple editing of pictures, such as adjusting the brightness, contrast, transparency, and file type, among other things
- Create borders or other effects
- Layer pictures and wrapping
- Create clickable hot spots
- Crop images

Table Tools

The Table Tools menu, shown in Figure 2-11, gives you more control over tables inserted onto a page. You can use this menu to insert more rows or columns, split or merge cells, format the table, and size and set the cell layout.

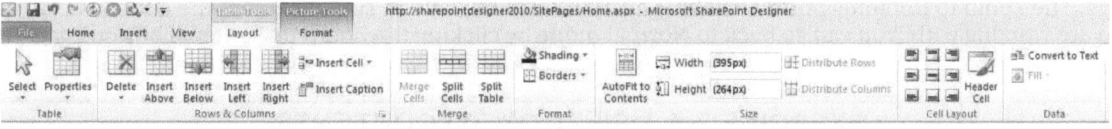

Figure 2-11. *Table Tools menu*

Layout Tab

Depending on the type of page you are editing, the Layout tab might display simple menu like the one shown in Figure 2-12, or it could display the Table Layout menu shown earlier in Figure 2-11. Figure 2-12 illustrates the basic Layout menu for a standard ASPX page. Most of the operations center around managing layers on a page. You can insert new layers and then set the position and hierarchy of the layers.

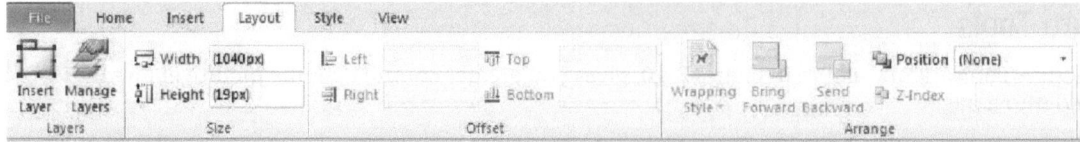

Figure 2-12. Layout tab

View Tab

We touched on the View tab (Figure 2-13) earlier in the "Task Panes" section. The View tab enables you to select the way you want to edit your page. You can choose to edit your page in Design mode, Code view, or Split view.

In addition to these options, the tab provides a couple of other buttons that offer some unique functionality: Zoom to Contents and Visual Aids. The tab also provides page layout tools in its Ruler and Grid section. These buttons and tools are detailed in the following sections.

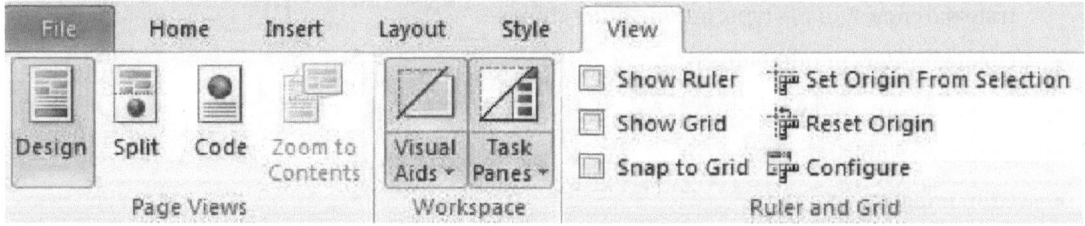

Figure 2-13. View tab

Zoom to Contents

Many times when you are working on a detailed web page, you want to focus on just one section of the page. The Zoom to Contents button will hide everything in the editing surface except the content section you are working with. You can go back to Normal mode by clicking the Zoom to Contents button again.

EXERCISE 2-5. USE ZOOM TO CONTENTS

Try out the Zoom to Contents button by following these steps:

1. Open the Home.aspx page in Design view.

2. Click the main content section.

3. Click the Zoom to Contents button. Notice how the noneditable parts of the page disappear.

4. Click the Zoom to Contents button again. Everything is back to normal!

Visual Aids

When you are working in Design view, SharePoint Designer 2010 provides several visual aids (Figure 2-14) that help illustrate the various components of the page you are editing. These visual aids enable you to see parts of the page that you would normally not see because they are hidden for display. Some examples are script blocks, anchors, and content placeholders. To turn off the different visual aids, select the item from the Visual Aids menu.

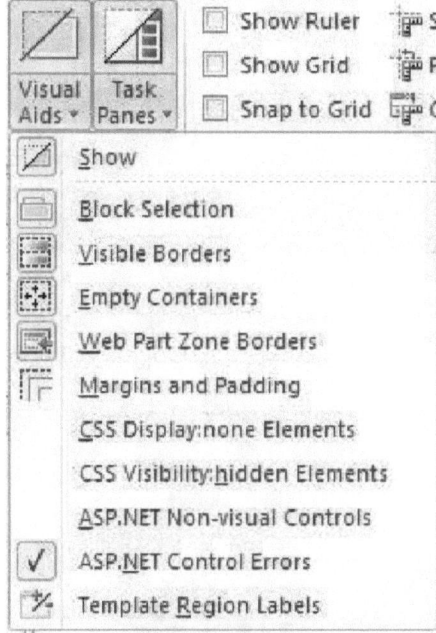

Figure 2-14. Visual Aids menu

EXERCISE 2-6. USE VISUAL AIDS

Turn on and off visual aids to investigate the different elements of a page:

1. Open Home.aspx from the Site Pages library.

2. From the View tab, click the Visual Aids button to access the Visual Aids menu. Click the Show menu item to quit showing all visual aids. Notice that the page is very near how it will render in the browser.

3. Open the Visual Aids menu again and click Show once more to turn on visual aids. Notice the dotted lines and the img tab above the picture.

4. Turn on all of the visual aids. All of the hidden elements of the page display, as shown in Figure 2-15.

5. Turn off the following aids to get back to the defaults:

   a.   Web Part Zone Borders

   b.   Margins and Padding

   c.   CSS Display: None Elements

   d.   CSS Visibility: Hidden Elements

   e.   ASP.NET Nonvisual Controls

   f.   Template Region Labels

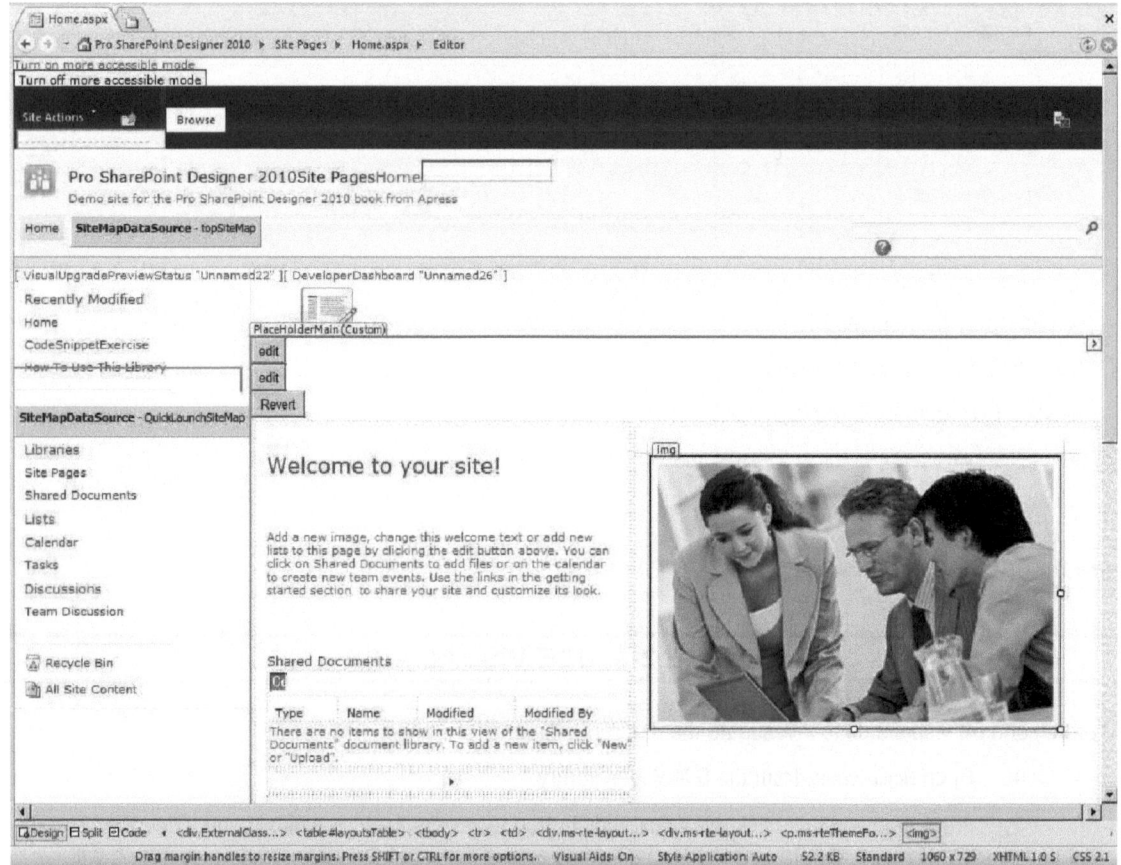

Figure 2-15. Home page with hidden designer elements

Page Sizes and Other Design Elements

To help you with your page layout, SharePoint Designer 2010 provides the following tools, accessed from the View tab, to assist you:

- *Show Ruler* shows a ruler on the top and side of the application.

- *Show Grid* overlays a grid on your editing surface. You can change the grid spacing in the Page Editor Options dialog box, shown in Figure 2-16.

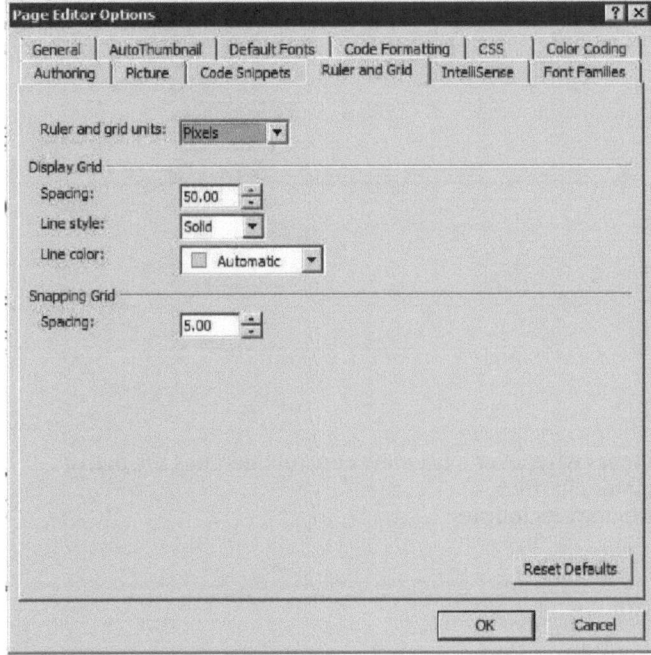

Figure 2-16. Page Editor Options dialog box

- *Snap to Grid* forces objects to snap to the grid. This makes it easy to keep objects on your page aligned.

- *Set Origin from Selection* reorients the ruler. Select an element on the page and then select this option, and the zero mark on the ruler will be the left boundary of the item selected.

- *Reset Origin* resets the origin of the ruler to the left edge of the page.

- *Configure* opens the Page Editor Options dialog box.

Page Sizes

When you are designing for a particular screen view or page size, it is helpful to be able to see how your work will look at different screen resolutions. The status bar on the bottom of the page has a menu item (Figure 2-17) that enables you to select different screen resolutions. You can select the predefined resolutions or you can edit the selections.

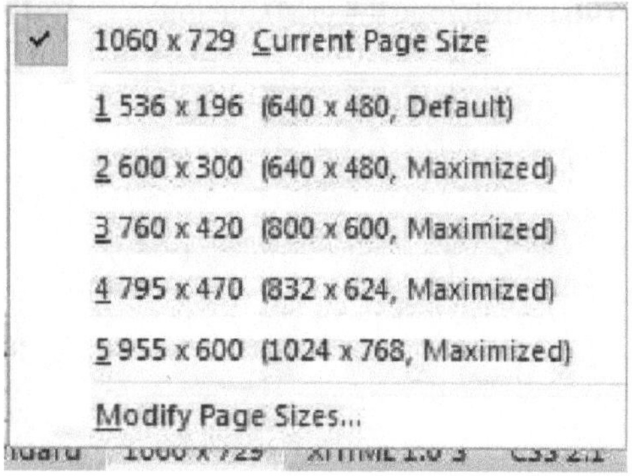

Figure 2-17. Page sizes

List View Tools

This special contextual menu (Figure 2-18) appears whenever a list view control becomes the active control on the page. You will use this menu in later chapters.

Some of the things you can do with the menu are as follows:

- Filter, sort, and group the data in the list view

- Set the paging settings for the control

- Add or remove columns that are viewable

- Enable the inline editing controls

- Work with data connections

- Change the style of the list view control

- Customize the XSLT in the list view

- Set the web part properties

- Perform actions on the table that displays the list (via the full Table Tools menu)

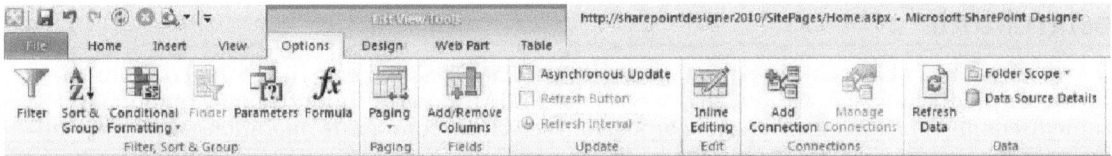

Figure 2-18. List View Tools menu

Editing Surface

The *editing surface* is where all of the magic happens. When you first open a page to edit, you are presented with the summary of the page, as shown in Figure 2-19. You use this page to view and manage settings for the file. You can set permissions on the file and see its version history. When you are ready to edit, click the Edit File link in the Customization pane.

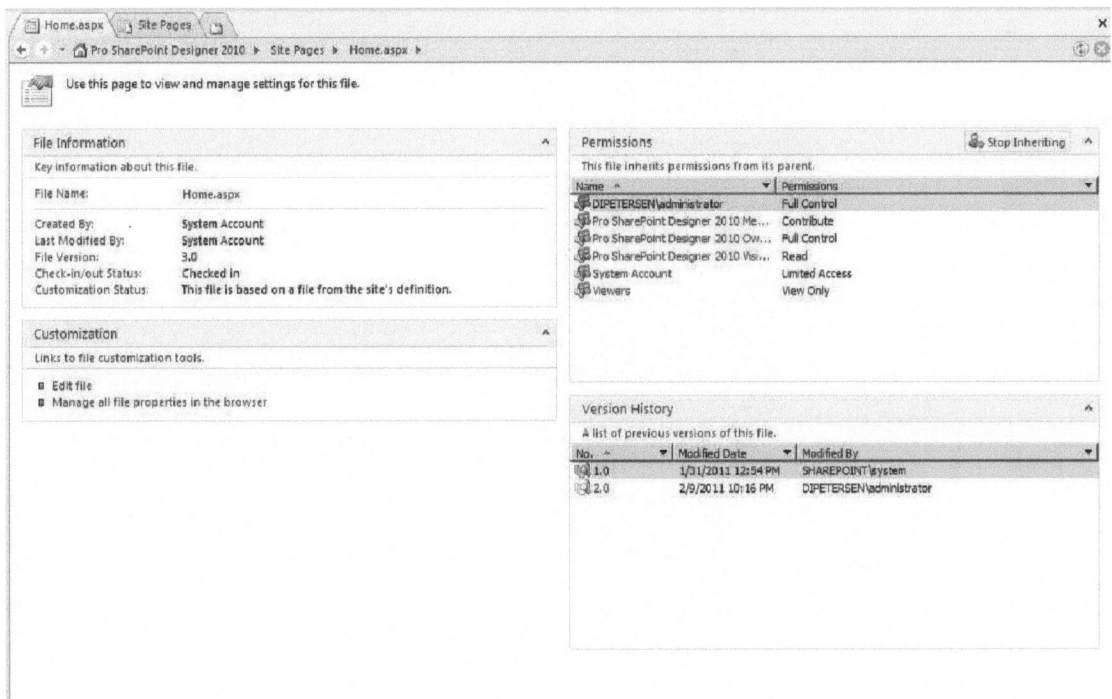

Figure 2-19. Page properties summary

When the file is open to edit, you have the option of editing in three different modes: Design mode, Code view, and Split view. These are covered in more detail next.

Design Mode

Design mode offers a what-you-see-is-what-you-get (WYSIWYG) editing experience. It allows you to create rich, dynamic websites without any knowledge of HTML code. It supports many traditional document-editing functions such as style editing, font selection, copy-paste operations, and drag-and-drop operations to move elements onto the editing surface.

Earlier sections of this chapter covered all of the menus and their functionalities plus all of the task panes that are available in Design mode. If you are comfortable using a word processor to create documents, you will feel comfortable using SharePoint Designer 2010.

Code View

Code view is for the more advanced users. SharePoint Designer 2010 has really grown up in this area. Figure 2-20 shows you what the Home.aspx page you have been working with looks like in Code view.

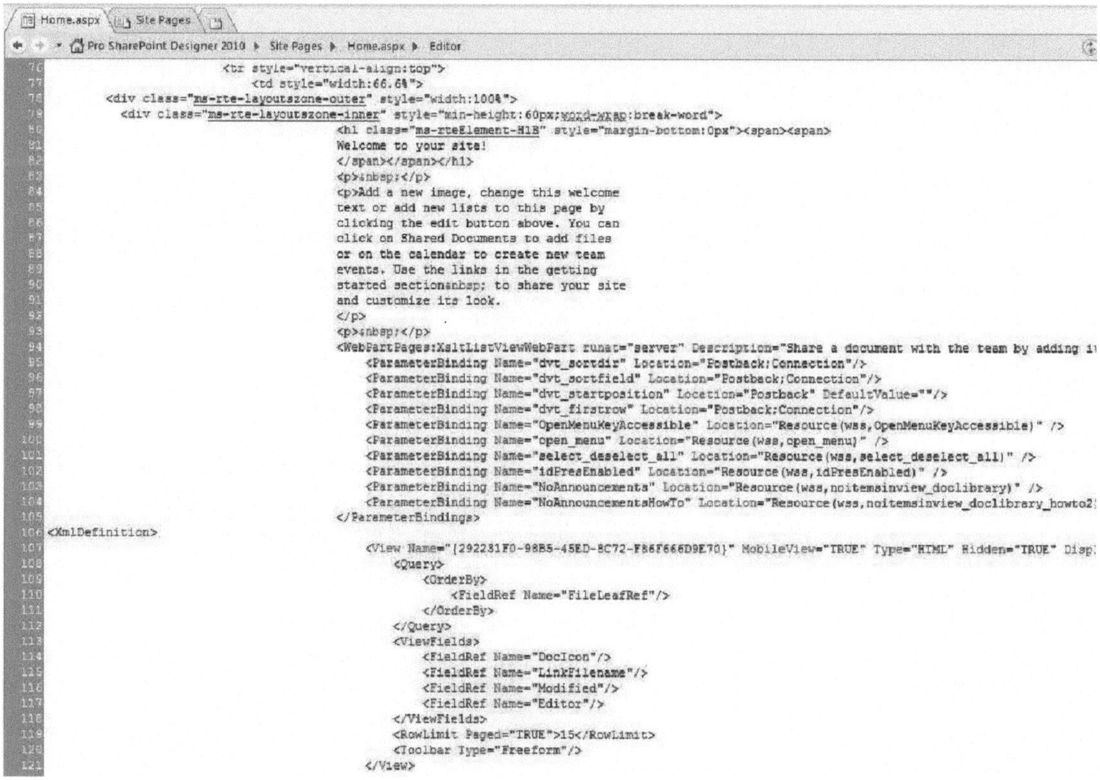

Figure 2-20. Code view

Instead of just providing a text editor for modifying the code for elements on the page, Code view uses color coding to help you recognize different code elements. In fact, Code view offers many of the same features available in modern development environments, including IntelliSense and code snippets.

IntelliSense

IntelliSense has long been part of the Visual Studio development experience. IntelliSense detects what you are typing and then pops up a suggestion for completing your operation. For example, if you were to begin to type the <img> tag, you would be prompted with a list of all properties available to that tag, as shown in Figure 2-21.

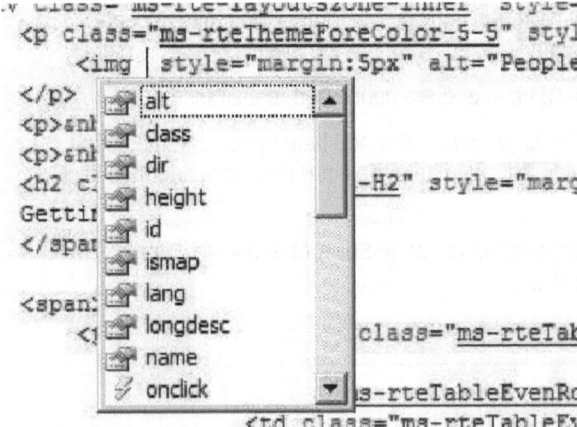

Figure 2-21. *IntelliSense menu*

The following are some of the things that IntelliSense does while you are editing a page in Code view:

- Completes programming code.

- Completes HTML tags.

- Completes CSS code.

- Closes tags and braces.

- Suggests parameters for HTML tags.

- Automatically codes hyperlinks, which enables you to Ctrl+click through to the source of the code. (For example, a hyperlinked CSS class name would link to a CSS file.)

- Highlights errors in code. If you have errors in your code, IntelliSense will show you the errors in the editor.

Code Snippets

One of the really cool things that you can do in SharePoint Designer 2010 Code view is create and use code snippets. Microsoft has supplied a lot of snippets for the major HTML elements, but if you find yourself typing the same piece of code over and over again, you can create your own code snippet. You can insert a snippet into your code by pressing Ctrl+Enter and selecting the snippet from the list that displays.

EXERCISE 2-7. CREATE AND USE A CODE SNIPPET

Let's say that you always use the same class for all paragraphs on your site. You could create a code snippet that inserts a paragraph tag with the class already defined. Here are the steps:

1. Make sure you have SharePoint Designer 2010 open and are connected to a site.

2. From the File menu, create a new blank HTML page. Select the Add Item option and then click the More Pages option. You will then see the HTML page item. Select HTML Page and then click Create.

3. In the New HTML Page dialog box that displays, name the page **Snippet** and save it in the Site Pages document library, as shown in Figure 2-22.

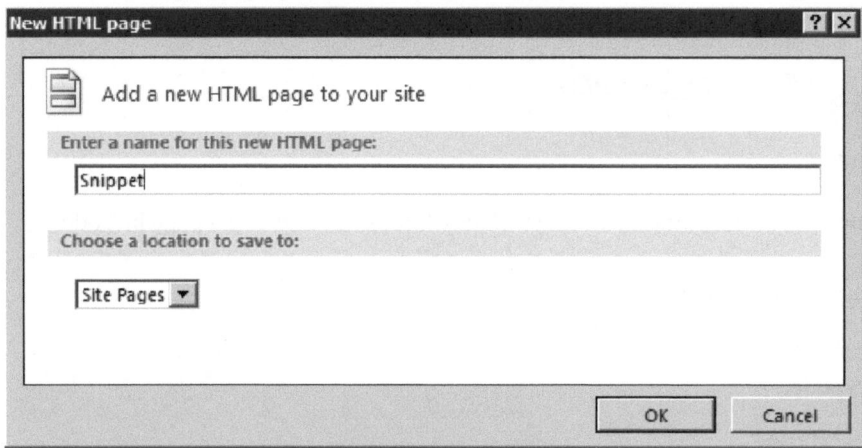

Figure 2-22. New HTML Page dialog box

4. After you open the HTML page, access Code view either by clicking Code View from the status bar at the bottom of the page, or by clicking the Code menu item on the View tab.

5. Place your cursor between the body tags and type **<p** and then a space. IntelliSense suggests the possible attributes you might need with your paragraph.

6. Select the class attribute and press Tab. IntelliSense finishes the class attribute for you and places the cursor between the question marks so you can type the class name.

7. Type **spd2010** as the class name. (This isn't really a name to a CSS class. This is just an example.) Finish by typing the **>** character after the class, and notice how IntelliSense closes the paragraph tag. When you create code snippets, you can use the single pipe character as a

prompt to indicate where to place the cursor when the snippet has been inserted into the code. If you use two pipe characters, it defines a highlighted section that you can use as a text prompt.

8. Place your cursor between the open and close paragraph tags and type the following:

```
<p class="spd2010">|Begin typing here|</p>
```

9. Highlight the whole paragraph tag and copy it to the Clipboard by pressing Ctrl+C.

10. On the Code View Tools menu item, click the Create button in the Code Snippet section. The Add Code Snippet dialog box pops up.

11. Type **spd2010para** in the Keyword box.

12. Type **SharePoint 2010 Designer paragraph** in the Description box.

13. Paste your code snippet into the dialog box by pressing Ctrl+V, as shown in Figure 2-23.

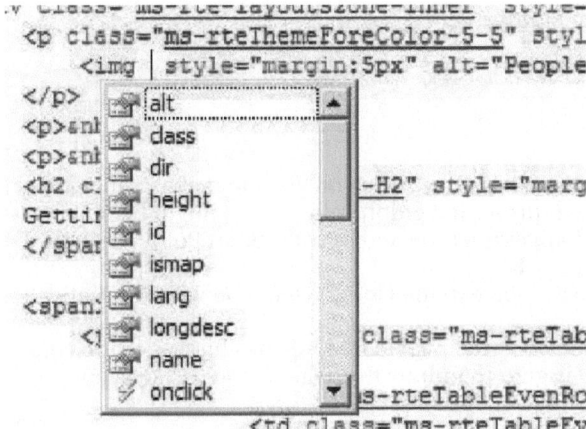

Figure 2-23. *Add Code Snippet dialog box*

14. Click OK.

Now you can test it.

15. Erase the paragraph line that you just created.

16. With your cursor between the body tags, press Ctrl+Enter

Begin typing **spd**. Your new code snippet should be highlighted.

17. Press the Enter or Tab key. Your new code snippet is added to your page, and a highlighted prompt appears, instructing you to begin typing:

```
<p class="spd2010">Begin typing here</p>
```

18. Start typing **SharePoint Designer 2010**.

```
<p class="spd2010">SharePoint Designer 2010</p>
```

19. Congratulations, you created your first code snippet!

Split View

Sometimes, when you are editing pages, you want to live in both worlds: you want to make changes in code, but you also want to see how those changes are represented graphically, or you might be making changes in Design view and want to see how those changes are reflected in code. SharePoint Designer 2010 gives you the option to see both views simultaneously:

Making changes in Design view. When you make a change in the Design view, you will automatically see those changes reflected in code.

Making changes in Code view. In Code view, when you are finished making the changes to the code, click in the Design View window to tell SharePoint Designer to redraw the page so you can see your changes.

Status Bar

At the bottom of the editing surface, the Status Bar provides you with a continuously updated status of contextual information on the page. It provides quick, one-click access to any object on the page. You can also switch between Design, Split, and Code views right on the Status Bar.

Creating New Pages

Now that you know what tools you have available, you can dive into creating pages. As you saw in Chapter 1, you can add new pages to your site through the Backstage area available from the File menu. From the Add Item option, you can create pages, lists, or work flows. Later chapters cover lists and workflows in more detail.

There are several kinds of page templates you can use to create new pages with Page Editor:

- Web part page

- New page from master

- HTML page
- ASPX page
- CSS page
- Master page
- JavaScript page
- XML page
- Text file

Using Libraries

Because you are creating new pages for a SharePoint site, you need a place to save the files you create. The common place to save site artifacts is in document libraries. For example, if you create a new site based on the Team Site template, two document libraries are created to store the site artifacts.

Site Pages Library

The Site Pages library is used to create and store pages on the site, including the following:

- Web part pages
- ASPX pages
- HTML pages

Site Assets Library

The Site Assets library is used to store files that are included on pages within the site, including these:

- CSS files
- JavaScript files
- XML files
- Text files
- Images

■ **Note** When you create HTML or ASPX pages, they don't have any regions that are editable in Safe mode, so they will all be opened in Advanced mode.

Web Part Pages

Web part pages are pages that have web part regions predefined. When you create a new web part page, you are presented with various layout choices. Figure 2-24 illustrates all of the different web part page layouts that are available. Each grayed-out area represents a web part zone and editable zones —places where you can put web parts, either by using SharePoint Designer or by using the web editing interface.

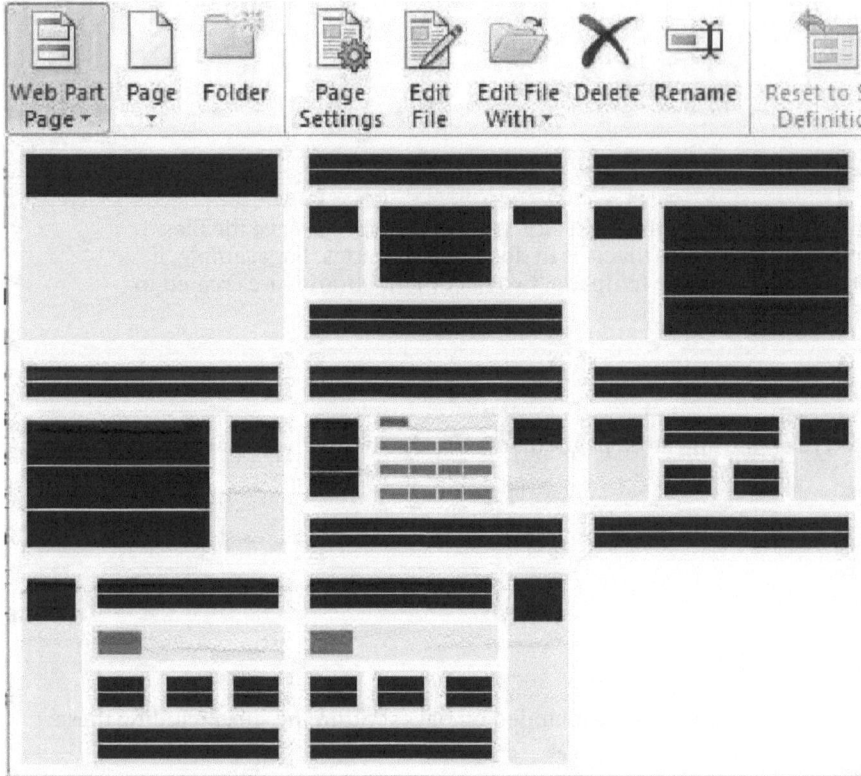

Figure 2-24. Web Part page selector

EXERCISE 2-8. CREATE PAGES AND ARTIFACTS

In this exercise, you will create and edit a new web part page in SharePoint Designer. You will then view the page in the browser and add another web part to the newly created page. You will be able to see how SharePoint Designer reflects changes made in the web editing interface, and how the web editing interface reflects changes made in SharePoint Designer.

Let's get started.

1. Make sure that you have a SharePoint site that you can create pages in.

2. From the File menu, click Add Item and then select Web Part Page.

3. Click the template labeled Header, Left Column, Body, as shown in Figure 2-25.

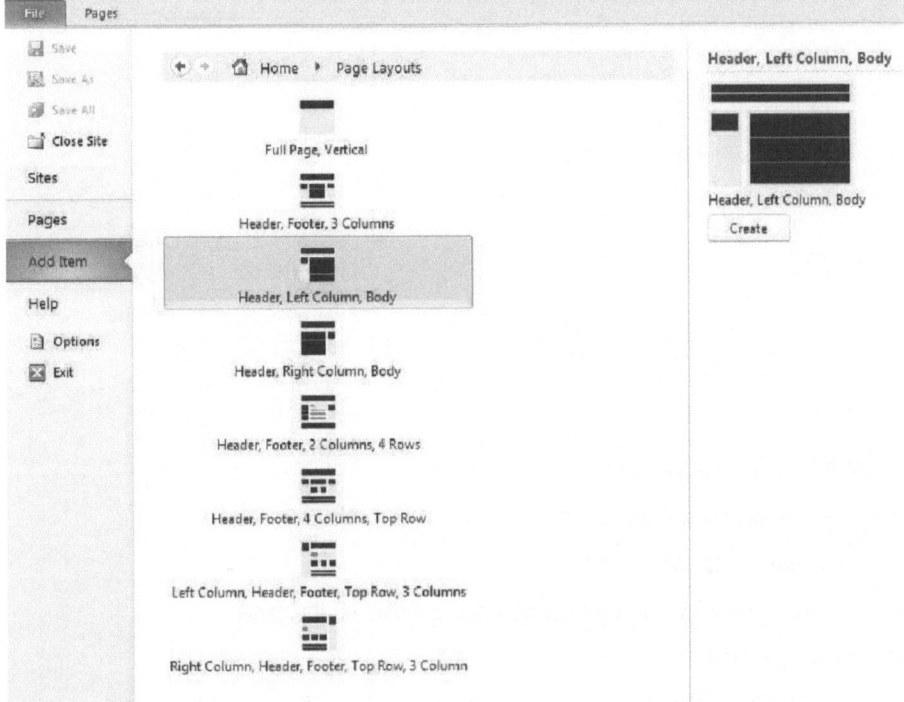

Figure 2-25. Add Item menu

4. Click the Create button to the right the page templates.

5. In the dialog box that pops up, type **Demo Web Part Page** as the filename.

6. Select Site Pages as the library to store the new file.

7. Click the Save button.

8. If SharePoint Designer is not already in Design view, click the Design View button on the status bar. You will see that the page has three web part zones. These are also regions that can be edited in Safe mode.

9. On the Home tab, click the Preview in Browser button. You will see a blank page in your site.

10. In the Site Actions menu item, click Edit Page. Notice the three web part zones, as shown in Figure 2-26. Also notice that the Ribbon menu is also available from the web editing interface.

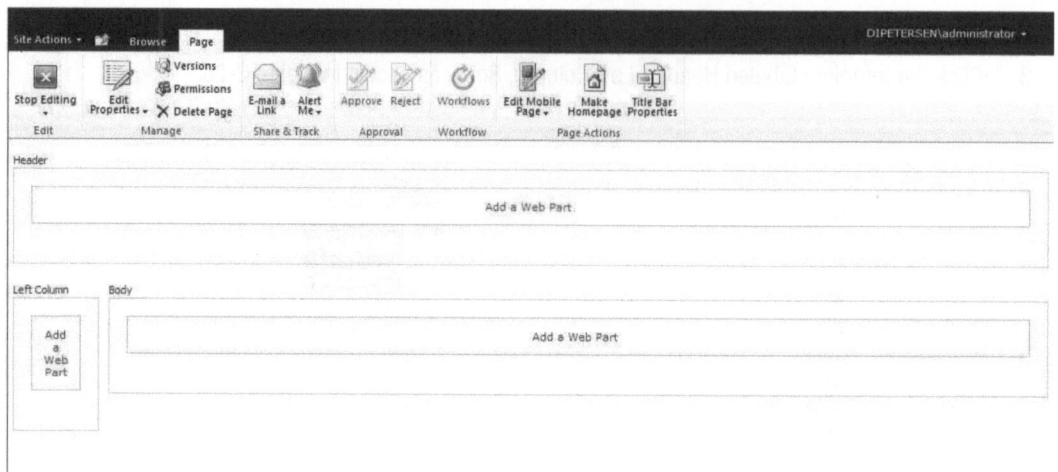

Figure 2-26. *Web part zones*

11. Click Add a Web Part in the top web part zone.

12. Select Lists and Libraries under Categories.

13. Select Announcements under Web Parts.

14. Click the Add button. A new Announcements web part appears on the page.

15. Click the Stop Editing option.

16. Now go back to SharePoint Designer and press F5 to refresh the editing surface. The web part you added in the web interface is now present in the SharePoint Designer editing surface.

17. Switch to Code view and take a look at the code for the web part, as shown in Figure 2-27.

```
67   <WebPartPages:XsltListViewWebPart runat="server" Description="Use this list to track upcoming events, status updates or other
68       <ParameterBinding Name="dvt_sortdir" Location="Postback;Connection"/>
69       <ParameterBinding Name="dvt_sortfield" Location="Postback;Connection"/>
70       <ParameterBinding Name="dvt_startposition" Location="Postback" DefaultValue=""/>
71       <ParameterBinding Name="dvt_firstrow" Location="Postback;Connection"/>
72       <ParameterBinding Name="OpenMenuKeyAccessible" Location="Resource(wss,OpenMenuKeyAccessible)" />
73       <ParameterBinding Name="open_menu" Location="Resource(wss,open_menu)" />
74       <ParameterBinding Name="select_deselect_all" Location="Resource(wss,select_deselect_all)" />
75       <ParameterBinding Name="idPresEnabled" Location="Resource(wss,idPresEnabled)" />
76       <ParameterBinding Name="NoAnnouncements" Location="Resource(wss,noXinviewofY_LIST)" />
77       <ParameterBinding Name="NoAnnouncementsHowTo" Location="Resource(wss,noXinviewofY_DEFAULT)" />
78   </ParameterBindings>
79   <XmlDefinition>
80       <View Name="{F94315A1-A9B2-4DBF-89CF-DBD59BEF6008}" MobileView="TRUE" Type="HTML" Hidden="TRUE" DisplayName="" Url="/Site
81           <Query>
82               <OrderBy>
83                   <FieldRef Name="Modified" Ascending="FALSE"/>
84               </OrderBy>
85           </Query>
86           <ViewFields>
87               <FieldRef Name="Attachments"/>
88               <FieldRef Name="LinkTitle"/>
89               <FieldRef Name="Modified"/>
90           </ViewFields>
91           <RowLimit Paged="TRUE">30</RowLimit>
92           <Toolbar Type="Freeform"/>
93       </View>
94   </XmlDefinition>
95   <DataFields>
96   </DataFields>
97   </WebPartPages:XsltListViewWebPart>
```

Figure 2-27. *Code view*

18. Switch back to Design view.

19. Close the web part page.

20. Click the Site Assets library.

21. On the Ribbon, click the Assets menu. From the Asset drop-down, select CSS to create a new CSS page.

22. Name the page `mystylesheet.css`.

23. Click the filename. The page's properties windows open.

24. Click Edit File in the Customization section of the property page. Notice that there is no Design view for CSS files.

25. Start typing **Table {'**. Notice how IntelliSense suggests different elements you can apply the style to. Notice how it also completes the bracket and then suggests style elements.

26. Continue typing other elements and notice that the code is color-coded.

27. Close the CSS page.

28. Experiment with other pages. Try an HTML page. Try a JavaScript file. Notice what menus are available.

Summary

This chapter covered all the tools SharePoint Designer provides when you create and edit pages as depicted in the figure below. You learned about

- Task Panes
  - Properties
  - Styles and Behaviors
  - Tools
  - Reporting
  - External Resources
- The Ribbon Menu
  - Home
  - Insert
  - Picture Tools
  - Table Tools
  - Layout
  - View
- Editing Views
  - Design View
  - Code View
  - Split View
- Creating Code Snippets
- Using the Quick Tag Editor

You also covered how to create a new web part page and other artifacts, and observed the interaction between the web editing environment and the editing surface in SharePoint Designer.

Editing Pages

Task Panes

Properties
Styles and Behaviors
Tools
Reporting
External Resources

Ribbon Menu

Home
Insert
Picture Tools
Table Tools
Layout
View

Editing Views

Design View
Code View
Split View
Quick Tag Editor
Code Snippets

CHAPTER 3

Using SharePoint to Store Data

SharePoint provides containers called *lists* to store information. Microsoft provides many predefined list templates that you can use to build powerful applications in SharePoint. SharePoint also has a generic list that can be customized to fit specific requirements. *Libraries* are special kinds of lists in which each list item refers to a file. Data in SharePoint is organized by creating different types of content that consists of columns or data. Once the data is stored in SharePoint, custom views of the data can be created.

This chapter covers the different types of lists and will take you through exercises in creating and customizing these. Mastering how to use lists to organize and store data will enable you to build robust web applications.

You will learn about the following topics in this chapter:

- Customizing lists and libraries

- Creating site columns and content types

- Adding custom actions

- Creating and modifying views

- Saving lists as templates

- Using Lists and Libraries

When you want to store data in SharePoint, you create a list. You can use one of the predefined lists or create one of your own. Lists contain columns (called *site columns*) of data. In database terms, each list (table) contains list items (rows) with one or more columns (fields). Libraries are a special type of list. Whereas a list contains list items, libraries contain files. A field in a list is more commonly referred to as *metadata* in a document library because it is used to describe the associated file. Although you can attach files to list items, the file is not the main point of the list item. It is just another piece of information associated with that list item. In a library, the file itself is the main piece of data in the library.

■ **Note** *Metadata* is data that describes other data. In a list, each column is considered a part of the data. In a document library, the file is the data, and the other properties (such as Title, Created By, and Modified Date) are the metadata that describes the data.

You can create most lists and libraries either in the browser or in SharePoint Designer 2010, but you have much more control of your list creations with SharePoint Designer. This chapter will help you determine when to use the browser and when to use SharePoint Designer.

List Templates

You create lists by using *templates*. Microsoft provides several templates that have common business or collaborative functionality. If a premade template does not fit what you need to do, you can use SharePoint's generic template, which allows you to build a list to your specifications. Once you create your own custom lists, you can save them as your own list templates, as you'll see later in this chapter.

Table 3-1 lists some of the supplied list templates and their uses.

Table 3-1. *List Templates*

Announcements	Used to track upcoming events, status updates, or other news.
Calendar	Used to keep informed of meetings, deadlines, and other important events. Can be synchronized with Microsoft Outlook or other compatible programs.
Contacts	A list of people your team works with, such as partners or customers. Can be synchronized with Microsoft Outlook or other compatible programs.
Custom	A blank list to which you can add your own columns and views. Use this template if none of the built-in list types are similar to the list you want to make.
Custom List in Datasheet View	A blank list that is displayed as a spreadsheet in order to allow easy data entry. You can add your own columns and views. This list type requires a compatible list datasheet ActiveX control, such as the one provided in Microsoft Office.
Discussion Board	A place to hold newsgroup or bulletin-board discussions on topics relevant to your team.
External	Creates an external list to view the data in an External Content Type.
Issue Tracking	A list of issues or problems associated with a project or item. You can assign, prioritize, and track issue status.
Links	Used to keep links to other web pages that you or your team might find useful.
Project Tasks	A list for team or personal tasks. This list provides a Gantt Chart view and can be opened by Microsoft Project or other compatible programs.

Survey	A list of questions that you would like to have people answer. Surveys allow you to quickly create questions and view graphical summaries of the responses.
Status	A place to track and display a set of goals. Colored icons display the degree to which the goals have been achieved.

Library Templates

As mentioned, a library is different from a list in that its focus is on the file contained in the library. Table 3-2 is a list of provided library templates.

Table 3-2. Library Templates

Asset Library	A place to share, browse, and manage rich media assets, such as image, audio, and video files.
Data Connection Library	A place where you can easily share files that contain information about external data connections.
Document Library	A place for storing documents or other files that you want to share. Document libraries allow folders, versioning, and checkouts.
Form Library	A place to manage business forms such as status reports or purchase orders. Form libraries require a compatible XML editor, such as Microsoft InfoPath.
Picture Library	A place to upload and share pictures. This is different from the Asset Library template in that it provides functionality to display the pictures.
Slide Library	Create a slide library when you want to share slides from Microsoft PowerPoint or a compatible application. Slide libraries also provide special features for finding, managing, and reusing slides.
Wiki Page Library	An interconnected set of web pages that can be easily edited and that can contain text, images, and web parts.

■ **Note** Microsoft also provides several lists and libraries with predefined functionality—but only if you first create a site from a specific site template. For example, if you create a Group Work Site, you will see Circulations, Holidays, Time Card, Phone Call Memo, and Whereabouts lists created for you. One of the reasons these are not supplied as templates is because of the dependencies between the different lists in the template. A Visio Process Repository site is another site template that contains a unique document library with the following six content types attached: Basic Flowchart (Metric), Basic Flowchart (US units), BPMN Diagram (Metric), BPMN Diagram (US units), Cross Functional Flowchart (Metric), and Cross Functional Flowchart (US units).

Creating Lists

As mentioned earlier in the chapter, you can create lists either in the browser or by using SharePoint Designer. After a list is created, you can do the following:

- Add, modify, or delete columns

- Modify list- or item-level permissions

- Add, modify, or delete content types

- Create custom views of the list data

- Create a list template from the customized list

EXERCISE 3-1. CREATE A LIST IN THE BROWSER

In this exercise, you will create a new list in the browser, add site columns and content types, and then view the list in SharePoint Designer. Make sure you have a fresh, blank site to begin with. If you need to create a new site, make sure you create it by using the Blank Site template. If you plan on completing the other exercises in this chapter, don't delete the list, because you will build on it as you progress through the chapter.

Follow these steps to create a list in the browser:

1. Open your site in the browser.

2. Click Site Actions ➤ More Options.

3. When you are prompted by the Create dialog box, click the Custom List icon.

4. In the Name field to the right of the icons, type **Purchases** and then click the Create button.

5. Once your new list is created, you will be automatically redirected to the All Items View page of your list. You will also notice the List Tools menu appear on the

Ribbon. Click the List Settings button. In the Columns area, click the Create Column.

6. Complete the form with the following values:

   - Column Name: Purchase Date

   - Type: Date and Time

   - Require That This Column Has Information: No

   - Enforce Unique Values: No

   - Date and Time Format: Date Only

   - Default Value: Today's Date

   - Add to Default View: Selected

7. Click OK.

8. Create a number column with all of the defaults:

9. Column Name: Quantity

10. Type: Number

11. Create a currency column with the name **Price** and keep all of the defaults:

12. Column Name: Price

13. Type: Currency

14. Click the Purchases List link in the left navigation pane. You will now see the default All Items view with all of the columns you defined.

EXERCISE 3-2. CREATE A LIST BY USING SHAREPOINT DESIGNER 2010

Using the same blank site that you started with in the preceding exercise, you will create a Contacts list to keep track of your contacts:

1. Open your site in SharePoint Designer.

2. From the Ribbon's Site menu , choose SharePoint List ➤ Contacts.

3. Type **Contacts** in the Name field.

4. Type A list to store our contacts' addresses in the Description field.

5. Click OK. The List Properties pane appears.

Configuring List Properties

After you create your list, you can configure and customize it. From permission settings to versioning, lists and document libraries are very flexible containers for storing information. With SharePoint Designer 2010, it is even easier than before to rapidly develop business applications without code.

As soon as you create a list in SharePoint Designer, you are presented with its settings page. As you can see in Figure 3-1, the page is divided into the following sections, which you can customize:

- List Information
- Customization
- Settings
- Content Types
- Views
- Forms
- Workflows
- Custom Actions

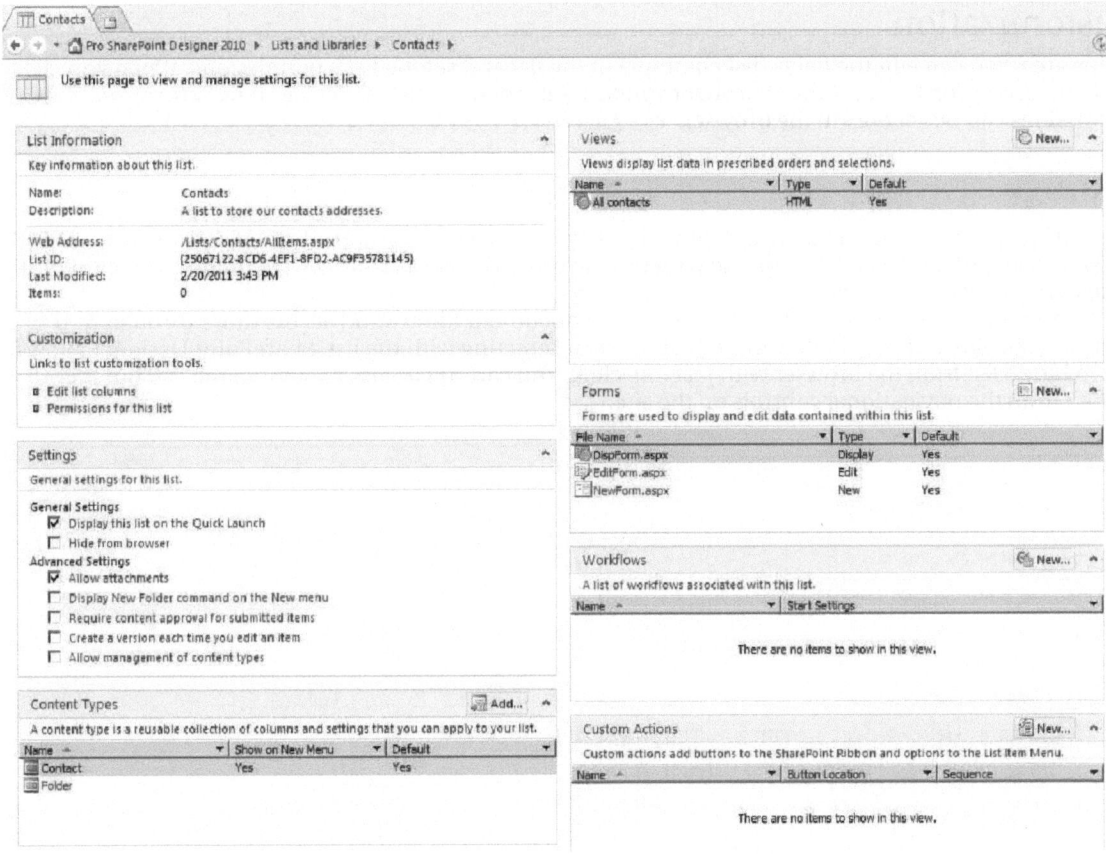

Figure 3-1. Contacts settings page in SharePoint Designer 2010

List Information:

The List Information area contains the name and description you gave the list when you created it. These can be edited by clicking the Name and Description links. This area also contains the following settings:

- *Web Address*: The site - relative URL of the default view (which is typically the All Items view)

- *List ID*: A number that uniquely identifies the list

- *Last Modified*: The date that an item or setting was last modified

- *Items*: A count of all items in the list, including folders

Customization

In this area, you can edit the fields (list columns) in the list and set the list's permissions. When you click the Permissions for This List link, a browser window will open to the List Permissions Settings window. Permissions can be set only in the browser.

Settings

The Settings pane, shown in Figure 3-2, provides a place to set general and advanced settings for the list. Although most of these settings can also be set in the browser, there is one setting unique to SharePoint Designer: Hide from Browser.

Suppose you want to store Form templates in a document library and access those through web parts on your site, but you don't want users directly interacting with the list. SharePoint Designer allows you to hide a list from the browser with just one click. You can still access content in the list, but it is hidden from the navigational controls on the site.

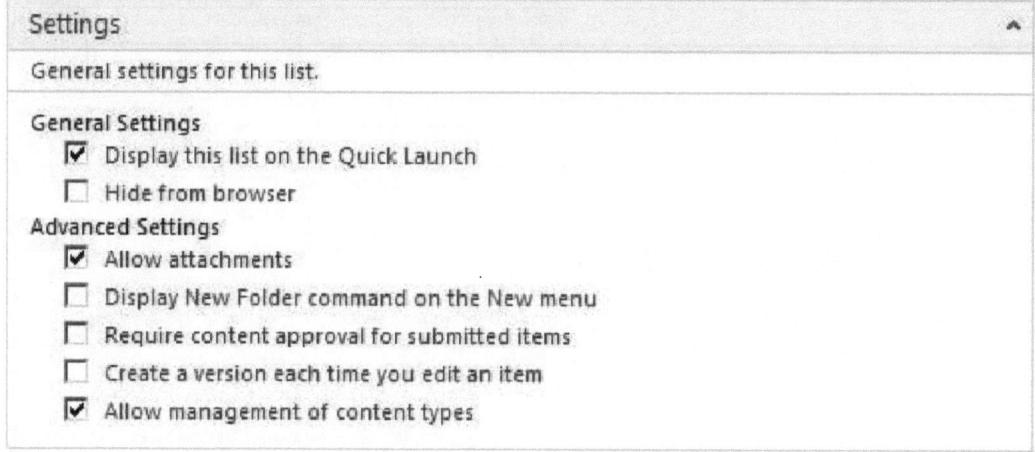

Figure 3-2. Settings pane.

EXERCISE 3-3. HIDE A LIST

In this Exercise, you will see the effects of the Hide From Browser setting.

1. If you are not at the Contacts list settings, click Lists and Libraries in the Navigation pane and then click the Contacts list.

2. Click the Preview in Browser button on the Ribbon menu.

3. The Contacts list opens in All Items view. Notice the Contacts list in the left navigational pane.

4. Copy the URL in the browser to your Clipboard by highlighting the URL and pressing Ctrl+C.

5. Go back to SharePoint Designer and in the Settings pane, deselect the check box labeled Display This List on the Quick Launch and select the Hide from Browser check box.

6. Click the Save icon on the menu or press Ctrl+S to save your changes.

7. Go back to your browser window and click the Home link in the breadcrumb.

8. Notice that the Contact list does not appear in the Quick Launch.

9. Click the All Site Content link. Notice that the Contacts list does not appear in the lists collection.

10. Paste the URL you copied into the browser's address bar and press Enter. The page still navigates to the All Items view of the Contacts list.

11. Go back to SharePoint Designer and deselect the Hide from Browser check box and select the Display This List on the Quick Launch check box. Press Ctrl+S to save your changes.

Browser Settings

Although you can set various advanced settings in SharePoint Designer, such as versioning or content type management, there are some that you can set only in the browser (for instance, audience targeting). SharePoint Designer provides an Administration Web Page button on its Ribbon menu to take you directly to the list's web settings page.

Managing Data

Because this chapter is about using SharePoint to store data, you will use the same scenario throughout this chapter, building on it as you move through the different features available to you in SharePoint to manage data through lists.

▪ **Scenario** The building maintenance department of the Black Box Company has decided to set up a SharePoint site to help manage the department's daily work orders and to provide the rest of the company information on the building maintenance services available to the company.

Using Content Types

Whenever you create a new Microsoft Word document, it contains various properties. These properties (for example, author, title, subject, keywords, and comments) are used to describe the Word document. These fields and more are present in every Word document. They are index fields that can be used for searching. In other words, they are the key fields to help locate the document during a search. Furthermore, these same fields also appear in every other Microsoft Office application document. Each application's document contains these same key fields. So, if you wanted to organize all of these documents that contain the same metadata but were each a different type of data, you could say that you have Word document types, Excel document types, and PowerPoint document types.

In SharePoint, a set of metadata about a piece of information is called a *content type*. Content types enable you to quickly replicate a set of site columns in a list or describe the properties of a document. By using content types, you can keep your data organized and structured. Content types, by definition, define the data they are associated with.

Microsoft defines a SharePoint content type as the attributes of a list item, a document, or a folder. Each content type can specify the following:

- Properties

- Metadata

- Workflows

- Information management policies

- Document templates

- Document conversions to make available

- Other custom features.

In our scenario, the Black Box Company's maintenance department wants to create a library to store all of their departmental documents. These include maintenance documents, repair instructions, schedules, and service contracts. Each type of document will contain the following common departmental key fields that will enable a search to find them faster:

- Author

- Publish Date

- Subject

- Category (for example, electrical or plumbing)

- Keywords

Even though all of the documents share these common fields, they also need other fields specific to their document type. For example, a repair instruction would need the name of the piece of equipment to repair, and a service contract would have a start and end date. How can we manage each type of information in the same library?

SharePoint allows us to create individual content types, which inherit from a parent content type. So in our example, you could create a Department Document content type that contained all of the specific site columns, and then create individual content types for each type of content stored in the library, that would inherit its base fields from the Department Document content type. So, if youwere to create a Service Contract content type, youwould set its parent as the Department Document and then add any additional site columns, such as Start Date and End Date, to make up a Service Contract content type.

Once you have created all of the content types, you can then assign them to a list. You can choose whether the content type will appear in the New menu in the list or library.

You can do many things with content types, including these:

- You can create special views of the list, filtering on content type.

- You can associate document templates with a content type.

- You can define a content type at a site collection level, and all subsites can inherit from that content type.

- You can set the content type as read-only so it can't be changed.

Adding and Modifying Content Types

SharePoint provides an easy way to add predefined content types to lists by including a Content Type Picker. To use the quick Content Type Picker, click the Add button on the Content Types pane in the settings window.

EXERCISE 3-4. CREATE NEW SITE COLUMNS.

For this exercise, you need to create a department list. To begin, you will create new departmental site columns and a content type called Department. For the Department content type, you want the following fields:

- Department Name

- Department Location

- Manager Name and Contact Information

- Mail Routing Code

- Comments

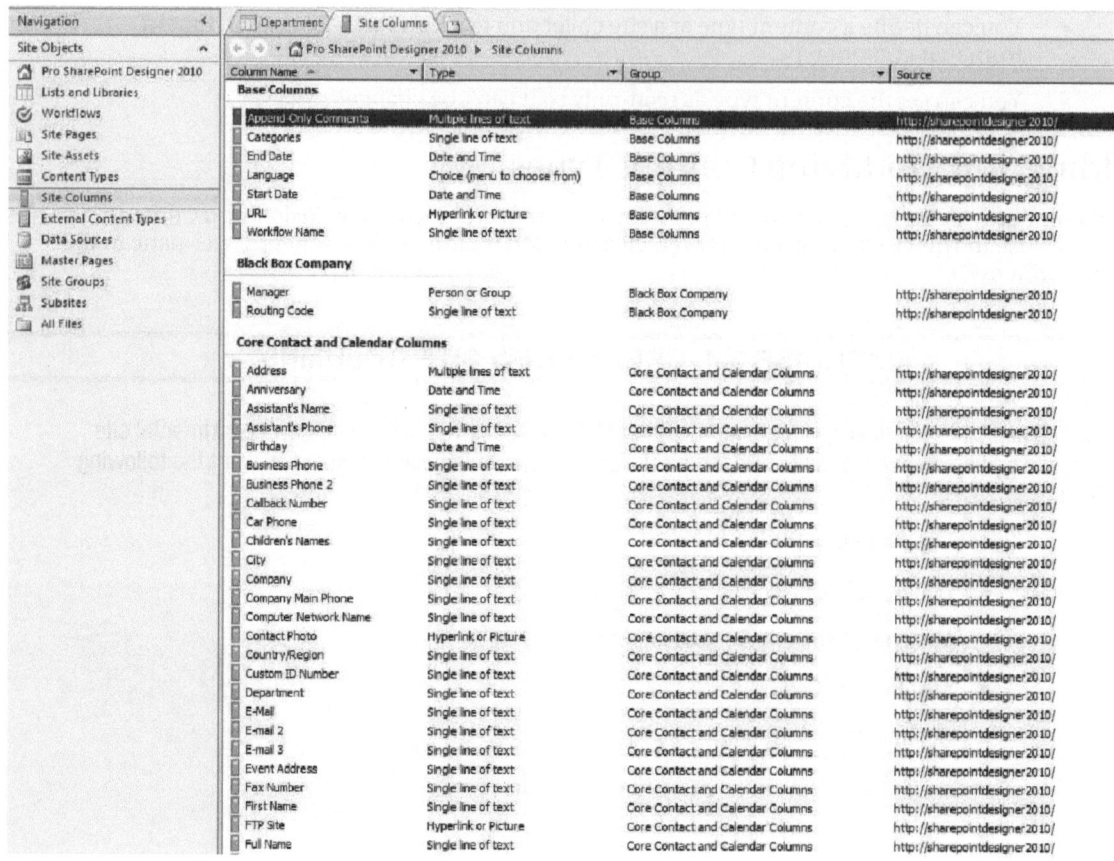

Figure 3-3. Site columns.

You can use some existing site columns, but there isn't an existing column for the mail routing code or manager name. So you will create new site columns to be used in the Department content type:

In the Navigation pane, click Site Columns.

1. Click New Column and then select Single Line of Text from the drop-down menu. The Create a Site Column dialog box opens, as shown in Figure 3-4.

2. Type **RoutingCode** (no space between words) in the Name field.

3. Type **The Black Box Company mail routing code.** in the Description box.

4. Because this is the first site column you have created, you will create a new site column group. Click the New Group radio button and then type Black Box Company in the text box.

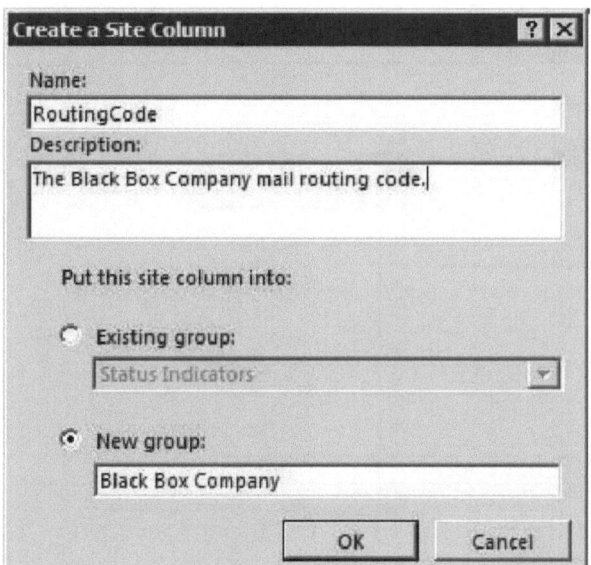

Figure 3-4. *Create a Site Column dialog box*

5. Click OK to save your new site column.

6. You should now see the new site column created with its name highlighted. If the name is not highlighted, click once on the name, and then click Rename from the Ribbon menu or press F2.

7. Add the space now between the words *Routing* and *Code* for display purposes.

8. Click anywhere outside the Column Name field to quit editing.

9. Click the Push Changes to List button on the Ribbon menu.

10. Click New Column and pick Person or Group.

11. Type **Manager** for the name.

12. Type **Black Box Co. Department Manager** in the Description box.

13. Because you have already created the new group, select Black Box Company from the Existing Group drop-down list.

14. Click OK to save.

15. Now that you have the Manager column created, you need to configure it to provide the functionality you need. Make sure the Manager field is selected and then press the Column Settings button on the Ribbon menu. The Column Editor dialog box opens, as shown in Figure 3-5.

16. Because you want this field to contain only manager contact information, change the Allow Selection Of option to People Only.

17. In the Choose From section, click All Users.

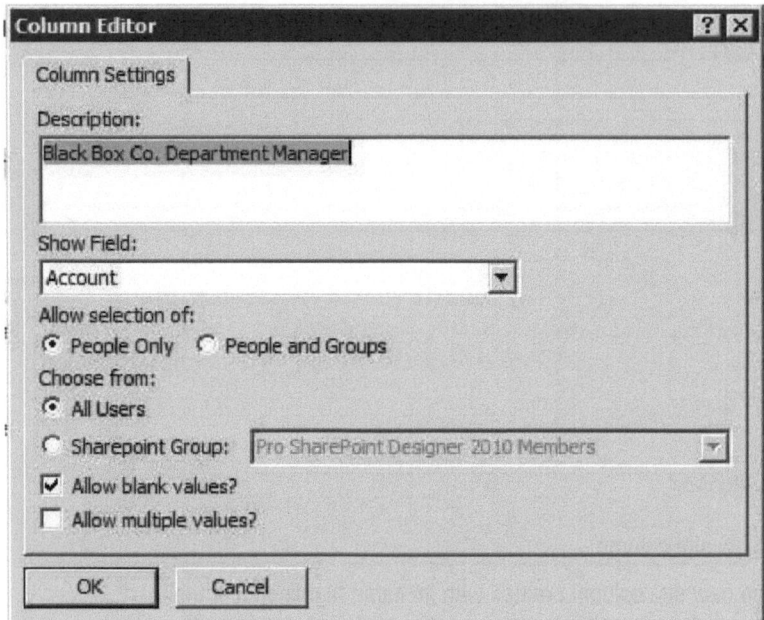

Figure 3-5. Column Editor dialog box

18. You want to allow blank values just in case you don't know who the manager is when you are setting up a new department, so select the Allow Blank Values check box.

19. Click OK to save.

20. Click the button labeled Push Changes to List to save your new site column.

Now that you have created the site column, you will create the new content type.

EXERCISE 3-5. CREATE THE NEW CONTENT TYPE

In this exercise, you will create a new department Content Type for the Black Box Company.

1. In the Navigation pane, click Content Types.

2. Click Content Type on the New section of the Ribbon Menu.

3. In the Create a Content Type dialog box that opens, type Department in the Name field.

4. Type Black Box Company department content type. in the Description box.

5. The parent content type is important because all content types inherit columns from their parents. Because this is a custom list, choose List Content Types from the first drop-down list, labeled Select Parent Content Type From. Choose the Item option from the second drop-down list, labeled Select Parent Content Type.

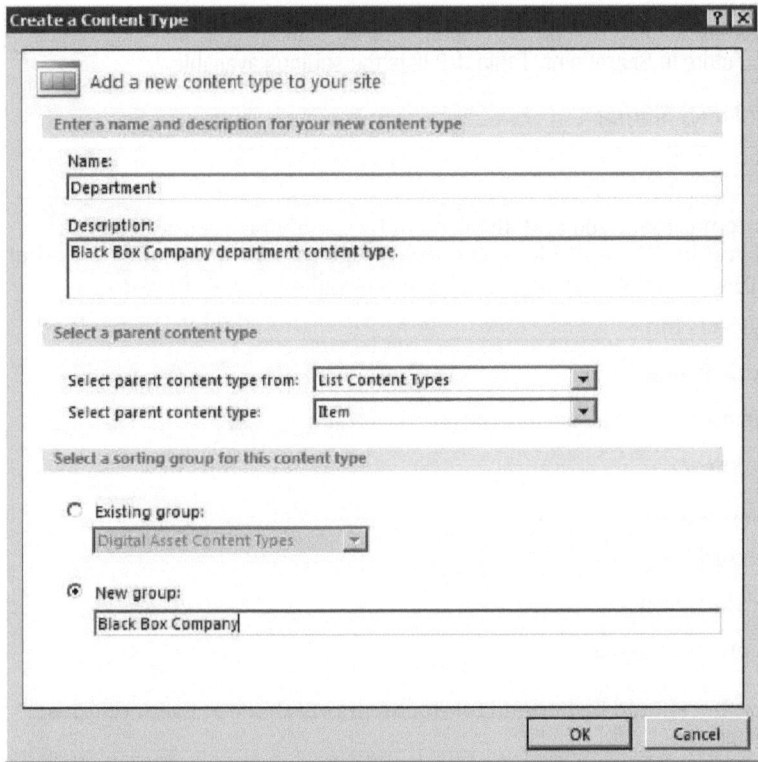

Figure 3-6. Create a Content Type dialog box

6. Because you are creating your own custom content types, you want to organize them into your own group. Click the New Group radio button and type **Black Box Company** in the box provided.

7. Press OK to save.

8. You should now see your content type under the Black Box group. Click the Department content type.

9. In the Customization pane, click Edit content type columns.

SharePoint Designer can't configure everything about a content type. Because of the architecture of SharePoint, some features are available only in the browser. If you select the Administration Web Page button on the Ribbon menu, you will see other features that are available to content types such as workflow settings and information management policy settings.

By being able to associate a workflow with a content type, you can ensure that business processes are initiated every time an item or document of that particular type is created. For example, you could require approval every time a new department is created. Associating an approval workflow with this content type would ensure that the requirement is met.

Other options available in the browser are the Information management policy settings. These settings can help you manage the information you store in SharePoint. Table 3-3 lists the settings available.

Table 3-3. Information Management Policy Settings

Policy	Description
Retention	Schedules how content is managed and disposed of by specifying a sequence of retention stages. If you specify multiple stages, each stage will occur one after the other in the order they appear on the settings page. Options available are as follows: • Move to recycle bin • Permanently delete • Transfer to another location • Start a workflow • Skip to next stage • Declare record • Delete previous drafts • Delete all previous versions
Auditing	Specifies the events that should be audited for documents and items. Event options include the following: • Opening or downloading documents, viewing items in lists, or viewing item properties • Editing items • Checking out or checking in items • Moving or copying items to another location in the site • Deleting or restoring items
Barcodes	Assigns a barcode to each document or item.

Policy	Description
Labels	Specifies a label that will be added to a document to ensure that important information about the document is included when it is printed. Document properties can be used in the label.

Now that you have created the content type, you need to add the columns that will make up the content type. You will use existing site columns and the ones you just created.

EXERCISE 3-6. ADD SITE COLUMNS TO THE CONTENT TYPE.

In this exercise, you will add Site Columns to the Department Content Type that you created previously.

1. In the Navigation pane, click Content Types.

2. Click the Department content type under the Black Box Company group heading.

3. In the Customization pane, click Edit Content Type Columns. You will use the Title field as the Department name and change the Display name later.

4. From the Ribbon menu, click Add Existing Site Column. The Site Columns Picker opens, as shown in Figure 3-7.

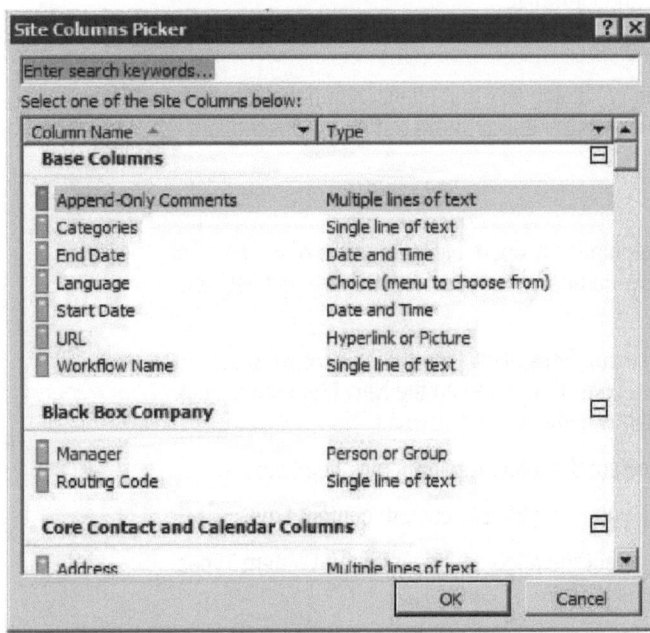

Figure 3-7. Sites Column Picker.

5. For this content type, you will use some fields from the Core Contact and Calendar Columns group. Click Location under the Core Contact and Calendar Columns section and then click OK to add the Location column.

6. For the manager's name, you will use your Manager site column. Find the Manager column under the Black Box Co. group, select the column, and click OK.

7. Click Add Existing Site Column.

8. Do the same thing with the Routing Code column.

9. For the comments section, use the Comments field from the Core Document columns. Hint: Type **Comments** in the search box to help you find the correct one.

10. After you have added all the columns to the content type, click the Push Changes to Sites and Lists button.

Now that you have your content type created, it is time to create the Department list.

EXERCISE 3-7. CREATE A CUSTOM LIST.

For this exercise, you will create a new Department list based on the Department Content Type that you created.

1. In the Navigation pane, click Lists and Libraries.

2. Click Custom List from the Ribbon menu.

3. In the "Create list or document library" dialog box that opens, name the list **Department** and type **Black Box Company department list** in the Description box.

4. Click OK to save.

5. If the settings window does not automatically open, click the name of the new list to open it. After the settings window comes up for your new Department list, you can begin to configure it.

6. You don't want folders in the list, so suppress displaying the new folder in the menu. Make sure the Display New Folder Command on the New Menu check box is deselected in the Advanced Settings section.

7. Under Advanced Settings, also deselect the Allow Attachments check box.

8. Now that you have created the list, you can add your custom content type.

9. In the Advanced Settings section, select the Allow Management of Content Types check box.

10. In the Content Types pane of the settings window, click the Add button.

11. Select Department and then press OK to add the Department content type to the list.

12. Now you have three content types in this list. You need only one. Highlight the Folder content type and click the Delete button on the Ribbon menu. Highlight the Item content type and click the Delete button again. (Remember, your Department content type is based on the Item content type.)

13. Press Ctrl+S to save your changes.

14. You have one more minor change to the list columns. Remember that you used the Title field as the Department name in your Department site collection. Now that you have created a list, you can modify the column name to make it more descriptive.

15. In the Customization pane, click the Edit List Columns link.

16. Click the Title column name. It should go into Edit mode.

17. Type **Department Name** in the Column Name field..

18. Click outside the field to exit Edit mode.

19. Edit the following column descriptions by highlighting the field name and clicking the Column Settings button.

Column Name	Description
Location	Example: 4th floor SW
Manager	Please select the manager for this department.
Routing Code	Example: 4-125
Comments	[Make the description blank]

20. Press Ctrl+S to save your changes. Your Department list is now ready to use.

■ **Note** Every list or document library has key identity and administrative fields that cannot be removed, such as Title, ID, Created By, and Modified By. In a document library, the Name field is created and refers to the name of the file. The Title field is special in that it contains a drop-down context menu that you can use to work with individual list items.

Browse to your site and look at the Department list. Open a New Item form and notice the fields and their descriptions, as shown in Figure 3-8. Go ahead and create a department list item and save it.

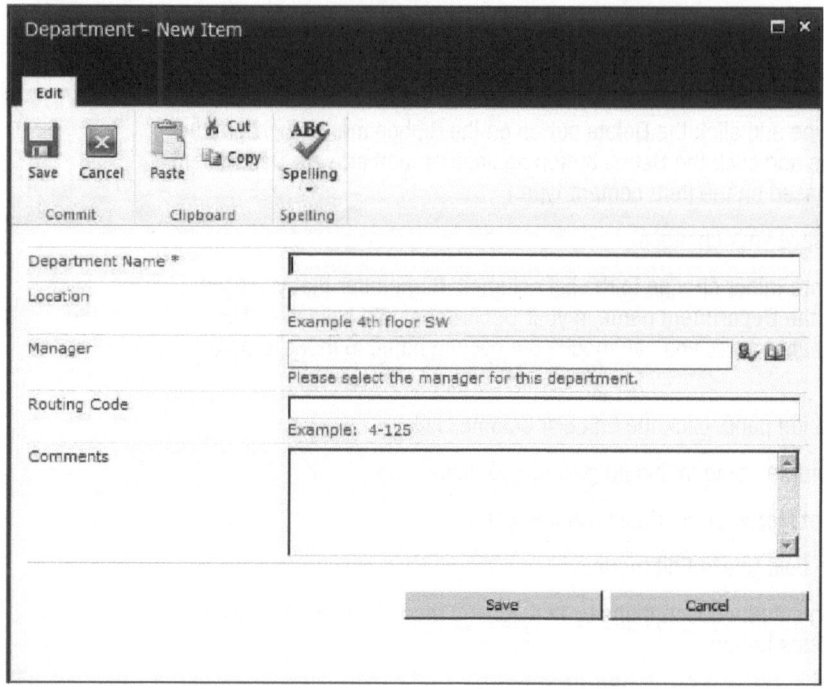

Figure 3-8. New Item form.

Using Special Site Columns

SharePoint provides a couple of Site Column types that have special functionality: the calculated column and the lookup column.

Calculated Columns

The *calculated column* is able to display data that is calculated from data already included in the list. It uses formulas similar to Excel and Access. Calculated columns can contain functions, column references, operators, and constants, as well as IF statements.

EXERCISE 3-8. CREATE A CALCULATED COLUMN

In this exercise, you will create a Calculated Column in the Purchases list to see how you can create dynamic data in your lists.

1. In SharePoint Designer, click Lists and Libraries in the Navigation pane.

2. Click the Purchases option.

3. In the Customization pane, click Edit List Columns.

4. On the Ribbon menu, make sure the Add to Default View button is highlighted.

5. You now want to create a currency column that will automatically calculate the total spent. Add a new Calculated column by clicking the Add New Column button and selecting Calculated (Calculation Based on Other Columns).

6. In the Column Editor that pops up, find the Quantity column name and select it.

7. Click the Add to Formula button.

8. In the Formula field, click after the field name and type *.

9. Click the Price column and click Add to Formula. Your formula should look like Figure 3-9.

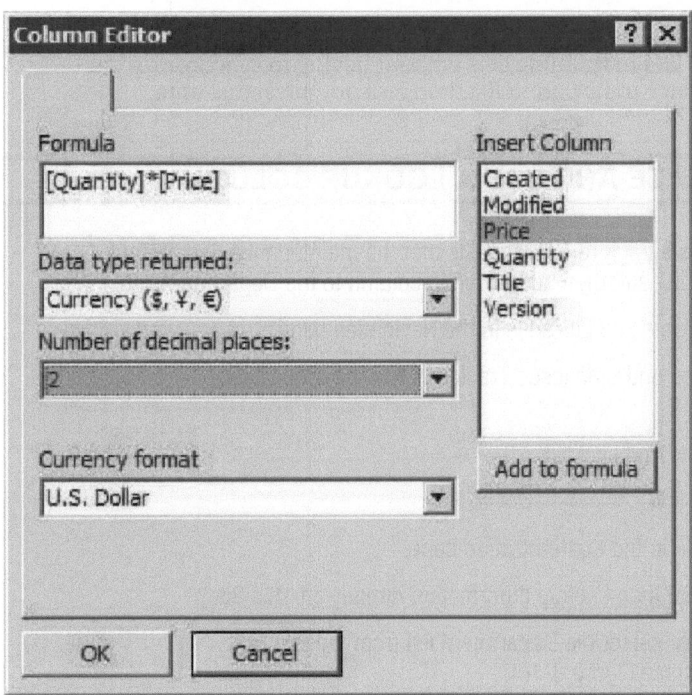

Figure 3-9. Calculated column

10. Change the Data Type Returned drop-down list to Currency.

11. Change the Number of Decimal Places drop-down list to 2.

12. Set the Currency Format drop-down list to U.S. Dollar.

13. Click the OK button.

14. Click the Column Name and change it to **Total Price.**

15. Press Ctrl+S to save your changes.

16. Close the list settings page and click the Preview in Browser button.

17. Click the Purchases link on the left Navigation and add a new purchase.

18. After you have added a few purchases, look at the All Items view of your Purchases list. Notice that the total has been calculated automatically.

19. Now, edit one of the list items. Change the price to something different.

20. Click Save. The total price for that item updates..

Lookup Columns

A *lookup column* is a Choice Column type that gets its values from another list. This makes lists more relational and allows you to use the same data in multiple lists without having to synchronize data manually. A lookup column stores a reference to its parent list item and not the actual data.

EXERCISE 3-9. CREATE AND USE A LOOKUP COLUMN

In this exercise, you will create a list that will track repair requests that the maintenance department receives. You will use the standard Issues list and then add a lookup column to the Department list.

1. In SharePoint Designer, click Lists and Libraries in the Navigation pane.

2. Click the SharePoint List button and then Issue Tracking from the drop-down menu.

3. Name the list **Repair Requests** and click OK.

4. Click the Repair Requests list link.

5. Click the Edit List Columns link in the Customization pane.

6. Click Add New Site Column and then Lookup (Information Already on This Site).

7. When the Column Editor opens, select the Department list from the List or Document Library drop-down (see Figure 3-10).

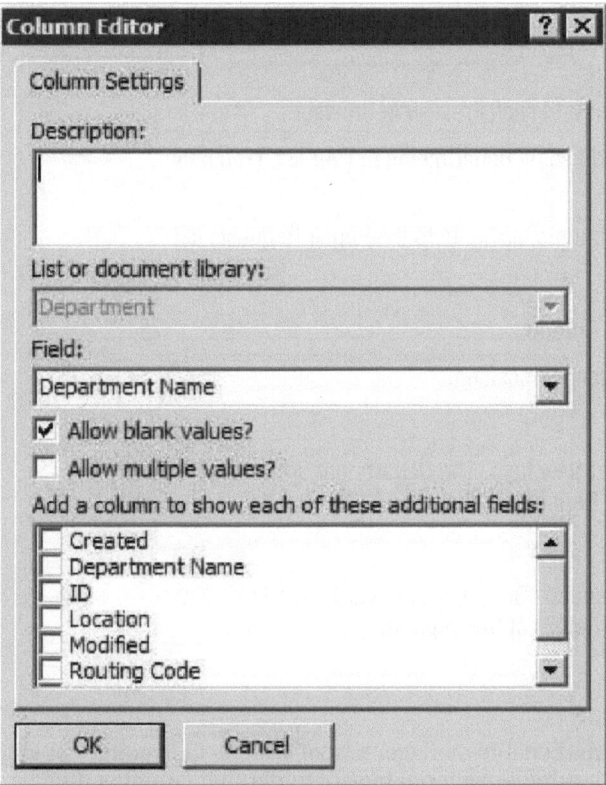

Figure 3-10. Column Editor

8. Select Department Name from the Field drop-down list..

9. Click OK.

10. Change the name to Department.

11. Click the Category.

12. Make the choices the following values:

    (1) General

    (2) Electrical

    (3) Plumbing

    (4) Maintenance

    (5) Preventive

13. Make (1) General the default.

14. Click OK.

15. Press Ctrl+S to save your changes.

16. Close the Repair Requests edit window and click Preview in Browser.

17. Navigate to the Department list and add some departments to your list. (You only need the Department name.)

18. Once you have finished adding departments, navigate to the Repair Requests list.

19. Click the List Settings menu item.

20. In the Columns section, click Column Ordering.

21. Move the Department column to the second position.

22. Click OK to save your changes.

23. Go back to view your list and click Add New Item. The Department drop-down list is populated with the values from the Department list.

24. Add a repair request and click Save.

25. Look at the view of the item you just added. The Department is a hyperlink. Click the Department link. You can see the details of the Department..

Using Document Sets

Document sets are new in SharePoint Server 2010 and enable management of a single deliverable, which can include multiple documents or files. A document set is a special type of folder that contains the unique attributes of the document set and the attributes and behavior of folders and documents. It has its own specific object model elements, metadata, and user interface. A common scenario for a document set would be a request for proposal (RFP) or a real estate contract.

An organization could create a special Document Set content type for each type of project they create. That content type would then define the approved content types for the project, common attributes, default items, workflows, information management policies, and so forth.

The following are some common considerations when deciding whether to use document sets:

- There is no limit on the number of documents that can exist in a document set. Knowing that, if you use the Send To feature with a Document Set, the sum for all documents in a document set cannot be larger than 50 MB. Even though there are no limits, page load times are greatly affected at a number 5,000 and over. Great care is needed to design sites in full knowledge of these limitations.

- There is no limit on the number of document sets that can exist in a document library, but the display of document sets is limited by the display threshold of about 5,000 items.

- If you use routing, document sets that are sent to a content organizer will remain in a drop-off library and be moved to the appropriate location by the content organizer's processing timer job.

To use document sets, you must have the Document Set feature activated. The Document Set feature is a site collection feature.

■ **Note** To enable the Document Set feature, go to the settings page and under Site Collection Administration, click Site Collection Features. Once the features page opens, find the Document Sets feature and click Activate.

Working with Views

Views are ways to look at the data stored in a list. When you create a list, a default view called All Items is created. This enables you to see all the items in your list. You may want to create different views of your data depending on your use for it or your audience.

Although you can create different public views in the browser, SharePoint Designer gives you more control over creating views of your SharePoint list data. In this section, you will learn about creating, sorting, filtering, and grouping data.

Creating Views

You can see the views that a list has by looking at its settings page in the Views pane. All lists come with a default view called All Items. You can create your own views by clicking the New button. A dialog box then appears, prompting you for the name of the view and asking whether you want it to become the default view. After naming your view, click the filename of the newly created view to customize the view in the View Editor.

When you are in the View Editor, you can add or remove columns from your view by selecting Add/Remove Columns from the Ribbon menu. In the Displayed Fields dialog box that opens, you can select the columns to display, as shown in Figure 3-11. The view in the Page Editor will then reflect your changes. You can also set limits on the number of rows displayed, in case your list is long.

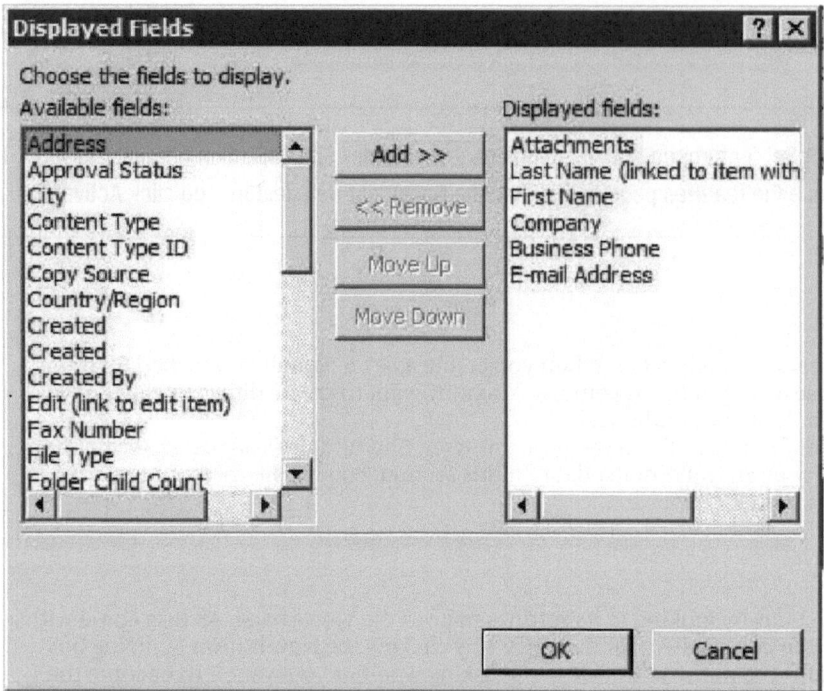

Figure 3-11. Adding and removing display fields

Sorting, Grouping, and Filtering

You can set the order that a list is displayed in your view by clicking the Sort & Group button on the Ribbon menu to access the Sort and Group dialog box, shown in Figure 3-12. Here you can sort a list based on any field that is available and can sort in ascending or descending order. You can also specify that you want the data displayed in groupings based on the sort order.

To filter your data, click the Filter button on the Ribbon menu. A dialog box assists you in creating filters. You can select a field to filter on and the criteria. You can combine fields by using And and Or.

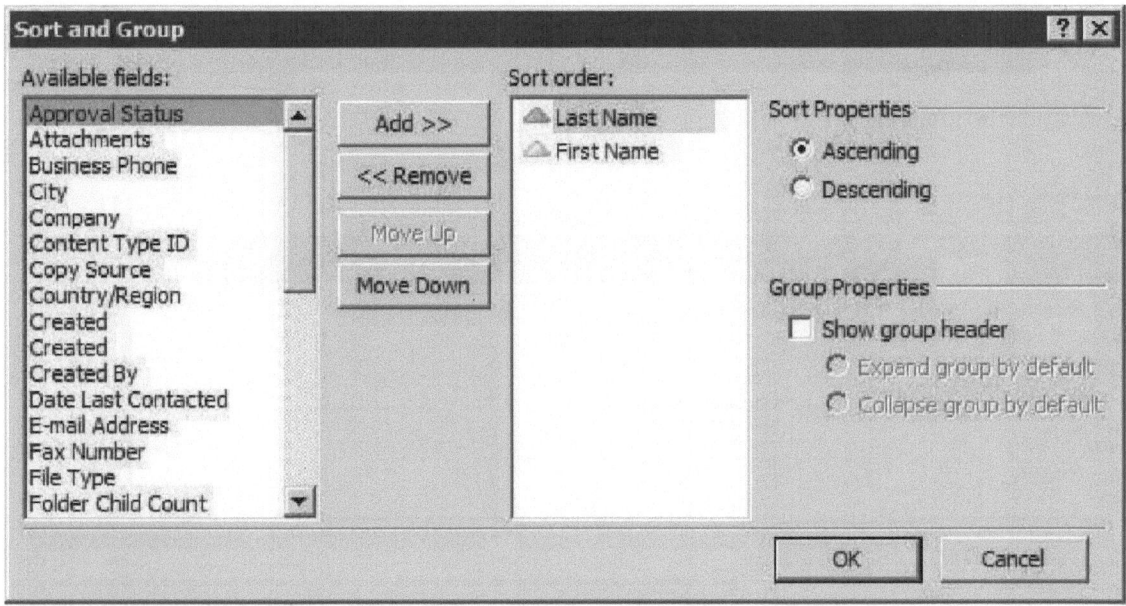

Figure 3-12. Sorting and grouping

EXERCISE 3-10. CREATE A CUSTOM VIEW

In this exercise, you will create a Custom View of the Purchases list called, Purchases by Month.

1. In SharePoint Designer, click the Purchases List in the Navigation pane.

2. In the settings page, find the Views pane and click New.

3. Name the view Purchases by Month.

4. Click the name of your newly created view to show the ASPX page in the View Editor.

5. If you are not in Design view, click Design View so you can see the changes as you go.

6. Click the main web part area so that the List View Tools menu becomes active.

7. Click the Add/Remove Columns button.

8. Make sure that the following fields are selected to display in the following order:

   • Title

   • Purchase Date

- Quantity
- Price
- Total Price

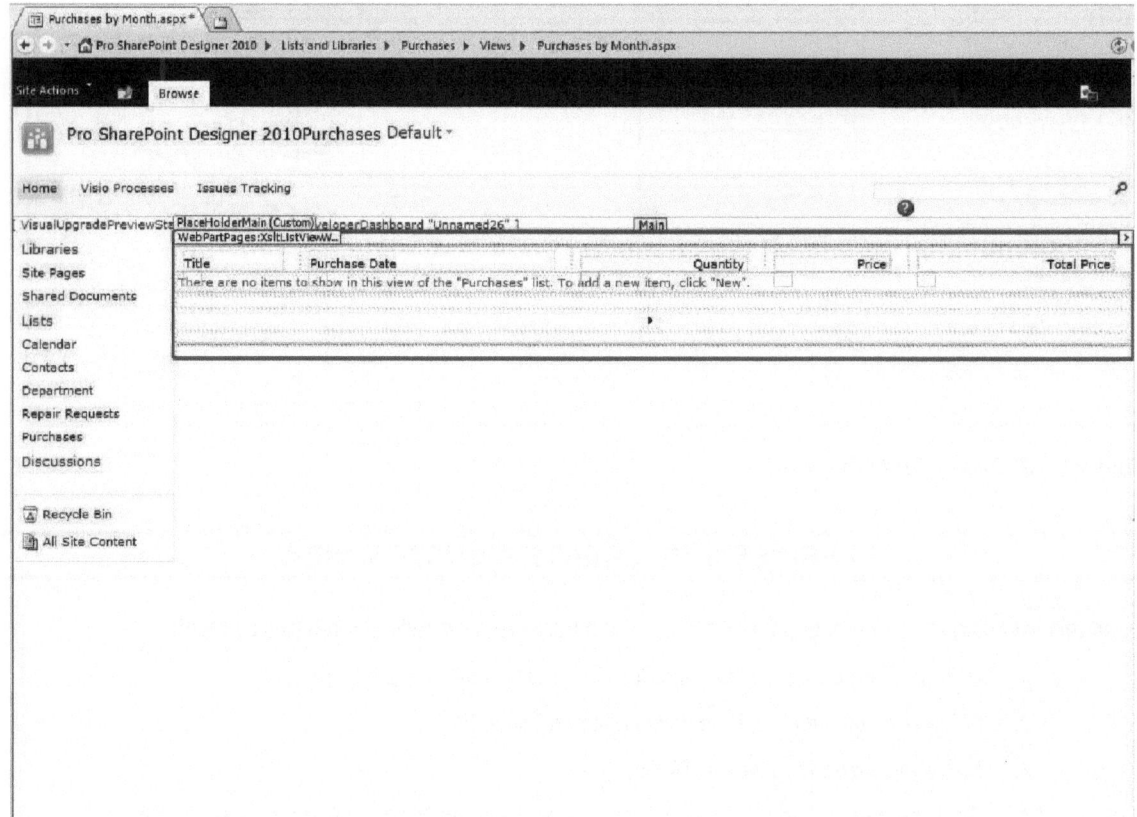

Figure 3-13. Creating a custom view

9. Click OK.

10. Click Sort & Group.

11. Select Purchase Date to Sort By.

12. Select Ascending.

13. Click Show Group Header and Expand Group by Default.

14. Click OK.

15. Press Ctrl+S to save your changes.

16. Open the browser and navigate to the purchases list.

17. Add some data, varying the month of purchase. Table 3-4 provides an example of some data.

Table 3-4. Sample data for the view

Title	Purchase Date	Quantity	Price
Garden Hose	1/23/2011	2	$14.56
Spray Nozzle	2/1/2010	5	$5.50
Fertilizer	4/13/2010	50	$1.26
Trash Liners	3/14/2011	6	$45.00
Paint	5/1/2010	3	$9.00
Cleaner	6/1/2011	6	$9.00
Mops	7/1/2010	2	$9.00
Paper	8/1/2010	7	$8.00
Light bulbs	9/1/2010	8	$7.00
Paper Towels	10/1/2011	59	$6.00
Glue	12/1/2010	2	$5.00
Markers	11/1/2010	7	$3.00
Paint	2/1/2011	9	$2.00
Spray Nozzle	4/1/2010	3	$3.00
Hose	6/1/2010	4	$3.00
Sponges	8/1/2011	5	$5.50
Wash Cloths	3/1/2010	2	$3.00

18. In the Ribbon menu, switch to the Purchases by Month view. Notice that the display is grouped by purchase date but not month.

19. You need to calculate the month so you can group only based on the month. Close the browser and go back to SharePoint Designer.

20. Click the Purchases list and then click Edit List Columns in the Customization pane.

21. You are going to create a new calculated field so you can sort on it. Click the Add New Column item on the Ribbon and then select Calculated. When the Column Editor dialog box opens, add the formula shown in Figure 3-14. In the Data Type Returned drop-down list, make sure you select Single Line of Text. Then click OK to close the dialog box.

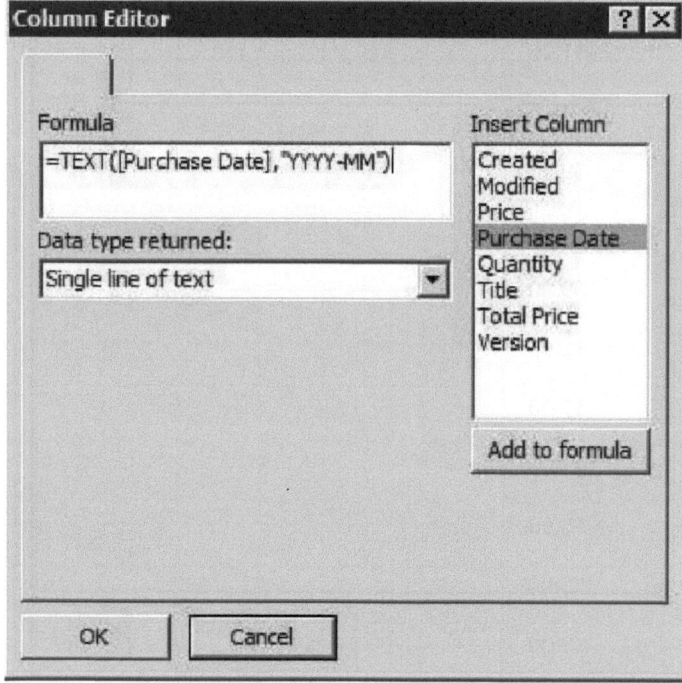

Figure 3-14. Adding a formula in the Column Editor

22. Click the name of the field you just created (usually NewColumn1). It should go into renaming mode. If not, right-click the filename and select Rename from the context menu. Name the field **PurchaseYearMonth**.

23. Press Ctrl+S to save the new column to the List.

24. In the breadcrumb navigation, click Purchases, as shown in Figure 3-15 to get back to the list settings screen. Then click the Purchases By Month View to open the View Editor.

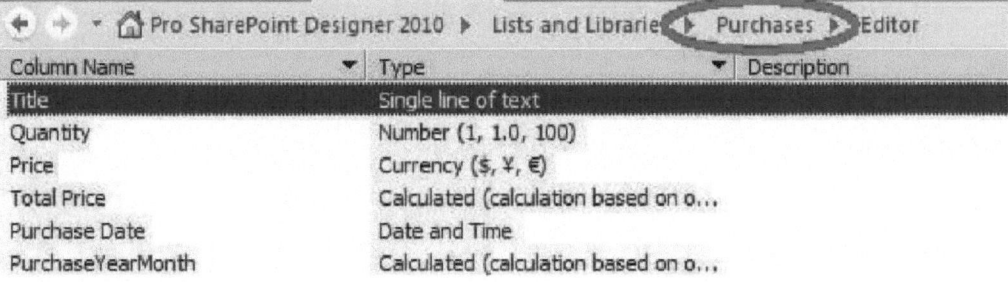

Figure 3-15. Breadcrumb navigation

25. After the View Editor opens, select Sort & Group from the Ribbon menu.

26. Remove the Purchase Date sorting choice.

27. Add PurchaseYearMonth as the Sorting field and then choose Ascending, Show Group Header, and Expand Group by Default, as shown in Figure 3-16.

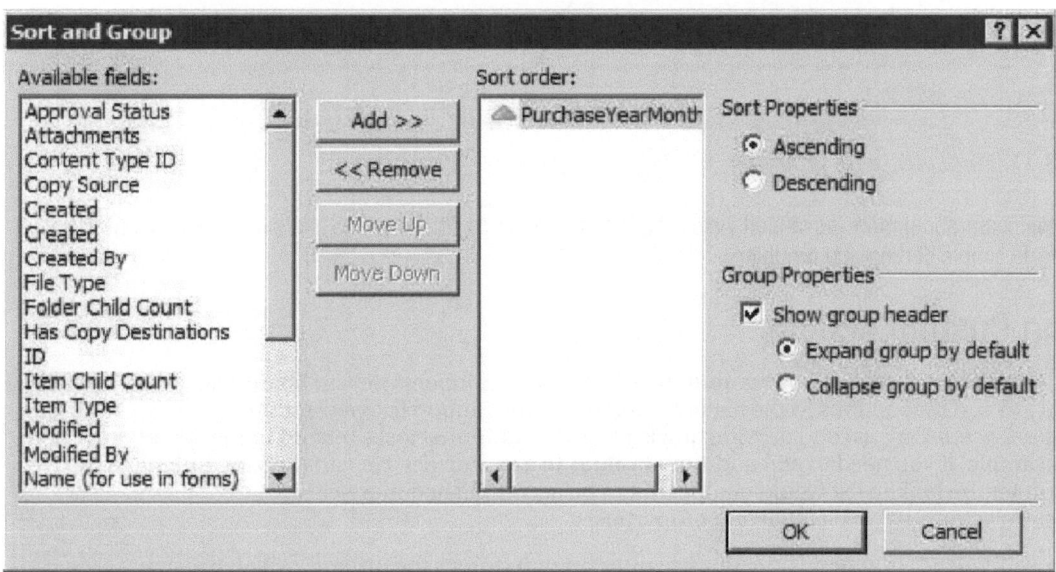

Figure 3-16. Grouping by PurchaseYearMonth

28. Click OK to save your grouping settings and then press Ctrl+S to save the changes to the view.

29. Go back to the browser and navigate to the Purchases by Month view, as shown in Figure 3-17. If you need to press F5 to refresh the page, do so. Notice how the purchases are grouped.

☐	◍	Title	Purchase Date	Quantity	Price	Total Price	PurchaseYearM
⊟ PurchaseYearMonth : 2010-01 (1)							
		Garden Hose	1/23/2010	2	$14.56	$29.12	2010-01
⊟ PurchaseYearMonth : 2010-02 (2)							
		Spray Nozzel	2/1/2010	5	$5.50	$27.50	2010-02
		Paint	2/1/2010	9	$2.00	$18.00	2010-02
⊟ PurchaseYearMonth : 2010-03 (2)							
		Trash Liners	3/14/2010	6	$45.00	$270.00	2010-03
		Wash Cloths	3/1/2010	2	$3.00	$6.00	2010-03
⊟ PurchaseYearMonth : 2010-04 (2)							
		Fertilizer	4/13/2010	50	$1.26	$63.00	2010-04
		Spray Nozzel	4/1/2010	3	$3.00	$9.00	2010-04
⊟ PurchaseYearMonth : 2010-05 (1)							
		Paint	5/1/2010	3	$9.00	$27.00	2010-05
⊟ PurchaseYearMonth : 2010-06 (2)							
		Cleaner	6/1/2010	6	$9.00	$54.00	2010-06
		Hose	6/1/2010	4	$3.00	$12.00	2010-06
⊟ PurchaseYearMonth : 2010-07 (1)							
		Mone	7/1/2010	2	$9.00	$18.00	2010-07

Figure 3-17. Final view with grouping

You will learn about more-advanced view creation in Chapter 5. This exercise is a simple one meant to illustrate simple sorting and grouping.

Adding Custom Actions

The ability to add custom actions without the need for a developer is new in SharePoint 2010. It refers to the ability to add new actions to the list item menu and the Ribbon list view menu.

Custom actions are used to provide quick access to additional tasks related to the list it is attached to. For example, if you need to add additional values to a lookup list, a custom action linking to the New Item form for the lookup list would enable that to be accomplished more easily.

Custom actions have the following properties:

- *Sequence number*: The sequence number determines the order in which the new custom action appears. Every menu item has a sequence number, and with a little experimentation, you will be able to determine what value to assign to your new custom action.

- *Rights mask*: You can use the empty mask or you can specify a rights mask that defines which users can see the custom action. The rights mask can contain any of the special base permissions from the SPBasePermission member names found at http://msdn.microsoft.com/en-us/library/microsoft.sharepoint.spbasepermissions.aspx.

EXERCISE 3-11. CREATE A CUSTOM ACTION

In this exercise, you will create a Custom Action on the ribbon menu of a New Form dialog.

1. Click Lists and Libraries in the Navigation pane.

2. Click the Repair Requests list created in Exercise 3-9, "Create and Use a Lookup Column."

3. In the settings page, click inside the Custom Actions area.

4. On the Ribbon menu, choose Custom Action -> New Form Ribbon.

5. In the Create Custom Action dialog box that opens, type **New Department** in the Name field.

6. In the area labeled Select the Type of Action, click the Navigate to URL radio button.

7. Click the Browse button and then in the Insert Hyperlink dialog box, browse to the NewForm.aspx page in the Department list, as shown in Figure 3-18.

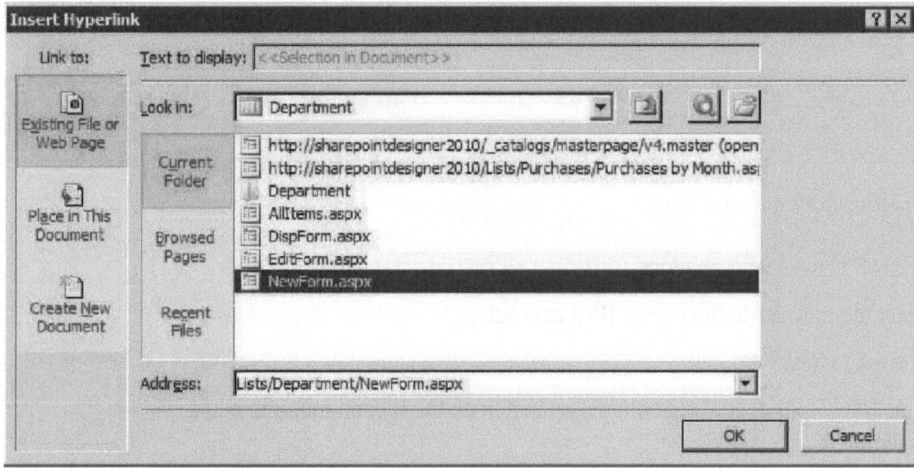

Figure 3-18. Selecting a new form in the Department list

8. In the Advanced Custom Action Options section of the Create Custom Action dialog box, enter the following paths for the icon, as shown in Figure 3-19:

- For the 16×16 image: `_layouts/images/sharepointdesigner16.png`
- For the 32×32 image: `_layouts/images/sharepointdesigner32.png`

9. In the Rights Mask text box, type **EmptyMask**.

10. In Sequence Number text box, type **150**.

11. Click OK.

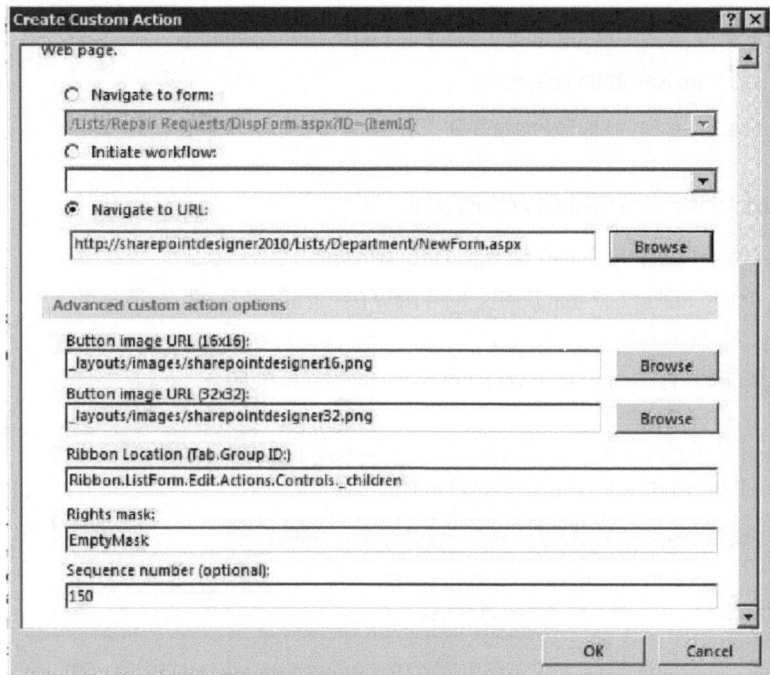

Figure 3-19. Create Custom Action dialog box

12. Press Ctrl+S to save your changes.

13. Now open the browser to the Repair Requests list.

14. Click the +Add New Item link.

15. When the New Form opens, notice the new button on the Ribbon menu to add a new department.

16. Click the New Department button.

17. The Add New Department form opens. Create a new department and save.

18. Click the +Add New Item link in the Repair Requests list again.

19. When the Add New form opens, notice that the department that you just created is now available in the drop-down list on the form.

Creating Your Own Template

SharePoint provides an easy way to replicate a customized list or library. Once you have finished customizing your list, you can save it as a *template* to use again on your site or on other sites.

You save the list as a template in the browser. SharePoint Designer provides a quick link on the Ribbon menu to the Save as Template page in the browser. Once you open the page, give your list template a filename, a descriptive template name, and a description. It is good practice to add detail in the Description field indicating the function of the list and any unique features. That way, when you create new lists in the future, you won't mistakenly duplicate your efforts.

You can also choose to include content in your template. This is helpful if you want to seed the list with sample values, form templates , or lookup values. It is important to remember that item security is not maintained in the template, so if you have any private information in the list, saving it as a template is not recommended. Once saved, the list template is a file stored in the list template gallery, accessed from Site Settings. From there, you can export the template to use on other sites.

EXERCISE 3-12. SAVE A LIST AS A TEMPLATE

In this exercise, you will save the Purchases list you have been working on as a template so you can duplicate it on other sites.

1. Open the Purchases list in SharePoint Designer by clicking the list name in the Navigation pane.

2. Click the Save as Template button. The browser window opens to the Save as Template page.

3. Fill in the form with the following values:

   - File Name: Purchases

   - Template Name: Purchases List

   - Template description: This list will track purchases made. It contains calculated columns for totals, month, and year. It also includes a custom view that groups purchases by year and month.

4. Select the Include Content option for the purposes of this exercise.

5. Click OK to save.

6. The Success dialog box displays, with a link to the list template gallery. Click the link to see the new template in the gallery.

7. Now, click Lists in the Quick Launch in the browser.

8. Click Create.

9. Select the filter by List and then select Blank & Custom.

10. Select the Purchases List and name it **New Purchases**.

11. Click Create. When the list creation is finished, you will be brought to the All Items view with all of the content displayed.

12. Change the view to Purchases by Month. Notice how the views and content came over from the original list.

13. Because this is just an example, you can delete this new list by refreshing your display in SharePoint Designer, highlighting the new list, and clicking the Delete button on the Ribbon menu.

Summary

This chapter explained the differences between a list and a library. The chapter used a scenario to illustrate key concepts of using these lists and libraries to store data in SharePoint. Some of the key points to remember are as follows:

- SharePoint stores data in a list or library.

- Metadata is data that describes other data.

- Site columns are specific types of data, such as date, number, or text.

- Content types are made up of site columns, workflows, document templates, and information management policies.

- More than one content type can be associated with a list or library.

- In SharePoint Designer, you can now add custom actions to the list item and Ribbon menu.

- Once you are finished creating a customized list, you can save it as a template, including its content.

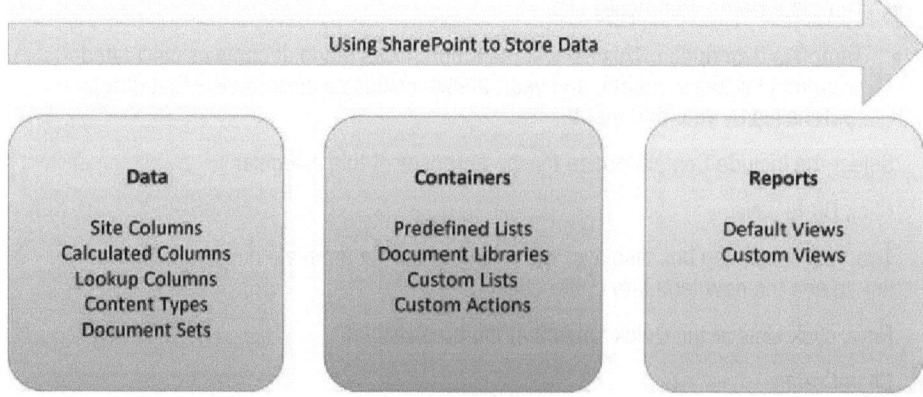

CHAPTER 4

Managing Web Parts

Web parts are an important piece for quickly creating dynamic and robust SharePoint sites. SharePoint 2010 provides several web parts to help you quickly get started. Although you can add web parts to web pages in the browser, it is much quicker and more efficient to create web part pages in SharePoint Designer.

You will learn about the following topics in this chapter:

- Creating Web part pages, master pages, and wiki pages

- Working with Web parts and controls

- Using the Web Part Gallery

- Adding and configuring web parts

- Using personal views vs. shared views

- Connecting web parts

- Exporting web parts

- Fixing broken pages

If lists are the foundation for the data stored in SharePoint, web parts are the foundation for the presentation of that data to the user. One of the great benefits of SharePoint is that it enables an end user to create portals and web sites without programming skills, by using only the web browser. By using lists to store content and preprogrammed web parts to display data, almost anyone can create dynamic, content-rich web sites.

Web parts are small applications that perform a specific function on a web page. You can have a web part that displays the contents of a list. You can have a web part that displays the status of a project. Web parts are self-contained so that they are portable, which enables them to be used multiple times in a web site. For example, you could have a List View web part display only the top five new items in the list on the welcome page of the site, but display all of the list items in a details page—same web part, different presentation.

This chapter covers the web parts available to users in the different versions of SharePoint 2010. You will learn about the pages that can and cannot contain web parts. You will also learn how to connect web parts to provide a richer user experience. Then finally, you'll see how you can export your web part configurations to reuse them on other sites.

Creating Pages for Web Parts

A discussion about web parts can't really begin without talking about the pages they can be placed on, and the pages they can't. SharePoint Designer 2010 provides the ability to create many types of files you can use on a web site:

- Web content pages
  - Master pages
  - Page layouts
  - Web part pages
  - Wiki pages
  - ASPX pages
  - HTML pages
- Artifacts
  - CSS
  - JavaScript
  - XML
  - Text files

This section covers the web content pages. Chapters 6–9 provide detailed discussions on the types of artifacts that you can create in SharePoint Designer 2010.

■ **Note** SharePoint sites come in two flavors: publishing and nonpublishing. The Publishing Site template, combined with the publishing features, contains specific functionality to manage the content publishing process, such as content approval, versioning, and publishing. It uses three files to create a web page: the master page, the page layout, and the content page. Publishing is covered in detail in Chapter 7.

Master Pages

In order to provide your site with a consistent look and user experience, SharePoint employs ASP.NET master pages. A *master page* defines the basic layout, structure, and functionality of the site content. The master page provides placeholders to indicate where content can go. When a new page is created based on the master page, the new page content and the master page are merged by replacing the placeholders with the page content. SharePoint 2010 uses one main master page called v4.master, but you can create your own master pages and use them as your default master page.

To create a new master page, you can click the All Files link in the Navigation pane and then select Blank Master Page from the New File menu on the Ribbon. It is important to remember that when you create a new master page in SharePoint, it is going to expect certain placeholders, such as

PlaceHolderMain, to exist in order to display the site content on the page. It is because of these requirements that most people begin with a copy of v4.master when making their own master page. Working with v4.master is covered more in Chapter 6.

Wiki Pages

Wiki pages are a new page type in SharePoint 2010. These special SharePoint web part pages contain a SharePoint embedded form field, or content editor. With this type of form field, you can edit the content either in SharePoint Designer or the browser. You can also add other web parts to the page. Although it's possible to create a wiki page in SharePoint Designer, it is much more efficient to create the page in the browser. A simple way of creating a new page in SharePoint Designer is to make a copy of an existing wiki page and then rename it.

EXERCISE 4-1. CREATE AND EDIT A NEW WIKI PAGE

1. Open the browser to a SharePoint team site. If you don't already have a team site to work with, create a new site called Chapter 4 by using the Team Site template.

2. From the Site Actions menu, select New Page.

3. Give the new page the name **Chapter 4**, as shown in Figure 4-1.

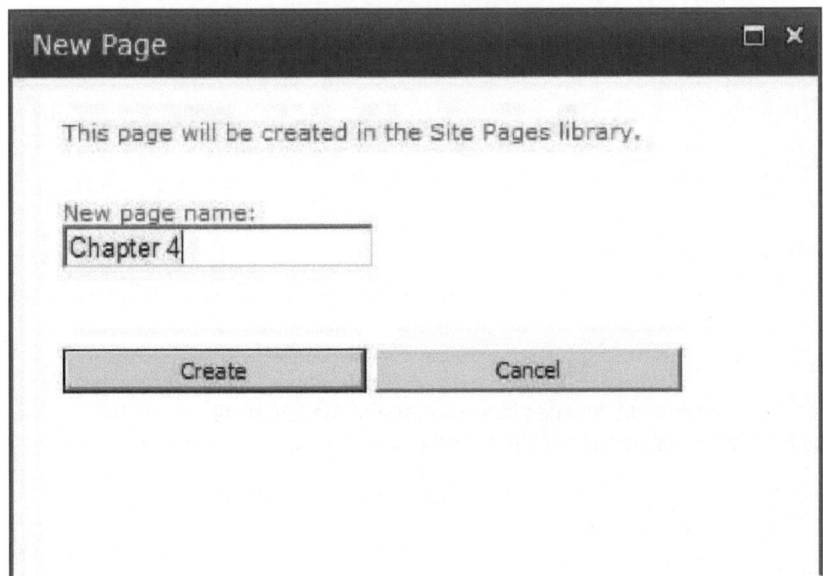

Figure 4-1. New Page dialog box

4. Your browser then displays the page in Edit mode. Click the different menu tabs on the Ribbon. Notice the different options you have for creating content.

5. Click your mouse in the main content area of the page.

6. On the Format Text menu, select Text Layout and then Two Columns, as shown in Figure 4-2.

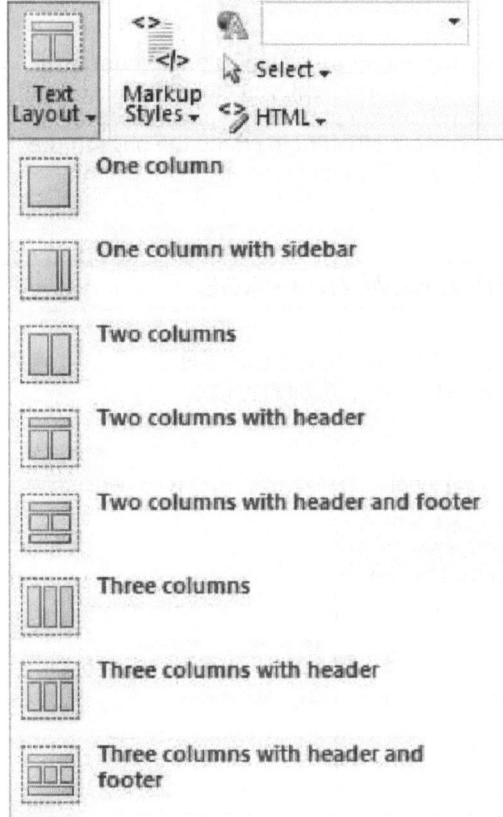

Figure 4-2. Text Layout menu

7. In the left column, type some content. You can use any of the formatting tools available to you on the Ribbon. In the right column, do the same thing.

8. When you are finished creating content in the two columns, save your changes by clicking the Page tab and then Save & Close.

9. Open the same site in SharePoint Designer.

10. Click Site Pages.

11. If the new page is not listed, press the F5 key to refresh the list display. Click the Chapter 4.aspx page.

12. When the page settings page comes up, click Edit File in the Customization section in the middle of the page.

13. Once the page opens in Edit mode, make sure you are in the Design view.

14. To make it easier to edit the content, either right-click in the content area and choose Zoom to Contents or choose it from the View menu on the Ribbon, as shown in Figure 4-3. This isolates the content area of the page.

Figure 4-3. *Zoom to Contents menu*

15. Click anywhere on the content of the page that you just added. Notice that you can edit the contents of the page.

16. Switch to Code view. The content area appears in `<div>` tags, as you can see in Figure 4-4.

```
RibbonCommand="Ribbon.WikiPageTab.EditAndCheckout.SaveEdit.Menu.SaveEdit.Revert"
        runat="server"
        Text="Revert"/>
    </SharePoint:VersionedPlaceHolder>
    <SharePoint:EmbeddedFormField id="WikiField" FieldName="WikiField" ControlMode="Display" runat="server"><div class="ExternalClassDA7
Lorem ipsum dolor sit amet, consectetur adipiscing elit. Vivamus sit
amet lorem magna<span style="text-decoration: underline">, tincidunt
dapibus lacus. Nullam sit amet ligula nisl, quis malesuada augue. Sed eu
sagittis odio. Nulla dui velit, auctor vel pellentesque nec, posuere non
odio. Sed</span> sodales sodales ante at sodales. Aliquam erat volutpat.
Nam ecem>t nunc libero, sed rutrum lorem. Praesent aliquet tempus magna,
quis lobortis enim porta ac. Cras lectus ante, varius id placerat sed,
consequat blandit libero. Praesent quis metus vel nunc lacinia congue.
Morbi at mauris nibh. Suspendisse eu vulputate nisl. Proin dictum, ipsum
sit amet dictum tempus, turpis m</em>agna placerat neque, a auctor metus
nulla in nulla. Nam tincidunt, velit eu porta mollis, lacus purus
volutpa<strong>t tortor, at posuere dolor m</strong>auris eu lacus. </p></div></div></td>
<td style="width:49.95%"><div class="ms-rte-layoutszone-outer" style="width:100%"><div class="ms-rte-layoutszone-inner"><div><div>
Lorem ipsum dolor sit amet, consectetur adipiscing elit. Vivamus sit amet
lorem magna, tincidunt dapibus lacus. Nullam sit amet ligula nisl, quis
malesuada augue. Sed eu sagittis odio. Nulla dui velit, auctor vel
pellentesque nec, posuere non odio<strong>. Sed sodales sodales ante at
sodales. Aliquam erat volutpat. Nam et nunc libero, sed rutrum lorem.
Praesent aliquet tempus magna, quis lobortis enim porta ac. Cras lectus
ante, varius id placerat sed, consequat blandit libero. Praesent quis metus
vel nunc lacinia congue. Morbi at mauris nibh. Suspendisse eu vulputate nisl.
Proin dictum, ipsum </strong>sit amet dictum tempus, turpis magna placerat
neque, a auctor metus nulla in nulla. Nam tincidunt, velit eu porta mollis,
lacus purus volutpat tortor, at posuere dolor mauris eu lacus. </div></div>
</div></div></td></tr></tbody></table>
<span id="layoutsData" style="display:none">false,false,2</span></div></SharePoint:EmbeddedFormField>
    <WebPartPages:WebPartZone runat="server" ID="Bottom" Title="loc:Bottom"><ZoneTemplate></ZoneTemplate></WebPartPages:WebPartZone>
    </ContentTemplate>
```

Figure 4-4. *Content area in Code view*

17. Switch back to Design view and position your cursor in a blank area of the left content section.

18. From the Insert menu on the Ribbon, select Web Part and then select Image Viewer under the Media and Content section (see Figure 4-5).

■ **Note** Although you are adding an Image Viewer web part to the wiki page, you could have added any web part in the Web Part list.

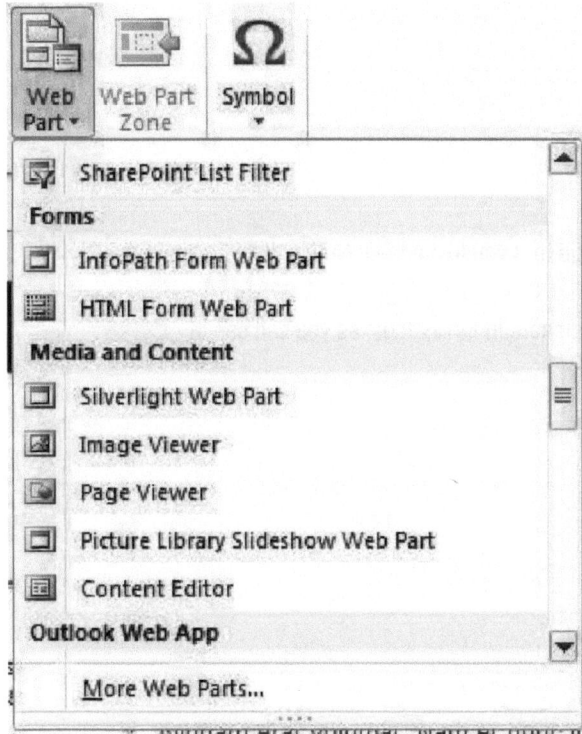

Figure 4-5. Web Part menu

19. Right-click the web part and select Web Part Properties.

20. In the Image Link box, type **/_layouts/images/homepageSamplePhoto.jpg** (see Figure 4-6). Type **Sample Homepage Picture** in the Alternative Text box. Then click OK.

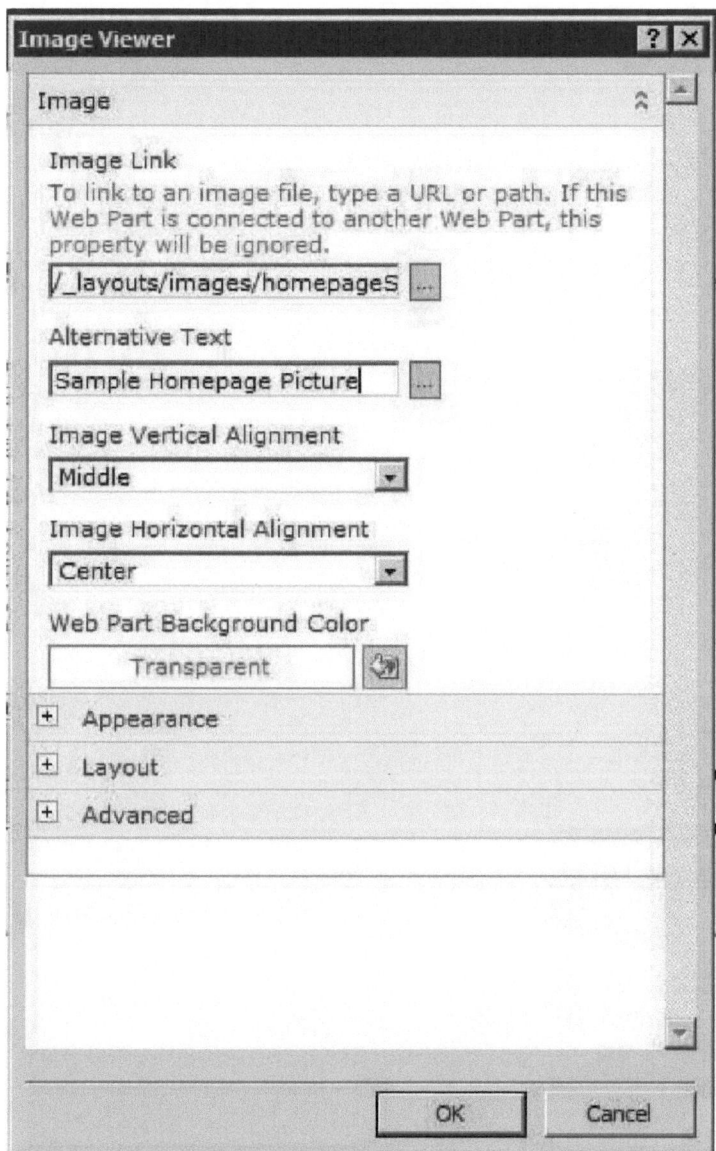

Figure 4-6. Image Viewer web part properties

21. From the File menu, choose Save.

22. Go back to your browser and refresh the page. You can see the changes that you made in the Designer (see Figure 4-7).

Figure 4-7. Final wiki page

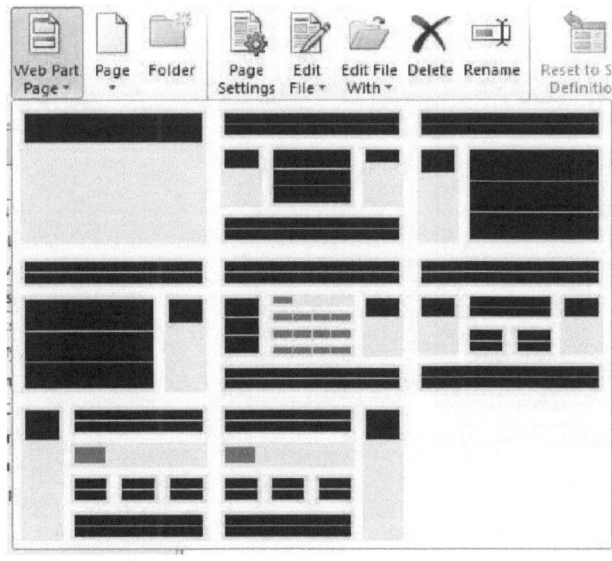

Figure 4-8. Web Part Page men

Web Part Pages

Web part pages are special web pages in that they specify different zones that can contain content. These zones allow end users to add web parts to pages and customize pages to their needs. SharePoint Designer provides web part page layout templates that you can select right out of the box, as you can see in Figure 4-8. You can also create your own layouts. Web part pages enable this functionality through the use of web part zones.

Although you can place web parts outside a web part zone when using SharePoint Designer in Advanced edit mode, web part zones are the only area that a user can edit in the browser. Web parts placed outside a web part zone are referred to *as static web parts*, and those web parts placed inside web part zones are *dynamic web parts* . Figure 4-9 shows web part zones on a page.

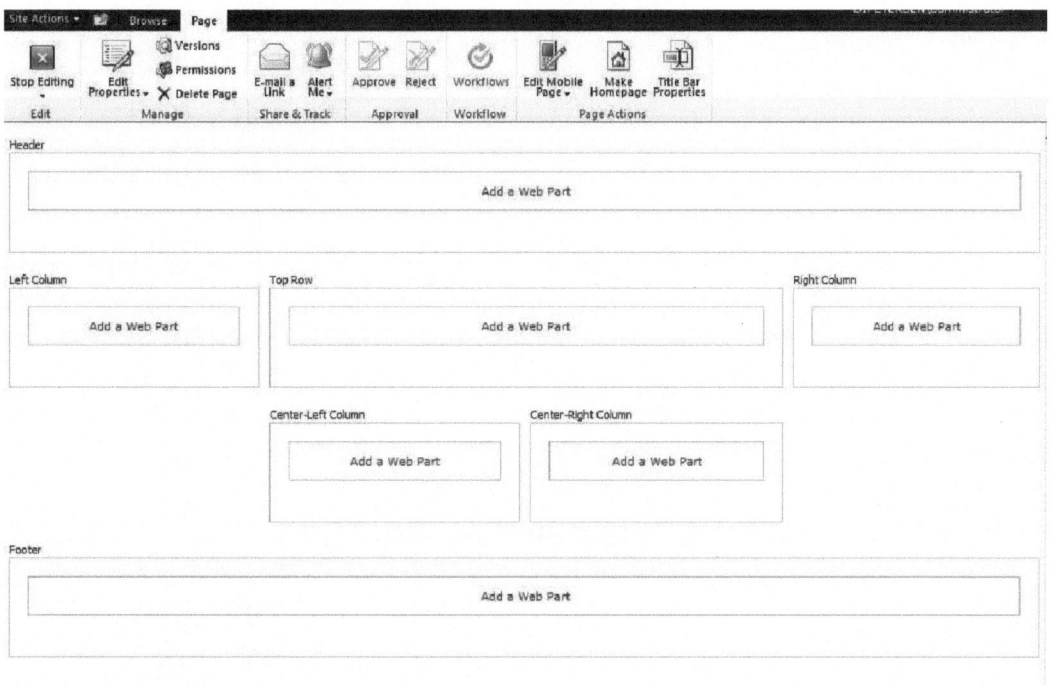

Figure 4-9. *Web part page showing web part zones*

ASPX and HTML Pages

SharePoint Designer 2010 provides the ability to create and edit ASPX pages and standard HTML pages. This functionality is provided in case there is a need to create or edit regular web pages as part of a site. These pages do not automatically inherit the site master page and can be edited only in Advanced mode. You cannot put web parts on them unless you manually add a web part manager and web part zones (thereby creating a web part page), which is beyond the scope of this chapter.

Using the Web Part Gallery

The *Web Part Gallery*, shown in Figure 4-10, is a special document library that resides at the root of the site collection and contains a list of all of the web parts that can be used for the site collection. You can upload new web parts here or you can export your other web part configurations and upload them here. An easy way to find the Web Part Gallery is to add /_catalogs/wp to the end of your site collection URL. For example, if your site collection is at http://sharepointdesigner2010, then the Web Part Gallery is at http://sharepointdesigner2010/_catalogs/wp.

□	Type	Web Part	Edit	Modified	☐ Modified By	Group	Recommendation Settings
		AdvancedSearchBox.dwp		1/31/2011 12:54 PM	System Account	Search	Search
		AuthoredListFilter.webpart		1/31/2011 12:54 PM	System Account	Filters	Filters; My Site: Middle Right; My Site: Middle Left; My Site: Bottom
		BusinessDataActionsWebPart.dwp		1/31/2011 12:54 PM	System Account	Business Data	My Site: Middle Right; My Site: Middle Left; My Site: Bottom
		BusinessDataAssociationWebPart.webpart		1/31/2011 12:54 PM	System Account	Business Data	My Site: Middle Right; My Site: Middle Left; My Site: Bottom
		BusinessDataDetailsWebPart.webpart		1/31/2011 12:54 PM	System Account	Business Data	My Site: Middle Right; My Site: Middle Left; My Site: Bottom
		BusinessDataFilter.dwp		1/31/2011 12:54 PM	System Account	Business Data	Filters; My Site: Middle Right; My Site: Middle Left; My Site: Bottom
		BusinessDataItemBuilder.dwp		1/31/2011 12:54 PM	System Account	Business Data	My Site: Middle Right; My Site: Middle Left; My Site: Bottom
		BusinessDataListWebPart.webpart		1/31/2011 12:54 PM	System Account	Business Data	Dashboard; My Site: Middle Right; My Site: Middle Left; My Site: Bottom
		CategoryResultsWebPart.webpart		1/31/2011 12:54 PM	System Account	Content Rollup	Site Directory
		CategoryWebPart.webpart		1/31/2011 12:54 PM	System Account	Content Rollup	Site Directory
		contactwp.dwp		1/31/2011 12:54 PM	System Account	Social Collaboration	Miscellaneous
		DateFilter.dwp		1/31/2011 12:54 PM	System Account	Filters	Filters; My Site: Middle Right; My Site: Middle Left; My Site: Bottom
		DualChineseSearch.dwo		1/31/2011 12:54 PM	System	Search	Search

Figure 4-10. Web Part Gallery

The exact web parts that in you have available to you are different depending on the version of SharePoint you have installed and the features you have activated. Microsoft does not provide a specific list of which web parts are in which version, but a quick search of the Internet turns up a couple of comprehensive lists.

To add a new web part to the Web Part Gallery, navigate to the Web Part Gallery by clicking Site Actions ➤ Site Settings ➤ Galleries ➤ Web Parts. Once there, click the Documents tab of the Ribbon and select New Document. A list of all available web parts registered with the web.config file will be displayed. Select the check boxes of the web parts you wish to install and click the Populate Gallery button.

■ **Note** To enable web parts in the site collection Web Part Gallery, the web parts must be properly installed and registered with the site collection's `web.config` file. This can be accomplished manually or by a deployment package, usually as part of a WSP file. More information on deployment can be found at
`http://technet.microsoft.com/en-us/library/cc261736.aspx`.

Adding and Configuring Web Parts on a Page

To use web parts, you first need to have a container to put them in. As mentioned earlier, SharePoint has page templates with web part zones already defined. When you create a web part page based on one of these templates, it is saved in a special document library called Site Pages that is created automatically when the site is created. You can also create web pages in other document libraries and in folders within those document libraries. Once you create a page, you can place web parts in defined web zones.

With SharePoint Designer, you can also add or delete web part zones. You can edit pages in Basic mode or Advanced mode. In Basic mode, you can add or remove web parts from a page but you can't modify layouts. In Advanced mode, you have full control over the page, but it is done at a price. When you edit pages in Advanced mode, you separate the file from its original site definition file that resides on the file system. Performance is affected because the modified file is stored in the content database. When the page is requested, it is read from the content database each time, which is slower. If you find that you accidentally modify a page in Advanced mode and you wish to go back to its original form, you can select Reset to Site Definition anytime to get rid of your changes.

EXERCISE 4-2. CREATE A WEB PART PAGE

In this exercise, you will create a new web part page in SharePoint Designer 2010 from the predefined templates provided. This page will then be used in the subsequent exercises.

1. If you don't already have a practice site to work with, create a new site called Chapter 4 by using the Team Site template.

2. From within SharePoint Designer, click the Site Pages link in the left Navigation pane.

3. From the Ribbon menu, choose New ➤ Web Part page, and then select the template that has a Header web part zone, a Left web part zone, and a Right web part zone, as shown in Figure 4-11.

Figure 4-11. Web part page

4. Name the page **WebPartPageDemo.aspx**.

5. When the file is created, click the filename to get to the Page Settings page and then click the Edit File link in the Customization pane.

6. Let's display the Announcements list on this page. Click inside the Right web part zone. Then, on the Ribbon, click Insert ➤ Data View ➤ Announcements (see Figure 4-12). You should see the default display of the Announcements list. You'll customize that later.

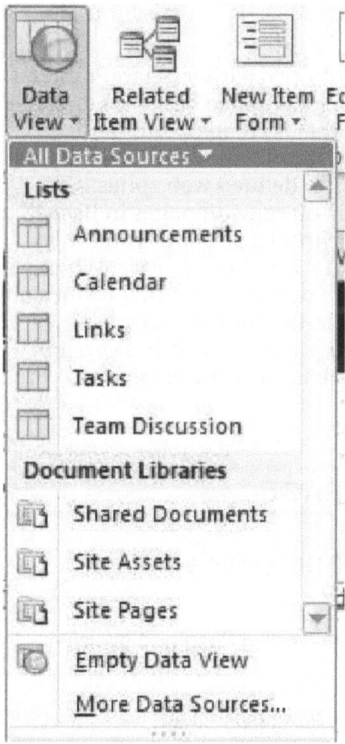

Figure 4-12. Data View menu

7. In the Header web part zone, type **Web Part Page Demo Page**. Use the formatting tools on the Ribbon to center the text and give it the Heading 1 style.

8. Switch to Split mode and notice that a WikiContentWebpart was added automatically for you in Basic editing mode (see Figure 4-13).

```
<WebPartPages:WikiContentWebpart frametype="none" chrometype="None" runat="server"
    <content>
    <h1 style="text-align: center">Web Part Page Demo Page</h1>
</content>
</WebPartPages:WikiContentWebpart>
</ZoneTemplate></WebPartPages:WebPartZone> </td>
```

Figure 4-13. *WikiContentWebpart in Code view*

■ **Note** The web part was automatically added because in Basic mode, you can configure and edit web parts only in web part zones. To have static text, you would have to place the page into Advanced editing mode, which would customize the page.

---

9. Switch back to Design mode and click in the Left web part zone.

10. On the Ribbon menu, choose Insert ➤ Data View ➤ Links.

11. When the Links web part is rendered on your page, choose Options from the List View Tools menu. Then select Add/Remove Columns.

12. Remove all fields except Notes (see Figure 4-14).

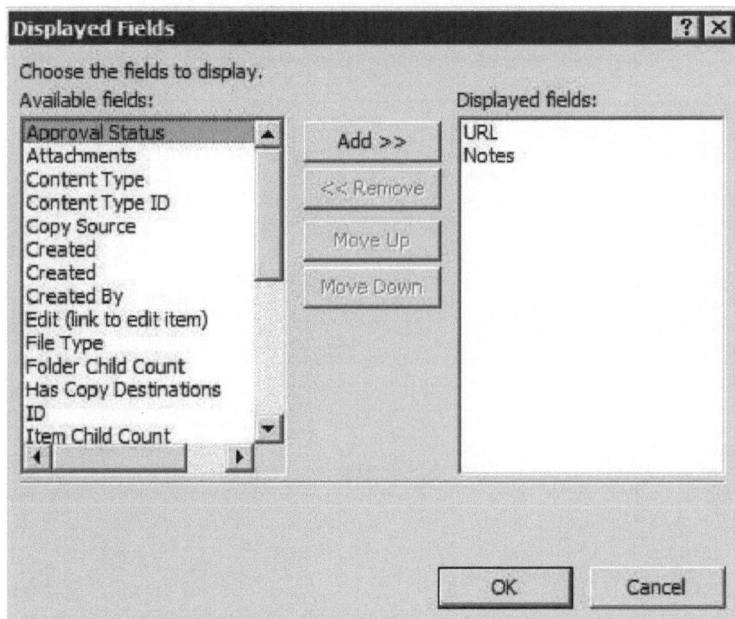

Figure 4-14. *Data view column picker*

13. Add the regular URL field back into the Displayed Fields list. Then move the URL field to the first position by clicking the Move Up button. Click OK.

14. Click the Design menu, and select the sixth display option, which looks like Figure 4-15.

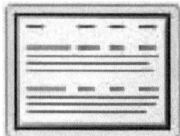

Figure 4-15. Data view display template

15. Right-click the web part and select Web Part Properties from the context menu.

16. In the Appearance section, under Width, type **300px** in the Width box of the web part and make sure Yes is selected. Click OK.

17. Save the page by clicking the Save button or by pressing Ctrl+S.

18. Press F12 or choose Home ➤ Preview in Browser from the Ribbon menu to see your new page in the browser.

This is a simple web part page, as you can see in Figure 4-16. You will customize it later in the chapter. For now, add a few links and a few announcements to give the page some content.

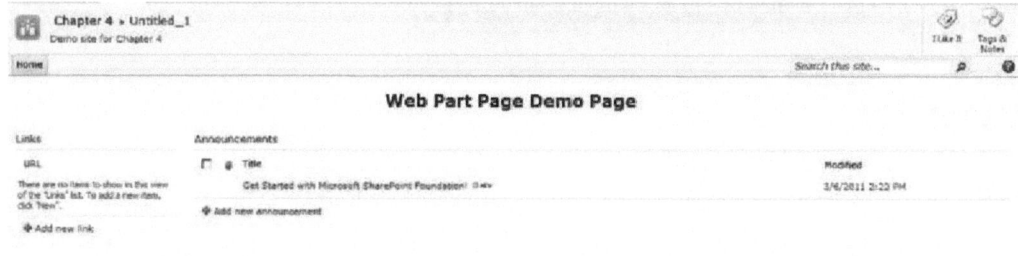

Figure 4-16. Final web part page

Working in a Personal View vs. a Shared View

Normally, when a user navigates to a web part page, that user is viewing the Shared view of the page. This view is the same view that everyone else sees. SharePoint provides a way for a user to customize the page and the different web parts on the page to give them a Personal view of the page. This is one of the powerful aspects of SharePoint. Each user can have a different experience, within limits, based on the web parts they decide to place on the web part page. This functionality is achieved through the Personal menu attached to the person's login name. All personal configuration information is stored separately for each user. Personalization can be done only from the browser, but you can enable or restrict some personalization features in SharePoint Designer. For example, a user might want to display an RSS feed that applies to his job, but you don't want users to be able to delete an RSS feed to your corporate site.

EXERCISE 4-3. CREATE A PERSONAL VIEW OF A WEB PART PAGE

1. In the browser, navigate to the WebPartPageDemo page you created in Exercise 4-2.

2. In the upper-right corner, click your login name. The Personalization drop-down menu shows, as you can see in Figure 4-17.

Figure 4-17. Personalization menu

3. Select Personalize This Page from the menu.

4. In the web editor, click in the left web part zone labeled Add a Web Part.

5. When the web part selector opens, select the RSS viewer from the Content Rollup category, as shown in Figure 4-18.

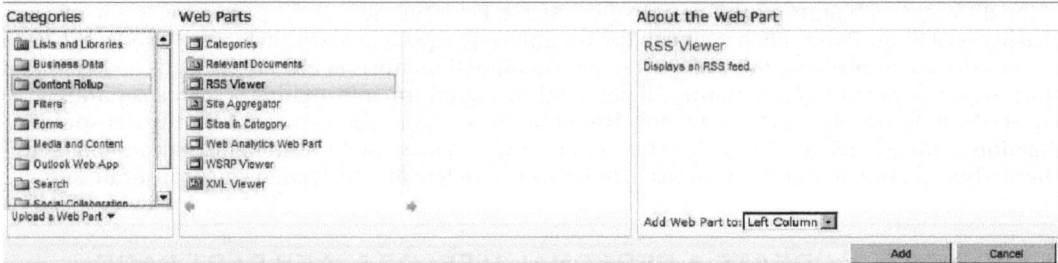

Figure 4-18. Web part selector

6. Make sure the Add Web Part To drop-down list displays Left Column, and then click the Add button.

7. In the RSS Viewer web part, click Open the Tool Pane Link to edit the settings of the web part (see Figure 4-19).

8. Type **http://www.apress.com/resource/feed/newbook** in the RSS Feed URL text box.

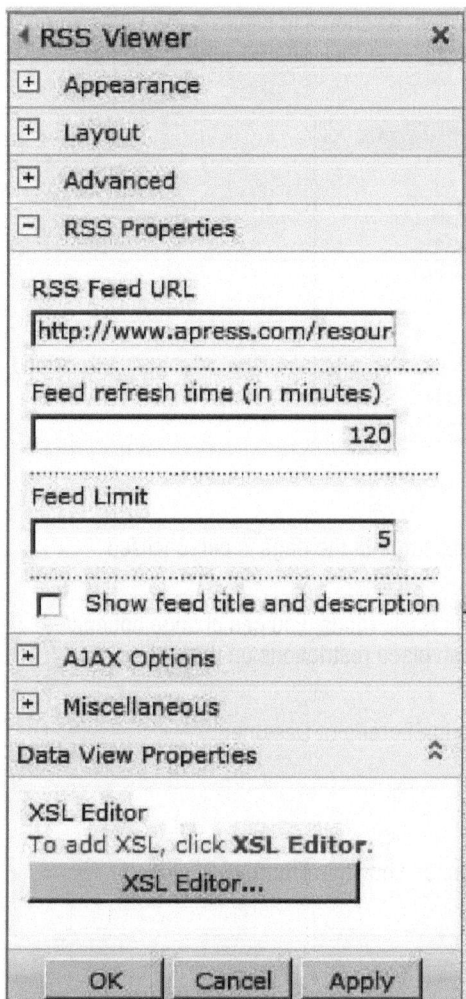

Figure 4-19. RSS Viewer web part properties

9. Accept all of the other defaults and click OK.

10. On the Ribbon menu, click the Stop Editing button. Your view of the page changes.

11. From the Personalization menu, select Show Shared View. The RSS Viewer web part does not display.

12. Now select Show Personal View in the Personalization menu. At any time, you can reset the page back to the Shared view.

13. From the Personalization menu, select Reset Page Content.

14. A dialog box opens, prompting you to confirm your selection, as shown in Figure 4-20. When you reset the page, all personalized web part settings will be reset to their shared values, and any private web parts will be deleted.

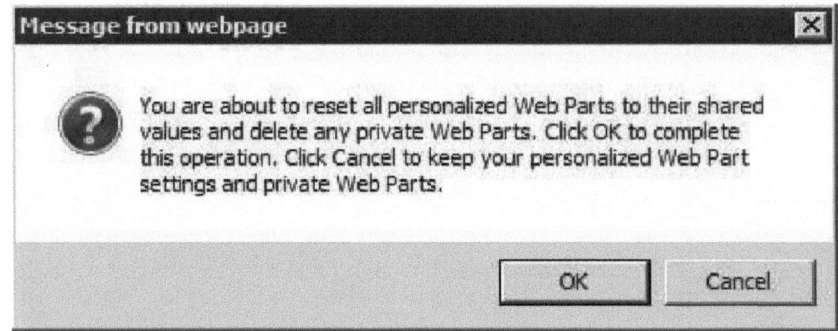

Figure 4-20. *Warning dialog box when resetting the web part*

Once you reset the page, the Show Personal View menu item is absent until the page is personalized again.

It is sometimes desirable to prevent certain customizations. In Basic mode, you can change options only on the web parts themselves. In Advanced mode, you can place restrictions on the web part zones.

1. Open the WebPartPageDemo page in Design mode in SharePoint Designer.

2. Click the Announcements web part.

3. On the Ribbon menu, click the Web Part tab.

4. In the Allow section, deselect all of the check boxes, as shown in Figure 4-21.

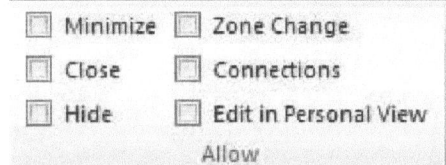

Figure 4-21. *Web part Allow settings*

5. Save your changes.

6. In the browser, navigate to the WebPartPageDemo page or refresh the page if you are already there.

7. Click the title bar of the Links web part. Notice that there is a drop-down menu that allows you to minimize or export the web part (see Figure 4-22).

Figure 4-22. *Edit My Web Part menu.).*

> 8. Click the title bar of the Announcements web part. Notice that the option to minimize or export the web part is not there (see Figure 4-23).

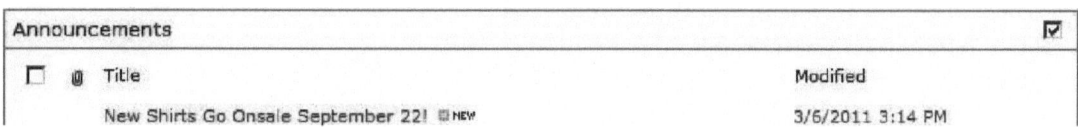

Figure 4-23. *Web part without edit menu*

> 9. Go back to SharePoint Designer.
>
> 10. Put the page in Advanced editing mode by clicking the Home tab and then clicking Advanced Mode under the Editing section.
>
> 11. Click in the right zone labeled Body.
>
> 12. In the status bar at the bottom of the page, locate the entry `<WebPartPages:WebPartZone#Body>` and right-click it (Figure 4-24).

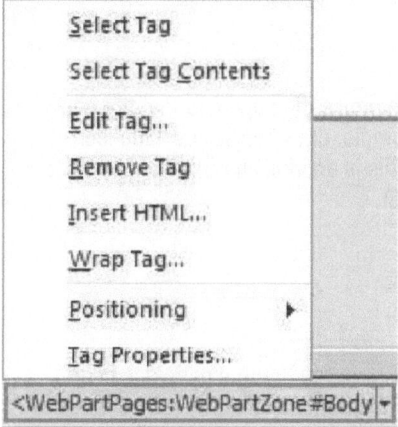

Figure 4-24. *Web part zone menu*

13. Select Tag Properties from the menu. Web Part Zone Properties dialog box pops up, as you can see in Figure 4-25.

14. In the Frame Style drop-down list, select None. At the bottom of the dialog box, deselect all three check boxes. Then click OK to close the dialog box.

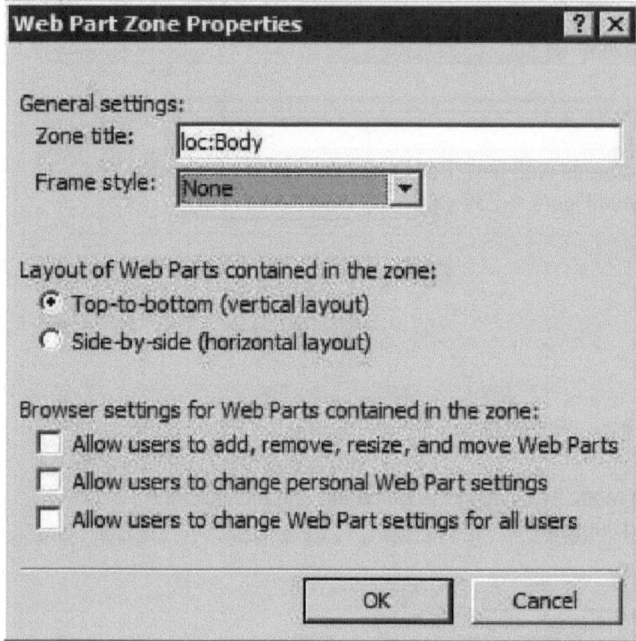

Figure 4-25. Web part zone properties

15. Click the Save button or press Ctrl+S.

16. A dialog box comes up, warning that you are about to customize the page and that the page will no longer be based on the site definition. For this example, click Yes. A new blue icon appears next to the page name in the Navigation pane. This is an indicator that the page has been customized from the site definition (see Figure 4-26).

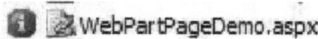

Figure 4-26. Customized indicator

17. Go back to the browser and refresh the page. (If you are prompted that the page has been modified, click Refresh This Page.) Notice that the Announcements web part does not have a title bar and that nothing changes in the Ribbon menu when you click it.

18. From the Personalization menu, select Personalize This Page. You still have web part zones in the Header and Left areas, but cannot edit the Body web part zone.

19. Click Stop Editing to return to Browsing mode.

20. Go back to SharePoint Designer.

21. In the Navigation pane, right-click the WebPartPageDemo page name and select Reset to Site Definition.

22. A dialog box displays, informing you that resetting to the site definition will replace the contents of this page with the original contents from the site collection, and that a backup copy of the current page will be created in the same folder. Click Yes to confirm that you want to do this. When the page refreshes in SharePoint Designer, the web parts will still be there, but the web part zone customizations that you made previously are reset.

23. Go back to the browser to verify the changes. (You may have to navigate to another page and then back to see your changes.)

Connecting Web Parts

Because web parts by design are meant to be portable, they are programmed to live on any page. But being able to place these web parts on a page by themselves would be boring. It would make web sites more interactive and more dynamic if the web parts could communicate with each other and share data. SharePoint provides that functionality with web part connections. Connecting web parts have the ability to provide values to another web part on the same page or another page or accept data from another web part. The data accepted can be used as filter data to further filter a list or as parameter values. Web parts can exchange single values or multiple values. Not all web parts can be connected, but for those that can, they can help create a rich user interface.

EXERCISE 4-4. CONNECTING WEB PARTS

In this exercise, you will create a page that utilizes the Filter web part and will connect web parts:

1. If you have not already created a practice site, create a new site based on the Team Site template and name it **Chapter 4**.

2. Now you're ready to create and use a new list. Create a new custom list called **Territory Sales** and add the fields shown in Figure 4-27.

Column Name ▼	Type
Title	Single line of text
Territory ID	Number (1, 1.0, 100)
Group	Single line of text
SalesYTD	Currency ($, ¥, €)

Figure 4-27. *Territory Sales field list*

3. When you have the list set up, add the values shown in Figure 4-28.

Title ▼	TerritoryID ▼	Group ▼	SalesYTD ▼
Northwest	1	North America	$5,767,341.98
Northeast	2	North America	$3,857,163.63
Central	3	North America	$4,677,108.27
Southwest	4	North America	$8,351,296.74
Southeast	5	North America	$2,851,419.04
Canada	6	North America	$6,917,270.88
France	7	Europe	$3,899,045.69
Germany	8	Europe	$2,481,039.18
Australia	9	Pacific	$1,977,474.81
United Kingdom	10	Europe	$3,514,865.91

Figure 4-28. *Territory list values*

■ **Note** It is easiest to add data quickly by placing the list in Datasheet view before adding the values.

---

4. From within SharePoint Designer, click the Site Pages library in the left Navigation pane.

Create a new web part page called `Connections.aspx`. Use the template shown in Figure 4-29.

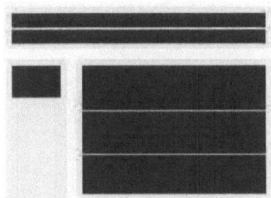

Figure 4-29. Web part page template

5. From within the editor, click in the left web part zone. From the Insert ➤ Web Part menu, choose a Choice Filter web part.

6. Right-click the inserted web part and choose Web Part Properties.

7. In the Filter Name text box, type **Group**.

8. In the Values box, type the text shown in Figure 4-30.

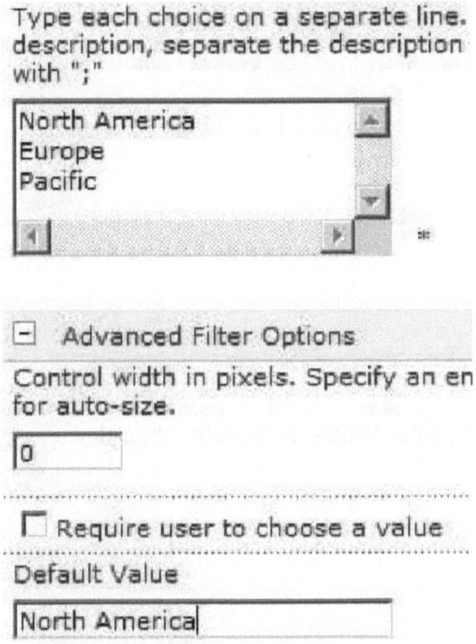

> Type each choice on a separate line.
> description, separate the description
> with ";"
>
> North America
> Europe
> Pacific

□ Advanced Filter Options

Control width in pixels. Specify an en
for auto-size.

`0`

☐ Require user to choose a value

Default Value

`North America`

Figure 4-30. Choice Filter web part settings

9. Open the Advanced Filter Options and type **North America** as the default value.

10. In the Appearance section, click the Yes radio button and type **300** in the text box indicating a fixed width, as shown in Figure 4-31. Then click OK.

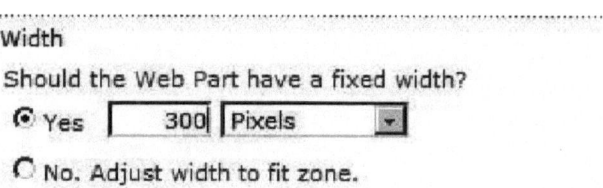

Width

Should the Web Part have a fixed width?

◉ Yes [300] [Pixels ▼]

○ No. Adjust width to fit zone.

Figure 4-31. Appearance settings

11. Click in the main Body web part zone.

12. From the Insert menu, insert a Data View web part of the Territory Sales list. Your page should look like Figure 4-32 in SharePoint Designer.

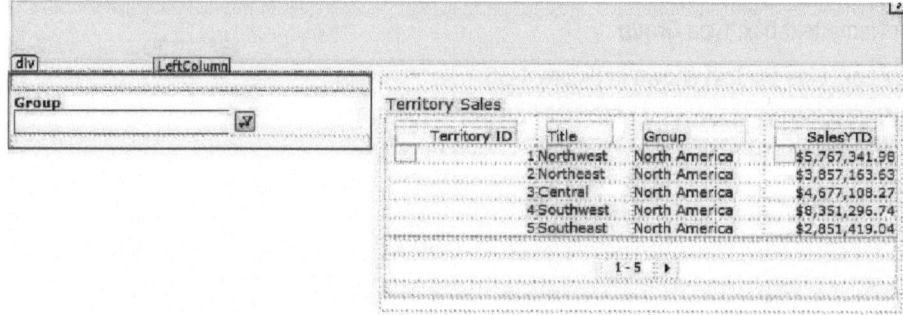

Figure 4-32. Group filter web part page

13. Click the Group web part.

14. Select Add Connection from the Web Part Tools menu.

15. When the Web Part Connection Wizard opens, select Send Filter Values To from the drop-down menu, as shown in Figure 4-33. Then click Next.

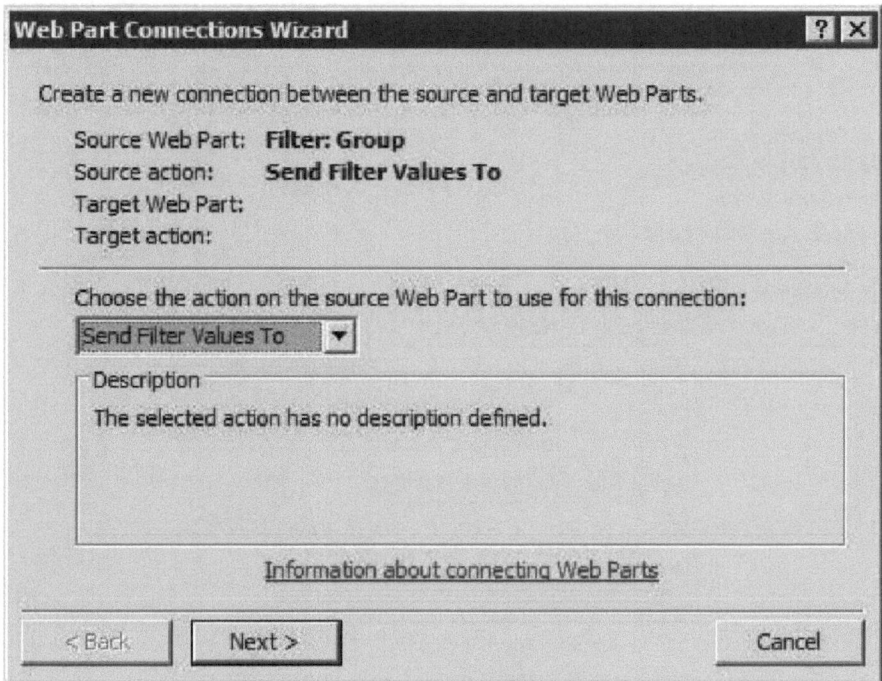

Figure 4-33. Web Part Connection Wizard's Send Filter Values To option

16. Accept the defaults and click Next again.

17. Select Territory Sales for the Target Web Part. Select Get Filter Values From for Target Action. Then click Next.

18. Click Choice Filter on the left and Group on the right (see Figure 4-34). Click Next.

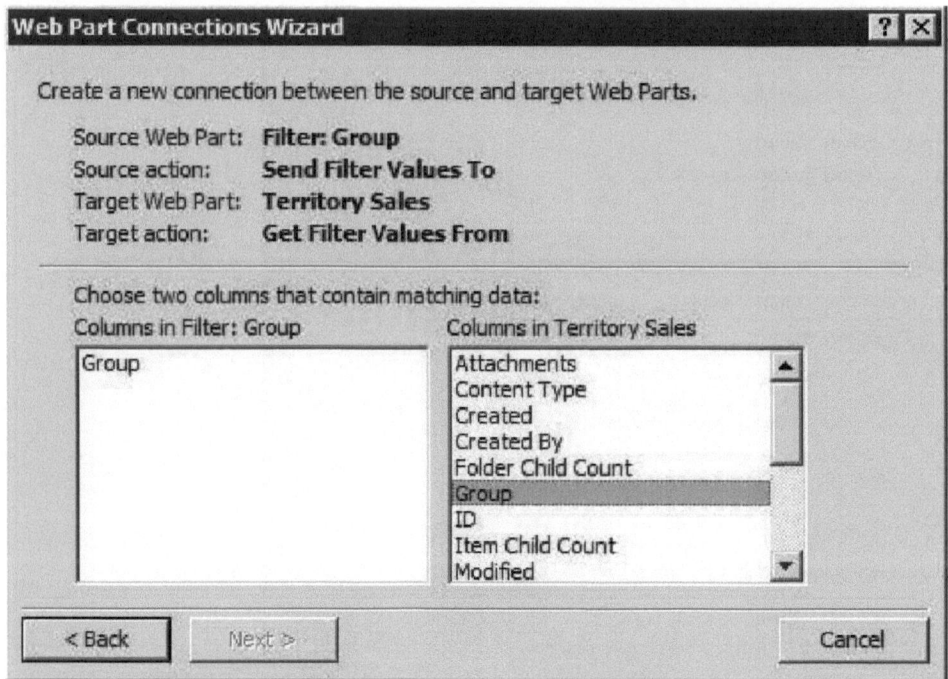

Figure 4-34. Web Part Connection Wizard

19. Click Finish.

20. Click the Save button or Ctrl+S.

21. On the Home menu, click Preview in Browser. You should see the page filtered for North America.

22. Click the filter icon and then pick the other filter options. The Data view is filtered based on your selection, as shown in Figure 4-35.

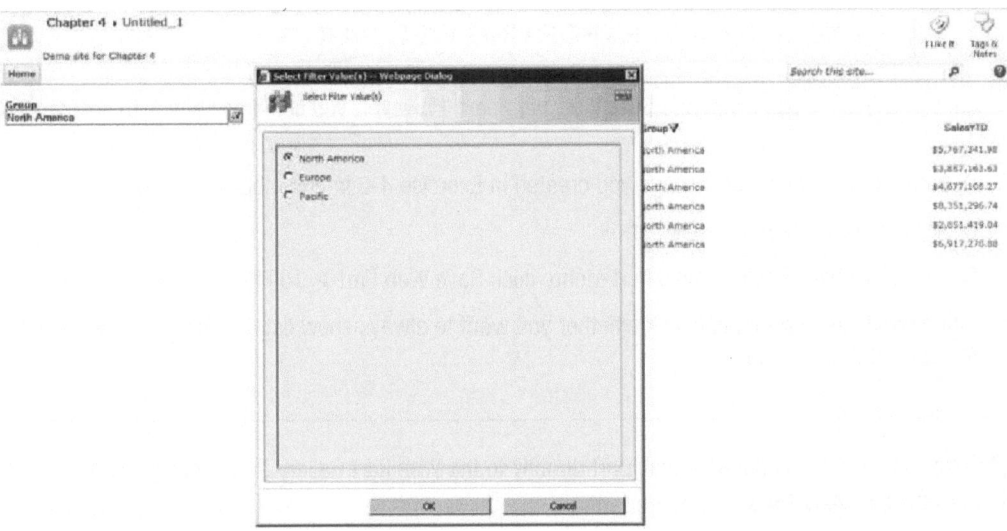

Figure 4-35. *Select Filter Value dialog box*

Exporting Web Part Configurations

Often times, you might want to save the configuration of a web part to use it on other pages. You can export the configuration of a web part and then import it into another page. You can also import it into another Web Part Gallery file.

To export a web part, open the web part page in SharePoint Designer. Select a web part and then click To Site Gallery on the Web Part tab. A dialog box will open, prompting you to supply a Name and Description for your configuration. It is important that the name be unique and the description detailed so you know exactly what configuration you are saving. Also, by giving it a unique name, you avoid future confusion when selecting web parts for a new page. The dialog box also gives you the opportunity to change the configuration before saving it to the Web Part Gallery.

Once the web part is exported to the Web Part Gallery, it will be available in the drop-down Web Part menu under Custom Web Parts. When you select that custom web part for another page, it will already be configured.

You can also export a web part configuration to a file by clicking the To File button on the Format tab. A Save As dialog box will prompt you to choose a location and filename to save the new web part configuration. It is important to remember that when you export to a file, you are saving only the configuration information. If the web part is not installed in the new environment, you won't be able to use the exported web part configuration.

■ **Note** If you were to open a `.dwp` or `.webpart` file, you would see that it is just an XML file storing the web part's configuration. Because it is an XML file, you can modify the configuration in the file if you are careful. Always remember to make changes only to a copy of the original.

EXERCISE 4-5. EXPORTING WEB PARTS

In this exercise, you will use a page with one Data View web part. However, you could use any web part for this exercise.

1. Open the WebPartPageDemo page you created in Exercise 4-2 in Edit mode.

2. Click the Links web part to select it.

3. From the List View Tools ➤ Web Part menu, click Save Web Part ➤ To File.

4. When the dialog box opens to ask whether you want to always show list data from the current web site, click Yes.

■ **Note** You can save the configured web part directly to the Web Part Gallery by selecting To Site Gallery from the List View Tools ➤ Web Part menu.

---

5. Close the web page.

6. Open the Site Collection settings in the browser and navigate to the Web Part Gallery.

7. On the Documents tab of the Library Tools menu, select Upload Document.

8. When the dialog box opens, fill out the form as illustrated in Figure 4-36. Then click Save.

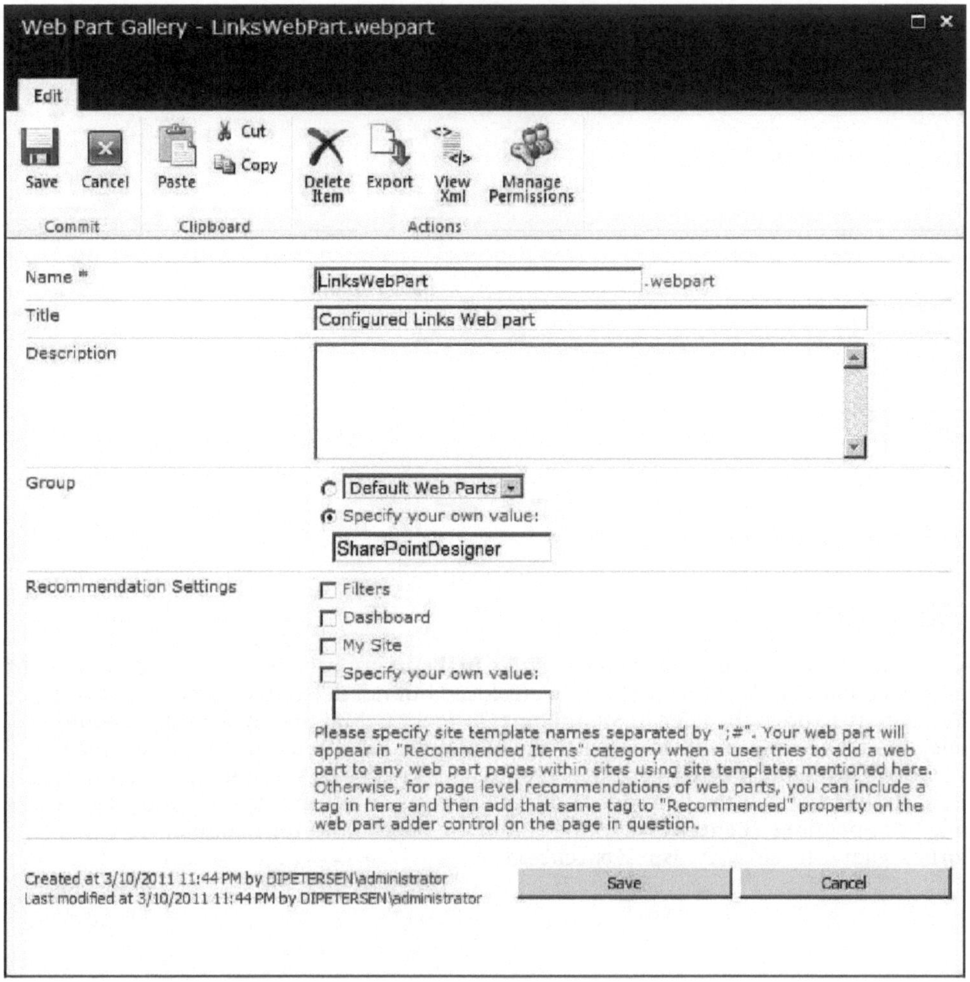

Figure 4-36. Export Web Part dialog box

9. Open another web part page for editing in SharePoint Designer and click an empty web part zone.

10. On the Insert Web Part menu, find the web part you just uploaded to the gallery. In the example here, it is listed in the SharePoint Designer group and is called Configured Links Web Part (see Figure 4-37). When the web part is inserted, it should look exactly like the original.

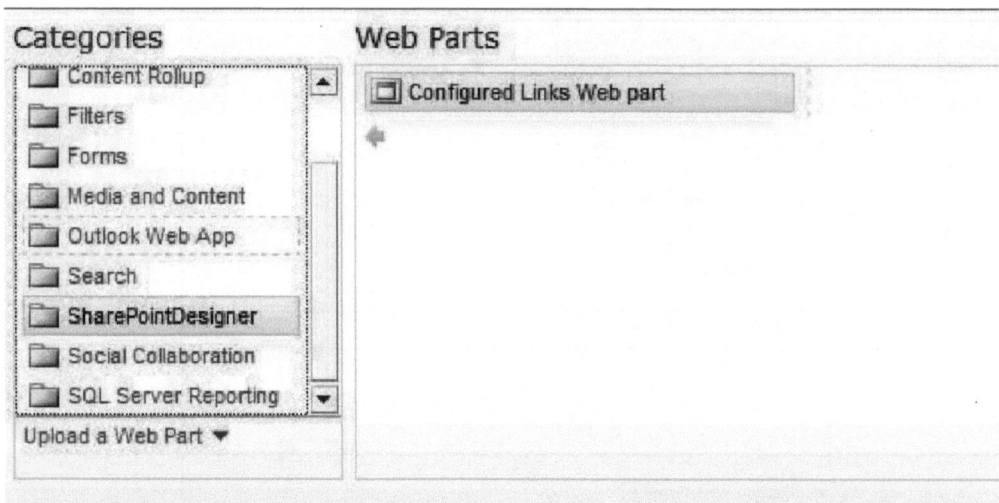

Figure 4-37. Selecting the exported web part

Fixing Broken Pages

At times you may need to recover a page after a code change makes it impossible to render, or you might have some orphaned web parts (web parts that have been closed but not deleted) on a page that you need to restore. You can try to open the page in SharePoint Designer in Maintenance mode. To enter Maintenance mode, open the browser and select the Page tab on the Ribbon menu. Then click the Edit Properties button. Once the menu changes, click the Open Web Part Page in Maintenance View link. If you are unable to reach that menu or the page does not render, you can attempt to open the page in Maintenance mode by appending **?Contents=1** to the end of the page URL—for example, http://SharePointDesigner2010/default.aspx?Contents=1.

Summary

This chapter covered how to manage web parts. You learned where you can place web parts and how to create the pages that can hold those web parts. You also learned about exporting and reusing your preconfigured web parts as well as creating web part connections. As you have seen, web parts make it possible to create all sorts of dynamic web sites quickly and with minimal effort.

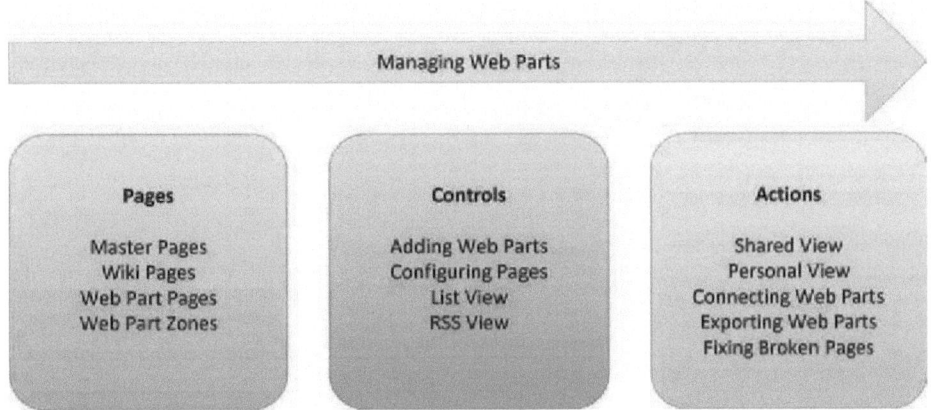

Managing Web Parts

Pages	Controls	Actions
Master Pages	Adding Web Parts	Shared View
Wiki Pages	Configuring Pages	Personal View
Web Part Pages	List View	Connecting Web Parts
Web Part Zones	RSS View	Exporting Web Parts
		Fixing Broken Pages

Advanced Site Customization

CHAPTER 5

Displaying Data

SharePoint Server 2010 is a platform that can be used to integrate data from many sources. Some of these sources reside within SharePoint itself, such as lists and libraries. Others are external data sources. These include Relational Database Management Systems (RDBMSs) such as Microsoft SQL Server or database products from other vendors such as Oracle and IBM. Data can also be retrieved from web services, Really Simple Syndication (RSS) and Representational State Transfer (REST) feeds, or from XML files. SharePoint's Business Connectivity Services (BCS) system is also a versatile way to access data.

This chapter focuses on the presentation of data. SharePoint Designer has some excellent tools for customizing the presentation of data—including capabilities to read, delete, and update data residing in various types of data sources. Because this chapter focuses on presentation, you will work only with data stored in SharePoint lists and libraries. For details about using other types of data sources, see Chapter 10.

You will learn about the following topics in this chapter:

- Accessing data within a SharePoint Page

- Understanding data sources in SharePoint Designer

- Creating site pages containing data list and form web parts

- Customizing the look and feel of data web parts

- Passing parameters to and between data web parts

- Knowing which web parts to use in different situations

Note The following software is required:

- SharePoint Server 2010 (Enterprise edition recommended)

- SQL Server 2008 (R1 or R2)

- SharePoint Designer 2010

Understanding Data Sources and Data Views

There are three primary considerations when displaying or updating data: the data itself, how the data is accessed, and how the data is presented. SharePoint provides a common platform for presenting data in a web-based format. SharePoint Designer leverages that platform to allow the designer to customize the retrieval and presentation of data from a variety of sources.

As noted earlier, in this chapter you will focus on data that is stored within SharePoint in the form of lists and libraries. As you saw in Chapter 2, lists in SharePoint can be thought of as tables of information. Each item in the list is a row in the table. Each value or attribute associated with the item is a column in the table. When accessing data from lists, it is helpful to think of lists as tables because that is usually how the presentation is formatted; Figure 5-1 shows an example. A SharePoint library is just a specific type of list that is designed to store a document along with each item.

□	⓪	Type	Title	☐ Assigned To	Status	Priority	Due Date	% Complete	Predecessors
		▯	Set up room		Not Started	(2) Normal			
		▯	Give it a rest		Not Started	(2) Normal			
✤ Add new item									

Figure 5-1. A task list as a table of information

The task of accessing data in SharePoint by using SharePoint Designer is divided into two components: a data source and a data view (or form). *Data sources* provide a description of where the information being displayed will come from. The data source also defines the form of the data, including what values and data types are associated with each field. A *data view*, or form, is a web part that can be placed on a SharePoint page, bound to a data source, and customized to render the data in precisely the way desired.

In the following sections, you will explore the types of data sources that are available. You will then move on to a description of the various web parts that are available for presenting this data and will learn how to customize their appearance. Finally, you will walk through some common scenarios for creating and customizing the presentation of data by using SharePoint Designer.

Working with Data Sources

As stated in the preceding section, a *data source* in SharePoint is an object that defines the parameters needed to connect to a particular set of data. For example, a data set might point to a list within SharePoint or to a table in an RDBMSS such as MS SQL Server or Oracle. In addition to retrieving data, data sources can also be configured to insert, update, or delete information from the underlying data source, if the user has the necessary security privileges.

A typical SharePoint site contains some data sources by default, and more can be added through SharePoint Designer. If you open your web site in SharePoint Designer and click Data Sources within the Navigation pane, the Data Sources Gallery displays. This window, shown in Figure 5-2, contains a catalog of all data sources available within the current site.

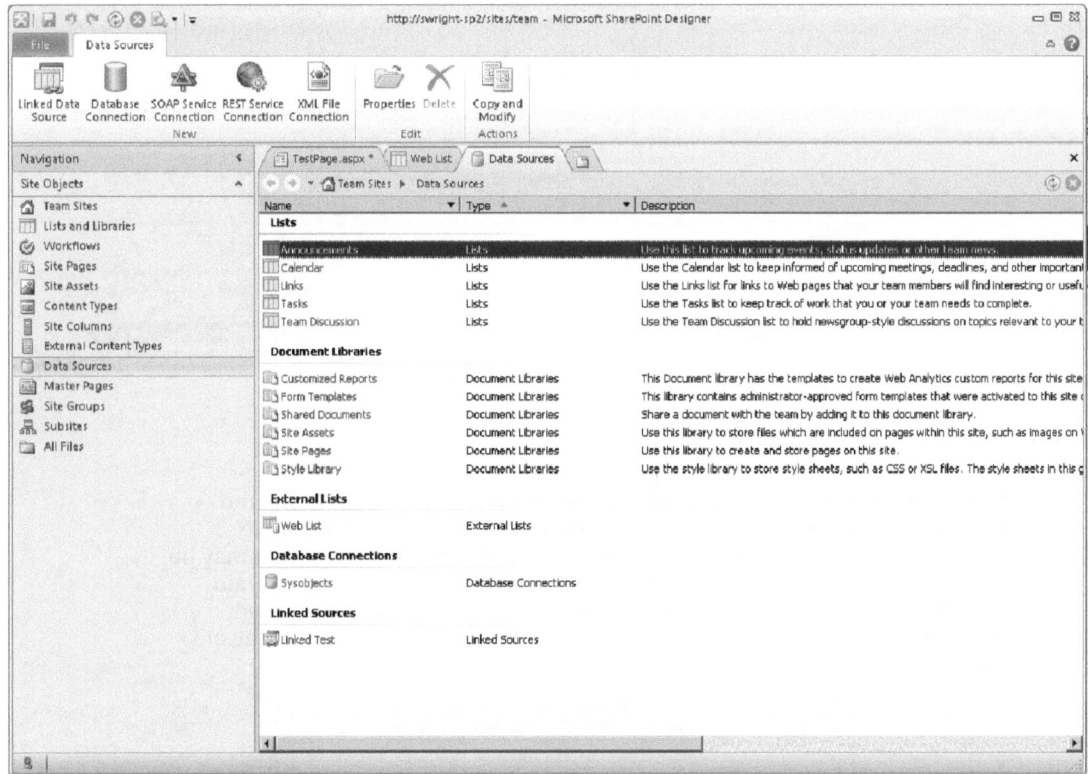

Figure 5-2. The Data Sources Gallery

Lists and Libraries

Data sources are created in one of two ways: automatically or manually. SharePoint Designer automatically exposes data sources associated with internal and external lists and with libraries that exist within the site. These data sources are configured to return all of the information from those sources and, where permitted, to support updates to items in those lists.

In most cases, it is not necessary to create new data sources for lists and libraries, but it can be done if necessary. The data source automatically created for a list cannot be altered except by changing the underlying list. However, to create a customized view of the data in a list, a new data source can be created and configured:

1. Open the Data Sources Gallery by clicking Data Sources in the Navigation pane.

2. Select the list you wish to use in the gallery page and then click Copy and Modify from the Actions group on the Data Sources tab on the menu, as shown in Figure 5-3.

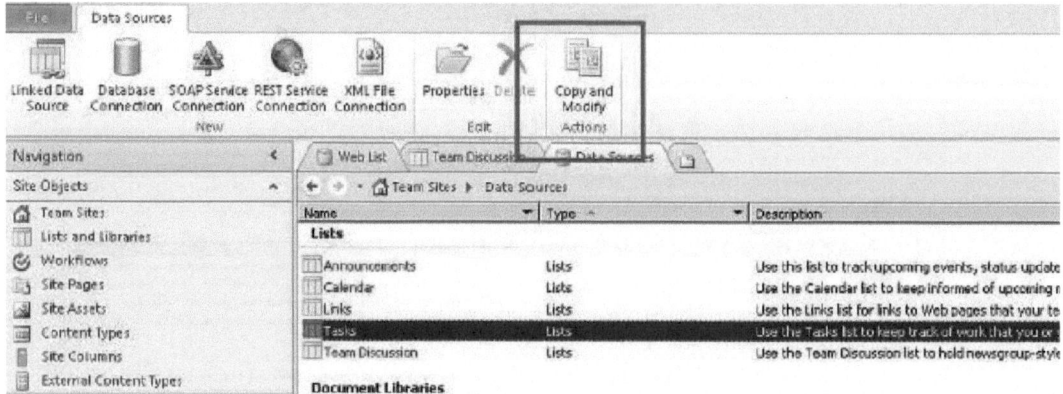

Figure 5-3. *The Copy and Modify action*

3. The Data Source Properties dialog box appears (see Figure 5-4). Using the options on the Source tab, you can select the fields to be made available through the data source, the sort order for the data, and any filters that may be needed to limit the items returned. Because lists and libraries may contain folders, there is also an option to select the scope of items to be returned. Leaving these options alone will create a new data source exactly like the old one.

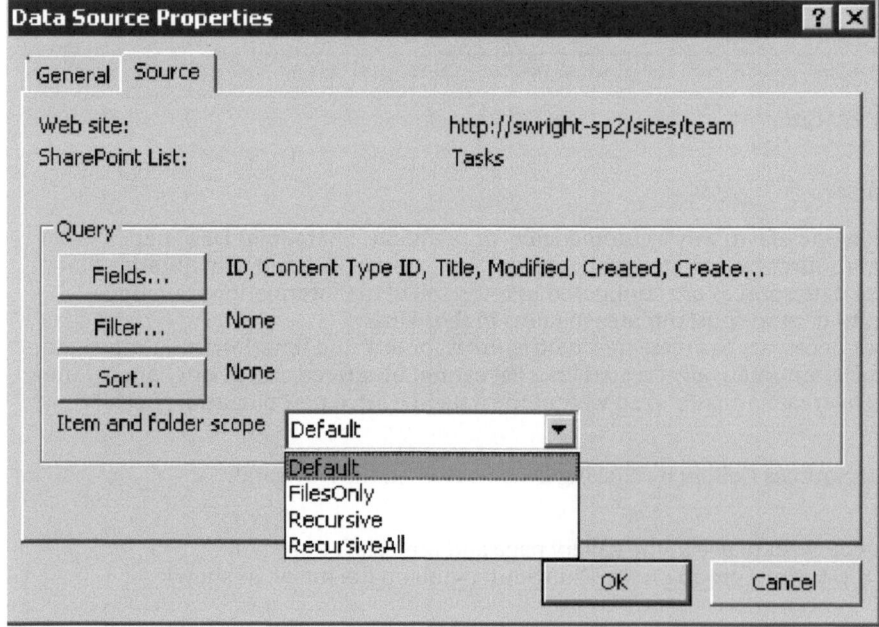

Figure 5-4. *Data Source Properties dialog box*

4. Click the General tab. Set the name and description for the new data source and then click OK to create it.

The new data source can now be used like any of the automatically created data sources except that it can be altered and deleted if necessary.

■ **Note** This technique for copying and modifying a data source is not unique to list data sources. Any data source can be copied and altered in the same way.

When you create a new data source, it appears in the Data Source Gallery. The gallery is just a conceptual container within SharePoint Designer, not a physical directory within the site. The data source you created was written as XML to a file in the web site. To work with this file directly, you can locate it in the All Files Gallery:

1. Click All Files in the Navigation pane. This displays a Gallery page that looks like Windows Explorer, as shown in Figure 5-5. These are the files and folders that are stored within the site.

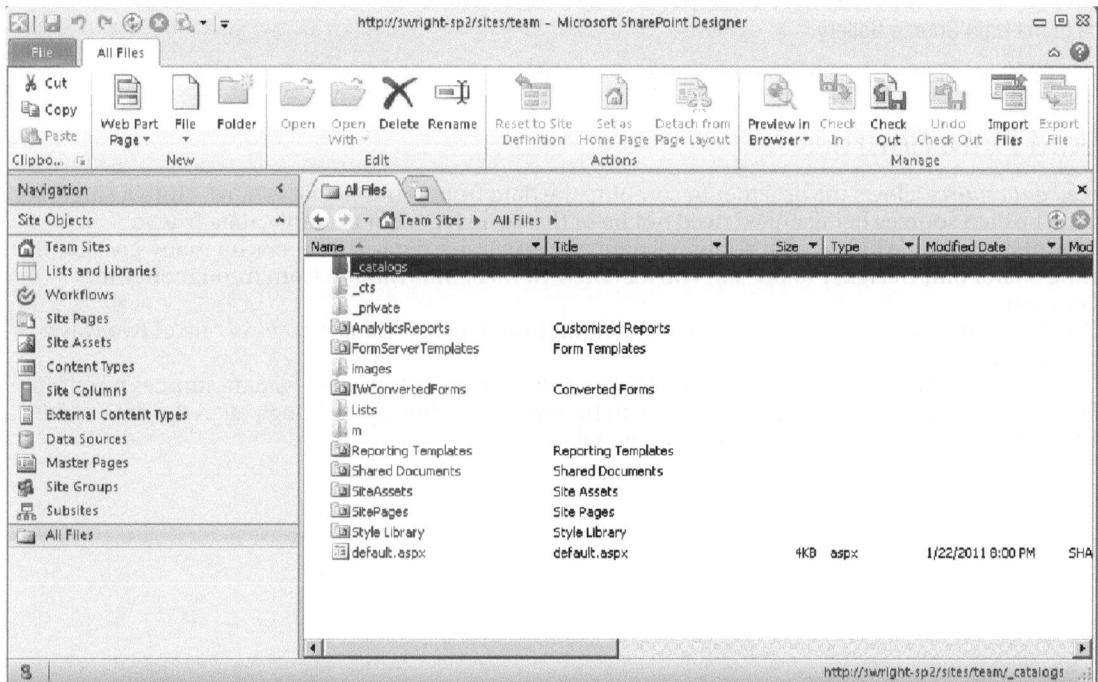

Figure 5-5. *The All Files Gallery page*

2. Click the _catalogs and then fpdatasources folders.

Figure 5-6. The fpdatasources folder

This folder contains all of the manually created data sources within the site. These are stored as XML files. These files can be exported to other locations or managed like any other file within SharePoint Designer. Any changes made to these files are automatically reflected in the Data Source Gallery.

■ **Caution** The XML in these data source files can be complex and difficult to understand. Use great care when attempting to edit these by hand. Where possible, use the built-in editors that are launched by clicking the data source in the Data Source Gallery.

Linked Data Sources

A *linked data source* allows the designer to combine the data from multiple data sources into a single set of data. The data sources being linked need not be of the same type. For example, data from a SharePoint list could be linked with relational data or web service data. This opens up many possibilities for using SharePoint Designer to present consolidated views of information from throughout the organization.

A linked data source can combine the information from a pair of data sources in one of two ways: merging or joining.

Merging data sources is like shuffling a deck of cards. The records of the two data sources are simply combined into a single list. The combined list can be sorted and filtered as though all of the data came from a single source. Figure 5-7 illustrates merging data.

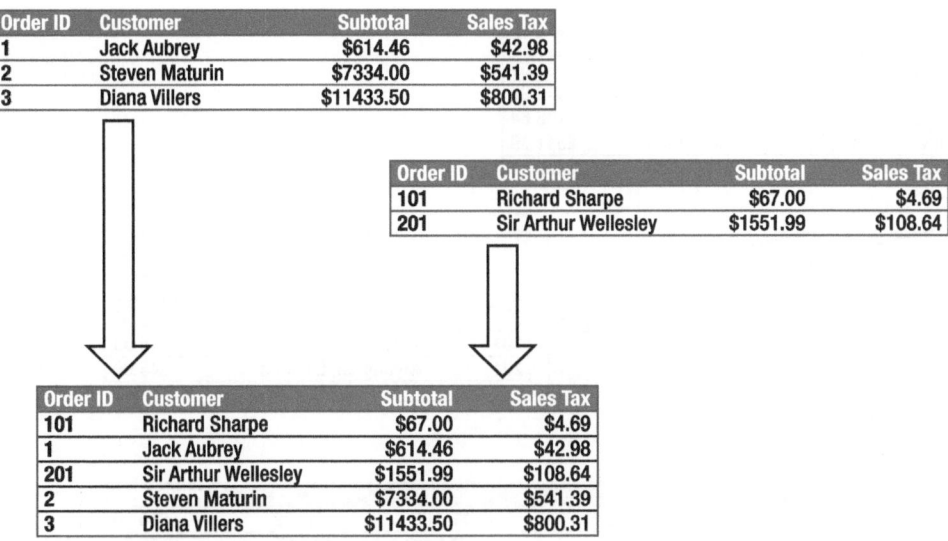

Figure 5-7. Linking data sets by merging data

The other option for linking data sources is to perform a *join* operation. Joining data involves creating new records by combining the fields of related records in the two data sources. Instead of having a list containing all of the entries of both lists, as in merging data, a joined data set will contain one entry for each combination of related records. This allows you to combine different types of information from different locations to produce new insights into the data. Figure 5-8 illustrates joining data.

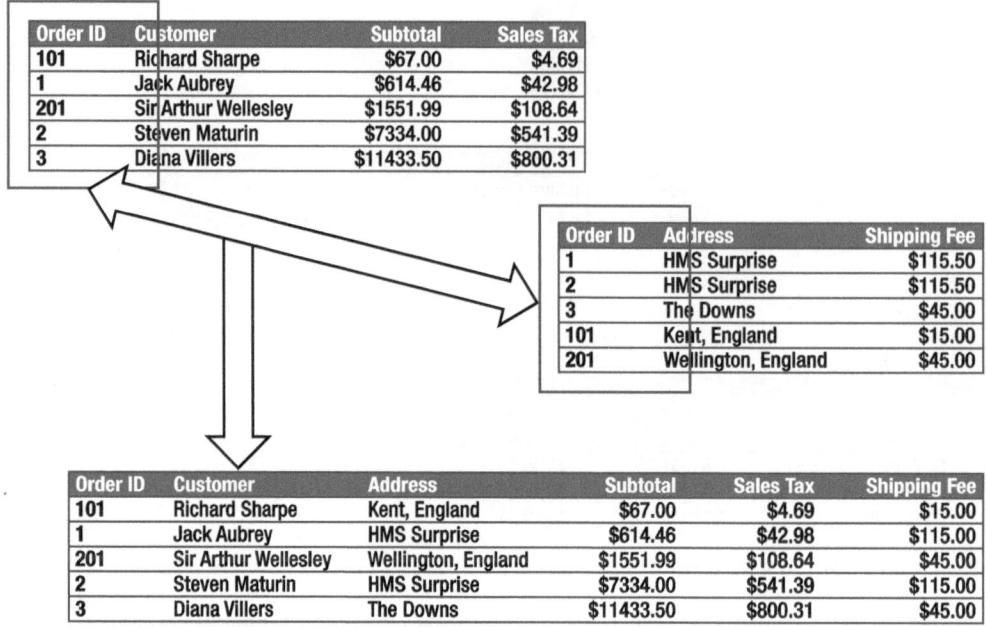

Order ID	Customer	Subtotal	Sales Tax
101	Richard Sharpe	$67.00	$4.69
1	Jack Aubrey	$614.46	$42.98
201	Sir Arthur Wellesley	$1551.99	$108.64
2	Steven Maturin	$7334.00	$541.39
3	Diana Villers	$11433.50	$800.31

Order ID	Address	Shipping Fee
1	HMS Surprise	$115.50
2	HMS Surprise	$115.50
3	The Downs	$45.00
101	Kent, England	$15.00
201	Wellington, England	$45.00

Order ID	Customer	Address	Subtotal	Sales Tax	Shipping Fee
101	Richard Sharpe	Kent, England	$67.00	$4.69	$15.00
1	Jack Aubrey	HMS Surprise	$614.46	$42.98	$115.00
201	Sir Arthur Wellesley	Wellington, England	$1551.99	$108.64	$45.00
2	Steven Maturin	HMS Surprise	$7334.00	$541.39	$115.00
3	Diana Villers	The Downs	$11433.50	$800.31	$45.00

Figure 5-8. Linking data sets by —joining data

External Lists

An *external list* is a special type of SharePoint list that stores its data outside of SharePoint Server. This data is accessed by using the BCS subsystem within the SharePoint server. To use BCS, you create an *external content type* that serves the function of defining the data that is being stored externally. An external list is then created by using the external type to give access to the data. An external list is just another list when used as a data source. It may or may not support writing changes back to the underlying data source, but can otherwise be used like any other list.

■ **Note** For additional details on using external lists and the other data source types described throughout this section, see Chapter 10.

Database Connections

RDBMSs are among the most common and versatile data storage systems used by most companies. The data stored in these databases is often used by various applications throughout the organization. SharePoint Designer allows this data to be queried and modified through data forms and views presented within a SharePoint site.

SharePoint Designer database connections can connect to most modern relational systems, including those supporting the Object Linking and Embedding, Database (OLE DB) and Open Database

Connectivity (ODBC) protocols. For additional functionality, performance, and ease of use, custom interfaces are provided for Microsoft SQL Server and Oracle databases.

When accessing data through a database connection, three methods are available for providing credentials. The simplest means is to provide a user ID and password with the required access privileges as part of the data source. You can also provide a complete, custom connection string as part of the data source's configuration. The problem with both of these options is that there is no way for the back-end database to enforce user-specific permissions because all access is made by using a single account. SharePoint Designer provides a further option to solve this problem. Using SharePoint's Secure Store Service (SSS), a database connection can be configured to access the back-end database using credentials that are specific to the user accessing the data. For more information on SSS, see the TechNet article at http://technet.microsoft.com/en-us/library/ee806889.aspx.

Beyond retrieving data, a database connection can also be configured to support the full range of create, read, update, and delete (CRUD) operations. The user can supply custom SQL or stored procedures to support inserts, updates, and deletes in addition to the default SELECT query.

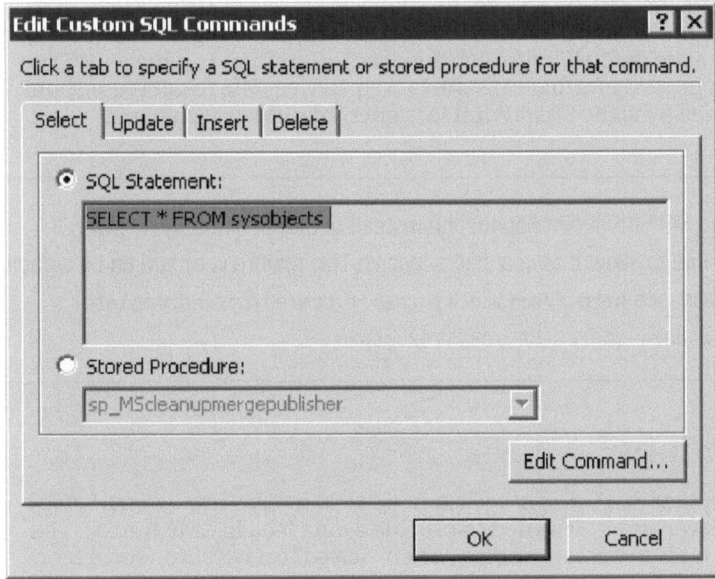

Figure 5-9 .Edit Custom SQL Commands dialog box

XML File Connections

An XML file connection allows XML-formatted data to be presented on a SharePoint site. The XML file may be stored locally within the site or accessed from another site by using a URL. When an XML file is added to the local site, it is automatically listed in the Data Sources Gallery. External XML files must be added manually.

When accessing local XML files, SharePoint enforces its normal access controls. When accessing remote XML files, it may be necessary to provide login credentials. This can be done either statically, by providing a fixed username and password, or dynamically, by using Windows Authentication or SSS.

XML files used as data sources are not required to have an associated Document Type Definition (DTD) or XSD schema definition. Therefore, these files can contain any valid XML markup.

Web Service Connections

A *web service* is a location on the network where a program can make a request and receive data in response. The interaction is similar to a web page, except that there is no user or web browser involved. A program makes a request from the web server behind the scenes. Web services are typically based on the SOAP protocol. SOAP, when it was originally created by Microsoft, stood for *Simple Object Access Protocol*, but that name is no longer used. SOAP is now a widely accepted Internet standard for web services. SOAP-based services exchange XML requests and responses over a network. SharePoint Designer web service connections allow this data to be presented within a site.

Secure web services may require the caller to provide login credentials. This can be done either statically, by providing a fixed username and password, or dynamically, by using Windows Authentication or SSS.

A web service may require parameters that can be passed into the data source by using a web part connection. This allows the caller to pass information as needed to access the data desired. The request and response required by the web service are defined in its Web Services Description Language (WSDL) file. SharePoint Designer uses this file to properly format calls into a web service. The result is a response XML document that can then be formatted by using SharePoint Designer's data view web parts.

■ **Note** If you are running your site by using MS SharePoint Foundation instead of SharePoint Server, you will need to update the `web.config` file for your site to allow it to use web services. This feature is turned on by default only when using the server product. For details, see `http://office.microsoft.com/en-us/sharepoint-designer-help/add-a-soap-service-as-a-data-source-HA010355752.aspx`.

Server-Side Script Connections

A server-side script connection is very similar to a web service connection in many ways. A *server-side script* is a program that runs on a web server and is designed to provide a data feed in XML format. The most obvious example of this type of script is a web log, or *blog*. When viewed in a web browser, a blog appears to be like any other web page, but behind the scenes, blogs provide a series of XML documents that are consumed by some other application.

The terminology gets somewhat confused because Microsoft also sometimes refers to these connections as *REST service connections*. REST is an architectural style for exposing web services in a simplified way. REST is only one type of server-side interface supported by SharePoint Designer. RSS feeds are also supported. RSS feeds are the traditional interface for blogs. However, many blogs also use REST and Atom Syndication feeds. These are all supported by SharePoint Designer.

In reality, a server-side script is just a program that accepts parameters and returns XML over a standard HTTP connection. Therefore, a basic service can be written by using almost any server-side technology such as ASPX, CGI, PHP, and so on.

When configuring a server-side script, it is important to have the following information beforehand:

- What is the URL of the script?

- What parameters are necessary?

- Does the service use the HTTP GET or POST protocol?

Unlike a SOAP web service, these services do not provide a WSDL file that can guide SharePoint Designer in preparing the correct parameters for the service.

▪ **Note** If you are running your site by using MS SharePoint Foundation instead of SharePoint Server, you will need to update the web.config file for your site to allow it to use server-side scripts as a data source. This feature is turned on by default only when using the server product. For details, see http://office.microsoft.com/en-us/sharepoint-designer-help/add-a-soap-service-as-a-data-source-HA010355752.aspx.

Using Data View Web Parts

SharePoint Designer presents data from a data source by using one of several data view web parts. There are several of these web parts, and each is tailored for use in certain situations. They all share certain attributes that make them easier to configure and customize.

The data web parts can be split into two classifications: list views and form views. *List views* display information as a table of information, as shown in Figure 5-10.

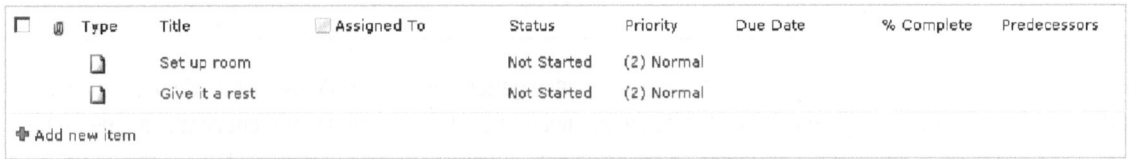

Figure 5-10. List view web part

Form views are most often used to display the details of a record or allow it to be inserted or updated, as shown in Figure 5-11.

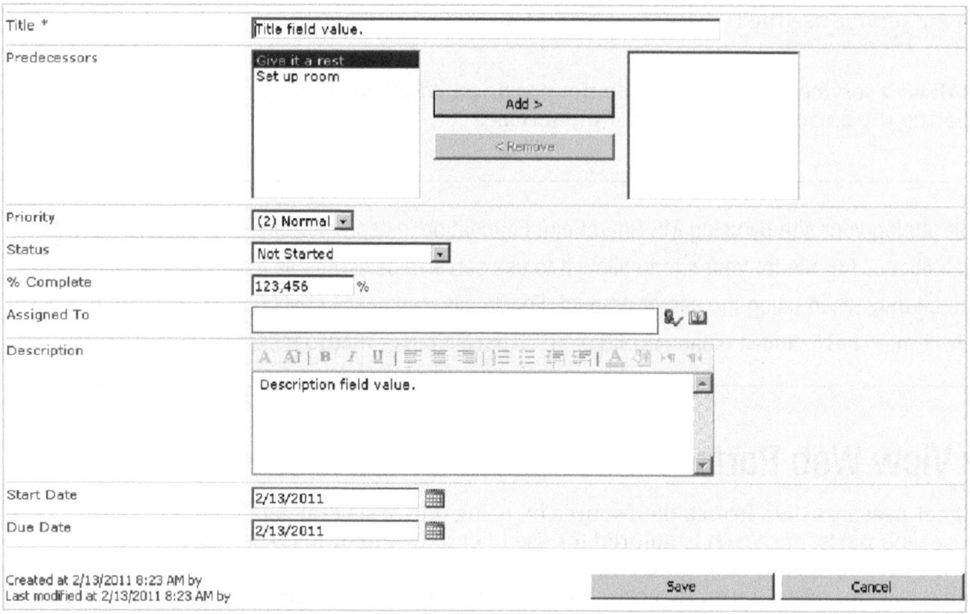

Figure 5-11. Form view web part

■ **Note** Unfortunately, the names of the data web parts have gotten very confusing over time. Some of the web parts can be used for more than one thing, leading to names that contain seemingly random combinations of the words *List*, *View*, *Data*, and *Form*. SharePoint 2010 introduced a new set of web parts with *XSLT* in the name. This has only added to the confusion, because these are not the only web parts that support XSLT formatting. A catalog of these web parts is presented later in this chapter. Be careful to note which web parts are used with which data sources and in which situations. Try not to get hung up on the names because they can be misleading. This is why they are frequently abbreviated with names such as *XLV* and *DFWP* that have little meaning on their own.

When working with data web parts, the Data Source Details task pane provides a view of the data that is being presented, as shown in Figure 5-12. The Data Source Details pane appears to the right of the main window automatically when a data web part is present on the page. If it does not appear when needed, it can be activated manually by selecting the View tab on the menu and then selecting the Data Source Details item from the Task Panes drop-down menu in the Workspace group.

Figure 5-12. Data Source Details task pane

Regardless of the type of data source being used, the data is always described in this task pane as an XML document. XML provides a standard form for describing the data being presented. The Data Source Details pane can be used to view data values, create additional related web parts, and add additional fields to an existing data web part by dragging and dropping fields onto the Page Editor.

The data view web parts can provide highly customized presentations because of their use of XML. The data values from the data source are passed to the web parts as an XML document. The web part then uses XSL Transformations (XSLT) to convert the XML into the HTML that is sent to the user's web browser.

In Figure 5-13, some HTML markup has been added to the XSLT associated with a DataFormWebPart. In the Page Editor's Split view, it is easy to see the result of your modifications in near real-time. Highlighting objects in one view panel causes them to be highlighted in the other. XSLT formatting allows for very tight control of the exact rendering of information in the data web parts, without sacrificing the functionality of the underlying data source.

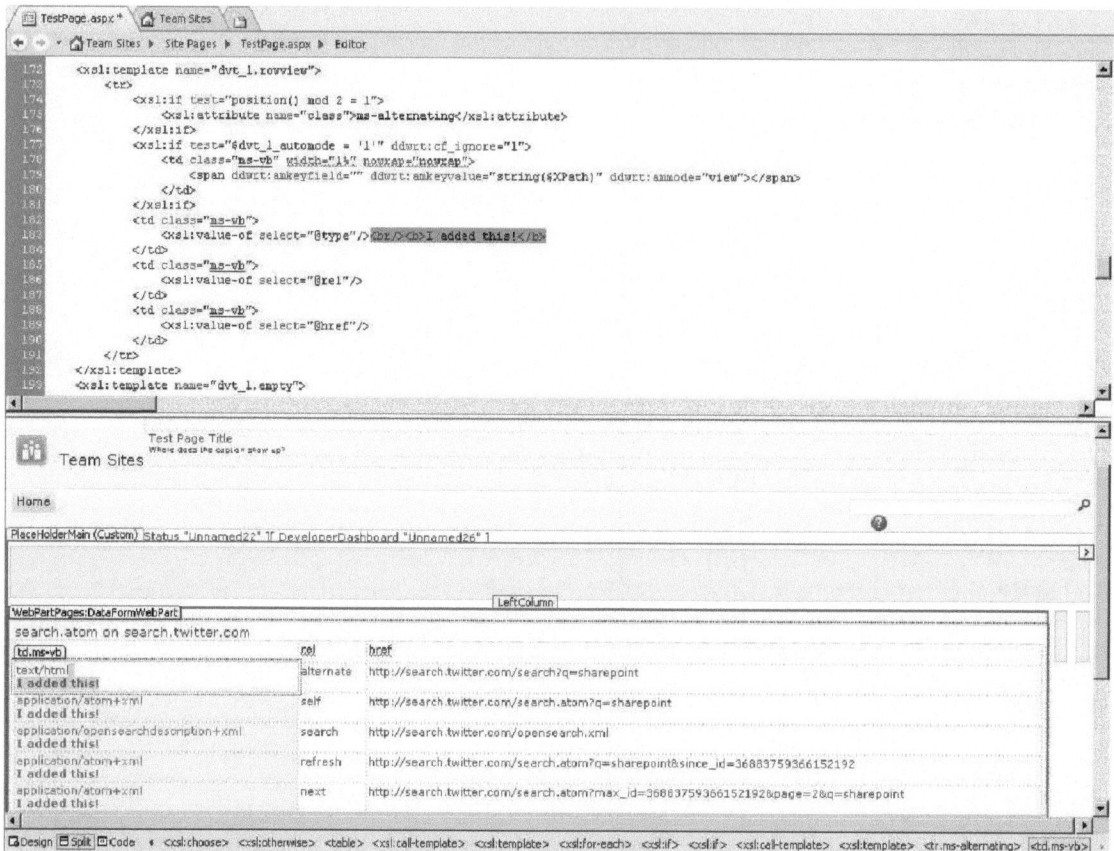

Figure 5-13. *XSLT formatting in the Page Editor (Split view)*

■ **Note** For those wanting to learn more about formatting data by using advanced XSLT markup, take a look at Jeni Tennison's *Beginning XSLT 2.0: From Novice to Professional* (Apress, 2005).

Data web parts are also designed to work together by passing parameters using web part connections. For example, a list of items can send an item's ID to a form view when an item is selected. These connections can also be used between pages when necessary.

List View Web Parts

List view web parts are primarily used to display lists of information from a data source. There are only two purely list-oriented web parts: the ListViewWebPart and the XsltListViewWebPart. Table 5-1 details the two list view web parts.

Table 5-1. *List View Web Parts*

Web Part	Description	When to Use
ListViewWebPart (LVWP)	The ListViewWebPart is an older web part that is used primarily for backward compatibility and highly customized views in SharePoint 2010. These customized views are part of the SharePoint product and include calendars and Gantt charts.	Not generally used by designers.
XsltListViewWebPart (XLV)	The XsltListViewWebPart is a customizable, easy-to-use web part for displaying lists of data. Many changes to the format can be made directly from the browser. Complex customizations can be made by using XSLT in SharePoint Designer. When SharePoint creates a new list view page, such as `AllItems.aspx`, an XLV is used to display the data. This web part is limited in the types of data sources it can use. XLV can receive data only from SharePoint lists (internal or external) and libraries. For other data sources, consider using the DataFormWebPart (DFWP).	For SharePoint lists and libraries, when easy customization is desirable.

Data Form Web Parts

Form-oriented web parts are primarily for displaying detailed data about an item. These forms can also be used to create and update items in some cases. Table 5-2 lists these data form web parts.

Table 5-2. *Data Form Web Parts*

Web Part	Description	When to Use
ListFormWebPart (LFWP)	The ListFormWebPart is a very simple web part that cannot be customized and is used to display data entry forms. This web part is placed on the default pages `DispForm.aspx`, `EditForm.aspx`, and `NewForm.aspx` generated by SharePoint when a list is created. In order to customize the appearance or functionality of the form, it must first be converted to a DataFormWebPart.	Generated by default when a SharePoint list or library is created.
DataViewWebPart (DVWP)	This web part is included in SharePoint 2010 only to support upgrades from earlier versions of SharePoint. It is no longer used for new sites.	Upgrades only. Do not use on new sites.

Web Part	Description	When to Use
DataFormWebPart (DFWP)	The DataFormWebPart is the most versatile of the data web parts in SharePoint Designer. DFWP can be used for either a form or a list view of data. It can also be used with any type of data source. The DFWP is most often used when inserting new web parts from the Data Source Details pane. It is also the default web part used when viewing data from sources other than SharePoint lists and libraries.	Use with any data source for presenting either lists or forms.
XsltListFormWebPart (XLF)	This web part is designed for manipulating data to external lists. There are no customization options available through the web browser. All modifications must be done in SharePoint Designer by using XSLT. Chapter 10 covers using external content types and lists with SharePoint Designer.	Use when creating data entry forms for external content types.
InfoPath Form Web Part (IFWP)	Microsoft InfoPath is an application used to create intelligent data entry forms. These forms can be used in place of the generated forms for editing list items. InfoPath forms are discussed in Chapter 11 along with an example of replacing a generated form. The IFWP is used to host the InfoPath form in this scenario.	Use when hosting an InfoPath-based data entry form.

Creating Data Pages in SharePoint Designer

Now that you are familiar with the data access components available through SharePoint Designer, let's try putting the pieces together.

In the following exercises, you will create a set of related lists within SharePoint. These lists will provide the information for your data pages. You will customize the views and forms that are automatically generated by SharePoint. You will then create two new web pages by using SharePoint Designer's data web parts. The first page will be a simple listing of orders that will allow you to subtotal your orders geographically. The second page will provide a means of filtering data, passing parameters, and entering data by using the data web parts.

EXERCISE 5-1. CREATE DATA LISTS

The first thing you need to do is establish some test data in a set of SharePoint lists. In a blank site, create three lists: States, Orders, and Order Lines. These lists will be related with lookup fields that will allow you to relate items in one list with items in the others.

SharePoint 2010 has improved the functionality of lookup fields to include features similar to foreign keys in relational databases. These fields are still somewhat limited compared to true foreign keys but they allow one important new feature that you will use here. This is the concept of projected fields. A *projected field* is a value taken from the lookup table and made available as a read-only field in the list. For example, if you do a lookup on a state's abbreviation (such as *CA*), you can also expose the full name of the state (*California*) as a read-only field in the list making the reference. You will walk through doing this in a moment.

1. Open SharePoint Designer and create a new blank site if necessary.

2. From the Navigation pane, select Lists and Libraries.

3. Select Custom List from the New group on the Lists and Libraries menu tab.

4. Type **States** for the name of the list and click OK.

5. Open the column list editor window for States.

6. Change the Title field to **State Abbr** and then create the other fields as shown in Figure 5-14.

Column Name	Type	Description	Required
State Abbr	Single line of text		Yes
State Name	Single line of text		
Sales Region	Single line of text		

Figure 5-14. States list definition

7. Save the new list definition.

8. Select Lists and Libraries from the Navigation pane.

9. Select Custom List from the New group on the Lists and Libraries menu tab.

10. Type **Orders** for the name of the list and click OK.

11. Open the column list editor window for Orders.

12. Change the Title field to **Order Number** and then create the other fields as shown in Figure 5-15.

Column Name	Type	Description	Required
Order Number	Single line of text		Yes
Customer	Single line of text		
City	Single line of text		
Taxes	Currency ($, ¥, €)		
Shipping	Currency ($, ¥, €)		
SubTotal	Currency ($, ¥, €)		
Total	Currency ($, ¥, €)		
Order Date	Date and Time		

Figure 5-15. Orders list definition (partial)

13. Finally, select Lookup (Information Already on This Site) from the Add New Column drop-down list in the New group on the Columns tab. The Column Editor opens, as shown in Figure 5-16.

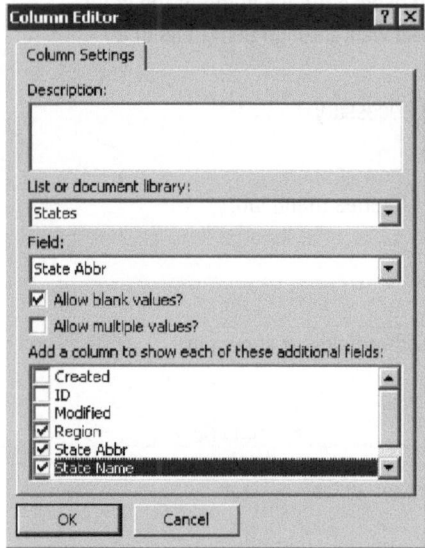

Figure 5-16. Column Editor (State field)

14. Select the States list and the State Abbr field.

15. At the bottom of the dialog box, select the check boxes for the Region, State Abbr, and State Name fields. This will make these fields appear in the Orders list as read-only columns.

16. Click OK and set the field name to State.

17. Save the new list definition. The region and state name fields appear only after the list definition is saved (see Figure 5-17).

ok—

Figure 5-17. Orders List definition (complete)

■ **Note** In Figure 5-17, it may seem strange that we have listed both State and State:State Abbr when they appear to contain the same information. The reason for this will be made clear later. In brief, the State field contains a reference to the ID field in the States list, whereas the State:State Abbr field contains the actual two-letter abbreviation of the state. When simply displaying this field, there is no difference. Both fields are rendered as the two-letter abbreviation. However, when accessing data for sorting, filtering, or joining lists, it is sometimes necessary to use the data value rather than the identifier column.

18. Select Lists and Libraries from the Navigation pane.

19. Select Custom List from the New group on the Lists and Libraries menu tab.

20. Type **Order Lines** for the name of the list and click OK.

21. Open the column list editor window for Order Lines.

22. Change the Title field to **Product ID** and then create the other fields as shown in Figure 5-18.

Figure 5-18. Order Lines list definition (partial)

23. Save the new list definition.

24. Select Calculated (Calculation Based on Other Columns) from the Add New Column drop-down list in the New group on the Columns tab.

25. Enter the formula to calculate the Line Total value as shown in Figure 5-19.

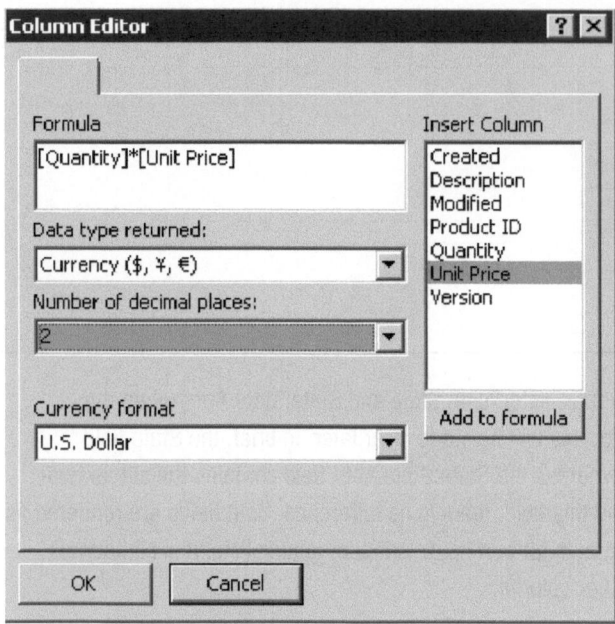

Figure 5-19. Column Editor (Line Total field)

26. Select Lookup (Information Already on This Site) from the Add New Column drop-down list in the New group on the Columns tab. The Column Editor opens, as shown in Figure 5-20.

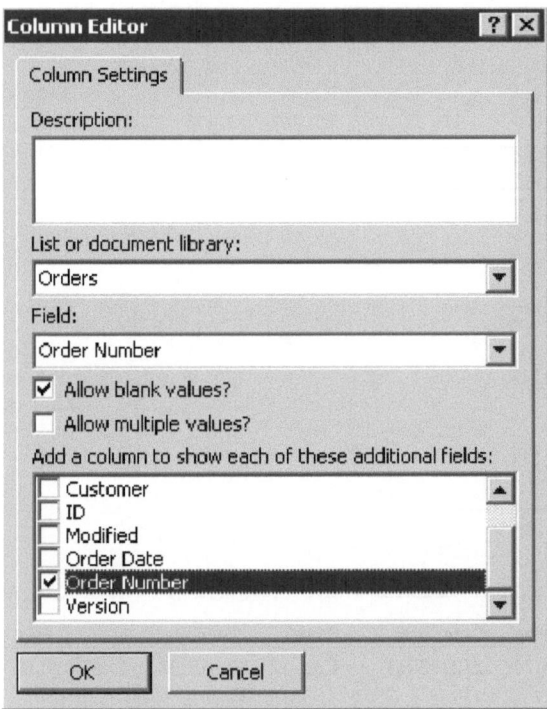

Figure 5-20. Column Editor (Order Number field)

27. Select the Orders list and the Order Number field.

28. Select the Order Number field under additional fields.

29. Click OK and set the field name to Order Number.

30. Save the new list definition.

Column Name	Type	Description	Required
Product ID	Single line of text		Yes
Description	Single line of text		
Quantity	Number (1, 1.0, 100)		
Unit Price	Currency ($, ¥, €)		
Line Total	Calculated (calculation based on other columns)		
Order Number	Lookup (information already on this site)		
Order Number:Order Number	Lookup (information already on this site)		

Figure 5-21. Order Lines list definition (complete)

Now that the lists have been created, you need to create some sample data in the lists to work with. You can do this by using the data entry forms available in SharePoint, through the Datasheet view (if available in your configuration) or through the SharePoint Workspace client application. The data you will use in the rest of this chapter is shown in Table 5-3, Table 5-4, and Table 5-5 and can be downloaded from this book's web site.

Table 5-3. *States List Items*

State Abbr	State Name	Sales Region
CA	California	West
IN	Indiana	Midwest
NE	Nebraska	Midwest
NY	New York	East
KY	Kentucky	Midwest
TX	Texas	West
IL	Illinois	Midwest
FL	Florida	East

Table 5-4. *Orders List Items*

Order Number	Customer	City	Taxes	Shipping	Order Date	State	SubTotal	Total
S0001	Jack Aubrey	South Hampton	$245.79	$73.74	2/21/2011	CA	$3,511.33	$3,830.86
S0002	Stephen Maturin	Kent	$548.34	$164.50	3/13/2001	NE	$7,833.48	$8,697.06
S0003	Diana Villers	Kent	$558.01	$167.40	4/23/2009	NE	$7,971.64	$8,697.06
S0004	Arthur Wellesley	London	$680.36	$204.11	3/5/2007	NY	$9,719.49	$10,603.96
S0005	Richard Sharpe	Plainfield	$579.83	$173.95	2/2/2002	IN	$8,283.23	$9,037.00

Table 5-5. *Order Lines List Items*

Product ID	Description	Quantity	Unit Price	Order Number	Total Price
w42345	Socks	5	$153.23	S0001	$766.15
e3462	Backpack	4	$427.32	S0002	$1,709.28
2342-25	MP3 Player	3	$1,709.41	S0003	$5,128.23
t423523	Table	2	$1,149.26	S0001	$2,298.52
25-345-6344	Sofa	1	$766.17	S0001	$766.17

EXERCISE 5-2. CUSTOMIZE GENERATED VIEWS AND FORMS

When a new SharePoint list or library is created, a set of ASPX pages are generated automatically. These correspond to the views and forms used to access the data in the list. By default, one view (`AllItems.aspx`) and three forms (`DispForm.aspx`, `EditForm.aspx`, and `NewForm.aspx`) are created. These can be seen by viewing the settings page for the list, as shown in Figure 5-22.

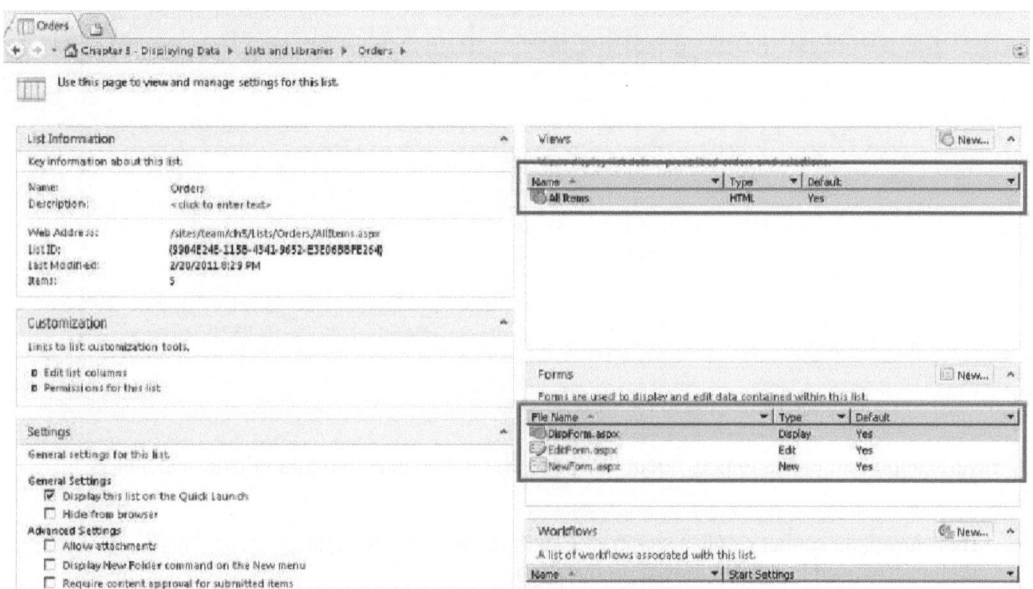

Figure 5-22. Order List settings page

In this exercise, you will explore and customize these views and forms.

1. Open the settings page for the Orders list and click the All Items view. This opens the Page Editor for the All Items view, as shown in Figure 5-23.

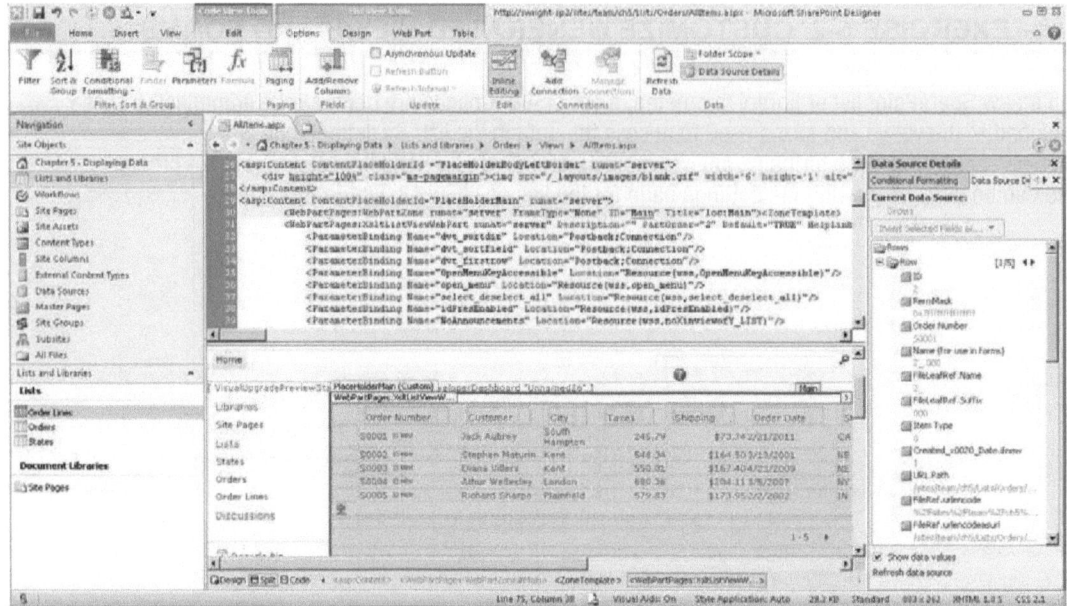

Figure 5-23. *All Items View Page Editor (Split mode)*

There are several important things to note about this page and the options that SharePoint Designer is presenting:

- This view page contains only a single web part: an XsltListViewWebPart (XLV). This web part is used to display the list on the page.

- In the top half of the Split view, the markup for the view is visible and can be directly edited.

- The markup highlighted in yellow is inherited from the page layout and is not editable except in Advanced mode (see Chapter 2).

- To the right of the Page Editor is the Data Source Details task pane, which displays all the data fields that are available for this view. If the Data Source Details pane does not appear automatically, it can be activated by using the Task Panes drop-down menu on the View tab of the menu.

- The List View Tools tab on the Ribbon menu contains many options for customizing the view without writing any HTML or XSLT markup. This toolbar is available whenever the XLV control is selected.

You will now use some of these options to customize the view in useful ways. Figure 5-24 illustrates the onscreen options.

2. The Order Date is currently aligned to the left, making it hard to read. Click one of the dates in the Order Date column.

3. On the Table tab under List View Tools, click the center button in the Cell Layout group.

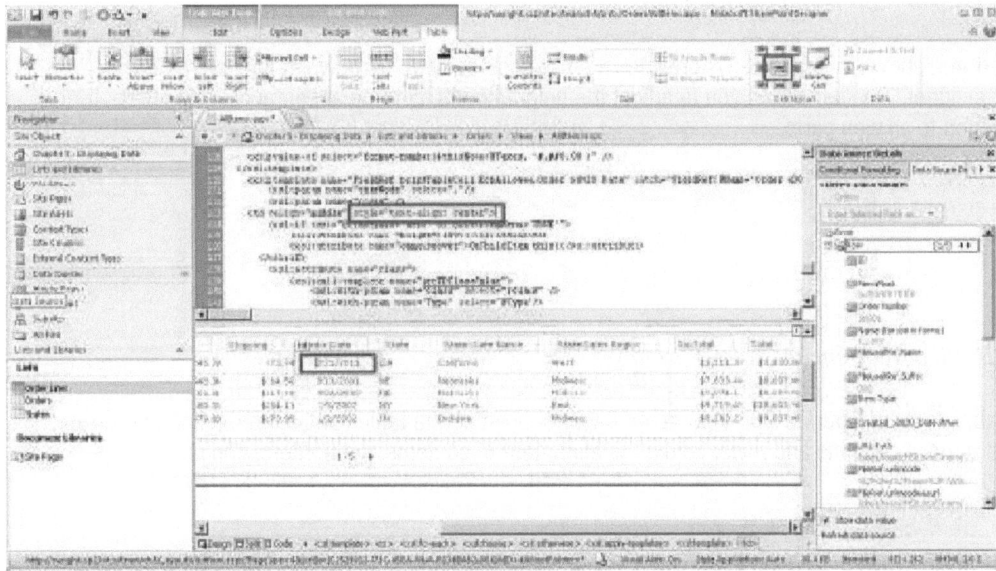

Figure 5-24. Centering Order Date in the All Items view

Let's look at some of the other options available to you on the Ribbon menu. The Options tab, shown in Figure 5-25, allows the designer to sort, group, and filter items and adjust the presentation of the list in other ways.

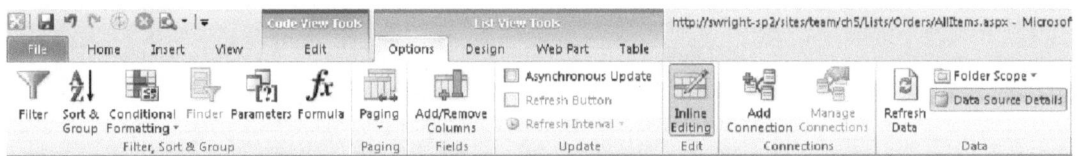

Figure 5-25. List View Tools menu—Options tab

The Design tab, shown in Figure 5-26, presents commands for radically changing the layout of the list items. You can also adjust the toolbar and add total rows.

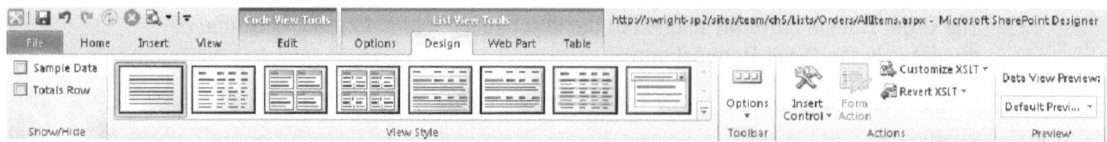

Figure 5-26. *List View Tools menu—Design tab*

The Web Part tab, shown in Figure 5-27, provides a set of tools for web parts when they are edited in SharePoint Designer. This tab allows you to adjust the height, width, chrome appearance, and other options common to all web parts.

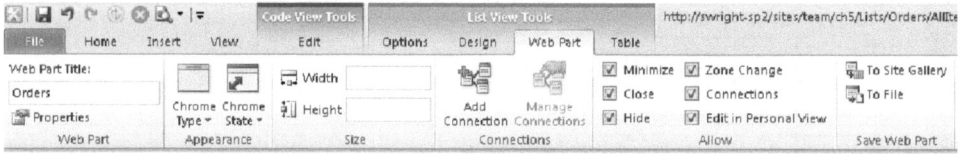

Figure 5-27. *List View Tools menu—Web Part tab*

The Table tab, shown in Figure 5-28, is targeted toward adjusting the table containing the list items. You can add and remove columns and rows, adjust the alignment of contents, set borders, and so on.

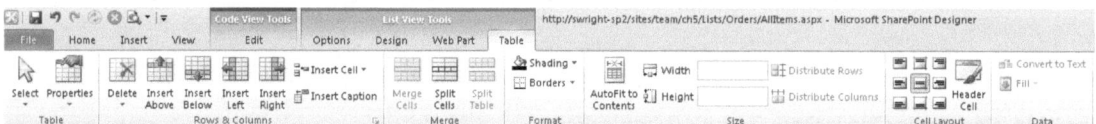

Figure 5-28. *List View Tools menu—Table tab*

Now you will customize the view by setting up paging and allowing inline editing. *Inline editing* is a feature that allows the user to enter data directly into fields rendered within the list view, as shown in Figure 5-29.

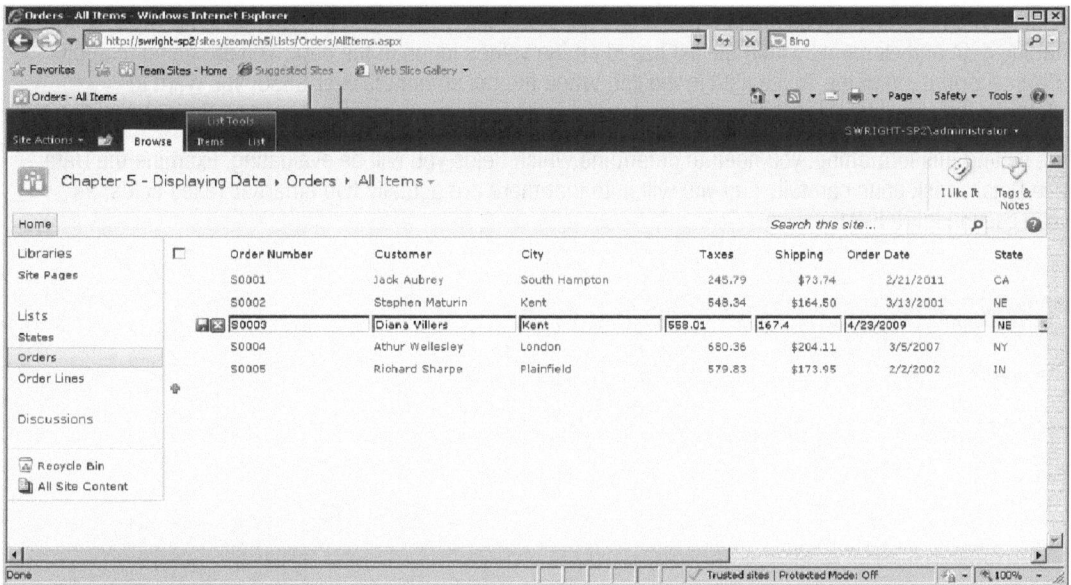

Figure 5-29. List View in Inline Editing mode

4. On the Options tab, open the Paging drop-down menu and select the Display Sets of 5 Items option, as shown in Figure 5-30. The pages displayed will now contain five items instead of the default of ten.

5. On the same tab, click the Inline Editing option in the Edit group. This enables the inline editing feature for the web part when it is viewed in the browser.

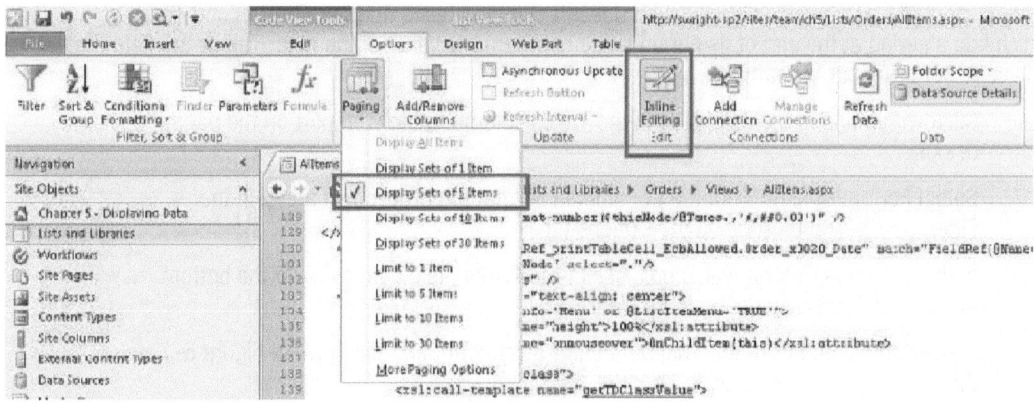

Figure 5-30. Set Paging and Inline Editing modes

Up to now, you have focused on options that affect the entire list. SharePoint Designer also has options for formatting data and elements within the list based on the values found in the data. You are going to apply *conditional formatting* to the Taxes field in the list. When the tax amount is over $550, you want to highlight the value by changing the background color on the cell.

Before setting this formatting, you need to determine which fields you will be evaluating. Examine the Data Source Details task pane carefully and you will note that there are actually two different Taxes fields, as you can see in Figure 5-31.

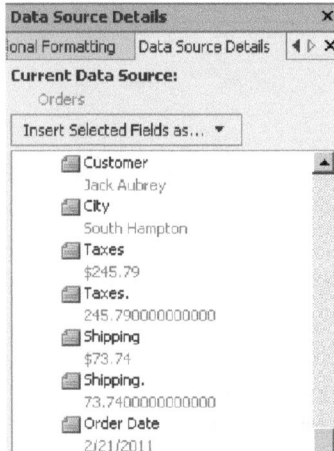

Figure 5-31. Numeric fields in the DSD task pane

The first Taxes field is a nicely formatted version of the currency field. This is useful for display purposes, but not for performing numeric logic, because it doesn't contain a valid number. The second Taxes field(which has a period at the end of its name) is the raw numeric value of the field. This is the field that you will use to perform your formatting.

6. Click within one of the data cells in the Taxes column in the web part on the page designer.

7. Select Format Column from the Conditional Formatting drop-down menu in the Filter, Sort & Group group on the Options tab.

8. In the Condition Criteria dialog box, select the Taxes. field by moving to the bottom of the field list and selecting More Fields.

9. Set the condition to Greater Than and enter a value of 550, as shown in Figure 5-32.

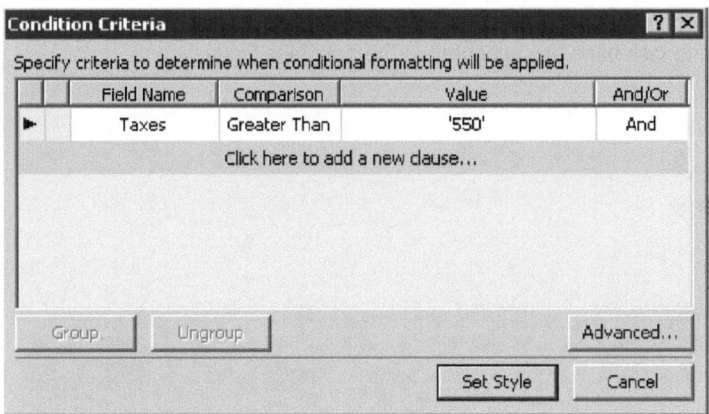

Figure 5-32. *Condition Criteria dialog box*

10. Click the Set Style button. The Modify Style dialog box opens, as shown in Figure 5-33.

11. Select the Background category and set the Background-Color option to your favorite color.

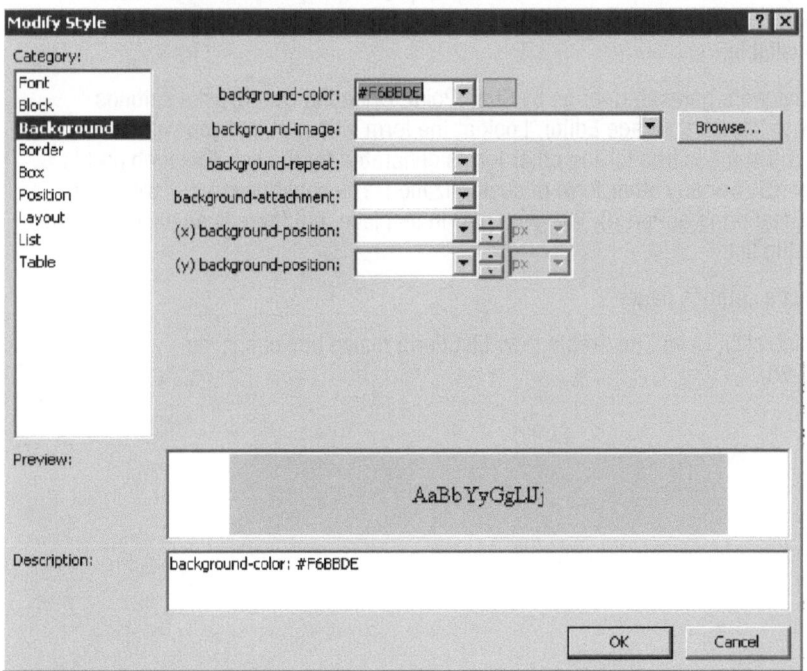

Figure 5-33. *Modify Style dialog box*

12. Click OK. Note that the list in the page designer has taken on the new style and that the Conditional Formatting task pane has appeared to the right (see Figure 5-34).

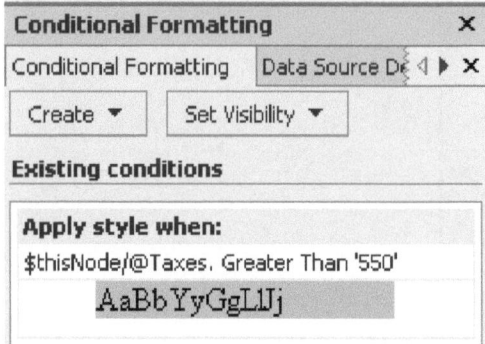

Figure 5-34. Conditional Formatting task pane

13. Save the page and view in the web browser.

Using conditional formatting, the XsltListViewWebPart (XLV) web part provides a powerful way to customize SharePoint views without resorting to coding XSLT by hand. Of course, that option is always available when the needed effect isn't available.

Now let's examine the forms that were generated for us by SharePoint. Open the Orders list's settings page and click EditForm.aspx to launch the Page Editor. Look at the form web part and you will see that it is a ListFormWebPart (LFWP). The same is true for the other forms generated for the list. This web part is very limited. It does not support XSLT or any other form of customization. You could delete this web part from the page and add a new DataFormWebPart (DFWP) web part in its place, but there is an easier way to create a customizable form for the list.

14. Open the Orders list's settings page.

15. Above the Forms list, click New. The Create New List Form dialog box opens, as shown in Figure 5-35.

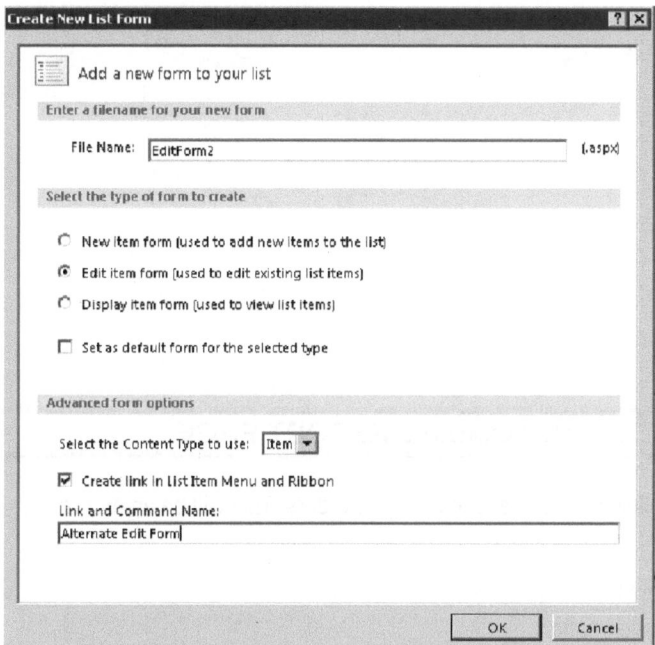

Figure 5-35. *Create New List Form dialog box*

16. In the File Name text box, type**EditForm2**.

17. Select the Edit Item Form radio button.

18. Select the check box labeled Create Link in List Item Menu and Ribbon.

19. In the Link and Command Line field, type **Alternate Edit Form**. Click the OK button.

Note that two new items have been created on the settings page: a new form and a new custom action. Open the new form in the Page Editor and you will notice that it is very similar to the original EditForm.aspx except that it uses the DFWP, which allows for a wide variety of customization similar to those for the XLV you examined earlier.

The new custom action appears on menus attached to items in the list. This menu item opens the new form you just created, as you can see in Figure 5-36.

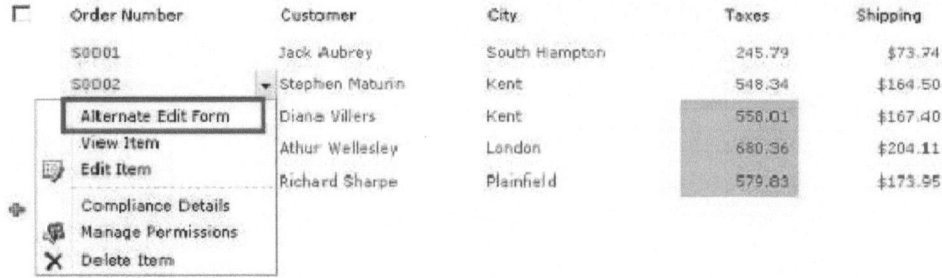

	Order Number	Customer	City	Taxes	Shipping
	S0001	Jack Aubrey	South Hampton	245.79	$73.74
	S0002	Stephen Maturin	Kent	548.34	$164.50
		Diana Villers	Kent	558.01	$167.40
		Athur Wellesley	London	680.36	$204.11
		Richard Sharpe	Plainfield	579.83	$173.95

Alternate Edit Form
View Item
Edit Item
Compliance Details
Manage Permissions
Delete Item

Figure 5-36. New custom form action

EXERCISE 5-3. CREATE A CUSTOMIZED REPORT PAGE

You are now going to create a page that will allow you to total some of your orders. This will be an ordinary site page, not a list view or form:

1. Open the site in SharePoint Designer.

2. Select Site Pages from the Navigation pane.

3. Select the first template from the Web Part Page drop-down menu on the Pages tab of the menu, as shown in Figure 5-37.

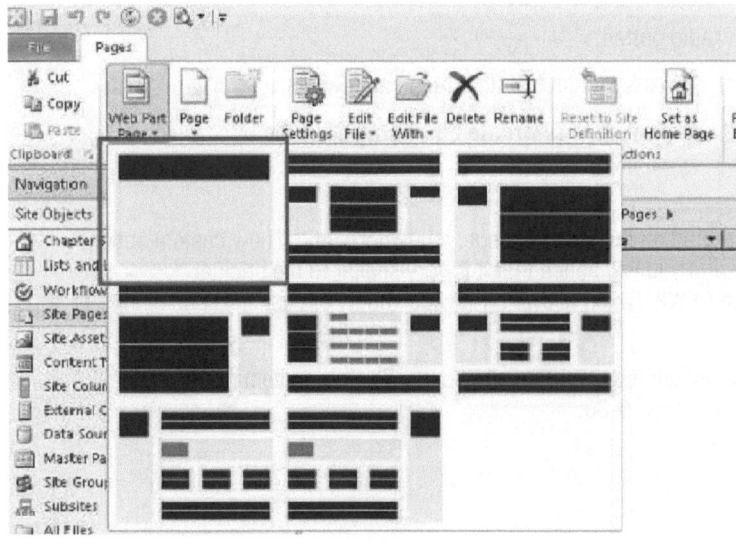

Figure 5-37. Web part page templates

4. Rename the new page OrderReport.aspx.

5. Open the new page in the Page Editor. Click the web part zone in the center of the page.

6. From the Data View drop-down menu in the Data Views & Forms group on the Insert tab of the menu, select Orders, as shown in Figure 5-38.

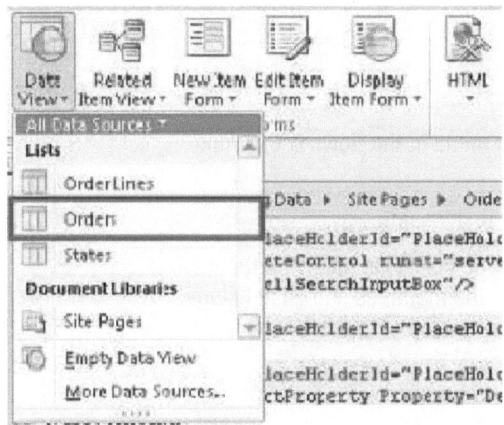

Figure 5-38. Insert the data view web part

7. Click Sort & Group from the Options tab on the List View Tools menu.

8. Add the State:Sales Region and State:State Name fields, selecting Show Group Header for both.

9. Add the Order Number field, but *do not* show the group header. Click OK.

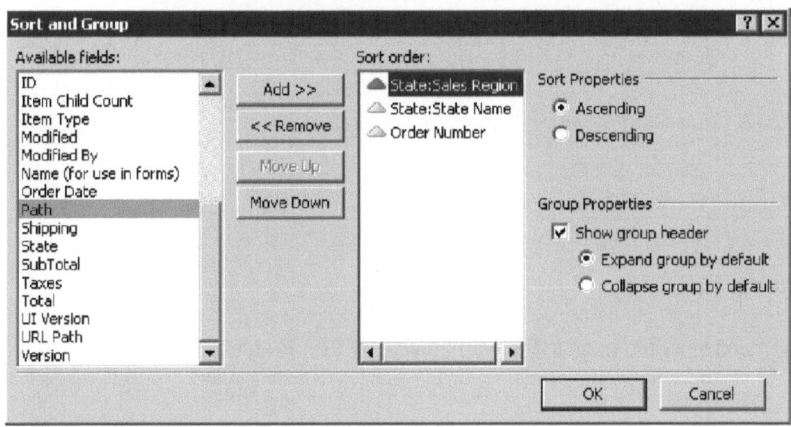

Figure 5-39. Sort and Group dialog box

10. Switch to the Design tab on the List View Tools menu and select Totals Rows. After a few moments, a row showing the totals for each group and subgroup appears.

11. You don't want to display all of the counts in the Totals row, so select each one and press Delete.

12. In the remaining totals fields, select the Sum= text and delete it, being sure to leave the total alone by itself in the cell.

13. Switch to the Table tab in the menu.

14. Select the top cell from the State:State Name column.

15. Select Delete Column from the Delete drop-down menu in the Rows & Columns group on the menu.

16. Remove State:State Abbr and State:Sales Region in the same way.

17. Select the total row cells that contain the totals to be displayed and click the Align Center Right button from the Cell Layout group on the menu, as shown in Figure 5-40.

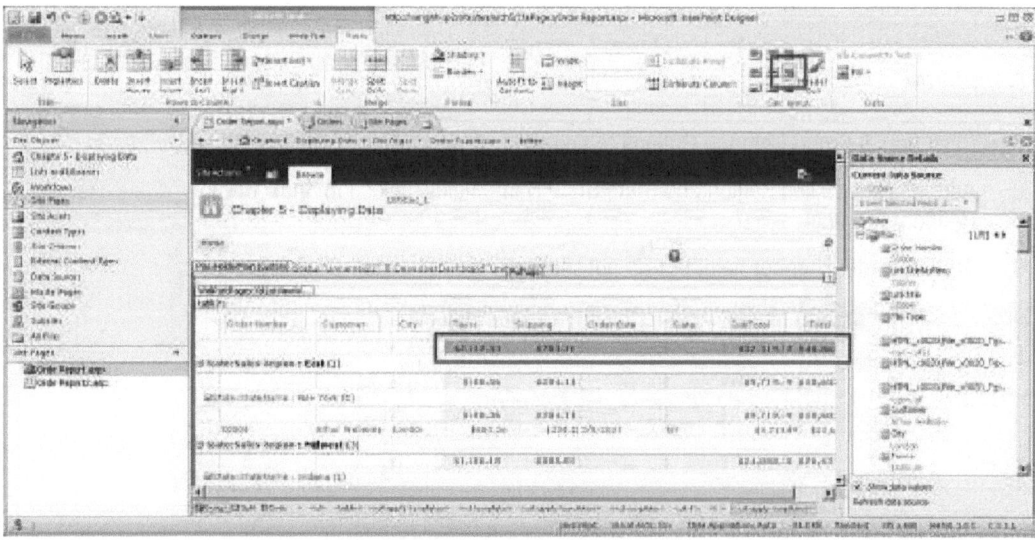

Figure 5-40. Page Editor (`OrderReport.aspx`)

18. Save the page (Ctrl+S) and view the page in the web browser (F12), as shown in Figure 5-41.

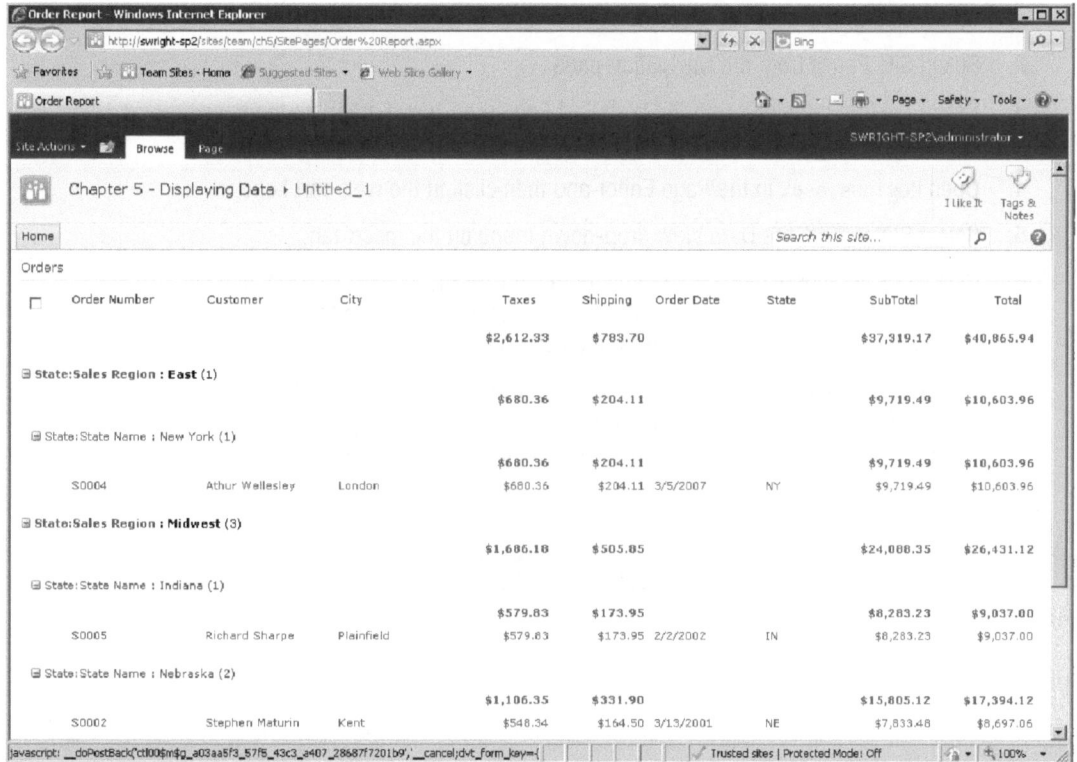

Figure 5-41. *Orders report page*

With just a few clicks, you have created a custom report based on the order data within these SharePoint lists. With further formatting and XSLT changes, the possible variations of this type of report are virtually limitless.

EXERCISE 5-4. CONNECT AND PARAMETERIZE DATA WEB PARTS

In this exercise, you will explore two important features of SharePoint Designer's data web parts: connections and parameters. Web part connections are not unique to the data web parts. *Connections* allow data to be passed from one web part to another, usually for the purpose of filtering the data displayed. *Parameters* serve a similar purpose, except that these can receive their data from sources other than web parts, including cookies, form and server variables, ASP.NET controls and, most commonly, from query string parameters on the page's URL.

In this example, you will create two pages. The first page will list the states in your system and present a filtered list of the orders for the selected state. The order number will link to the second page, passing the order number in the URL. This page will show the selected order's details and line items.

1. Open the site in SharePoint Designer.

2. Select Site Pages from the Navigation pane.

3. Select the first template from the Web Part Page drop-down menu on the Pages tab in the menu. Name the new page Regions.aspx.

4. Open Regions.aspx in the Page Editor and then click in the web part zone.

5. Select States from the Data View drop-down menu on the Insert tab.

6. Click in the web part zone beneath the data view for the States list. This may be easier to do if you use Split mode in the Page Editor. Select the States list and then move the cursor after the web part in the code window.

7. Select Orders:State from the Related Item View drop-down menu on the Insert tab. If this option is grayed out, be sure you are not still on the list control itself. You need to have your cursor in the web part zone, but not on the list.

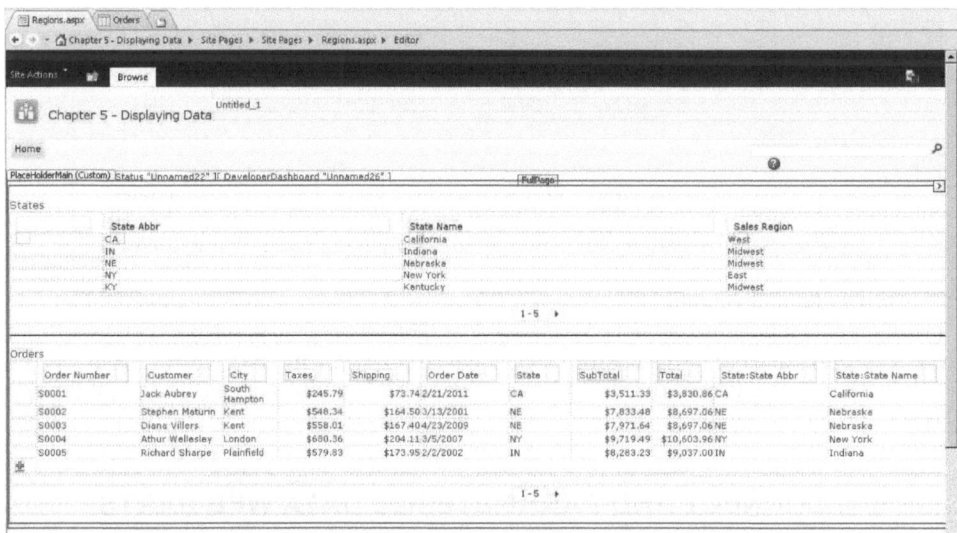

Figure 5-42. Regions page with connected web parts

8. Save the page (Ctrl+S) and view the page in the web browser (F12).

9. Click the double-arrow icon at the beginning of the Nebraska line, as shown in Figure 5-43. This will refilter the list of orders to show those from Nebraska.

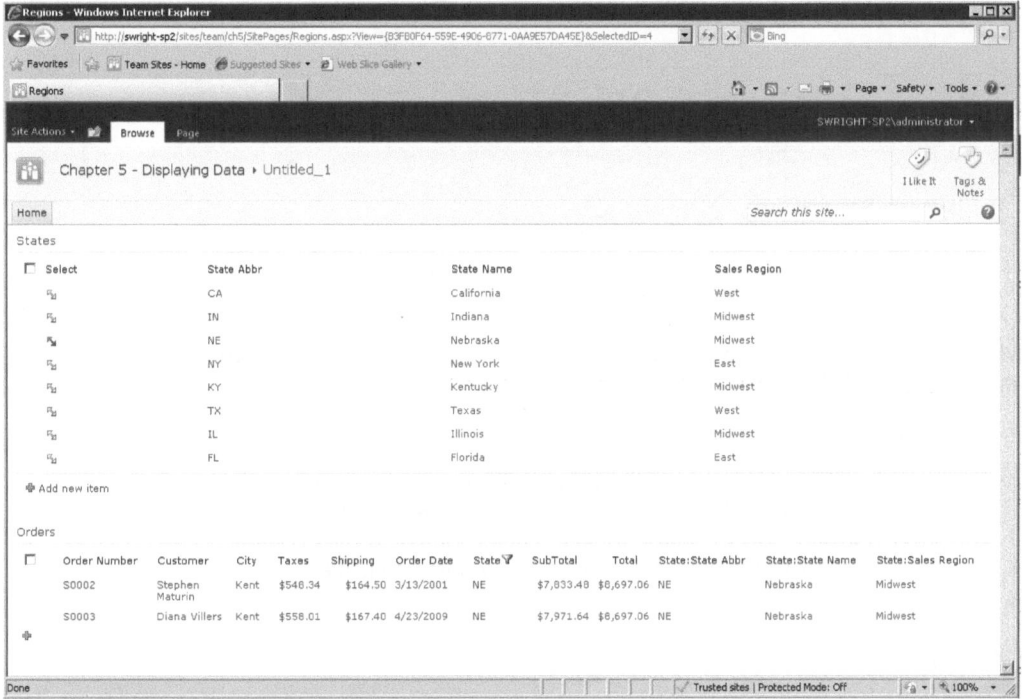

Figure 5-43. Regions page (web browser)

At this point, there are two XSLT list view web parts on the page. The Related Item View option has automatically configured a connection between these views. To see how this connection is configured, right-click either of the web parts and select Manage Connections.

10. Select Site Pages from the Navigation pane.

11. Select the first template from the Web Part Page drop-down menu on the Pages tab of the menu.

12. Name the new page OrderDetails.aspx.

13. Open OrderDetails.aspx in the Page Editor and then click in the web part zone.

14. Select Orders from the Display Item Form drop-down menu on the Insert tab.

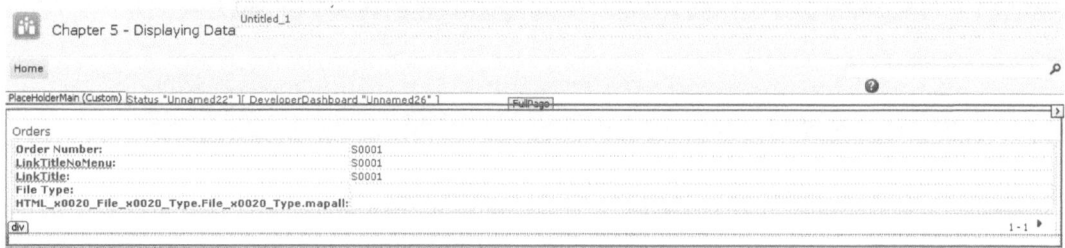

Figure 5-44. *Default form for displaying items*

The default item form contains only a few fields that do not suit our purposes. Instead, you will remove it and use the Data Source Details pane to create a more appropriate form.

15. Select the form and press Delete.

16. In the Data Source Details (DSD) task pane, select only the fields to be displayed in the form: Order Number, Order Date, Customer, City, State:State Abbr, Taxes, Shipping, SubTotal, and Total. Be sure to select the formatted versions of the numeric fields. Those are the fields without periods after the name.

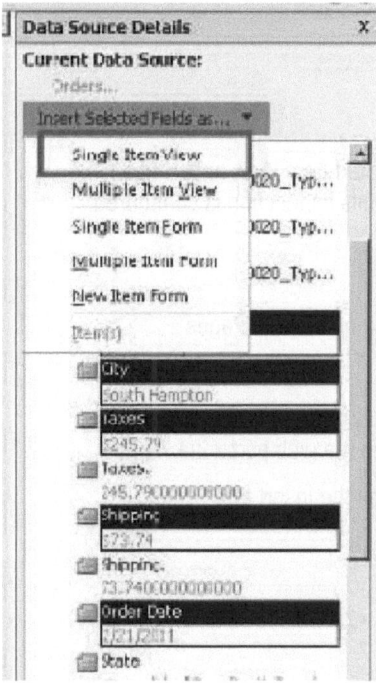

Figure 5-45. *Data Source Details task pane*

17. From the Insert Selected Fields As drop-down list at the top of the DSD pane, select Single Item View.

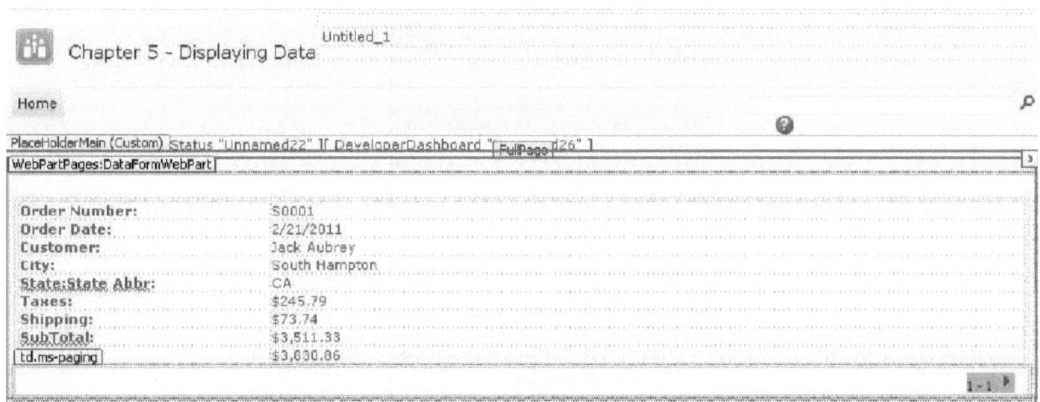

Figure 5-46. Display form for order details

18. Select Parameters from the Filter, Sort & Group group on the Options tab of the Data View Tools menu.

19. The ListID parameter has already been set and should not be altered. Add a new parameter called OrderNumber.

20. Set the Parameter Source to Query String and the Query String Variable name to ord.

21. Set the Default Value to S0001. This default value will allow you to view and manipulate the view in SharePoint Designer instead of seeing a message indicating that the view is empty.

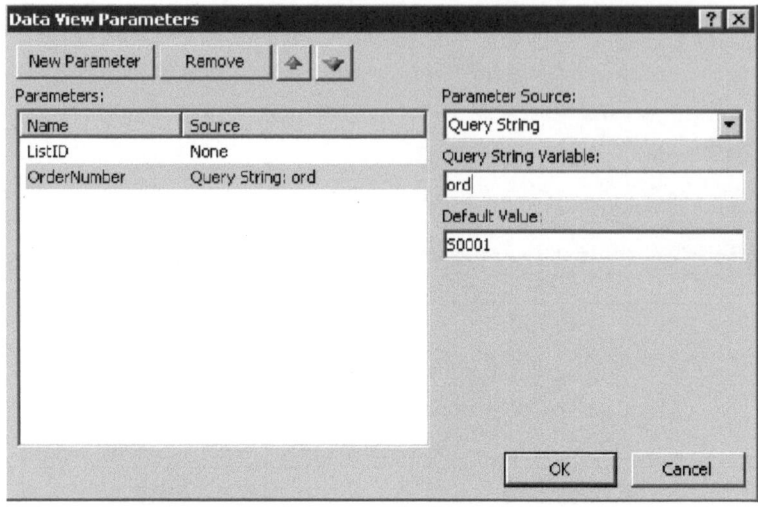

Figure 5-47. Data View Parameters dialog box (order form)

22. Click OK.

23. Select Filter from the Filter, Sort & Group group on the Options tab of the Data View Tools menu.

24. Select the Order Number field and leave the comparison as Equals.

25. Select [OrderNumber] from the Value drop-down list, as shown in Figure 5-48. This refers to the parameter you just created. Then click OK.

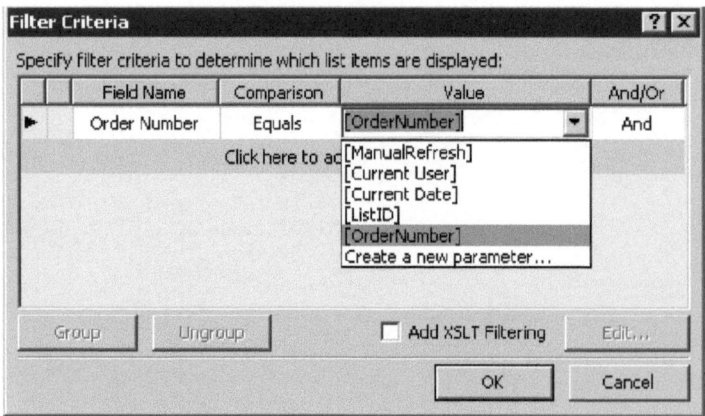

Figure 5-48. Filter Criteria dialog box (order form)

The data view you have just created accepts a parameter from the ord parameter on the page's URL and uses it to find the single order item to be displayed. Now you will create another data view that will display the line items for the order. It will use the same parameter and filter properties that were used in the previous example.

26. Click in the web part zone beneath the data view for the order details. Again, this may be easier to do using Split mode.

27. Select Order Lines from the Data View drop-down menu on the Insert tab.

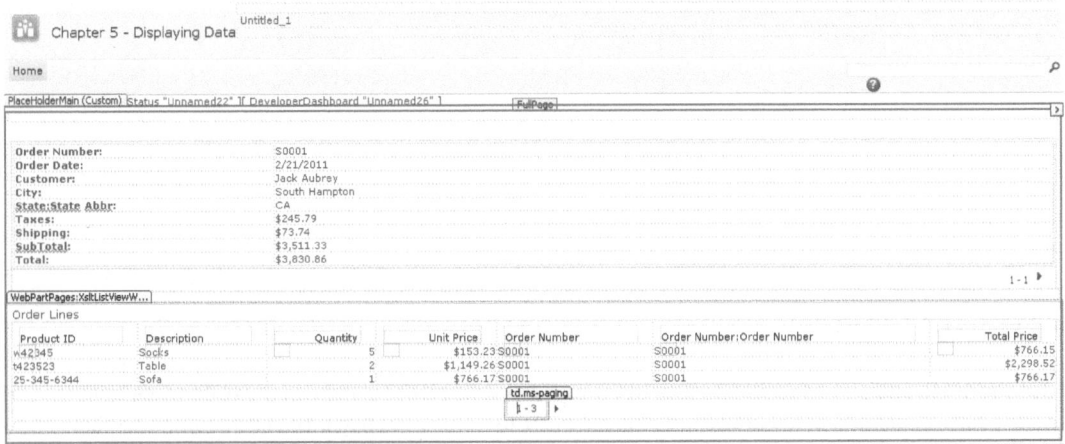

Figure 5-49. Order details web parts

28. Select Parameters from the Filter, Sort & Group group on the Options tab of the Data View Tools menu.

29. The ListID parameter has already been set and should not be altered. Add a new parameter called OrderNumber.

30. Set the Parameter Source to Query String, the Query String Variable name to ord, and the Default Value to S0001. Click OK.

31. Select Filter from the Filter, Sort & Group group on the Options tab of the Data View Tools menu.

32. Select the Order Number:Order Number field and leave the comparison as Equals.

33. Select [OrderNumber] from the Value drop-down list. Click OK.

34. Save the page (Ctrl+S) and view the page in the web browser (F12), as shown in Figure 5-50.

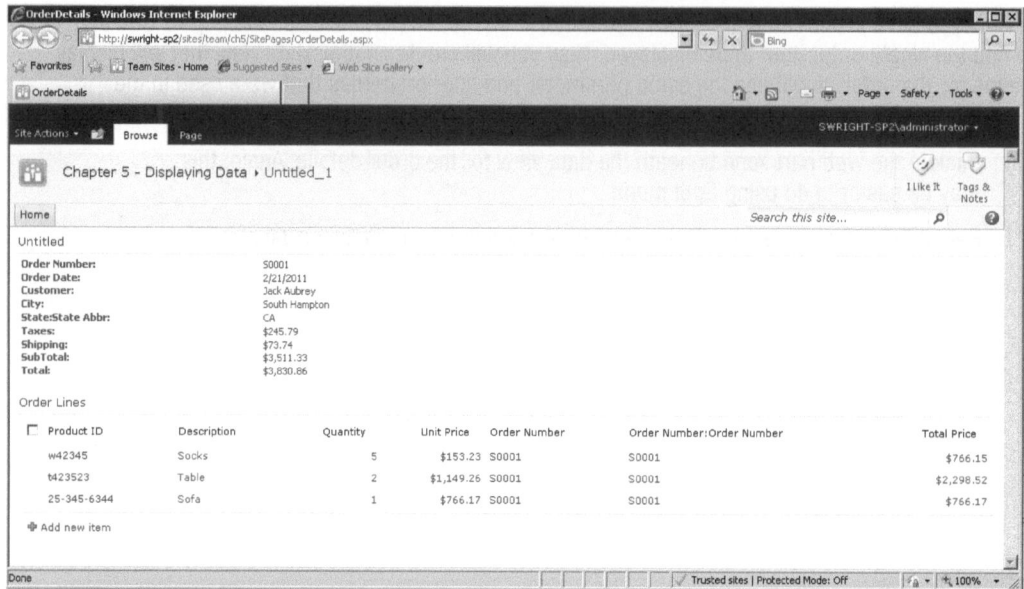

Figure 5-50. *Order details page*

Because you set the default parameter values to S0001, that is the order shown on the page by default. Add `?ord=S0002` to the URL in the browser and press Enter to refresh the page. Details for order number S0002 should now be shown in both web parts.

■ **Note** The web parts on this page (see Figure 5-50) are not connected to one another as they were on the `Regions.aspx` page. Instead, they are both filtering based on the same query string parameter.

You have one more step to complete your solution. If you go back to the `Regions.aspx` page, you will see that the order number is a link, but that when clicked, that link opens the default display form for the order. You need to update the page to link to your custom page instead, passing in the order number on the URL. To do this, you will directly edit the XSLT for the orders list.

35. Open `Regions.aspx` in the Page Editor and then click in the cell next to the order number S0001.

36. From the DSD task pane, select the OrderNumber field.

37. From the Insert Selected Fields As drop-down list, select Item(s). This causes the order number to appear twice in that cell, as shown in Figure 5-51.

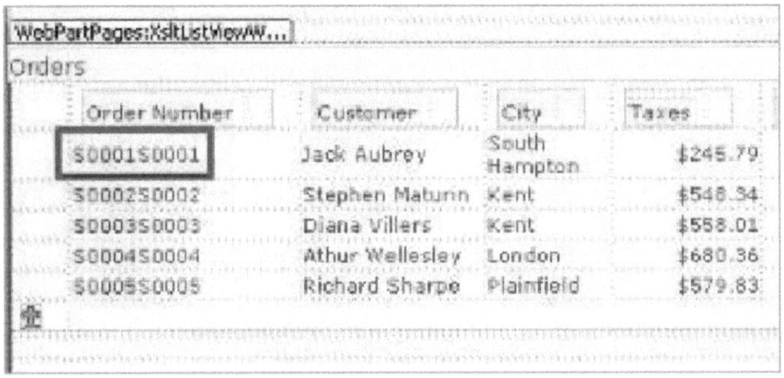

Figure 5-51. Order Number cell in Design view

38. Switch the Page Editor to either Split view or Code view and then find the markup for the Order Number cell, as shown in Figure 5-52.

Figure 5-52. Original markup for the Order Number cell

39. Replace that markup with `<a href="OrderDetails.aspx?ord={$thisNode/@Title}"><xsl:value-of select="$thisNode/@Title" /></a>`. The resulting section of XSLT should look like Figure 5-53.

■ **Note** The field name used in the XSLT markup is `@Title` because the list's original Title field was renamed and is being used for the Order Number field. Order Number is the display name for the field, but the internal name is still Title.

Figure 5-53. Final markup for the Order Number cell

40. Save the page (Ctrl+S) and view the page in the web browser (F12).

41. Click an order number. The corresponding order should now appear on the new page.

Summary

In this chapter, you have

- Introduced Data Access using SharePoint Designer
- Explored the Data Sources Available in SharePoint Designer
- Examined Which Web Parts to use in Different Situations
- Created and Customized Data Pages Using Data Web Parts
- Enabled the Passing of Parameters Between Data Web Parts

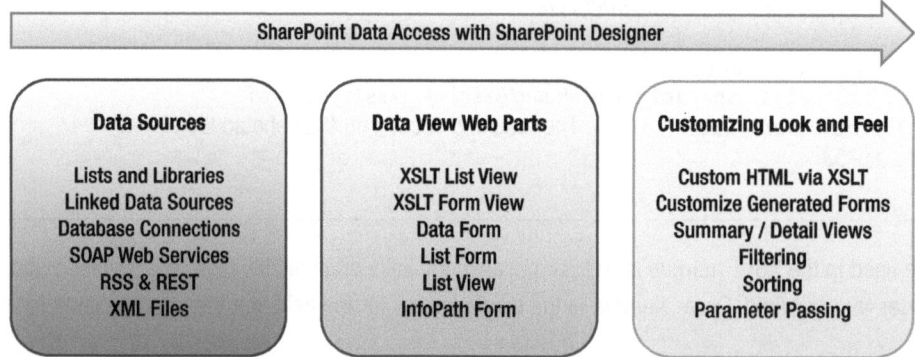

Figure 5-54. Road map to accessing data with SharePoint Designer

CHAPTER 6

Styles and Themes

Throughout my years of helping different businesses and business units plan and implement SharePoint, the most requested requirement is to make a SharePoint site look *not* like SharePoint. SharePoint's look is bland for a reason. It emphasizes function over form. It provides a basic road map, so to speak, to get you where you want to go. I always tell people that SharePoint is a platform with enormous functionality that is just waiting to be the foundation of your own creation! This chapter covers the main areas in customizing your own SharePoint look, or brand, with the use of styles and themes.

You will learn about the following topics in this chapter:

- Understanding SharePoint branding

- Knowing the differences between SharePoint 2007 and SharePoint 2010

- Working with the different levels of SharePoint branding

- Creating a new theme

- Modifying an out-of-the-box master page

What Is Branding?

Throughout the world, ranchers mark their livestock by permanently placing their brand on their animals. There are also some organizations in which the members brand themselves. The brand, when seen by others, provides a unique identity to the rancher or that organization. As it relates to commerce, *branding* is the creation of a mark or identity that uniquely identifies a company or product. Think of the logos of Target, McDonald's, and Pepsi, and you instantly recognize and associate a product with a brand without even needing words to describe it.

For web sites, branding entails creating a look and feel by using colors, styles, graphics, fonts, and logos. The SharePoint branding brand helps the user identify the web site and, if successfully done, promotes and encourages user adoption. When we talk more specifically about branding SharePoint, most people choose to brand to either make it unique to them, improve usability, or a combination of both. Most people are familiar with the bland user interface that comes with SharePoint. It was done that way on purpose. When we work with clients, we always say that SharePoint, while delivering a lot of functionality out of the box, is meant to be a platform for creating and developing your own solutions. It provides the foundation—you provide the walls and paint. The paint is your brand.

Site Type Considerations in Branding

How you approach branding is dictated by the type of SharePoint installation you have: intranet, Internet, or extranet. Each type of installation has its own specific characteristics and requirements.

■ **Tip** A great resource for viewing web sites that use custom-branded SharePoint is `www.topsharepoint.com`.

Intranet

An intranet installation is typically for an authenticated, internal audience and controlled by the IT department. You will have more control over the platforms you have to support. Since the intranet is also meant for internal communication and collaboration, more emphasis is usually placed on function over form: the main page has a focus on communication, and subsites have a focus on collaboration. From a branding standpoint, an intranet site is easier to brand than other types of sites because you are usually able to standardize on one browser. You will also find that the most frequent site template used is the Team Site template.

Internet

On the other end of the spectrum is a public-facing Internet site. With Internet sites, the audience could be anyone who visits your site. Consequently, you will have to support more kinds of browsers, on different platforms. Internet sites are also typically owned by the marketing department of the company and tend to be visual. A premium is placed on form as well as function. An Internet site typically is used to communicate information to the visitor with very little collaborative content. There is typically no authentication requirement, and all visitors will browse the site anonymously. These sites take longer to implement because of the extra effort needed to test for browser compatibility.

Extranet

An extranet site lives in that happy middle between an intranet and the Internet. The extranet's audience is typically the customers of the company and can be a mixture of anonymous and authenticated users. Parts of the extranet are for disseminating information to the customer. Other areas of the site, after authentication, will then key on a collaborative function, such as managing orders, collaborating with internal users, or retrieving reports. Branding an extranet is also somewhere between an intranet, with its utilitarian requirement for collaboration, and the highly stylized branding of an Internet site. Like an Internet site, the extranet site will typically need to support different browsers and platforms, and that is what makes security the most challenging aspect of an extranet.

Branding in 2007 vs. 2010

Much has changed from 2007 to 2010 as it relates to branding. Microsoft Office SharePoint Server 2007 (MOSS 2007) introduced master pages and page layouts. This made standardizing an overall look and feel much easier. SharePoint Server 2010 continues using master pages and page layouts, and has added quite a few new features. These new features also make branding a SharePoint 2010 site much easier than branding a MOSS 2007 site.

Themes

MOSS 2007 themes worked by overlaying the theme's XML and CSS over the top of the default master page and CSS. They were normally stored in the 12 hive. In SharePoint 2010, themes are created with Microsoft Office clients and then loaded into SharePoint 2010 sites to be applied to any site by the site owner. The SharePoint Server 2010 version also allows a site owner to modify themes directly in the web interface.

Master Pages

Whereas MOSS 2007 came with only one master page for collaborative sites and one for a publishing site, SharePoint 2010 comes with several built-in master pages, including the following:

- v4.master: This is the default master page.

- nightandday.master: This master page is available only on SharePoint Server 2010 sites with the publishing feature enabled.

- minimal.master: Unlike the minimal.master pages that were produced as a base point for custom branding in MOSS 2007, in SharePoint 2010, the minimal.master page is meant to be used by pages that have their own navigation or need additional space. It wouldn't be a good starting point for a custom branding master page because it lacks some important SharePoint controls.

Master pages in SharePoint 2007 applied only to the site and not the settings page. SharePoint 2007 had an application.master master page that was separate from the default.master. Modifying the application.master was not supported by Microsoft. In SharePoint 2010, the master page is a dynamic page so that each site has a defined master page. That master page is used on all pages.

SharePoint 2010 provides fall-back-to-default functionality. If something creates an error in a custom master page, SharePoint will automatically fall back to the default v4.master page.

Wiki Pages

In MOSS 2007, the most popular site created was the team site. The wiki site was a separate template that was used as a special type of site. In SharePoint 2010, the wiki functionality is included as part of the Team Site template. With the new functionality, it is easier for team members to collaborate and create content. While wiki pages are available in both SharePoint Foundation 2010 and SharePoint Server 2010, the ability to create and use page layouts with wiki pages is available only in SharePoint Server 2010 (Figure 6-1).

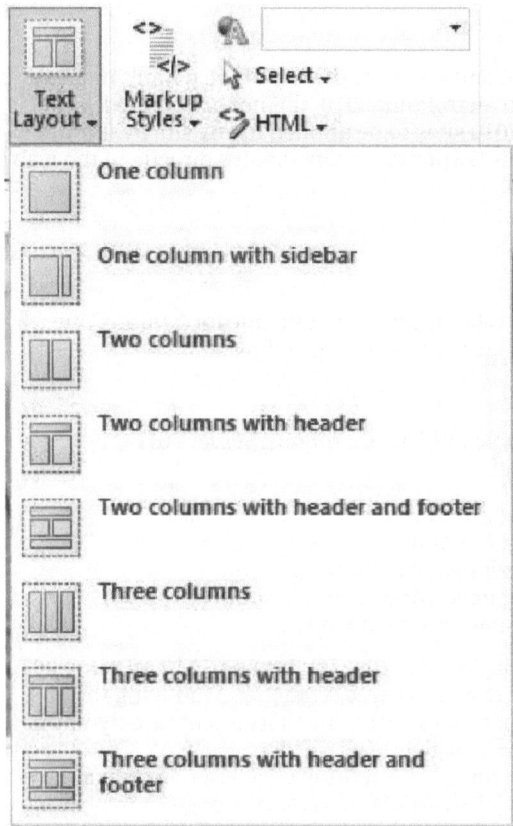

Figure 6-1. Text Layout menu

CSS

In MOSS 2007, there was one large CSS file called core.css that was loaded with each page, whether all of the CSS was really needed or not. It made page loading times longer than they sometimes needed to be. SharePoint 2010 splits the default CSS among several smaller CSS files, which are loaded only as they are needed. SharePoint Server 2010 also has the ability to use *alternate CSS* files that are applied over the top of any out-of-the-box CSS files.

Multilingual User Interface

In MOSS 2007, multilingual support was provided with a feature called *variations*, which basically created a new site for each language you wanted to support. In SharePoint 2010, variations are still there, but multilingual user interface (MUI) support changed so that you can specify multiple languages for only one site. When a user browses to a SharePoint 2010 site that has MUI enabled, SharePoint automatically checks which language is specified in the user's browser and then serves up the page in the user's language if present in the SharePoint site.

What's New in SharePoint 2010

If you are familiar with SharePoint 2007, you will notice that there have been some significant changes to the user experience in SharePoint 2010. The most significant change comes in the form of the Ribbon. The Ribbon made its appearance in Microsoft Office 2007 as a way to allow users to perform different tasks without leaving the context they were in. As Microsoft released new products, the Fluent UI (or Ribbon) became more and more prevalent. You can now see the Ribbon used in all Office applications, the Windows 7 apps such as Paint and WordPad, and now in SharePoint 2010. Because of the Ribbon, the Site Actions menu was moved from the upper-right corner to the left side of the page. Like all new interfaces, it will take users a little while to get used to, but usually, common tasks will be more accessible.

New Controls

To enable some of the new features in SharePoint 2010, new controls were created that you can use in your master pages. Table 6-1 lists a few of the new controls and their purposes as they relate to customizing a master page. A complete list can be found at http://msdn.microsoft.com/en-us/library/microsoft.sharepoint.webcontrols.aspx.

Table 6-1. New Controls in Sharepoint 2010

Control	Description
CssRegistration	Tells SharePoint to insert a CSS link
SPRibbon	Adds the Ribbon to the page
Popout Menu	Adds the breadcrumb menu that shows the current location
PageStateActionButton	Adds the Edit/Save button to a page
AspMenu	Represents the ASP menu control
WarnOnUnsupportedBrowsers	Displays a warning to users who are using an unsupported browser, such as Internet Explorer 6

Themes

Themes provide an easy way to change the look of a SharePoint site, by changing the colors and fonts used on a site. As mentioned earlier, new themes can be created in Microsoft Word or PowerPoint and even in the browser in SharePoint Server 2010 (Figure 6-2).

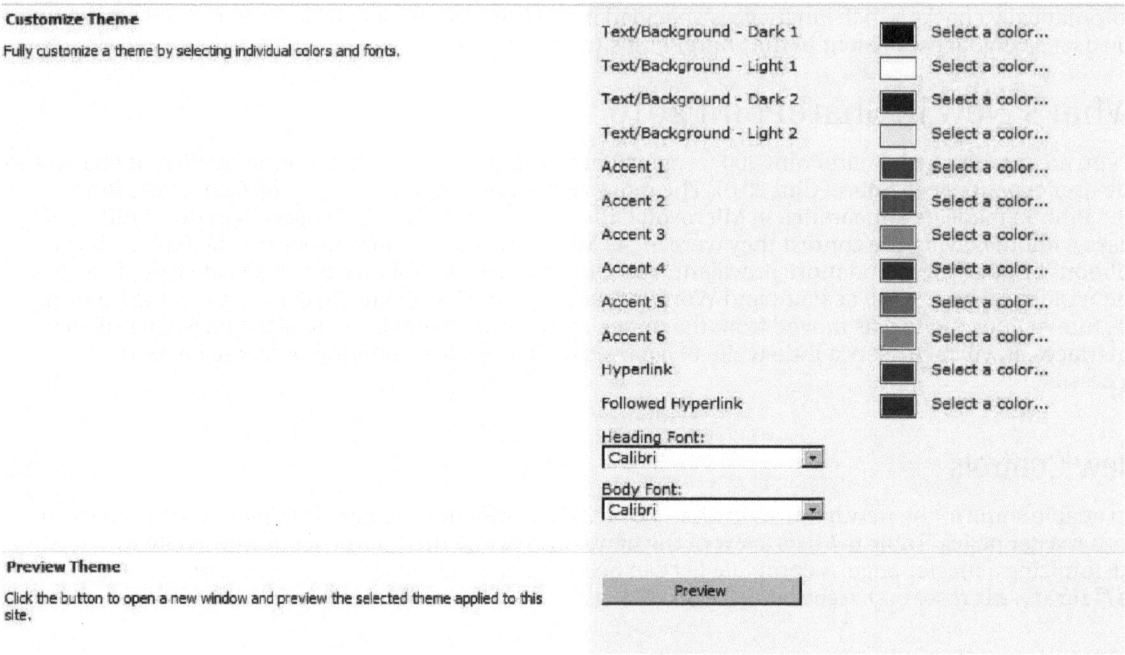

Customize Theme

Fully customize a theme by selecting individual colors and fonts.

Text/Background - Dark 1	■	Select a color...
Text/Background - Light 1	□	Select a color...
Text/Background - Dark 2	■	Select a color...
Text/Background - Light 2	□	Select a color...
Accent 1	■	Select a color...
Accent 2	■	Select a color...
Accent 3	■	Select a color...
Accent 4	■	Select a color...
Accent 5	■	Select a color...
Accent 6	■	Select a color...
Hyperlink	■	Select a color...
Followed Hyperlink	■	Select a color...

Heading Font:
Calibri

Body Font:
Calibri

Preview Theme

Click the button to open a new window and preview the selected theme applied to this site.

[Preview]

Figure 6-2. Browser theme selector

SharePoint 2010 introduces a new theme engine. The theme engine uses the same THMX file that is already used by Microsoft Word 2010 and Microsoft PowerPoint 2010. This OpenXML file format can be created and then imported into SharePoint to allow the user to change the look and feel of a SharePoint site.

To create a new theme, the user picks 12 colors and two fonts that work together. If you have ever created a new theme for a PowerPoint presentation, you can use that same theme in SharePoint.

EXERCISE 6-1: IMPORT A NEW THEME FROM POWERPOINT

A site owner has asked to have a custom theme created for her company's site. The company uses a theme for all of its slide presentations and would like to create a theme for the site that uses the same colors as the slide theme.

Because SharePoint uses the same theme engine that the other Microsoft Office products use, you can export a theme from PowerPoint and import it into SharePoint to be used on a site:

1. Open PowerPoint 2010. If the program doesn't begin a project by default, create a new blank slide presentation.

2. On the Ribbon menu, click Design.

3. From the theme selector, select a theme that you like, as shown in Figure 6-3.

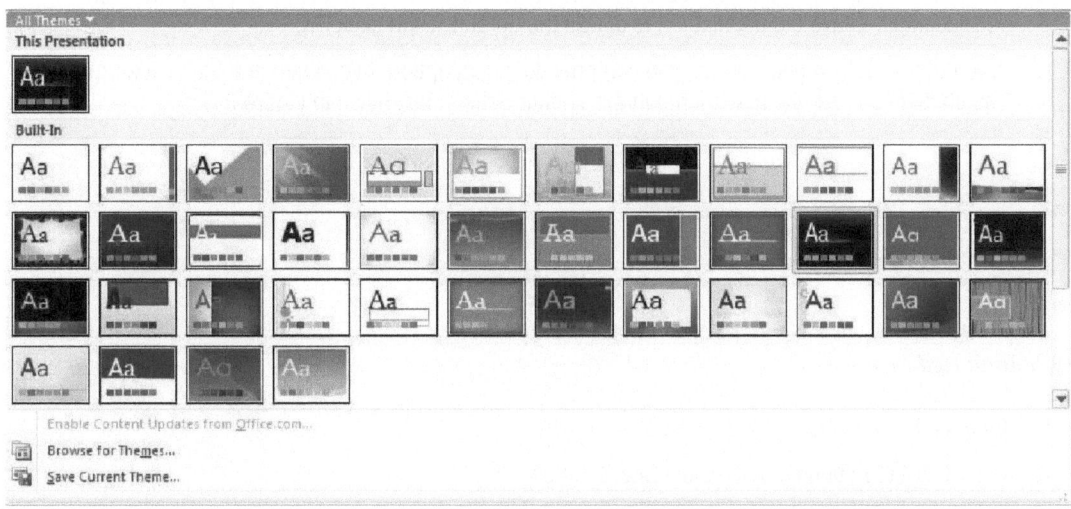

Figure 6-3. *Theme selector*

4. Click the theme selector drop-down menu and select Save Current Theme.

5. Save the theme on your desktop as **PowerPointTheme**.

6. Close PowerPoint 2010 without saving the presentation.

7. Open the root site of the SharePoint site collection in your browser.

8. From the Site Actions menu, select Site Settings.

9. The settings page opens. If you don't see the Theme Gallery listed under Galleries, make sure you are in the Site Collection Settings menu by selecting Go to Top Level Site Settings.

10. From the Galleries section, click Themes (Figure 6-4).

Figure 6-4. *Themes link in Galleries section*

11. From the Documents menu, click Upload Document.

12. When the dialog box opens, click Browse and select the PowerPoint theme that you saved on your desktop. Leave the destination folder as the default. Then click OK.

13. When the next dialog box opens, you can provide a description if you want and then click Save. You should now see the new theme in the Theme Gallery, as shown in Figure 6-5.

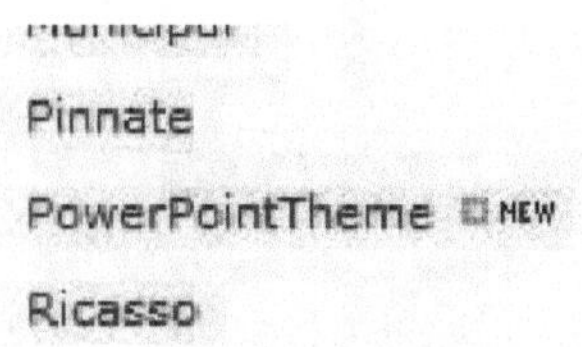

Municipal

Pinnate

PowerPointTheme ▢ NEW

Ricasso

Figure 6-5. Imported theme

14. Go back to your site.

15. From the Site Actions menu, select Site Settings.

16. From the Look and Feel group, click Site Theme.

17. Find your PowerPointTheme theme and select it. Notice that all of the colors and fonts are selected (Figure 6-6).

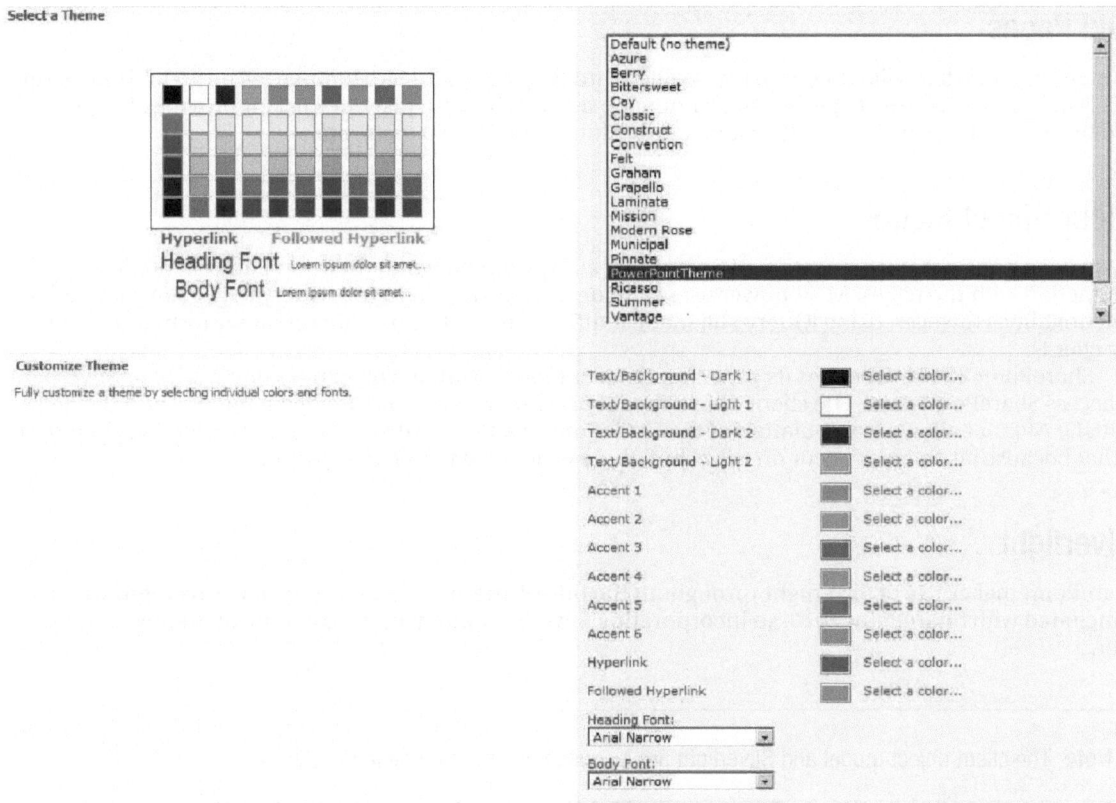

Figure 6-6. *New theme in the theme selector*

18. Click the Apply button.

19. Once your theme has been applied, click your home link to view your site with the new theme.

20. For even more fun, go back to the browser theme editor by selecting Site Settings from the Site Actions menu.

21. From the Look and Feel group, select Site Theme.

22. Change colors and then select Preview to see how your changes affect your theme. If you don't want to save your changes, click Cancel.

23. To put your site back to the default theme, open the theme settings again and select Default (no theme) from the selection list and then click Apply.

Wiki Pages

As mentioned earlier, wiki functionality is rolled into the new Team Site template. The great thing about this is that users can now begin editing content on a team site with just one click. It provides the power and flexibility of a wiki site with the collaborative functionality of a team site.

Client Object Model

If you have done any customization of SharePoint 2007, you know that there isn't any client-side interaction with the pages. Most power users and developers began to use jQuery to get some client-side functionality. However, using jQuery still made it difficult to update any SharePoint information from the client.

SharePoint 2010 introduces its own client object model. With it, you can use JavaScript or Silverlight to access SharePoint data. The client object model provides a simple create, read, update, and delete (CRUD) API that allows manipulation of the SharePoint data without any compiled code. The great part is that because all changes occur on the client, there is no need for a page refresh.

Silverlight

SharePoint makes use of Silverlight throughout the out-of-the-box templates. A new Silverlight web part is included with SharePoint 2010, so incorporating Silverlight into your SharePoint sites is easier than ever.

■ **Note** The client object model and Silverlight are discussed in more detail in Chapter 9.

Digital Asset Management

In today's world, media, in the form of audio and video files, is becoming more and more prevalent. This could include training videos or podcasts or customer informational videos. SharePoint 2010 has made improvements in its Asset library. A new Silverlight media player allows videos to be played directly from a SharePoint site. The Content Query web part (CQWP) also provides some new functionality specifically for media, allowing a file to stream instead of having to download the complete file before playing.

Accessibility

The W3C's Web Content Accessibility Guidelines (WCAG) were developed to make web content more accessible. By more closely following web development standards, SharePoint makes it possible to have a more WCAG-compliant web site.

Standard Compliance

In SharePoint 2007, browser compatibility was painful. It took a lot of effort to make sure that customizations would render properly in different browsers. With its emphasis on more closely following web development standards, SharePoint 2010 produces cleaner HTML and fewer tables. While not fully XHTML compliant, the new version has made branding much easier.

High-Level SharePoint Branding

Branding a SharePoint site basically entails creating or modifying a few key web elements. At its most basic level, a SharePoint site consists of a master page, CSS, and page content. The following items are key elements of SharePoint branding:

- *Themes*: Developing a custom theme is the easiest way to create a new brand for your site. As mentioned previously, you can create a new theme by using Microsoft Office or Microsoft PowerPoint.

- *Master pages*: Every SharePoint site requires a master page. It is not possible to render a SharePoint page without a master page. SharePoint 2010 provides some master pages out of the box that you can modify to create your own branded master page.

- *Content pages*: Master pages define the structure of a page, and the content pages define the body. Depending on the type of site you are creating, you will have different types of content pages.

- *Wiki pages*: These pages enable users to quickly create and edit content on the page. Because these pages can be modified by any number of users, they tend to be informal content pages. Typical uses for these are knowledge bases or a place where users can collaborate.

- *Web part pages*: A web part page is a more structured page. By definition, it provides a place for a user to place web parts in defined web part zones. Any user with the appropriate permissions can create a web part page and place web parts on them.

- *Publishing pages*: Publishing pages are available only after enabling the publishing feature in SharePoint Server 2010. The publishing feature enables authors to create pages that have an approval workflow so that the page content can be reviewed and approved before being published. Publishing pages use templates called *page layouts* that define the content areas. When creating content, users can select a specific page layout template that meets the user's needs.

- *Cascading Style Sheets*: CSS on a web site is like paint on a house. CSS defines the style, look, and feel of the web site. SharePoint 2010 makes wide use of CSS. All of the controls that are loaded in a master page are styled by CSS. Because CSS is so important in SharePoint, a thorough understanding of CSS is critical to branding a SharePoint site.

Levels of Effort

Each branding project can be classified by who normally does the branding, what skills are required to complete the branding project and the level of effort requred. Projects typically fall into one of the following three levels of effort.

Low Effort

This is typically the branding that an end user could perform. Examples include adding logos to the top of every page, selecting themes or master pages, and even creating a custom theme.

Medium Effort

This is typically the level of branding done by using SharePoint Designer. It entails making changes to CSS and HTML. In medium-effort projects, you might create additional web part zones on a page or modify an out-of-the-box master page by making a copy of an existing master page and customizing it. This level of effort is usually performed by a power user.

High Effort

The most extensive effort is usually done with other web development tools. In a high-effort project, you would likely be creating custom master pages, page layouts, and CSS. This level of effort is usually performed by a developer or designer experienced in web site design and also in ASP.NET and SharePoint. This is the level of effort typically required for highly stylized public Internet sites.

Before You Begin

While beyond the scope of this chapter, several considerations need to be taken into account before you begin branding any site. In addition, you can use other tools along with SharePoint Designer to help in your branding efforts. Both topics are covered in this section.

Considerations

The decisions you make based on the following considerations will dictate the level of effort required in your branding project:

- Targeted audience
  - Is this an intranet, extranet, or the Internet?
- Targeted browsers
  - Remember that IE6 is not supported out of the box.
  - Only 32-bit IE7 and IE8 on Windows are fully supported without limitations.
  - Other browsers are supported with some limitations.

- Version of SharePoint
    - SharePoint Foundation
    - SharePoint Server
- Screen resolution
    - The most common resolution now is 1024×768.
    - Will your users require something different?
- Questions to ask
    - What is the time frame to create the brand?
    - Is this a new design or one based on an existing design?
    - Does this require any custom web parts or third-party web parts?
    - What navigation is required?
        - Horizontal
        - Vertical
        - Breadcrumb
- Wireframes (Figure 6-7)
    - They define the skeleton of a site.
    - They define the layout and flow of a web site.
    - They promote ideas without distracting with colors.

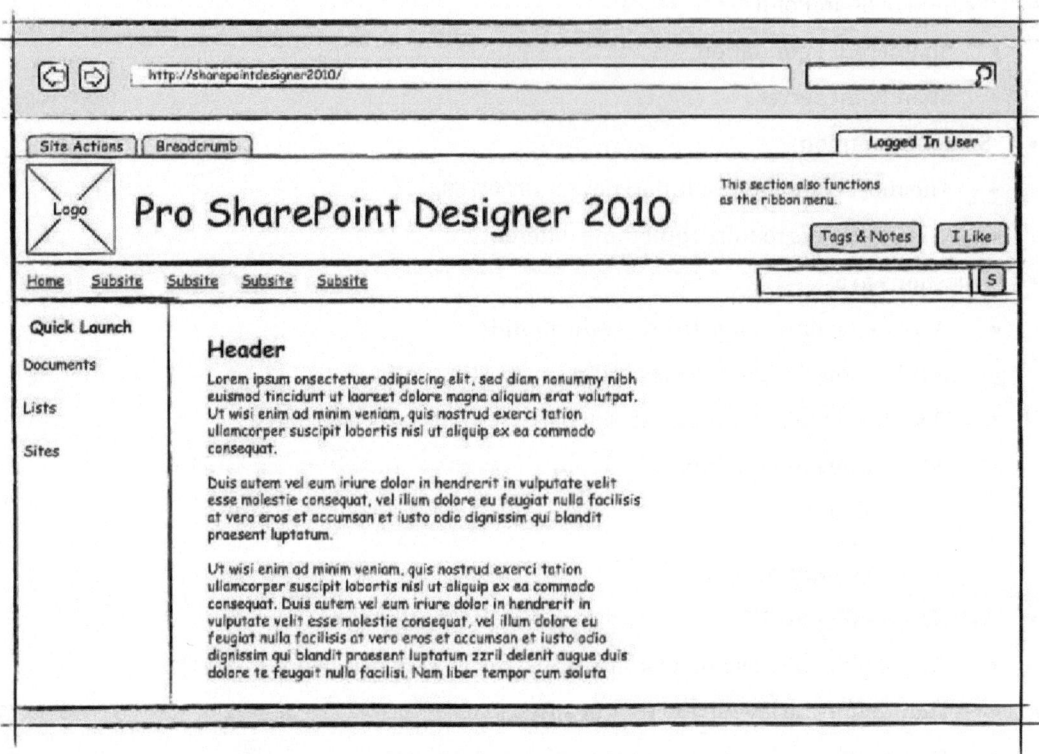

Figure 6-7. Wireframe example

- Great prototyping tools include Microsoft Visio and Microsoft Expression Studio's SketchFlow (www.microsoft.com/expression/products/SketchFlow_Overview.aspx).

- DOCTYPES

  - SharePoint's master pages are set to use the XHTML 1.0 Strict DOCTYPE.

  - If you are going to use another DOCTYPE, make sure that SharePoint controls will render correctly.

- IE8 compatibility mode

  - Each major release of IE has added features that increase security and more closely support standards. As each feature is released, there is always a risk that older web sites will not display correctly. The X-UA-Compatible header indicates the version of IE that the page is coded for. By default, all SharePoint 2010 pages come with compatibility mode set to IE=8.

- Tableless design

  - Modern web site design uses CSS to define layout. SharePoint 2007 used tables to define its structure. In SharePoint 2010, Microsoft has embraced the tableless design. CSS is used to define layouts, and tables are used to display tabular data.

- Testing

  - How much time will be dedicated to testing?

  - What browsers are being used for testing?

Other Tools Used in Branding

Along with SharePoint Designer, other tools can play an important part in your branding exercise and can help making branding that much easier.

Visio 2010

In previous versions of Visio, software developers could prototype software by using the Windows XP stencils. This made prototyping a new software application much easier than had been possible before. In SharePoint 2010, Microsoft made it much easier to prototype web applications with their Wireframe stencil set. These are interactive stencils that allow you to quickly create a wireframe of a new site and present it to a user.

Visio is also the place where you can create new themes to use in SharePoint. The theme engine in SharePoint is shared in the Microsoft Office family, so any theme you create in Visio 2010 or PowerPoint 2010 can be used on a SharePoint site. Creating themes is covered later in this chapter.

PowerPoint 2010

As mentioned earlier, you can use PowerPoint 2010 to create new themes for SharePoint. It is also a tool you can use to create a wireframe if you don't have Visio or another tool like it.

Image Editors

If you are the resident designer, you most likely already have an image editor you like to use. If you don't, the following are a couple of open source or freeware applications I like to use:

- *IrfanView*. This lightweight graphic viewer can open just about any graphic and then save it in another. It has a lot of great features that make this a Swiss-Army-knife graphic utility. It's great for format conversion, resizing, and even screen captures. It even plays MP3 files! You can find this program at www.irfanview.com.

- *GIMP*. The GNU Image Manipulation Program is a multiplatform, multilingual program for creating, manipulating, and retouching images. See www.gimp.org.

Branding with SharePoint Designer

When branding SharePoint sites, SharePoint Designer is most likely the first place everyone turns. In many cases, it is the only tool used to develop custom branded sites. Because of this, Microsoft has put a lot of work into making SharePoint Designer a very useful branding tool. You can create master pages, page layouts, and CSS pages. This section covers how you go about branding a SharePoint site with SharePoint Designer. You will start with a simple branding and lead up to developing a custom-branded master page. You will not be trying to create a new Ferrari.com site, but you will see examples that will get you started creating your own personally branded SharePoint site.

Simple Branding

All simple branding tasks can be done in the web editor. This includes creating custom-branded content pages, modifying themes, changing the logo for the site, and, on the publishing site, creating an alternate CSS. It is important to know what can be done in the browser before you start branding your site with SharePoint Designer.

EXERCISE 6-2: CREATE A SIMPLE CUSTOM-BRANDED SITE

As a site owner in the Systems Support department, you want to create a custom look for your site without a lot of effort. You want to use your own department logo and a different theme. Unfortunately, you do not have authority to use SharePoint Designer to make any changes to your site. In this exercise, you will use the browser to create a simple branded site. You will create a new SharePoint team site and then apply some simple branding to make it look unique:

1. Open a Site Collection root site in the browser.

2. Click the All Site Content link in the Quick Launch menu.

3. Click Create and then select the Team Site template.

4. Give the site the name **Support Team** and the URL support.

5. Leave all other settings to their default settings.

6. Click Create.

7. As soon as your site is rendered, select Site Settings from the Site Actions menu.

8. In the Look and Feel group, select Title, description, and icon, as shown in Figure 6-8.

Figure 6-8. *Title, description, and icon*

9. When the page opens (Figure 6-9), type the following URL in the Logo URL box: **/_layouts/images/AccessAssets.png**.

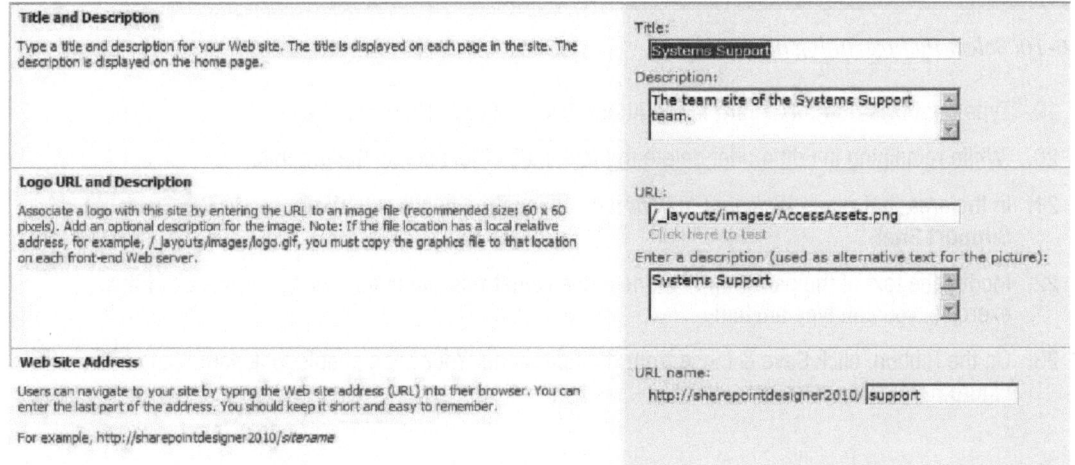

Figure 6-9. *Title, description, and icon settings*

10. Type **Systems Support** in the textbox that is labeled, *Enter a description (used as alternative text for the picture):*.

11. Click OK to save your changes. Your site should now have a custom site logo.

12. While remaining on the Site Settings page, select Site Theme from the Look and Feel section.

13. Select the Municipal theme and click Apply.

14. Go back to the home page by clicking the Home link on the top navigational bar.

15. From the Site Actions menu, choose Edit Page.

16. Click the graphic of the people collaborating.

17. From the Picture Tools menu, choose Change Picture from Address.

18. When the Select Picture dialog box opens, replace the filename in the Address field with **officialfile.jpg**, as shown in Figure 6-10.

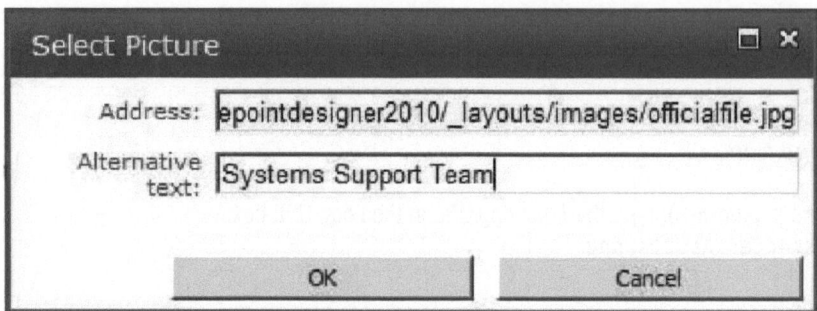

Figure 6-10. Select Picture dialog box

19. Type **Systems Support Team** in the Alternative Text box. Then click Save.

20. While remaining in Edit mode, delete the few lines of text below the graphic.

21. In the area that reads *Welcome to your site*, change the heading to **Welcome to the Systems Support Site!**

22. Modify the text of the paragraph that describes what this site is for. For the purposes of this exercise, you can type anything.

23. On the Ribbon, click Save & Close from the Edit menu. Your page should look something like Figure 6-11.

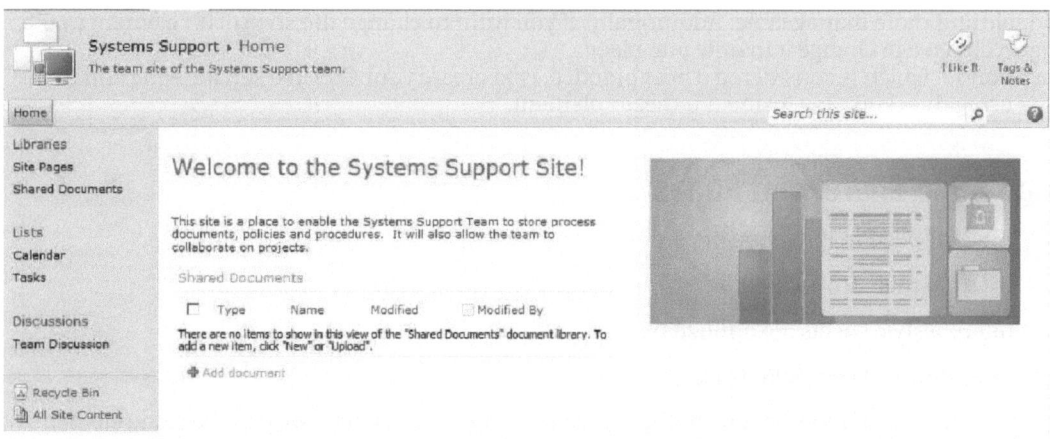

Figure 6-11. *Your page with the new picture*

Beyond the Browser

With SharePoint Designer, you have code-level access to the SharePoint site. With that level of access, you can create a completely custom SharePoint site. You can begin by modifying the CSS of the site to create a new look to the existing interface, or you could make your own master page or layout page. The options are almost unlimited.

In the next few exercises, you will use SharePoint Designer to perform branding functions. You will use the same site and keep building on it until you achieve a completely custom-branded SharePoint site.

To begin these next few exercises, you will use the team site that you just used in Exercise 6-2. If you didn't complete that exercise, go back and complete it so you will have a base for the next few exercises.

Modifying CSS

CSS is prevalent in SharePoint 2010. If you were to look at a SharePoint page with CSS disabled, you would see a plain page with a bunch of text on it—no form or function at all. The CSS provides the structure. This is a great aspect of SharePoint 2010. Whereas SharePoint 2007 used tables to provide structure, SharePoint 2010 uses CSS to provide the structure. This makes it that much easier to customize the user interface.

There are a couple of ways that you can add CSS to a SharePoint site. You can apply CSS to each element inline by using the style attribute of the HTML tags. This is easy, but it isn't the most desirable way to add style to an HTML page. By adding CSS to each element, the pages become quite large and hard to manage. If you want to apply the style used in one element, you would have to apply it to each element.

A better strategy is to add a <style></style> section in your HTML page. This is sometimes called an *internal style sheet*. Best practice and the XHTML Strict DOCTYPEs specify that the style element be placed inside the <head></head> element. The benefits of this are that it makes your document much more readable and more manageable. Additionally, if you want to change the style of an element in the whole page, you have to change it in only one place.

A third option, which is considered a best practice, is to create your CSS in a separate file and then link to it by using the `<link>` tag inside the `<head>` element.

Applying CSS in SharePoint Pages

In general, CSS is applied in the following order:

1. External rules are applied first.

2. Internal style sheets are applied next.

3. Any inline style is applied last.

It is important to remember that if conflicts arise by defining a different style in the same element, the style that is loaded last supersedes any previously defined style. That means that any inline style defined on an element will always take precedence in an element.

If there are no conflicts, the style is just added to the previous definition. For example, you can define a font for a paragraph in an external style sheet and define the color in an internal style sheet. Because the two styles don't conflict, they will both be applied. If you use inline CSS to define the color, the inline style will overwrite the color defined in the internal style sheet.

EXERCISE 6-3: ADD AN INTERNAL STYLE SHEET TO A SHAREPOINT PAGE

You want to illustrate some sales figures in a graph and display it on your web site. You don't have a lot of charting tools and you want your users to be able to view the graph quickly on your site. In addition to creating web part pages, SharePoint Designer can create regular ASPX pages. This is perfect for quickly creating a web page that can be viewed and styled individually. You decide to create an ASPX page and style it by using an internal style sheet. If you downloaded the code for this chapter, the page code is available in the file Chapter6CssDemo.txt.

1. Open a team site in SharePoint Designer.

2. Select Site Pages from the Navigation pane.

3. Choose Page > ASPX from the Ribbon menu, as shown in Figure 6-12.

Figure 6-12. New Page menu

4. Once the new page is created, rename the file to **Chapter6CssDemo.aspx**.

5. Open the new file in Edit mode.

6. A dialog box opens, asking whether you want to edit the page in Advanced mode. Click Yes, as shown in Figure 6-13.

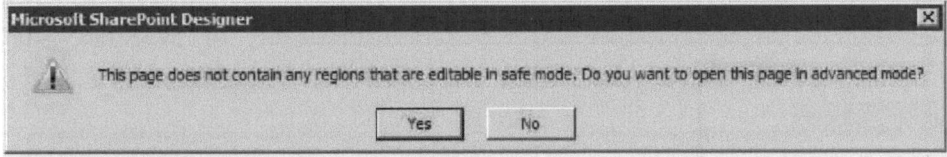

Figure 6-13. Advanced mode caution dialog box

7. If you aren't already in Code mode, switch to Code mode.

8. Delete the `<form>` tags.

9. Add the following code between the `<body>` tags:

```
<div id="chart">
  <div id="east">East<br/>
    <div class="red bar" style="width: 160px"></div ></div>
  <div id="west">West<br/>
    <div class="blue bar" style="width: 180px"></div ></div>
  <div id="north">North<br/>
    <div class="green bar" style="width: 120px"></div ></div>
  <div id="south">South<br/>
    <div class="yellow bar" style="width: 130px"></div ></div>
</div>
```

10. Add the following style code in the `<head>` section, just before the end tag.

```
<style type="text/css">
  body  {
    font-family: Arial, Helvetica, sans-serif;
    font-size: 10px;
  }

  div {
    display: block;
  }

  #chart {
    width: 200px;
    border: 2px black double;
    padding: 5px 5px 5px 5px;
  }
  .bar { height: 15px; }
  .red { background-color: red;  }
  .blue { background-color:blue; }
```

```
    .green { background-color:green; }
    .yellow { background-color:yellow; }
</style>
```

11. Save the page.

12. Click Preview in Browser to view how the style is applied to your HTML. Figure 6-14 shows the graph.

Figure 6-14. *Output of the ASPX example*

Modifying SharePoint CSS

As mentioned previously in this chapter, the main CSS file loaded by a SharePoint page is called `corev4.css`. It is found in the 14 folder. Its path is `<Program Files Dir>\Common Files\Microsoft Shared\Web Server Extensions\14\TEMPLATE\LAYOUTS\1033\STYLES\Themable\corev4.css`. Best practices dictate that you don't modify any internal SharePoint files but that you make copies of the files you want to modify and make your changes on those files. From a purely safety standpoint, it goes without saying that if something breaks in a copy of any native SharePoint file, you can always roll back to the original.

Microsoft also takes precautions when you modify pages in SharePoint Designer. When you open a page in Code view, you can see hyperlinks for all of the CSS classes in the code. When you Ctrl+click one of those links, SharePoint opens a copy of the associated CSS file. When you save your changes, a link to your new CSS pages is placed in your file so that it refers to the new CSS file instead of the core file.

When you make CSS changes on a page, they apply only to that page. In fact, any changes you make on a web page will apply only to that page. CSS changes will be stored in a copy, and the SharePoint page is separated from its site definition. If you want those changes to be reflected across the whole site, you need to make changes to the underlying master page.

Master Pages and CSS

Master pages were first introduced in .NET 2.0, and have been used in both SharePoint 2007 and SharePoint 2010. You can use your SharePoint 2007 master pages with SharePoint 2010 by doing an in-place upgrade, but this is really meant as a temporary solution. There are a number of new features in the SharePoint 2010 interface that were not present in earlier versions. One glaring example is the Ribbon. Because of these differences, you should upgrade your master page as soon as you can.

If you have the publishing feature enabled, you will also be able to use layout pages. This concept was introduced in SharePoint Server 2007 publishing sites. By using layout pages, you can define multiple layout templates that your users can use to create content. Page layouts control the inner layer of content on a page. When a page is requested from a web server, the layout page is generated first, and then the master page referenced by the layout page is rendered. This process is better illustrated in the diagram shown in Figure 6-15.

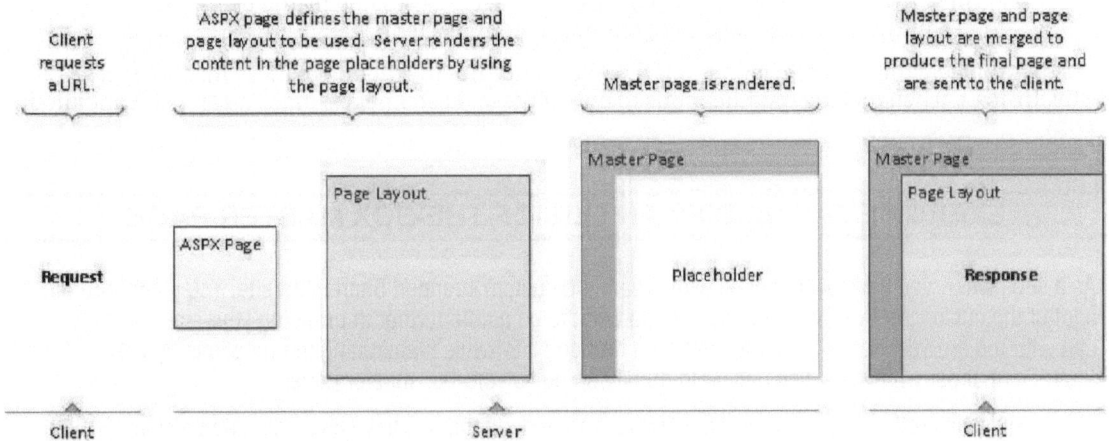

Figure 6-15. *Page layout flow diagram*

Modifying a Master Page

Because master pages define the outer shell of all the web pages in a site, almost all branding done in SharePoint Designer involves working with a master page. One of the easiest ways of creating your own brand is to modify a copy of one of the master pages provided by Microsoft. In SharePoint 2010, you store any custom master pages in the Master Page Gallery.

You already learned about some of the out-of-the-box master pages earlier in this chapter. The complete list of the out-of-the-box master pages you can begin your branding project with are as follows:

- `v4.master`: This is the default master page for a majority of all pages served in SharePoint 2010.

- `MWSDefaultv4.master`: This is the default master page for the Meeting Workspace.

- `simple.master`: This is the master page used for the error and login pages.

- `nightandday.master`: This is available only in SharePoint Server 2010 publishing sites. This master page is a good starting point for public-facing sites.

- `default.master`: This master page is used only when upgrading a SharePoint 2007 site to SharePoint 2010. It will make the site look almost identical to a SharePoint 2007 site. This can be used only when SharePoint 2010 is in SharePoint 2007 mode using Visual Upgrade.

- `minimal.master` : This master page is used by SharePoint sites that need more screen real-estate, have their own navigation, or are special applications. This master page should not be confused with what was commonly called a *minimal master page* in SharePoint 2007. That master page was created by the user-communityas a starting page for creating custom master pages.

As mentioned earlier in the chapter, it is a best practice not to edit one of these master pages directly. Instead, when making modifications to one of these master pages, make a copy of it and modify the copy.

EXERCISE 6-4: MODIFY AN OUT-OF-THE-BOX MASTER PAGE

As a site owner, you have been tasked with creating a custom-branded SharePoint site. You want to retain a lot of the out-of-the-box functionality, but you want to go a little further in branding your site than you can with the browser itself. To create your own branded site while maintaining the functionality that SharePoint already provides, you decide to modify an out-of-the-box master page.

This exercise is pretty long. In order make it easier to understand, we have divided it into sections.

Make a copy of an existing Master Page

1. If you didn't create the Team Site in the previous exercises, create a new site based on the Team Site template.

2. On the Navigation pane click the Master Pages menu item.

3. In the list of the master pages, right-click the `v4.master` and select Copy from the menu.

4. Right-click a blank area in the list of master pages and select Paste from the context menu.

5. You should see a new file called `v4_copy(1).master`, as shown in Figure 6-16.

Figure 6-16. Copy master page

6. Click the filename `v4_copy(1).master`, and the page properties window opens.

7. On the filename area of the property page, click the filename and rename your copied master page to **chaptersix.master**, as shown in Figure 6-17.

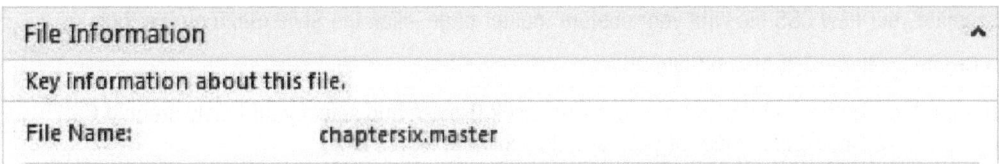

Figure 6-17. Renaming the file.

8. When the properties page comes up, click Edit File in the Customization section. You'll need to be in Edit mode to customize the master page.

9. Best practices dictate that you not modify the main CSS file that ships with SharePoint named `corev4.css`. You will create a new CSS file instead and use that.

10. In the Navigation pane, click Site Assets.

11. On the Ribbon menu, select CSS from the New ➤ Asset menu item, as shown in Figure 6-18.

Figure 6-18. Asset menu

12. Name your CSS file **chapter6.css** , as shown in Figure 6-19.

Figure 6-19. Filename of new CSS file

13. Now that you have an empty CSS file, you can associate it with your custom master page.

14. Go back to your master page by clicking the tab labeled `chaptersix.master`. If you have two tabs labeled the same, make sure you are on the tab where you can see your master page, and not the properties tab.

15. To associate your new CSS file with your custom master page, click the Style menu on the Ribbon.

16. In the Create section, click Attach Style Sheet.

17. When the Attach Style Sheet dialog box comes up, click Browse and select your newly created CSS file located in the Site Assets folder of your site, as shown in Figure 6-20.

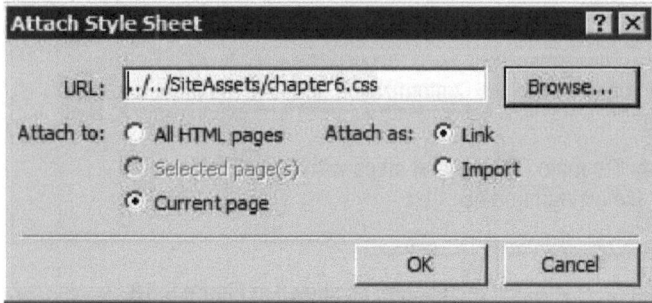

Figure 6-20. Attach Style Sheet dialog box

18. Make sure the Attach To option is set to Current Page and the Attach As option is set to Link. Then click OK.

19. Save by clicking the Save button or by pressing Ctrl+S.

20. If a dialog box pops up warning that you are customizing the page and that it will no longer be based on the site definition, click Yes to continue saving your modifications (Figure 6-21).

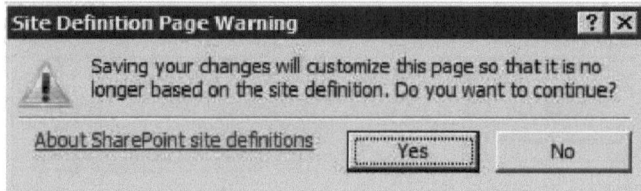

Figure 6-21. Site Definition customization warning

21. If you look at the code of your master page, you should see the entry shown in Figure 6-22 right before the ending </head> tag.

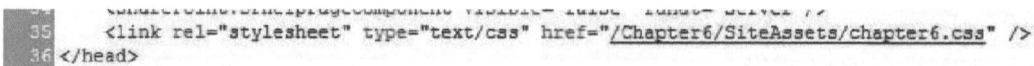

Figure 6-22. Linked style sheet code

22. Now, to make sure you can see the effects of your customizations, you need to make your custom master page the default master page. In the Navigation pane, click Master Pages.

23. When the list of master pages opens, right-click your custom master page, chaptersix.master, and in the context menu that opens, select Set as Default Master Page, as shown in Figure 6-23.

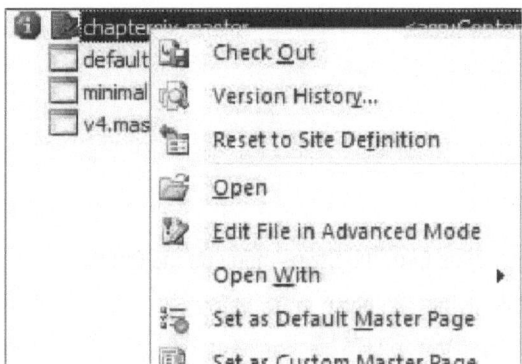

Figure 6-23. Set as Default Master Page menu item

Hide the Recycle Bin and All Site Content link

One of the most common things people want when they modify the master page is to hide the Recycle Bin or the All Site Content link from the Quick Launch pane. It's fairly easy to accomplish this. Make sure your edit window is in Split mode, and then click the Recycle Bin at the bottom of the Quick Launch pane, as shown inFigure 6-24.

Figure 6-24. Quick Launch pane

1. Look at the code that is highlighted. It should be ClusteredSPLinkButton, as you can see in Figure 6-25. If you look a few lines above that list control, you will see that it is part of an unordered list (UL)

that has the class s4-specialNavLinkList. This is the class you will want to override.

```
<ContentTemplate>
    <ul class="s4-specialNavLinkList">
        <li>
            <SharePoint:ClusteredSPLinkButton
                runat="server"
                NavigateUrl="~site/_layouts/recyclebin.aspx"
```

Figure 6-25. Code where the Recycle Bin is located

2. If your Manage Styles pane is not open, select Manage Styles from the Styles menu on the Ribbon.

3. Locate the s4-specialNavLinkList class in the list of CSS styles, as shown in Figure 6-26.

CSS styles:
- .s4-ql a.selected
- .s4-ln-sel a
- .s4-ln-sel a:hover
- .s4-specialNavLinkList li > span
- .s4-specialNavLinkList a
- .s4-specialNavIcon
- .s4-specialNavIcon + .ms-splinkbutton-tex.
- .s4-specialNavLinkList a:hover > span.ms-
- .s4-specialNavLinkList
- .s4-ql
- .s4-specialNavLinkList
- .s4-specialNavLinkList li
- .s4-ql li
- .s4-rcvd

Figure 6-26. CSS style for the s4-specialNavLinkList class

4. Right-click the style name and select New Style Copy.

5. When the New Style dialog box opens, delete the word Copy from the end of the Selector name so that the class has the same name as the original, as shown in Figure 6-27.

New Style

Selector: `.s4-specialNavLinkList`   ☐ Apply new style to document selection

Define in: Existing style sheet   URL: chapter6.css

Figure 6-27. New Style dialog box

6. From the Define In list box, choose Existing Style Sheet.

7. Select the URL of your new `chapter6.css` file from the drop-down.

8. From the Category options, select Layout.

9. For Visibility, select Hidden.

10. Click OK. This makes an entry in your `chapter6.css` file for the class.

11. If you don't already have the `chapter6.css` file open in Edit mode, open it and notice the new entry, as you can see in Figure 6-28.

```
7  .s4-specialNavLinkList {
8      visibility: hidden;
9  }
```

Figure 6-28. Visibility set to hidden

12. Because you are going to hide that section, you can then delete all of the other lines in that CSS class except the `visibility` line.

13. Click Save and then go back to your master page. In the Design part of the view, you should see the bottom section empty.

Add a Footer to a Master page

Another common request for modifying the master page is to add a footer for the site. This usually provides a copyright or even a site menu. You'll add a footer next.

1. In the master page code view, locate the tag `<SharePoint:DeveloperDashboard runat="server" />`. It us usually somewhere around line 624.

2. Right before that tag, add the footer code shown in Figure 6-29.

```
624    <div class="siteFooter">&copy; Copyright 2011 Bob's Bicycle Shoppe, Anytown, USA</div>
625    <SharePoint:DeveloperDashboard runat="server"/>
```

Figure 6-29. Code to insert footer

3. Click Save.

4. Because you haven't defined the footer CSS class, you need to do that. Open the `chapter6.css` file for editing, and add the following CSS class code:

```
.siteFooter {
        Clear: both;
        Background-color: #99CCFF;
        Padding: 5px;
}
```

5. Click Save.

6. Open your site in a browser and view how your site is beginning to change, as you can see in Figure 6-30.

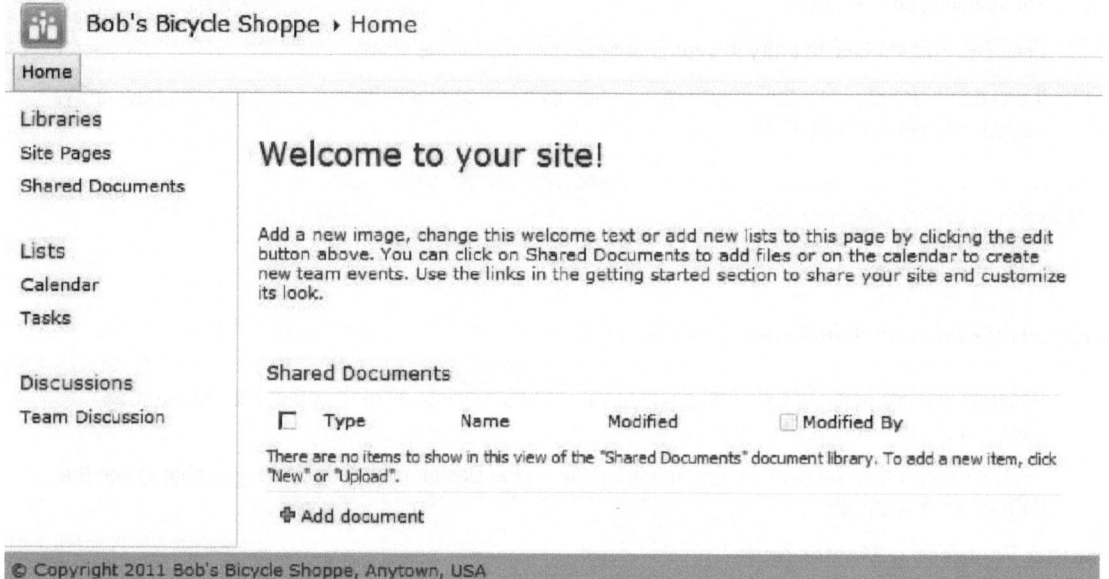

Figure 6-30. Site reflecting changes to CSS

If you start navigating around your site and you get to a page that opens a dialog box, notice that your footer also appears in the dialog box, as shown in Figure 6-31. This is because in SharePoint 2010, instead of navigating to a new page to add a new list item or document, they encapsulate that page in a dialog box.

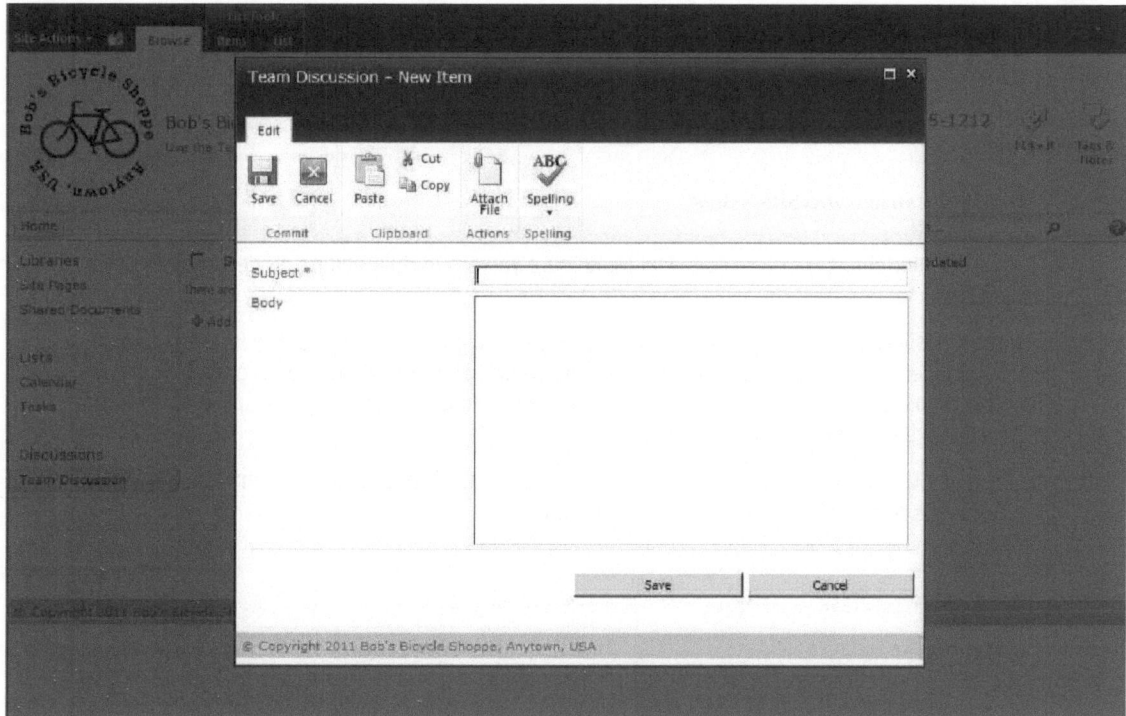

Figure 6-31. *Dialog box with the footer*

7. Because SharePoint still uses the master page to create the look and layout of the dialog box, it provides a class called `.s4-notdlg` to use on any element that you don't want to appear in a dialog box. So, in this footer example, you need to change the class attribute as shown in Figure 6-32.

```
<div class="siteFooter s4-notdlg">
```

Figure 6-32. *Add s4-notdlg to the class*

Create Custom Header

The next part that most organizations want to customize is the logo or site name in the header. This can be done through the browser, but you are still restricted to the basic layout of the default template. In this exercise, you will replace the header with the Bob's logo along with a custom title.

1. The first thing you need to do is to get your image assets in your Site Assets folder. From the Navigation pane, click the Site Assets link.

2. Click Import Files and then Add File, and locate the `bicycleshoplogo_120.png` file (from the downloaded chapter code), as you can see in Figure 6-33. Click OK to close the Import dialog box.

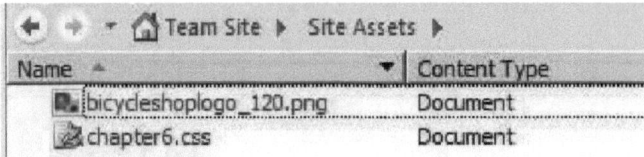

Figure 6-33. Files imported into Site Assets

3. Go back to your `chaptersix.master` file. Make sure you are in Split editing mode on your custom master page.

4. Click the existing logo. You should see the logo code highlighted. Notice that the logo image is a special `SharePoint:SiteLogoImage` control. This control allows a site owner to change the logo from the web interface. Because you are creating a custom master page, you want to remove that capability so the logo cannot be changed.

5. You can use CSS to make this change. In the `<td>` declaration that the logo is part of, Ctrl+click on the `class="s4-titlelogo"` link, shown in Figure 6-34.

```
301  <td class="s4-titlelogo">
302      <SharePoint:SPLinkButton runat="server" NavigateUrl="~site/" id="onetidProjectPropertyTi
303          <SharePoint:SiteLogoImage name="onetidHeadbnnr0" id="onetidHeadbnnr2" LogoImageUrl="
304      </SharePoint:SPLinkButton>
305  </td>
```

Figure 6-34. *s4-titlelogo code*

6. This should open `corev4.css` to the `s4-titlelogo` class declaration. This is the class you will override in your custom CSS. Copy the three declarations for `s-4-titlelogo` from `corev4` and paste them at the end of your `chapter6.css` file:

```
.s4-titlelogo{
        padding:12px 10px 12px 0px;
        text-align:center;
        vertical-align:middle;
}
.s4-titlelogo > a > img{
        vertical-align:middle;
}
.s4-titlelogo > img{
        vertical-align:middle;
}
```

7. Notice that the class deals with the positioning of the logo. If your second command merges the last two entries as shown in Figure 6-35, you will need to divide them.

```
2635 .s4-titlelogo > img,.s4-titlelogo > a > img{
2636 vertical-align:middle;
2637 }
```

Figure 6-35. s4-titlelogo image code

8. You will use the background-image command to place your logo into that same `<td>`. In your chapter6.css file, locate the first s4-titlelogo declaration that you just pasted into the CSS file. Modify the declaration as shown in Figure 6-36.

```
12 .s4-titlelogo{
13     background-image: url(bicycleshoplogo_120.png);
14     background-position:left center;
15     background-repeat: no-repeat;
16 }
```

Figure 6-36. Code to add logo

Notice that you are putting only the filename as the logo. Because the logo file resides in the same folder as the custom CSS, the URL is relative and you have to include only the name.

In the next declaration, you can see that the rule will apply to any img tag that resides in an 'A' tag that is assigned the .s4-titlelogo class. If you look at the master page code, this is where the following line of code is.

```
<SharePoint:SiteLogoImage name="onetidHeadbnnr0" id="onetidHeadbnnr2"
LogoImageUrl="/_layouts/images/siteIcon.png" runat="server"/>
```

9. Because you are going to use the background-image CSS command, you want to hide the actual logo. Setting visibility to hidden will make the original logo file invisible, but you will still be able to click the link.

10. Figure 6-37 shows the change you need to make to the .s4-titlelogo > a > img command.

```
18 .s4-titlelogo > a > img{
19     visibility: hidden;
20     width: 120px;
21     height: 120px;
22 }
```

Figure 6-37. Setting to hide current logo

What does this do? First, it makes the original image invisible while still maintaining the space it would have taken on the page. This is important because you still want to be able to click the link that will take you to the root of the site. Second, you need to make sure that you set the width and height to the dimensions of the logo file. That will provide the space required to view the background image.

11. Save your work and view the site. You should now see your new logo, as shown in Figure 6-38. If you go to the Site Actions menu in the browser and try to change the logo from the site settings menu, it will have no effect on your CSS logo modification.

Figure 6-38. Custom page with new logo

Customize the Header

Bob also wants the header to look different from other SharePoint sites. He wants his site name larger and he wants a contact number in the header.

1. Click the header of the master page and notice the code that is highlighted. If you look at the whole \<tr\> row, you will see that the row contains the logo, the site name, a secondary title, a page description, and the social media controls.

■ **Note** The social media controls will appear on pages when the administrator has ratings and tags turned on. If this is a feature that you will want in your site, it is best to take the delegate control, GlobalSiteLink3, into consideration. On a regular site page, this control is pretty large and could get in the way of a custom header. One way of providing this functionality while giving yourself some room to customize the header is to use an alternate GlobalSiteLink3 control called GlobalSiteLink3-mini. This provides the same functionality in a smaller format.

If you look at the page, you can see the social media control, the search control, and the help control. To provide as much room as possible for the header, you are going to move the social media tags between the search control and the help control.

2. Locate the piece of code around line 323 that is shown in Figure 6-39.

```
<SharePoint:DelegateControl ControlId="GlobalSiteLink3" Scope="Farm" runat="
```

Figure 6-39. GlobalSiteLink3 code

3. Cut the whole line of code from the table cell.

4. Scroll down until you find the search area, at about line 332.

5. Right after the ContentPlaceHolder for the SmallSearchInputBox, paste the line of code for the GlobalSiteLink3.

6. Add **-mini** to the GlobalSiteLink3 control ID name. Your code should look like that in Figure 6-40.

```
331    <a name="startnavigation"></a>
332    <div id="s4-searcharea" class="s4-search s4-rp">
333        <asp:ContentPlaceHolder id="PlaceHolderSearchArea" runat="server">
334            <SharePoint:DelegateControl runat="server" ControlId="SmallSearchInputBox" Version="4"/:
335        </asp:ContentPlaceHolder>
336        <SharePoint:DelegateControl ControlId="GlobalSiteLink3-mini" Scope="Farm" runat="server"/>
337        <span class="s4-help">
338            <span style="height:17px;width:17px;position:relative;display:inline-block;overflow:
339        </span>
```

Figure 6-40. Edited code for GlobalSiteLink3

7. Because the title is really just one `<table>` element, you can delete the cell that contained the delegate control.

8. If you click around the site, you will notice that the site title is also used for breadcrumb navigation. A link to the site root is always available by clicking the site name, so you should keep that. You will notice that a page description is also present underneath the breadcrumb navigation. This provides a hint to the user about what the page is used for (Figure 6-41).

Figure 6-41. Adding breadcrumb navigation

9. To make the site title more visible, you will add a row to the site table and separate the title from the other navigation. Start by adding the CSS classes to the chapter6.css file, as shown in Figure 6-42.

```
.customSpacer {
    width: 25px;
    float: left;
}

.customHeader {
    vertical-align: bottom;
}
.customHeader > H1 > a {
    font-size: 3em;
    padding-left: 5px;
}
```

Figure 6-42. CSS code for the header

10. Locate the Title table at about line 298. If you have downloaded the chapter code, open the file TitleTable.txt, shown in Figure 6-41. Select all and paste the code between the <tbody> tags. If you haven't downloaded the code, type the code snippet shown in Figure 6-43 between the <tbody> tags.

```
300   <tr>
301       <td class="s4-titlelogo" rowspan="2">
302           <SharePoint:SPLinkButton runat="server" NavigateUrl="~site/" id="onetidProjectPropertyTitleGraphic">
303               <SharePoint:SiteLogoImage name="onetidHeadbnnr0" id="onetidHeadbnnr2" LogoImageUrl="/_layouts/images/siteIcon.png" runat="server"/>
304           </SharePoint:SPLinkButton>
305       </td>
306       <td class="customHeader sr-titletext">
307           <h1 name="onetidProjectPropertyTitle">
308               <asp:ContentPlaceHolder id="PlaceHolderSiteName" runat="server">
309                   <SharePoint:SPLinkButton runat="server" NavigateUrl="~site/" id="onetidProjectPropertyTitle">
310                   <SharePoint:ProjectProperty Property="Title" runat="server" /></SharePoint:SPLinkButton>
311               </asp:ContentPlaceHolder>
312           </h1>
313       </td>
314   </tr>
315   <tr>
316       <td class="s4-titletext">
317           <div class="customSpacer"> </div>
318           <span id="onetidPageTitleSeparator" class="s4-nothome s4-bcsep s4-titlesep">
319           <SharePoint:ClusteredDirectionalSeparatorArrow runat="server"/> </span>
320           <h2>
321               <asp:ContentPlaceHolder id="PlaceHolderPageTitleInTitleArea" runat="server" />
322           </h2>
323           <div class="s4-pagedescription" tabindex="0" >
324               <div class="customSpacer"> </div>
325               <asp:ContentPlaceHolder id="PlaceHolderPageDescription" runat="server"/>
326           </div>
327       </td>
328   </tr>
```

Figure 6-43. TitleTable.txt

11. Save your changes and view the site in a browser.

12. Click the different links and notice that you still have the breadcrumb navigation.

13. Click the Lists link in the Quick Launch pane. Your site should look like Figure 6-44.

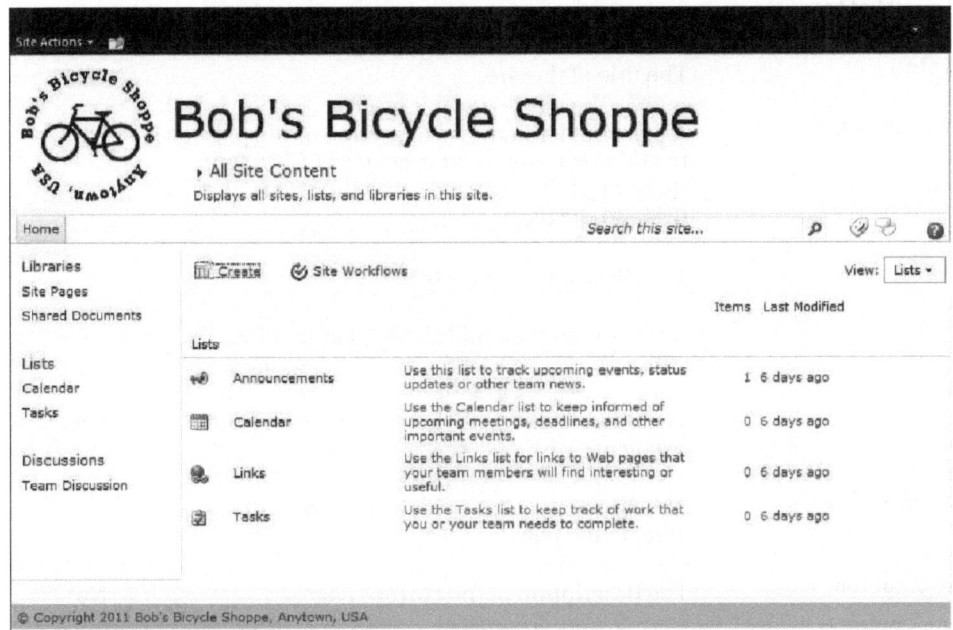

Figure 6-44. Finished customized site

Creating Your Own Custom Master Page

The branding that requires the most effort begins by creating your own custom master page. Although creating a master page from scratch is beyond the scope of this book, there are some things that we can cover here to get you started.

When designers create a completely custom master page, they usually create it in another application, such as Microsoft's Expression Blend or Adobe Photoshop. A master design is created and then the content placeholders are added based on the functionality that is desired for the site. When a site is highly customized, a lot of the built-in controls and placeholders will not be used. If you want to retain some of the functionality, such as breadcrumb navigation, horizontal navigation bar, search, and so on, the designer will need to plan for those items and then include them in the code of the master page.

Regardless of how highly customized the site design is, when you create your own master page, placeholders are required for SharePoint to operate properly. When you create a custom master page, it is important to include in your code all of the 33 required placeholders listed in Table 6-2.

Table 6-2. *SharePoint 2010's Required Placeholders*

Placeholder Control	Description	New In 2010
PlaceHolderQuickLaunchTop	The top of the Quick Launch menu.	Yes
PlaceHolderQuickLaunchBottom	The bottom of the Quick Launch menu.	Yes
PlaceHolderPageTitle	The title of the site.	No
PlaceHolderAdditionalPageHead	A placeholder in the head section of the page used to add extra components such as ECMAScript (JavaScript, JScript) and Cascading Style Sheets (CSS) to the page.	No
PlaceHolderBodyAreaClass	The class of the body area.	No
SPNavigation	A control used for additional page-editing controls.	No
PlaceHolderSiteName	The name of the site where the current page resides.	No
PlaceHolderPageTitleInTitleArea	The title of the page, which appears in the title area on the page.	No
PlaceHolderPageDescription	The description of the current page.	No
PlaceHolderSearchArea	The section of the page for the search controls.	No

Placeholder Control	Description	New In 2010
PlaceHolderGlobalNavigation	The breadcrumb control on the page.	No
PlaceHolderTitleBreadcrumb	The breadcrumb text for the breadcrumb control.	No
PlaceHolderGlobalNavigationSiteMap	The list of subsites and sibling sites in the global navigation on the page.	No
PlaceHolderTopNavBar	The container used to hold the top navigation bar.	No
PlaceHolderHorizontalNav	The navigation menu that is inside the top navigation bar.	No
PlaceHolderLeftNavBarDataSource	The placement of the data source used to populate the left navigation bar.	No
PlaceHolderCalendarNavigator	The date picker used when a calendar is visible on the page.	No
PlaceHolderLeftNavBarTop	The top section of the left navigation bar.	No
PlaceHolderLeftNavBar	The Quick Launch bar.	No
PlaceHolderLeftActions	The additional objects above the Quick Launch bar.	No
PlaceHolderMain	The main content of the page.	No
PlaceHolderFormDigest	The container where the page form digest control is stored.	No
PlaceHolderUtilityContent	The additional content at the bottom of the page. This is outside the form tag.	No
PlaceHolderTitleAreaClass	The class for the title area. This is now in the head tag. Any customizations that add a web part zone in a content tag to this placeholder will cause an error on the page.	No
PlaceHolderPageImage	Not used in 2010 but needed for backward compatibility.	No
PlaceHolderTitleLeftBorder	Not used in 2010 but needed for backward compatibility.	No

Placeholder Control	Description	New In 2010
PlaceHolderMiniConsole	Not used in 2010 but needed for backward compatibility.	No
PlaceHolderTitleRightMargin	Not used in 2010 but needed for backward compatibility.	No
PlaceHolderTitleAreaSeparator	Not used in 2010 but needed for backward compatibility.	No
PlaceHolderNavSpacer	Not used in 2010 but needed for backward compatibility.	No
PlaceHolderLeftNavBarBorder	Not used in 2010 but needed for backward compatibility.	No
PlaceHolderBodyLeftBorder	Not used in 2010 but needed for backward compatibility.	No
PlaceHolderBodyRightMargin	Not used in 2010 but needed for backward compatibility.	No

In addition to these controls, you also need to plan for the server ribbon. More details and the ribbon code can be found at http://msdn.microsoft.com/en-us/library/ee539981.aspx.

Hiding Placeholders

What do you do if some of the required placeholders are not necessary for your design? Hide them. They still need to be listed in your code, or you will receive an error when the server tries to render them. The best place to do this is inside an <asp:Panel> control right before the closing </form> tag, and then set the visible attribute to false.

The following is an example of hiding placeholders:

```
<!-- Hide Placeholders -->
<asp:Panel visible="false" runat="Server">
    <asp:ContentPlaceHolder id="PlaceHolderSearchArea" runat="server" />
    <asp:ContentPlaceHolder id="PlaceHolderHorizontalNav" runat="server" />
    <asp:ContentPlaceHolder id="PlaceHolderPageTitleInTitleArea" runat="server" />
    <asp:ContentPlaceHolder id="PlaceHolderPageDescription" runat="server"/>
    <asp:ContentPlaceHolder id="PlaceHolderLeftNavBarDataSource" runat="server" />
    <asp:ContentPlaceHolder id="PlaceHolderCalendarNavigator" runat="server" />
    <asp:ContentPlaceHolder id="PlaceHolderLeftActions" runat="server" />
    <asp:ContentPlaceHolder id="PlaceHolderLeftNavBarTop" runat="server"/>
    <asp:ContentPlaceHolder id="PlaceHolderLeftNavBar" runat="server" />
    <asp:ContentPlaceHolder id="PlaceHolderQuickLaunchBottom" runat="server" />
    <asp:ContentPlaceHolder id="PlaceHolderGlobalNavigation" runat="server" />
```

```
      <asp:ContentPlaceHolder id="PlaceHolderTitleBreadcrumb" runat="server" />
      <asp:ContentPlaceHolder id="PlaceHolderGlobalNavigationSiteMap" runat="server"
Visible="false" />
      <asp:ContentPlaceHolder ID="SPNavigation" runat="server">
    </asp:Panel>
    <!-- End Hide Placeholders -->
```

Starter Master Pages

If you do a search for *StarterMasterPages*, you will find a CodePlex project at http://
startermasterpages.codeplex.com that was created by a SharePoint Server MVP. He has created master
pages with all of the required placeholders that you can use as a starting point for your custom master
pages. This helps ensure that you will have all required elements for a functional SharePoint 2010 master
page.

Branding Considerations

There are considerations that should be made when creating your own master pages. Because
SharePoint is a complex platform with lots of moving parts, great care should be taken when creating
your own custom master pages. Take into consideration that SharePoint 2010 includes certain features
that make it appealing to users—for example, the page editing features or the Ribbon. Removing or
limiting this functionality could hinder the user experience and could hinder widespread user
acceptance.

You also have to think about the amount of time testing your custom master page will require.
Microsoft has taken care to test all aspects of the user experience to ensure proper functionality with its
included master pages. Proper testing of your master page will need to be done to ensure that all default
SharePoint functionality (adding web parts, for one) actually works and that all default web parts (data
grids, calendars, and explorer views) work in your custom master page.

When Things Go Wrong

When you create your own master page, inevitably something will go wrong. Creating your own master
page is difficult because of all of the parts that make SharePoint such a powerful platform. There are
some common problems that could cause your master page to break. Consider the following when
debugging your master page:

- *Required placeholders*: As mentioned previously, SharePoint requires placeholders
  to function properly. This is why it is suggested that you begin with a copy of an
  out-of-the-box master page.

- *Missing controls*: In addition to the required placeholders, controls are required
  for SharePoint to function correctly. Check the following:

  - The SPPageManager control needs to be placed in the <head> element and is
    used to route commands to page components.

  - The ScriptLink control needs to be placed in the <head> element also. It
    creates a reference to the SharePoint client-side script libraries.

- The `ScriptManager` control needs to be placed in the <body> element. It manages all client-side script functions on the page and controls communication between the browser and server without having to refresh the page.

- *Duplicate placeholders*: Make sure that all placeholders are on the page only once. SharePoint Designer will throw an error if a duplicate placeholder exists on a page.

- *Typographical errors*: Make sure all control names, placeholder names, and other required elements are spelled correctly. It is advisable to copy and paste elements from a working master page instead of manually typing these.

Summary

This chapter has covered SharePoint branding and the different levels of effort required to create your own branded SharePoint site when using SharePoint Designer 2010. The top take-aways from this chapter are as follows:

- The main master page used by SharePoint 2010 is called `v4.master`, and the main CSS file is called `corev4.css`.

- Never modify the included SharePoint pages directly. Instead, make a copy of them first and then edit the copy.

- If you don't know CSS, you can still use the tools provided by SharePoint Designer to style your site.

- If you are going to create a custom master page, it is important to remember to include the 33 required placeholders in your code, even if you aren't planning on using them.

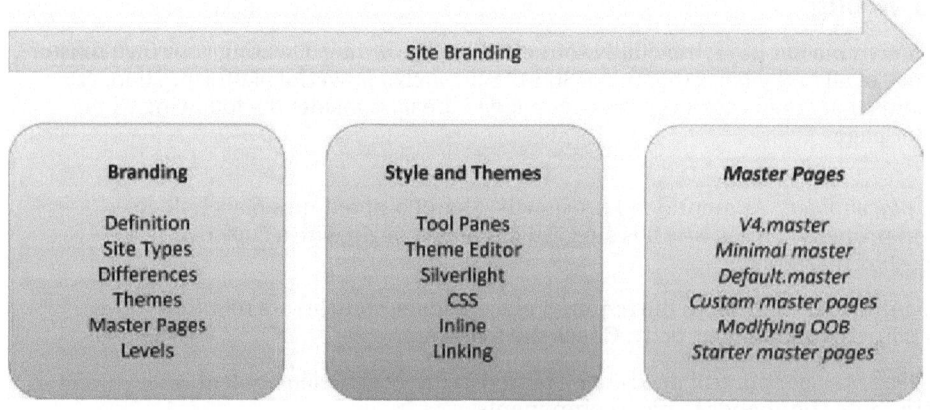

CHAPTER 7

Managing Publishing Sites

The publishing features of SharePoint Server 2010 provide a sophisticated web content management (WCM) architecture for SharePoint-based sites. Publishing sites use a multilayered page structure that allows for tight control over and efficient maintenance of web content. Pages are created and published based on a common data management and approval workflow. Content can be managed centrally or through a series of content repositories that allow for the staging of content.

In this chapter, you will explore the concepts and procedures used to manage web content via SharePoint's publishing features. You will examine the security and workflow for publishing content and learn about the construction of publishing sites. You will see the SharePoint features that enable the publishing functionality.

You will learn about the following topics in this chapter:

- How to create web content by using SharePoint's publishing features

- How to manage the approval workflow

- How to schedule site changes to be applied and withdrawn on a predefined schedule

- How to design the master pages, page layouts, and content pages to produce the desired visual effect and maintenance experience

- The importance of additional publishing features such as navigation, site variations, and content deployment

Exploring the Publishing Process

SharePoint Server 2010 Enterprise's publishing features provide a complete WCM solution for sites built on the SharePoint platform. When a change is made to a publishing site, it is not immediately visible to all users of the site, as is the case with non-publishing SharePoint sites. Published pages must go through an approval process before they are visible to the site's general audience. They can also be scheduled for release at a later time.

User Roles and Permission Levels

Publishing sites use the same security mechanisms as any other SharePoint site. When the publishing features are enabled, a set of SharePoint permission levels and groups are created that allow users to perform content editing and publishing tasks.

The permission levels for publishing include the following:

- *Approve*: Users with this level of permissions can edit and approve published items including pages, documents, and list items.

- *Manage Hierarchy*: This level allows users to create new publishing sites as well as edit published content.

- *Restricted Read*: Users with this permission can view published items but cannot access any of the publishing metadata behind them such as revision histories.

These permission levels are deployed to a standard set of roles represented by these SharePoint groups:

- *Approver*: The members of this group have the right to edit and approve published items including pages, documents, and list items.

- *Designer*: The Designer role is intended for those users who are responsible for the look and feel of the site. These users create page layouts and other publishing artifacts that control the appearance of the site.

- *Site Member (a.k.a. Contributor)*: Each site has a default group for members of the site. Site members are generally those users who contribute content to the site. They can edit pages and submit them for approval.

- *Site Collection Administrator*: This role is not deployed as a SharePoint group but is built in to the SharePoint Foundation. In the context of publishing, site collection administrators are responsible for approving changes to page layouts and master pages by default. This is because changes to these files do not affect a single site, but every site in the site collection.

Publishing Workflow Overview

The publishing of content is controlled through a SharePoint workflow that manages the state of each published item throughout its life cycle. In this section, you will examine the flow of content items from creation through final publishing.

Workflow Sequence

Figure 7-1 depicts the typical publishing workflow for a published item.

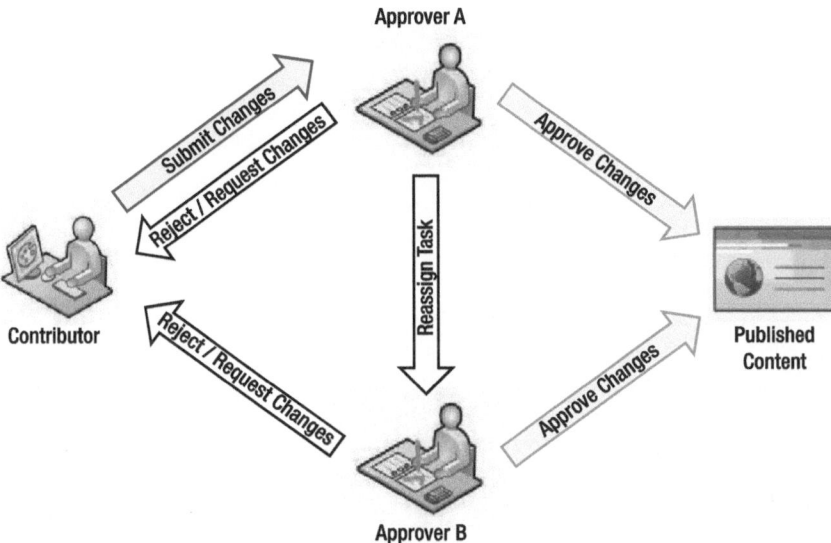

Figure 7-1. Page publishing workflow

The first step in the process is the submission of the changes by a site member or contributor. This initiates the publishing workflow and assigns a task to a set of designated approvers. By default, this task is assigned to the Approvers group for the site.

Approvers have several actions they can take with regard to the approval task:

- *Approve*: This action accepts the changes and publishes them to the site.

- *Reject*: This action rejects the changes and returns the draft to the contributor for possible resubmission at a later time.

- *Request change*: This action allows the approver to provide feedback to the contributor without terminating the publishing workflow. The contributor can make changes to the item and send the changes back to the approver for review.

- *Reassign task*: This action transfers the approval task to another user or group. This might be used, for example, when an organization wants to have all changes managed by a central group that is responsible for routing the changes to the correct department for approval.

Once an approver has approved or rejected the changes, the publishing workflow ends. SharePoint maintains a detailed log of all actions taken during a workflow, as you can see in Figure 7-2. This log can be accessed through the Status item on the Publish menu tab for a page.

Workflow Information

Initiator: SWRIGHT-SP2\aapprover	Document: default
Started: 3/6/2011 10:16 AM	Status: In Progress
Last run: 3/6/2011 10:19 AM	

= Cancel all Approval tasks

Tasks

The following tasks have been assigned to the participants in this workflow. Click a task to edit it. You can also view these tasks in the list Workflow Tasks.

Assigned To	Title	Due Date	Status	Related Content	Outcome
Approvers	Please approve default ⊠ NEW		Completed	default	
Steve Wright	Please approve default ⊠ NEW		Not Started	default	

Workflow History

The following events have occurred in this workflow.

Date Occurred	Event Type	User ID	Description	Outcome
3/6/2011 10:16 AM	Error	System Account	The e-mail message cannot be sent. Make sure the e-mail has a valid recipient.	
3/6/2011 10:16 AM	Error	System Account	The e-mail message cannot be sent. Make sure the e-mail has a valid recipient.	
3/6/2011 10:16 AM	Workflow Initiated	SWRIGHT-SP2 \aapprover	Approval was started. Participants: Approvers	
3/6/2011 10:16 AM	Task Created	SWRIGHT-SP2 \aapprover	Task created for Approvers. Due by: 1/1/0001 12:00:00 AM	
3/6/2011 10:19 AM	Task Completed	SWRIGHT-SP2 \aapprover	Task assigned to Approvers was delegated by SWRIGHT-SP2\aapprover. Comments: Please review	Delegated by SWRIGHT-SP2\aapprover to Steve Wright
3/6/2011 10:19 AM	Task Created	SWRIGHT-SP2 \aapprover	Task created for Steve Wright. Due by: 1/1/0001 12:00:00 AM	

Figure 7-2. *Workflow status and history page*

Versioning and Statuses

The most common type of item that is published in SharePoint is a web site page. Other items such as list items, images, and documents can also follow the publishing process, but our examples are pages. Just remember that a page is a type of document, and a document is a type of list item. SharePoint treats all items the same when publishing is enabled and approval is required in the list or library.

Each page in the site has a version history associated with it. the This is a record of each set of changes that the page has gone through over time. A *major version* is one that has been released to the general user community, or *published*. A *minor version* is one that has not been published. A page may go through several minor revisions before being published or republished. Each version has a number associated with it, such as 3.2. The whole number represents the published version, and the decimal represents the draft version. Whole-numbered versions, such as 3.0, are published versions of the page. Other versions are drafts based on the previously published version. A history of all versions of a page can be accessed by viewing the Version History for a page, shown in Figure 7-3.

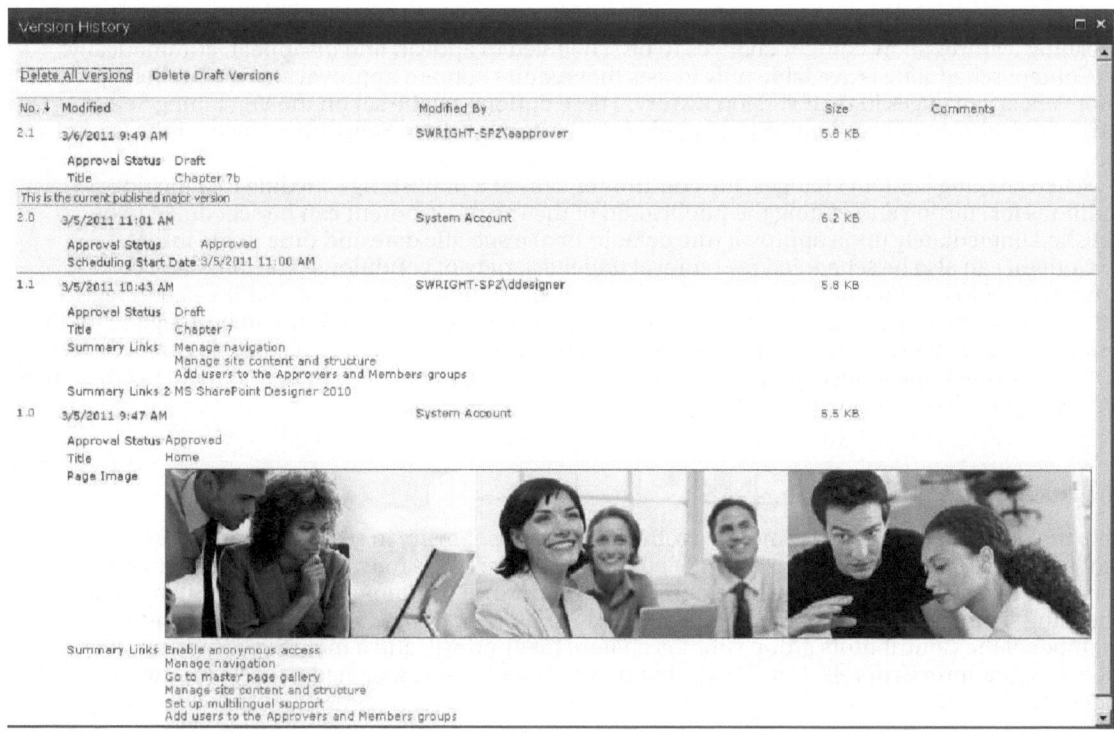

Figure 7-3. *Version History dialog box*

As a page goes through the publishing process, it has a different *approval status* depending on the last action taken with respect to that page. The types of approval status are as follows:

- *Draft*: A draft version of this page has been created. A draft version can be viewed by users authorized to review drafts depending on whether it is checked in or not.

  - A *checked-in draft* can be seen by all reviewers.

  - A *checked-out draft* can be seen only by the user to whom it is checked out. All other reviewers will see the previously checked-in version.

- *Pending*: When a page is submitted for publishing, its status becomes Pending.

- *Approved*: Once a draft version is approved, it becomes a major version and its status becomes Approved.

Scheduling Content

By default, when a draft is approved, it becomes visible to site visitors immediately. In some cases, this is not desirable. For example, when preparing the web site content for a new product release, the entire content creation and approval cycle may need to be complete weeks ahead of time. SharePoint's publishing features allow content changes to be scheduled to appear, and disappear, automatically.

Content scheduling is available only in lists that require content approval and maintain major and minor versions of pages in their version history. These options can be set on the Versioning Settings page for the list or library. Scheduling can be enabled on the Manage Item Scheduling page for the list or library.

When creating content changes, the contributor can set a publishing schedule that includes conditions for starting and ending the publication of the version. Content can be scheduled to be published immediately upon approval (the default) or at a specific date and time in the future.

Content can also be scheduled for removal under a variety of conditions. The item may be configured not to be automatically removed, but instead a reminder can be sent to the page's registered contact user for review on a periodic basis. Alternately, a specific date and time can be assigned for the version to be automatically removed. An optional notification can be sent to the page's contact user to warn them of the impending expiration of the page. By default, published changes remain in effect until they are superseded by a later version.

Simple Moderation

While the publishing workflow provides a robust review mechanism, in some cases a full review process is not necessary or desirable. If the group of content authors is the same as the group of content approvers, there would seem to be little point in a full approval workflow. In this case, SharePoint publishing supports a lite publishing process called *simple moderation*. In simple moderation approval, a member of the Contributors group submits an item for approval, and a member of the Approvers group simply approves or rejects it. There are no workflows or tasks assigned to users in simple moderation.

Publishing Templates

The publishing features of SharePoint are very versatile in that they can be applied to any site or list. By enabling the publishing features and configuring options such as versioning and content approval, the publishing process can be tailored in many ways. Additionally, Microsoft has provided a set of templates to create sites specifically designed for managing published content. This simplifies the configuration of these sites dramatically.

Out of the box, SharePoint provides two templates at the site-collection level. When one of these is used to create a new site collection, publishing is automatically enabled for both the site collection and the root site. By default, only publishing site templates are available for creating new sites under a publishing site collection root site. This default can be altered by the site collection administrator if desirable. The two templates are as follows:

- *Publishing Portal*: This is a general-purpose publishing site that uses all of the publishing features including workflow. The site contains lists and libraries for pages, reusable content, images, and more. This template is ideal for public-facing Internet sites or internal intranet sites.

- *Enterprise Wiki*: This template provides a customized wiki authoring environment that includes SharePoint's publishing features. Unlike a team wiki site, this template requires that content changes be approved.

Once a publishing site collection is created, the following set of site templates can be used to manage content in subsites:

- *Publishing Site with Workflow*: This template creates a subsite that employs all publishing features including workflow.

- *Publishing Site*: This template does not enable the publishing workflow. Sites created with this template use simple moderation for approval, as described earlier.

- *Enterprise Wiki*: This template is designed for creating subsites within an Enterprise Wiki site collection.

Understanding Published Pages

Site pages that appear in publishing sites have a different structure than those contained in nonpublishing sites. In this section, you will examine what makes publishing pages unique.

Anatomy of a Publishing Page

In a nonpublishing site, pages are essentially normal ASP.NET pages that contain two layers: a master page and a content page. The master page contains the markup that defines the structure and general layout of the page. This usually includes headers, footers, menus, and content placeholder controls. The content page is then created by defining content to be placed in each of the content placeholders in the designated master page.

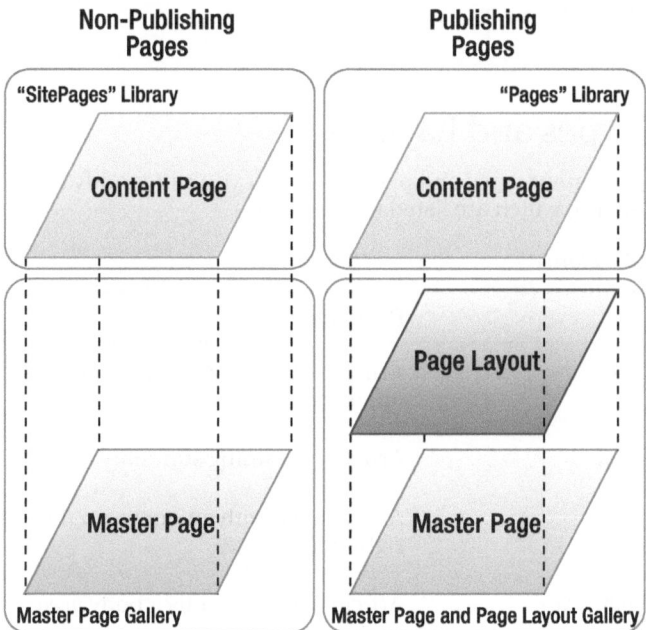

Figure 7-4. Comparative web page anatomy

Publishing pages are based on the same framework as nonpublishing pages, but the content page layer is split into two sublayers: the page layout and the content. A page layout (a.k.a. a layout page) defines the content that goes into the placeholders defined in the underlying master page. The page layout also defines its own controls that act as placeholders to be filled in by the content page.

At first glance, this may seem to be an unnecessary complication of the page structure. Why should adding a third layer make any difference? The answer is found in the mechanism used to deliver the content to the controls in the layout page.

Publishing Content Types

Each page layout is associated with a SharePoint content type. Recall that content types allow us to define the data fields associated with list items in SharePoint. The content types used with page publishing always derive from a base type named Page. These types, creatively called *page content types*, contain fields that support the publishing and scheduling mechanisms of publishing sites.

The content type for a particular page layout contains fields, in addition to those associated with the Page type, that represent the content that should appear on the site page. As a result, the content changes for a web page are reduced to simple data fields, making them much easier to manage than the HTML and ASP.NET markup that make up a nonpublishing content page.

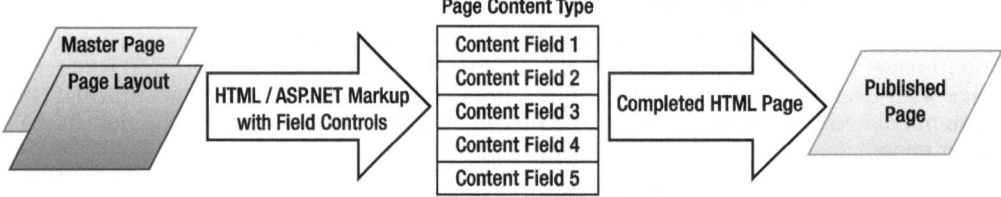

Figure 7-5. Page content types

Standard Publishing Content Types and Layouts

As a site designer, you can create your own page content types and page layouts or you can modify one of the standard components provided by SharePoint, which are listed in Table 7-1.

Table 7-1. Out-of-the-Box Publishing Types and Layouts

Page Content Type	Page Layout	Description
Article page	ArticleLeft.aspx	Article page with an image on the left of the page.
	ArticleLinks.aspx	Article containing summary links.
	ArticleRight.aspx	Article page with an image on the right of the page.
	PageFromDocLayout.aspx	Article page with only a body area.
Enterprise Wiki page	EnterpriseWiki.aspx	A basic wiki page.

Page Content Type	Page Layout	Description
Project page	ProjectPage.aspx	A wiki page for project information.
Redirect page	RedirectPageLayout.aspx	A page that redirects to a configured URL.
	VariationsRootPageLayout.aspx	A page the redirects based on the detected site variation needed. See the "Variations" section later in this chapter.
Welcome page	BlankWebPartPage.aspx	One main content area with a variety of web part zones.
	WelcomeLinks.aspx	Contains one image and content area, two lists of links, and web part zones.
	WelcomeSplash.aspx	Contains one image, a content area, and web part zones.
	WelcomeTOC.aspx	Contains one image, a content area, a Table of Contents web part, and web part zones.

Page layouts are not stored in the site but in the Master Page Gallery associated with the site collection. This is important because it changes how page layouts are managed. When a page layout is modified, it affects the entire site collection, not just one site. Therefore, the security and approval requirements for page layouts are more like those for master pages than for ordinary site pages in nonpublishing sites.

■ **Note** Because of the importance of page layouts to the stability of the web site, it may be beneficial in some environments to disable the ability to edit them. This can be done by using the SharePoint Central Administration web site.

Field Controls

Page layouts are composed of three major components: HTML markup, field controls, and web part zones.

The *HTML markup* that appears in a page layout is simply rendered to the final site page. It is important to remember that the final output from the page must be valid HTML. All HTML in the master and layout pages must be consistent when the final page is rendered.

In Chapter 4, you learned how to use web parts and web part zones in your site pages. The concepts are the same for layout pages. By placing web part zones in your layout pages, you make them available to your site page authors. Remember that because web parts are not stored in your page content type, they are not versioned with the rest of the page.

Field controls are the key to managing content when using layout pages. Field controls are ASP.NET controls that are designed to read and manage data fields in the content page's underlying content type. Depending on the type of data the field contains (an image vs. rich text, for example), a different field control will be used. In SharePoint Designer, you simply drag the field onto the Page Editor, and the correct field control is created automatically.

The magic of field controls happens when the page is viewed in editing mode in the web browser. In normal page-viewing mode, a field control simply renders the content stored in the page's data field. In Edit mode, the field control renders an on-page content editor that the user can use to create or modify the content in the field.

A special type of field control is the *edit mode panel*. This type of field control is visible only in Edit mode. This control allows the page author to update page fields that do not appear directly on the page. A common example is shown in Figure 7.6; the edit mode panel is making the page title available for editing.

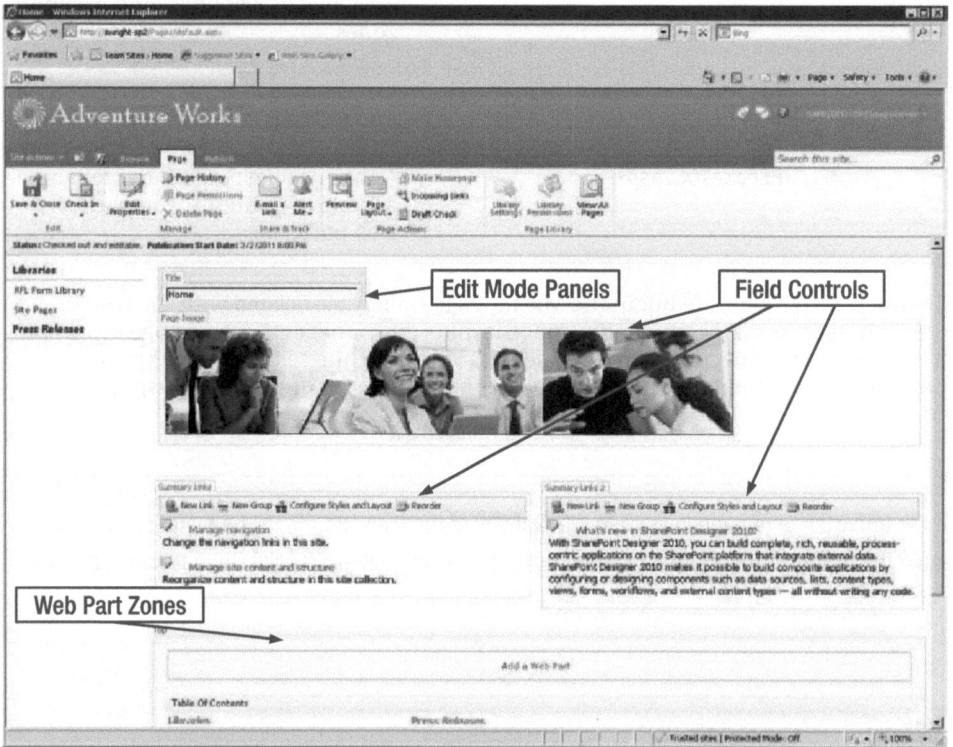

Figure 7-6. Field controls in Edit mode

Using Additional Publishing Site Functionality

Beyond the ability to publish web pages and other documents, the publishing features of SharePoint allow users to manage other aspects of publishing web sites. This section introduces these features, but a full exploration of them is beyond the scope of this book.

Navigation

In standard nonpublishing sites, navigation is handled by the global navigation bar across the top and the Quick Launch menu on the left of the page. In publishing sites, the Quick Launch bar is replaced by a menu called Current Navigation, which serves a similar purpose but behaves differently.

The Global and Current Navigation bars can be extensively customized by using the Navigation link that is added to the Site Settings page when publishing is enabled. The navigation bars can be configured to show or hide subsites and site pages. They can be sorted, grouped, and have items added or hidden as needed.

The navigation controls for publishing sites are sensitive to the pages that are published in the Pages library as well as their status. For example, a page that is not yet published will not appear in the navigation menu for users who cannot see the page yet.

■ **Tip** In some cases, it is desirable to have certain pages in a site show up in the menu and others to be hidden. A simple means to accomplishing this is to place the hidden pages inside a folder within the Pages library. Such pages are automatically hidden, whereas those in the root folder are automatically shown in the menu.

Variations

Site *variations* are sets of publishing sites that are designed to be very similar to one another but with certain well-controlled differences. Variations allow a number of sites to share some content while allowing for slight modifications between sites.

A single root site is created with the content that is common to all sites. Then, variants of that site are created based on the specific needs of the site. When a user navigates to the root site's URL, that user is redirected to the correct site variant automatically.

The most common use for site variations is to create multilingual web sites. The root variation site might contain the site's content in English. Each additional variant would be for a specific additional language. It is even possible to create multiple levels of variation sites for different dialects of the same language. SharePoint contains site translation workflows to help organize the generation of site variations in different languages. When a user enters the root site's URL in a web browser, the default welcome page detects the language being used by the visitor's browser and redirects that user to the correct site variation.

Variations can also be used to route visitors to content that is specific to the user in ways other than their language. For example, site variations can be used to customize content for different brands, mobile devices, or geographic locations. Essentially, anything a web page can detect about the user could be used to select a site variation.

Content Deployment

Content deployment refers to the process of moving published content from one site collection to another. The most common use of content deployment is to allow designers and content contributors to work in a nonproduction environment. Only after content is approved for publication does it move into the production server farm.

Content deployment is carried out by a series of timer jobs that can be scheduled or run manually. It is important to use the correct type of deployment job to get the desired effect. The jobs are as follows:

- *Full*: Moves all content from the source collection to the destination. Any existing content in the destination collection is *not* removed prior to copying over the new content. Therefore, deletions that have occurred in the source will not be reflected in the destination after a Full deployment.

- *Incremental*: Moves only new changes from the source to the destination. Any added, updated, or removed content items in the source will be reflected in the destination. An Incremental job will perform a Full deployment the first time it is run to ensure that all content is initially moved. Subsequent runs will move only updates.

- *Quick Deploy*: Moves only items that have been specified for quick deployment. This timer job generally runs more often than Incremental or Full jobs. This type of job is ideal for patching content that has been found to be incorrect in a staging or production environment. .

In software development, it has long been standard operating procedure to develop in one environment, test in another, and operate production on yet another set of servers. Content development in SharePoint can benefit from a similar approach. The advantages of this approach revolve around allowing only certain types of operations in each environment. There are also different numbers of users and network infrastructures to consider, as follows:

Authoring Environment	Small number of users and servers, SharePoint Designer access enabled, content authoring allowed
Stage Environment	Small number of users and servers, no authoring or designer access, receives deployed content from the authoring environment, used for performing final reviews of new content
Production Environment	Full complement of servers, no authoring or designer access, receives deployed content from the stage environment, used to serve web pages to the end-user community

By using SharePoint's content deployment feature, these environments can be separate site collections within the same server farm. As a best practice, at least the production environment should be a separate SharePoint farm. Three common designs for content deployment are one-, two-, and three-farm topologies.

In a *single-farm topology*, shown in Figure 7-7, authoring is performed in one site collection, and content is deployed to production in a second. There could also be a third site collection for staging if desired. The weakness of this approach is that many of SharePoint's security controls are applied at the farm level and therefore cannot protect against accidental changes in this configuration.

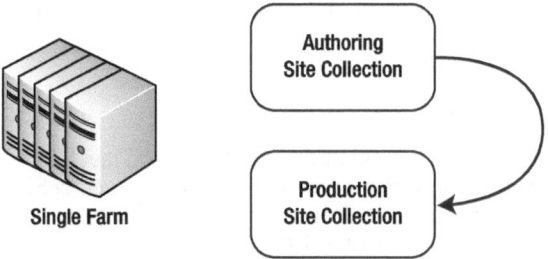

Figure 7-7. *A single-farm topology*

In a *two-farm topology*, shown in Figure 7-8, authoring is performed in one SharePoint farm, and content is deployed to production in a second. The authoring farm need not contain as many servers as the production farm, because it will presumably have far fewer users.

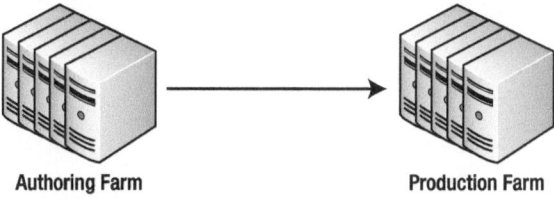

Figure 7-8. *A two-farm topology*

A *three-farm topology*, shown in Figure 7-9, adds an intermediate staging environment that can be used for a detailed review of the completed content before final deployment to production. There are two ways to handle production deployment in this topology. Content can be deployed to production either from the stage farm or directly from the authoring farm.

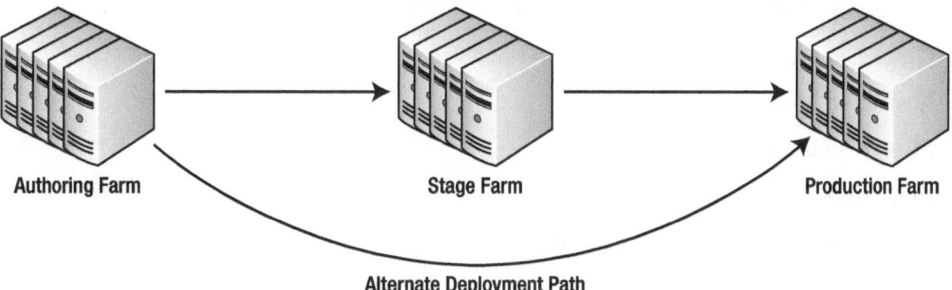

Figure 7-9. *A three-farm topology*

Enabling Publishing Features

SharePoint's publishing site functionality is implemented in a pair of features that can be enabled in any site or site collection. A third feature implements the publishing workflow. When using the publishing site and site collection templates provided by SharePoint, these features are automatically enabled. If you want to use them in an existing site, you need to activate them manually. This section describes the contents of these features and how to control them.

SharePoint Server Publishing Infrastructure

The SharePoint Server Publishing Infrastructure feature can be activated at the site collection level. In the root site of the collection, select Site Settings from the Site Actions menu. On Site Settings, select Site Collection Features under Site Collection Administration. Find the SharePoint Server Publishing Infrastructure feature in the list. The feature can be activated or deactivated from this page.

When the publishing infrastructure is activated in a site collection, a large number of artifacts are added to the SharePoint environment, including the following:

- Site templates
  - Publishing Site with Workflow
  - Publishing Site
  - Enterprise Wiki
- Permission levels
  - Approve
  - Manage Hierarchy
  - Restricted Read
- SharePoint groups
  - Approvers
  - Designers
  - Hierarchy Managers
  - Quick Deploy Users
  - Restricted Readers
  - Style Resource Readers
- Site settings links
  - Options to manage content structure
  - Options to manage navigation
  - Site collection actions for managing page layouts and site variations
- Navigation changes
- Master pages and page layouts
  - New master pages
  - New page content types and page layouts

- Site collection lists and libraries
  - Style library
  - Content and Structure
  - Reusable Content
  - Site Collection Documents
  - Site Collection Images
- Web parts
  - Summary Links web part
  - Table Of Contents web part
  - Content Query web part
  - Media web part

Publishing Approval Workflow Feature

The Publishing Approval Workflow feature provides the publishing workflow used with publishing sites. This feature should generally be activated at the site collection level whenever publishing is in use.

SharePoint Server Publishing Feature

The SharePoint Server publishing feature is activated at the site level. On the Site Settings page of the site, select Manage Site Features under Site Actions. Find the SharePoint Server Publishing feature in the list. The feature can be activated or deactivated from this page.

When the publishing site feature is activated, the following additions are made to the site:

- Site settings links
  - Control site output caching
  - Apply master pages and CSS styles
  - Control available page layouts and site templates
  - Set the site welcome page
  - The Save Site as Template link is removed because this feature is not available on publishing sites.
- Site lists and libraries
  - Documents: Contains site-specific document files
  - Images: Contains images for use within the site
  - Pages: Contains the site's publishing content pages

- Workflow Tasks: Used by the publishing workflow to manage approval tasks

- Other site configurations

  - Published item scheduling is enabled.

  - Document versioning is set to create major and minor versions.

  - Draft items are made available only to users who can edit them.

  - Pages are set to require a check-out operation prior to being edited.

Exercises

In this section, you will explore the functionality of SharePoint's publishing sites by creating and modifying content. SharePoint's publishing features are an enormous subject that could easily fill a book on their own. Because this book focuses on SharePoint Designer, these examples focus on using SharePoint Designer within the context of publishing. Please don't make the mistake of thinking that what you see here is all there is to publishing in SharePoint.

You will begin by deploying a standard publishing template. Then, you will experiment with the workflow that governs the publishing of content pages. The key value of SharePoint Designer in publishing comes into play when designing page layouts. You will continue by modifying one of the default page layouts. Finally, you will create an entirely new kind of page by defining a new page content type and a page layout to go with it.

EXERCISE 7-1. SET UP A PUBLISHING SITE

Although any existing site can be converted to a publishing site by enabling the SharePoint publishing features, for this exercise, you will take the simpler approach of deploying one of SharePoint's standard publishing templates.

Note You will need to have Farm Administration privileges on the SharePoint server in order to perform this exercise. If not, you will need to work with your farm administrator to deploy the publishing template to a site collection in your environment.

---

1. Open the SharePoint 2010 Central Administration site in a web browser.

2. Select Application Management from the menu at the left, as shown in Figure 7-10.

3. On the Application Management page, select Manage Web Applications from the Web Applications group.

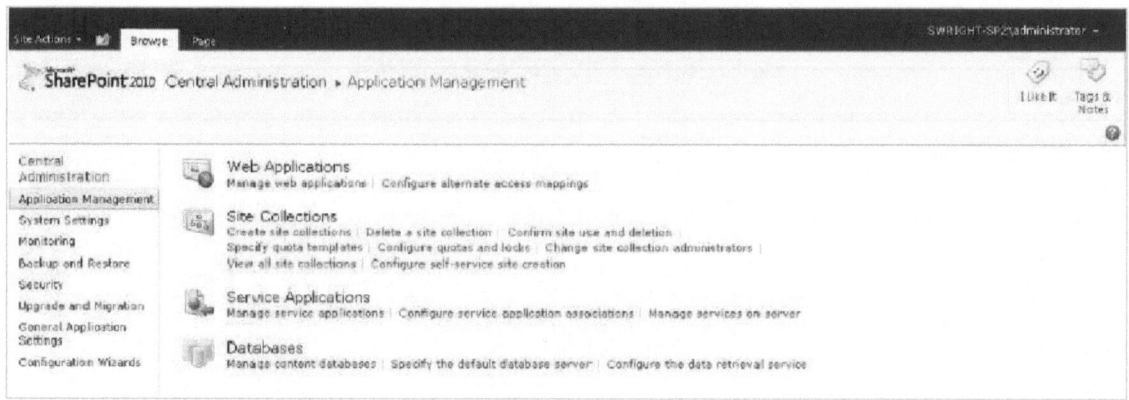

Figure 7-10. *Application management*

4. On the Web Applications Menu tab, click New in the Contribute group.

5. Create the new application by using Classic Mode Authentication and the NTLM provider.

6. Create a new IIS web site, and enter **80** for the port number, or another port if another web application already exists on this port

7. Because this will be a public web site, you will also enable Anonymous users.

8. For this exercise, you can set the web application's application pool identity to NETWORK SERVICE. In a production environment, the identity should be set to a managed service account for security reasons.

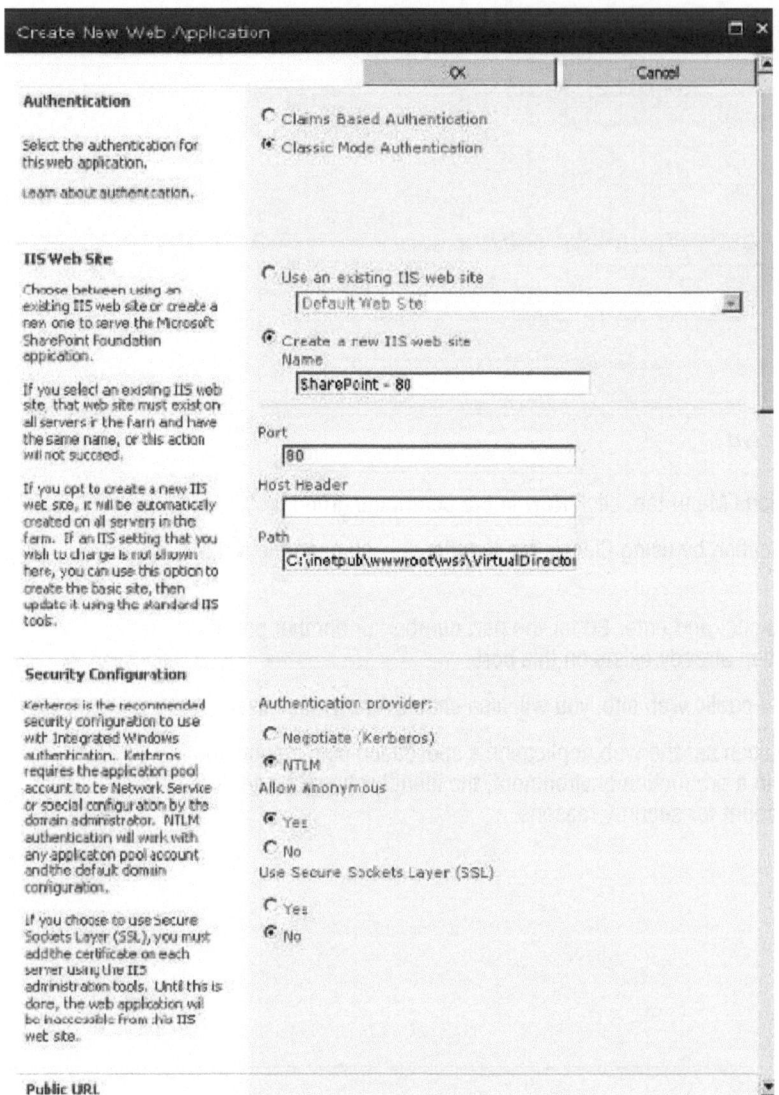

Figure 7-11. Creating a new web application

9. Click OK. It will take a few minutes for the new web application to be provisioned.

10. Return to Application Management in the Central Administration site.

11. Under Site Collections, select Create Site Collection.

12. Select the previously created web application from the drop-down list.

13. Enter a site title and description.

14. In the Select a Template section at the bottom right of the page, click the Publishing tab and select Publishing Portal.

Figure 7-12. Creating a site collection

15. Select Site Collection Administrator Users and then click OK. Once the site collection is provisioned, open the site in a web browser and log in as a Site Collection Administrator.

At this point, only a site collection administrator can access the site. You need to give other users access.

For this exercise, you will use three user accounts to demonstrate the different roles within the publishing workflow: *aapprover* will be an approver, *ddesigner* will be the site designer, and *administrator* will represent the site collection administrator. Any authorized user account could be used in place of these names, but they need to be different accounts in order to see the effect of the publishing roles.

16. From the Site Actions menu, choose Site Permissions.

17. On the Permission Tools tab of the menu, select the Anonymous Access option from the Manage group.

For this exercise, select the Entire Web Site option and then click OK, as shown in Figure 7-13.

18. Anonymous users can now see published content on the web site.

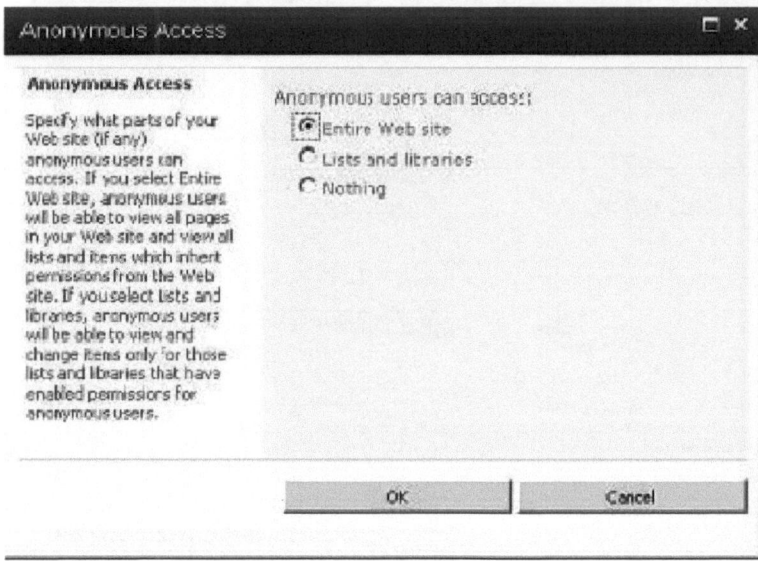

Figure 7-13. Enabling anonymous access.

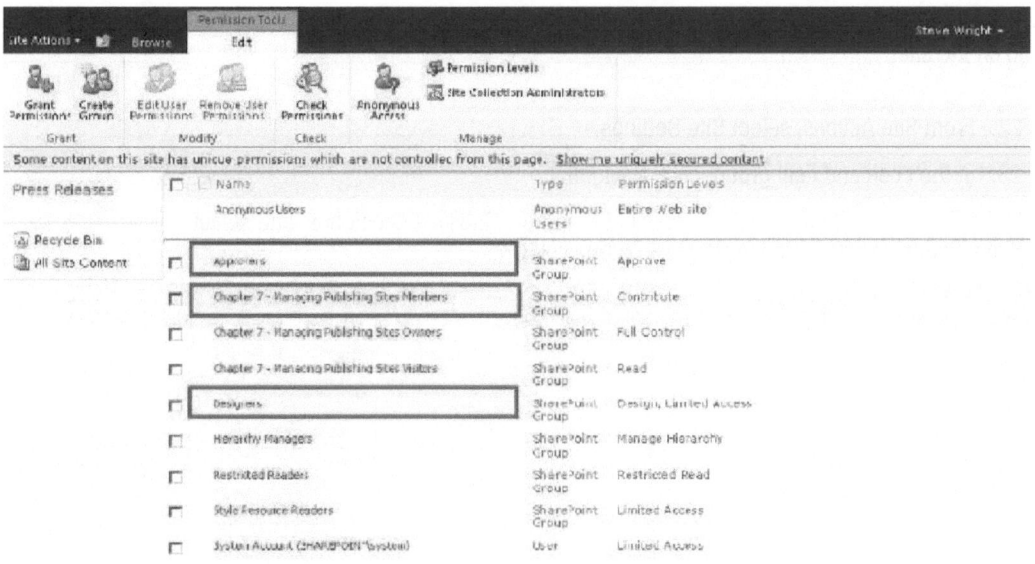

Figure 7-14. SharePoint groups for publishing.

19. Add **aapprover** to the Approvers SharePoint group.

20. Add **ddesigner** to the Designers SharePoint group.

21. Add **ddesigner** to the <Site Name> Members SharePoint group for the site.

Question: Why did we use the Members group instead of just the Designers group?

Adding the ddesigner user to the Designers group allows the user to design site artifacts such as page layouts in SharePoint Designer but not to actually access the site. In most cases, the Contributor role provides the appropriate set of permissions for a user updating content pages in the site. This is the level of access given to the site's Members group. The Designer role gives the user only the minimal set of permissions needed for designing artifacts. These permissions are usually combined with other levels to allow the user to access the site as needed. A user doing both content and layout design in a site should be added as a member of both of these groups, as we are doing here.

You have now set up security for the site. The last item on our agenda is to alter the navigation that is displayed on the site:

22. From Site Actions, select Site Settings.

23. In the Look and Feel group, click Navigation.

In the Current Navigation section, deselect the Show Subsites check box and select Show Pages, as shown in Figure 7-15. Then click OK.

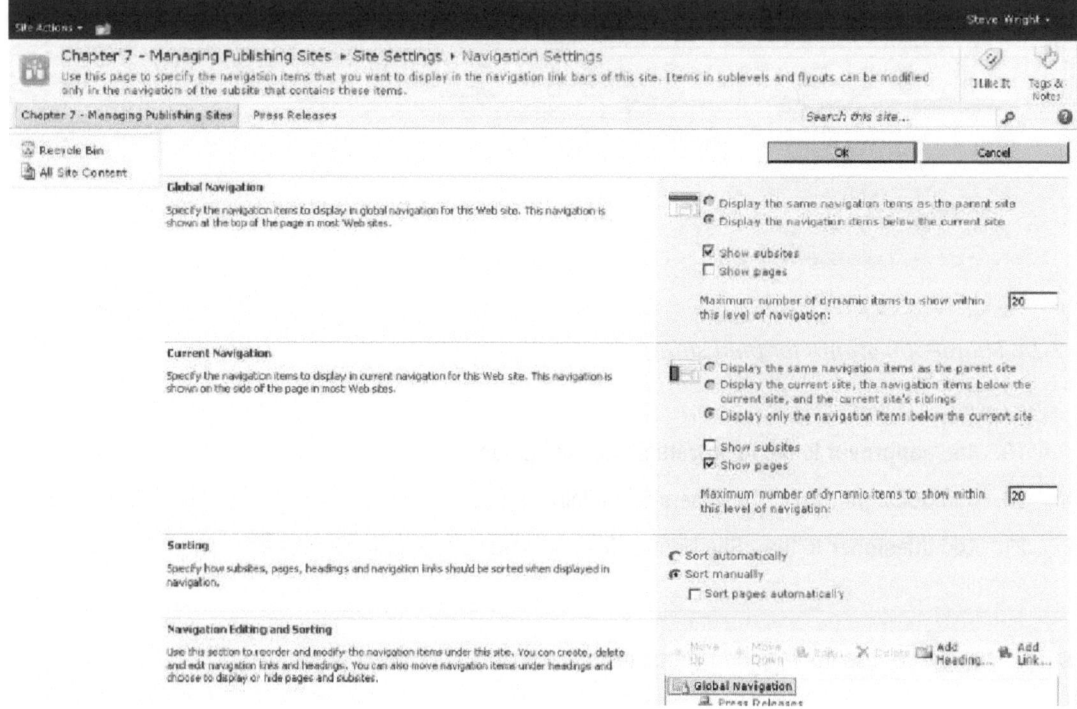

Figure 7-15. *Navigation settings*

EXERCISE 7-2. EDIT A CONTENT PAGE

In this exercise, you will make minor changes to the content on the home page of your site. You will then examine the effects of those changes as you go through the publishing workflow.

1. Open the site in a web browser and log in as ddesigner.

2. On the Page tab of the menu, select Edit in SharePoint Designer from the Edit drop-down list in the Edit group.

3. Once SharePoint Designer loads, the dialog box in Figure 7-16 displays. Click the
    Cancel button and close SharePoint Designer.

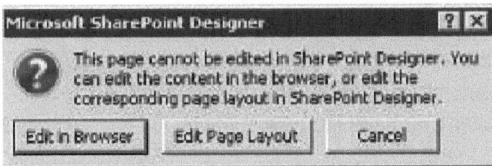

Figure 7-16. SharePoint Designer content page warning

■ **Note** Although it might seem obvious that a designer would edit content pages in SharePoint Designer, this is
not possible. You will use SharePoint Designer for page layouts and content types, but content pages can be edited
only in the browser.

---

4. Back in the browser, click the Edit button on the menu. This checks out the
    content page and puts it into Edit mode in the browser, as shown in Figure 7-17.

5. Make some visible changes to the content of the page. For this example, you will
    set the page title and rearrange some of the links from the summary links areas.

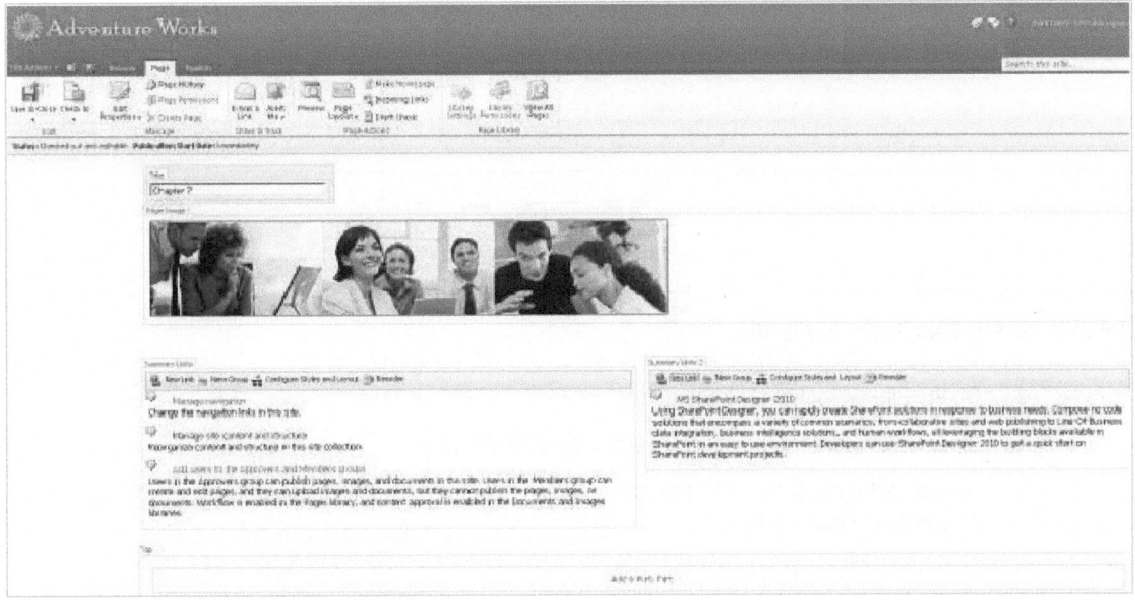

Figure 7-17. Content Page in Edit Mode

6.   On the Page tab of the menu, click Check In in the Edit group.

7.   In the Check In dialog box, enter a comment and then click Continue.

At this point, your changes are checked in. This means that site members and administrators can see the changes, but nonprivileged users cannot. Try opening the site anonymously and then as aapprover. The anonymous user sees the original version, whereas the aapprover user sees the new content.

1.   As ddesigner, switch to the Publish tab on the menu and select Schedule.

2.   Enter a date and time for the Start Date that is sometime in the future, as shown in Figure 7-18. Then click OK to close the dialog box.

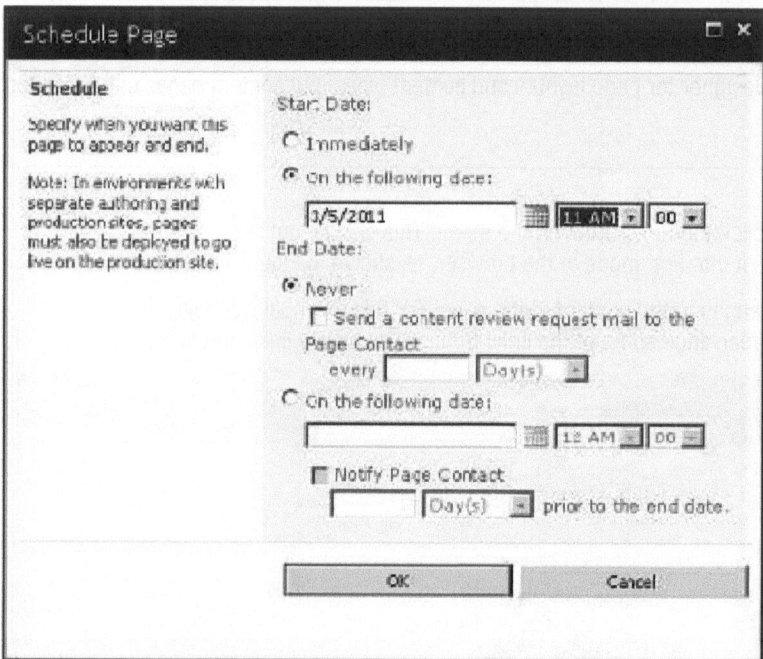

Figure 7-18. Schedule Page dialog box

3.   On the Ribbon menu, click Submit.

4.   Enter a comment for the approval and then click Continue.

5.   On the next form displayed, enter the initiation data for the publishing workflow, as shown in Figure 7-19.

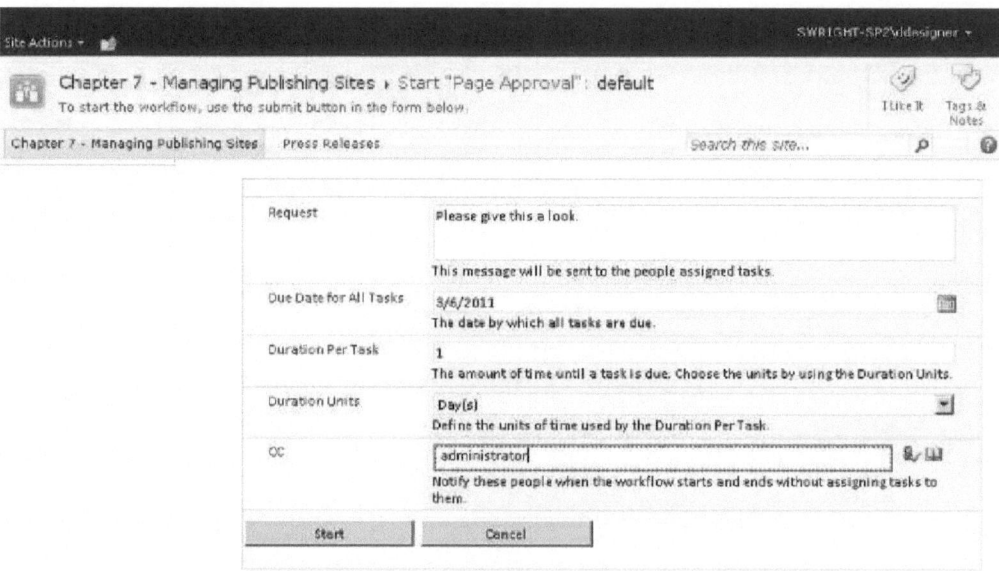

Figure 7-19. Workflow initiation form

6. Reopen the web site and log in as aapprover.

7. On the Publishing tab of the menu, select View Tasks from the Workflows group, as shown in Figure 7-20.

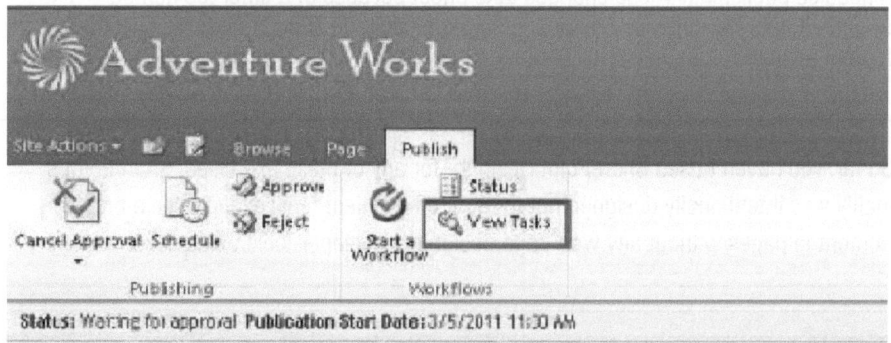

Figure 7-20. View Tasks menu item

8. The approval task form that opens allows the approver to request changes and reassign approval tasks as well as accept or reject the changes, as you can see in Figure 7-21. Click the Approve button at the bottom of the form.

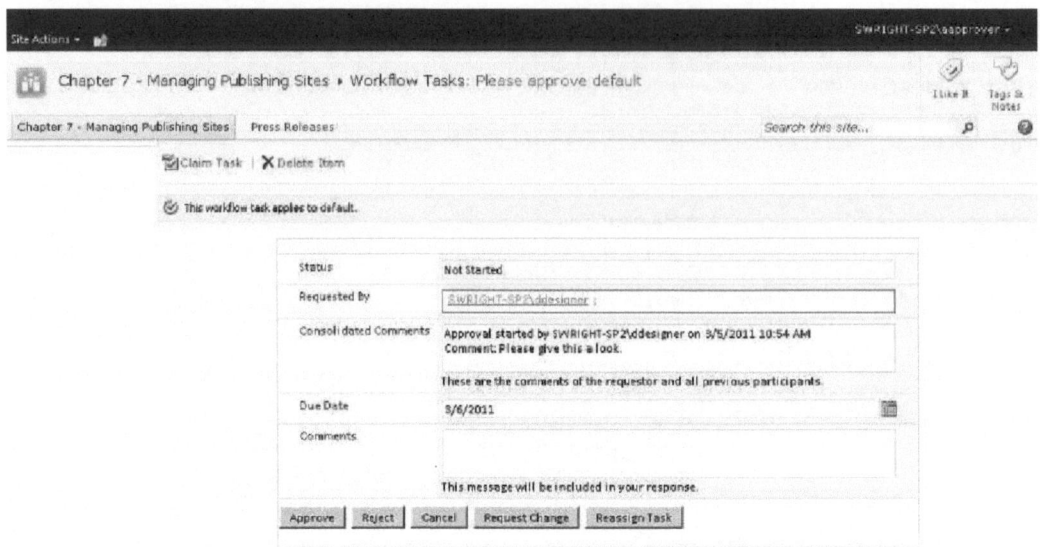

Figure 7-21. *Publishing task form*

At this point, your changes are fully published. If you reopen the site as an anonymous user, you may not see the changes right away. Remember, you scheduled the publishing of the changes to start at a future time. Until that time comes, anonymous users will continue to see the original page content. Even when the time comes, there may be a small delay before the new content appears. This is due to the way SharePoint manages scheduled publishing. These changes take effect because of a timer job named Scheduled Approval. By default, this job runs once a minute, so there could be a lag of up to 60 seconds before the published content appears.

■ **Note** Did you notice? So far, you haven't used SharePoint Designer for any of these exercises. SharePoint's content publishing functionality was intentionally designed not to require any client tools except a web browser. End users can contribute content to pages without any web page design or developer tools whatsoever.

EXERCISE 7-3. PUBLISH A PAGE LAYOUT CHANGE

Now you will move from simple content authoring into the realm of site design. Specifically, in this exercise, you are going to modify one of SharePoint's built-in page layouts. Ordinarily, the preferred approach is to copy the built-in page layout to a new file and alter it there, leaving the original unchanged. We are doing it this way only for simplicity.

The default publishing rules for page layouts and master pages is a little different than for content pages. There is no explicit workflow involved. These artifacts use the simple moderation approval method described earlier in this chapter.

1. Open the site in a web browser and log in as ddesigner.

2. On the site's home page, click the Page tab of the menu. From the Edit drop-down menu in the Edit group, select Edit in SharePoint Designer.

3. Once SharePoint Designer loads, a warning dialog box appears, indicating that you cannot edit the content page in SharePoint Designer. In this case, you want to edit the page's layout, not its content. To do this, click the Edit Page Layout button.

4. The next dialog box asks whether you want to check out the page layout file, WelcomeSplash.aspx. Click Yes.

In the Page Editor, you will make some visible changes to the page layout. However, at the moment, you cannot edit anything on the page. This is because the version of the WelcomeSpash.aspx file that you are viewing is the same one that is part of the SharePoint installation. SharePoint Designer protects you from inadvertently customizing files like this by mistake. Once you customize this file, any changes made to it in a future service pack will not take effect in your sites. In order to continue with your changes, you first must switch the editor to Advanced Mode. See Chapter 2 for more details about Advanced mode.

5. On the Code View Tools tab of the menu, click Advanced Mode in the Editing group.

6. In the Code view of the page layout, find the string splashLinkFrame. This CSS class is used to format tables on the page layout. Search for the second instance of splashLinkFrame from the top of the page.

7. Select the first table using this class by clicking the table tag.

8. On the Table Tools menu tab, find the Format group and select All Borders from the Borders drop-down menu, as shown in Figure 7-22.

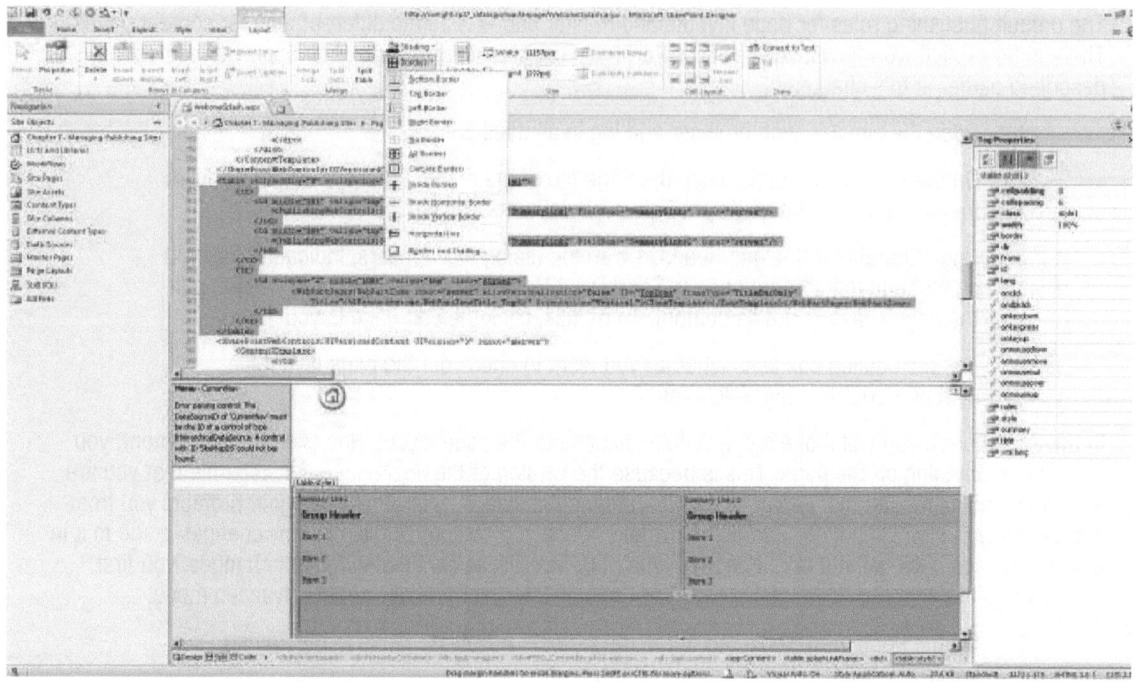

Figure 7-22. *Modifying the* `WelcomeSplash.aspx` *page layout*

9. Save the page layout.

10. Return to the web browser, still logged in as ddesigner, and refresh the site's home page. Note that the borders are added to the table, as you can see in Figure 7-23.

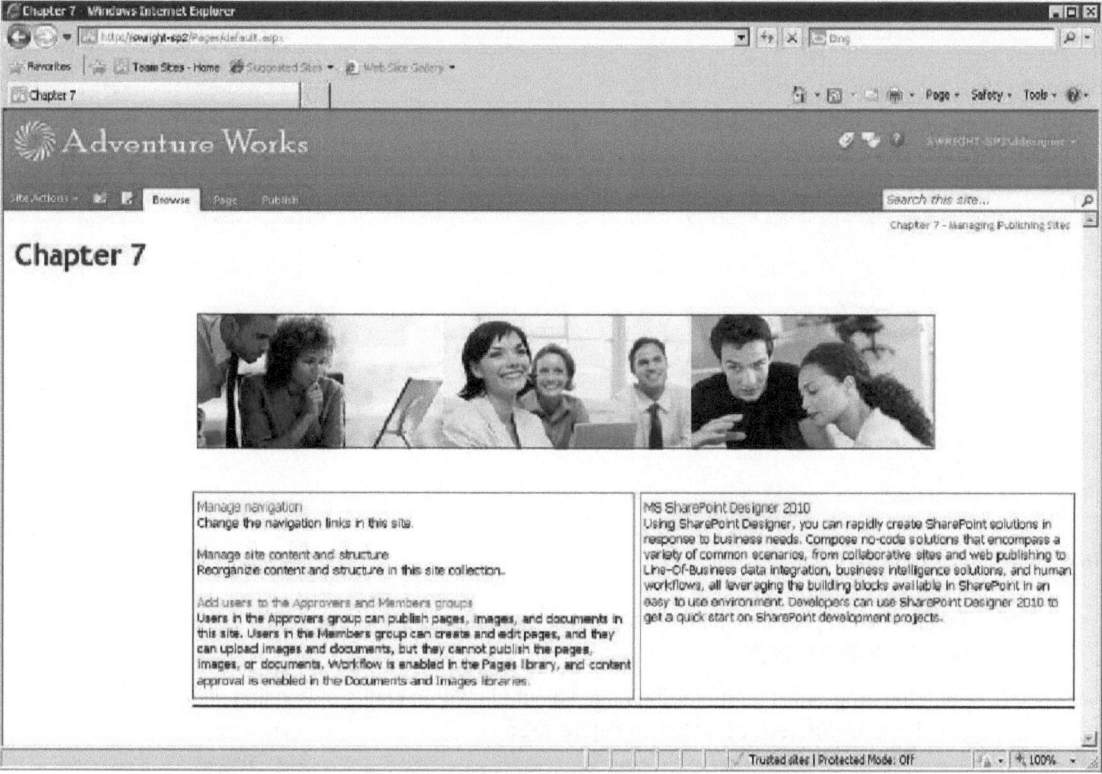

Figure 7-23. Viewing draft changes in the web browser

11. Reopen the page as an anonymous user and verify that the change is not visible.

12. In SharePoint Designer, select the Page Layouts Gallery from the Navigation pane.

13. The green check mark next to the `WelcomeSplash.aspx` file indicates that this change is checked out. Right-click the file and select Check In.

14. In the Check In dialog box, select Publish a Major Version and then add a comment, as shown in Figure 7-24. Click OK.

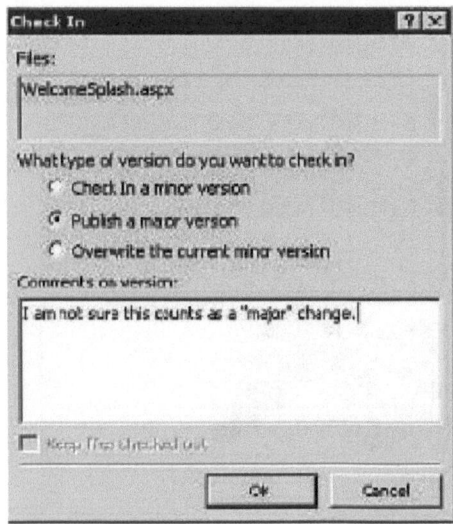

Figure 7-24. Check In dialog box

15. A dialog box appears, indicating that this content requires approval. Click Yes to open the approval page.

16. Open the drop-down menu for the page layout file with a status of Pending and select Approve/Reject, as shown in Figure 7-25.

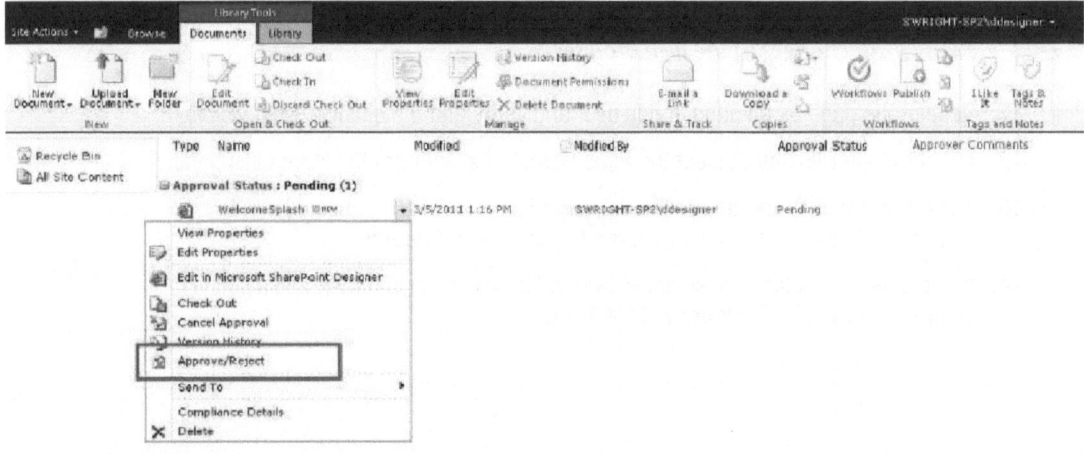

Figure 7-25. Approving a pending layout change

17. In the Approve/Reject dialog box, select Approved for the Approval Status and then enter a comment, as shown in Figure 7-26. Click OK.

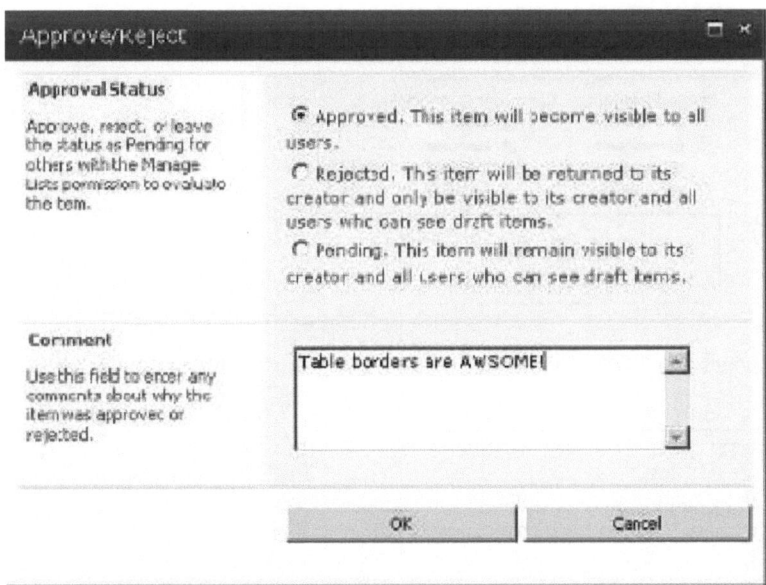

Figure 7-26. *Approve/Reject dialog box*

18. Return to the web browser as an anonymous user and note that the change is now visible.

The publishing process used in the Master Pages and Page Layouts Gallery is an example of simple moderation without the publishing workflow. If the full workflow is desired for these changes, it can be enabled for this library in the same way as any other workflow, by using the library's Workflow Settings page.

EXERCISE 7-4. CREATE A NEW PAGE CONTENT TYPE AND PAGE LAYOUT

For this exercise, our organization has decided to publish product information on the web site. These pages will all have a similar type of content that will be customized for each product we sell. The page will look like the wireframe in Figure 7-27.

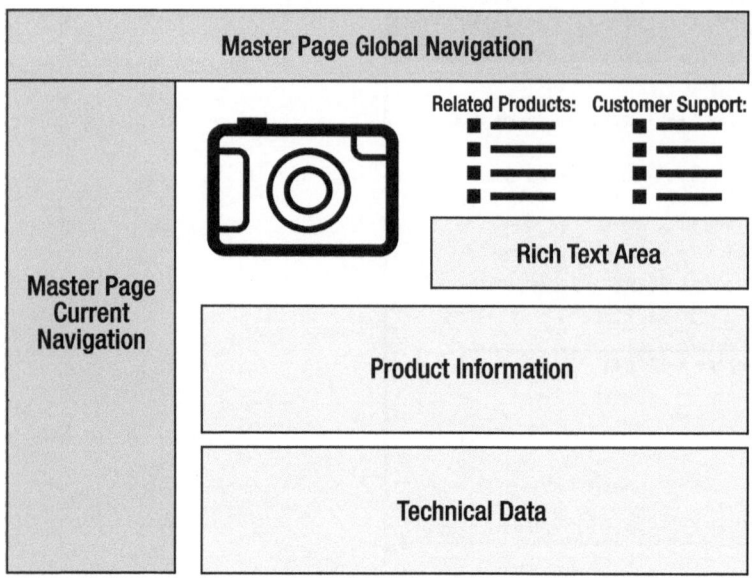

Figure 7-27. Product information page design (wireframe)

In creating a reusable page layout, you will be performing the following steps:

- Creating site columns for each of the content areas on your layout

- Creating a page content type containing these site columns

- Creating and publishing a page layout ASPX file

- Creating a product page and adding content to it

- Publishing the new page to the web site

1. Open the site in a web browser and log on as ddesigner.

2. From the Site Actions menu, select Site Settings.

3. Under Galleries, select Site Columns.

4. From the Show Group drop-down menu, select Page Layout Columns, as shown in Figure 7-28.

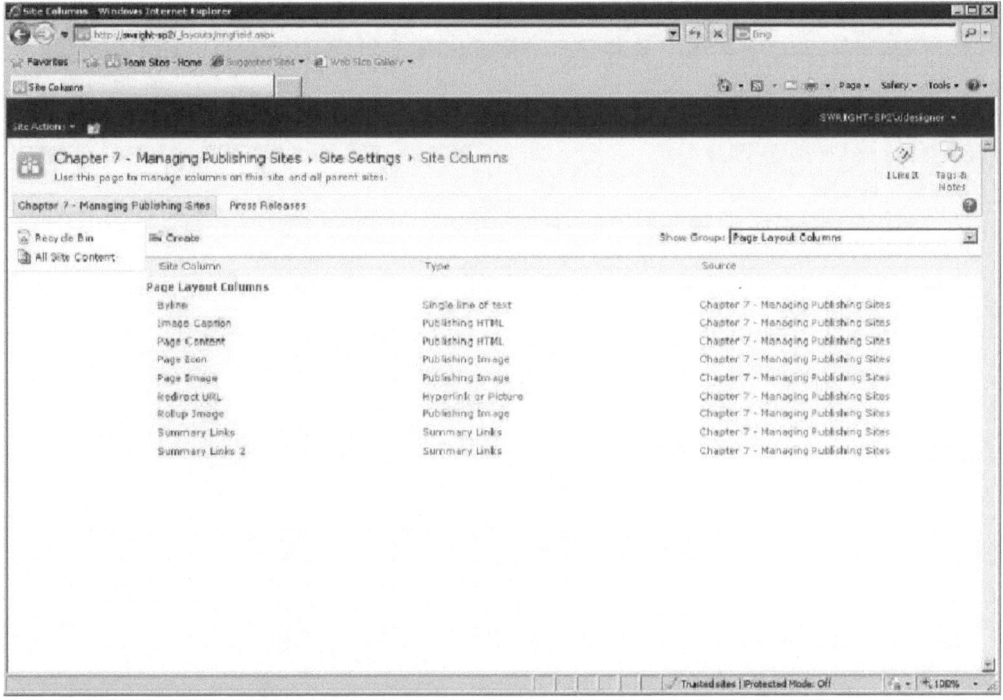

Figure 7-28. *Site Columns gallery page*

5.   Click the Create link.

6.   On the New Site Column page, enter **Product Information** as the column name and select Full HTML Content with Formatting as the field type (see Figure 7-29).

7.   Select the Page Layout Columns group (or create a separate group for your own columns).

8.   Under Additional Column Settings, select Yes to require the field to contain information. Then click OK.

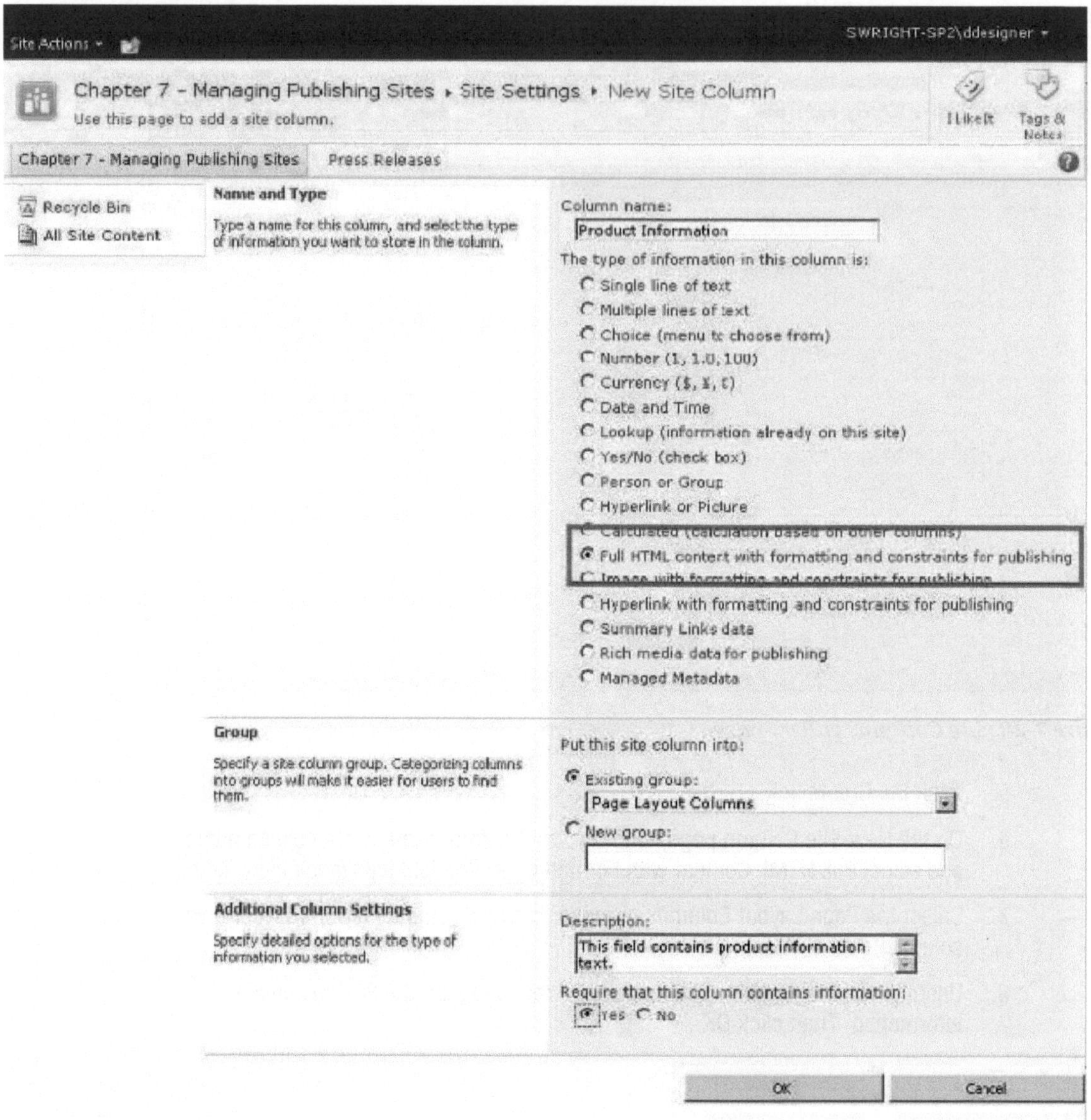

Figure 7-29. Creating a Site Column page

Question: Why aren't we using SharePoint Designer to create site columns?

While SharePoint Designer is perfectly capable of creating ordinary site columns, it does not contain the property editors to handle custom column types such as the publishing column types. If we were using standard column types such as Number or Multi Lines of Text, we could use SharePoint Designer.

9. Repeat steps 5 through 8 to create a second HTML site column called Technical Data.

10. Repeat steps 5 through 8 to create two additional columns called Related Products and Customer Support, using the Summary Links Data type.

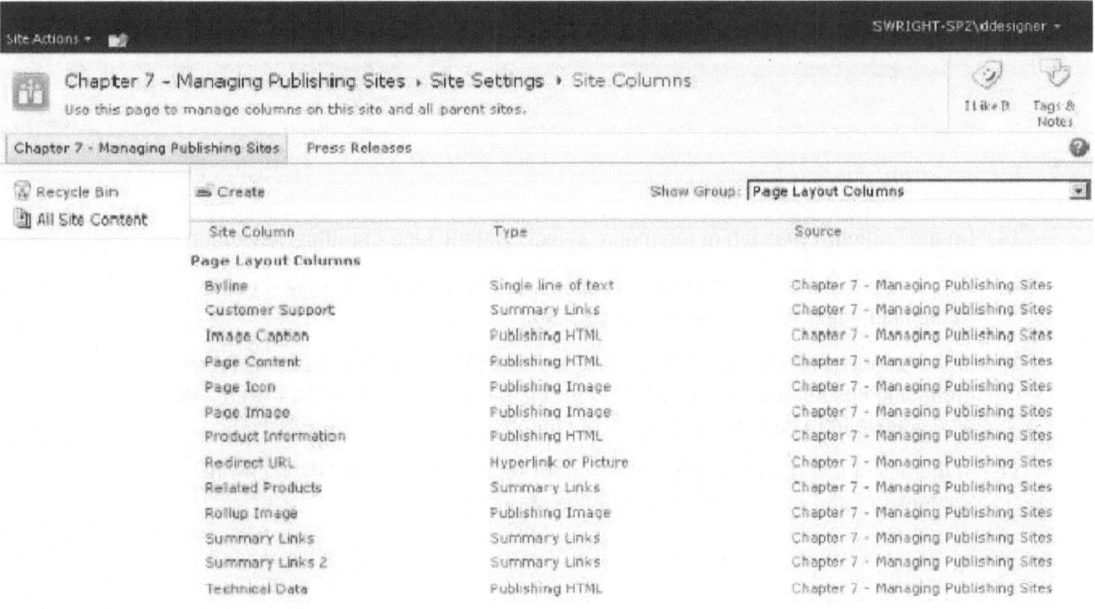

Figure 7-30. Site Column Gallery (with new site columns)

Now that all of the site columns you need have been created, you will proceed to create a page content type on which your new page layout will be based.

11. Open the site in SharePoint Designer as ddesigner.

12. In the Navigation pane, click Content Types.

13. Note the Page Layout Content Types group in the gallery window (see Figure 7-31). These are the content types associated with the out-of-the-box page layouts.

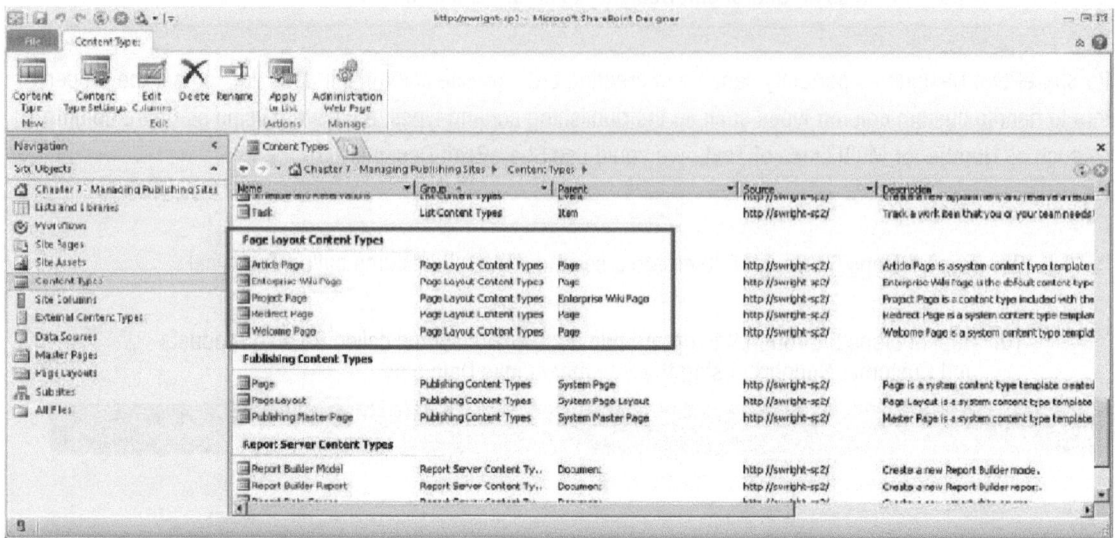

Figure 7-31. Page layout content types

14. On the Content Types tab of the menu, select Content Type from the New group.

15. The Create a Content Type dialog box opens, as shown in Figure 7-32. In the Name field, enter **Product Information Page**.

16. In the Select a Parent Content Type section, select the Publishing Content Types group and ensure that Page is selected for the parent type. All publishing content types derive from Page either directly or indirectly.

17. In the Select a Sorting Group for This Control Type section, select Page Layout Content Types. Then click OK to create the new content type.

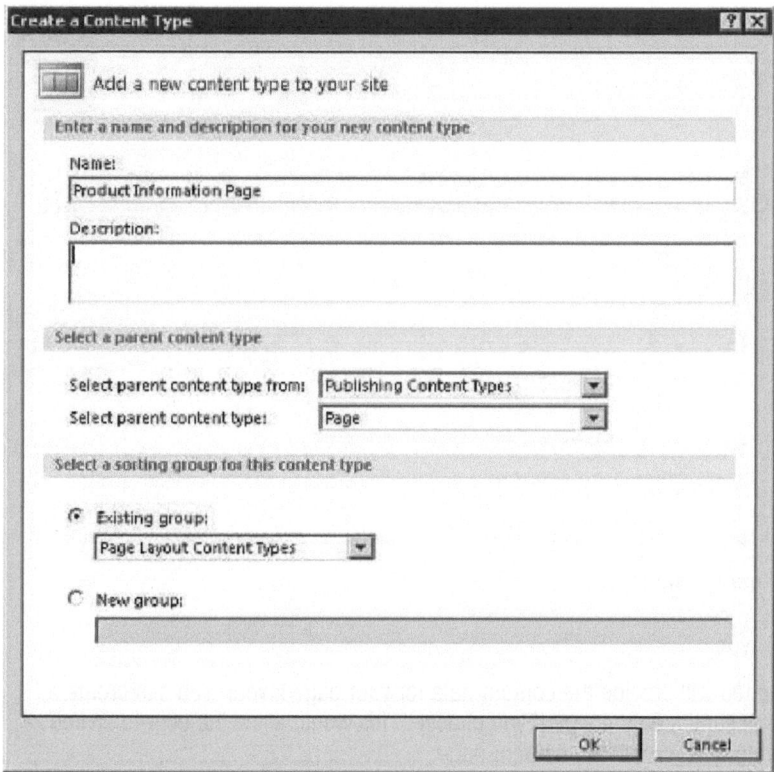

Figure 7-32. Create a Content Type dialog box

18. Click the Product Information Page link in the gallery to open the settings page for the type.

19. Under Customization, click the Edit Content Type Columns link.

20. Using the Add Existing Site Column option on the menu, add the following site columns to the page:

- Page Image: Image (built-in site column)

- Page Content: HTML (built-in site column)

- Product Information: HTML

- Technical Data: HTML

- Related Products: Summary Links

- Customer Support: Summary Links

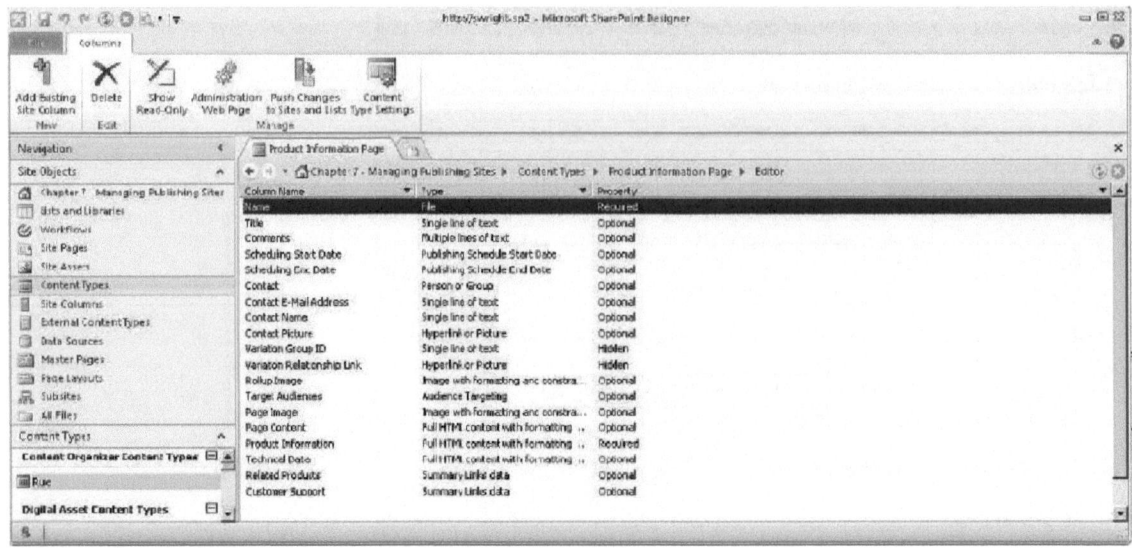

Figure 7-33. *Column Editor for the new content type*

21. Save the new content type.

The content type you have just created will provide the content data for your page layout. You can create a variety of page layouts based on this same content type if you choose. This would allow the user to switch between page layouts without having to re-create the content page.

22. From the Navigation pane, select Page Layouts.

23. From the Page Layouts tab on the menu, select New Page Layout.

24. The New page layout dialog box is displayed. From the Content Type Group options, select Page Layout Content Types. For the Content Type Name, select Project Information Page. Set the other fields as shown in Figure 7-34 and then click OK.

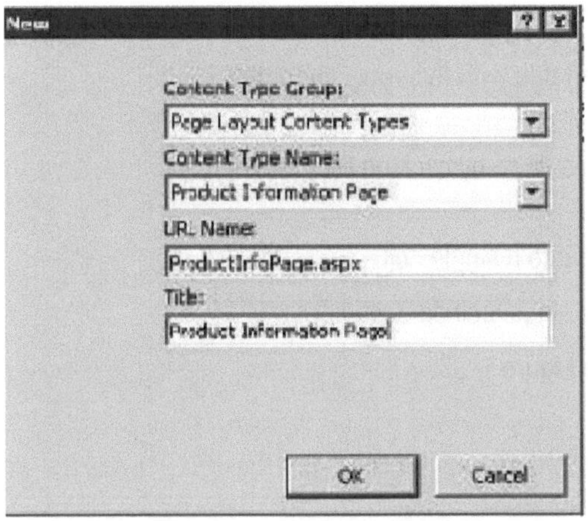

Figure 7-34. *New page layout dialog box*

The page layout created contains two content placeholders. The first allows you to display the page's title on the page. The second area (PlaceHolderMain) is where most of the layout markup will be placed.

25. Switch to Split mode if you aren't already using it.

26. In the code window, add the following markup *before* the PlaceHolderMain content tag. This markup causes the page title to be displayed in the page header.

```
<asp:Content ContentPlaceholderID="PlaceHolderPageTitleInTitleArea"
  runat="server">
<SharePointWebControls:UIVersionedContent UIVersion="4" runat="server">
    <ContentTemplate>
        <SharePointWebControls:FieldValue FieldName="Title"
          runat="server"/>
    </ContentTemplate>
</SharePointWebControls:UIVersionedContent>
</asp:Content>
```

27. In the code window, add the following markup *inside* the PlaceHolderMain content tag. This markup adds a hidden field control, an edit mode panel, that will allow the content editor to change the page's title when the page is in Edit mode.

```
<SharePointWebControls:UIVersionedContent UIVersion="4" runat="server">
    <ContentTemplate>
        <div class="welcome welcome-splash">
            <PublishingWebControls:EditModePanel runat="server"
              CssClass="edit-mode-panel">
                <SharePointWebControls:TextField runat="server"
                  FieldName="Title" />
            </PublishingWebControls:EditModePanel>
        </div>
    </ContentTemplate>
</SharePointWebControls:UIVersionedContent>
```

28. Move the cursor beneath the markup you just added.

29. Switch to the Insert tab on the menu and insert a table with five rows and three columns.

30. Select the first cell in the first two rows and merge them by clicking Merge Cells on the Table Tools tab on the menu.

31. In the second row, merge the rightmost two cells into a single cell.

32. In the last three rows, merge all three cells into a single cell on each line.

33. The `PlaceHolderMain` area should now look like Figure 7-35.

Figure 7-35. `PlaceHolderMain` content area layout

34. In the Toolbox pane, find the Content Fields section under SharePoint Controls. If the Toolbox pane is not visible, you can open it by switching to the View tab and selecting it from the Task Panes drop-down menu.

35. Drag the Page Image field into the upper-left cell of the table.

36. Drag the Related Products field into the second cell in the first row.

37. Drag the Customer Support field into the third cell in the first row. It may be hard to see because it is very narrow at this point. If necessary, you can also drag the field to the code view and drop it between `<td>` and `</td>` for the cell.

38. To even out the columns, select all three of the cells into which you have placed fields.

39. On the Table Tools tab on the menu, enter **33%** into the Width text box, as shown in Figure 7-36.

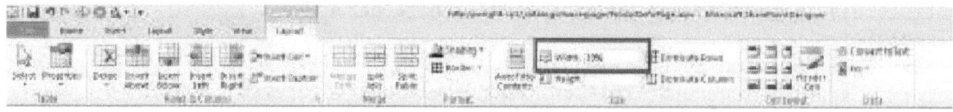

Figure 7-36. Setting column widths via the menu

40. Drag the Page Content field into the cell in the second row.

41. Drag the Product Information field into the cell in the third row.

42. Drag the Technical Data field into the cell in the fourth row.

43. Click on the last row of the table in the Design view.

44. From the Insert tab on the menu, select Web Part Zone from the Web Parts group. This creates a zone at the bottom of the page where content editors can add arbitrary web parts as needed.

Figure 7-37. Completed page layout design

Your page layout is now complete. Feel free to add any finishing touches by using either the designer options or by putting HTML directly into the code view. Now you need to publish your page layout:

45. Save the page layout.

46. In the Navigation pane, select Page Layouts.

47. Right-click the new page layout and select Check In.

48. In the Check In dialog box, select Publish a Major Version and click OK.

49. Open the content approval page in the browser when prompted and approve the new page layout.

Now that you have a page layout published, it is time to create a content page that uses that layout. Again, SharePoint Designer isn't the tool for creating content pages, so you will be going back into the web browser.

50. Open the web site in the browser and log in as ddesigner.

51. From the Site Actions menu, select the (rather vaguely named) option labeled More Options.

52. The Create dialog box that opens allows you to create numerous types of artifacts. From Installed Items, select Publishing Page, as shown in Figure 7-38.

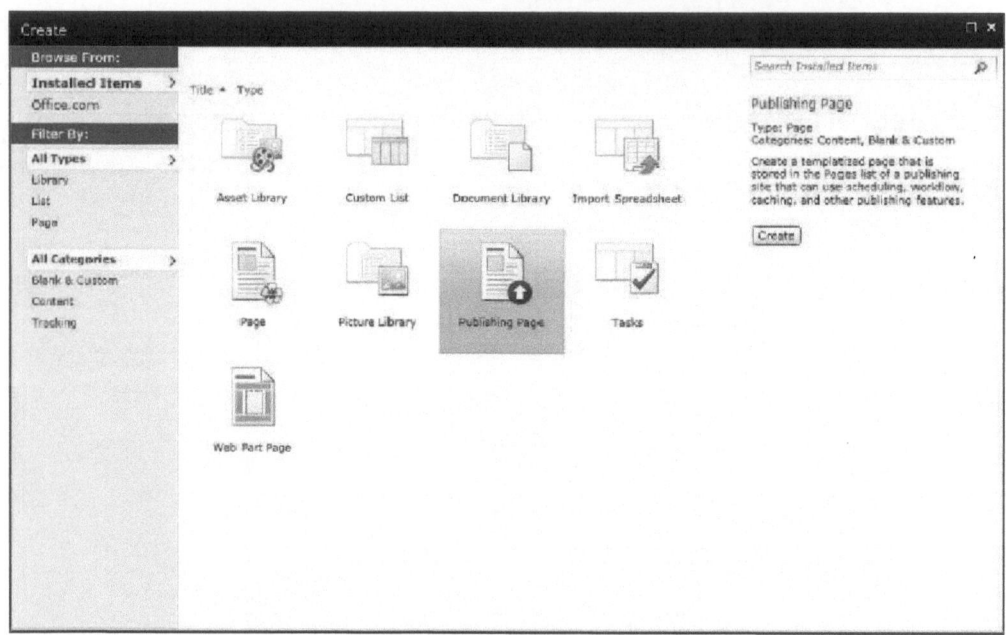

Figure 7-38. Create dialog box

53. Click the Create button on the right side of the dialog box.

54. On the Create Page page, enter a page title and URL.

55. From the Page Layout list, select the Product Information Page option.

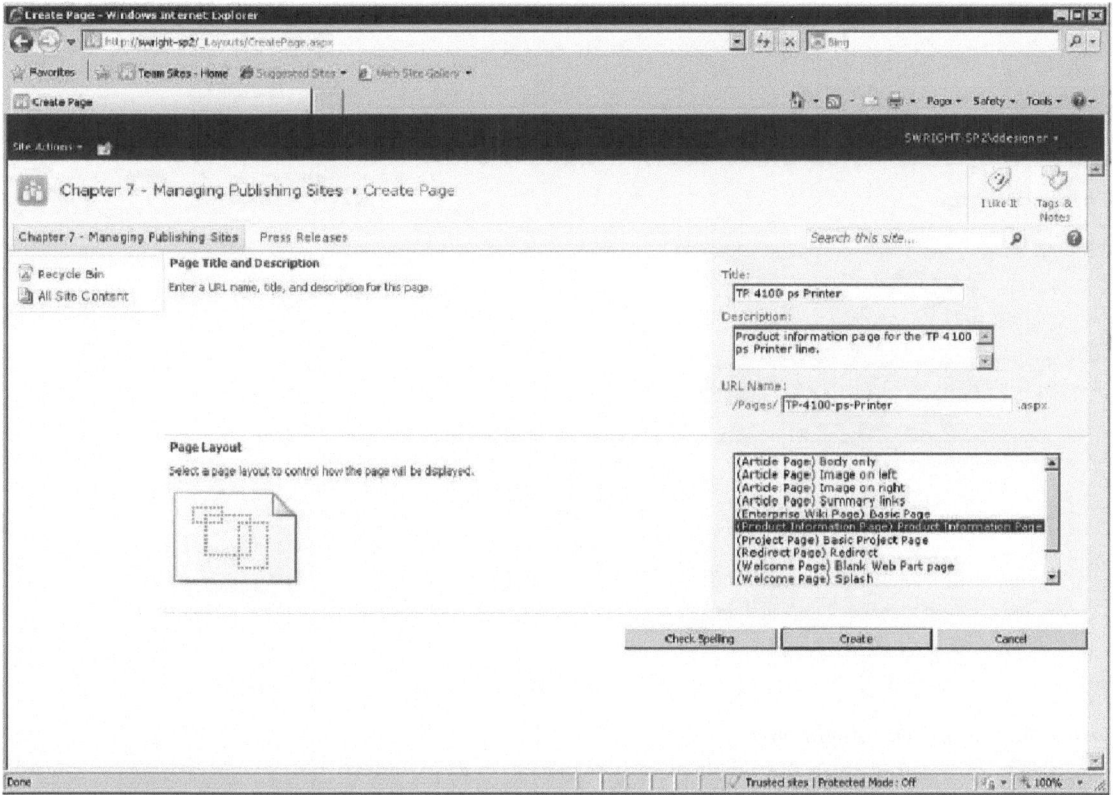

Figure 7-39. Creating a publishing page

56. Click the Create button. The page is created and placed into Edit mode to allow the content fields to be updated.

57. Enter your own content into the content areas.

58. Once the content is complete, click Check In on the Page tab on the menu.

59. Publish the content page by using the same steps you used before.

Now you have created and published all of the artifacts necessary to use a custom page layout. Content editors can now create and modify as many of these pages as needed without fear of creating nonstandard pages or causing problems in the HTML markup of any of your pages.

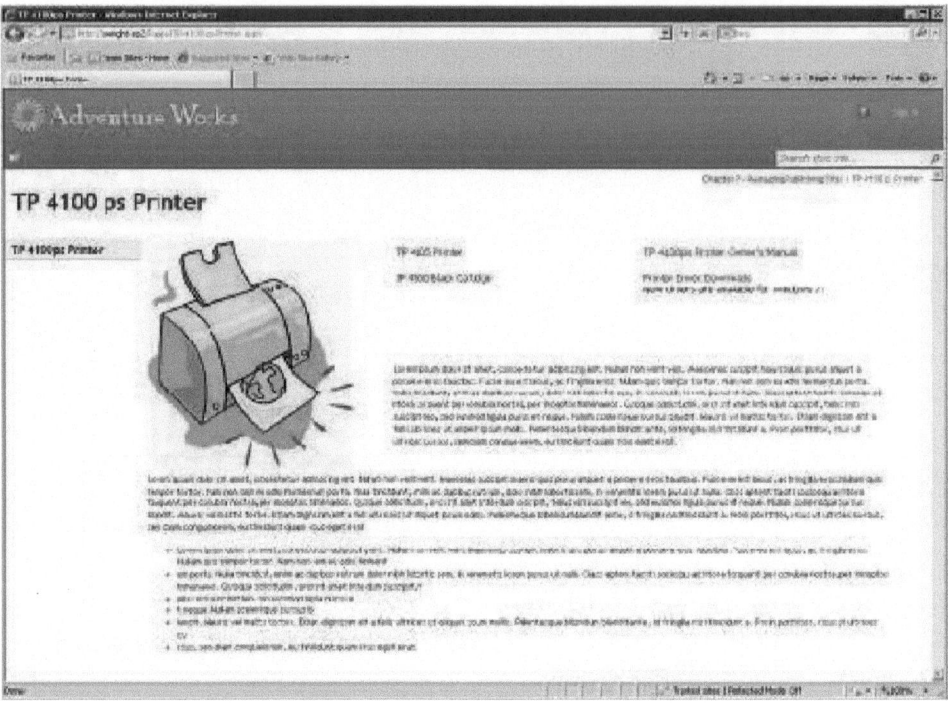

Figure 7-40. *Completed content page*

Notice that, when you published your product page, it appeared in the left-hand navigation control for the site. This happened because of the changes you made to the navigation configuration for the site in the first exercise in this chapter.

Summary

In this chapter, you have

- Configured SharePoint's publishing features and created a full-featured publishing site

- Created and approved web content changes by using the approval workflow

- Explored the relationships between master pages, page layouts, and content pages

- Examined advanced publishing techniques including custom navigation, site variations, and content deployment

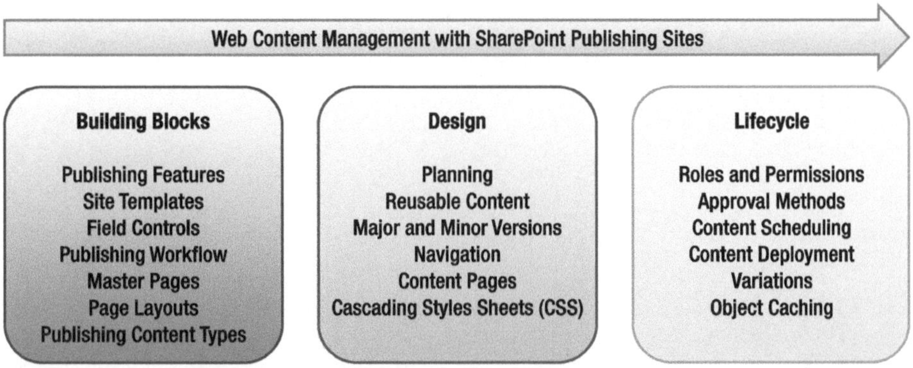

Figure 7-41. SharePoint publishing road map

CHAPTER 8

Advanced Site Customizations

Now that you have explored creating content for your sites and tailoring their appearance, you will look at some more advanced topics for creating a rich, easy-to-use web site. Specifically, in this chapter, you will focus on customizing the search and site navigation features available in SharePoint.

You will learn about the following topics in this chapter:

- How ASP.NET is used to provide a structure for SharePoint's navigation system

- What components to use to create an intuitive site navigation structure

- How to customize the out-of-the-box controls and web parts to improve the search and navigation experience of your site

- How to present search criteria and results in a way that aids users in finding the content that is most relevant to them

Navigation in SharePoint Sites

Creating a useful and efficient Navigation system is a major contributor to the usability of a site. Navigation links and menus help the user understand the structure and layout of the site and their current location within that structure. SharePoint 2010 provides a set of navigation controls that can be customized to provide a wide range of navigation experiences.

The default site templates provided by SharePoint contain a set of navigation controls that fall into one of three broad categories depending on their purpose and where they appear on the web page (see Figure 8-1).

At the top of most pages is the area known as the *global menu*. This is usually a menu with various tabs referring to sites within the site collection. The global menu is designed to provide the user with feedback concerning their position within the site collection as a whole.

To the left of most standard page layouts is the *local (or current) menu* area. The controls that appear in this area lead the user to resources within the current SharePoint site. These controls are depicted vertically and may contain links to lists and libraries within the site, subsites, or other resources in a tree view.

The third navigation area, and the one that varies the most from site to site, is the *content area* in the center of the web page. The controls in this area generally provide access to resources in, or related to, the local site and can be configured in different ways depending on the type of control used.

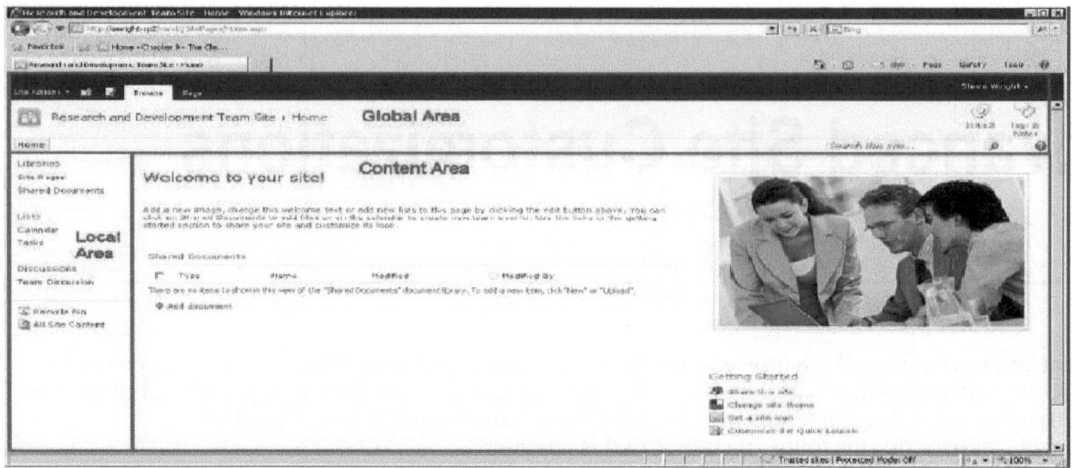

Figure 8-1. *Navigation areas for a typical site layout*

In this section, you will look at the types of controls that are available and how you can use them to customize the menus in your SharePoint sites.

ASP.NET Navigation

The basic technology used in SharePoint 2010 for rendering menus is inherited from the .NET Framework's ASP.NET menu system. These are the same concepts and controls used to create menus and tree views within any ASP.NET site. Let's do a quick review of these concepts.

Any site navigation control renders links, buttons, or icons that navigate the user's browser to a certain URL. The information associated with each of these links is called a *menu node*. The ASP.NET navigation objects are designed to create a flexible system for gathering and delivering a set of menu nodes to the page. The components used to do this build on one another to create a rendered HTML menu.

Site map providers are components that access some source of menu node information. These nodes could come from a database, an XML file, a file directory structure, or an application-specific data repository, such as a SharePoint content database. The site map provider is responsible for determining which menu nodes to provide and what information (URL, label, and so on) goes with each node. The site's site map providers are generally configured in a web site's configuration files.

The menu nodes from the site map provider are passed to a site map. The *site map* consolidates nodes from one or more site map providers for the site and manages this information as an in-memory database of navigation information.

A *site map data source* is an ASP.NET control that allows other controls to bind to the in-memory hierarchy of menu nodes. A data source control can be configured to control which nodes are bound from which providers by using a given set of criteria.

Finally, the navigation controls bind to the data source controls to retrieve the list of menu nodes to be rendered to the user. Each control renders the information differently depending on its intended purpose.

SharePoint Navigation

When creating SharePoint navigation solutions, the location of the navigation controls is critical in determining how navigation is controlled and customized. By default, the global and local menus are defined in the site's master page. This ensures that all pages in the site use a consistent set of core navigation controls. In some cases, it may be appropriate to suppress some of these controls, but when they appear, they should be made consistent.

Navigation controls that appear in the content area vary quite a bit depending on the design of the individual page or page layout. In publishing sites, it is common to place lists of summary links and tables of contents on certain page layouts. This creates a common template for these pages while allowing some flexibility to the page author. For maximum flexibility, many of these controls are implemented as web parts so that they can be added to any page that has an open web part zone. If greater control is needed, these web parts may be restricted by using permissions assigned to them in the Web Part Gallery.

One of the most important navigation features in SharePoint is concerned not with showing menu nodes, but with hiding them. This is called *security trimming*. Security trimming in SharePoint navigation causes menu nodes for resources that the user cannot access to vanish from their menus. For example, if a user visits a site containing a document library that the user does not have access to, that user will not see a link to that library in the menu. This is important for two reasons. First, it avoids help desk calls from angry users who keep seeing *Access Denied* every time they try to get a look at the good stuff. Second, it avoids advertising the existence of sensitive content to (perhaps anonymous) users who should not see it.

Navigation Controls

In this section, you will take a brief look at the main navigation controls used by SharePoint. A more complete description of these controls can be found on MSDN at `http://msdn.microsoft.com/en-us/library/ms476607.aspx`.

Common Controls

The default global and local menus are rendered by using the `AspMenu` control. This control is derived from the ASP.NET `Menu` class. It can be used vertically or horizontally, as shown in Figure 8-2 . It can display multiple levels of static menu links or dynamic fly-out menus. This control is designed to be dramatically customized by using Cascading Style Sheets (CSS).

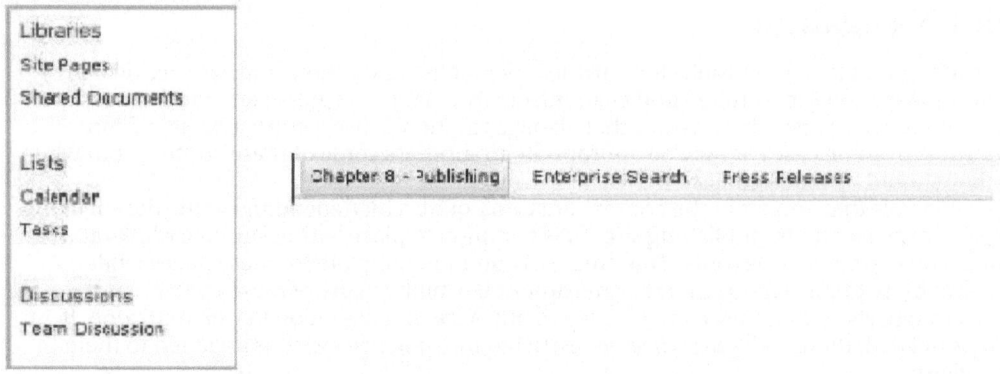

Figure 8-2. AspMenu in vertical and horizontal modes

The SPTreeView control, shown in Figure 8-3, is a specialized version of the ASP.NET TreeView control. It displays a tree of nodes that represent the content in the site. Using metadata on the content items in the site, this control can also be used to navigate and filter items on custom metadata.

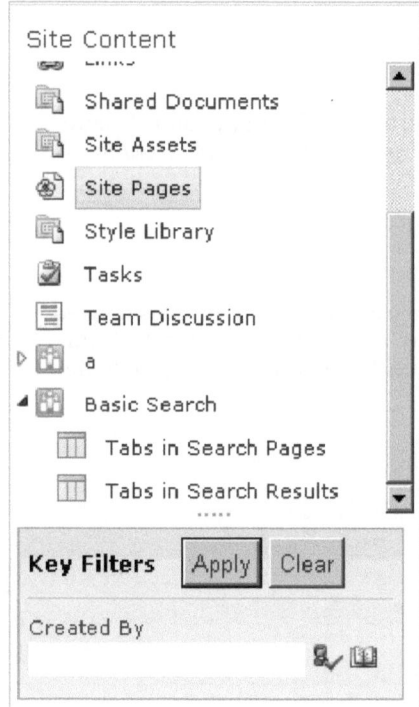

Figure 8-3. SPTreeView control

Breadcrumbs are useful when a site has a large number of pages and a deep directory structure. This control renders the levels of the web site as a series of links. In SharePoint, breadcrumbs are rendered by using the ListSiteMapPath control. This is derived from the ASP.NET SiteMapPath control. The breadcrumb control can also render the views or pages available in the current location as a drop-down list, as shown in Figure 8-4.

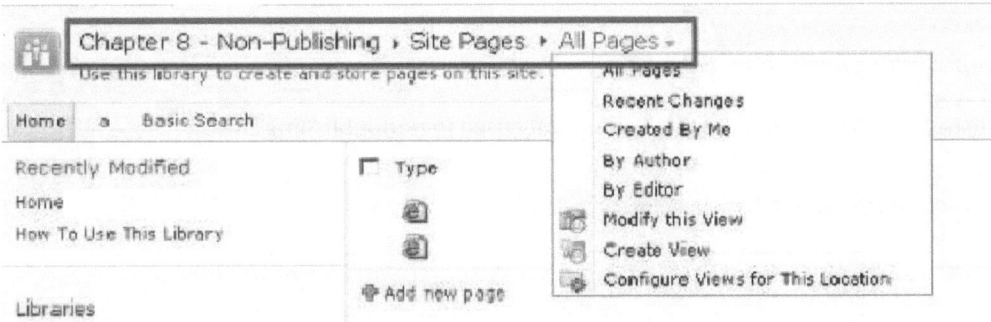

Figure 8-4. ListSiteMapPath *control*

The menu, tree view, and breadcrumb controls are present in most SharePoint sites by default, but several additional web parts are provided that can be added as well. These fall into two categories, publishing and nonpublishing, depending on the type of site they are intended for use in. You will review these in a moment. While these web parts are intended for use in a certain type of site, they can still be used in other kinds of sites.

Another important set of navigation controls are those that are created by a developer for custom rendering needs. These controls are simply ASP.NET web controls, as are the controls provided by SharePoint. Because these controls require coding in Visual Studio, not SharePoint Designer, we do not cover them here.

Nonpublishing Sites

In nonpublishing sites, the global (top) menu is called the *top link bar*. The local (left-side) menu is referred to as the *Quick Launch menu*. These are both AspMenu controls provided by the v4.master master page.

In Site Settings, these menus can be configured by using the Quick Launch and Top Link Bar links in the Look and Feel submenu, as shown in Figure 8-5. The Tree View link can be used to show or hide the Quick Launch menu and the tree view control that can optionally appear beneath it. By default, the Quick Launch menu is shown and the tree view is hidden.

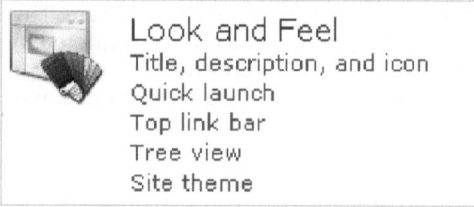

Figure 8-5. Nonpublishing navigation settings

Table 8-1 lists the web parts that are most commonly used in nonpublishing sites.

Table 8-1. Nonpublishing Content Area Web Parts

Web Part	Category	Description
Categories	Content Rollup	Displays a list of site categories from the site directory.
Sites in Category	Content Rollup	Displays sites within a category in the site directory.
Site Aggregator	Content Rollup	Displays the documents, forms, and other content items from a set of sites that are rendered as tabs on the control. Selecting the tab for a site renders a listing of the site's contents. This control is designed for use in a user's My Site.
Tag Cloud	Social Collaboration	Renders a set of links that indicate the popularity of subjects based on the social networking tags associated with them.

Publishing Sites

In publishing sites, the global and local menus are also AspMenu controls provided by the site's master page. In Site Settings, these menus can be configured by using the Navigation link in the Look and Feel submenu, as shown in Figure 8-6. The Tree View link can be used to show or hide the Quick Launch menu and the tree view control that can optionally appear beneath it. Note that the Quick Launch and tree view controls are not exposed on some publishing page layouts and will not appear even if enabled.

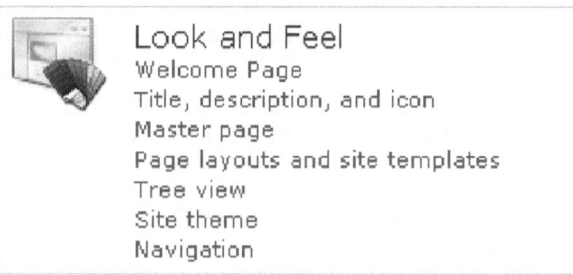

Look and Feel
Welcome Page
Title, description, and icon
Master page
Page layouts and site templates
Tree view
Site theme
Navigation

Figure 8-6. Publishing navigation settings

Table 8-2 lists the web parts that are most commonly used in publishing sites.

Table 8-2. Publishing Content Area Web Parts

Web Part	Category	Description
Summary Links	Content Rollup	This web part can be manually configured to contain a set of links including descriptions. Summary Links can also be stored in a content column for a page layout if desired (see Chapter 7).
Table of Contents	Content Rollup	This control displays a table of links to content within the local site collection. The filtering and presentation of these links is highly customizable.
Content Query	Content Rollup	The Content Query web part is often used to generate lists of navigation links in publishing sites. This control provides great flexibility in querying and rendering content links. Note that, while this web part is often used for navigation purposes, it is not a navigation control in the sense that it does not use the site map or site map providers.

Customizing Site Navigation

In the following exercises, you will walk through performing some common customizations to the navigation of two sites. One will be a publishing site, and the other will be a standard nonpublishing team site. On the nonpublishing site, you will explore the tree view and metadata navigation. On the publishing site, you will customize the navigation for the site by using both Site Settings and a custom master page.

You may notice that you will not be using SharePoint Designer much in these examples. This is because SharePoint 2010 includes more navigation configuration options in the web user interface.

EXERCISE 8-1. CUSTOMIZE THE MENUS ON A TEAM SITE

In this exercise, you will look at some of the ways that the menus for a team site can be configured. You will start with a standard team site. You will replace the normal Quick Launch menu with a tree view and then add metadata navigation elements to the tree.

1. Create a new site using the Team Site site template in a site collection that does not have the SharePoint publishing features activated.

2. In your web browser, select the Shared Documents library.

3. Create several folders and upload a few documents into each folder. The names and contents of these files and folders is not important.

4. From the Site Actions menu, select Site Settings.

5. From the Look and Feel group, select Tree View.

6. Deselect the Enable Quick Launch check box, shown in Figure 8-7 .

7. Select the Enable Tree View check box. Then click OK.

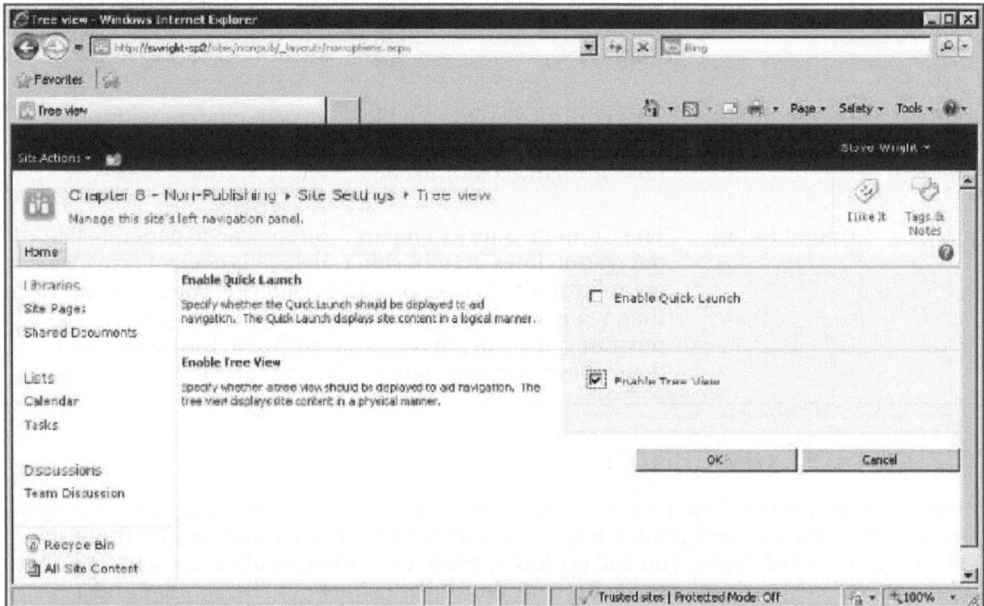

Figure 8-7. Tree View settings page

8. Click Shared Documents in the tree view at the left of the page, as shown in Figure 8-8.

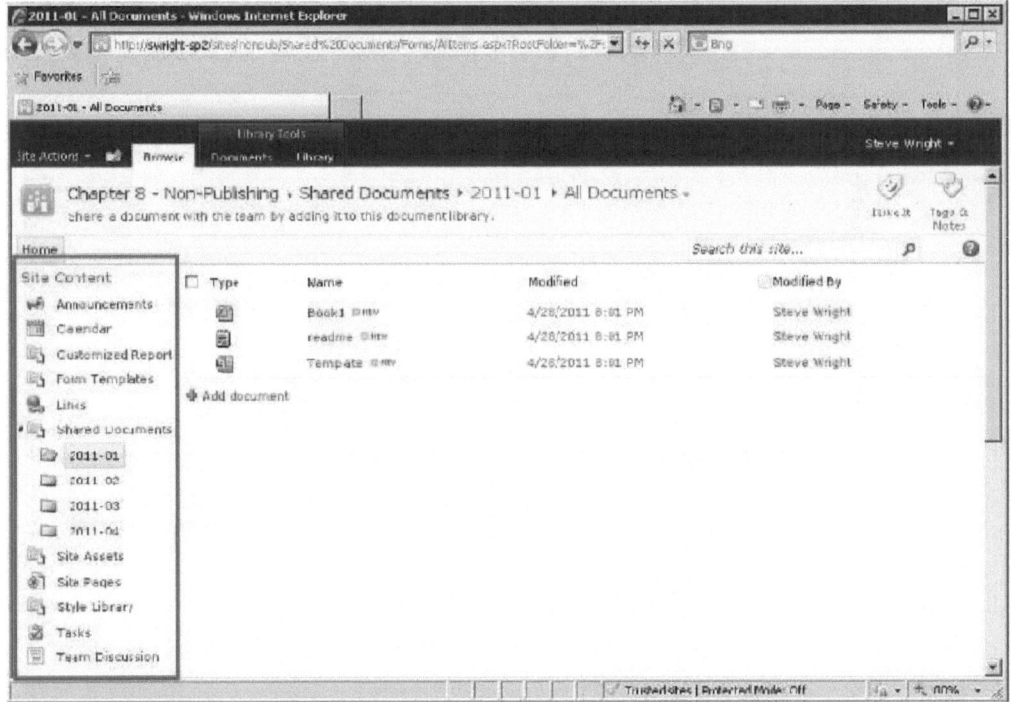

Figure 8-8. *Tree view menu*

In the tree view, beneath Shared Documents, you will see the folders that you created earlier. Clicking one of these links will display the documents in that folder.

9. On the Library tab on the menu, select Library Settings.

10. Under General Settings, select the Metadata Navigation Settings link.

11. Add Content Type to the Select Hierarchy Fields list. Note that Folders was already selected, causing the folders to appear in the tree view in Figure 8-8.

12. Add Modified By and Modified to the Selected Key Filter Field list, as shown in Figure 8-9. Then click OK.

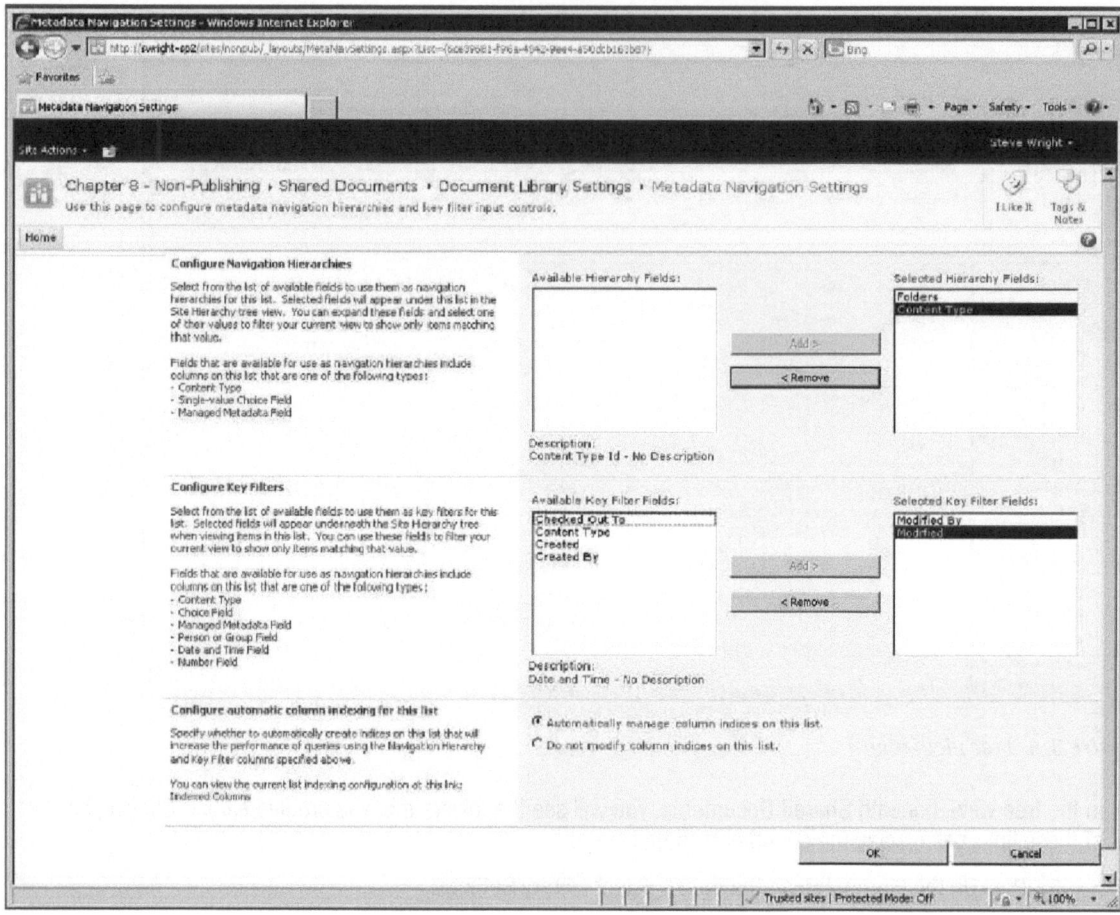

Figure 8-9. *Metadata Navigation Settings page*

> **13.** Click Shared Documents in the tree view, as shown in Figure 8-10.

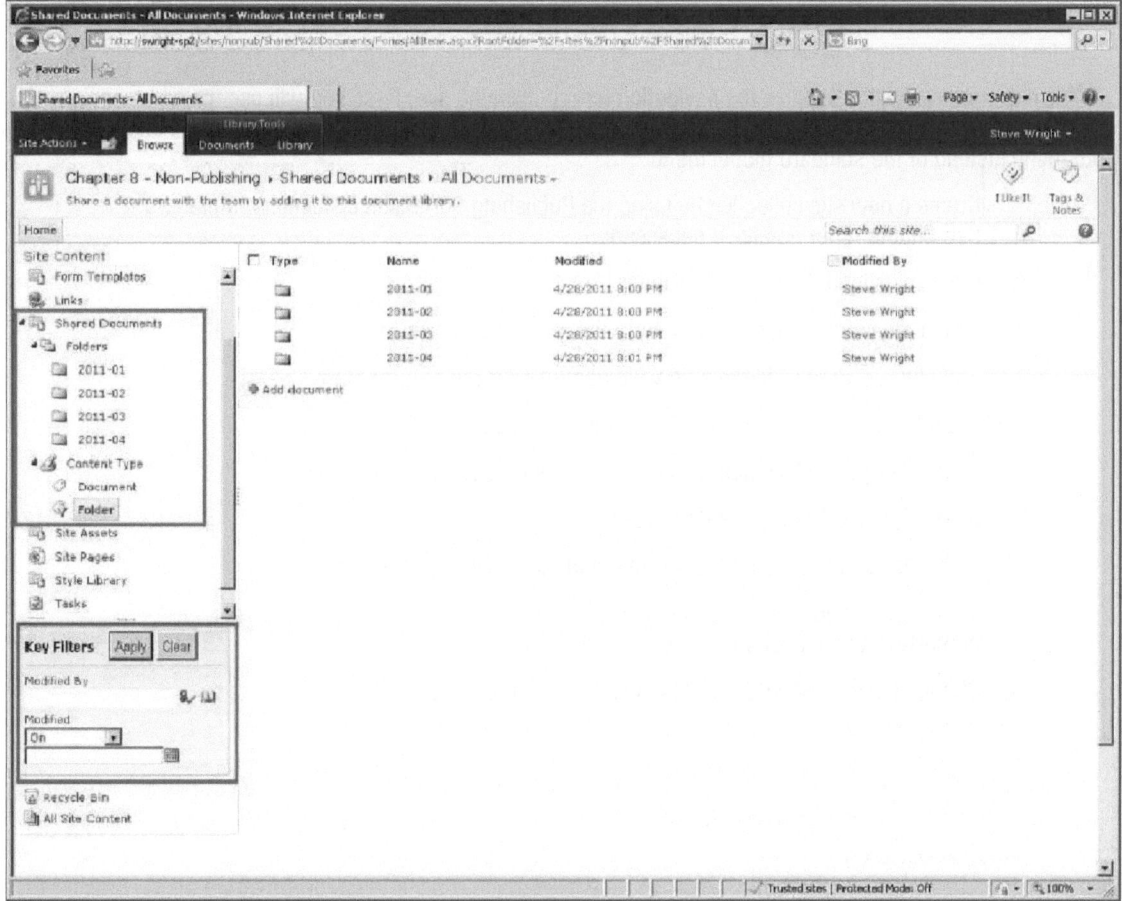

Figure 8-10. *Tree view with metadata navigation*

The tree view now contains a hierarchy for both folders, which was enabled by default because this is a document library, and content types. If a list or library is altered to contain other metadata fields, these could be used in navigation as well. By using the Managed Metadata service within SharePoint, you can define hierarchies of terms that can be used as metadata fields. These fields allow the tree view to display a custom hierarchy of objects filtered by their metadata values.

The key filters you selected are made available in the Key Filters pane at the bottom of the tree view. This feature allows users to further refine the filter to find just what they are looking for.

EXERCISE 8-2. CUSTOMIZE THE MENUS ON A PUBLISHING SITE

In this exercise, you will customize the navigation for a publishing site. First, you will use the web user interface to configure the menus for the site. Then, you will create a new master page that will use a fly-out menu instead of the standard global menu.

1. Create a new site collection by using the Publishing Portal site collection template. See Chapter 7 for details, if necessary.

2. Open the site in SharePoint Designer.

3. Select the Master Pages Gallery from the Navigation pane.

4. Copy the v4.master file to a new file named **custommenu.master**.

5. Open the custommenu.master file in the Page Editor.

6. When Designer asks whether you want to check out the file, click Yes.

7. Select Split mode from the Page Editor.

8. In the Design panel, click the horizontal menu at the top of the page.

9. In the Code panel, shown in Figure 8-11, change the StaticDisplayLevels property of the AspMenu tag to 1.

10. Change the MaximumDynamicDisplayLevels property of the AspMenu tag to 2.

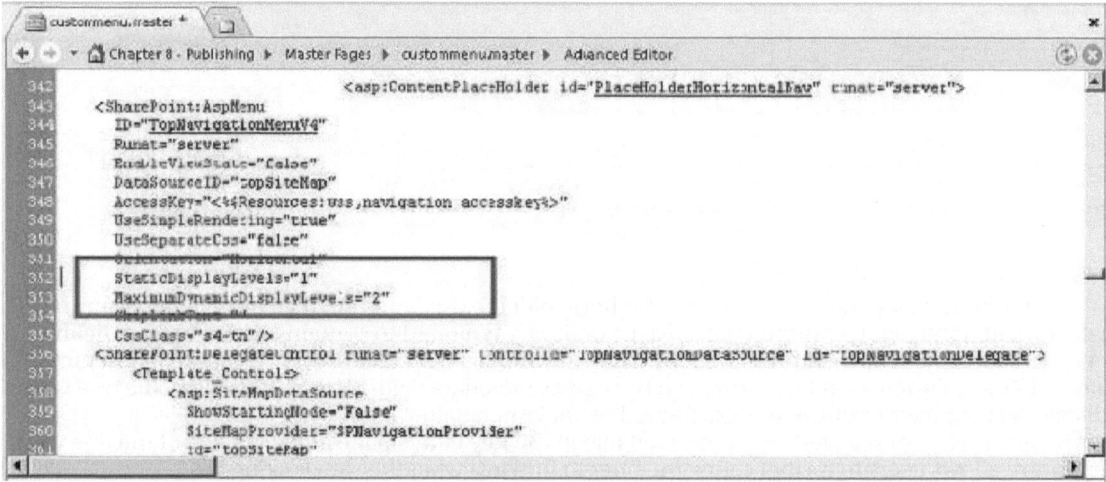

Figure 8-11. Customized AspMenu control on the master page

11. Save the page changes.

12. Click Yes in response to the Site Definition Page Warning dialog box that appears.

13. Select the Master Pages Gallery from the Navigation pane.

14. Right-click the `custommenu.master` file and select Check In.

15. Select Publish a Major Version and then click OK.

16. Click Yes to begin document approval.

17. Once the web browser opens, select Approve/Reject from the drop-down menu for the master file you have created.

18. Select Approved and then click OK.

19. Return to SharePoint Designer.

20. Right-click `custommenu.master` again and select Set as Custom Master Page.

21. In the web browser, open the site or refresh the home page.

Figure 8-12. Customized global menu

By changing the properties of the `AspMenu` control in the master page, you have converted the typical horizontal menu into a fly-out menu. However, this change has taken effect only on site pages. These are the pages that you explicitly create content for. Other pages, such as Site Settings or list and library forms, use a separate master page called the System master page. You will switch that setting to your new master page in a moment. Then, you will customize the links that appear on the menu.

22. From the Site Actions menu, select Site settings. Note that the Site Settings page is still using the original master page because it is an application page.

23. Select the Master Page link under Look and Feel.

24. Select `custommenu.master` in the System Master Page drop-down list.

25. Select the check box labeled Reset All Subsites to Inherit This Site Master Page Setting in both the Site Master Page and System Master Page sections. Then click OK.

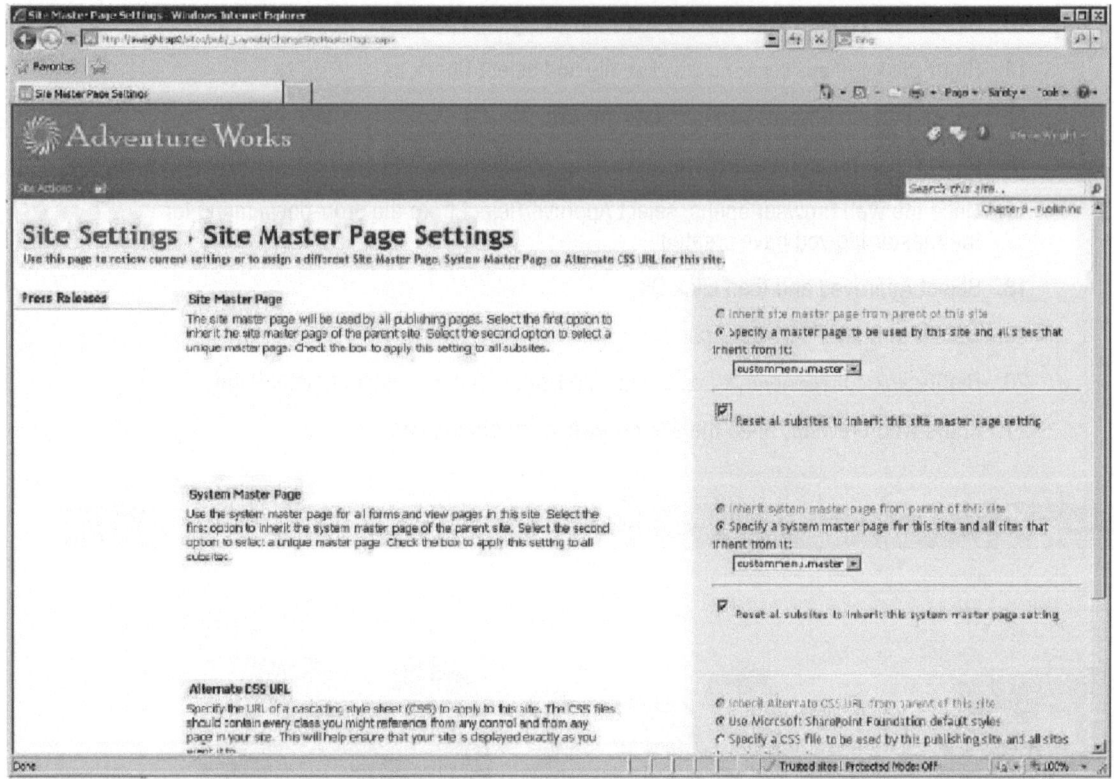

Figure 8-13. Master page settings page

26. Select the Navigation link under Look and Feel.

27. Under Navigation Editing and Sorting, select the Search (Hidden) item.

28. Click the Show button on the toolbar and then click OK.

29. Return to the site's home page and note that the Search site is now visible in the menu.

The Navigation Settings page allows the user to modify the contents of the global and current navigation areas of the site. You can include sites and/or pages in either menu, alter the maximum items to show, create submenu headings, add links, and arrange the menu items as needed.

SharePoint 2010 Search

Searching for content is a key feature in many web sites. SharePoint 2010 has several different solutions for searching content. Which solution is available depends on which version of SharePoint you are using. Configuring the search service in SharePoint is well beyond the scope of this book, but it is helpful to understand the options available.

Microsoft SharePoint Foundation (SPF) 2010 contains a simple search functionality that indexes and searches the content of the local SharePoint sites. Because SPF is a free add-on to Windows, the search service included is very limited. Most important, it can index only content stored within SharePoint's content databases and can perform searches only within the local site collection. The SPF search engine is designed to support small- to medium-scale farms containing fewer than 10 million documents per search server.

SharePoint Server 2010 contains an enterprise-grade search solution designed for scalability and extensibility called *SharePoint Enterprise Search*. This search engine can index content from various external sources, federate results from other search crawlers, and support most very large enterprises by scaling up to about 100 million documents. There are three different product SKUs that use this search engine.

In addition to SharePoint Server 2010, *Microsoft Search Server 2010 Express* is a free product that supports SharePoint Server's search functionality only on a very small scale. Search Server Express is limited to a single application and database server. It can even run using the free version of SQL Server, called SQL Server Express; however, this limits its scalability even further.

The third product using the enterprise search engine is *Microsoft Search Server 2010*. This product contains the full search features of SharePoint Server 2010 without supporting the rest of the functionality of SharePoint. A *people search* capability is not included with Search Server because it depends on other services within SharePoint Server that are not available.

The last type of search available in the SharePoint family of products is called *FAST Search Server 2010 for SharePoint*. This is a new set of features in the SharePoint 2010 release. FAST search is based on technology that Microsoft acquired in 2008 when it purchased FAST Search and Transfer ASA of Norway. The FAST technology is designed for high-performance and massive scale, to half a billion documents or more.

■ **Note** For more information on the SharePoint search options available, see these online resources:

SharePoint Search Getting Started Guide:

www.microsoft.com/downloads/en/details.aspx?FamilyID=96663b95-e9f5-48c8-beb9-a15ad119c499&displaylang=en

Search Feature Comparison Diagram:

www.microsoft.com/downloads/en/confirmation.aspx?displaylang=en&FamilyID=d7c0091e-5766-496d-a5fe-94bea52c4b15

This section focuses on the Enterprise Search features of SharePoint Server 2010 because that is the version most commonly used by enterprises. Many of the concepts presented will transfer to SPF and FAST search technologies as well. As noted before, the configuration of any of these technologies is beyond the scope of this book. Contact your SharePoint administrator to discuss configuring the search services in your environment.

All content that is indexed by SharePoint is categorized into scopes. A *scope* is a subset of all of the content available that is applicable to a certain set of users or sites. When conducting a search in SharePoint, a scope is always used to limit the results of the search. The two most commonly used scopes are All Sites and the local context. All Sites applies the query to the entire index of the server farm.

The local context may be a site, list, or library, depending on where the search is run from. In most cases, when the user doesn't explicitly select a scope, the current context scope is used.

SharePoint Server 2010 also exposes a People scope that refers to all the users of the farm. Running a search against the People scope will return a list of relevant users instead of documents. Queries for people can return results based on a person's name, department, job title, expertise, and so forth.

Once a search is complete, SharePoint supports the refinement feature. Essentially, *refinement* refers to searching with the results of a previous search. For example, if the user has performed a search that returned thousands of documents, refinement can be used to drill into those results by attributes such as the author or age of the document.

Search results are automatically security trimmed, where feasible. This means that if a user doesn't have the necessary permissions to open a document, that document will not appear in that user's search results. There are limitations to security trimming. When content is indexed against external sources that do not provide detailed permission information, or when search results are received from federated search services, security trimming may not be possible. A *federated search service* is one that exists outside the local SharePoint farm but has been configured to provide search results within SharePoint.

The search functionality of SharePoint 2010 also includes new features as compared to the 2007 version. One often-requested feature that has finally appeared in SharePoint search is the ability to use wildcard characters in search terms. Unfortunately, SharePoint supports wildcards only at the end of a word, not at the beginning or in the middle. For example, using *custom** as a search term would match *custom*, *customer*, and *customized*. However, using **stomer* would, most likely, not match anything because the asterisk (*) would not be seen as a wildcard in this case. SharePoint also supports a new query syntax in search terms that allow AND, OR, and NOT conditions to be used. For example, *sharepoint NOT foundation* would match items that contain *sharepoint*, excluding those that also contain *foundation*.

Search Web Parts

The search experience in SharePoint is created SharePoint 2010 by using a set of web parts specifically designed for handling search functions. These web parts are usually provisioned by creating a site based on one of the Search Center site templates provided by SharePoint. These templates are described in the next section. In this section, you will learn about the web parts available.

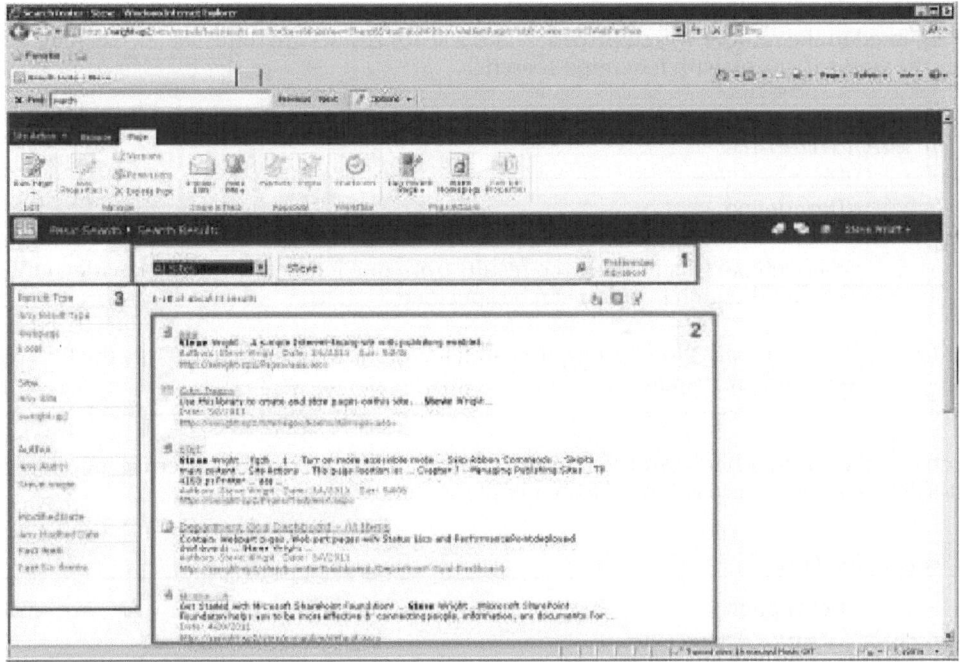

Figure 8-14. Basic Search Center web parts

The most common use of search is to find pages and documents that have been indexed by SharePoint. Table 8-3 lists the web parts used to enter a search query and display search results.

Table 8-3. Standard Search Web Parts

Web Part	Description
Search Box	This web part manages the entry of search queries and the selection of scopes and preferences. See box 1 in Figure 8-14.
Advanced Search Box	This is an expanded form of the Search Box that allows more detailed search queries to be composed. The page containing this search box is generally reached by clicking the Advanced Search link on the standard search box.
Search Core Results	This web part displays the results of the last search. The presentation of these results can be customized by using CSS and XSLT. See box 2 in Figure 8-14.
Refinement Panel	This web part presents options for refining the last search by using additional criteria. See box 3 in Figure 8-14.

As described earlier, federated searches are those that are performed by external search providers. The search query is passed to the remote search provider, and a set of results are returned and displayed. Table 8-4 describes the web parts used with federated searches.

Table 8-4. Federated Search Web Parts

Web Part	Description
Federated Results	This web part displays search results from one federated search provider. Only one federated search location can be specified.
Top Federated Results	This web part allows multiple search locations to be searched. Only the first results received are displayed.

A people search is used to find other SharePoint users based on their name, title, expertise, or other attributes. Table 8-5 lists the web parts used to perform people searches.

Table 8-5. People Search Web Parts

Web Part	Description
People Search Box	This web part is used to enter a search query for people.
People Search Core Results	This is the people search results web part.
People Refinement Panel	This web part is used to refine a people search.

The remaining search web parts display information about a set of search results or control the display of search results. Table 8-6 lists these web parts.

Table 8-6. Additional Search Web Parts

Web Part	Description
Search Action Links	This web part displays a set of actions the user can take related to the displayed search results. These include sorting by date or relevance, setting an alert, creating a favorite, or subscribing to an RSS feed. This web part is typically displayed above and to the right of the search results.
Search Paging	This web part displays a set of page links for navigating through a large set of search results. By default, the paging control is shown beneath the search results list.

Web Part	Description
Search Statistics	This web part is displayed to the left, above the search results, by default. It displays various types of information about the search results, which may include the range of currently displayed results, the total number of results, and the amount of time spent doing the search.
Related Queries	This web part normally appears on the right side of the search results page. It displays queries that have been used in the past and that are similar to the current query. Only frequently used queries that produce useful results will appear in this list.
Search Summary (a.k.a. "Did you mean?")	This web part typically appears immediately below the search box. It will occasionally display a message when an alternative search term is recommended. For example, a search for *goale* may result in a message such as "Did you mean goal?" (where goal is a link that will rerun the query with the corrected spelling).
Search Best Bets	This web part displays "best bet" links that have been associated with the keywords used in the search.
Search Visual Best Bet	This web part is a more advanced form of the Search Best Bets web part that is designed to provide a richer user interface. This web part is available only when using FAST search.

Search Site Templates

SharePoint Server 2010 comes with three site Partstemplates that are designed to provide a complete search user interface. Each one contains a set of search pages and search results pages that are prepopulated with a group of configured search web parts. These sites can be easily deployed and then customized as needed.

The *Basic Search Center template* is a simple search site that consist of a simple search page (default.aspx) containing nothing but a Search Box web part. There is also an advanced search page (advanced.aspx) that uses an Advanced Search Box instead. Search results from either of these pages are displayed on the Search Results page (results.aspx). The Basic Search Center is designed for use in site collections that do not use publishing or other enterprise features.

The *Enterprise Search Center template* is similar to the basic site except that the pages in this site contain a tabbed control that allows for multiple search and result pages to be deployed into one search solution. It contains the same three pages as the basic site plus search and results pages for people searches. The site contains two tabs by default: All Sites and People. Additional search and result pages can be added as needed. See Exercise 8-4 later in this chapter for an example of adding tabs to this site template.

The third search site template is called the *FAST Search Center*. As its name indicates, it is designed to work with the FAST Search Server 2010 for SharePoint search engine. Once FAST search is configured, this search center is similar to the Enterprise Search Center except that it contains enhancements for displaying results from the FAST search service.

Customizing the Search Experience

In the following exercises, you will explore the user interface components that are available for customizing the SharePoint search experience. You will use both the Basic and Enterprise Search Center templates. As you did when looking at site navigation, you will do one example in a nonpublishing site and the other in a publishing site.

In order to follow these exercises, you will need to meet the following conditions:

- You will need to have at least site owner privileges in the sites you will be working with.

- You will need to have the right to create new subsites.

- Your SharePoint farm administrator will need to have configured the search service in your environment.

EXERCISE 8-3. DEPLOY AND CUSTOMIZE A BASIC SEARCH CENTER

This exercise will walk you through the process of deploying the Basic Search Center site template in a nonpublishing environment. You will then configure the site to use the Scope drop-down list, which is not normally available in this type of site.

1. Open your web browser to the nonpublishing site you used for the first navigation exercise or create a new site using the Team Site template.

2. Create a new subsite by using the Basic Search Center site template, shown in Figure 8-15.

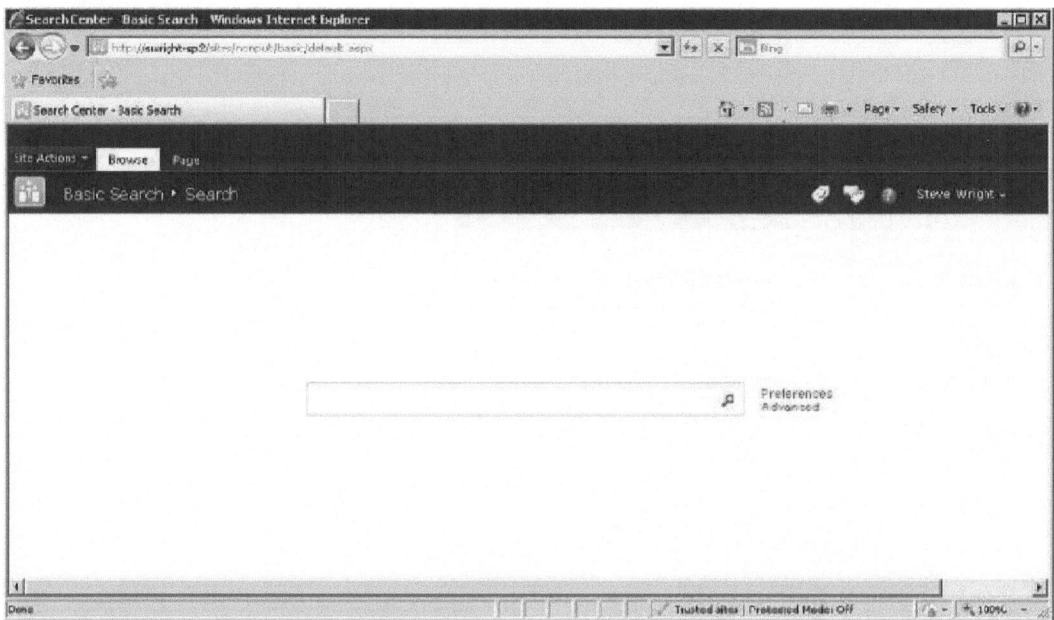

Figure 8-15. Basic Search Center site template

3. On the default.aspx page of the search center, select Edit Page from the Page tab on the menu.

4. Select Edit Web Part from the drop-down menu for the Search Box web part.

5. Expand the Scopes Dropdown category in the configuration panel. From the Dropdown Mode list, select Show, and Default to 's' URL Parameter, as shown in Figure 8-16. Click OK.

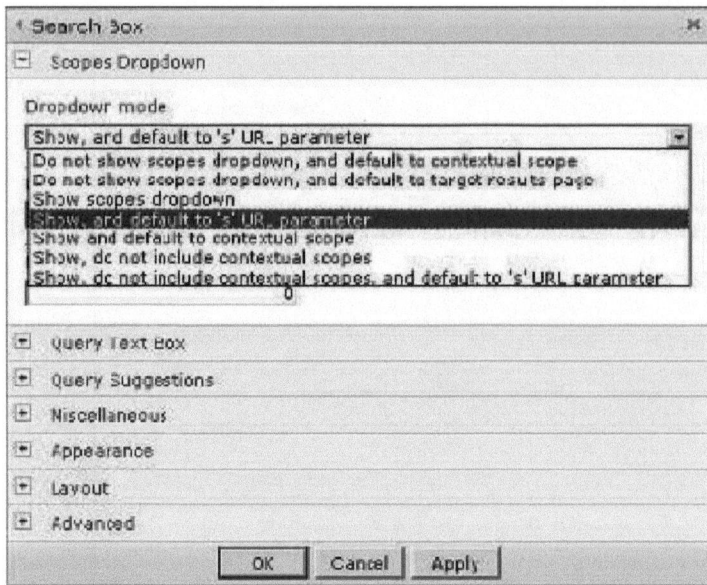

Figure 8-16. Configure Scope Dropdown Mode

6. Switch to the `results.aspx` page for the site and repeat steps 3 through 5 on the results page.

7. Select People in the scope drop-down and type your first name into the search box.

8. Press Enter or click the magnifying glass to the right of the search box.

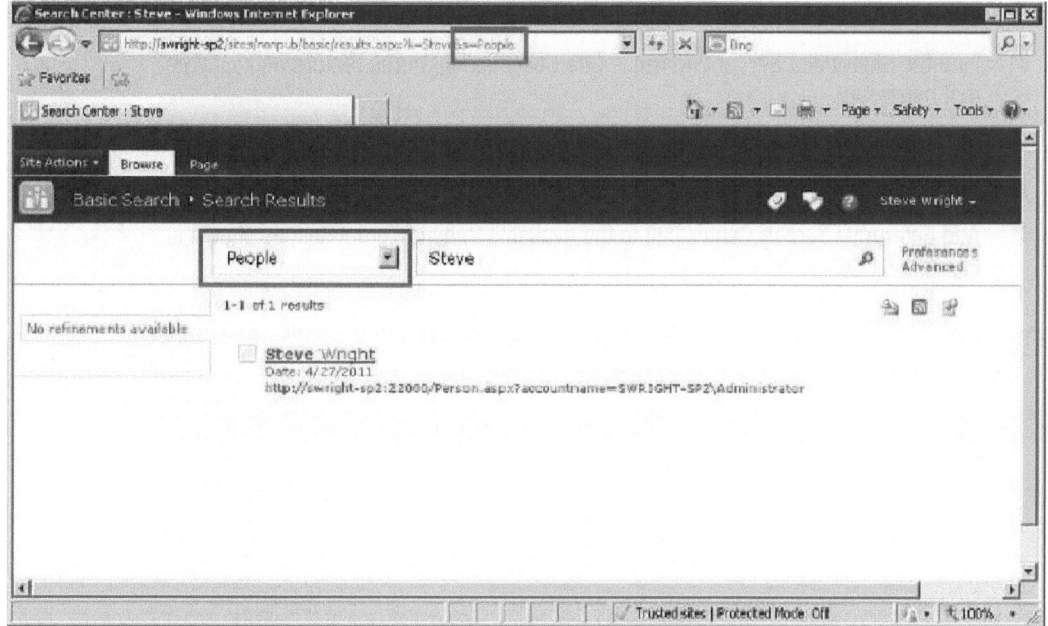

Figure 8-17. *Customized Search Results page with a scope drop-down control*

The scope drop-down list is used to select the search scope to use for the search. By default, the scope drop-down is not shown, and the search is limited to the current context. Turning on the scope drop-down allows the user to expand the search to include other scopes or to search for people. The scope selected is passed from page to page by using the s parameter on the URL. The setting you selected causes the scope drop-down to automatically display the selected scope when the page is rendered.

■ **Tip** Take some time to explore the options available on the other web parts that are part of the standard results.aspx page. The variations available are extensive.

EXERCISE 8-4. DEPLOY AND CUSTOMIZE AN ENTERPRISE SEARCH CENTER

In this final exercise, you will deploy and customize the Enterprise Search Center template in a publishing environment. Once the site is created, you will add a new tab to the site that performs a customized query.

1. Open your web browser to the publishing site you used for the second navigation exercise or create a new site collection by using the Publishing Portal template.

2. From the Site Actions menu, select Site Settings.

3. Under Site Collection Administration, select the Site Collection Features link.

4. Find the SharePoint Server Enterprise Site Collection Features feature and activate it, if necessary.

5. Select Site Settings from the Site Actions menu.

6. Under Look and Feel, select the Page Layouts and Site Templates link.

7. Add Enterprise Search Center (All) to the available Subsite Templates, as shown in Figure 8-18. Click OK.

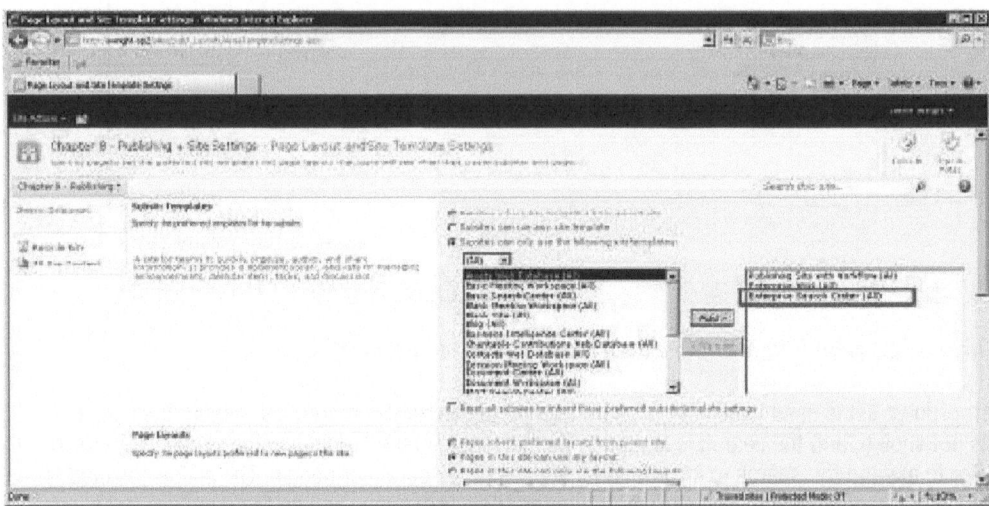

Figure 8-18. *Page Layout and Site Template Settings page*

The reason you had to turn on the Enterprise feature and select the site template is that the Publishing Portal site collection template contains only the minimum set of features needed for a publishing site. The Enterprise feature makes the Enterprise Search Center site template available. It is then necessary to explicitly include it in the list of allowed templates. Otherwise, it would not appear as an option when creating a subsite.

8. From the Site Actions menu, select New Site. Create a new subsite by using the Enterprise Search Center site template, shown in Figure 8-19.

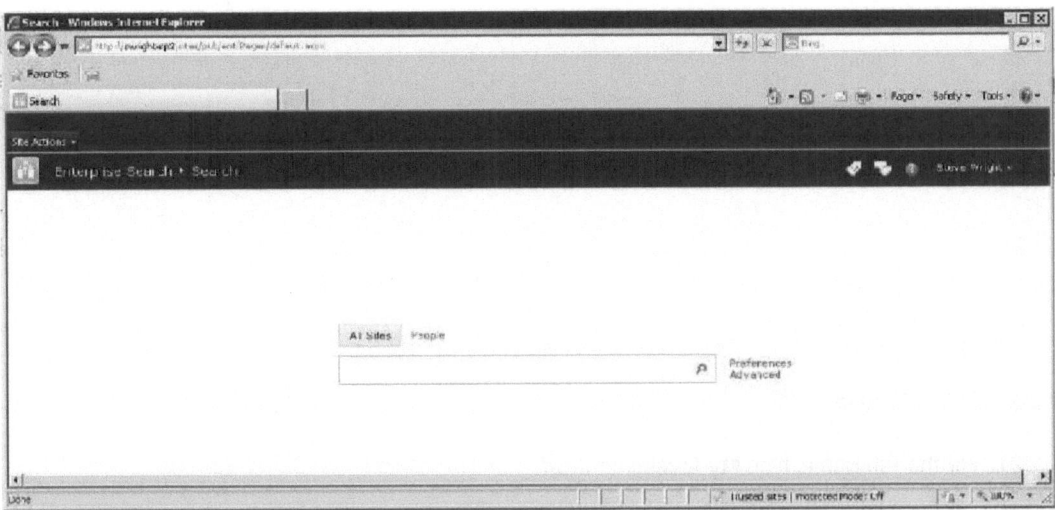

Figure 8-19. Enterprise Search Center site template

9. From the Site Actions menu, select Edit in SharePoint Designer.

10. From the Navigation pane, select All Files.

11. From the All Files gallery window, select the Pages library.

12. Copy the `default.aspx` page to a new page named **mystuff.aspx**.

13. Double-click the `mystuff.aspx` page to open it in the Page Editor.

14. Select Edit in Browser when prompted to open the page or page layout.

15. Click Yes in the source control pop-up box.

16. Select Edit Web Part from the Search Box web part's drop-down menu.

17. Open the Query Text Box category in the configuration panel.

18. In the Additional Query Terms text box, type **Author:"Steve Wright"**, substituting your own name. Note that the string should include double-quotes around your name because it (most likely) contains a space. Click OK.

19. Click the Add New Tab link above the Top Zone web part zone, as shown in Figure 8-20.

287

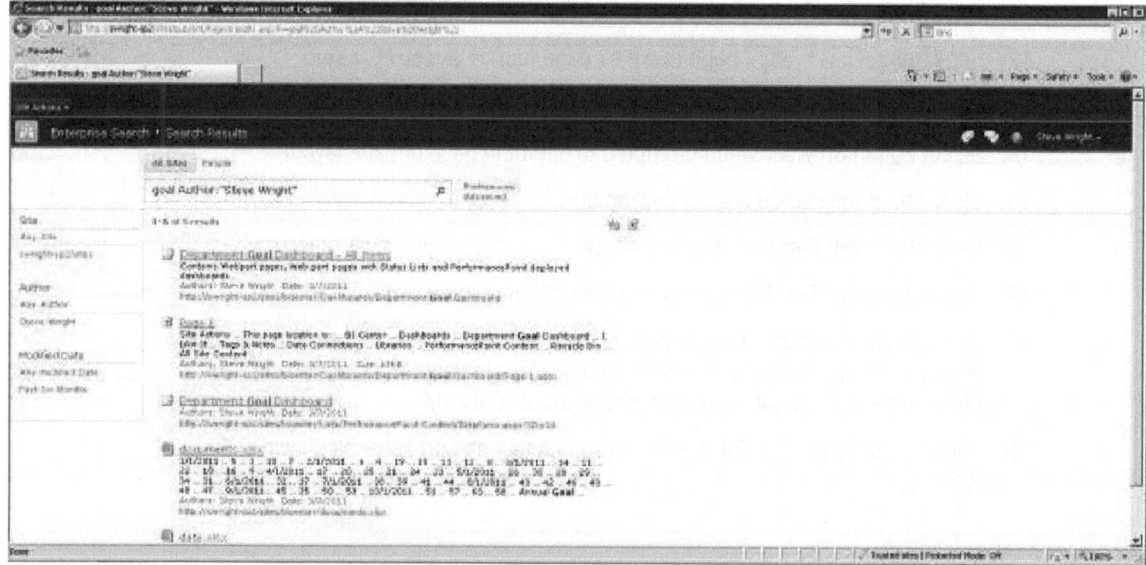

Figure 8-20. *Add New Tab link*

20. For the Tab Name, type **My Awesome Stuff**.

21. For the Page, type `mystuff.aspx`.

22. Click Save.

23. Press F5 to refresh the page in the browser. This causes the new tab to appear.

24. Type a search term in the search box and press Enter.

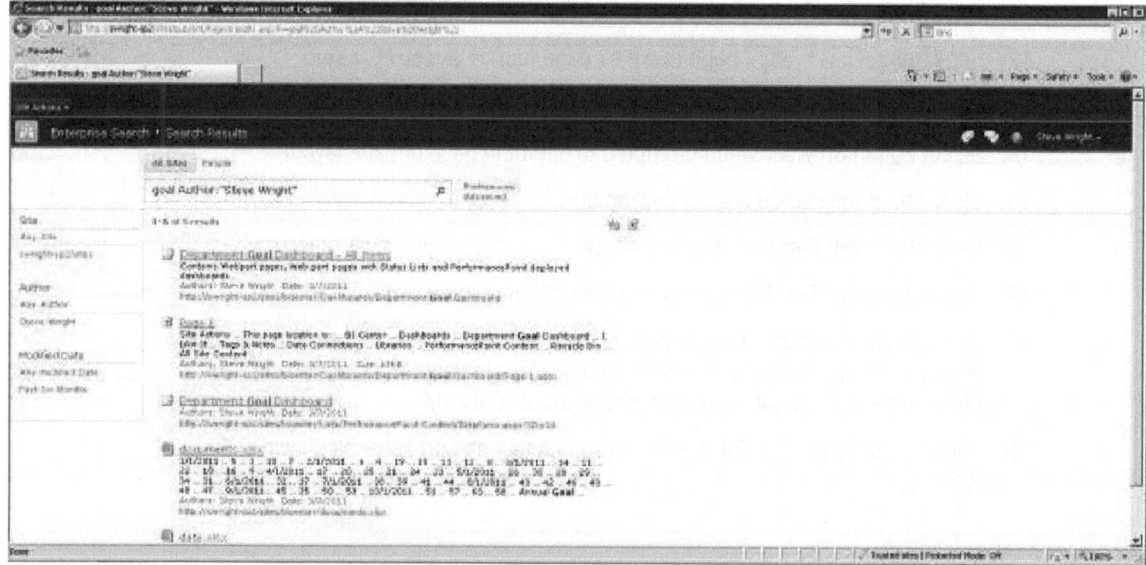

Figure 8-21. *Customized search results*

Note that the Author search term was added to the search term you entered before the search was run. Also, the tab you added is no longer visible on the results page. This is because there are separate sets of tabs for search pages (such as default.aspx) and results pages (such as results.aspx). To add a corresponding tab on the results pages, you would copy the existing results.aspx page and make the same changes to the search box. You would then add a tab from the results page by using the same procedure you used before.

Summary

In this chapter, you have

- Examined the .NET technologies used to implement SharePoint's navigation system

- Described the visual components used to create an intuitive site navigation structure

- Customized the out-of-the-box pages, controls, and web parts to implement customized site navigation and search

- Customized the search web parts to improve the search relevancy and flexibility

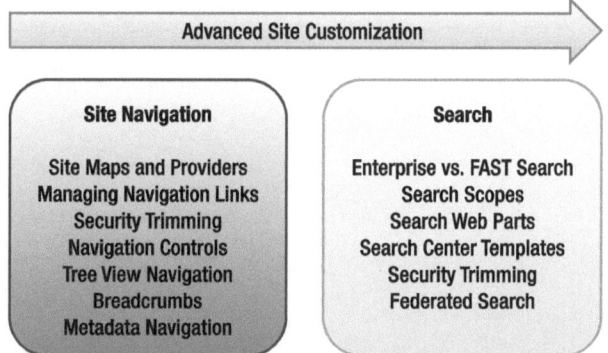

Figure 8-22. Advanced site customization road map

CHAPTER 9

Client-Side Programming

At this point, you are going to take a slight detour from building the visual components of your sites into the magical realm of code writing. As you have seen throughout this book, some amazing things can be accomplished with SharePoint Server 2010 and SharePoint Designer 2010 without ever writing a line of code. However, in order to build the richest of user experiences, it is sometimes necessary to crack open the toolbox and pull out the power tools.

In this chapter, you will take a brief look at some of the tools that are available for writing high-performance client-side behaviors in SharePoint. This is not intended to be a comprehensive discussion of client-side programming in SharePoint. The purpose of this chapter is simply to make you aware of the tools that are available. Many excellent resources are available online, including on MSDN, and more are appearing all the time. The SharePoint client object models described here are catching on very rapidly, and a great deal of interest has been generated among developers who write blogs.

Note Unlike the rest of this book, this chapter assumes that the reader has a certain familiarity with writing code that runs in a web browser. This includes technologies such as JavaScript, HTML, DOM, AJAX, and WCF. If these terms are foreign to you, don't feel too bad. You are in good company (with most of the human race) and should feel free to skip this chapter.

You will learn about the following topics in this chapter:

- How SharePoint 2010 exposes server functionality by using client-side object models (CSOMs).

- Why Microsoft felt this was an important feature to provide

- Why writing code that runs in the client browser is sometimes preferable to code that runs on the server

- How to make the browser interact with the server more efficiently

- Why we all love writing code so much!

Understanding Client- vs. Server-Side Programming

In previous versions of SharePoint, we had two interfaces for accessing the objects and content stored within SharePoint: API calls or web services.

If our code was destined to run on the SharePoint server—for example, in a web part or event receiver—we could use the SharePoint API (a.k.a. the SharePoint server object model). This allowed us to create, read, update, and delete (CRUD) objects such as SPSite, SPWeb, SPList, and SPListItem. We could set permissions, configure features, and manipulate just about anything in the SharePoint environment as long as we had the necessary credentials. We could also write code against the API that would run as an add-on to the SharePoint Administration tool (STSADM) or in a .NET application. The only restriction was that it had to run *on the SharePoint server*. This interface still exists in SharePoint 2010, along with a new set of PowerShell commands that can be used for many of the same purposes.

If our SharePoint 2007 code needed to run on a computer other than the SharePoint server, we had to use SharePoint's web services interface. This interface was not as rich as the full server API, but it suited many scenarios well enough. The problem with the web services interface was that it worked well for the situations Microsoft designed it for, but not at all in most other cases. The web service method you needed either existed, or it didn't—and you were out of luck.

Many developers, me included, began routinely deploying custom web services within our SharePoint sites to allow client applications to perform actions not supported by the web services interface. Using AJAX-style code in the web browser, these services could be used to provide a richer user experience that did not require as many time-consuming page posts to the web server. JavaScript code running in the web browser would call the custom web service to carry out a server-side function, returning data objects to the browser. The script would then update the currently displayed page without posting the entire page to the server. Unfortunately, these services often performed poorly and affected scalability by transferring logic that could be done on the client side to the server.

Another approach to the problem was to redefine the *client* application as a *server* application. For example, integrating SQL Server Reporting Services (SSRS) with SharePoint 2007 required the SQL server to have SharePoint installed locally so that SQL could use the SharePoint API to communicate with SharePoint. This was true even if there was no plan to render pages or run any other SharePoint server processes on the SSRS server. Although this did not have a large impact when using the free Windows SharePoint Services (WSS) package, this could get very expensive once you started deploying Microsoft Office SharePoint Server (MOSS).

As Microsoft began developing the next version of SharePoint, they were flooded with requests for additional web services to be added to the interface. More and more web sites have the need for a flexible client-side programming interface to support rich browser interfaces and mobile web applications. At some point, Microsoft came up with a more elegant solution than continuing to add new SharePoint web services ad infinitum.

Working with the SharePoint Client Object Model

SharePoint 2010 contains a new set of features called the *SharePoint Foundation 2010 client-side object model* (CSOM) or just the *client object model*. Note that I am using the abbreviation *CSOM* instead of *COM* to avoid confusing it with the old component object model. The purpose of the CSOM is to provide a client-side subset of the SharePoint API that can be used from a variety of platforms. The object model is available for .NET Framework applications, Silverlight applications, and web sites using ECMAScript-compatible scripting languages such as JScript and JavaScript.

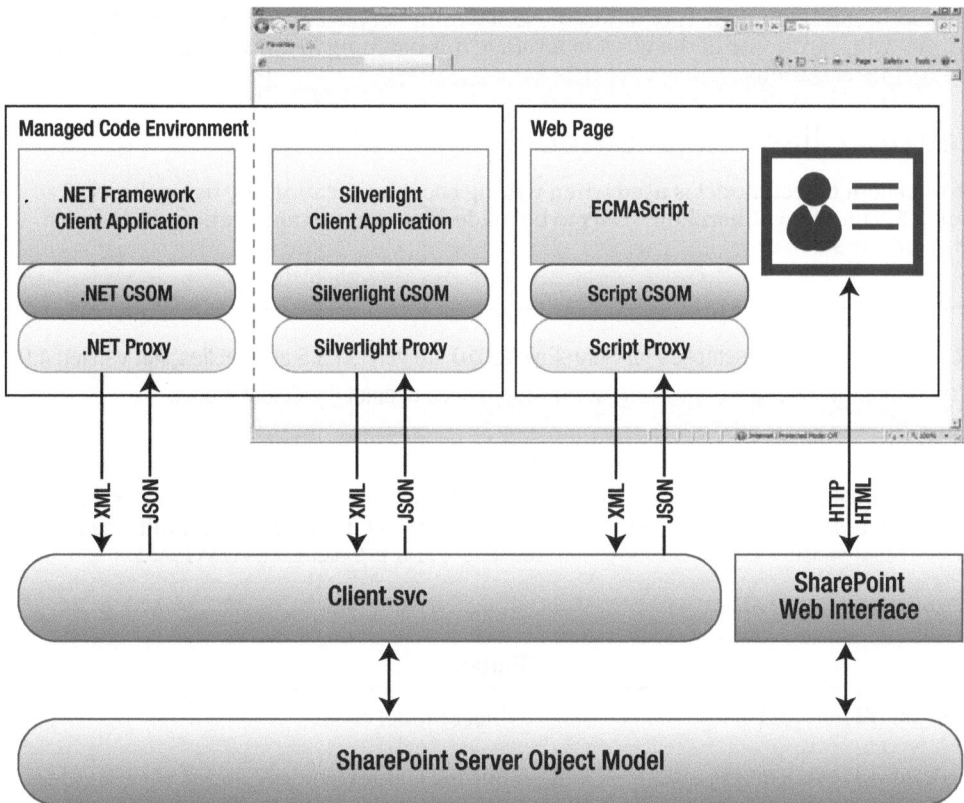

Figure 9-1. Client-side object model components

Each version of the client object model has a similar component structure. The specifics of each environment are presented in a later section. For now, you will look at the architecture that is common to them all (see Figure 9-1).

On the SharePoint server, there is a new component called Client.svc. As the name suggests, this is a Windows Communication Foundation (WCF) service. This service acts as a façade for the SharePoint Server object model running on the server. The client service receives client requests in XML form, executes the request against the server API, and returns objects to the caller in JavaScript Object Notation (JSON) format.

Each client object model implementation consists of two layers. The first layer is the client-side object model classes. These classes map directly in most cases to a corresponding SharePoint Server object model class. For example, the SPSite server object is represented by the Site object in each client object model.

The second layer of the implementation consists of a proxy layer, or *runtime*. The purpose of the proxy component is to streamline the passing of requests and responses to and from the server. A key difference between the server and client object models is the effect of the proxy layer. When a call is made to the client object model, that request is not immediately processed on the server. The proxy batches the requests until the client application explicitly tells it to contact the server. At that point, all of the outstanding requests are processed in order, and the results are returned to the client. This makes writing good client-side SharePoint code very different from writing server-side code. In the "Using Best Practices" section, you will learn some of the ways to leverage this batching behavior to dramatically improve performance and scalability.

.NET Framework Client Object Model

The .NET Framework client object model is used when writing client applications by using the .NET Framework version 3.5. This allows SharePoint calls to be made from console applications, Windows applications, and Windows services.

■ **Note** The .NET client object model assemblies for SharePoint 2010 are version 3.5 assemblies, not version 4.0. Be sure to select the correct .NET Framework version when writing code against the object model.

There are two assemblies to be referenced when building SharePoint client applications in .NET, as shown in Table 9-1. Both assemblies can be found in the 14 hive's ISAPI directory. By default, the full path is C:\Program Files\Common Files\Microsoft Shared\Web Server Extensions\14\ISAPI.

Table 9-1. .NET Framework CSOM Files

Filename	Purpose
Microsoft.SharePoint.Client.dll	Object model classes
Microsoft.SharePoint.Client.Runtime.dll	Runtime classes

Silverlight Client Object Model

The Silverlight client object model is used when writing Silverlight applications. These applications may be hosted in a variety of environments, from mobile phones to SharePoint sites, using the Silverlight web part.

Again, two assemblies need to be referenced when building SharePoint client applications. Both assemblies can be found in the 14 hive's TEMPLATE\LAYOUTS\ClientBin directory. SharePoint's 14 hive is the location to which SharePoint installs the content files and executables that are deployed as part of a SharePoint site. The full default path to these files is C:\Program Files\Common Files\Microsoft Shared\Web Server Extensions\14\TEMPLATE\LAYOUTS\ClientBin. There is also an Extensible AJAX Platform (XAP) file containing both dynamic-link libraries (DLLs). Table 9-2 lists the files.

Table 9-2. Silverlight CSOM Files

Filename	Purpose
`Microsoft.SharePoint.Client.Silverlight.dll`	Object model classes
`Microsoft.SharePoint.Client.Runtime.Silverlight.dll`	Runtime classes
`Microsoft.SharePoint.Client.xap`	Precompiled Silverlight package containing both DLLs

ECMAScript Client Object Model

The ECMAScript client object model is used when writing JavaScript code within web pages. The method of delivering the script to the web page may vary. It could be included in a Content Editor web part or other standard control, as you will see in our example. It could also be emitted by a custom web control or embedded in a .js script file.

In this case, only one file is needed for the client object model. All of the object and proxy logic is included in a single JavaScript file called sp.js. This file is commonly loaded at runtime by using a script statement like the one shown in Listing 9-1.

Listing 9-1. JavaScript Reference for the sp.js File

```
<script type="text/javascript">
        ExecuteOrDelayUntilScriptLoaded(MyFunction, "sp.js");
</script>
```

This causes the sp.js file to load before running the MyFunction routine, which can then use the client object model. This file is compacted and difficult to read. For debugging purposes, you may want to use the sp.debug.js file. It is easier to work with but is 40 percent larger than the production file. Table 9-3 lists the ECMAScript CSOM files.

Table 9-3. ECMAScript CSOM Files

Filename	Purpose
sp.js	Production script file
sp.debug.js	Debug version of the script file

The ECMAScript object model has some limitations because of the environment in which it executes. Objects created with the model can access only the local site collection. In the server API or the other client object models, you can create a Site (or SPSite) object that points to any SharePoint site collection anywhere on the network. Because script objects exist within a certain web page, any attempt to access another site collection would be considered a cross-site scripting attack and is therefore prevented.

The proxy layer in any of the client object models can batch multiple requests destined for the server. When the client application wants to send the batch, it calls either ExecuteQuery or

ExecuteQueryAsync. The former call blocks the current thread until the results are returned. The latter registers callback routines that are called asynchronously after the request is completed. Because blocking the browser's user interface thread can cause the browser to freeze, only asynchronous requests are permitted. The ExecuteQuery method is not even included in the script object model.

The ECMAScript version of the client object model is the one that we can use from within SharePoint Designer 2010, so we will limit our discussion to it for the rest of this chapter.

SharePoint Object Model Comparison

All of the client object models are a subset of the server object model. Some of the objects, properties, and methods available within the server API are not available on the client side. That being said, most of the objects commonly used by SharePoint developers are available in a very similar form. Table 9-4 lists some of the most common objects and their client equivalents.

Table 9-4. Comparing Objects in the Object Models

Server API	.NET CSOM	Silverlight CSOM	ECMAScript CSOM
SPContext	ClientContext	ClientContext	ClientContext
SPSite	Site	Site	Site
SPWeb	Web	Web	Web
SPList	List	List	List
SPListItem	ListItem	ListItem	ListItem
SPField	Field	Field	Field

Using Best Practices

This section covers some best practices around using client-side script with SharePoint solutions. You will examine the most common use cases for which client-side programming is useful or preferable. Then you will look at some of the architectural considerations that affect performance and scalability of a SharePoint farm when using server-side vs. client-side logic. For those familiar with AJAX-style programming, many of these points will seem obvious.

The two main reasons for moving logic to the client are to improve site performance and create a richer user experience. The key is to remember that moving logic to the client side improves the scalability of the SharePoint farm by removing that processing from the server. Eliminating unneeded full-page post-backs is good for both the user experience and reducing load on the server.

User Experience

The new client object model is a powerful new tool for building SharePoint solutions, but when should it be used, and when is it best to avoid client-side scripting? It is important to understand what types of things can be done effectively from the client side. SharePoint server provides web parts and pages that handle most routine tasks by presenting a form to the user and receiving the data posted back from the form. Client-side forms allow more-complex behaviors to be created that make the user interface respond more quickly and interactively.

For example, in SharePoint 2007, when the user clicked the *+Add Document* link in a document library, the entire page was replaced by an upload form. Starting in SharePoint 2010, the same link will open a modal dialog box form to upload the document, as shown in Figure 9-2. Forms like this one are loaded without posting the entire page back to the server. When the form is submitted, the page behind it is redisplayed and updated only as necessary. This creates a much smoother interface.

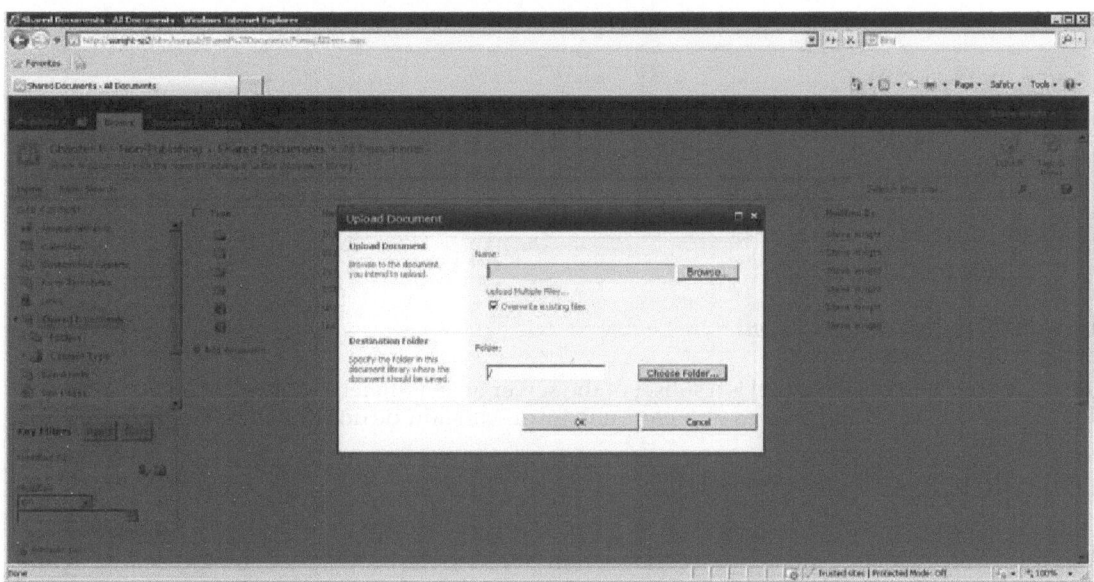

Figure 9-2. Modal dialog box form

The client object model contains a set of classes for displaying this type of modal dialog box easily from within client-side script. The dialog box can accept input, perform actions such as posting data back to the server, and return status and data elements to the calling client script.

Client-side scripts can also be used to update the elements on the current web page. A common scenario is to execute a Collaborative Application Markup Language (CAML) query against SharePoint server by using the client object model and then to render the results to controls already present on the web page. As you will see in the example later in this chapter, it is also simple to retrieve and update information about individual content objects that exist within the site. These objects can include web sites, lists, libraries, list items, and documents.

Using SharePoint Designer, it is also possible to create *custom actions* within the SharePoint site, as you can see in Figure 9-3. These are menu items that can launch a form, start a workflow, or navigate to a specific URL. By adding a JavaScript call to the custom action's URL, this feature can be used to run arbitrary client-side script when the menu item is selected.

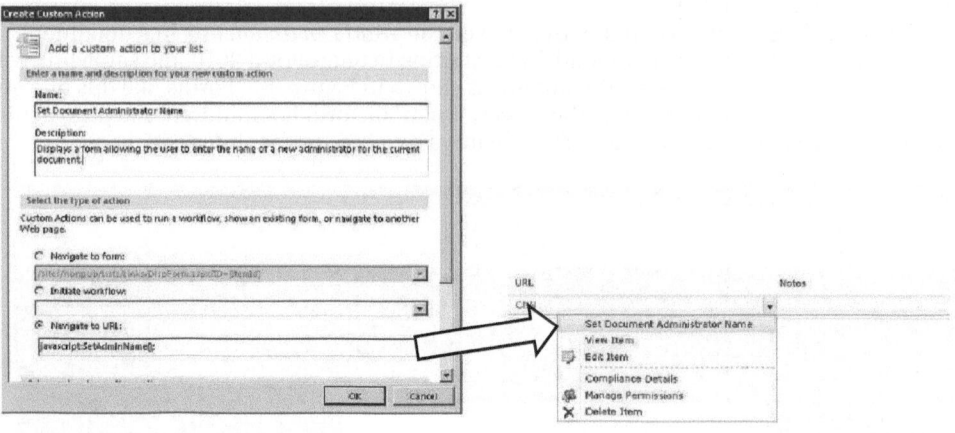

Figure 9-3. *Client-side custom actions*

Because the client object model is a subset of the server object model, many of the tasks traditionally performed within a site's web parts and forms can now be done on the client side.

Performance and Scalability

Performance and scalability are two sides of the same coin. What the user experiences as performance from your web site is dependent on how quickly actions taken in the browser are communicated to the server and then reflected back in the browser. As additional users place additional load on the server, it naturally responds more slowly. SharePoint server farms are intended to provide scalability by providing additional servers to handle the load. However, the design of your application will determine how effectively those server resources can be used.

Getting the best performance possible requires balancing the functionality of the application against the capabilities of the hardware supporting it. The SharePoint client object models are designed to allow some of the processing that might have occurred on the servers to be performed on the client side of the network connection. This frees up server capacity and improves scalability.

Consider all of the logic that goes into a SharePoint application. This might include querying, reading, formatting, and updating data. It might also include time-consuming calculations or repetitive tasks. Some of these have to be done, at least in part, on the server side because they involve accessing SharePoint's databases. When designing functionality for the SharePoint environment, consider which pieces of logic can be done on the client and which cannot. Of those that can be moved to the client side, consider the savings in terms of server resources that could be gained by doing so.

Your goal is to reduce the physical load on the servers in terms of CPU time, memory usage, disk I/O, and network traffic. Because SharePoint is an IIS-based application, you also need to consider the worker threads allocated within IIS as a limited resource to be managed and conserved. Performing calculations and formatting tasks on the client side can help reduce CPU and thread usage. Carefully managing the volume of data being sent to and received from the server can make a big difference when network capacity is at a premium. Of course, having pages load faster is a boost to the user experience even when the servers are lightly loaded.

The following are some concrete suggestions for improving performance and scalability when using the client object model.

Update Only a Small Portion of the Page

Using client-side script, you can retrieve information from the server and display it in the controls and display elements within the current web page instead of posting back and re-rendering the entire page. This eliminates the need to re-render those parts of the page that are not changing. For example, if you are adding an item to a list, there is no need to regenerate the page's navigation controls including all of the security checks and HTML creation that goes with them. Additionally, the network bandwidth consumed will be greatly reduced because there will be less redundant data to transmit.

Carefully Design Request Batches Submitted to the Proxy Layer

When using the client object model, the proxy layer records the requests made to the objects in the ClientContext object. It sends those requests to the server only when explicitly instructed to do so via the ExecuteQueryAsnyc() method. At that time, it packages the requests into an XML document, establishes a connection to the server, and transfers the data. The server then transmits the response data back to the proxy layer as JSON objects. The amount of time and network bandwidth used sending and receiving data is proportional to the amount of data being sent. The overhead associated with the call (connecting, error correcting, and so forth) is fairly consistent for all calls made, no matter how big or small.

To maximize the efficiency of the interaction between the client and server, try to reduce the number of calls by planning the request batches that will be sent to the proxy layer. Each batch should contain as many requests as possible. In some cases, the results of one operation are needed as inputs to the next one. Those operations will have to be in separate batches, but the client object model was designed to minimize this type of dependency. It is possible to open a webpage, find a list, and create list items, all before sending anything to the server.

In short, remember to keep your interactions *chunky*, not *chatty*. A few large data transfers are more efficient than many small ones.

Minimize Data Volume by Limiting the Items and Fields Returned

Wait a minute! Didn't we just say to make your request and response batches *bigger*? Yes—but only as big as they need to be.

When you retrieve an object by using the server-side SharePoint API, you generally expect the object to be populated with all of the properties for the object. In the client object models, you can specify which properties you are interested in so that none of the others need to be retrieved. If you are generating a list of documents in a library, you may be interested in its name and URL, but not its status, creation, and modification information. The size of the response sent from the server to the client can be greatly reduced by carefully selecting only those properties that you are actually going to use after the object is loaded. The concept is similar to writing SQL statements that avoid using SELECT * FROM to retrieve all of the fields in a table. If you cannot list all of the fields in the object, you probably do not need all of their values in the response.

It is also worth mentioning that you should limit the number of items being returned as well. Querying the properties of objects is one operation that is much better done on the server side. Imagine looking for a particular document in a library of a million items by pulling the entire list into the client web browser and then looping through it. The CAML query object is ideal for retrieving only those items and fields that are actually needed.

Use Modal Dialogs Instead of Launching Forms on a New Page

As described earlier in the subsection "User Experience" and shown in Figure 9-2, the client object model contains utility classes, such as `SP.UI.ModalDialog`, for creating modal dialog boxes within the current page. Although this may seem quite trivial at first, just consider how that same interface would probably have appeared in SharePoint 2007. A full-page post-back would be executed to load a form into the web browser. Then, the form data would be posted to the server. The form data would be processed, and then the user's browser would be redirected to a new page that would have to be completely generated from scratch. By presenting the form in a dialog box, we have turned two complete round-trips to the server into a couple of small requests for HTML and posting data. The rest of the current page remains in the browser, ready for use.

Client-Side Anti-Patterns

Just as it is important to know when to use the client object model, you also need to consider cases in which using it might not be desirable. The dangers introduced by using the client object model are similar to the risks that have always been associated with browser-based scripting.

The most obvious reason *not* to use client-side scripting is that it might not be available. All modern browsers support ECMAScript, but older browsers may not. Also, some organizations limit or disable scripts when they come from the Internet. Consider the network environment and required browser support when moving to client-side scripts. When creating a public-facing Internet site, your site needs to degrade gracefully when faced with old, or intentionally crippled, browsers.

When you write a client-side script and place it on a web page, you are essentially releasing your source code to the public. Anyone can view and copy the scripts associated with a web page. Never put proprietary logic into the scripts on a web page. Most client-side logic is fairly straightforward, so exposing it isn't really an issue. If your company's secret sauce is algorithms, such as a search technique or financial analysis process, keep it inside the firewall by keeping it on the server.

Remember too that there is nothing to keep hackers from writing their own client object model code or altering the code you include in your web page. Always make sure that the objects within your sites are properly secured against access and modification. Just because you don't provide an interface to access or modify something, doesn't mean that an intruder using a well-known interface, such as the client object model, couldn't do so.

Creating a Client-Side Script

Now you will walk through a few examples using the client object model. You will start with simply reading an object. Then you will write to that object and verify that the change has taken effect. Finally, you will perform a CAML query against a list and display the results.

■ **Note** The source files for these exercises can be downloaded from the book's web site at www.apress.com.

Creating a Test Environment

The first step in your exploration of the client object model will be to create a test page in which you can run your scripts. For simplicity's sake, you will your scripts within a Content Editor web part. The script files will be stored in a library on the site. Here are the steps:

1. Create a new site by using the Blank Site template.

2. Open the site in SharePoint Designer 2010.

3. From the Navigation pane, select Lists and Libraries.

4. From the New group on the menu, click the Document Library drop-down and select Document Library.

5. Name the new library **Scripts** and then click OK.

6. In the Navigation pane, click All Files.

7. Click the Scripts link in the file listing.

8. From the All Files tab on the menu, click the File drop-down in the New group and select HTML.

9. For the filename, type **ListWebTitle.html**and then press Enter.

10. Open the ListWebTitle.html file in the Page Editor.

11. Replace the default HTML with the code in Listing 9-2. The contents of the script are detailed in the next section.

Listing 9-2. List Web Title Script

```
<script type="text/javascript">
    ExecuteOrDelayUntilScriptLoaded(GetProperties, "sp.js");
    var web;

    function GetProperties() {
        var ctx = new SP.ClientContext.get_current();
        web = ctx.get_web();
        ctx.load(web);

        ctx.executeQueryAsync(
            Function.createDelegate(this, this.onLoadSuccess),
            Function.createDelegate(this, this.onLoadFail));
    }
    function onLoadSuccess(sender, args) {
        document.getElementById('output').innerText =
            'Current Web Title: ' + web.get_title();
    }
    function onLoadFail(sender, args){
        document.getElementById('output').innerText =
            'Failed to get the web. Error:' + args.get_message();
    }
```

```
</script>
<h1 id="output"></h1>
```

12. Save the file in SharePoint Designer.

13. Open the site's defa he Web-Part drop-down and select Content Editor.

14. Right-click the new web part and select ult.aspx file in the Page Editor.

15. Select the web part zone labeled Left.

16. From the Insert tab of the menu, click t

17. Web Part Properties.

18. In the Content Link text box, type **scripts/ListWebTitle.html** and then click OK, as shown in Figure 9-4.

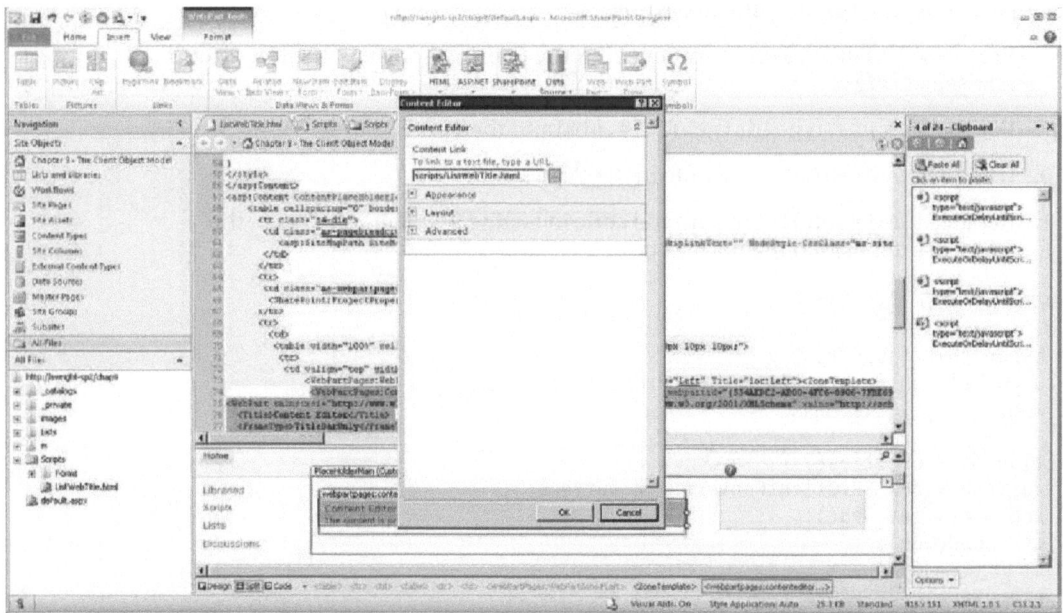

Figure 9-4. Linking a script to a Content Editor web part

19. Save the default.aspx page.

20. Press F12 to launch the page in a web browser.

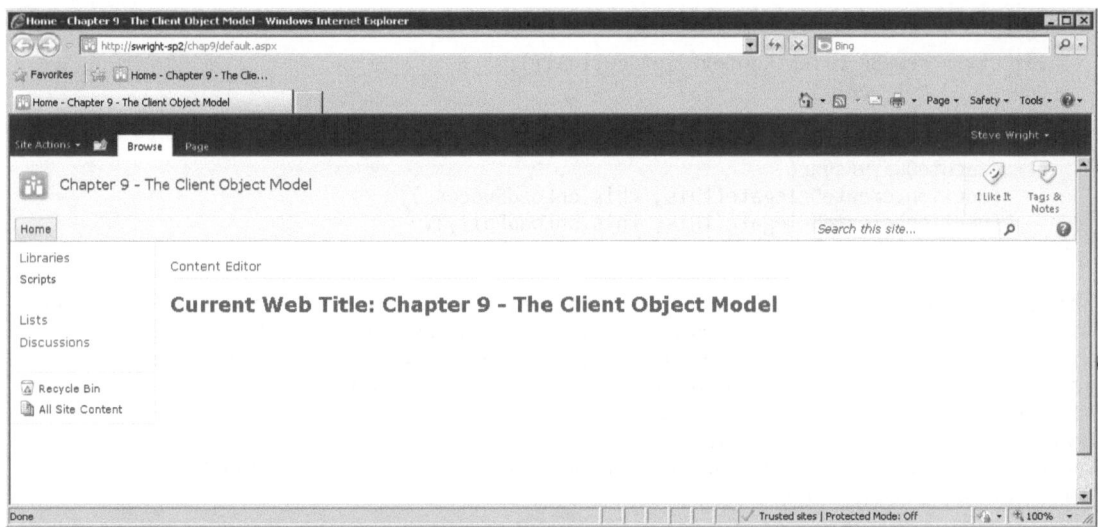

Figure 9-5. *Home page with client script*

At this point, you have a web part on the home page of your site that reads its contents from a file in the Scripts library. The script currently linked to the web part reads the current site's title property and displays it on the page, as shown in Figure 9-5.

Reading and Writing Object Properties

Loading and manipulating SharePoint objects are probably the most common operations performed when using the SharePoint server object model. It is reasonable to assume that the same will be true for the client-side models. Let's take a closer look at the code in Listing 9-2.

At the highest level, you have a `<script>` tag followed by an `<h1>` header tag. The `<h1>` tag has an ID of output so that you can write into it by using JavaScript. Starting at the top, you can see that the script starts out by loading the `sp.js` file containing the ECMAScript client object model components:

```
ExecuteOrDelayUntilScriptLoaded(GetProperties, "sp.js");
var web;
```

You use `ExecuteOrDelayUntilScriptLoaded` to ensure that your CSOM code doesn't begin running before the library is loaded. Once loading is complete, you will run the `GetProperties` method. Next, you declare a global variable that will contain a reference to the site's web object. Remember that site collections are called `SPSite` or `Site` in the object models, and sites are `SPWeb` or `Web`.

The `GetProperties` method begins by retrieving a reference to the current client context object. Because this is ECMAScript, the current context is the only one available. You cannot connect to other site collections. Next, you get a reference to the local web object and tell the context to load the properties for it. Looking at the code, you might expect the web object to be ready to use, but you would be wrong. Remember, the proxy layer batches all requests until you explicitly tell it to send them. Up to this point, you have not sent any requests or data to the server whatsoever.

```
function GetProperties() {

    var ctx = new SP.ClientContext.get_current();
    web = ctx.get_web();
    ctx.load(web);

    ctx.executeQueryAsync(
        Function.createDelegate(this, this.onLoadSuccess),
        Function.createDelegate(this, this.onLoadFail));
}
```

The last statement in this routine calls the executeQueryAsync method. This causes a request to be sent to the server containing all outstanding requests. In this case, that consists of a request to load the current web site's property values into the object referenced by the web global variable. When the response is received, the proxy layer will populate the objects received and then call either onLoadSuccess, if the call succeeded, or onLoadFail, if it failed.

Both of the onLoad routines perform similar actions. They write a message into the <h1> tag for display on the web page. In the case of success, the object reference saved in the global web variable is used to retrieve the web site's title:

```
function onLoadSuccess(sender, args) {
    document.getElementById('output').innerText =
        'Current Web Title: ' + web.get_title();
}
function onLoadFail(sender, args){
    document.getElementById('output').innerText =
        'Failed to get the web. Error:' + args.get_message();
}
```

■ **Note** If this is the only thing you are going to do with the web object, this code is wasteful. The web object contains many properties that will also be returned by this code, which wastes bandwidth. This example would work just as well if you used the following statement to load the web object:

ctx.Load(web, 'Title'); // Load only the "Title" property

Now that you have seen how to read an object, let's look at updating one. In this example, you will add code to the script that will read the web's title, allow you to update it, and then reread it to ensure that it worked:.

1. Create a second HTML file in the Scripts library called **UpdateWebTitle.html**.

2. Replace the file's contents with Listing 9-3.

3. Edit the default.aspx page and replace the ListWebTitle.html reference with UpdateWebTitle.html.

4. Save both files.

Listing 9-3. Update Web Title Script

```
<script type="text/javascript">
    ExecuteOrDelayUntilScriptLoaded(GetProperties, "sp.js");
    var web;

    function GetProperties() {
        var ctx = new SP.ClientContext.get_current();
        web = ctx.get_web();
        ctx.load(web, 'Title');

        ctx.executeQueryAsync(
            Function.createDelegate(this, this.onLoadSuccess),
            Function.createDelegate(this, this.onLoadFail));
    }
    function onLoadSuccess(sender, args) {
        document.getElementById('output').innerText =
            'Current Web Title: ' + web.get_title();
        document.getElementById('txtTitle').value = web.get_title();
    }
    function onLoadFail(sender, args) {
      document.getElementById('output').innerText =

            'Failed to get the web. Error:' + args.get_message();
    }

    function UpdateTitle() {
        var ctx = new SP.ClientContext.get_current();
        web = ctx.get_web();
        web.set_title(document.getElementById('txtTitle').value);
        web.update();

        ctx.executeQueryAsync(
            Function.createDelegate(this, this.onUpdateSucceed),
            Function.createDelegate(this, this.onUpdateFail));
    }
    function onUpdateSucceed(sender, args) {
        alert('The title was updated, but you have to refresh the page to see it in the site
header.');
        GetProperties();
    }
    function onUpdateFail(sender, args) {
        alert('Unable to update the title. Error: ' + args.get_message());
    }
</script>
<h1 id="output"></h1>
<p>
New Site Title:
<input type="text" id="txtTitle" value="" size="50" />
</p>
<p>
<input name="btnUpdate" type="button" value="Update Title"
```

```
        onclick="javascript:UpdateTitle();" />
</p>
```

5. Press F12 to launch the default.aspx page in your web browser.

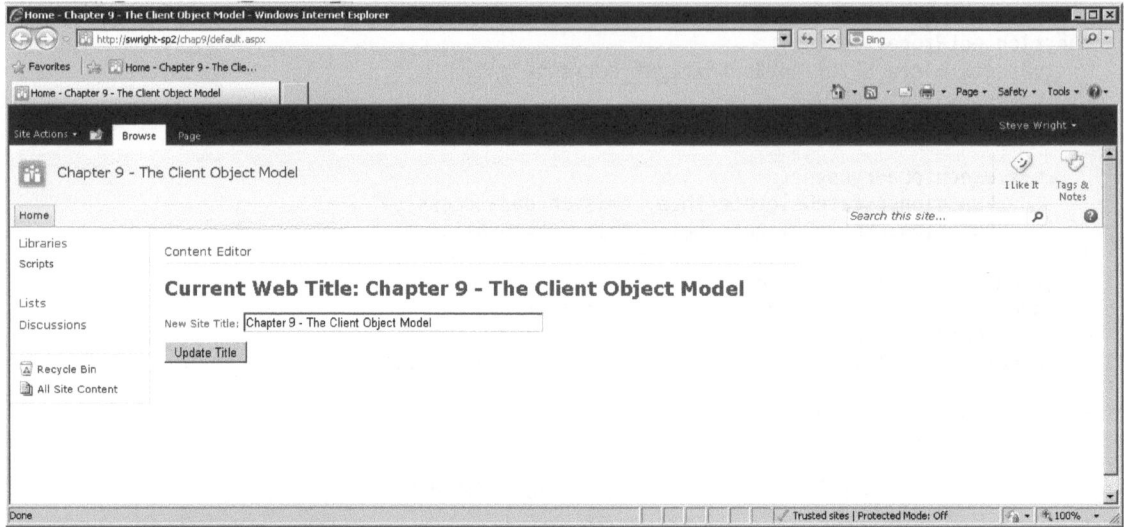

Figure 9-6. Home page with title

6. Type a new title for the web site into the text box, as shown in Figure 9-6.

7. Click the Update Title button. An alert dialog box displays, as shown in Figure 9-7.

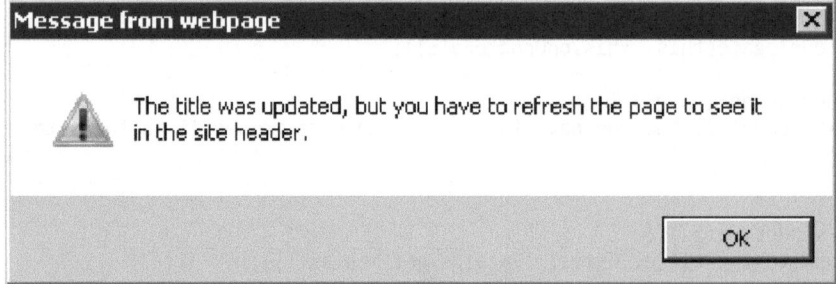

Figure 9-7. Alert dialog box

8. Click OK.

9. Note that the site title at the top of the page no longer matches the one in the <h1> tag. This is because the title at the top of the page is updated only when the full page is retrieved from the server.

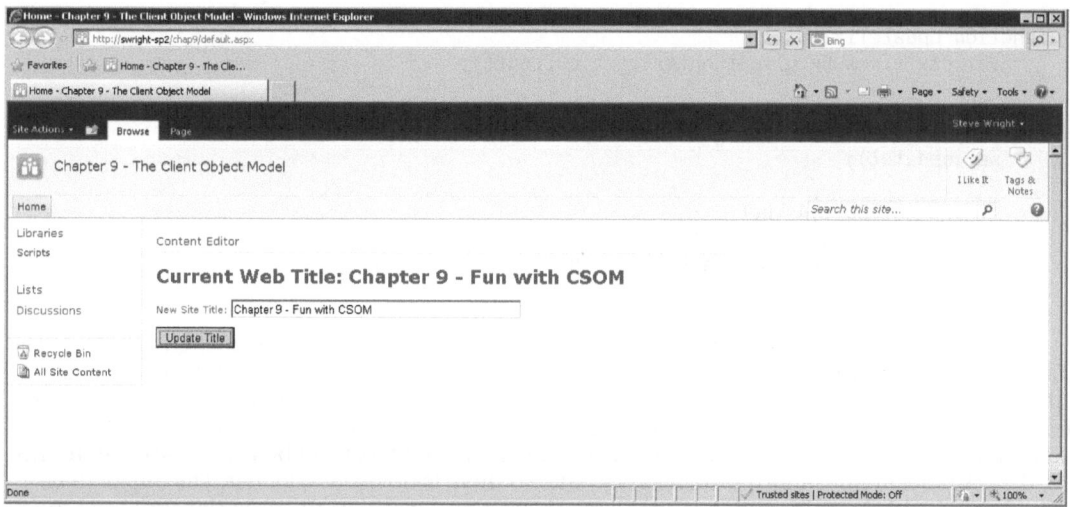

Figure 9-8. home page with new title (not refreshed)

10. Click the Refresh button on your web browser.

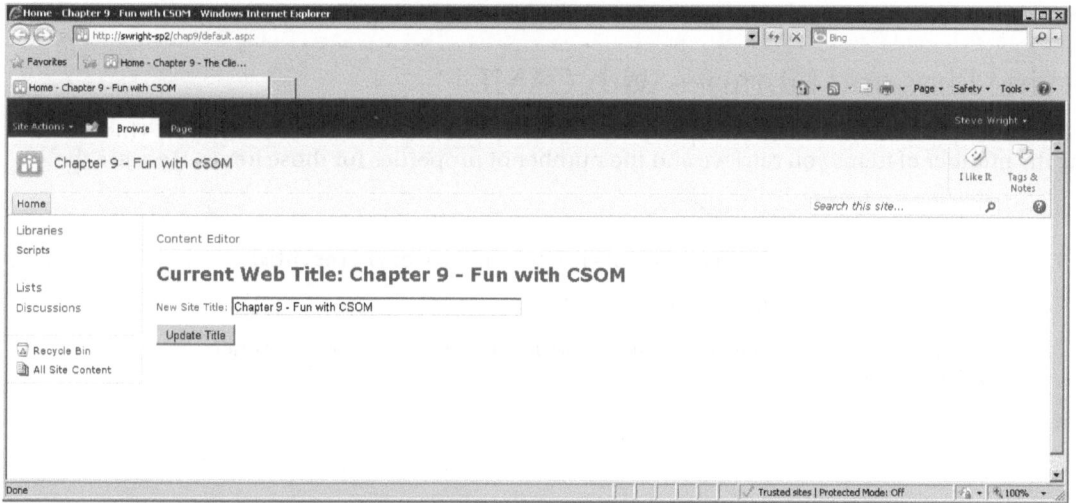

Figure 9-9. Home page with title (refreshed)

The new elements in this page are a text box, an input button, and some additional script. When the page loads, the title is loaded into the text box. The user can then update the title and click the Update Title button. This executes the UpdateTitle method:

```
function UpdateTitle() {
    var ctx = new SP.ClientContext.get_current();

    web = ctx.get_web();
    web.set_title(document.getElementById('txtTitle').value);
    web.update();

    ctx.executeQueryAsync(
        Function.createDelegate(this, this.onUpdateSucceed),
        Function.createDelegate(this, this.onUpdateFail));
}
```

At first glance, this method looks similar to the GetProperties method you looked at before. The difference is that you are setting the title instead of loading it. Take a close look at the code. You get the context and web objects and then you set the title *without loading the web object from the server first.* This is an important difference between loading and updating objects. Because of the way the CSOM handles the identity of objects, it is not always necessary to load an object before updating it. In this case, the web object represents the current web site, so there is no need to load it. The object to be updated has already been identified. The call to web.Update() instructs the proxy layer to send the changes to the web object to the server. Again, the request batch is sent only when you call executeQueryAsync.

If you needed to, you could create, update, and delete several objects before sending anything to the server. This makes the passing of requests and responses very efficient because the overhead of the call is shared among multiple requests.

Querying Lists and Libraries with CAML

In our final example, you will see how to query the SharePoint content database efficiently. This includes limiting the number of items you retrieve and the number of properties for those items. Here are the steps:

1. Create another HTML file in the Scripts library called **QueryFiles.html**.

2. Replace the file's contents with Listing 9-4.

3. Edit the default.aspx page and replace the UpdateWebTitle.html reference with QueryFiles.html.

4. Save both files.

Listing 9-4. Query Files Script

```javascript
<script type="text/javascript">

ExecuteOrDelayUntilScriptLoaded(LoadPages, "sp.js");

var ctx;
var web;
var list;
var itemCollection;

function LoadPages()
{
    ctx = new SP.ClientContext.get_current();

    web = ctx.get_web();
    ctx.load(web);

    list = web.get_lists().getByTitle("Scripts");
    ctx.load(list);

    var qry = new SP.CamlQuery();

    qry .set_viewXml(
        "<View>"
        + "<ViewFields><FieldRef Name='ID' /><FieldRef Name='FileLeafRef' /><FieldRef
Name='Modified' /></ViewFields>"
        + "<RowLimit>50</RowLimit>"
        + "</View>");
    itemCollection = list.getItems(qry);
    ctx.load(itemCollection);

    ctx.executeQueryAsync(
        Function.createDelegate(this, this.onQuerySuccess),
        Function.createDelegate(this, this.onQueryFailed));
}

function onQuerySuccess(sender, args)
{
    var s = '';

    var itemEnumerator = itemCollection .getEnumerator();
    while (itemEnumerator .moveNext())
    {
        var item = itemEnumerator .get_current();

        s = s + item.get_item('FileLeafRef')
                + ' modified on ' + item.get_item('Modified') + "<br />";
    }
```

```
        document.getElementById('output').innerHTML = s;
}

function onQueryFailed(sender, args)
{
        alert('Query failed.');
}
</script>
<div id="output"></div>
<p>
<input name="cmdRefresh" type="button" value="Refresh" onclick="javascript:LoadPages();"/>

</p>
```

5.   Press F12 to launch the default.aspx page in your web browser (see Figure
      9-10).

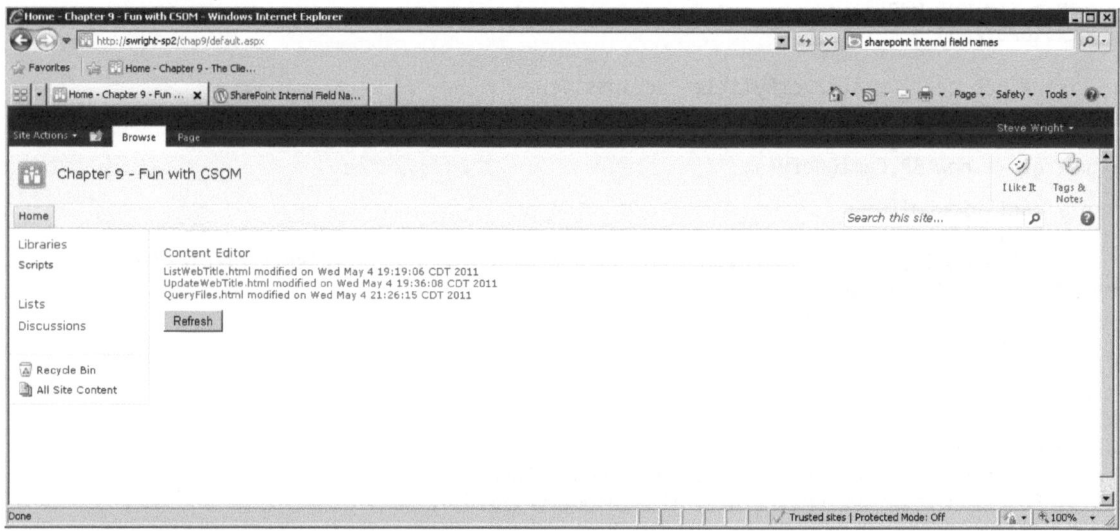

Figure 9-10. Home page with query results

When this script runs, the LoadPages method creates a CamlQuery object that defines the data that you want to retrieve. This is represented by a CAML view definition. In this case, you specify that you want only the ID, FileLeafRef, and Modified fields for up to 50 items. You then use the query to retrieve items from the Scripts document library.

```
        var qry = new SP.CamlQuery();
        qry .set_viewXml(
            "<View>"
            + "<ViewFields><FieldRef Name='ID' /><FieldRef Name='FileLeafRef' /><FieldRef
Name='Modified' /></ViewFields>"
            + "<RowLimit>50</RowLimit>"
            + "</View>");
```

```
itemCollection = list.getItems(qry);

ctx.load(itemCollection);
```

■ **Warning** You may have noticed that one of the fields listed in this query is called `FileLeafRef`. Unfortunately, SharePoint fields have two different names: display names and internal names. The display name for a field is the one you see on your web site. The internal field name is used…well…internally. CAML uses internal field names in its queries. `FileLeafRef` is the internal name for the Name column in a document library. There is no rhyme or reason to the internal names in many cases. For example, the `Modified` field is called Editor. The Web provides several lists of mappings from display to internal names. Here is one that I use:

```
http://sharepointmalarkey.wordpress.com/2008/08/21/sharepoint-internal-field-names
```

When the query completes, the data returned is placed into a collection of objects that can be enumerated and used to access the data returned, as shown here:

```
var itemEnumerator = itemCollection.getEnumerator();
while (itemEnumerator.moveNext())
{
    var item = itemEnumerator.get_current();

    s = s + item.get_item('FileLeafRef')
          + ' modified on ' + item.get_item('Modified') + "<br />";
}
```

CAML queries in SharePoint can do more than just return a certain number of items. They can include a <query> tag that allows the criteria for filtering items to be extensive. A CAML query can also be used to sort the returned items. This gives CAML a level of flexibility similar to that seen in SQL.

Summary

In this chapter, you have

- Explored the various client-side object models exposed by the SharePoint `Client.svc` service

- Discussed the best practices for writing ECMAScript client-side code that leverages the client object model

- Considered why running code on the client may be preferable to running it on the server in some cases

- Examined the client object model code for loading, updating, and querying SharePoint objects

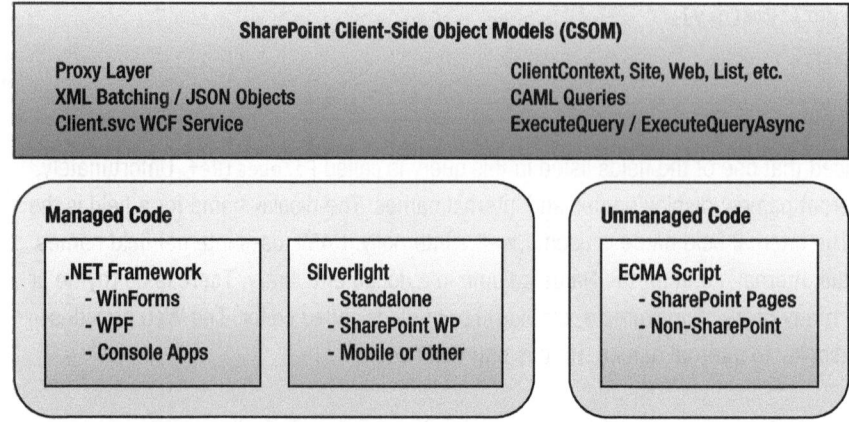

Figure 9-11. SharePoint client object model concepts

PART III

■ ■ ■

Integrating SharePoint

CHAPTER 10

Consuming External Data

SharePoint is very good at enabling you to store data and present it on the Web, but most organizations have data in many different areas and systems that they would like to present in a web format. In previous chapters, you learned how to create data sources of internal data stores. In this chapter, you will learn how to connect to external sources of data and present that data on your SharePoint site. This chapter also covers SharePoint's new Business Connectivity Services, which makes it easier to surface your line-of-business data on your SharePoint site.

You will learn about the following topics in this chapter:

- Working with the different data sources that connect to external data

- Connecting to external data sources

- Using Business Connectivity Services

- Creating an external content type

- Interacting with external data by using external lists

- Incorporating external columns in standard SharePoint lists

- Leveraging external content in Microsoft Office applications

---

■ **Note** This chapter covers accessing stored data from an external source. To complete the exercises using Business Connectivity Services (BCS), you will need to download and install the AdventureWorksLT2008R2 sample database provided by Microsoft and found at http://sqlserversamples.codeplex.com/.

Why External Data?

As you read in Chapter 5, SharePoint is and has been a great platform to store and then present data in a web-based format. The challenge for most organizations is that they have a lot of data stored in other line-of-business (LOB) systems such as SAP, Microsoft Dynamics, and Oracle's Siebel and PeopleSoft products. Because SharePoint made it so simple to create web interfaces, users began to want to integrate and display their LOB data on the SharePoint platform.

While Chapter 5 dealt with surfacing data by using data sources of data in internal lists, this chapter covers how to consume and display data from external sources. SharePoint provides two basic ways of accessing external data: the data source interface and the Business Connectivity Services (BCS) interface. Both ways can help you build robust web applications in SharePoint—and with SharePoint Designer, you can accomplish this without writing code.

External Data Sources

In Chapter 5, you were introduced to the various data sources available to you via the Data Source menu on the Ribbon. Many times, data from external sources are delivered dynamically via the Web. SharePoint Designer provides for three types of external data sources that you can use in your site: an XML file connection, REST services, and SOAP services.

XML

Numerous web sites and services produce XML data to be used by other applications. SharePoint Designer provides an easy way to create a data source with the URL of the XML file. You can retrieve the XML anonymously or you can provide login credentials.

■ **Note** It is important to remember that the XML file does not have to be static. It can change over time, which provides great advantages in being able to provide fresh content to your site. Also, the URL does not have to end in .xml. SharePoint is concerned only that the content of the URL contains valid XML.

EXERCISE 10-1. CREATE AND USE AN EXTERNAL XML DATA SOURCE

Perhaps the most popular type of XML data are RSS feeds. Every SharePoint site can produce an RSS feed of its list data. Other sites also produce RSS feeds that you can leverage to provide content for your site. In this exercise, you will create an XML data source from an external RSS feed and display it on a web part page:

1. Open a SharePoint site in SharePoint Designer.

2. From the Navigation pane, click Data Sources.

3. From the Ribbon, click XML File Connection.

4. Type **http://research.microsoft.com/rss/news.xml** in the Location box of the Source tab.

5. Click the General tab.

6. Type **Microsoft Research News** in the Name text box and then click OK to save. You now have a new XML data source called Microsoft Research News.

7. In the Navigation pane, click Site Pages.

8. From the Ribbon, click the Pages menu and then click Web Part Page to create a new web part page.

9. Name the file **XMLExample.aspx**.

10. Click the filename and then click Edit File to open the new web part page in Edit mode.

11. Make sure that you are in Design mode and click in the main web part zone.

12. On Ribbon's Insert tab, click Data View and then select Empty Data View.

13. In the web part zone, click the Click Here to Select a Data Source link.

14. Find the newly created Microsoft Research News data source, select it, and then click OK.

15. In the data source details pane, you will see two folders, one called channel and the other called item.

16. Ctrl+click the Title and Description fields under the channel folder and drag them to the web part zone.

17. Ctrl+click on the description, link, and pubDate fields under the item folder and drag them to the web part zone. Your page should look something like Figure 10-1.

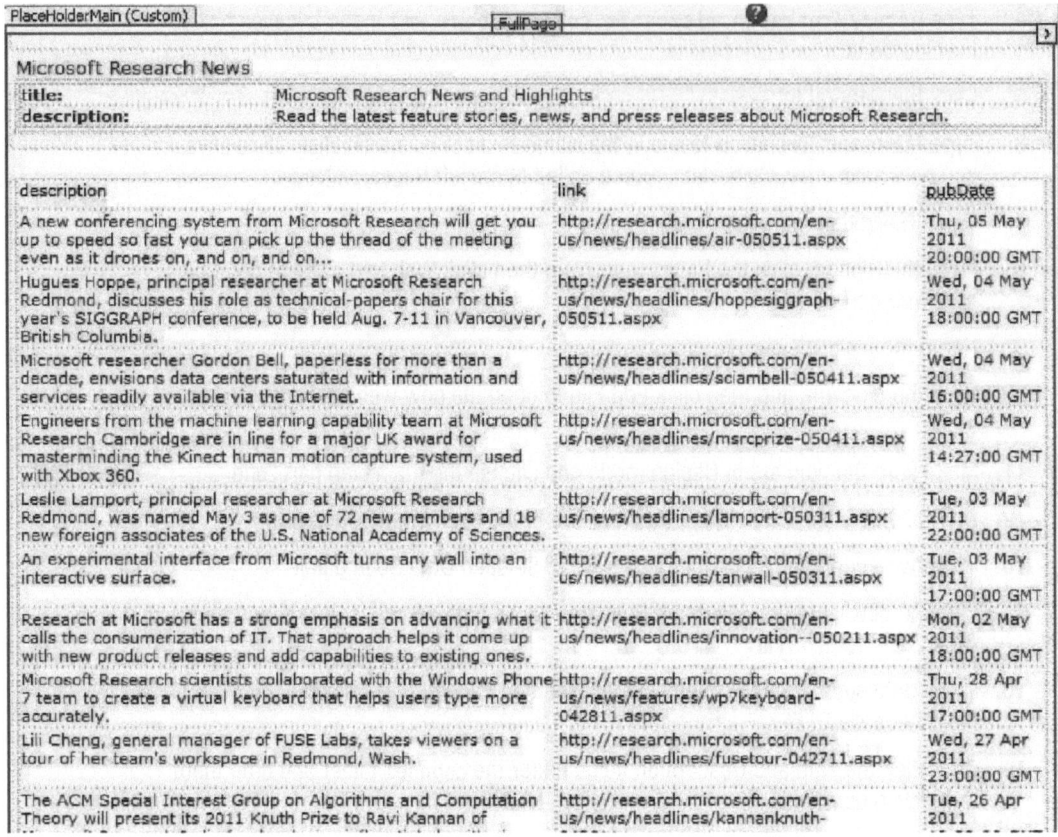

Figure 10-1. XMLExample.aspx

18. Click the title and description fields at the top of the web part and fix the capitalization to *Title* and *Description*, respectively.

19. Click the lower Data View web part. In the Tag Properties pane (usually on the right-hand side of SharePoint Designer), locate the Appearance section and change the chrome type to None.

20. With the web part still highlighted, click Add/Remove Columns on the Ribbon menu.

21. When the dialog box opens, change the order of the fields to link, description, pubDate and then click OK to save your changes.

22. On the header row of the DataView, rename the link field to **Title**, change description to **Description**, and change pubDate to **Publication Date**, as illustrated in Figure 10-2. You place the fields into Edit mode by clicking each field name.

Title	Description	Publication Date
http://research.microsoft.com/en-us/news/headlines/air-050511.aspx	A new conferencing system from Microsoft Research will get you up to speed so fast you can pick up the thread of the	Thu, 05 May 2011 20:00:00 GMT

Figure 10-2. Editing headers

23. Click a link in the first row of the first column and open the Common xsl:value-of-Tasks menu (see Figure 10-3). From the Format As drop-down list, select Hyperlink. When the dialog asks you to confirm, click Yes.

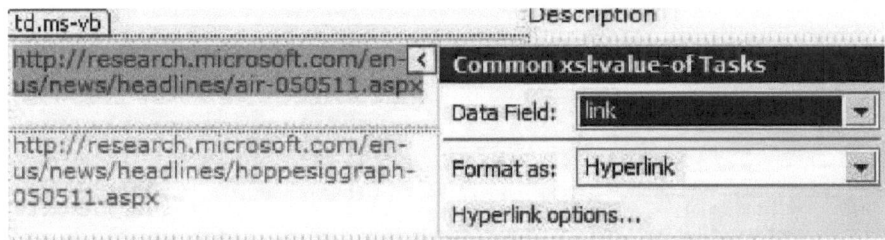

Figure 10-3. Common xsl:value-of-Tasks menu

24. In the Edit Hyperlink dialog box, change the Text to Display text box entry from {link} to **{title}**, as shown in Figure 10-4. Click OK to save your changes.

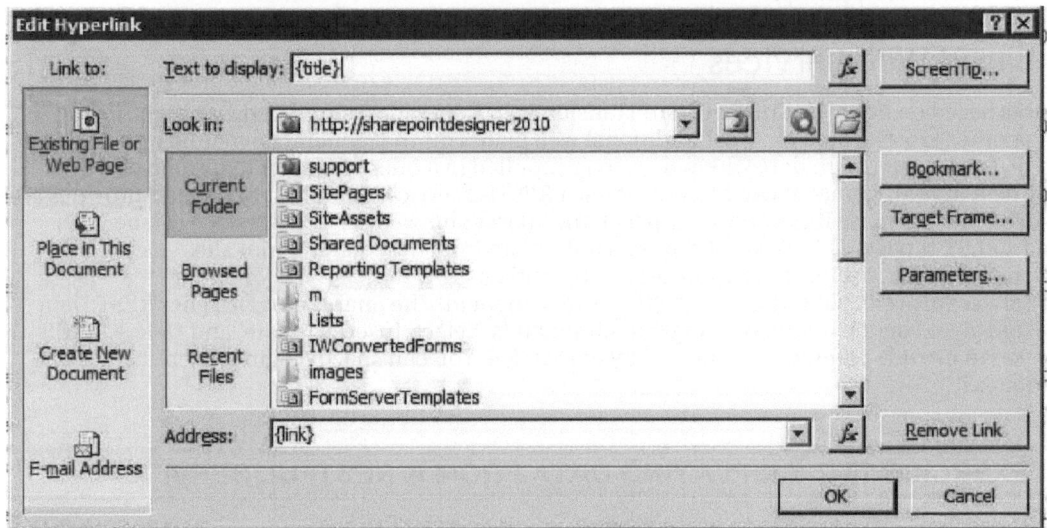

Figure 10-4. Edit Hyperlink properties

25. Press Ctrl+S to save your changes, and click Preview in Browser from the Home tab on the Ribbon. Your page should look like the Figure 10-5.

Microsoft Research News

| Title: | Microsoft Research News and Highlights |
| Description: | Read the latest feature stories, news, and press releases about Microsoft Research. |

Title	Description	Publication Date
If You Doze During a Meeting, Microsoft's Got Your Back	A new conferencing system from Microsoft Research will get you up to speed so fast you can pick up the thread of the meeting even as it drones on, and on, and on...	Thu, 05 May 2011 20:00:00 GMT
Interview: SIGGRAPH Technical Papers Chair Hugues Hoppe	Hugues Hoppe, principal researcher at Microsoft Research Redmond, discusses his role as technical-papers chair for this year's SIGGRAPH conference, to be held Aug. 7-11 in Vancouver, British Columbia.	Wed, 04 May 2011 18:00:00 GMT
Online 24/7: 'Life Logging' Pioneer Clarifies the Future of Cloud Computing	Microsoft researcher Gordon Bell, paperless for more than a decade, envisions data centers saturated with information and services readily available via the Internet.	Wed, 04 May 2011 16:00:00 GMT
Microsoft Cambridge Kinects to Further Glory	Engineers from the machine learning capability team at Microsoft Research Cambridge are in line for a major UK award for masterminding the Kinect human motion capture system, used with Xbox 360.	Wed, 04 May 2011 14:27:00 GMT
Lamport Elected as Member of the U.S. National Academy of Sciences	Leslie Lamport, principal researcher at Microsoft Research Redmond, was named May 3 as one of 72 new members and 18 new foreign associates of the U.S. National Academy of Sciences.	Tue, 03 May 2011 22:00:00 GMT
Talking to the Wall	An experimental interface from Microsoft turns any wall into an interactive surface.	Tue, 03 May 2011 17:00:00 GMT
At Microsoft, Future Growth Rides on Research, Innovation	Research at Microsoft has a strong emphasis on advancing what it calls the consumerization of IT. That approach helps it come up with new product releases and add capabilities to existing ones.	Mon, 02 May 2011 18:00:00 GMT
Windows Phone 7: A Better Keyboard	Microsoft Research scientists collaborated with the Windows Phone 7 team to create a virtual keyboard that helps users type more accurately.	Thu, 28 Apr 2011 17:00:00 GMT
Video: FUSE Labs with Lili Cheng	Lili Cheng, general manager of FUSE Labs, takes viewers on a tour of her team's workspace in Redmond, Wash.	Wed, 27 Apr 2011 23:00:00 GMT
Microsoft Researcher to Receive ACM SIGACT Knuth Prize	The ACM Special Interest Group on Algorithms and Computation Theory will present its 2011 Knuth Prize to Ravi Kannan of Microsoft Research India for developing influential algorithmic techniques aimed at solving long-standing computational problems.	Tue, 26 Apr 2011 19:28:00 GMT

1 - 10 ▶

Figure 10-5. Final XMLExample.aspx

REST-Based Web Services

Web-services based on Representational State Transfer (REST) provide a simplified way of retrieving data from another external system. Most traditional web platforms that generate dynamic web pages, such as PHP or ASP, can return data with parameters supplied in a query string. If that same platform returns the data in XML format, it can be considered a RESTful service. SharePoint Designer provides an interface to connect to these REST services. In fact, the SharePoint web service interface can be considered a REST service. This makes it easy to display data from other SharePoint sites, even if they aren't in your farm. You just need the appropriate credentials.

REST services also can allow data to be written back to them. The SharePoint Designer REST Data Source Wizard gives you the option of using four commands: Select, Insert, Update, and Delete. It will also allow you to provide parameters expected by the service. You can specify login credentials if the service requires it.

EXERCISE 10-2. DISPLAYING DATA FROM A RESTFUL SERVICE

In this exercise, you will create a data source based on a RESTful service and display the data on a web part page.

1.   Open a SharePoint site in SharePoint Designer.

2.   In the Navigation pane, click the Data Sources menu.

3. From the Ribbon's Data Sources menu, click REST Service Connection.

4. When the Connection Wizard opens, make sure you are on the Source tab and then configure the data source by using the following options, shown in Figure 10-6:

   a. HTTP Method: HTTP Get

   b. Command: Select

   c. Connection Info:
      `http://api.twitter.com/1/statuses/user_timeline.xml`

5. Add the following parameter by clicking the Add button:

   d. Name: screen_name

   e. Value: ApressBooks

   f. Click OK to save the parameter. (Note that the wizard will add your parameters to the query string so you don't have to.)

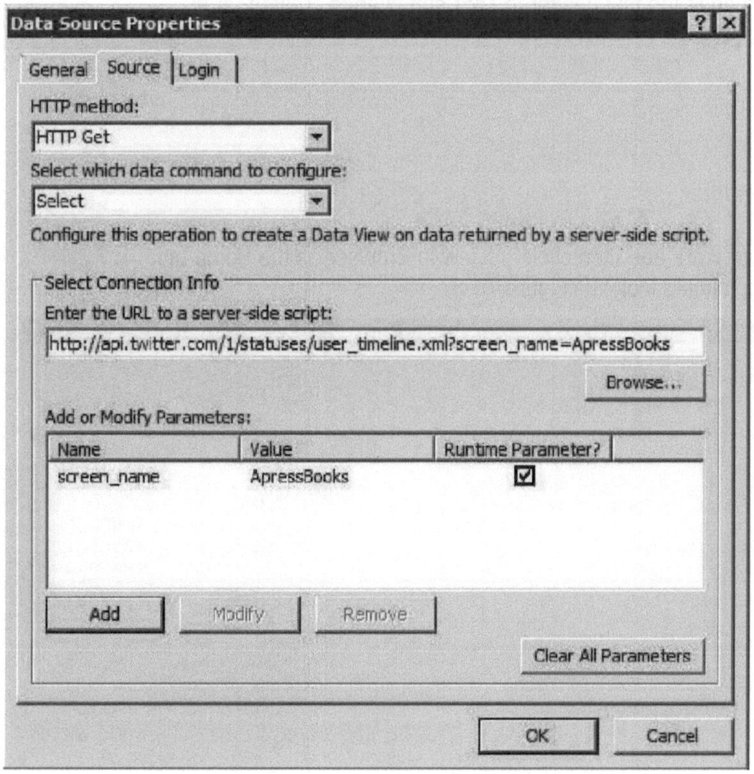

Figure 10-6. REST service properties

6. Click the General tab.

7. Type **Apress Books Twitter Status** for the name and click OK to save your data source.

8. In the Navigation pane, click Site Pages and create a new web part page called **RESTExample.aspx**.

9. Click the filename and click Edit File again to put the page in Edit mode.

10. Ensure you are in Design mode and click the main web part zone.

11. From the Ribbon's Insert menu, click Data View and select Empty Data View.

12. Click the data view link to select a data source.

13. Select Apress Books Twitter Status from the Data Sources Picker. Click OK.

14. In the Data Source Details pane, Ctrl+click *text* and *created_at* and drag them into the web part zone.

15. Edit the headings and change the text header to **Text** and change created_at to **Date**, as shown in Figure 10-7.

Figure 10-7. Editing headings in Data view

16. Press Ctrl+S to save your work and then click Preview in Browser on the Home tab of the Ribbon. Your page should look like Figure 10-8.

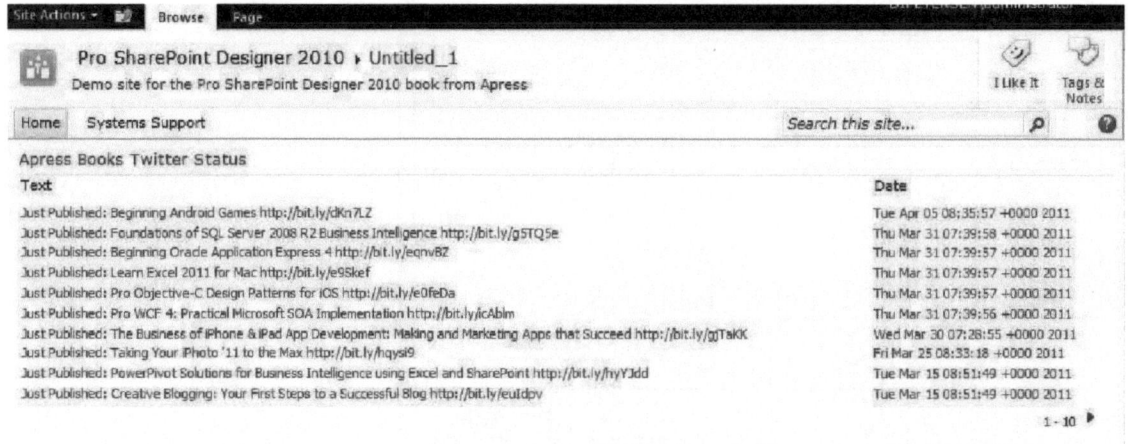

Figure 10-8. RESTExample.aspx

SOAP-Based Web Services

SOAP-based web services are a widely accepted standard web service, and they can provide a lot more functionality than REST services. REST services are limited to four commands, but SOAP-based services specify all of the operations that can be called by the client application in a service description file. The SOAP Connection Wizard provides the ability to create connections and to call all of the different operations provided by the service.

To find out what methods are available to a calling application, SOAP-based services provide a Web Services Description Language (WSDL) definition file that describes how to use the web service.

EXERCISE 10-3. CONNECT TO A SOAP-BASED SERVICE AND DISPLAY THE RESULTS ON A WEB PART PAGE

In this next exercise, you will connect to a SharePoint-provided SOAP web service. Because the configuration of the SOAP-based service is slightly more complicated than the other data sources, this exercise describes in detail the different sections of the wizard.

1. In the Navigation pane, click Data Sources. From the Ribbon, click the SOAP Service Connection menu item. The Data Source Properties dialog box opens with the following SOAP-specific configuration options:

    a. *Service Description Location:* This is the URL to the service description (WSDL) file. You specify this by adding a **?WSDL** to the end of the service URL. You can view the WSDL file by pasting the same URL in a browser and viewing the page that is returned. Type **http://[SharePoint Site URL]/_vti_bin/lists.asmx?wsdl** (where SharePoint Site URL is the URL to your SharePoint site). Click Connect Now so SharePoint Designer can retrieve the description file.

    b. *Data Command:* Like a REST service connection, this box identifies the command that your data source is going to be configured to run. If the web service supports all of the commands, a separate data source will have to be configured for each command. Most of the time, you would use only Select.

    c. *Port:* If the web service supports multiple interfaces, they will be listed here. The default port will be selected.

    d. *Operation:* When the Connect Now button is clicked, the wizard retrieves the WSDL file, which defines all of the operations that can be performed on the web service. If you click the drop-down list and look at the Lists service, you can see that some operations have required parameters and some don't. For this exercise, select GetListCollection from the drop-down menu.

    e. *Parameters:* As mentioned previously, if the operation selected in the previous step requires parameters, those will be listed. You can modify the values of the parameters. Parameters with an asterisk (*) are required. For this exercise, there are no parameters.

2. The wizard has two other tabs that are the same as the other data sources. The Login tab can be used to set default login credentials. For this exercise, you will use the default credentials. The General tab is used to provide a description of the data source configuration. Click the General tab and type **Site List Collection** for the name and click OK to save your new data source.

3. As you did in the previous two exercises, create a new web part page, this time named **SOAPExample.aspx**, and open it in Edit mode.

4. Click in the web part zone, and then from the Ribbon, click Data View and find the newly created Site List Collection data source.

5. Your page should now be filled with a listing of all of the lists contained in your site. Click Add/Remove Columns from the Ribbon menu.

6. Remove all columns except the DefaultViewUrl column and click OK.

7. Click the first list item, select Hyperlink, and then confirm Yes.

8. In the Edit Hyperlink dialog box, change the Text to Display text box to **{@Title}**, as shown in Figure 10-9. Then click OK.

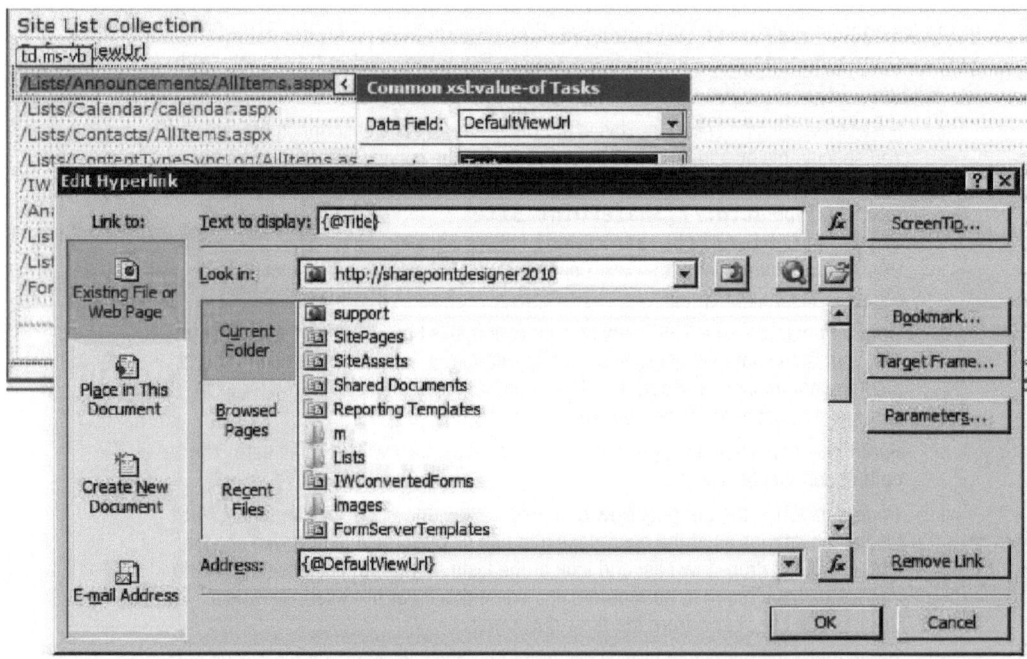

Figure 10-9. DefaultViewUrl hyperlink properties

9. Press Ctrl+S to save your changes and then click Preview in Browser from the Home tab. You should see a page displaying a list of all of the SharePoint lists in your site. Clicking the links should take you to the default view of that list.

Business Connectivity Services (BCS)

Beginning with the Enterprise CAL of Portal Server 2003, Microsoft introduced a capability to surface external data in SharePoint. That was the first release of the Business Data Catalog (BDC), and not only was it was very code intensive, it allowed only read access to the data. In Microsoft Office SharePoint Server (MOSS) 2007, the BDC was greatly improved, but it was still code intensive and required an Enterprise CAL to use it. One big improvement was the ability to not only read LOB systems but to write back to those systems, albeit at a very primitive level that did not meet industry standards. In SharePoint 2010, Microsoft builds on the capabilities of the BDC with Business Connectivity Services (BCS). BCS allows simple, read/write access to external data with even the base, Microsoft Foundation, platform.

Common BCS Terminology

When discussing BCS, here are some common terms to be familiar with:

- *Business Connectivity Services (BCS)* describes a broad range of technologies that are used to bring data from external systems (such as SAP, Oracle, Siebel, and PeopleSoft) to SharePoint 2010 and Office 2010.

- *Business Data Connectivity (BDC)* is the new term used instead of the Business Data Catalog used in Microsoft Office SharePoint Server 2007. Business Data Connectivity refers to the connectivity runtime for both SharePoint Server and the Office clients.

- *External content type (ECT)* is a very important concept to understand with the BCS. It is the building block of any BCS solution. The ECT is SharePoint's representation of the external data entity, such as sales, orders, or customers. It is a reusable collection of metadata that describes the connection information, data definitions, and behaviors of the data. All ECTs are stored in a dedicated database called the Business Data Connectivity Service database.

- *External List* is a new list template in SharePoint 2010. This provides the same look and feel as regular SharePoint lists to external systems, including support for CRUD operations.

- *External data column* is a column that is bound to an external system and can be added to an existing list or document library.

- *External data web parts* are available only in the Enterprise version of SharePoint. The five web parts (Item, List, Related List, Actions, and Item Builder) can be added to any web part page to display external data.

Features by Version

SharePoint 2010 includes a majority of the BCS functionality in its base, Microsoft Foundation version. This is important because previous versions of SharePoint restricted this functionality to only the Enterprise version. Table 10-1 illustrates the differences in the versions of SharePoint 2010.

Table 10-1. *BCS Features by Version*

BCS Feature	SharePoint Foundation	SharePoint Standard	SharePoint Enterprise
External data column	X	X	X
External lists	X	X	X
Connectors (ADO, WCF, .NET)	X	X	X
Central Admin BDC admin pages	X	X	X
BDC multitenant	X	X	X
BDC Admin object model	X	X	X
Runtime object model	X	X	X
Secure store		X	X
BDC web parts			X
Profile pages			X
Packaging			X
Rich client extensions			X
InfoPath forms			X

SharePoint Designer Support for BCS

SharePoint Designer 2010 provides robust support for working with BCS. You can accomplish almost all BCS operations in SharePoint Designer 2010 except create custom connectors or WCF services, which require Visual Studio 2010. Through the rest of this chapter, you will learn the different ways to work with BCS in SharePoint Designer, building on the knowledge of the previous sections. Exercises along the way will reinforce each topic.

■ **Note** The following exercises utilize connections to the AdventureWorksLT2008R2 database, as explained at the beginning of this chapter. If you do not have access to the database, you will not be able to complete the exercises in the rest of this chapter.

Creating External Content Types

As previously mentioned, the main building block for BCS is the *external content type*. Any solution that you build to display external data requires that you define the external content type.

To create an external content type, you need to complete a few steps. Fortunately, there is a wizard to guide you.

EXERCISE 10-4. CONNECT TO AN EXTERNAL SYSTEM

To create a new external content type, click the External Content Types link in the Navigation pane and then click External Content Type from the Ribbon. You will be shown a page that requires you to configure your new external content type. You can give it a name by clicking the Name hyperlink. The display name will change automatically. You can change the display name if you don't want it the same as the external content type name.

After you have named it, the next step is to determine what Office Item Type it will be. The selector defaults to Generic List, but you can choose Appointment, Contact, Task, or Post if they are closer to the type of content you will be connecting to. Offline Sync is enabled by default. This setting allows mobile devices to disconnect from the network and still perform operations on the list and then sync back up when they are connected. If you are performing only read operations, this setting doesn't apply.

The next setting is selecting the external system you will be connecting to. When you click the hyperlink, the Operation Designer window opens. When you click the Add Connection button, you are presented with three options, as shown in Figure 10-10:

- .Net Type
- SQL Server
- WCF Service

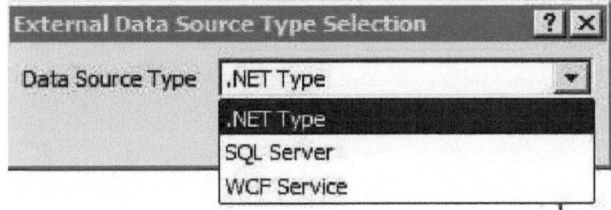

Figure 10-10. External data source type selector

Even though the most common choice is SQL Server, let's take a closer look at how to create a connection to each of these systems.

.NET Type

The .NET Type is a custom connector that has to be developed in Visual Studio. If you or someone in your organization has already developed a .NET connector in Visual Studio, SharePoint Designer 2010 will allow you to make a connection to that interface.

If you choose .NET Type, you will be presented with the dialog box shown in Figure 10-11.

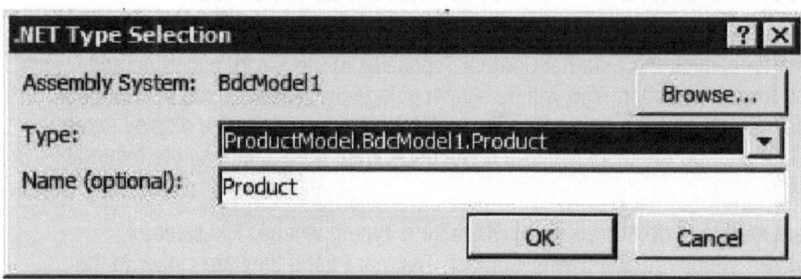

Figure 10-11. .NET type selector

To configure a connection to a .NET type, you select the .NET assembly from those that have already been deployed. You will then see all of the operations that the custom connector offers. If you do not specify a name, it will use the assembly name. When you save your connection, you will be shown all of the methods that are available to you (see Figure 10-12).

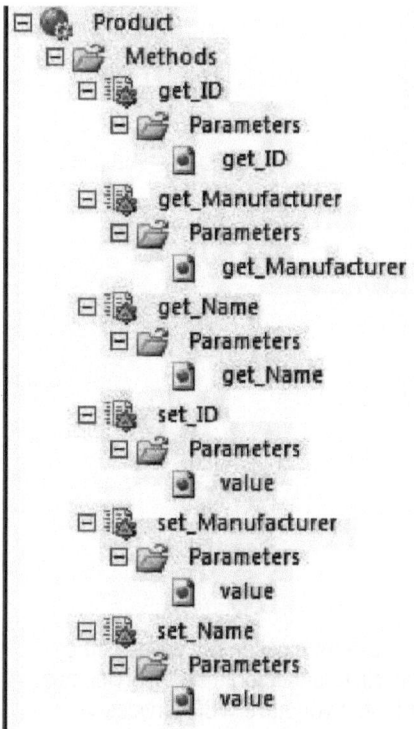

Figure 10-12. .NET connector methods

SQL Server

When you select SQL Server, you define the database server name, the database name, and the credentials you will use to connect to the database (see Figure 10-13). The default option is to use the user's identity. This option is important because it ensures that the user of your SharePoint site will be able to view only the data that user has access to. You can also use credentials stored in the secure store if you are using the Standard or Enterprise version of SharePoint. The *secure store* is a special location in Central Administration that stores usernames and passwords for accessing external systems through SharePoint. Finally, if you don't specify a name, the connection wizard will use the database name as a reference.

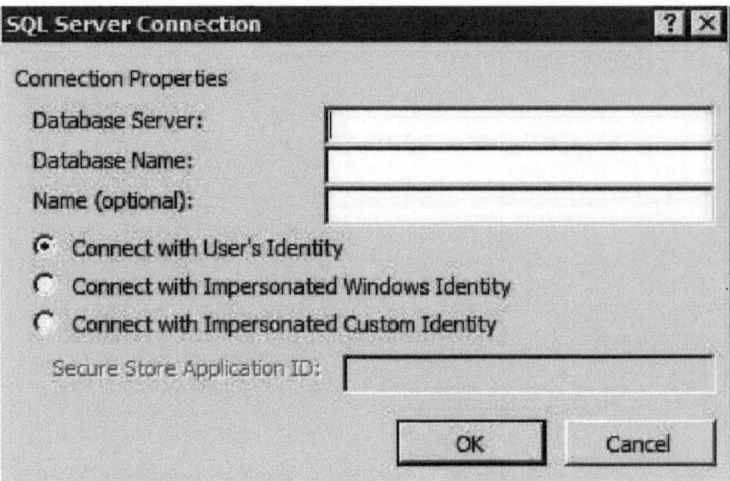

Figure 10-13. SQL Server Connection dialog box

WCF Service

A Windows Communication Foundation (WCF) service is the new service communication API developed by Microsoft and has to be created by developers in Visual Studio. Like the .NET connector, a WCF service has to be developed and deployed to a web server before you can connect to it. If you have WCF services deployed in your organization, SharePoint Designer can enable you to connect to it.

If you choose WCF Service as the connection, you will be presented with the dialog box shown in Figure 10-14 to configure your WCF service connection.

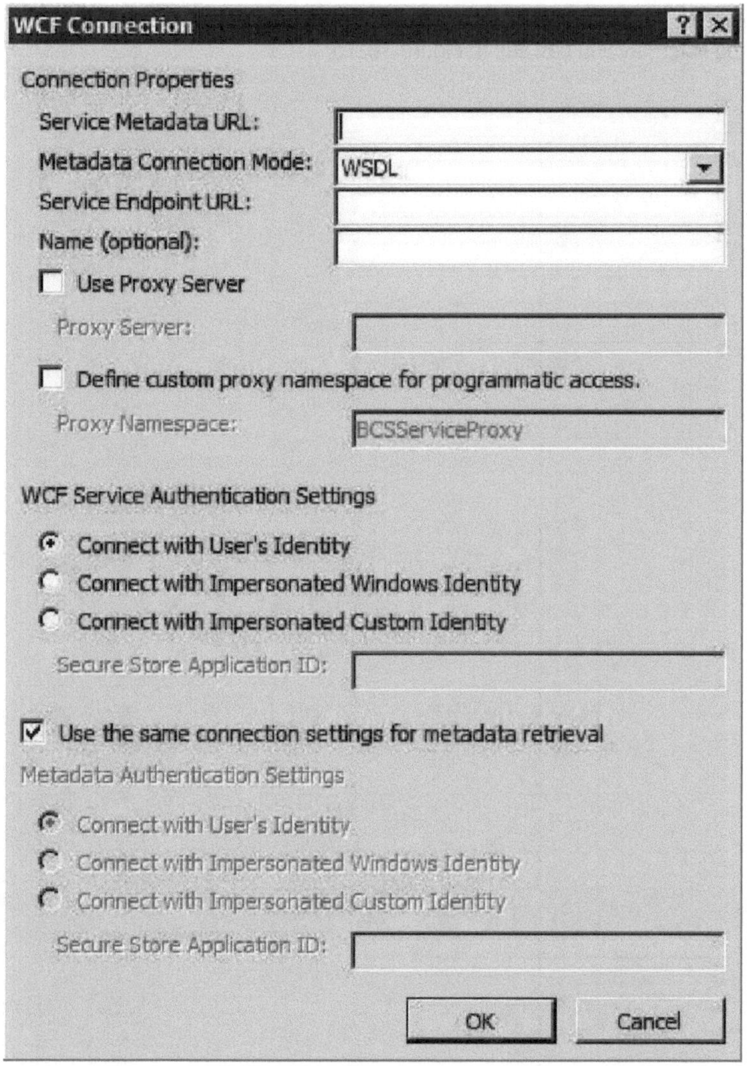

Figure 10-14. WCF Connection dialog box

To configure the WCF connection, you enter the service metadata URL to allow the service to retrieve the service description file. You have an option to use either WSDL or Metadata Exchange mode to retrieve the metadata. The service endpoint is similar to the metadata URL except that the endpoint URL is the URL that SharePoint will use to communicate with the service. If you are required to use a proxy to access the web service, the proxy server address can be entered as well. The authentication settings are similar to the SQL Server authentication options.

When you save your WCF connection settings, a new Connection entry will be visible, and all of the methods provided by the service will be listed, as you can see in Figure 10-15.

Figure 10-15. WCF web methods listing

Create Operations

After you have created your connections, you have to define the operations you want to perform on the connected external systems.

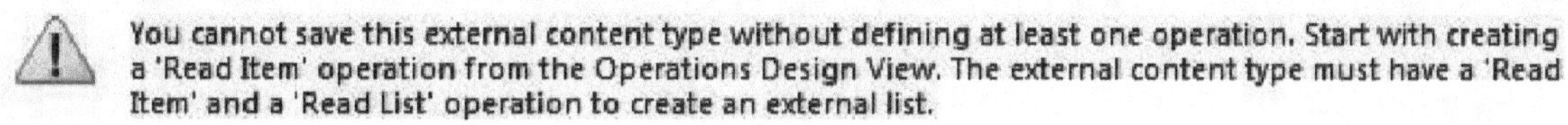

 You cannot save this external content type without defining at least one operation. Start with creating a 'Read Item' operation from the Operations Design View. The external content type must have a 'Read Item' and a 'Read List' operation to create an external list.

Figure 10-16. Operations warning

As the warning indicates (Figure 10-16) you cannot save an external content type without defining one operation. All external content types must have a Read Item and a Read List operation if you are going to use it to create an external list.

When you make a connection to an SQL server, the tables will be listed in a folder labeled Tables. The views will be in a folder labeled Views, and the user-defined stored procedures will be in a folder labeled Routines. In a WCF connection, all methods provided by the service will be listed as illustrated earlier in Figure 10-15.

To define an operation, select the object you want to perform the operation on and right-click it. A context menu will appear, allowing you to create All Operations or any specific CRUD operation, as shown in Figure 10-17.

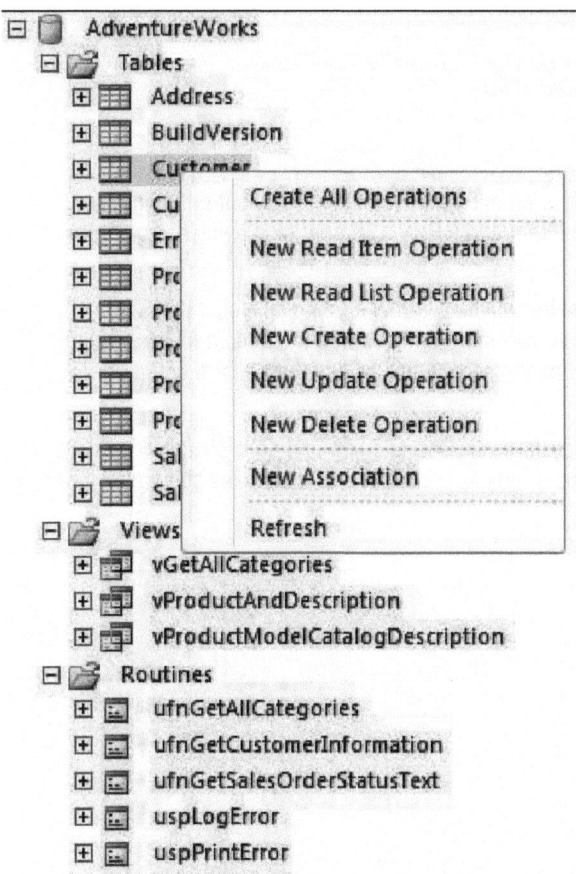

Figure 10-17. Create Operations context menu

When you select an operation to create, the Create Operation Wizard, shown in Figure 10-18, will pop up and lead you through the process of creating the operations you selected.

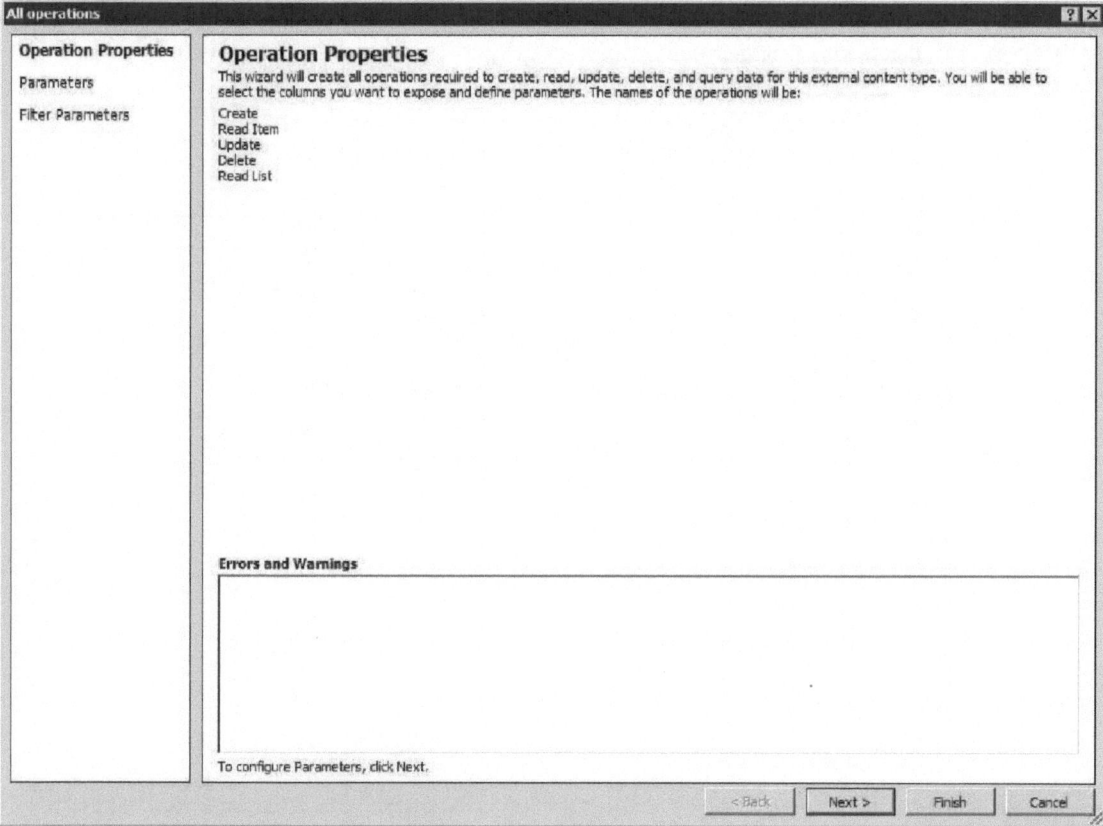

Figure 10-18. Create All Operations Wizard

When you click Next, you are able to map the fields to properties. You will also be shown any errors that exist that you can correct (see Figure 10-19). One of the options you can configure is which fields to display in the picker. The picker is a dialog box much like the People Picker from SharePoint that will provide a quick lookup of valid values to assist your user in entering the correct values. You can set these values by highlighting the fields and then configuring the field settings on the right.

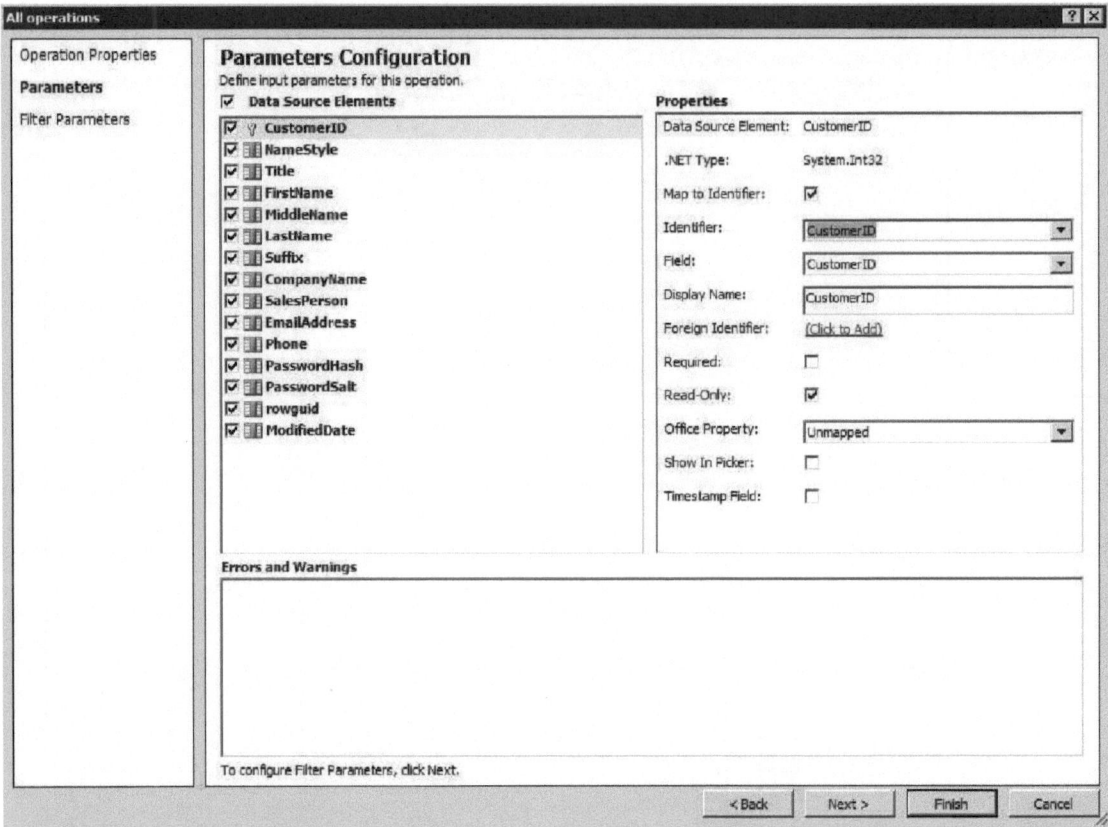

Figure 10-19. External field mapping dialog box

Creating an External List

After you have clicked Finish to create your external content type, you can choose to create lists and forms from the external content type that you just defined. This can be accomplished by clicking Create Lists & Form from the Ribbon menu. A dialog box will open, prompting you to specify the List Name, Read Item Operation, System Instance, and Description for the list, as you can see in Figure 10-20. You can also elect to have InfoPath forms automatically created with the list.

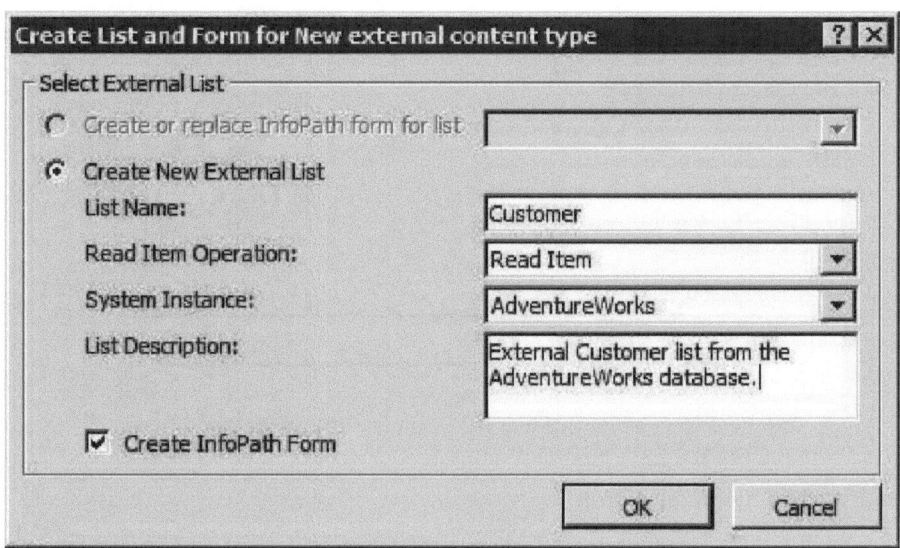

Figure 10-20. Create List and Form dialog box

EXERCISE10-5. CREATE AN EXTERNAL CONTENT TYPE AND EXTERNAL LIST

For this exercise, you will create an external content type and list so that you can interact with it in SharePoint:

1. From the Navigation pane, click External Content Type. From the Ribbon menu, click External Content Type.

2. Click the Name hyperlink and change the name to **Customer**.

3. From the Office Item Type drop-down list, select Contact (see Figure 10-21).

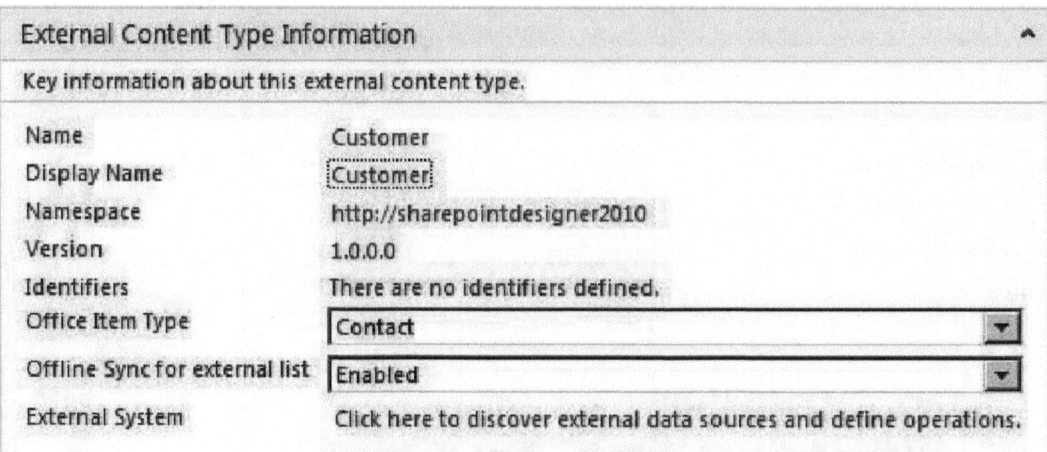

Figure 10-21. *New external content type information*

4. Click the hyperlink to discover external data sources and define operations.

5. Click Add Connection and select SQL Server.

6. When the dialog box opens, type the name of your SQL Server and **AdventureWorksLT2008R2** as the database. Give it a name of **AdventureWorks**. Leave the identity settings to Connect with User's Identity. Click OK.

7. In the Data Source Explorer, right-click the Customer table and select New Read List Operation from the context menu.

8. Click Next until you get to the Return Parameter Configuration window.

9. We aren't going to do anything with the passwords, so you can deselect PasswordHash, PasswordSalt, and rowguid.

10. Click CustomerID. In the Properties pane, select Map to Identifier, and if not already selected, select CustomerId as the identifier. Make sure that the Read-Only check box is selected.

11. For the FirstName, LastName, and CompanyName fields, select Show in Picker in the Properties pane.

12. Click Finish to save.

13. Right-click Customer again and select New Read Item Operation.

14. Click Next until you get to the Return Parameter window.

15. You will see a couple of warnings indicating that your FirstName and LastName fields are not mapped to an Office property. Make the mappings shown in Table 10-2 to your fields.SharePoint:

Table 10-2. Field Mappings

Field	Office Property
FirstName	First Name (FirstName)
LastName	Last Name (LastName)
CompanyName	Company Name (CompanyName)
EmailAddress	Email 1 Address(Email1Address)
Phone	Primary Telephone Number (PrimaryTelephoneNumber)

16. Click Finish to save.

17. Right-click the Customer table and select New Update Operation.

18. When the Update operation dialog box opens, just accept all of the defaults and click Finish to save. Your external content type should look like Figure 10-22.

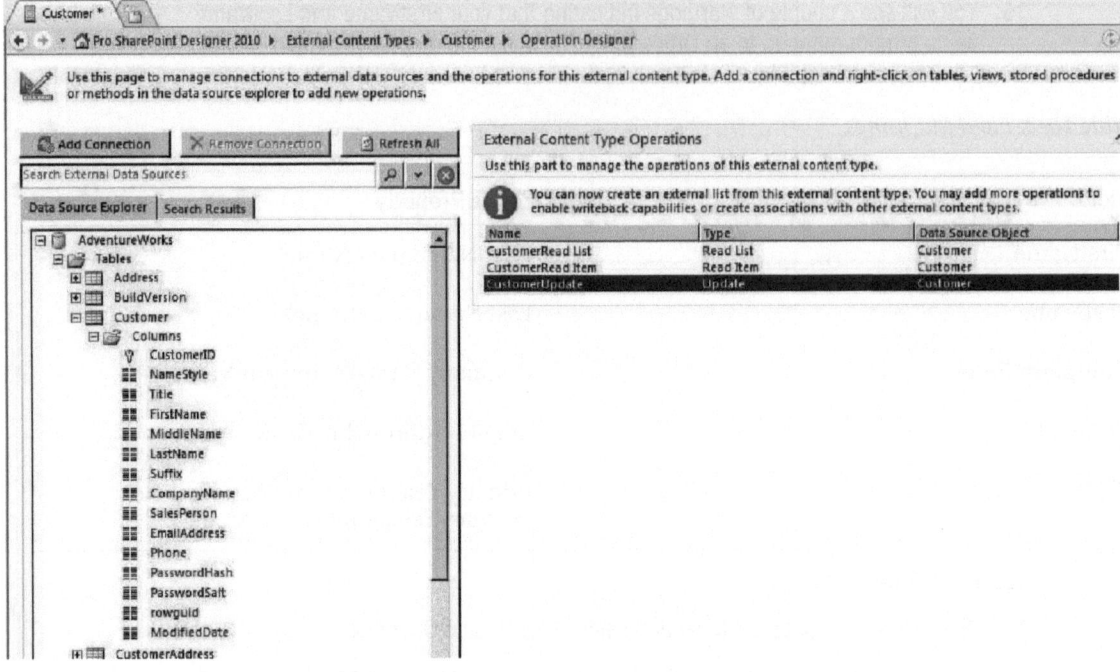

Figure 10-22. Customer external content type with operations defined

19. Press Ctrl+S to save.

20. Once your external content type is created, you can let SharePoint Designer create your external lists. Click the Create Lists and Forms button on the Ribbon menu.

21. When the Create List and Form for Customer dialog box opens, name your list **AdventureWorksCustomer** and give it a description, as illustrated in Figure 10-23.

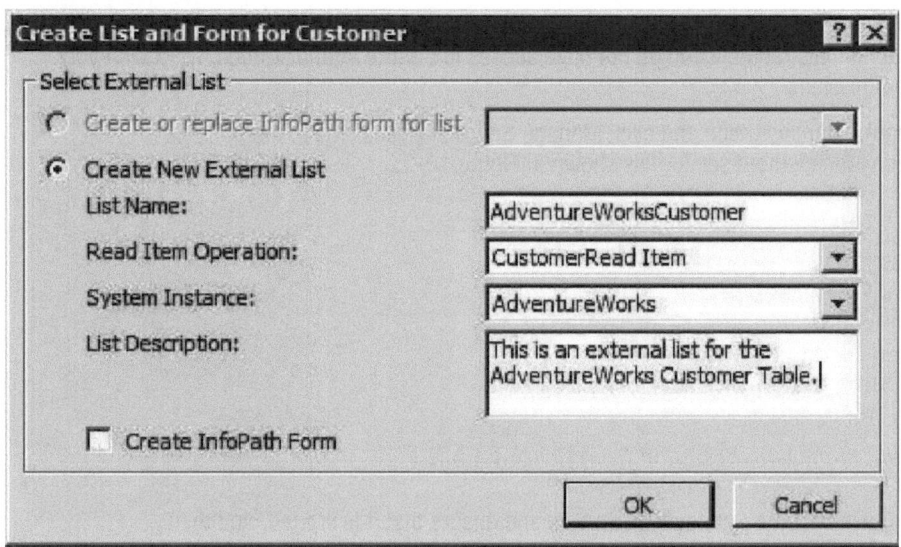

Figure 10-23. Create List and Form for Customer dialog box

22. Click OK. Your new external list will be created.

23. From the Navigation pane, click Lists and Libraries. In the External Lists section, you should see your newly created list. Click the list name and then click Preview in Browser. The browser should open and display your list (see Figure 10-24). Click the CustomerID and see that you can view an individual item. Click the Edit Item option to view how the form changes to an Edit form. Edit the name of one of the contacts, save it, and notice how it updates the data.

CustomerID	NameStyle	Title	FirstName	MiddleName	LastName	Suffix	CompanyName	SalesPerson	EmailAddress	Phone	ModifiedDate
1	No	Mr.	Orlando	N.	Gee		A Bike Store	adventure-works\pamela0	orlando0@adventure-works.com	245-555-0173	7/31/2005 7:00
2	No	Mr.	Keith		Harris		Progressive Sports	adventure-works\david8	keith0@adventure-works.com	170-555-0127	7/31/2006 7:00
3	No	Ms.	Donna	F.	Carreras		Advanced Bike Components	adventure-works\jillian0	donna0@adventure-works.com	279-555-0130	8/31/2005 7:00
4	No	Ms.	Janet	M.	Gates		Modular Cycle Systems	adventure-works\jillian0	janet1@adventure-works.com	710-555-0173	6/30/2006 7:00
5	No	Mr.	Lucy		Harrington		Metropolitan Sports Supply	adventure-works\shu0	lucy0@adventure-works.com	828-555-0186	8/31/2006 7:00
6	No	Ms.	Rosmarie	J.	Carroll		Aerobic Exercise Company	adventure-works\linda3	rosmarie0@adventure-works.com	244-555-0112	8/31/2007 7:00
7	No	Mr.	Dominic	P.	Gash		Associated Bikes	adventure-works\shu0	dominic0@adventure-works.com	192-555-0173	6/30/2006 7:00
10	No	Ms.	Kathleen	M.	Garza		Rural Cycle Emporium	adventure-works\josé1	kathleen0@adventure-works.com	150-555-	8/31/2006 7:00

Figure 10-24. AdventureWorks customer external list

If you get an access denied message, you have to configure permissions to access the new external content type in Central Administration. If you do not have access to Central Administration, work with your administrator to set permissions.

24. Open Central Administration and click Manage Service Applications in the Application Management section, as shown in Figure 10-25.

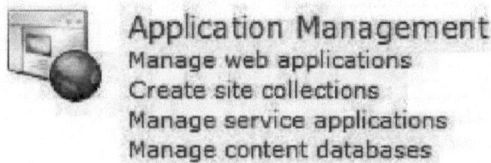

Figure 10-25. Application Management section from Central Admin

25. Find the Business Data Connectivity Service and ensure that it is started, and then click the hyperlink (see Figure 10-26).

| Business Data Connectivity Service | Business Data Connectivity Service Application | Started |
| Business Data Connectivity Service | Business Data Connectivity Service Application Proxy | Started |

Figure 10-26. Business Data Connectivity Service links in Central Admin

26. You should see your external content type listed. Click Set Permissions from the context menu, as shown in Figure 10-27.

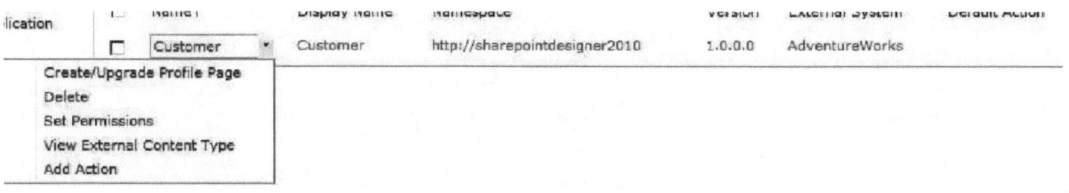

Figure 10-27. Set Permissions context menu

27. In the dialog box, search for your login ID or a group that you are a member of. The best practice is to always assign permissions to groups. Click Add and then OK.

28. Click your login name and then assign the appropriate permissions you want to allow on this external content type (see Figure 10-28).

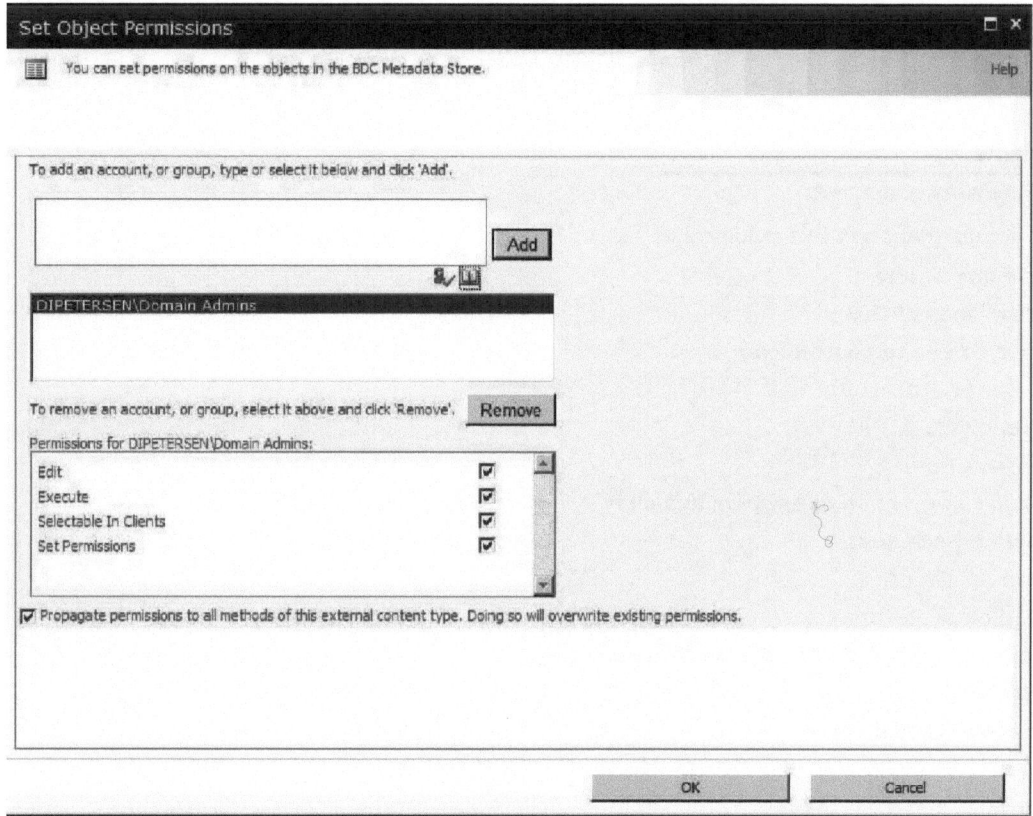

Figure 10-28.Set Object Permissions dialog box

    29. Click OK and now go back to your list to view it.

Using External Columns

After you create an external column type, you can use the columns in regular SharePoint lists. A great example is using the AdventureWorks Customer content type in your Customer Correspondence document library.

1.   Open the browser to your site and click the Libraries link. Create a new document Library called **Customer Contacts**. Accept the defaults.

2.   Open your new library in the browser and on the Ribbon menu, select Library Settings.

3.   Click the Create Column option. In the Column Name field, enter **AdventureWorksCustomer**, as shown in Figure 10-29.

4. Select the External Data radio button. Then in the external content type, use the selector to locate the Customer external content type you just created.

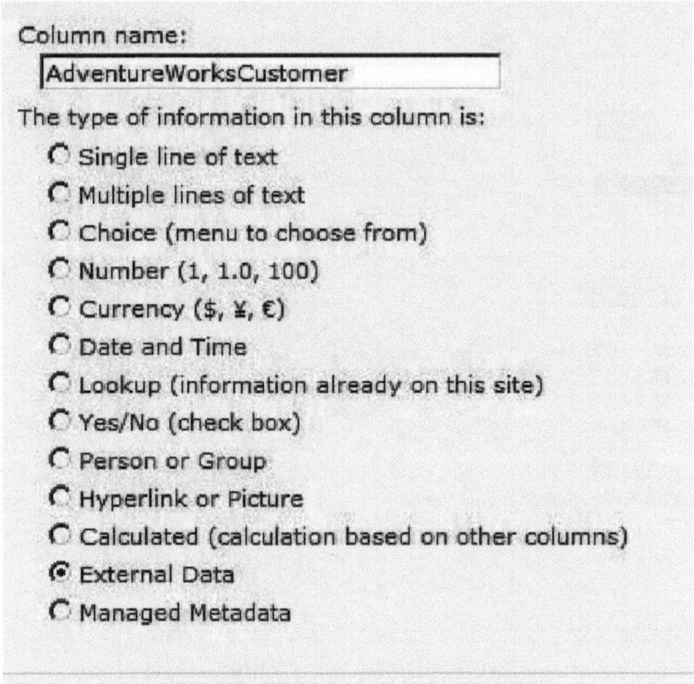

Column name:

AdventureWorksCustomer

The type of information in this column is:

- ○ Single line of text
- ○ Multiple lines of text
- ○ Choice (menu to choose from)
- ○ Number (1, 1.0, 100)
- ○ Currency ($, ¥, €)
- ○ Date and Time
- ○ Lookup (information already on this site)
- ○ Yes/No (check box)
- ○ Person or Group
- ○ Hyperlink or Picture
- ○ Calculated (calculation based on other columns)
- ● External Data
- ○ Managed Metadata

Figure 10-29. External data site column

5. In the drop-down list that asks which field you want to show on this column, select CompanyName.

6. In the field selector check boxes, select CustomerID, EmailAddress, FirstName, LastName, MiddleName, Phone, SalesPerson, Suffix, and Title, as shown in Figure 10-30.

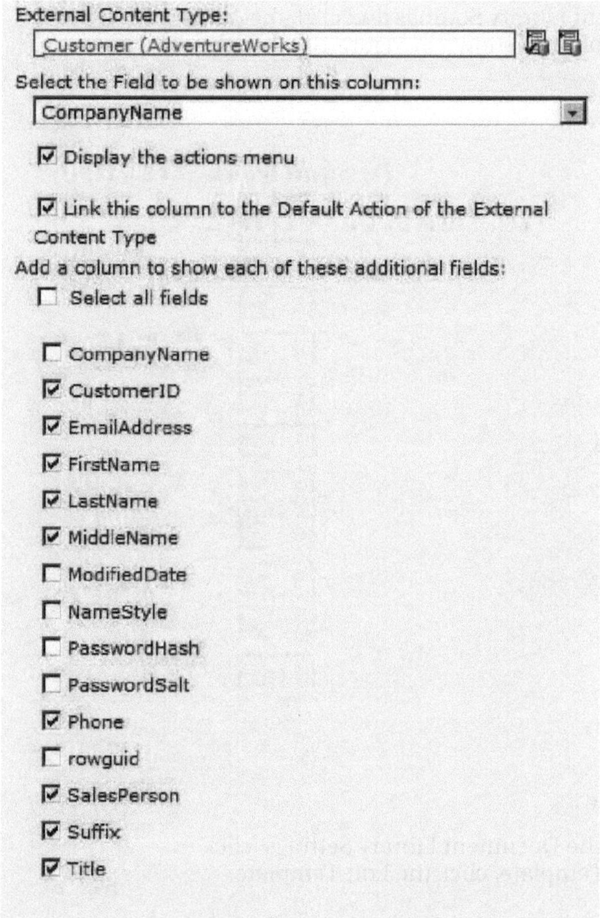

External Content Type:

Customer (AdventureWorks)

Select the Field to be shown on this column:

CompanyName

☑ Display the actions menu

☑ Link this column to the Default Action of the External
Content Type

Add a column to show each of these additional fields:

☐ Select all fields

☐ CompanyName

☑ CustomerID

☑ EmailAddress

☑ FirstName

☑ LastName

☑ MiddleName

☐ ModifiedDate

☐ NameStyle

☐ PasswordHash

☐ PasswordSalt

☑ Phone

☐ rowguid

☑ SalesPerson

☑ Suffix

☑ Title

Figure 10-30. *Selecting additional fields to display*

7. Click OK to save. Your columns should look like Figure 10-31.

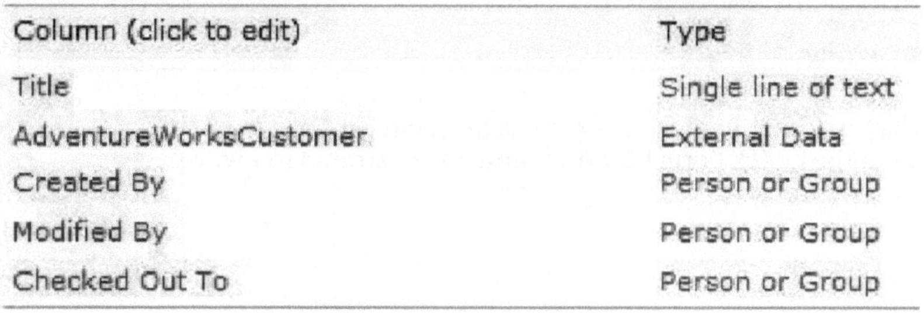

Column (click to edit)	Type
Title	Single line of text
AdventureWorksCustomer	External Data
Created By	Person or Group
Modified By	Person or Group
Checked Out To	Person or Group

Figure 10-31. *Customer contact site columns*

8. Go to the Views section of the Document Library Settings and click the All Documents view to edit it. Select the columns shown in Figure 10-32 to display.

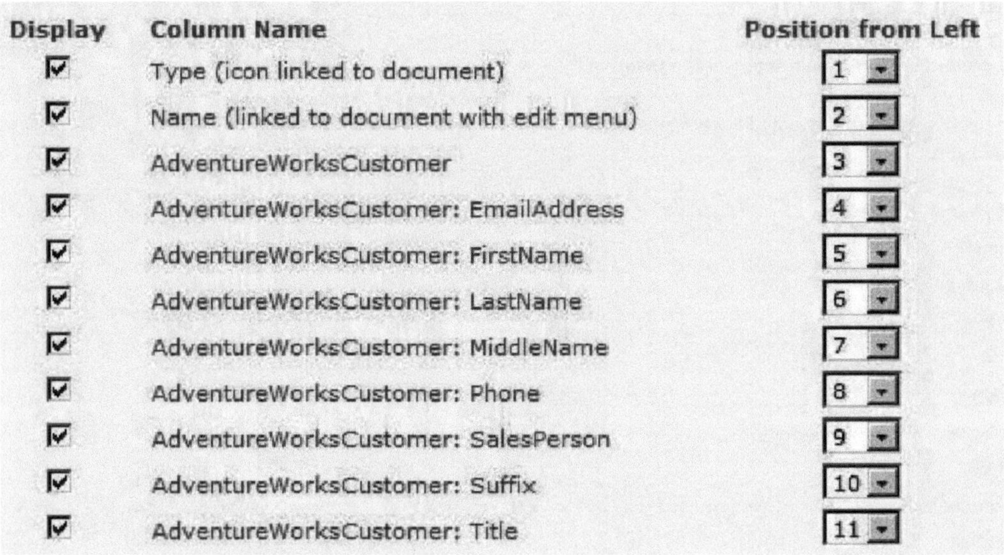

Display	Column Name	Position from Left
☑	Type (icon linked to document)	1 ▾
☑	Name (linked to document with edit menu)	2 ▾
☑	AdventureWorksCustomer	3 ▾
☑	AdventureWorksCustomer: EmailAddress	4 ▾
☑	AdventureWorksCustomer: FirstName	5 ▾
☑	AdventureWorksCustomer: LastName	6 ▾
☑	AdventureWorksCustomer: MiddleName	7 ▾
☑	AdventureWorksCustomer: Phone	8 ▾
☑	AdventureWorksCustomer: SalesPerson	9 ▾
☑	AdventureWorksCustomer: Suffix	10 ▾
☑	AdventureWorksCustomer: Title	11 ▾

Figure 10-32. All Documents view field selector

9. Click OK to save the changes to the view.

10. Now you will create your template. In the Document Library Settings, click Advanced Settings. Under Document Template, click the Edit Template hyperlink, as shown in Figure 10-33.

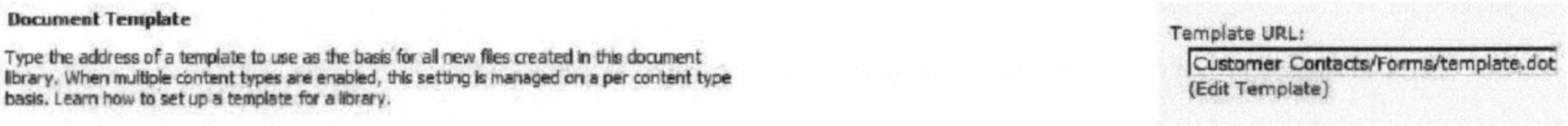

Document Template

Type the address of a template to use as the basis for all new files created in this document library. When multiple content types are enabled, this setting is managed on a per content type basis. Learn how to set up a template for a library.

Template URL:

Customer Contacts/Forms/template.dot

(Edit Template)

Figure 10-33. Document Template setting

11. To add AdventureWorksCustomer fields to your Word template, choose Document Property from the Quick Parts Ribbon menu, as illustrated in Figure 10-34.

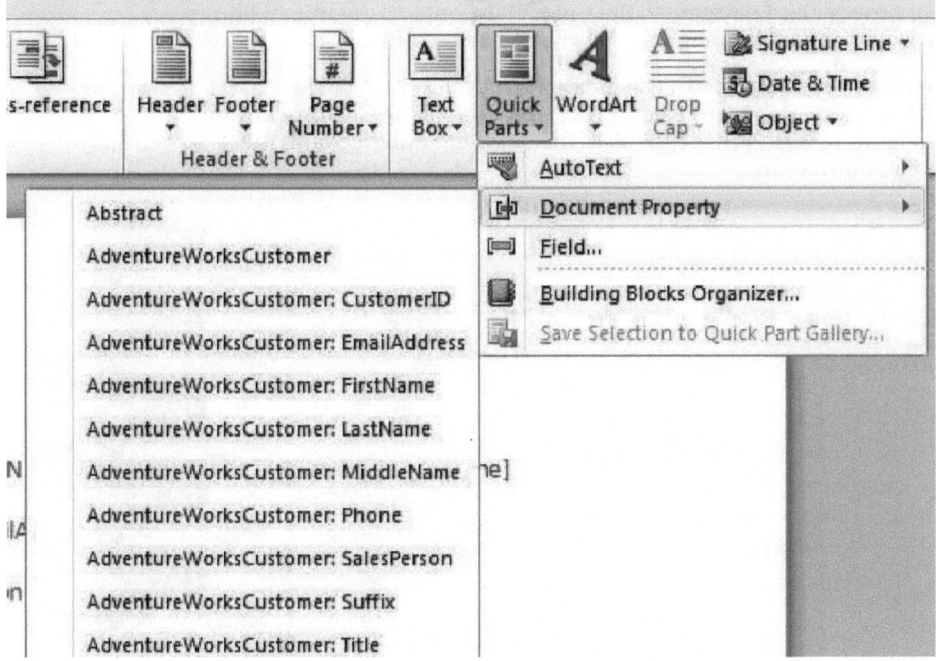

Figure 10-34. Inserting document properties with Quick Parts

12. Edit the template as shown in Figure 10-35, inserting the appropriate fields from the Quick Parts menu. Press Ctrl+S to save your changes and then close Word.

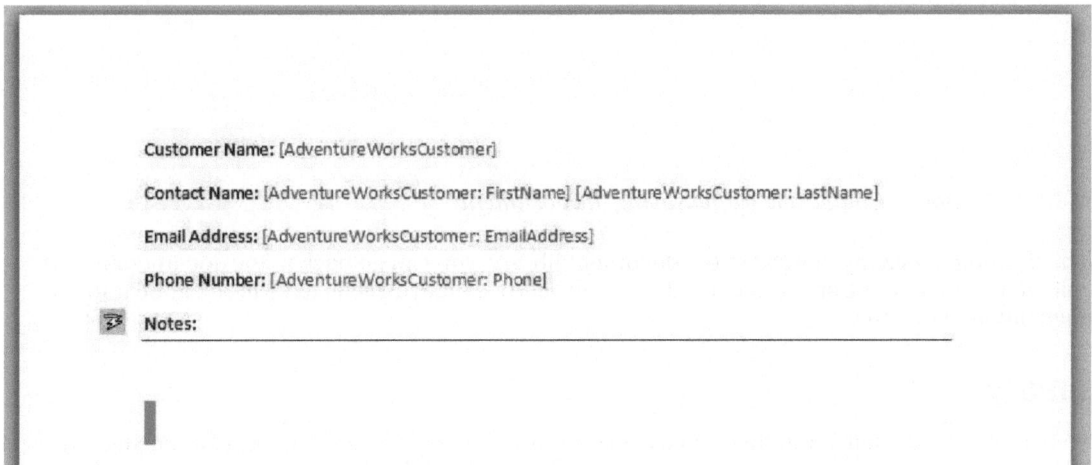

Figure 10-35. Customer Contacts template

13. Open your browser and navigate to the Customer Contacts document library. From the Documents Ribbon menu, select New Document.

14. When the new document opens, use the Customer Picker to select Metropolitan Sports Supply by clicking the right side of the Customer Name field (see Figure 10-36). Notice how all of the fields are updated with the appropriate information.

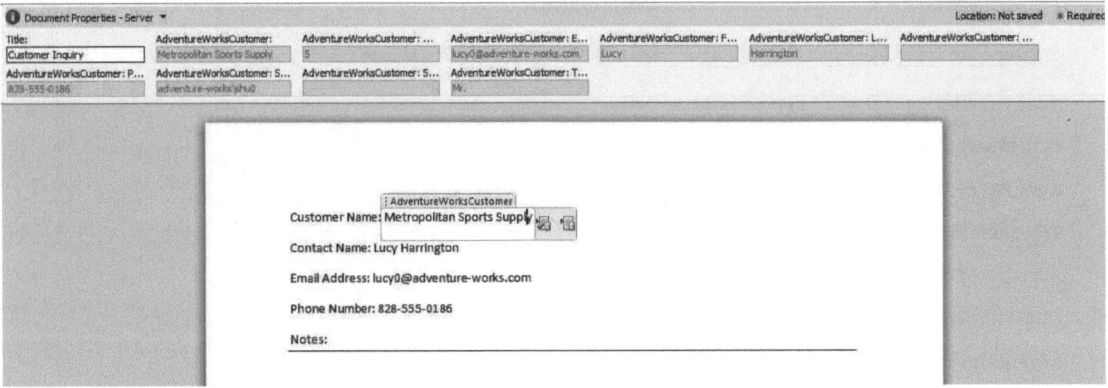

Figure 10-36. New customer contact document

15. In the Title property, type **Customer Inquiry**.

16. Save to the document library. Notice that the fields are populated, as shown in Figure 10-37.

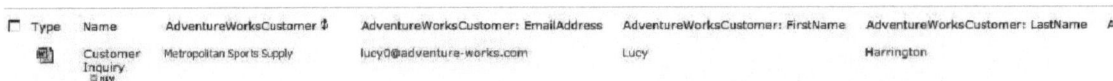

Figure 10-37. Customer Contact view after saving the document

If you have problems saving directly to the document library, you can go back to the document library and upload the document from your computer. All properties that you selected will still appear in the document library columns.

Summary

In this chapter, you learned about how you can use SharePoint Designer to connect external data to SharePoint and use that data in your SharePoint sites. You learned that SharePoint Designer supports connecting to external data sources and also learned about the powerful new Business Connectivity Services. It is important to remember the following about BCS:

- External content types are the building blocks of the BCS.

- You must first create an external content type before you can use any of the external data.

- You can create external lists from the external content types, and you can interact with the external lists in the same way that you use internal SharePoint lists.

- You can add individual external columns to regular SharePoint lists and libraries.

- By mapping an external column to a document library, the external columns become part of the document roperties.

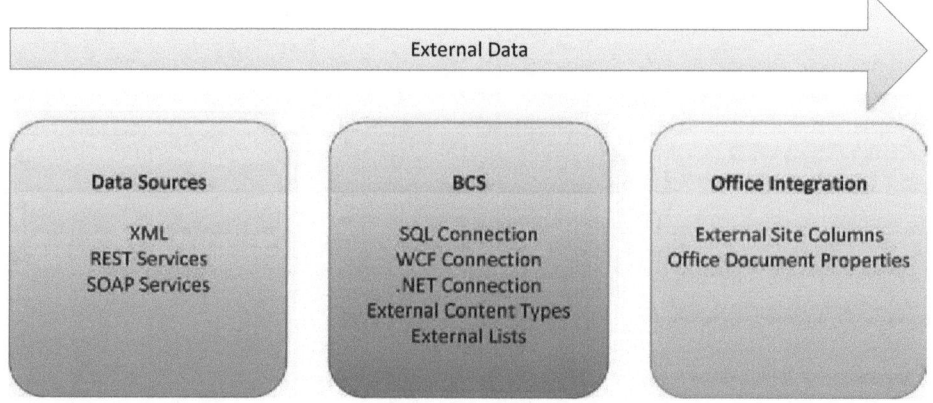

Using InfoPath Forms

InfoPath forms allow designers to create rich, custom forms that can create and consume data from a variety of sources including SharePoint. In this chapter, you will explore the features of InfoPath forms that make them well-suited to inclusion in a SharePoint-based solution. You will examine the concepts and security considerations to be addressed when working with InfoPath forms in SharePoint. You will then learn the process for building and publishing different types of forms for use within SharePoint.

You will learn about the following topics in this chapter:

- The basics of creating web-enabled forms by using InfoPath 2010

- The limitations placed on web-based forms in terms of security and functionality

- How to control the deployment of form templates in a SharePoint environment

- How to customize SharePoint list forms by using InfoPath form templates

- How to integrate custom document information panels with Microsoft Office applications such as Word or Excel

Introduction to InfoPath

Let's start off our discussion of InfoPath by pointing out that this book is about SharePoint Designer, not InfoPath. Why then is this chapter called "Using InfoPath Forms"? That's a good point...*on to Chapter 12*!

Just kidding. The reason for discussing InfoPath here is that data entry forms occur naturally in many situations when designing SharePoint sites. InfoPath and SharePoint are designed to work well together, and some interesting features can best be leveraged by using both technologies together. This chapter will not attempt to teach you everything there is to know about designing InfoPath forms. There are many good books on that subject already. The purpose of this chapter is to introduce the concepts of InfoPath and to explore the situations for which a SharePoint site designer may find using InfoPath forms helpful.

The Form-Filling Environment

When Microsoft released InfoPath as part of MS Office 2003, it saw slow adoption because of the way users had to fill out forms. The MS InfoPath 2003 client application was used to both create form templates and fill out forms. In order to get InfoPath, most organizations had to sign up for volume licensing and more-expensive editions of MS Office. Although integration with SharePoint was considered a valuable feature, there was no way to create a web-based data entry form in InfoPath.

Because most users did not have InfoPath on their desktops, deploying an InfoPath form in any but the most controlled internal-facing scenario was impractical.

Compare this situation with InfoPath's competitors such as Adobe's Acrobat forms. Acrobat forms can be designed using the full Acrobat client application, but they can be filled out using the Acrobat Reader application, which is available as a free download. The lack of an equivalent form-filling environment caused many organizations to reject InfoPath as a solution.

When InfoPath 2007 was released, it provided the capability to create web-based forms. These form definitions were designed to run within SharePoint's InfoPath Forms Services subsystem. Forms Services was included in the Enterprise license of MOSS 2007 or as a separate product called SharePoint Forms Services 2007. This strategy eliminated much of the restriction on InfoPath's adoption, but web-based forms have certain security limitations that prevent them from being used in all cases.

■ **Tip** The fact that a form template is deployed to SharePoint does not require that it be web-based. A non-web-based form opened from SharePoint will open in InfoPath Designer or InfoPath Filler if available. Only if InfoPath is not available will this type of form fail to open.

With the release of InfoPath 2010, Microsoft has adopted a three-pronged strategy for filling out forms. InfoPath forms can now be used in three distinct environments:

- *InfoPath Designer 2010*: This Windows-based client application is used to design or fill out InfoPath form templates. This is the authoring environment for forms.

- *InfoPath Filler 2010*: This Windows-based client application is used to fill out forms based on form templates designed in the designer application. This application allows forms to use the same security model as forms running in InfoPath Designer.

- *InfoPath Forms Services 2010*: This is a subsystem within SharePoint Server 2010 Enterprise Edition that hosts web-based InfoPath forms. This allows a user to complete and submit forms without installing any client application, but with more-restricted functionality.

■ **Note** Unfortunately, the new InfoPath Filler application is not the revolution it seems to be. Microsoft did not see fit to release it as a free download like Acrobat's Adobe Reader application. In fact, under the covers, this application runs the same executable as the InfoPath Designer. It just runs in a different mode. As such, users still need to buy an upscale edition of MS Office in order to use it. The same barriers to adoption exist for InfoPath 2010 that were present in the 2007 version.

What's New in InfoPath 2010?

The 2010 release of InfoPath contains new features to make forms easier to design, more functional to use, and more versatile to host and deploy. These new features can be divided into three main categories, as follows:

- Designing form templates

    - *Page layouts*: Allow the designer to apply a variety of standard layouts to a form view.

    - *New controls*: Include picture buttons, date/time pickers, person/group pickers, digital signatures and managed metadata pickers.

    - *Improved rules engine*: New types of rules allow the quick creation of complex behaviors without coding. Also includes an improved rule management interface.

    - *Quick Publish button*: This option allows the designer to republish a previously published form without going through the entire publishing wizard again.

- SharePoint integration

    - *SharePoint list forms*: The new display and edit forms generated for a SharePoint list can be replaced with an InfoPath form template for added control and functionality.

    - *SharePoint workspace integration:* SharePoint lists and libraries taken offline using SharePoint Workspace (previously known as Groove) can still leverage InfoPath forms. Forms entered offline are synchronized with SharePoint when a new connection is made.

- Web-based forms

    - *More supported controls*: Includes lists, list and combo boxes, picture buttons, hyperlinks, pickers, and sections.

    - *InfoPath Form web part*: This web part allows any InfoPath web-enabled form to be hosted on a web page in SharePoint, including connecting the form to other web parts via web part connections.

    - *Browser standards compliance*: The new version is compliant with XHTML 1.0 and Web Content Accessibility Guidelines 2.0 (WCAG 2.0) AA.

InfoPath Integration with SharePoint

InfoPath integrates with SharePoint in several ways, but the underlying technology supporting that integration is the InfoPath Forms Services subsystem. This component is part of the Enterprise edition of SharePoint Server 2010.

Forms Services is configured in SharePoint's Central Administration site. Unlike other SharePoint services, such as Excel Services or PerformancePoint Services, Forms Services is not a service application configured under Application Management. To configure Forms Services, select the General Application Settings link in the left-hand menu and look for the InfoPath Forms Services group.

To enable InfoPath Forms Services features within SharePoint site collections, you have to activate the SharePoint Server Enterprise Site Collection feature. This feature activates the web parts and menu actions necessary to host InfoPath forms within the site collection.

After you have configured and enabled Forms Services in the site collection, you can use the InfoPath form templates in various ways. InfoPath forms are XML-based. This means that all of the data entered is encoded into an XML document that is then submitted to a data store of some kind. The most basic use of InfoPath forms in SharePoint is to use a SharePoint document library as a repository for storing completed forms. SharePoint provides several features that are useful when working with forms, including versioning, access security, and workflow processing.

A form template can be integrated with a library in two ways. The simplest way to surface a form in a library is to publish the form template as a document template in the library. The problem with this method is that the form template is stored specifically for this library and isn't usable elsewhere in the site. A better approach is to associate a form template with its own content type. Adding the form's content type to a library allows forms to be filled out and stored in the library. The advantage is that the content type becomes a centralized location for managing the form template. You will explore creating a form content type in Exercise 11-1 later in this chapter.

The next most common use for InfoPath within SharePoint is for creating customized forms for workflows. SharePoint workflows allow users to perform controlled business processes managed by the Windows Workflow Foundation (WF) engine hosted within SharePoint. The WF engine can assign tasks, send e-mails, or perform a number of other activities in order to complete a business process. At each step in the process, user input may be required. The forms for entering this data are called *task forms*. InfoPath can be used to create highly customized templates for the forms. You will explore this type of form in Chapter 12 when you examine SharePoint's workflow features.

A new feature in InfoPath and SharePoint Server 2010 is the ability to create custom list forms in InfoPath. When a list or library is created in SharePoint, a set of default data entry forms is created. These forms create new items and edit or display existing items. A site designer can now customize these forms by using InfoPath form templates more easily than using the other methods available. You will customize list forms in Exercise 11-2 later in this chapter.

The final scenario where InfoPath forms are useful to site designers is when using SharePoint in conjunction with other MS Office client applications such as Word or Excel. Office applications allow the document author to set document properties such as the author, title, keywords, and so on. These properties can be viewed in the document information panel (DIP). In Word 2010, this panel can be displayed by selecting File from the Ribbon and then selecting Show Document Panel from the Properties drop-down to the right of the Backstage area. InfoPath and SharePoint can be used to create custom DIPs that will appear in Office applications when a document is opened from within SharePoint. Data entered into these panels can be stored as metadata with the document in SharePoint. You will create a custom DIP later in this chapter.

Understanding Security Considerations

Security is a complex topic when working with InfoPath forms because a form will often touch many resources outside the form. InfoPath forms can contain data sources that retrieve data from databases, web services, or other locations. Each of these interfaces may require its own authentication and authorization mechanism in order to function properly. Form templates may also contain managed .NET code that can access files on the user's system or perform other potentially dangerous actions.

To control the use of these features, InfoPath has *form security levels*. Each security level places a different set of restrictions on what actions the form template can perform. The form-filling environment also affects what actions a form can take. Forms running in InfoPath Designer or Filler have greater freedom than those running in a web browser. A comprehensive discussion of the rules governing the restrictions placed on forms at different security levels is beyond the scope of this book, but a general description of these levels follows.

Restricted Level

Forms running in Restricted mode cannot communicate with resources outside the form template's definition. This is the most secure, but least functional, mode in which a form can run. There are many InfoPath features that will not function in a Restricted mode form. The following is a partial list of the features that can't be used in this mode and a brief description of why they are not allowed:

- *ActiveX controls*: These controls run in a nonmanaged execution environment, where their actions cannot be limited.

- *Roles*: Role definitions require information about the user that is not part of the form's template.

- *Data connections*: Data connections access information that is external to the template. An exception to this rule is when submitting a form via e-mail. Submitting a form via e-mail is allowed because e-mail forms are the primary use of restricted forms.

- *Workflow forms*: Data must pass in and out of workflow forms, which violates the restriction.

- *.NET managed code*: Managed code will not load in a Restricted form because the .NET runtime is not available. The form will still load, but none of the .NET code will execute. No error will be displayed. This allows a template to use .NET code when running in InfoPath Filler while still functioning without code in a web-based form.

Because any form template that is deployed to SharePoint is, by definition, communicating with SharePoint, Restricted mode forms cannot run in SharePoint. Restricted mode forms are generally used for e-mail forms, where security limitations are extremely tight.

Domain Level

The Domain security level is the most commonly used mode for InfoPath forms in SharePoint. This level is an intermediate step between Restricted forms and those requiring Full Trust (which you'll learn about next). Domain mode forms can access external data as long as that data is accessible according to the domain's security zone as defined by Windows Internet Explorer.

■ **Note** It is important to recognize that InfoPath's use of the word *domain* is not the same as a domain in Active Directory or in Internet web addresses. For example, the Internet addresses www.microsoft.com and office.microsoft.com may or may not represent different security domains depending on the configuration of zones in IE on the user's system.

When a form is opened from a SharePoint list or library, it is running as a URL-based form. The URL used to open the template is checked against the security zones defined on the user's desktop to determine whether it is in the Internet or Local Intranet zone. In Domain mode, external resources are restricted based on their zone relative to the zone of the form template.

InfoPath's security model also defines a URN-based form that maps to the Local Computer zone. However, SharePoint-based forms are always URL-based, so we don't cover URN-based forms in this book.

Full Trust

The most permissive level of security for an InfoPath template is Full Trust. In Full Trust mode, a form can access any resources that the person filling out the form can access. This may include databases, files on the local hard drive, and Registry settings. Obviously, Full Trust forms should be used only when absolutely necessary because of their potential for unintended impacts to the user's system.

The good news is that forms cannot get Full Trust just by asking for it. In fact, it can be quite difficult to get a form template installed in a way that allows Full Trust. In order to run a form in SharePoint using Full Trust, the form must be digitally signed using a trusted root certificate and it must be installed by a farm administrator through SharePoint's Central Administration site. The form can't be directly published by the designer.

Note that Full Trust does not eliminate any of the limitations on a web-based form. A web-based form running in Full Trust must still refrain from using features that are not supported in such forms. Making a form require Full Trust simply opens up new communication options.

Configuring Security Levels

A form's security level is configured in the InfoPath Designer application when it is designed. By default, InfoPath determines the correct security level for the form based on the features used in it. When the designer adds a data source, for example, the form will automatically be promoted out of Restricted mode.

To set a specific security level for a form, select the File tab in the Ribbon to open the Backstage area. Select Form Options and go to the Security and Trust area in the Form Properties dialog box. This panel allows the designer to set the security level and, if desired, sign the form template.

Creating Form Templates

InfoPath forms run the gamut, from very simple forms that collect a few fields, to highly complex data entry applications with multiple views, data connections, and complex business rules. This section presents the things to consider when creating forms for use in SharePoint.

Planning

The first step is, of course, to plan the form you are going to create. Taking a few extra minutes up front to organize the presentation and functionality of a form can make a big difference to the end user.

Security and Filling Environments

When designing a form, you have to consider the security level that the form will need to run at and the environment the user will be expected to use when filling out the form. For security levels, Table 11-1 lists some rules of thumb.

Table 11-1. *Security-Level Rules*

Level	Consider Using For	Not Appropriate For
Restricted	• E-mail forms	• SharePoint forms
		• Forms that access data
Domain	• Data connections to internal organization data sources	• .NET managed code that requires Full Trust
	• Forms that store data in SharePoint	
	• Forms maintained by low-privilege users	
	• .NET managed code running inside the "sandbox"	
Full Trust	• Forms that access data outside the organization	• Forms maintained by low-privilege users
	• Forms deployed by farm administrators	
	• .NET managed code that requires Full Trust	

Remember to consider the desktop environment of the user who will be filling out the form and the features required by the form. If the user does not have InfoPath Filler on their desktop, your form must be web-enabled and forgo using any features not supported in web-based forms.

Data Connections

As with any data entry application, when designing InfoPath forms, you must consider where data is coming from and where it is being stored. In InfoPath, these become the data sources or connections.

The form's primary data source is the XML document that represents the data entered into the form. The data for this form generally gets written to a data store when the form is saved or submitted. In the case of SharePoint forms, the primary data connection is usually to a document in a document library or a list item.

Secondary data connections may retrieve data from databases, web services, or other SharePoint locations. The important thing is to ensure that whatever security credentials are needed to access that data are available in the intended filling environment. For example, a SQL Server connection string for a database connection can contain a password only if InfoPath Forms Services has been configured to allow it. A best practice for data connections is to use a data connection library to house a set of shared connections. These connections provide a level of trust that makes it easier to move and reconfigure form templates in SharePoint.

Using form templates in SharePoint also introduces two new data considerations: promoted values and web part parameters. When a form is published to a form library, it can expose some of the values from the form to the SharePoint environment. This allows users in the SharePoint environment to search and sort on data within the form without the need to open each form in the library. Using the new InfoPath Form web part on a web part page allows the form to interact with other web parts on the page through web part properties. When publishing a template, form values can be exposed as input, output, or input/output parameters from the web part the form is hosted in. This allows other web parts to feed data into an InfoPath web form and to receive values from it.

Roles

InfoPath *roles* are similar to *audiences* in SharePoint Server. Using a set of rules, the user filling out the form is assigned to a set of roles. Depending on which roles the user has, the form can be customized to show a different view or set of functionality.

Roles are not intended as a security feature because the user still has the ability to view the raw XML document after it is stored. Hiding information on the form template won't protect it after it is written to a form library or a disk file.

Another limitation of roles is that they work only in InfoPath Designer or Filler. Web-based forms cannot use roles. This limits their usefulness in SharePoint sites where web-enabled forms are preferred.

Views

InfoPath form templates can contain multiple pages, called *views*. Every template starts out with one default view. Additional views can be added that present the form's data in different ways. Each view can have its own layout and style. A view does not need to display all of the form's data. Like roles, views should not be used as a security feature. Some common reasons for using multiple views in forms include the following:

- To simplify a large form by splitting it up into more-manageable pages

- To create a print-friendly view of the report

- To show different data to different users based on their role or the current state of a business process

Adding Behavior

In this context, *behavior* refers to any action taken by the form that isn't a direct response to a user action. This includes field validations and calculations that occur within the form beyond the controls' normal abilities to accept input. InfoPath contains multiple mechanisms for implementing custom behavior in forms.

The simplest way to implement behavior in a form is to use rules. *Rules* are a declarative way to indicate what the form should do in response to certain events. Rules are either validation, formatting, or action rules. A rule may have a condition that must be met and a set of actions to take in response to the event. For example, a rule could be triggered when the Budget field is greater than $100,000. The resulting action could be to set the Approver field to CFO. InfoPath also contains a formula language that can be used to define calculations directly in some situations instead of using rules.

There are some types of logic that need to be written in a full-featured programming language. InfoPath supports writing managed code, using VB.NET or C#, that runs in the .NET runtime. Forms that run .NET code must run in either the Domain or Full Trust security level. Because .NET code has the ability to do a great deal of damage and consume a lot of server resources, InfoPath has been designed to control its use by using SharePoint's "sandbox" approach.

■ **Caution** Previous versions of InfoPath supported writing business logic in scripting languages such as JScript and VBScript. This functionality is now deprecated in favor of managed .NET code.

SharePoint Server 2010 contains a new system for hosting untrusted code in a safe, reliable way. Code running "inside the sandbox" is executed in a separate process from the rest of SharePoint. This prevents it from interfering with the server's basic functions and allows the farm administrator to limit the amount of server resources such code can consume. Sandboxed code can access only a subset of the .NET Framework that has been designed to prevent untrusted code from causing problems. This subset excludes connecting to databases, accessing files, or calling unmanaged code. For a more complete discussion, see the TechNet article at http://technet.microsoft.com/en-us/library/ee704541.aspx.

Web-enabled InfoPath forms always have to be able to run in the sandbox. They run in Domain security mode and can access only SharePoint resources that are within the site collection where they are deployed. Any .NET code they contain must adhere to the limitations of a sandboxed application. .NET code in InfoPath can access the InfoPath object model through a set of API calls. There are two versions of the DLLs containing these calls. One is a subset of the other and contains only those features that are valid for use in a sandboxed form. The references to these DLLs are set correctly depending on the compatibility settings for the form. A form that is set to be web-compatible will automatically bind to the more limited object model and .NET Framework classes.

■ **Tip** There is a subtle but important difference between a form running sandboxed .NET code and one running *no* code at all. A form running without code runs within the security context of the user accessing the web site. A form running sandboxed code runs in a separate sandbox service process. As a result, such a form will be unable to access the identity of the user after the form is open. The InfoPath `username()` function is designed to resolve this problem. It will return the correct username even when the form is running in the sandbox.

A form that cannot live within the restrictions of a sandboxed form can still be used within SharePoint. In that case, the form must be set to Full Trust and be published by a farm administrator. Also, because web forms must be sandboxed, Full Trust forms must be filled out by using InfoPath Filler, not a web browser. As a result, the fully trusted code runs on the user's desktop, not on the SharePoint server.

Publishing Templates

After the form template is complete, it needs to be published. A published form is more than just a copy of the form in a particular location. Think of publishing a form as compiling a computer program. After the template is published, it is ready to be used for filling out forms.

There are various ways to publish InfoPath forms, including publishing to network file shares, local directories, and as installable executable files (MSI). However, these do not apply to SharePoint and therefore are not discussed here. The options for publishing form templates to SharePoint include publishing to form libraries, content types, and farm deployments.

When a form is published directly to a SharePoint document library (called a *form library* when using forms), the template becomes the document template for the library. When the user creates a new document in the form library, the form is launched for the user. The form template is stored in the site directory housing the library. The template is used only by that library and is maintained separately from any other form templates in the SharePoint environment.

Instead of publishing directly to a form library, the template can be deployed as a content type in SharePoint. In addition to the form template, the site content type can define data fields, workflows, and information management policies such as retention rules. A content type can be used multiple times throughout the site collection. This simplifies maintenance for a widely used template because there is only one central copy to be updated when a change is made.

A form template can also be published at the farm level by a farm administrator. This places the template in a centralized, trusted, farmwide repository. Deploying form templates at the farm level allows them to access certain capabilities that are not available to templates at the site collection level. A farm-level template can be used by a library or content type housed in any site collection in the farm. Only a farm-level template can run in Full Trust mode, allowing it to access any data source and execute unrestricted .NET code.

Building InfoPath Forms for SharePoint

Now you will do some hands-on work, using InfoPath forms to augment the design of your SharePoint site. You will create a web-enabled form, customize the data entry forms for a list, and create a document information panel for a new project management office within your organization.

Before proceeding through these exercises, be sure to do the following:

- Ensure that InfoPath Forms Services is up and running in your SharePoint environment.

- Create a new site to work in. Any site template will work. This example uses a blank team site in a new site collection.

- Be sure that the SharePoint Server Enterprise Site Collection Features option is activated in your site collection.

- Install the InfoPath Designer 2010 client application on your workstation.

■ **Tip** For more information on configuring InfoPath Forms Services, see the TechNet article at http://technet.microsoft.com/en-us/library/cc262263.aspx.

EXERCISE 11-1. CREATE AN INFOPATH FORM FOR USE IN A FORM LIBRARY

In this exercise, you will create a simple form for entering data. When the user submits the form, it will be placed into a SharePoint library, where an approval workflow will be started automatically. First, you will create a form template in InfoPath Designer. You will publish the form to a new content type in SharePoint. You will enable the standard approval workflow for the content type and create a library to host your forms.

1. Open InfoPath Designer.

2. From the Backstage New area, select the SharePoint Form Library template.

3. Click the Design Form button to the right, as shown in Figure 11-1.

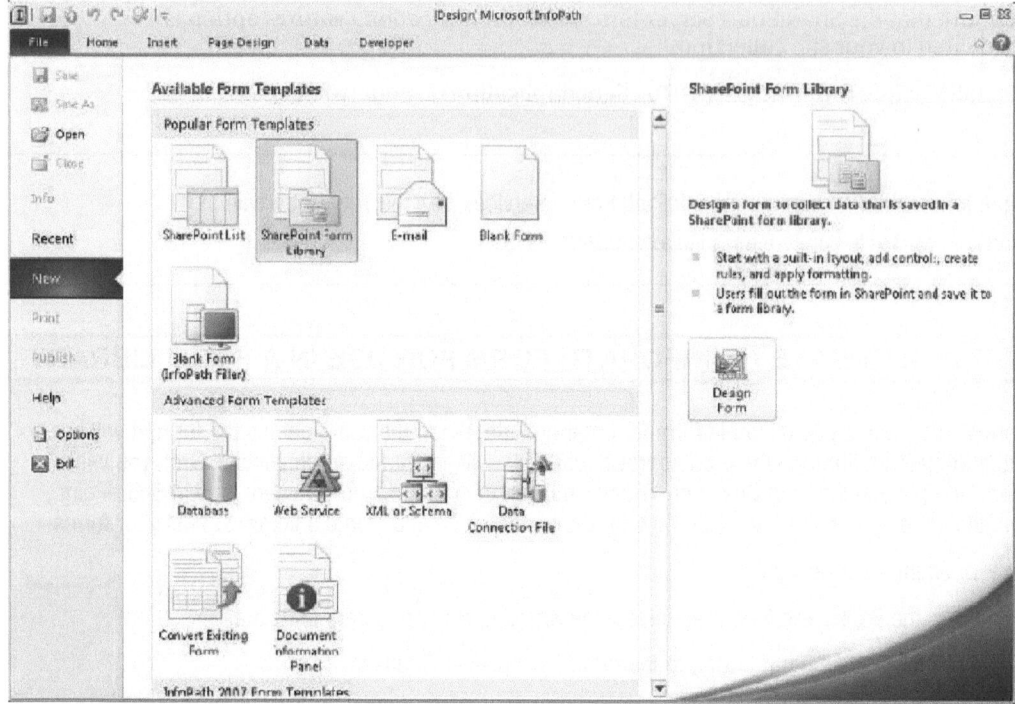

Figure 11-1. *Selecting a form template*

The default form template provided contains a title area and two table layouts. You can add or remove any of these elements as desired. First, you will define the data you want to capture:

4. In the Fields pane, shown in Figure 11-2, right-click myFields and select Add.

5. In the Add Field or Group dialog box, enter **ProjectName** for the field name and select the Cannot Be Blank check box. Leave the field type as Text. Then click OK.

6. Repeat step 5 to create a **ProjectManager** field.

7. Create a **BudgetEstimate** field with a type of Decimal (Double).

8. Create a **StartDate** field with a type of Date (Date).

9. Create an **EndDate** field with a type of Date (Date).

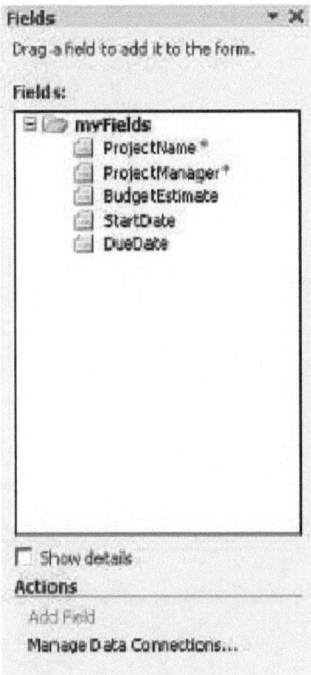

Figure 11-2. The Fields pane

These fields define the XML document that will be used to store the form's data. Now you will remove one of the table layouts and populate the form with controls:

10. Click in the top panel that currently reads Click to Add Title and type Project Initiation.

11. Click the table handle for the lower table, as shown in Figure 11-3. This selects the entire table.

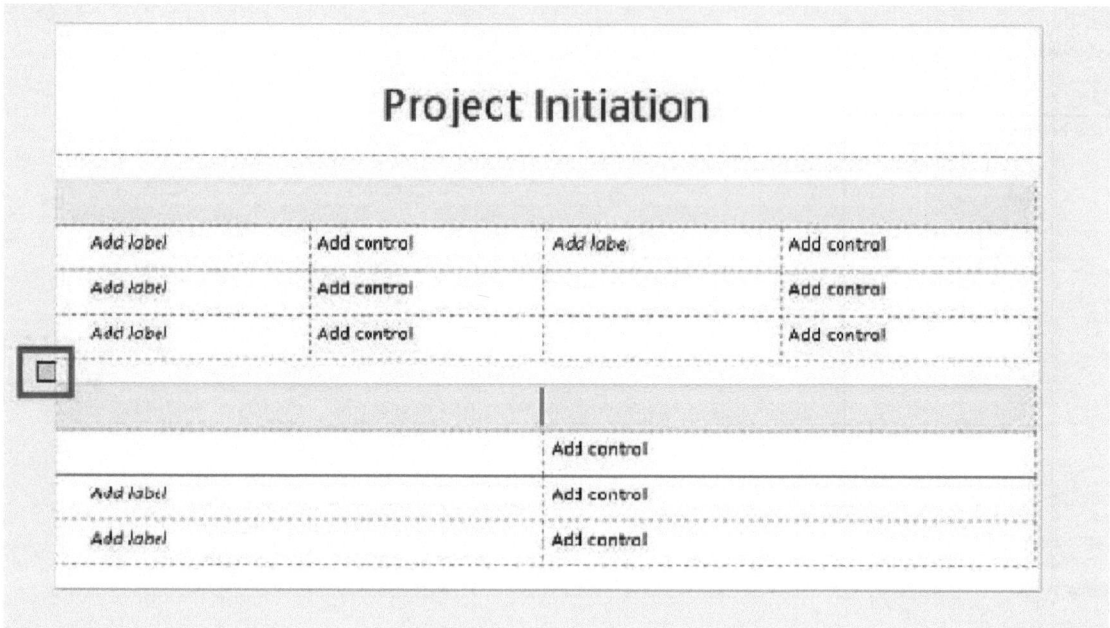

Figure 11-3. *Removing the second table layout*

12. Press the Delete key. This removes the second table layout from the form.

13. Select the second, third, and fourth cells in the first row of the remaining layout table.

14. From the Ribbon's Layout tab, select Merge Cells from the Merge group.

15. Merge the same cells in the second row.

16. Drag the ProjectName field from the Fields pane to the first row of the table. Put the label in the first cell and the text control in the second.

■ **Tip** InfoPath will try to help put the label and control in the correct place. When dragging the field, watch how the cells are highlighted before you drop the field. If you drop the field while both cells are highlighted, InfoPath will put the label in the first cell and the text control in the second. InfoPath even adds a space between *Project* and *Name* for you.

---

17. Drop the ProjectManager field in the second row in the same way.

18. Drop the BudgetEstimate field in the first two cells of the third row.

19. Click in the lower-right cell in the table and press Tab. This is an easy way to add a new row to the table.

20. Drop the StartDate field on the first two cells of the fourth row.

21. Drop the DueDate field on the last two cells of the fourth row.

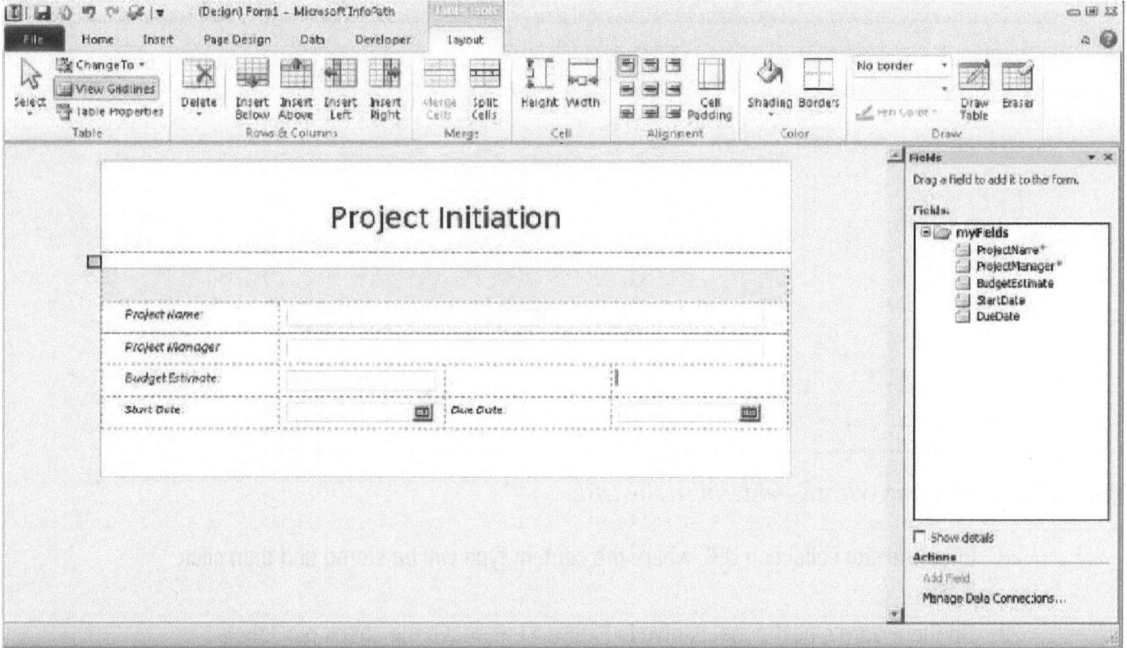

Figure 11-4. Completed form template in InfoPath Designer

22. Select the File tab from the Ribbon to activate the Backstage area.

23. Click the Publish button.

24. Click the SharePoint Server button.

Before publishing the form for the first time, InfoPath requires you to save the unpublished form. This version will be used to update the form template in the future. You will save it to the desktop for simplicity:

25. In the Save As dialog box, click the Desktop link.

26. Type **ProjectInitiation** as the filename.

27. Click the Save button. The Publishing Wizard is displayed, as shown in Figure 11-5.

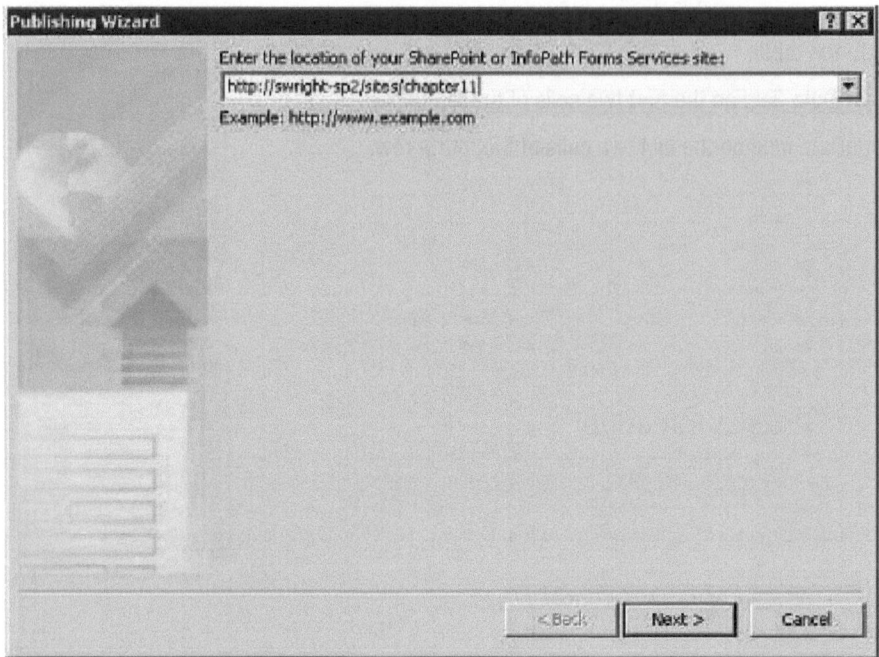

Figure 11-5. Publishing Wizard—entering a site URL

28. Enter the site collection URL where the content type will be stored and then click Next.

29. On the wizard's next page, shown in Figure 11-6, leave the check box labeled Enable This Form to Be Filled Out by Using a Browser selected.

■ **Note** If this option is missing, the probable causes are (1) InfoPath Forms Services is not configured correctly or (2) the SharePoint Enterprise site collection feature is not activated in the site collection where you are trying to publish the form.

---

30. Select the Site Content Type (Advanced) radio button and then click Next.

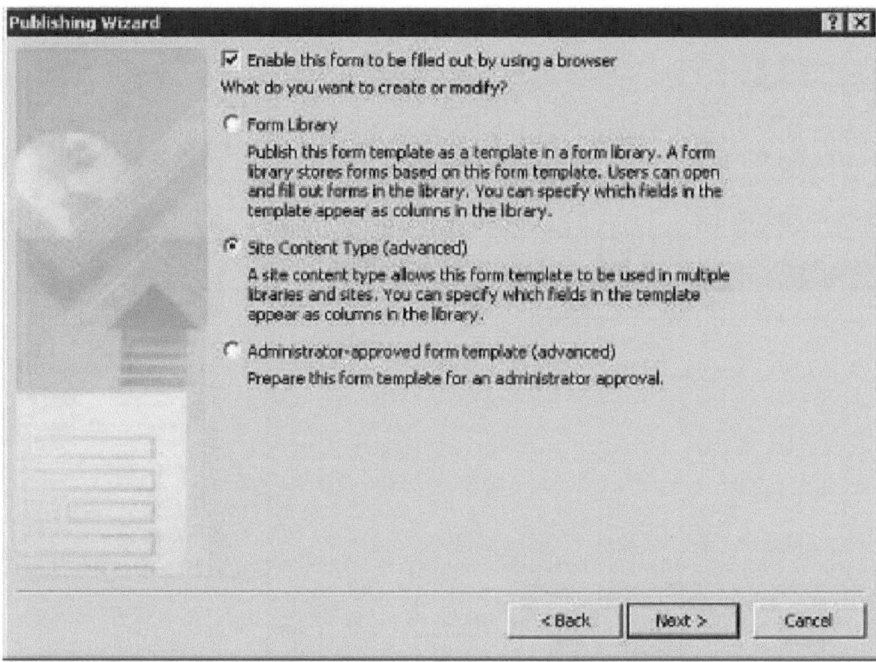

Figure 11-6. Publishing Wizard—setting the destination type

31. On the wizard's next page, shown in Figure 11-7, select the Create a New Content Type radio button.

32. In the Base This Content Type On list, select Form and then click Next.

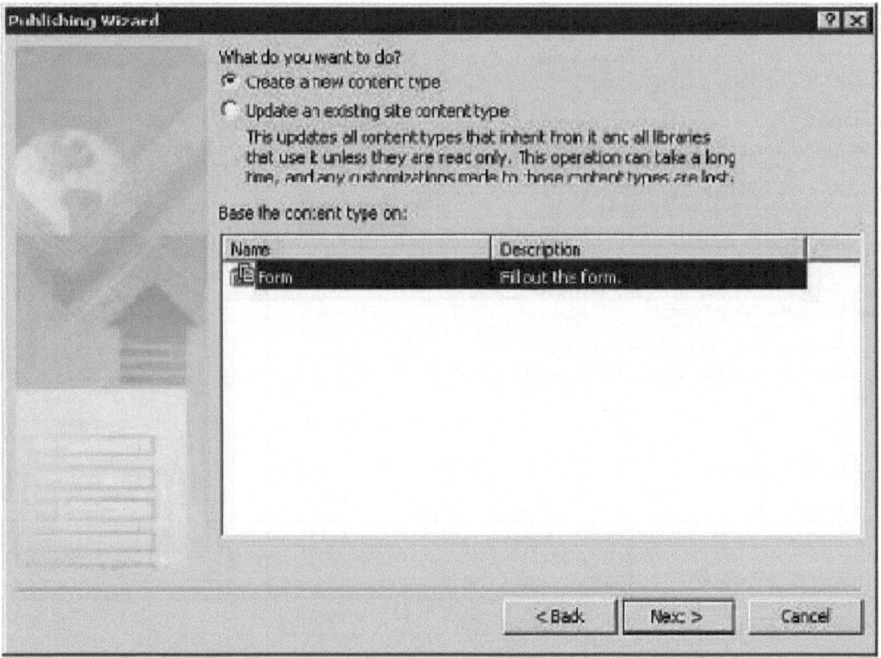

Figure 11-7. Publishing Wizard—creating a content type

33. On the wizard's next page, shown in Figure 11-8, enter the name and description for the form and then click Next.

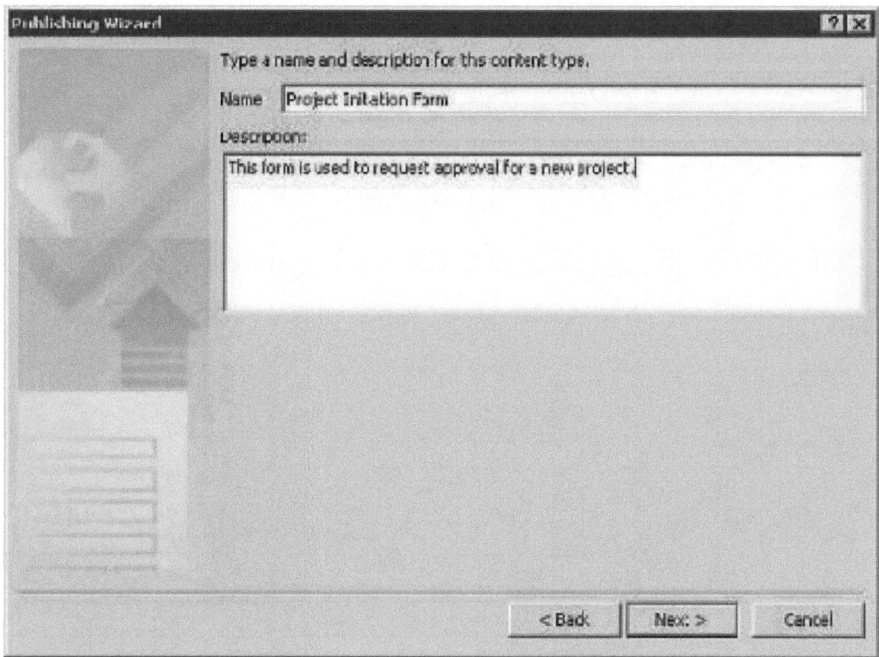

Figure 11-8. Publishing Wizardnaming the content type

The form used by a content type must be published to a location in the site. You can create a new document library or use an existing one. In this case, you will use the FormServerTemplate library that already exists in the site:

34. On the wizard's next page, shown in Figure 11-9, click the Browse button.

35. Double-click the document library to store the template in the list displayed.

36. Enter **ProjectInitiation** for the template filename and then click Save. Back in the wizard, click Next.

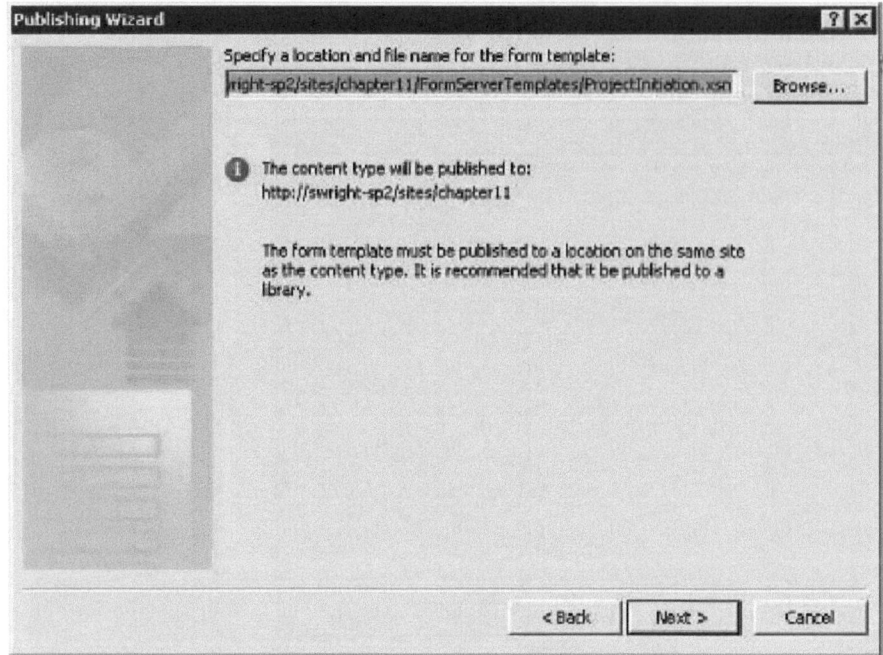

Figure 11-9. Publishing Wizard—setting the template location

The next step of the wizard is used to designate which fields in the XML form will be made visible to the content type as fields. You also have the option of exposing fields as parameters for connecting web parts. You will want to promote those fields that are useful for searching and sorting.

37. Click the Add button near the top of the dialog box.

38. Select the ProjectName field from the list, as shown in Figure 11-10, and then click OK.

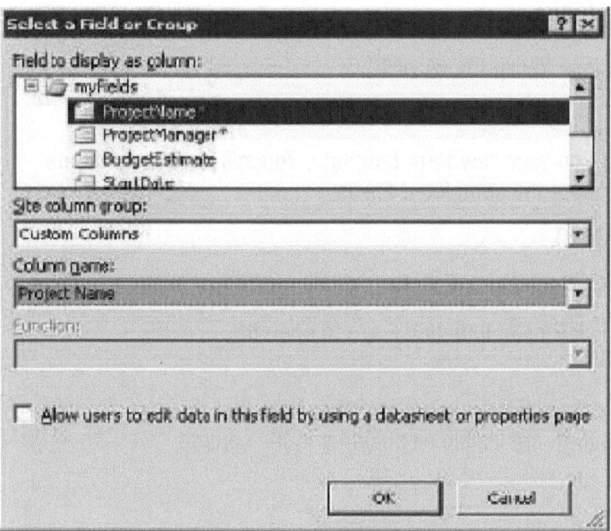

Figure 11-10. Adding a promoted field

39. Add the ProjectManager and StartDate to the list of promoted fields as well, as shown in Figure 11-11. Then click Next.

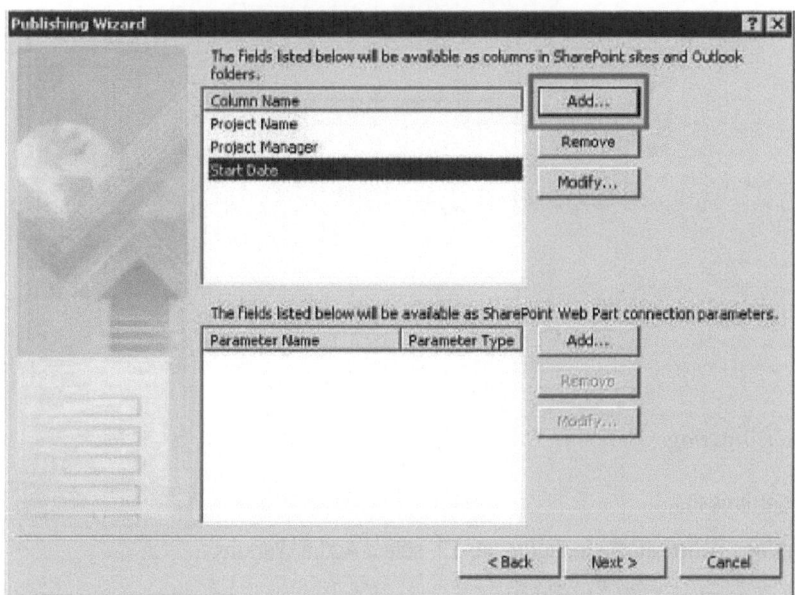

Figure 11-11. Publishing Wizard—adding promoted fields

40. Click Publish to complete the process.

41. When the process is complete, click Close to exit the wizard.

42. Close InfoPath Designer.

At this point, you have created a content type based on your new form template. You still have to configure the approval workflow and create a form library to store the completed forms:

43. Open the site in SharePoint Designer 2010.

44. From the Navigation pane, select the Content Types Gallery.

45. Under the Microsoft InfoPath group, click Project Initiation Form to open the content type's settings page.

46. From the Ribbon's Manage group, select Administration Web Page. Note that the three columns you promoted from the form are visible as columns in the content type, as shown in Figure 11-12.

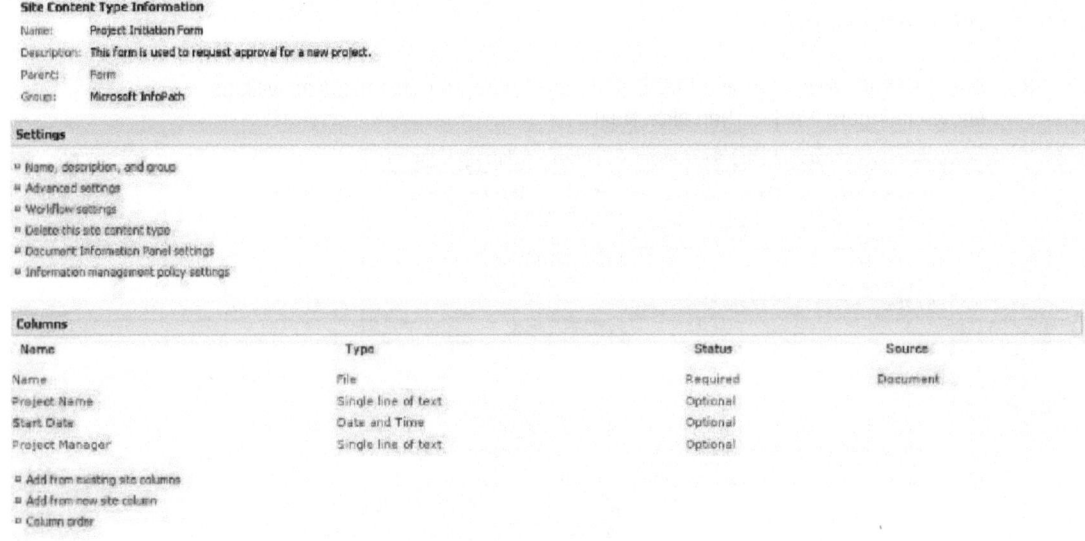

Figure 11-12. Form content type settings page

47. Click the Workflow Settings link.

48. On the Workflow Settings page, shown in Figure 11-13, select Add a Workflow.

49. Select the Approval—SharePoint 2010 workflow.

50. Enter **Project Approval** for the workflow name.

51. Under Start Options, select the check box labeled Start This Workflow When a New Item Is Created.

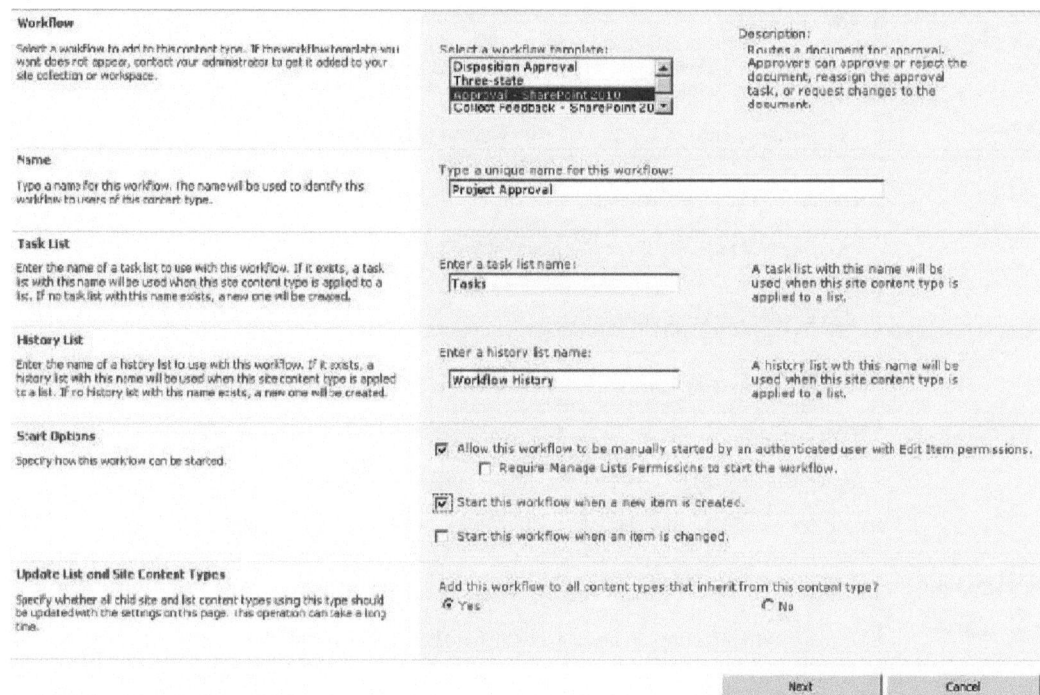

Figure 11-13. Workflow settings page

52. Accept all other defaults and then click Next.

53. The next form, shown in Figure 11-14, is for configuring the workflow. Enter a set of approvers and any other parameters as appropriate. Then click Save.

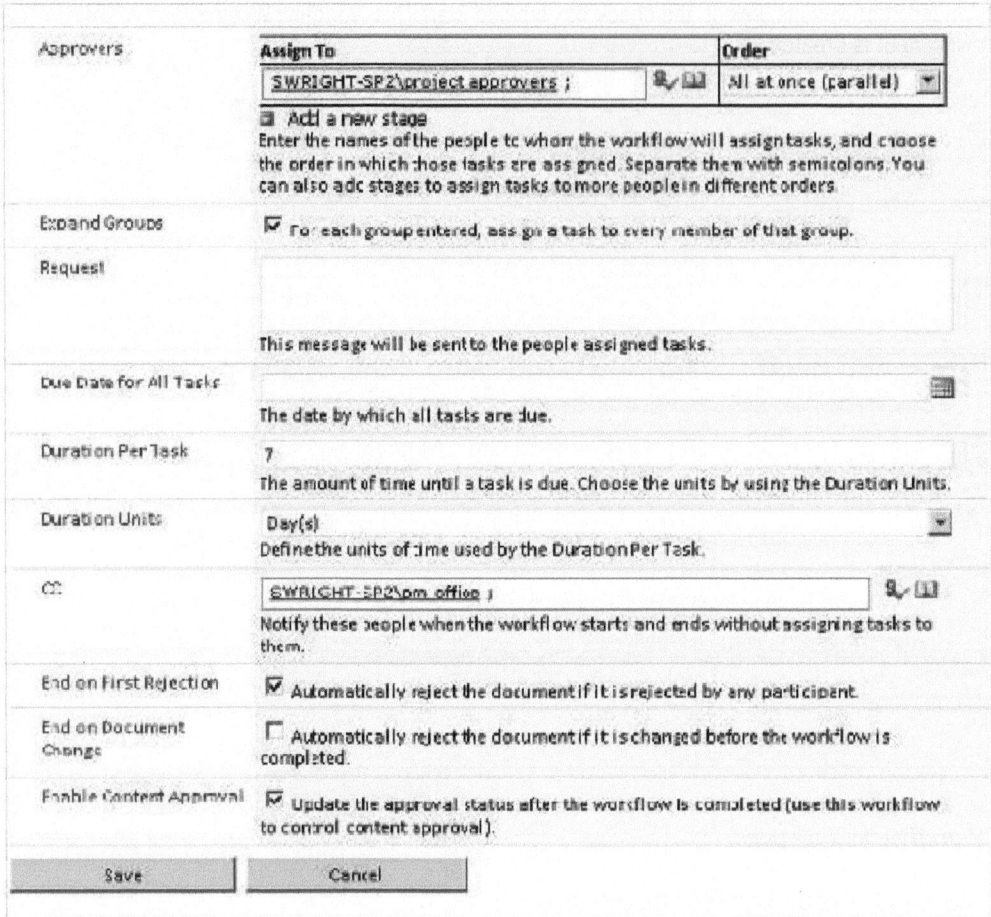

Figure 11-14. Approval workflow configuration

The setup of the content type is now complete. Finally, you will create a new form library to host the content type:

54. In SharePoint Designer 2010, select Form Library from the Document Library drop-down list in the New group on the menu.

55. Enter **Project Forms** for the name and then click OK.

56. In the List and Libraries Gallery, click the Project Forms link.

57. On the settings page, select the check boxes labeled Allow Management of Content Types and Require Content Approval for Submitted Items.

58. Save the changes to the list (Ctrl+S).

59. In the Content Types pane, click Add.

60. In the Content Types Picker, under Microsoft InfoPath, select Project Initiation Form, as shown in Figure 11-15. Then click OK.

Figure 11-15. Content Types Picker

61. In the Content Types list, select Form.

62. On the menu, deselect Show on New Menu in the Actions group. Only the Project Initiation form will be configured to show on the new menu.

Your form is now ready to be used. The form library you have created has inherited the promoted fields, form template, and approval workflow directly from the content type you created.

63. Open the list in a web browser (F12).

64. Click the Add Document link.

65. Enter data into the Project Initiation form displayed, as shown in Figure 11-16. Then click Save.

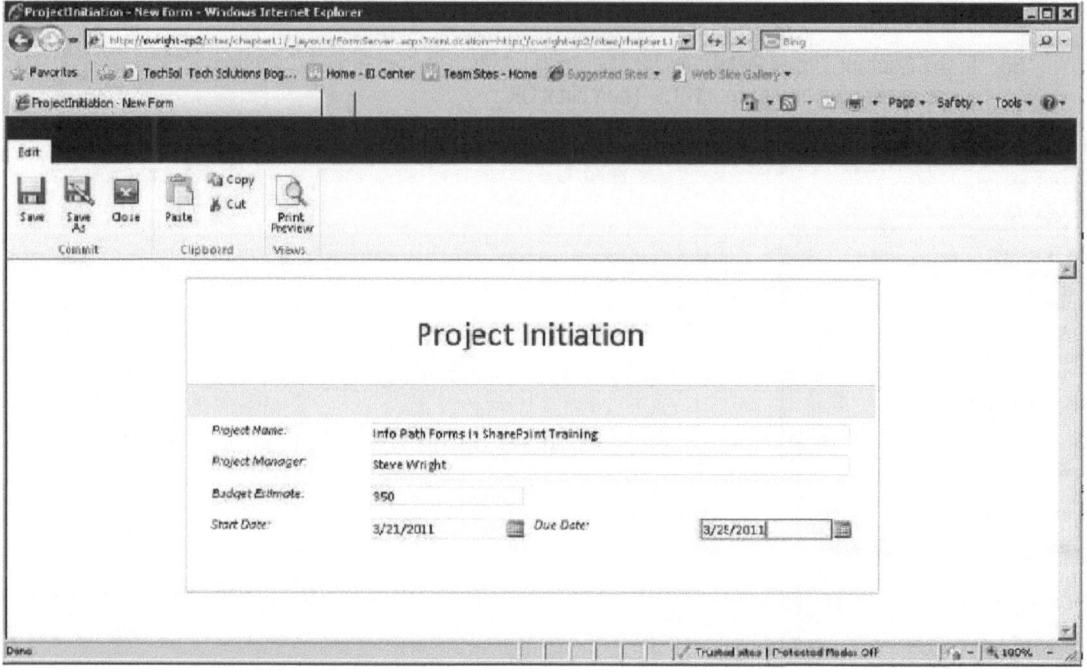

Figure 11-16. InfoPath form in the web browser

66. Enter a name for the file. Click Save.

67. From the menu, click Close.

The form you entered has been added to the form library, and the approval workflow has been started. The same content type can be used in multiple form libraries, and multiple form types can be hosted within this library. The value of using form content types is seen when it is necessary to update the form template. By updating the template associated with the content type, that update is automatically seen by all libraries that use the content type.

EXERCISE 11-2. CUSTOMIZE LIST FORMS BY USING INFOPATH

Tracking issues during a project is a common task performed by using lists in SharePoint. You will start with the standard issue list template available in SharePoint. Then you will create a custom InfoPath form for entering, updating, and viewing issues to suit your specific needs.

1. Open the site in SharePoint Designer 2010.

2. From the Navigation pane, select Lists and Libraries.

3. From the SharePoint List drop-down menu in the New group, select Issue Tracking, as shown in Figure 11-17.

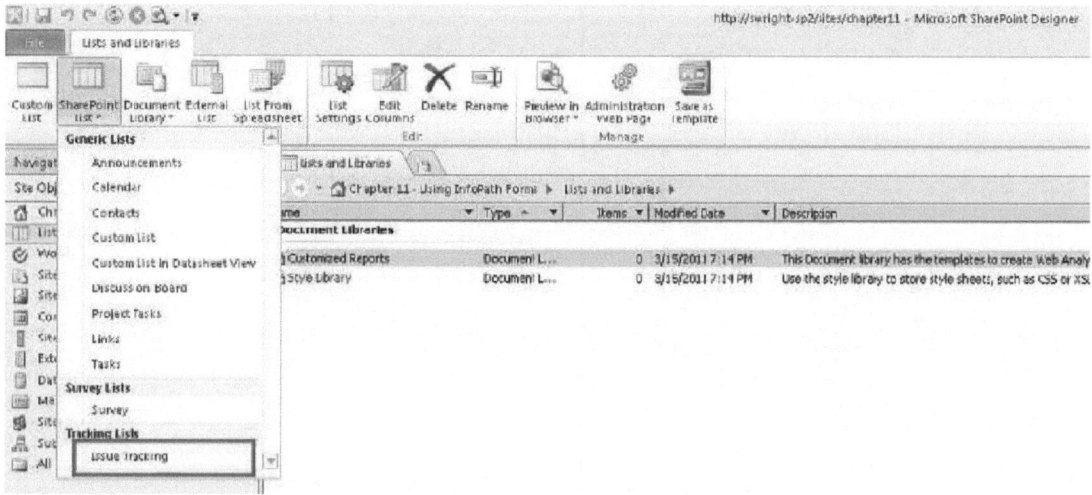

Figure 11-17. *Creating the Issue Tracking list*

4. Name the new list **Issues** and click OK.

5. Click the Issues list to go to the settings page.

6. Press F12 to view the list in the web browser.

7. Click the Add New Item link. This displays the default New Item dialog box for the list, as shown in Figure 11-18.

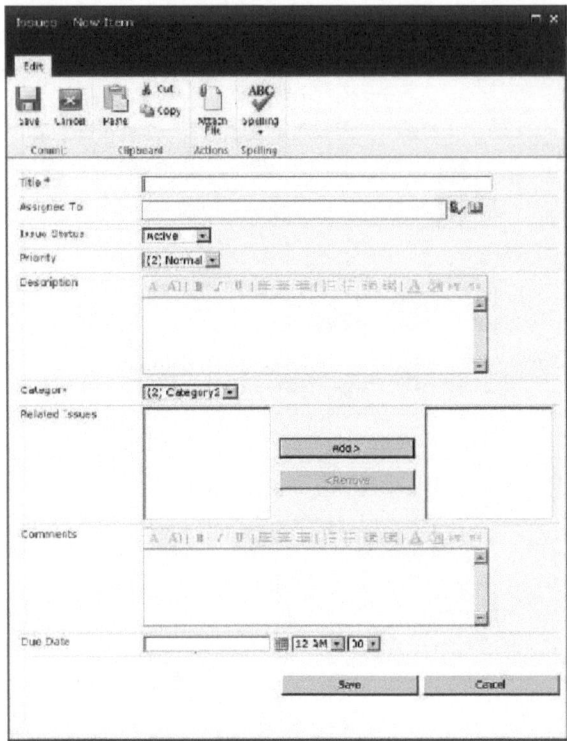

Figure 11-18. Default New Item form

8. In SharePoint Designer, on the Ribbon, select the List tab under List Tools.

9. Click the Customize Form button in the Customize List group of the menu, as shown in Figure 11-19.

Figure 11-19. Customize Form menu item

■ **Tip** If the Customize Form button is missing, it is probably because you forgot to activate the SharePoint Enterprise features in the site collection.

A new form template, shown in Figure 11-20, launches in InfoPath Designer 2010. This form is a replica of the default form generated by SharePoint. The fields in the pane to the right represent the columns in the list. These are the data elements for the form. Now you will remove and rearrange the fields in your form.

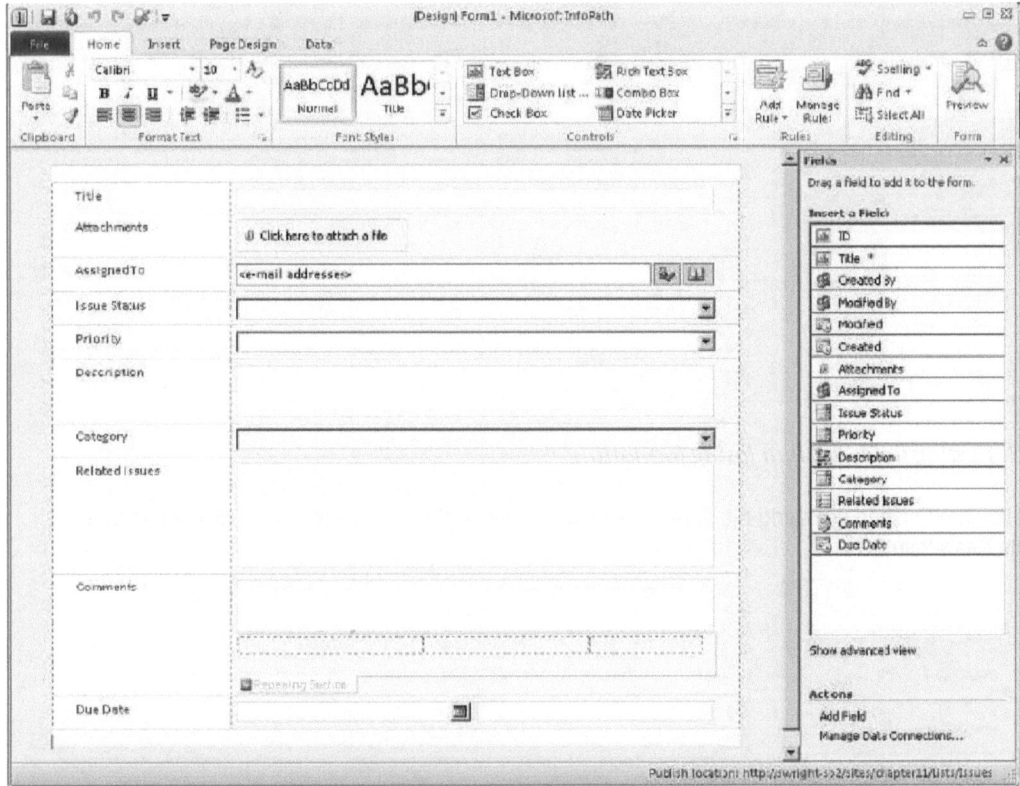

Figure 11-20. Default InfoPath list form

10. Right-click the Attachments row and select Delete ➤ Rows.

11. Right-click the Related Issues row and select Delete ➤ Rows.

12. Right-click the Category row and select Cut.

13. Click in the leftmost part of the cell containing Issue Status.

14. Right-click and select Paste Options: (Keep Source Formatting), as shown in Figure 11-21.

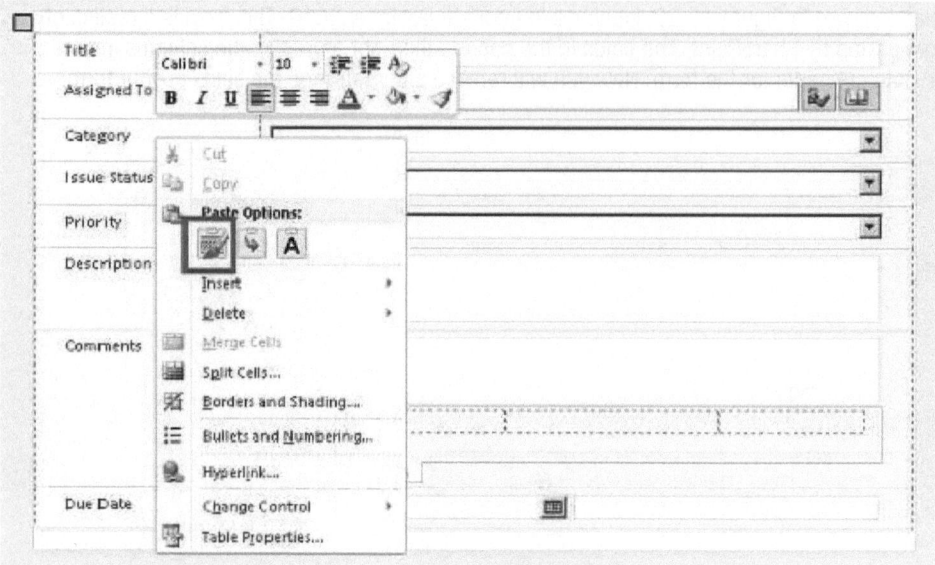

Figure 11-21. *Pasting fields without losing formatting*

Now that you are finished changing the appearance and behavior of the data entry form, you must publish it back into SharePoint.

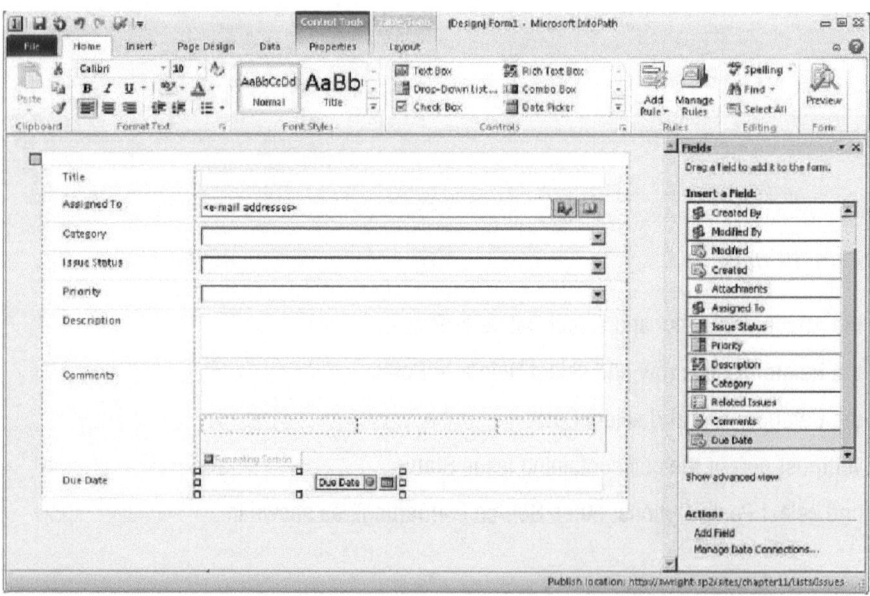

Figure 11-22. *Finished list form template*

15. From the Ribbon, click the File tab and select Quick Publish.

■ **Note** There is no need to tell InfoPath where or how to publish the form template because it was created specifically for your issues list. Quick Publish simply publishes it back to that location and installs it for you.

---

16. In a few moments, a dialog box appears, indicating that your form template was published successfully. Click OK.

17. Close InfoPath Designer.

18. Back in the web browser, you are still on the All Items view on the Issues list (see Figure 11-23). Click the Add New Item link again. The New Item form is now rendered by using your form template.

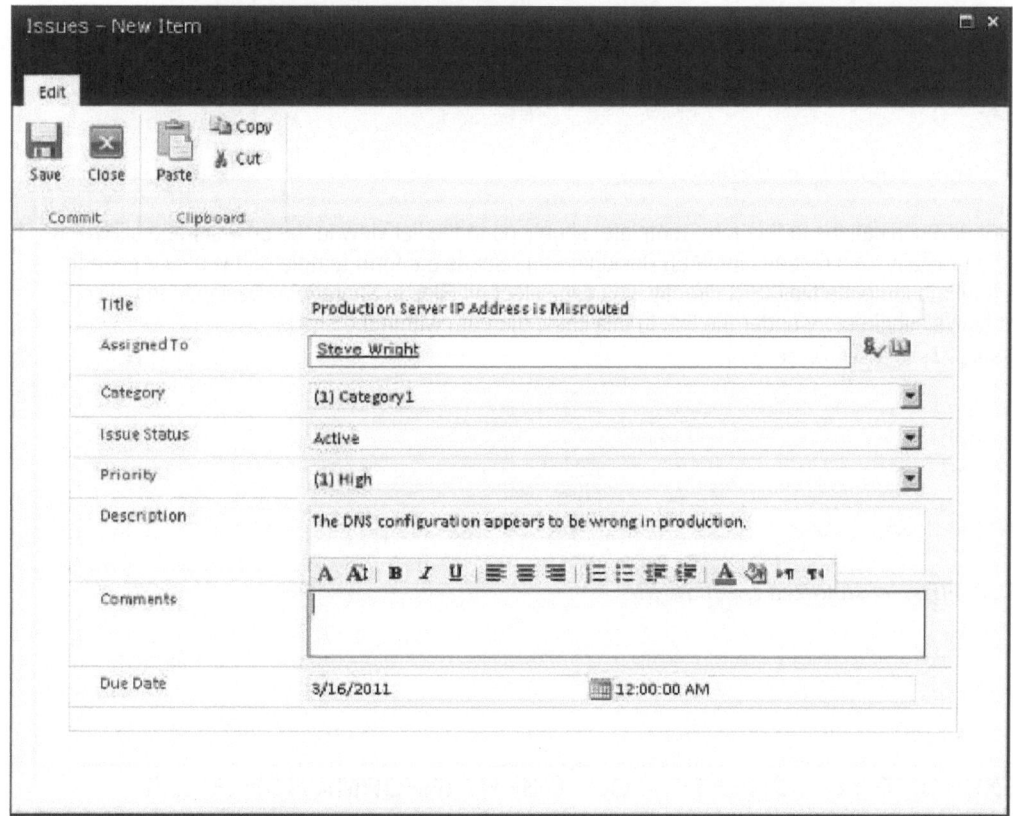

Figure 11-23. Customized list form in the browser

19. Enter some data and then click Save to submit it to the list.

20. The item now appears in the Issues list. Clicking the title opens your new form in Display mode.

21. In SharePoint Designer, open or refresh the settings page for the Issues list.

Three new forms have been added to the Forms pane: `displayifs.aspx`, `editifs.aspx`, and `newifs.aspx`, as you can see in Figure 11-24. If you open these pages in the Page Editor, you will see that they use the `BrowserFormWebPart` control to display the form template in the necessary mode (New, Edit, or Display). This control is the InfoPath Form web part, which uses Forms Services to display the form.

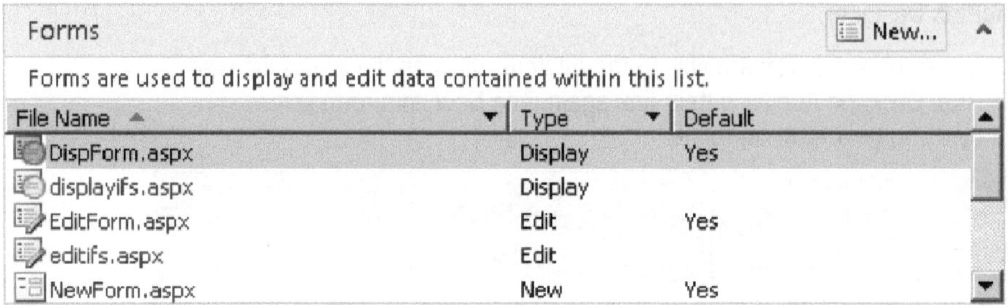

Figure 11-24. Customized forms in theIList

To make further modifications to this form template, simply go to the list view in the browser and click Customize Form again. This reopens InfoPath Designer and reloads the form template. If you ever need to access the InfoPath template file (XSN) directly, you can select All Files in SharePoint Designer and look in the content type's subdirectory under the list. In this case, the path within the site is `/Lists/Issues/Issue/template.xsn`.

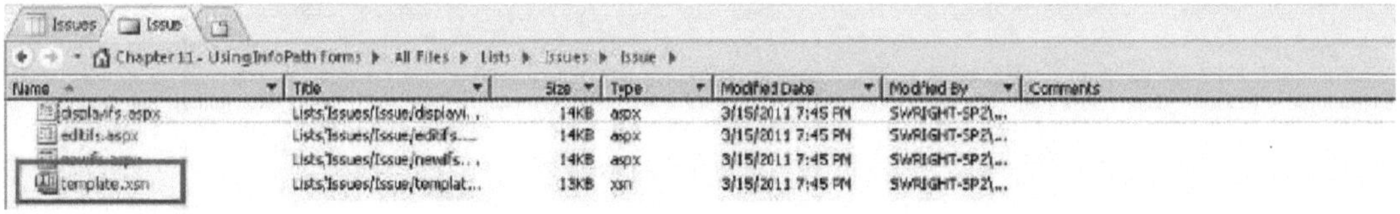

Figure 11-25. All Files—customized template file

EXERCISE 11-3. CREATE A DOCUMENT INFORMATION PANEL

In our final InfoPath exercise, you will create a document library for storing project documents such as requirements, designs, and project schedules. The documents in this library will have additional metadata fields defined in a content type. You will create a DIP for this content type that will integrate these metadata fields into whatever MS Office application is used to edit these documents.

1. Open the site in SharePoint Designer.

2. In the Navigation pane, click Site Columns.

3. From the menu, click the New Column drop-down and select Single Line of Text.

4. Enter **Project Name** for the column name, as shown in Figure 11-26. Then click OK.

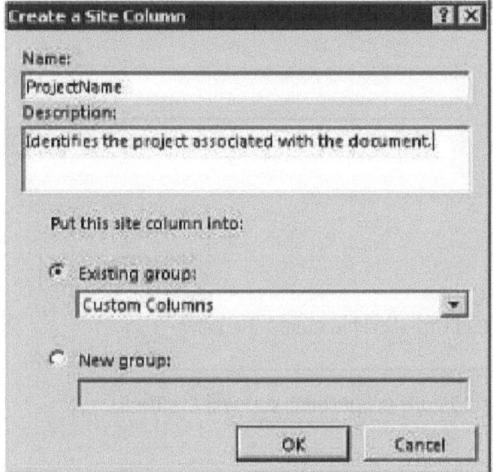

Figure 11-26. Creating a site column

5. From the menu, click the New Column drop-down and select Choice.

6. Enter **Document Type** for the column name and then click OK.

7. Double-click the Document Type site column in the gallery list.

8. In the Column Editor dialog box, enter **Requirements**, **Designs**, **Schedules**, and **Other** for the choices, as shown in Figure 11-27.

9. Set the Default Value option to **Other**. Then click OK.

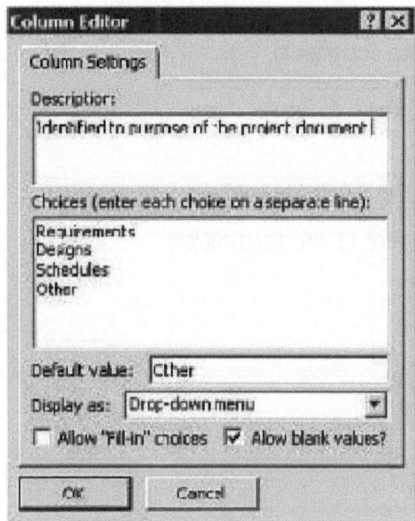

Figure 11-27. *Creating a choice column*

10. Click the Save button in the window title bar or press Ctrl+S. This saves the new site columns to SharePoint.

Now that you have created the site columns that will store your custom properties, you will create a content type to represent the document itself:

11. In the Navigation pane, click Content Types.

12. Select Content Type from the New group in the menu.

13. Enter **Project Document** in the name field.

14. From the Select Parent Content Type From drop-down list, select Document Content Types.

15. From the Select Parent Content Type drop-down list, select Document.

16. Under Existing Group, select Document Content Types. Click OK.

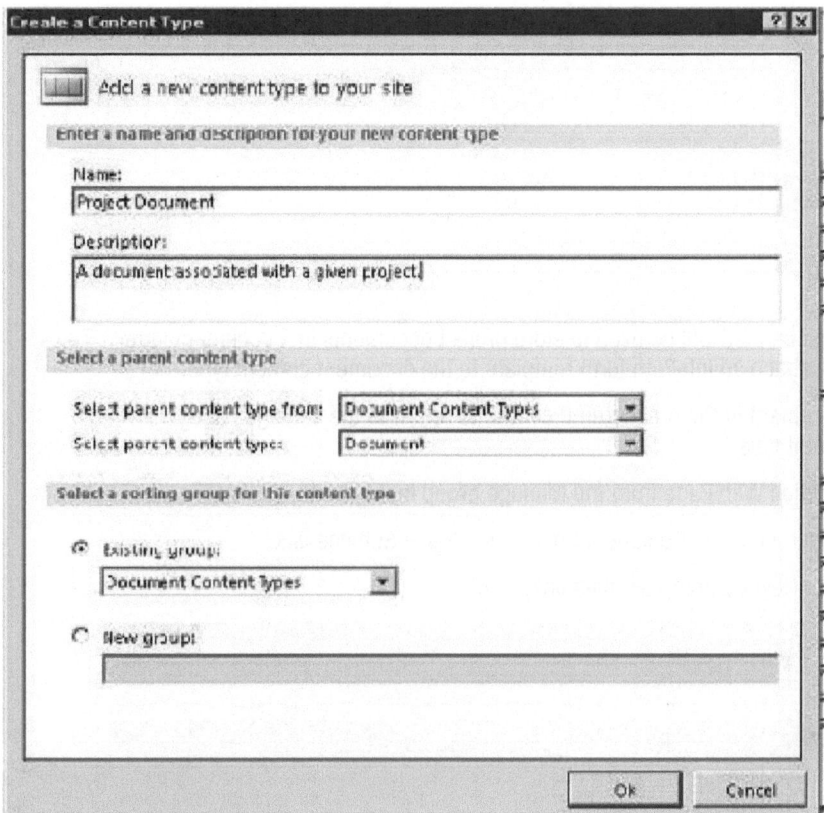

Figure 11-28. Creating a content type

17. In the Content Types Gallery, click the Project Document link.

18. On the settings page, click the Edit Content Type Columns link under Customization.

19. On the menu, select Add Existing Site Column from the New group.

20. Select Project Name and then click OK.

21. On the menu, select Add Existing Site Column from the New group.

22. Select Document Type and then click OK.

23. Click the Save button in the window title bar or press Ctrl+S. This saves the new content type to SharePoint.

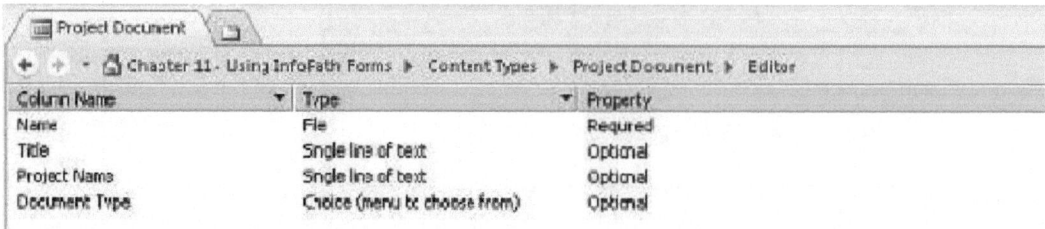

Figure 11-29. *Content Type Editor*

The content type you have just created will be used to store project documents in a document library. To implement the DIP, you must attach an InfoPath form template to the document content type.

24. Click Project Document in the breadcrumb control to return to the settings page for the new content type.

25. Select Administration Web Page from the Manage group in the menu.

26. In the web browser, click the Document Information Panel Settings link.

27. Click the Create a New Custom Template link.

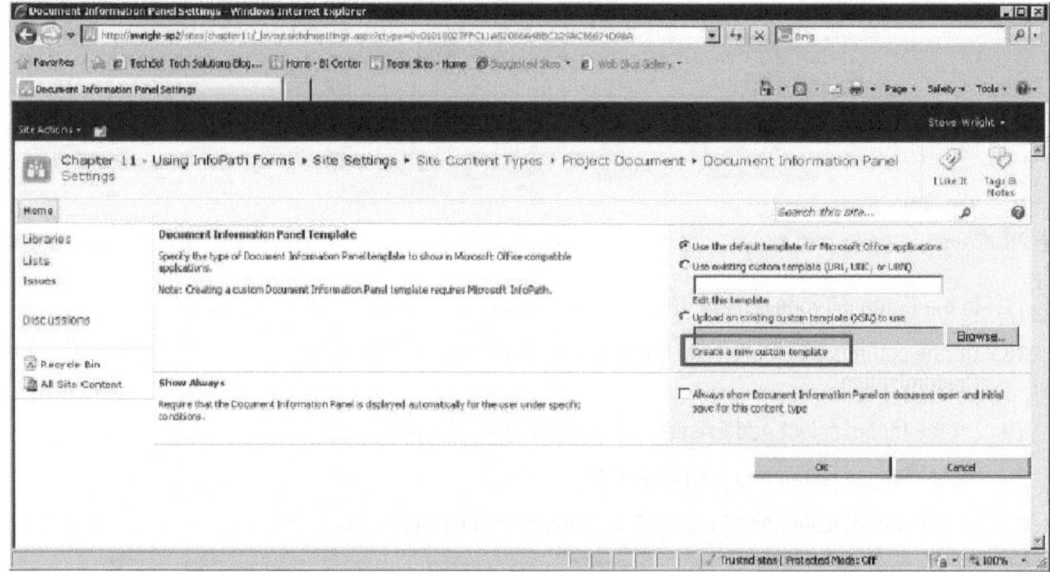

Figure 11-30. *Document Information Panel Settings page*

28. InfoPath Designer opens to an informational dialog box. Click Finish.

29. InfoPath displays a default DIP form based on the fields in the content type, as you can see in Figure 11-31.

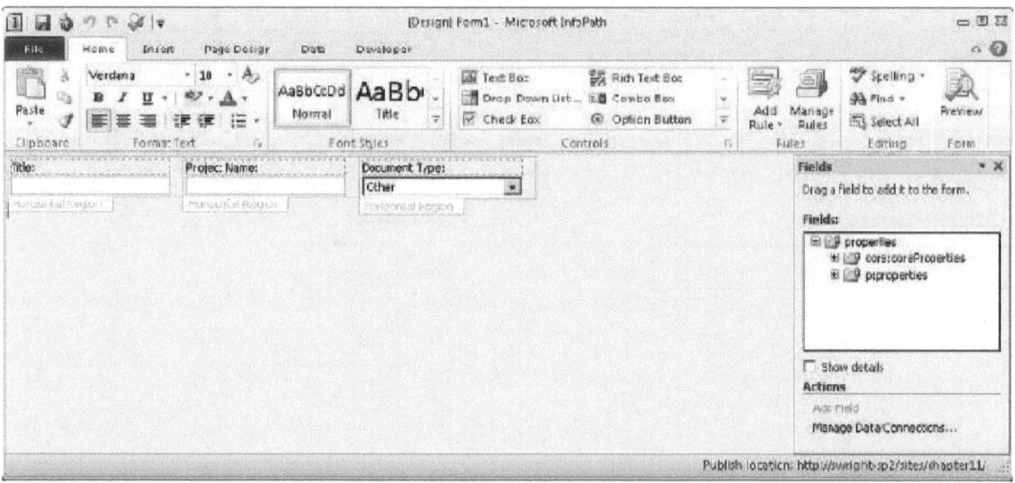

Figure 11-31. Default DIP form template

■ **Note** The Title field is included, but the Name field is not. The filename cannot be changed from a DIP form because this type of form is used when the file is open.

---

30. Make some changes to the layout of the form.

31. Click the File tab of the menu and select Quick Publish from the Backstage area.

■ **Note** As you saw for a custom list form, there is no need to tell InfoPath where or how to publish the form template. In this case, however, SharePoint Designer will insist that you save your unpublished DIP form template outside SharePoint before it publishes it to SharePoint. Future changes to the DIP template should be made in the saved file. The template is then republished to SharePoint.

---

32. In the Save As dialog box, save the unpublished form template to your hard drive.

33. In a few moments, a dialog box appears, indicating that your form template was published successfully. Click OK.

34. Close InfoPath Designer.

35. In the web browser, use the link provided to return to the DIP settings page (see Figure 11-32). Note the location of the DIP template stored in SharePoint.

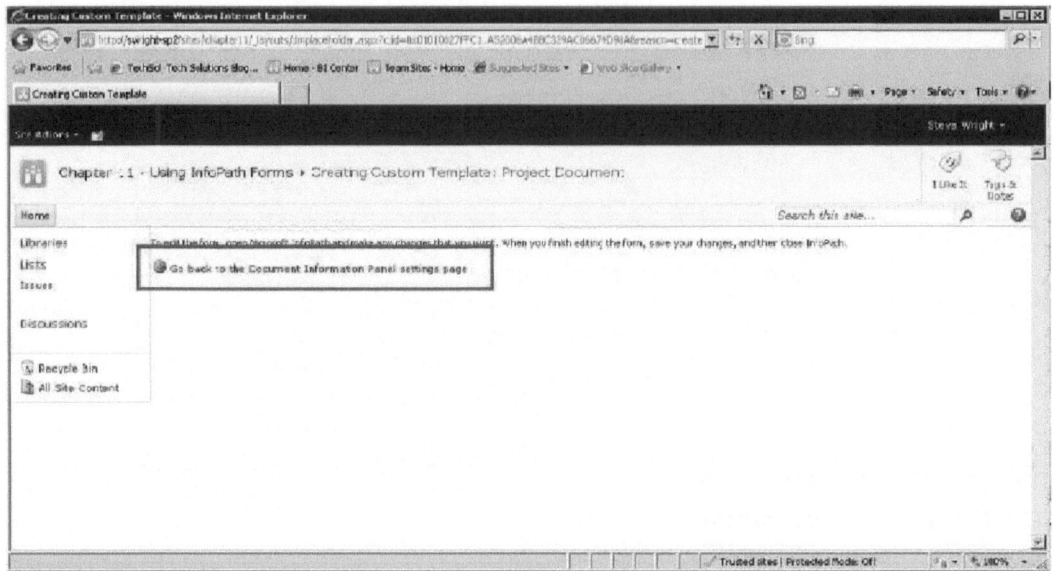

Figure 11-32. DIP settings page link

36. At the bottom of the page, select the check box labeled Always Show Document Information Panel. Click OK.

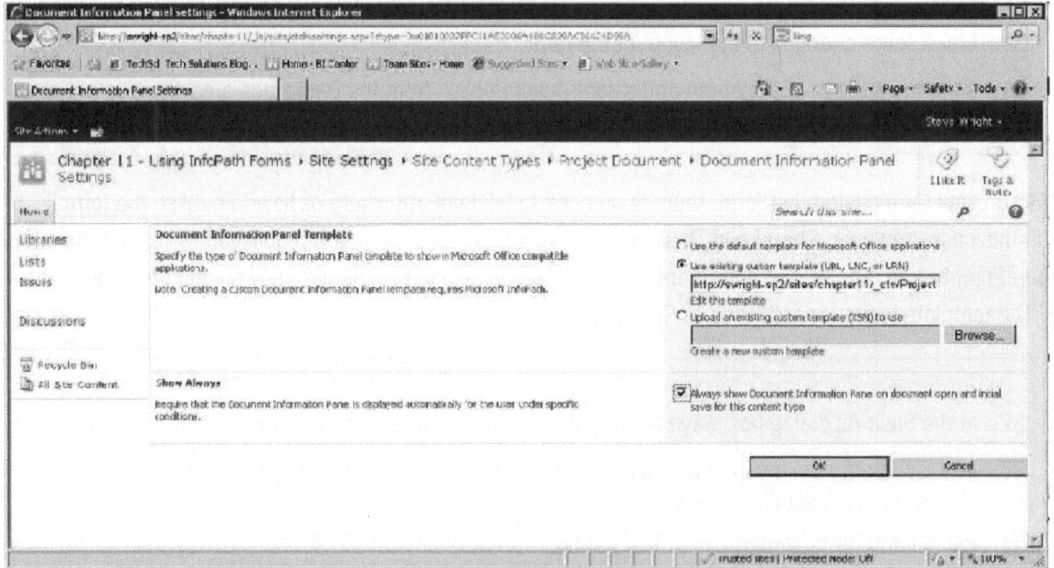

Figure 11-33. DIP Settings page

■ **Note** A DIP form template must be published to the same security domain as the document that will use it in order to function correctly. In our example, the template is being published to a document library within your site collection. This is a good practice to prevent security issues when dealing with these panels. If the form template is stored elsewhere, be certain that users can access it without crossing domains.

At this point, you have only created a content type for your documents and the document information panel you want to use. You still have to create a library and associate your content type with it:

37. In SharePoint Designer, select Lists and Libraries from the Navigation pane.

38. Select Document Library from the Document Library drop-down in the New group in the menu.

39. Name the new library **Project Documents**. Click OK.

40. In the Lists Gallery, click the Project Documents link to open the library's settings page.

41. In the Settings panel, select the check box labeled Allow Management of Content Types.

42. Save the changes by pressing Ctrl+S.

43. In the Content Types panel, click the Add button.

44. Select Project Document from the picker and then click OK.

45. Select the Project Document type in the Content Types list. Click the Set as Default button in the Actions group on the menu.

46. Select the Document type in the Content Types list. Click the Show on New Menu button in the Actions group on the menu.

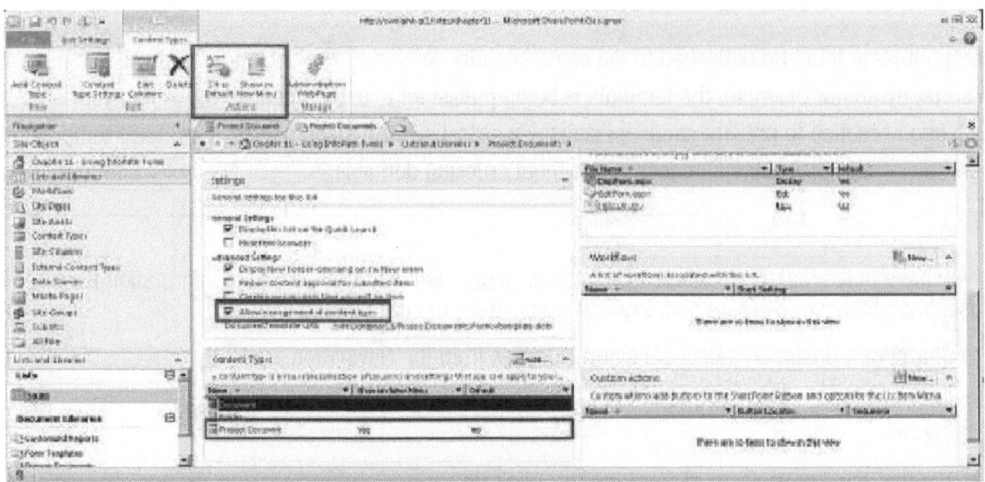

Figure 11-34. *Project Documents library settings*

The document library has been configured to contain either a document or a project document. You can't remove Document as a content type, but you have removed it from the New menu so users won't see that option anymore (see Figure 11-35).

47. Press F12 to open the list in the web browser.

48. On the menu, select the Documents tab under Library Tools.

49. Select the Project Document option under the New Document drop-down.

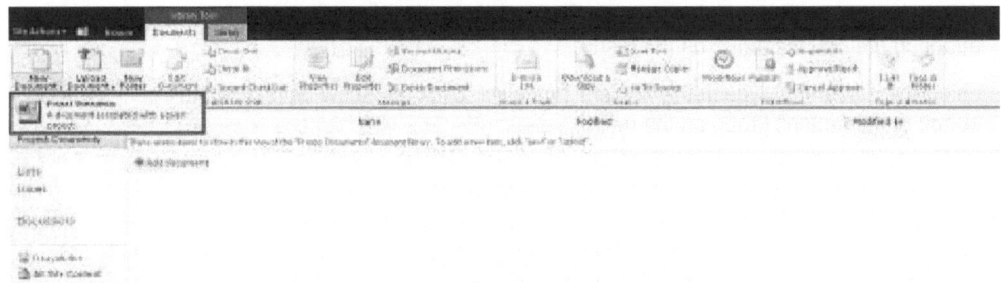

Figure 11-35. *Creating a new project document*

50. Type some content into the new Word document and save it to SharePoint. After the file is saved, the document information panel appears, as shown in Figure 11-36.

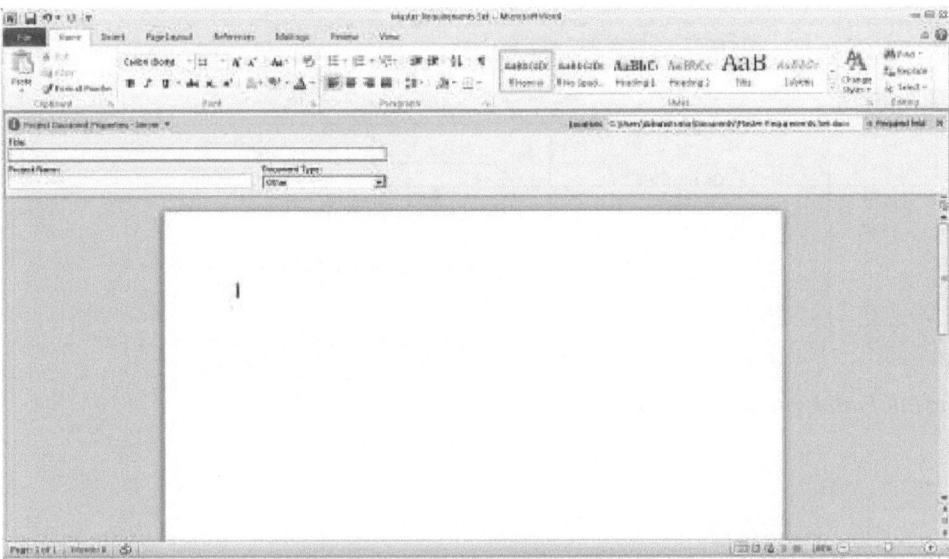

Figure 11-36. The document information panel in Word

51. Enter data in the DIP form and save the document and save it again.

In the library list, select View Properties from the document's drop-down menu. Note that the properties you entered are now part of the document's metadata. You can add as many properties as needed by using DIPs. You can also add other behaviors to the form by using InfoPath's other features such as roles, views, and rules.

Summary

In this chapter, you have

- Explored the concepts of InfoPath 2010 forms

- Examined the security and functionality considerations associated with browser-enabled forms in InfoPath

- Learned how to create and deploy InfoPath forms to a SharePoint environment

- Customized the new, display, and edit forms for a SharePoint list by using InfoPath

- Created a document information panel and deployed it in SharePoint to collect custom document metadata

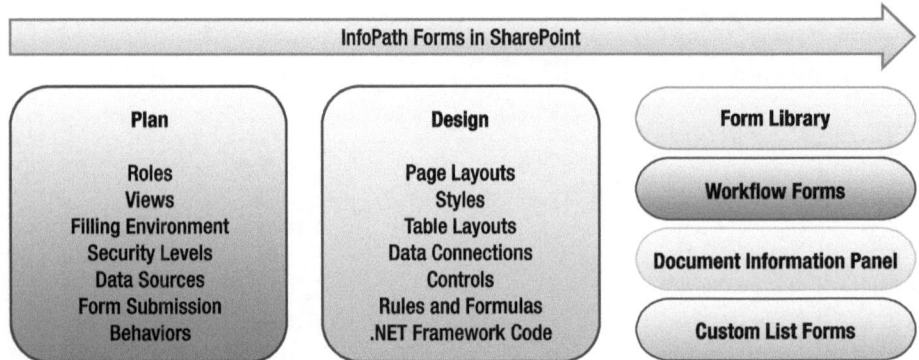

Figure 11-37. Using InfoPath forms in SharePoint

CHAPTER 12

Automating with Workflows

SharePoint Server 2010 contains a powerful workflow engine based on the .NET Framework's Workflow Foundation. Using SharePoint Designer, you can leverage this engine to automate many business processes quickly and easily.

In this chapter, you will explore the concepts and tools used to build and customize workflows in SharePoint Designer 2010. You will begin with the basic ideas behind the workflow engine. Then, you will learn about the components that are available to create new workflows. Finally, you will go through a series of exercises designed to touch on the most important use cases, where workflows can add value to a SharePoint solution.

You will learn about the following topics in this chapter:

- Using the concepts and building blocks available within SharePoint Designer to automate processes with workflows

- Using mechanisms to control security in workflows

- Understanding the collection and storage of data within a workflow instance

- Creating flexible, reusable workflow definitions

- Customizing the built-in workflows that come with SharePoint Server 2010

- Customizing the end-user experience by using InfoPath forms

- Creating all-new workflows with SharePoint Designer

- Automating SharePoint maintenance with site workflows

Introduction to Workflow

With version 3.0 of the .NET Framework, Microsoft introduced a standard infrastructure for creating and hosting custom business processes called the *Windows Workflow Foundation (WF)*. WF is a set of libraries that contain a complete in-process workflow engine and associated classes. The workflow engine manages the instances of a workflow that are running within the process.

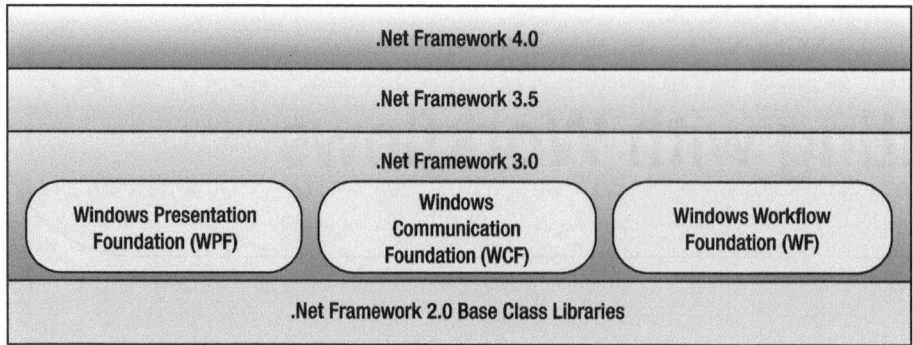

Figure 12-1. *Windows Workflow Foundation in the .NET stack*

Although the engine is designed to be hosted within any .NET application, SharePoint Server 2010 provides a wide variety of tools for designing, deploying, and managing workflows within a SharePoint server farm. Workflows are defined by using a designer, typically either SharePoint Designer 2010 or Visual Studio 2010. The workflow definition is then deployed to the SharePoint environment and associated with a list, a content type, or a site. An instance of the workflow may be started based on the creation of a document, a manual action, or the action of a program.

A workflow running in SharePoint has access to many of SharePoint's resources and can perform actions such as checking files in and out, creating or moving list items, setting item permissions, and so on. The most common actions taken by workflows are to send e-mail notifications and to assign tasks to users. SharePoint maintains the state of the workflows and provides the interface for managing instances. SharePoint also maintains a detailed log of all workflow actions and results.

As stated earlier, the tools most commonly used to create workflows in SharePoint are SharePoint Designer and Visual Studio. SharePoint Designer places certain restrictions on the types of workflows that can be created. For example, SharePoint Designer does not support custom .NET code, looping constructs, or state machine workflows. Even so, most common business processes can be modeled very well with the workflow features that are available in SharePoint Designer. Those that cannot are generally complex enough that a development team should be engaged to create the best implementation possible. These highly customized workflows should be created through a development tool such as Visual Studio. This chapter focuses on the features available to site designers and power users in SharePoint Designer.

As with other aspects of SharePoint Server, workflow could easily fill its own book, or several of them. To get a more in-depth look at workflow development, see *Beginning WF: Windows Workflow in .NET 4.0* by Mark Collins (Apress, 2009) and *Pro WF: Windows Workflow in .NET 4.0* by Bruce Bukovics (Apress, 2010).

What's New in SharePoint Designer 2010 Workflows?

In SharePoint Designer 2007, the scenarios available to workflow developers were limited by several barriers that have been removed in SharePoint Designer 2010. It is now much easier to create and deploy a wider variety of workflows from entirely within SharePoint Designer. There is far less need to abandon designer-based workflows in favor of Visual Studio. The introduction of the Ribbon menu and improvements to the designer interface have made SharePoint Designer a more productive workflow design environment as well.

Here is a list of some of the more important changes that have been made in the latest release:

- More-flexible workflow definitions

    - *Reusable workflows* are associated with a content type instead of a specific list.

    - *Site workflows* are associated with a site and not a specific list or item in a list.

    - *SharePoint's out-of-the-box workflows* can now be customized by using SharePoint Designer.

    - *Association columns* can be defined in a workflow and are automatically added to a list that uses the workflow.

    - *Solution files (WSP)* can be generated by exporting a workflow through SharePoint Designer. These can then be imported into another farm.

    - *InfoPath forms* are generated by SharePoint Designer for association, initiation, and task forms. These forms can be customized by using InfoPath Designer.

- Workflow step and action improvements

    - *Parallel blocks* allow the workflow designer to create multiple simultaneous paths through the workflow instead of all steps occurring in a strict sequence.

    - *Nested steps* allow for more-sophisticated workflow structures.

    - *Document set actions* can be used to control a document set and the documents within it as a unit.

    - *Impersonation steps* enable workflows to manage security permissions on list items by using the credentials of the workflow author instead of the user who started the workflow.

    - *Set Workflow Status* is a new action that allows the workflow designer to set an arbitrary status string for the workflow.

    - The *Task Process action* supports the creation of complex task sequences with rules for completing and continuing a series of tasks within a workflow.

    - *Start Approval Process* and *Start Feedback Process* are customized instances of the Task Process action that implement the standard approval and feedback workflows. These actions allow the default workflows to be customized.

- Improved workflow visualization

Microsoft Visio 2010 can now be used to create the overall structure of a workflow. That structure can then be imported into SharePoint Designer for implementation.

The *Workflow Status page* can contain a visual representation of the current state of a running workflow in a Visio diagram embedded in the page.

Workflow Concepts

In this section, you will explore the concepts on which SharePoint workflows are built. You will start by looking the security context of your workflows. Then you will look at the different types of workflows that SharePoint can host. A workflow instance contains various data elements and often has forms associated with it that provide an interface for data entry. Finally, you will learn about the tools available to create and customize workflow definitions, with an emphasis on choosing the right tool for the job.

Security

When a user starts a workflow instance, either intentionally or as a side effect to some other action, that instance will execute using that user's credentials. Even if the workflow continues to run long after the user has left the site, the workflow engine will still use those credentials. Any permissions (such as file or list item access rights) associated with the initiating user will be applied to the instance when it is running.

This security context has often proven too restrictive for some proposed workflow designs. For example, say a user creates a vacation request and saves it in a document library. As a result, an approval workflow is started. Once the request is approved, you want to move it into a protected archive for approved requests. Because the user who initiated the workflow doesn't have access to the protected archive, the workflow can't move the request into it.

One of the most important workflow improvements in SharePoint 2010 was created specifically to deal with this type of situation. A new type of workflow step, called an *impersonation step*, can be added to a workflow just like any other step. The difference is that the security context for the impersonation step is not that of the initiating user but of the workflow's author. The workflow's author is generally the user who last updated the workflow's definition. That user can be given the necessary permissions to perform the needed actions that the initiator may lack.

An impersonation step can contain conditions and actions like any other step, but the following set of actions can appear only within an impersonation step:

- Add List Item Permissions

- Remove List Item Permissions

- Replace List Item Permissions

- Inherit List Item Parent Permissions

These actions are designed to provide the workflow designer with greater flexibility when working with items and document permission settings. This enables SharePoint Designer to create workflows that have far more sophisticated security requirements.

Types of Workflows

One of the most common reasons for not using SharePoint Designer 2007 for building workflows had to do with way designer workflows were associated with lists. When designing a workflow, the user had to identify the one unique SharePoint list with which the workflow was to be associated. This was useful in that it gave the workflow access to all of the fields associated with the list, but it made it impossible to reuse workflow definitions between lists. Creating a list-independent workflow definition required Visual Studio.

In SharePoint Designer 2010, the site designer can create a *list workflow* as described in the preceding paragraph or a *reusable workflow* that is not tied to a specific list. Instead, a reusable workflow is designed using a SharePoint content type. The content type acts as a template for the eventual list item that will be associated with an instance of the workflow. Because content types inherit from one another, a workflow designed for one content type can also be used for any content type that is derived from it. Because all list and library items in SharePoint ultimately derive from the Item content type (called All in the SharePoint Designer interface), a workflow designed against that type can be used with any list or library item.

Reusable workflows can also be configured as part of the content type's definition. Whenever the content type is used in a SharePoint list, the workflow is automatically configured. This is a powerful means of standardizing processes across your SharePoint farm, because content types can also be shared between site collections in SharePoint Server 2010.

Another useful new type of workflow in SharePoint 2010 is the *site workflow*. In SharePoint 2007, all workflows had to be associated with a list or library item. What if the workflow process you are automating doesn't naturally correspond to a single content item in the site? In the previous release of SharePoint, this meant that a document or list item had to be created just to allow the execution of a workflow.

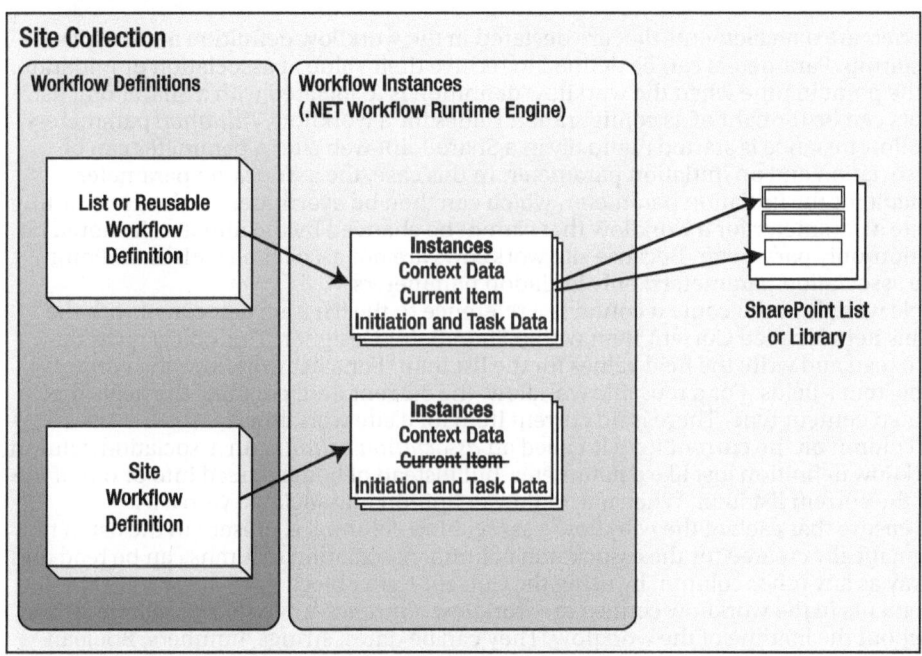

Figure 12-2. *Workflow instances in SharePoint*

A site workflow definition runs at the site level, so it has no *current item* associated with it. However, a site workflow is a normal workflow in most other respects. It can create list items, check files in or out, send e-mails, and take any other action that does not require an associated list item.

■ **Tip** The actions that operate against the current workflow item, and are therefore not usable in a site workflow, often have *Current Item* in their name.

Workflow Context Data

A workflow instance stores data that controls the processing of the workflow. There are several classifications of this data, depending on how it came to be associated with the workflow. Together, the data and status information for a workflow instance is referred to as its *context*. Most actions within a workflow have parameters that can be set by using values from the workflow context.

The workflow context contains status values related to the running of the instance. These include the current status of the workflow, when the workflow was started, and which user initiated the workflow. These values are set automatically by the workflow engine and can be used throughout the workflow.

Workflow *parameters* are data elements that are declared in the workflow definition and are passed into the workflow at startup. Parameters can be defined to receive their value at association or initiation. *Association* refers to the point in time when the workflow definition is associated with a SharePoint list. Association parameters can be thought of as configuration values for a workflow. *Initiation* parameters are set when the workflow instance is started manually in a SharePoint web site. A parameter can be defined as both an association and an initiation parameter. In this case, the association parameter setting becomes a default for the initiation parameter, which can then be overridden by the user starting the workflow. To create a parameter for a workflow that cannot be changed by the initiator, it should be created as an association-only parameter. Because site workflows are not associated with SharePoint lists, they do not have association parameters, only initiation parameters.

In a list or reusable workflow, the context contains a reference to the list item associated with the workflow instance. This item is called Current Item within SharePoint Designer. This object gives the workflow the ability to read and write the field values for the list item. For a list workflow, the current item contains all of the item's fields. For a reusable workflow, the current item contains the fields that are part of the associated content type. There is no current item for a site workflow.

A special type of column on the current item is called an *association column*. An association column is declared in the workflow definition just like a parameter, but instead of being passed into or out of the workflow, it is part of the current list item. When a workflow definition is associated with a list, SharePoint checks to ensure that each of the workflow's association columns is present in the list. If not, a new column is automatically created for the association column. Association columns can be read and written in the same way as any other column, by using the Current Item object.

The final data elements in the workflow context are workflow *variables*. These are simple variables that store data throughout the lifetime of the workflow. They can be dates, strings, numbers, Boolean values, or list item IDs. These values are retained until the workflow terminates. They are used to store transient data that will not be needed after the workflow completes.

Workflow Forms

During the execution of a workflow, SharePoint often needs to collect information from a user. To accomplish this, a form is rendered on the web site that collects the data and adds it to the workflow's context. There are three types of workflow forms distinguished by the workflow action that causes them to be displayed:

- *Association forms* are displayed when the workflow definition is attached to a SharePoint list. This form collects the values of the workflow's association parameters.

- *Initiation forms* are displayed when a user manually starts a workflow instance. This form collects initiation parameters.

- *Task forms* are designed to collect data during the processing of a workflow task. The data collected is generally written to the current item, to the History list, or to a workflow variable.

■ **Tip** It is easy to get confused about which data fields should appear on which workflow form. Remember that the audience is different for each form. The *association form* is filled out by the administrator who configures the workflow. The *initiation form* is seen by the user initiating the workflow instance. A *task form* is presented to the user assigned to the task.

Workflow forms can be implemented in a variety of ways but, historically, the most popular types have been ASP.NET and InfoPath forms. In the past, ASP.NET forms have held two big advantages. First, many developers are more familiar with ASP.NET development than InfoPath development. Second, InfoPath has imposed restrictions with regards to security and the edition of the SharePoint server product required.

■ **Annoying but True** An initiation form appears only when a workflow is started *manually*, not when it is started automatically as an item is created or changed!

This seemingly odd behavior occurs because the web browser is only *one* way a workflow could be started. Imagine a workflow starting automatically when an item is created by another program or workflow instance. Where would the initiation form be displayed? When a workflow is started automatically, the initiation parameters will be set to their default values. These could be set in the workflow definition or be inherited from the values set on the association form. A workflow that has a required initiation parameter without a default value cannot be started automatically.

In SharePoint 2010, InfoPath forms are much easier to use because of automated form generation and sandboxing. Sandboxing, described in Chapter 11, involves the ability to execute .NET Framework code within a secure InfoPath form template.

SharePoint Designer 2010 makes using InfoPath forms almost trivially easy. When you create a workflow in SharePoint Designer, you declare the association and initiation parameters along with the data for each type of task. SharePoint Designer automatically creates basic InfoPath data entry forms for entering this data, as shown in Figure 12-3. As you will see in a later exercise, the workflow designer can open these form templates in InfoPath Designer and customize them as needed.

File Name	Type	Modified Date
Approval with Design Review.xsn	Association...	4/3/2011 12:10 PM
Approval _x0028_4_x0029_.xsn	Task	4/3/2011 12:07 PM
Approval _x0028_3_x0029_.xsn	Task	4/3/2011 12:07 PM

Forms

A list of the forms used by this workflow.

Figure 12-3. Workflow Forms list in SharePoint Designer

Workflow Components

SharePoint Designer 2010 workflows are built from a set of basic building blocks. Although these components seem quite simple at first, they provide a wide range of options for managing data and processes.

Steps

All workflows created in SharePoint Designer 2010 are known as *sequential workflows* in Windows Workflow Foundation parlance. This means that they are structured as a series of steps that are executed in sequence. Branching logic is limited to if-then-else conditions, and looping is not supported. If looping or advanced flow control logic (for example, a State Machine workflow) is needed, the workflow will need to be constructed using Visual Studio.

When a new workflow is created, a single step is added to the work surface. A workflow must always contain at least one step. Additional step objects are added to the workflow by using the Step button in the Insert group of the menu bar, as shown in Figure 12-4. Objects will always be inserted at the point designated by the flashing orange cursor. This cursor can be moved by clicking another location on the workflow design surface.

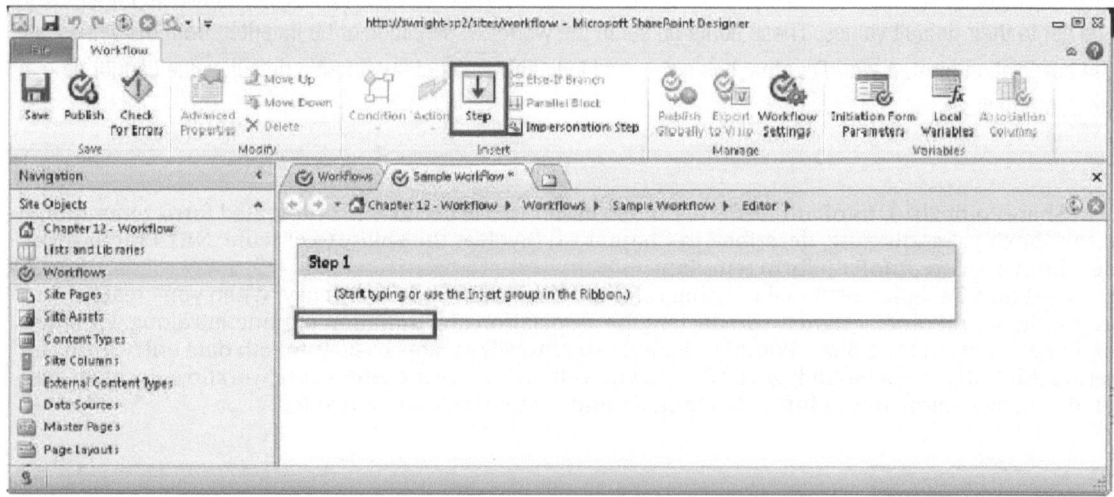

Figure 12-4. Workflow Designer (initial view)

A new feature in SharePoint Designer 2010 is the ability to create nested steps (see Figure 12-5). The nesting can be as deep and complex as needed.

Figure 12-5. *Nested workflow steps*

Another useful new feature in SharePoint Designer 2010 allows steps to be executed along multiple simultaneous paths by using the parallel block. The steps or actions within a parallel block will run in parallel with one another, creating two or more independent paths of execution. The workflow will pause at the bottom of the parallel block until all of the blocks inside have completed. Figure 12-6 depicts a parallel block with steps embedded within the block, but any action can be used within a parallel bock, whether enclosed in nested steps or not.

```
Step 1
  The following actions will run in parallel:
    Step 2
      The following actions will run in sequence:
    Step 3
      The following actions will run in sequence:
    Step 4
      The following actions will run in sequence:
```

Figure 12-6. *A parallel block with embedded steps*

The last type of workflow step is new to SharePoint Designer 2010. This is the impersonation step described in the "Security" subsection earlier in this chapter. This type of step executes its actions in the security context of the workflow author instead of the initiator. Impersonation steps are different from other steps in that they do not support nesting or being nested within other steps.

Conditions and Actions

Within the steps of a workflow are a series of conditions and actions. A *condition* provides the ability to perform conditional branching within the workflow. *Actions* are components that perform an action on behalf of the workflow initiator.

Conditions can be chained together to create if-then-else logic. Adding additional conditions can also create else-if logic, as shown in Figure 12-7.

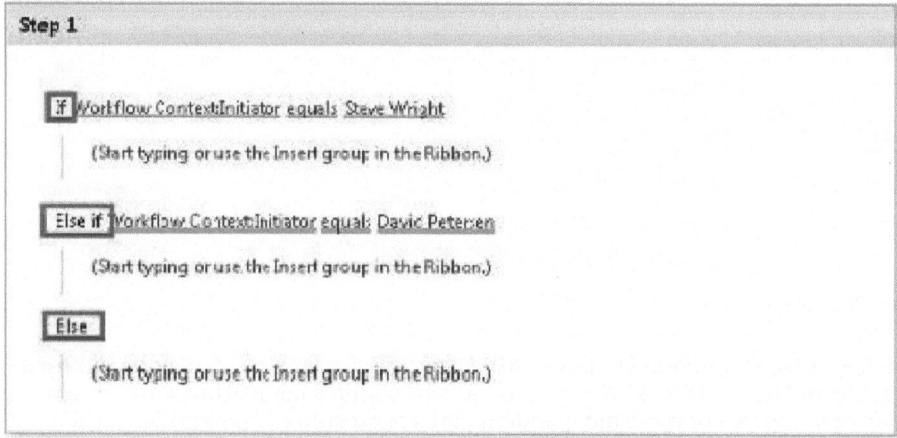

Figure 12-7. Conditional blocks

Conditional blocks can be nested inside other conditional blocks, creating sophisticated logical structures.

Action shapes in a workflow represent the work that is to be accomplished by the workflow. See the upcoming section "SharePoint Server Built-In Components" for a complete listing of the actions available within SharePoint Designer. Note also that new actions (a.k.a. *custom activities*) can be created using Visual Studio and used from within SharePoint Designer workflows.

When an action is added to the workflow design surface, its parameters are rendered as a set of hyperlinks, as shown in Figure 12-8. Clicking one of these parameters will launch an editor specific to that parameter. Most actions have at least one parameter. Many have more than one. Becoming familiar with the parameters and options associated with each available action is the key to creating powerful workflows in SharePoint Designer.

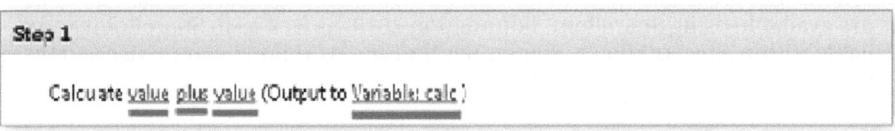

Figure 12-8. Action parameters

SharePoint Server Built-In Components

SharePoint Server 2010 comes with many built-in objects to enable the creation of workflows.

Workflow Definitions

The out-of-the-box workflows can be used as is or they can provide a starting point for creating customized approval processes. These include the following:

- Approval—SharePoint 2010

- Collect Feedback—SharePoint 2010

- Collect Signatures—SharePoint 2010

- Publishing Approval

The first three workflows are updated versions of the workflows that were included in SharePoint Server 2007. The fourth is the enhanced approval process used in SharePoint publishing sites. The Publishing Approval workflow may not be present if the publishing feature is not in use. The difference between these workflows in SharePoint 2010 and their 2007 counterparts is that they can now be copied and customized in SharePoint Designer 2010. Although it is possible to edit the SharePoint-provided versions of these workflow definitions, it is considered a best practice to make a copy and modify the copy.

Actions

SharePoint Designer 2010 comes with a large number of built-in actions that can be used to build most common business processes. When selecting the actions for a workflow, remember that some actions are not available in certain situations.

Many of the available actions are straightforward in their purpose and configuration. However, SharePoint 2010 has introduced a new action called the *Task Process action* that is a bit different. This action is a container for an entire task-oriented process such as an approval sequence. This action is almost a workflow within a workflow, but it is specifically designed to manage a process consisting of many tasks routed based on a set of rules instead of a simple sequence. The standard Approval, Collect Feedback, and Collect Signatures workflow definitions are all based on a single instance of this action. There is an entire subset of actions, called *Task Behavior actions*, that are designed to be used within the Task Process action shape.

SharePoint Foundation 2010 is a subset of the functionality that is available in SharePoint Server 2010. Therefore, it is reasonable to expect that the actions available in SharePoint Foundation would be a subset as well. Generally, the actions that are not available in SPF are those that use features that do not exist in that product. For example, the Declare Record action is not available in SPF workflows because record management is a feature of SharePoint Server 2010, not SPF.

Table 12-1 lists the actions that are available out of the box with SharePoint Server 2010. The table indicates which actions are available using SharePoint Foundation 2010, as well as in SharePoint Server 2010, and which are available within site workflows. Remember that site workflows cannot use actions that require a Current Item.

Table 12-1. SharePoint Designer Workflow Actions

Action Name	Available in SharePoint Foundation	Available in Site Workflows	Description
Workflow Control Actions			
Add a Comment	X	X	This action is used to add annotations to the workflow design. The task itself does not perform any action. It is just for adding information to the workflow design, making it easier to understand and maintain.
Log to History List	X	X	This action is used to log additional information to the History list.
			Each instance of a workflow creates an audit trail in the History list configured for the workflow. This list can be viewed during or after the execution of the workflow to see which users performed which actions and any other information the workflow chooses to log.
Pause for Duration	X	X	This action suspends the processing of the workflow for a given period of time. Once the period has elapsed, the workflow will resume after the next expiration of the timer job in SharePoint. Because the timer job's default interval is 5 minutes, there may be up to a 5-minute lag between the expiration of the Pause action and the actual resumption of the workflow.
Pause until Date	X	X	This action suspends the processing of the workflow until a given date and time.
Send an Email	X	X	This action is used to send e-mails from within the workflow. The destination addresses, subject line, and message body can be dynamically generated by using data from within the workflow. This action can be used to send notifications, reminders, and so on. The e-mail is sent by using the SharePoint outgoing e-mail process, which must be configured.

Action Name	Available in SharePoint Foundation	Available in Site Workflows	Description
Set Workflow Status	X	X	This action sets the status of the workflow to a value provided by the workflow designer. Typical statuses include Pending, Approved, Rejected, and Canceled. Using this action, you can define and set custom workflow statuses.
Set Workflow Variable	X	X	This action copies data into a workflow variable from another value in the workflow, including the current item's fields or workflow initiation values.
Stop Workflow	X	X	This action terminates the workflow and logs the given message into the History list. The final status of the workflow is the last value set by a task action or the Set Workflow Status action.
Data Manipulation Actions			
Add Time to Date	X	X	This action is used to perform date arithmetic in a workflow. For example, this action could be used to add a week to the current date for setting a deadline. The output of the calculation is stored in a workflow variable.
Do Calculation	X	X	This action is used to perform numerical arithmetic in a workflow. Numbers can be added, subtracted, multiplied, or divided. The output of the calculation is stored in a workflow variable.
Extract Substring from End of String	X	X	Extracts the last N characters from a string.
Extract Substring from Index of String	X	X	Extracts the end of a string, starting at character N.
Extract Substring from Start of String	X	X	Extracts the first N characters from a string.
Extract Substring of String from Index with Length	X	X	Extracts N characters from a string, starting at a given position.

Action Name	Available in SharePoint Foundation	Available in Site Workflows	Description
Find Interval Between Dates	X	X	This action is used to find the difference between two date/time values. The value can be calculated in minutes, hours, or days. The result is stored in a workflow variable.
Set Time Portion of Date/Time Field	X	X	This action sets the time part of a date/time value and stores it in a workflow variable. For example, this action could be used to remove the time portion from a value when only the date is needed, by setting the time portion to midnight.

List Item Actions (These actions also apply to documents.)

Action Name	Available in SharePoint Foundation	Available in Site Workflows	Description
Check In Item	X	X	This action checks an item into a document library, including supplying a check-in comment.
Check Out Item	X	X	This action checks out an item from a document library. The item must be checked in before this action can run successfully.
Copy List Item	X	X	This action makes a copy of an item in a separate list. This is generally used for archiving items or organizing large sets of items. For example, a workflow could evaluate an item to determine which list it should be routed to. This action would be used to perform the final routing step.
Create List Item	X	X	This action creates a new item in a list. The new item takes its field values from this action, and the ID of the new list item is returned and stored in a workflow variable for later reference. This action could be used for creating calendar entries, publishing announcements, or adding people to a contact list as part of a workflow.
Delete Item	X	X	This action deletes an existing item from a list.
Discard Check Out Item	X	X	This action removes the check-out from a library item, discarding any changes that have been made.

Action Name	Available in SharePoint Foundation	Available in Site Workflows	Description
Set Content Approval Status	X		This action is used to set the content approval status for the list item associated with the workflow. In order to set the approval status for an item, the list must be configured to enable content approval.
Set Field in Current Item	X		This action sets a field in the current list item for the workflow.
Update List Item	X	X	Use this action to update a list item. You can specify the fields and the new values in those fields.
Wait for Field Change in Current Item	X		This action suspends the workflow until a field in the current list item is changed. You can specify a specific condition to wait for in the field.
			Note: This action does not set the value. It waits for some other process to change it.

Document and Document Set Actions

Action Name	Available in SharePoint Foundation	Available in Site Workflows	Description
Capture a Version of the Document Set			This action is used to set a comment on a specific version of a document set. This includes recording the major and minor versions of all documents within the set.
Declare Record			This action identifies an item as a *record*. SharePoint Server 2010 allows the definition of rules regarding how documents designated as records can be accessed, edited, and deleted. Records can also be subjected to a retention policy. This action identifies an item as a record and enables the enforcement of these rules.
Delete Drafts			This action is displayed in workflow steps as Delete All Drafts (minor versions) of the item. It deletes the draft or minor versions of the current item, if any. There are no parameters to set for this action.
			Note: Versioning with minor versions needs to be enabled on the SharePoint list.

Action Name	Available in SharePoint Foundation	Available in Site Workflows	Description
Delete Previous Versions			This action is used to clear the version history for a document. The current version is preserved, but all previous versions (minor or major) are purged. This action applies only when versioning is enabled in the library.
Send Document Set to Repository			This action submits a document set to a document repository. While that repository may be a simple SharePoint library, this action is commonly used to submit document sets to sites by using the Content Organizer feature to route documents.
Set Content Approval Status of the Document Set			This action is used to set the content approval status for a document set. In order to set the approval status for an item, the list must be configured to enable content approval.
Start Document Set Approval Process			This action assigns approval tasks, on both the document set and the documents within the set, to a set of approvers.
Undeclare Record			This action removes the identification of an item as a record, thus disabling the record management policies currently associated with it.
Basic Task Actions			
Assign a Form to a Group	X	X	This action assigns a task to a given group of users by using a customized task form. The form may collect data from the end user, and that data will be added to the current item or workflow as appropriate.
Assign a To-Do Item	X	X	This action assigns a simple to-do task to a group of users. The users will simply signify that the task is complete. They will not provide any data to the workflow.
Collect Data from a User	X	X	This action is similar to Assign a Form to a Group except that it outputs a list item ID to an output workflow variable. This is the ID of the associated task that was assigned. Capturing the task ID allows the workflow to extract data from the task form completed by the user.

Action Name	Available in SharePoint Foundation	Available in Site Workflows	Description
Task Process Actions			
Start Approval Process		X	This action is a customized version of the Start Custom Task Process action. This task action behaves in the same way as the standard SharePoint approval workflow. The standard workflow can be customized by creating a workflow using this action and changing the settings provided.
Start Feedback Process		X	This action is a customized version of the Start Custom Task Process action. This task action behaves in the same way as the standard SharePoint feedback workflow. The standard workflow can be customized by creating a workflow using this action and changing the settings provided.
Start Custom Task Process		X	This action provides support for customized multiphase tasks such as approvals and data collection. Logic can be added to the action to control the flow and nature of the process. This action provides the basis for the standard approval and feedback workflows. See the Start Approval Process and Start Feedback Process table entries.
Task Behavior Actions (Used within Task Process actions)			
End Task Process		X	This action terminates the enclosing Task Process action and returns control to the workflow.
Task Process Item Updates			
Note: The Task Process Item may be different from the workflow item.			
Set Content Approval Status (as author)		X	This action sets the approval status by using the credentials of the workflow author. This is necessary because the impersonation step is not available within a Task Process action. This allows the workflow to automatically approve items when appropriate, because the workflow initiator likely does not have the necessary permission to do so.

Action Name	Available in SharePoint Foundation	Available in Site Workflows	Description
Wait for Change in Task Process Item		X	This action suspends the task process until a value in the task process's item is updated.
Wait for Deletion in Task Process Item		X	This action suspends the task process until a value in the task process's item is deleted.

Task Setup Actions

Set Task Field		X	This action is used during the Before Task is Assigned stage of the task process to place data into the task being created.

Task Control Actions

Rescind Task		X	This action cancels a pending task without setting an outcome.
Append Task		X	This action is used to add a task to the end of the current chain of approval tasks.
Delegate Task		X	This action rescinds a task and assigns *one new task* to a different user or group. To assign a separate task to each member of a group, use Forward Task instead.
Escalate Task		X	This action reassigns a task to the manager of the user currently assigned to the task.
Forward Task		X	This action rescinds a task and assigns a new task to a different user or a new *set of tasks* to the members of a group. To assign a single task to the group, use Delegate Task instead.
Insert Task		X	This action creates a new approval stage after the current stage and sets the specified user as the sole participant.
Reassign Task		X	This action reassigns a task to a different user without rescinding it first.

Action Name	Available in SharePoint Foundation	Available in Site Workflows	Description
Request a Change		X	This action requests a user to make a change. Once the change is completed, a new approval task is created for this user.
Send Task Email		X	This action causes a task notification e-mail to be sent that contains task buttons.
Relational Actions			
Lookup Manager of a User		X	This action is used to look up a user's manager from Active Directory. The result is written to a workflow variable. This information is useful when routing or escalating workflow tasks.
Impersonation Actions (Used only within an impersonation step)			
Add List Item Permissions		X	This action adds a set of permissions for a set of users to the selected list item.
Inherit List Item Parent Permissions		X	This action removes any unique permissions that exist for an item and sets the item to inherit permissions from its parent list or library.
Remove List Item Permissions		X	This action revokes a set of permissions for a set of users from the selected list item.
Replace List Item Permissions		X	This action replaces the current item permissions with a new set of permissions for a set of users.

Building Workflows with SharePoint Designer

Now that you have a firm grasp of the concepts behind workflows in SharePoint Designer, let's walk through some real-world examples. In the exercises that follow, you will create and customize workflows by using SharePoint Designer. First, you will customize one of the built-in workflows. After that, you will customize the InfoPath forms generated for that workflow. Then you will create your own reusable workflow from scratch. Finally, you will create and deploy a site workflow.

EXERCISE 12-1. CUSTOMIZE A BUILT-IN WORKFLOW

In this exercise, you will create a workflow definition that customizes the behavior of the built-in approval workflow. You will prevent the approver from reassigning approval tasks, prevent the initiator from altering the configured approver(s), and add logic to log the elapsed time in the History list when the workflow completes.

Because your task is to create a workflow definition that is very similar to a built-in workflow, you will use that workflow as a starting point. You will make a copy of the built-in workflow (because we do not recommend altering those delivered by Microsoft) and make the changes necessary to create the desired behaviors. You will then publish the workflow to our site, associate it with a list, and then run a workflow instance to verify its behavior.

1. Open the site in SharePoint Designer 2010.

2. In the Navigation pane, select Workflows.

3. Select the Approval – SharePoint 2010 workflow definition in the gallery list.

4. Click Copy & Modify in the Manage group on the menu, as shown in Figure 12-9.

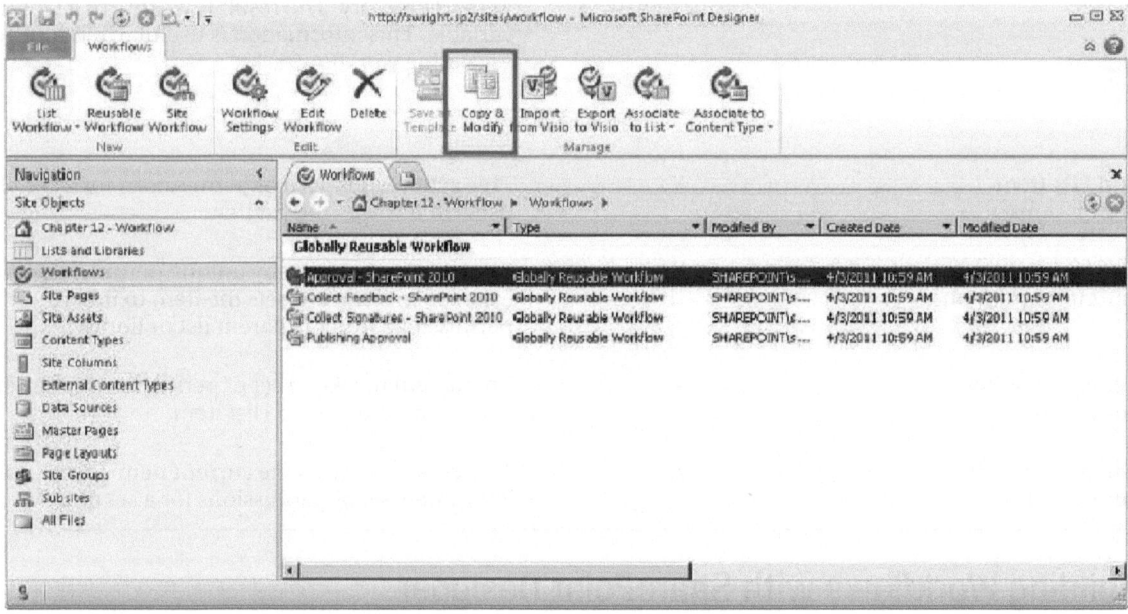

Figure 12-9. Copying and modifying a built-in workflow eefinition

5. In the Create Reusable Workflow dialog box that opens, enter **Custom Approval Process** for the name and click OK (see Figure 12-10).

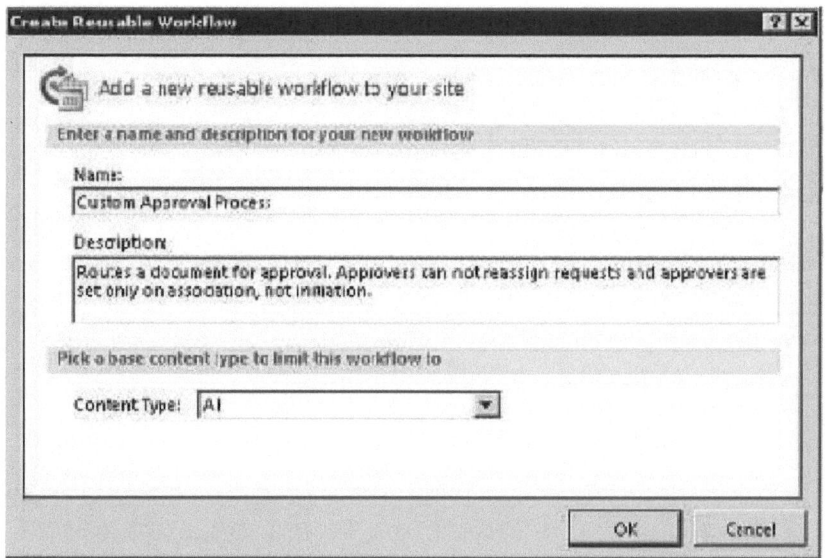

Figure 12-10. Creating a reusable workflow

6. In step 1, click theApproval Workflow Task (en-US) Copy 1 link, as shown in Figure 12-11.

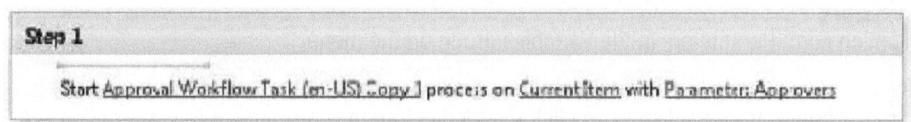

Figure 12-11. Default approval workflow

The action in step 1 is a Task Process action. Because you copied it from the built-in workflow definition, it is already configured to perform the entire approval process. Take a few moments to explore the options in the Customization panel. This will give you an inside look at how the task process operates. You will use this screen to disable the task reassignment feature.

1. Turn off the Reassignment check box, as shown in Figure 12-12.

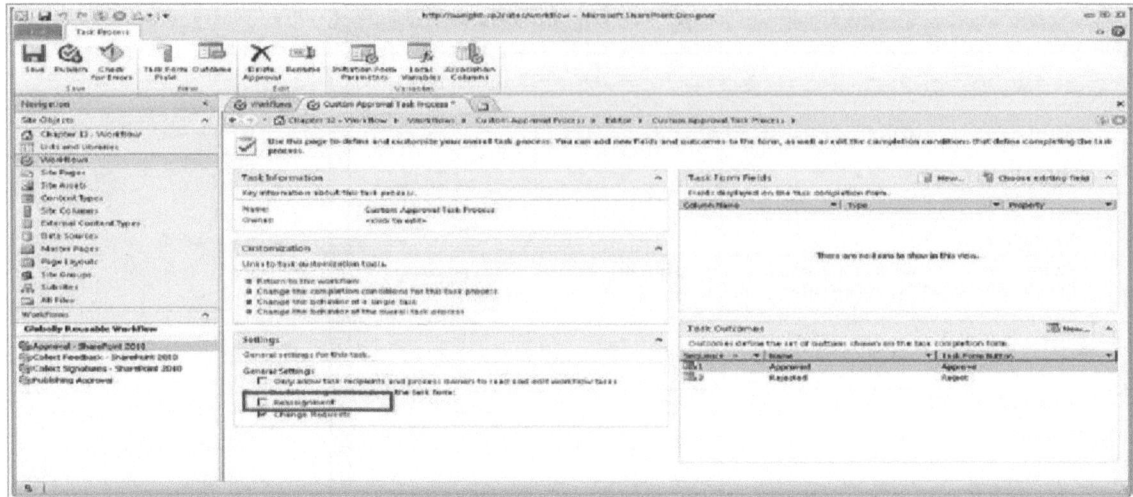

Figure 12-12. *Task Process action settings page*

2. In the Customization panel, click the Return to the Workflow link.

Note that the last parameter on the action reads Parameter: Approvers. This means that the workflow parameter called Approvers will be used to route the approval tasks. One of our requirements is that this parameter be set only when the workflow is associated, not initiated.

3. Click Initiation Form Parameters in the Variables group on the menu.

4. In the Association and Initiation Form Parameters dialog box that opens, select the Approvers parameter from the list. Then click the Modify button.

5. In the Modify Field dialog box, select Association (Attaching to a List) from the Collect from Parameter During drop-down box. Then click Next.

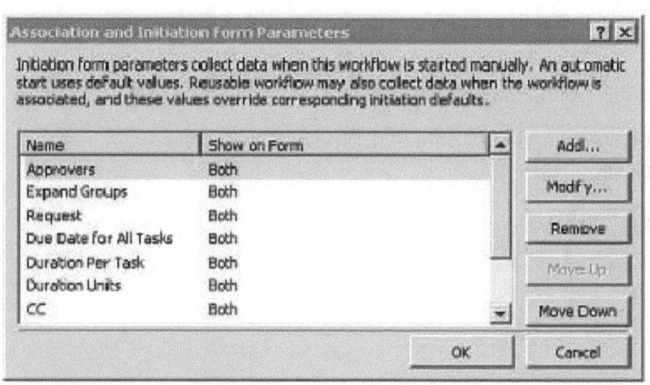
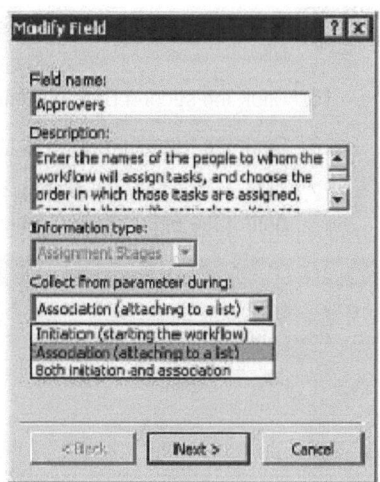

Figure 12-13. Initiation form parameters (Approvers field)

6. Click Finish.

7. Verify that the Approvers parameter now indicates Association below Show on Form. Click OK.

8. Now you will add an action to log the elapsed time in hours to the History list:

9. Click beneath the existing action but inside the Step 1 box. This moves the orange insertion point indicator after the approval process is complete.

10. From the Action drop-down list in the Insert group on the menu, select Find Interval Between Dates.

11. Click the Minutes link and select Hours.

12. In the action that was added, click the first Date link. This changes the link into a text box followed by an ellipsis button and a function button, as shown in Figure 12-14.

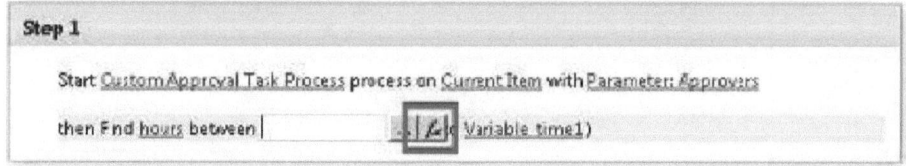

Figure 12-14. Function Editor button

13. Click the function button to launch the lookup dialog box.

14. Select Current Item for the data source. Select Modified for the field. Then click OK.

15. Click the second Date parameter.

16. Click the function button to launch the lookup dialog box.

17. Select Workflow Context for the data source. Select Date and Time Started for the field. (See Figure 12-15.)Then click OK.

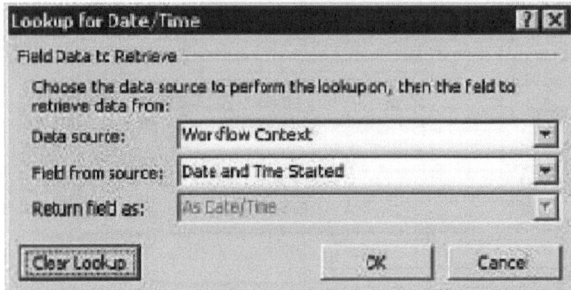

Figure 12-15. Lookup workflow start date and time

18. Click the link after Output To.

19. Select Create a New Variable from the drop-down list.

20. Enter **Elapsed Hours** for the variable name and **Number** for the type. Click OK.

21. From the Action drop-down list in the Insert group on the menu, select Log to History List, as shown in Figure 12-16.

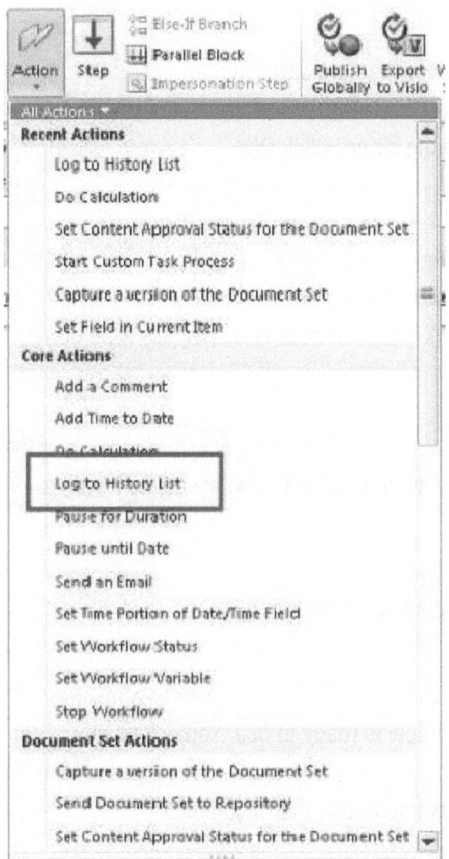

Figure 12-16. Action drop-down list

22. Click the This Message link.

23. Click the ellipsis button, shown in Figure 12-17. This opens the string builder dialog box.

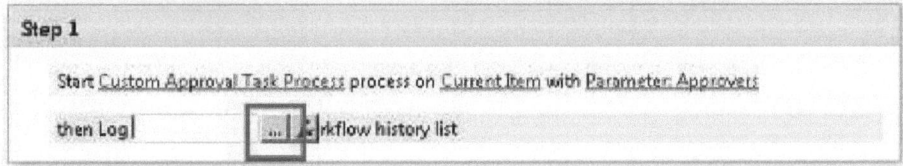

Figure 12-17. Launching the string builder (ellipsis)

1. Type The approval process was completed in in the text box.

2. Click the Add or Change Lookup button.

3. Select Elapsed Hours from the Workflow Variables and Parameters data source. Then click OK.

4. Append Hours after the lookup field that was added to the string. Click OK.

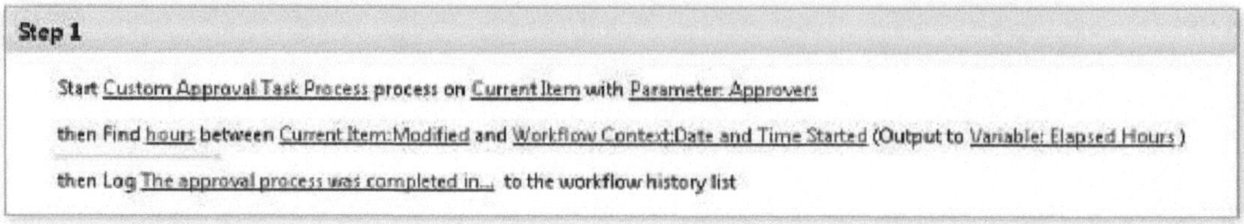

Step 1

Start Custom Approval Task Process process on Current Item with Parameter: Approvers

then Find hours between Current Item:Modified and Workflow Context:Date and Time Started (Output to Variable: Elapsed Hours)

then Log The approval process was completed in... to the workflow history list

Figure 12-18. Completed workflow

Your customized approval workflow is now complete. You need to save it, publish it, and associate it with a list:

1. On the menu, click the Check for Errors button.

2. If all goes well, a dialog box stating that the workflow contains no errors appears. Click OK to dismiss the dialog box.

3. Click the Save button and then the Publish button.

A progress window appears. When the process completes, the workflow is ready to use. You will now associate the workflow with a list and run the workflow:

1. Create a list or document library in your site. For this example, use the Documents library.

2. In SharePoint Designer, select the Custom Approval Process from the Workflows Gallery page.

3. In the Manage group in the menu, select Documents from the Associate to List drop-down, as shown in Figure 12-19.

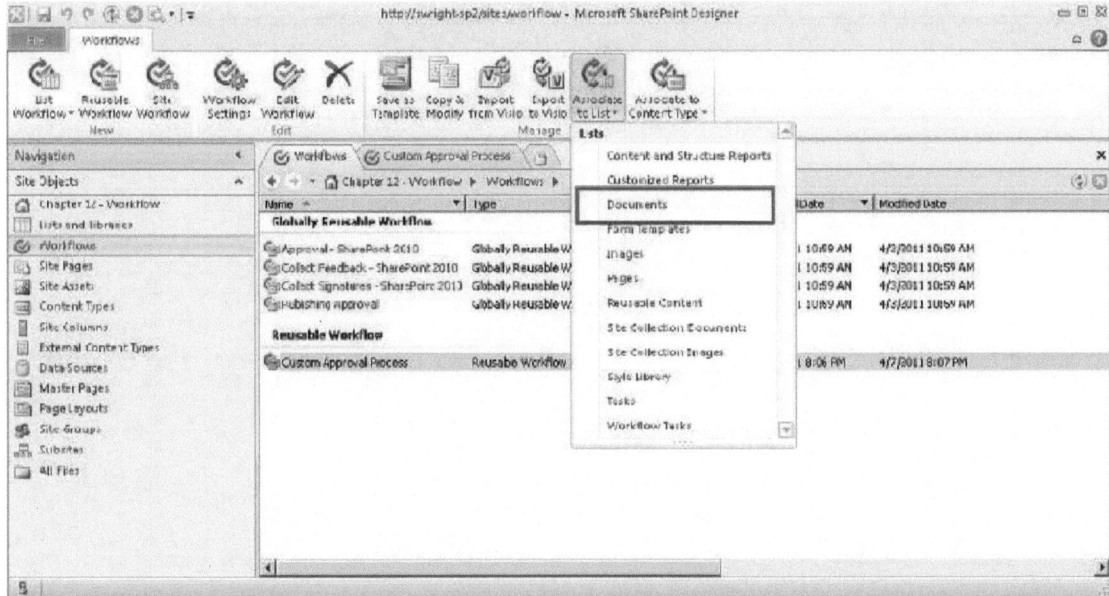

Figure 12-19. Associate to List

4. The workflow configuration form is now launched in the web browser (see Figure 12-20). Click the Next button.

Figure 12-20. Workflow configuration page

5. This shows the workflow's association form (see Figure 12-21). Set the Approvers field and any other desired settings. Then click Save.

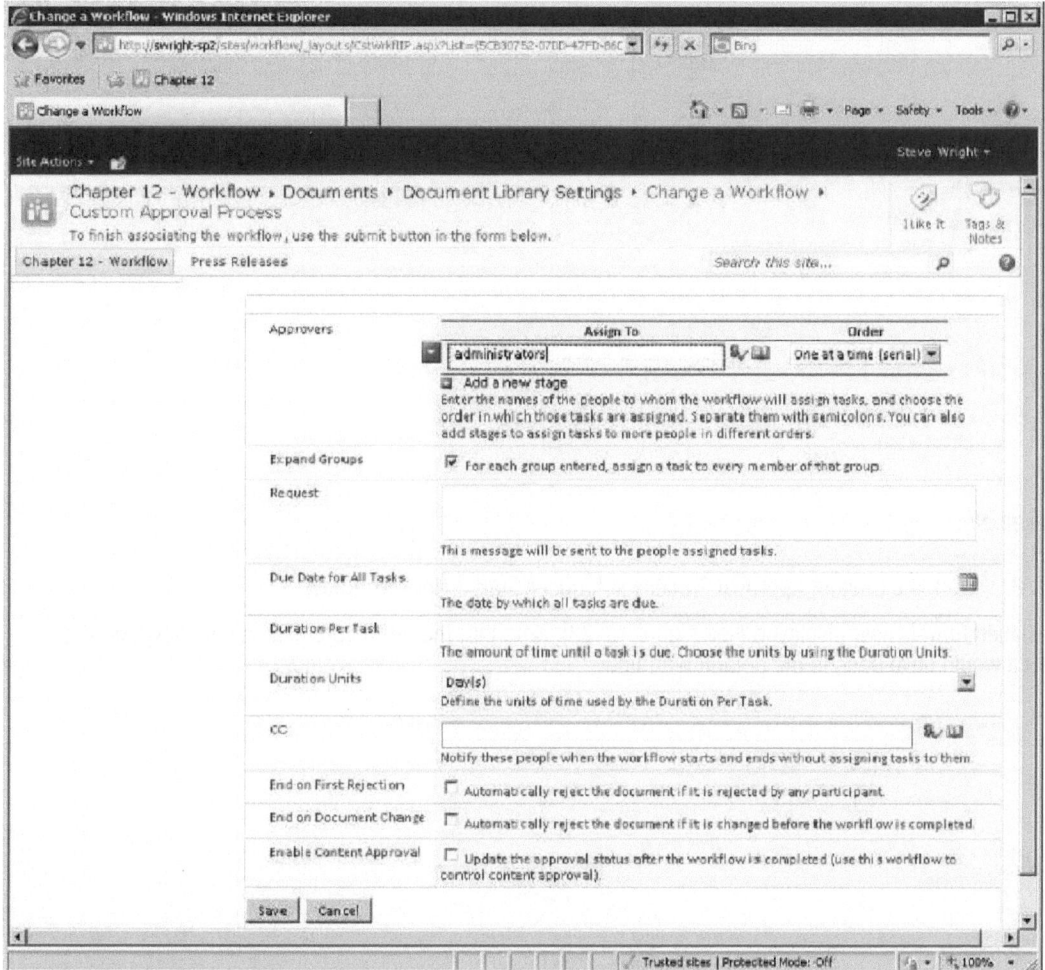

Figure 12-21. Association form

6. Navigate to the list in your web browser and upload a document or create a list item.

7. Open the drop-down menu associated with the item you added and select Workflows, as shown in Figure 12-22.

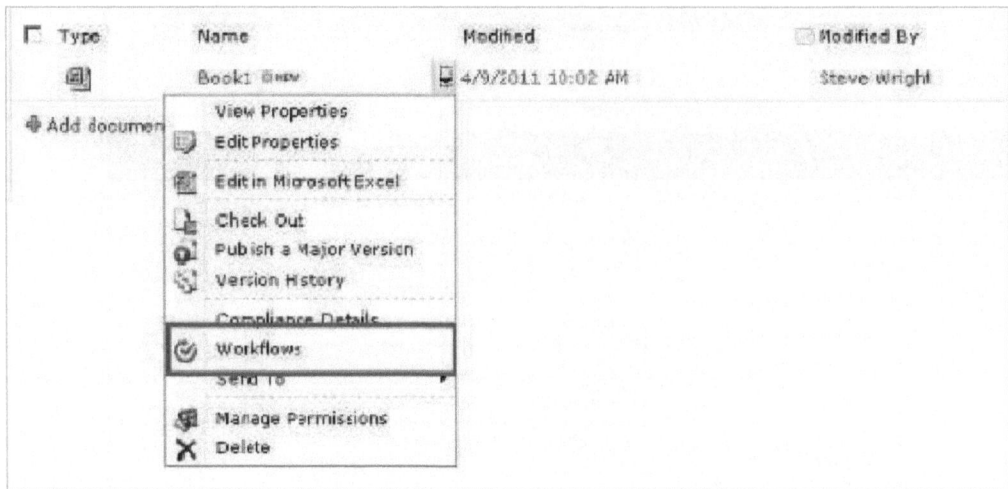

Figure 12-22. Starting a workflow manually

8. Click the Custom Approval Process link under Start a New Workflow.

The initiation form is now displayed (see Figure 12-23). Note that the Approvers field is not shown on this form as it would have been in the default workflow.

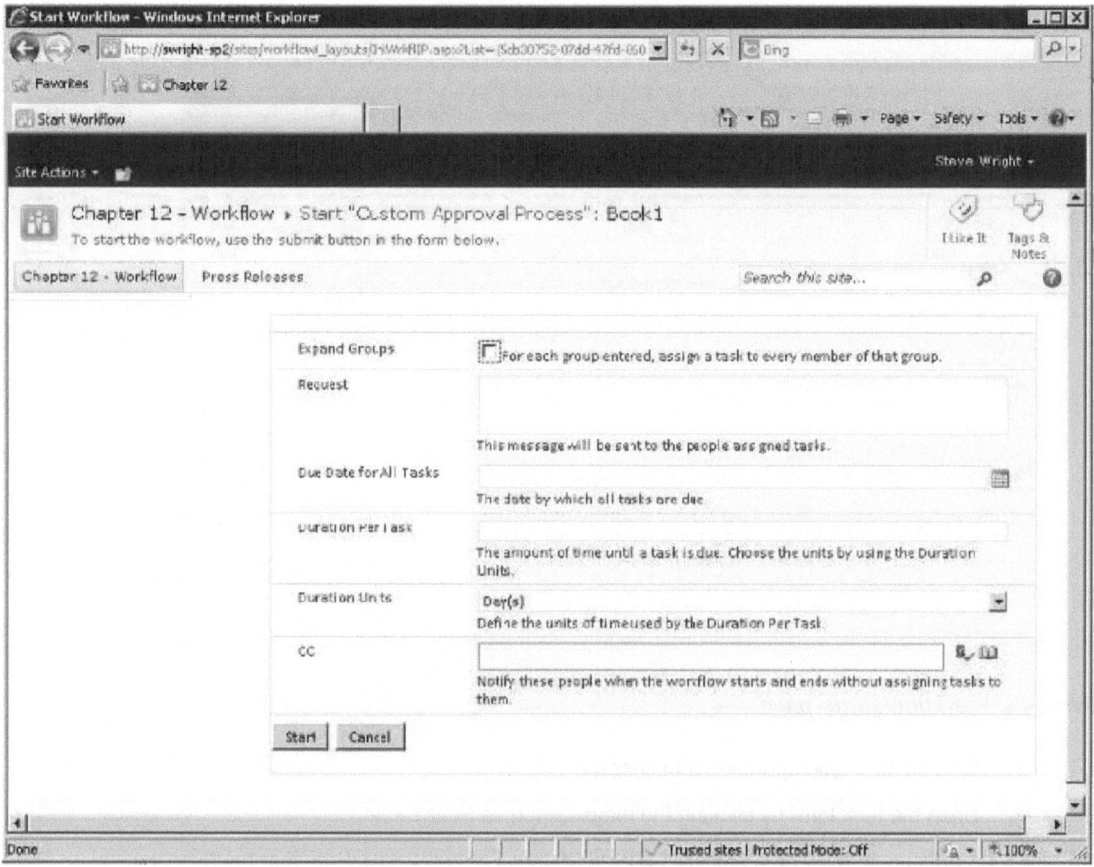

Figure 12-23. Start a Workflow Manually

1. At the top of the page, deselect the check box labeled "For each group entered, assign a task to every member of that group." Then click the Start button at the bottom of the page.

2. Open the drop-down menu associated with the item you added and select Workflows.

3. Click the Custom Approval Process link under Running Workflows.

The workflow status page, shown in Figure 12-24, provides details of a workflow during or after execution. The Tasks section shows all of the tasks created by the workflow, who they were assigned to, and their current statuses. In this case, there is a single task.

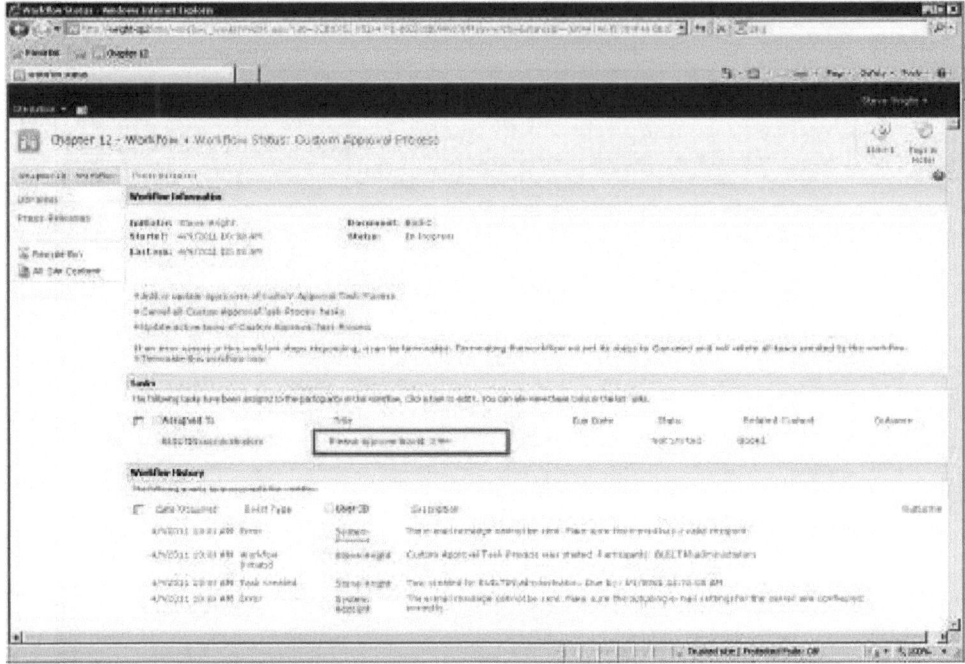

Figure 12-24. Workflow status page

1. Sign on as a valid approver, if necessary.

2. Open the task form by clicking the Please Approve Book1 link.

The task form appears in the web browser at this point (see Figure 12-25). Note that the Reassign Task button is missing because you turned off that option in the workflow definition.

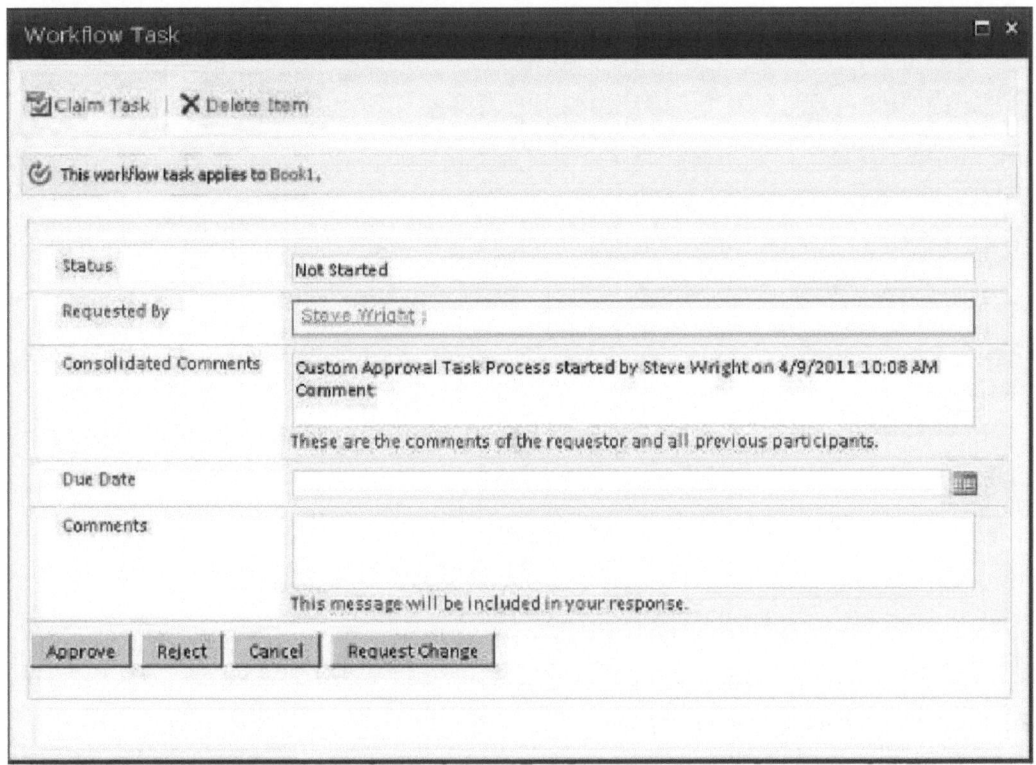

Figure 12-25. Workflow task form

    3.   Click theApprove button.

On the workflow status page, you can see the audit trail recorded in the History list. Note that the elapsed time was appended to the log because of the changes you made to the workflow definition (see Figure 12-26).

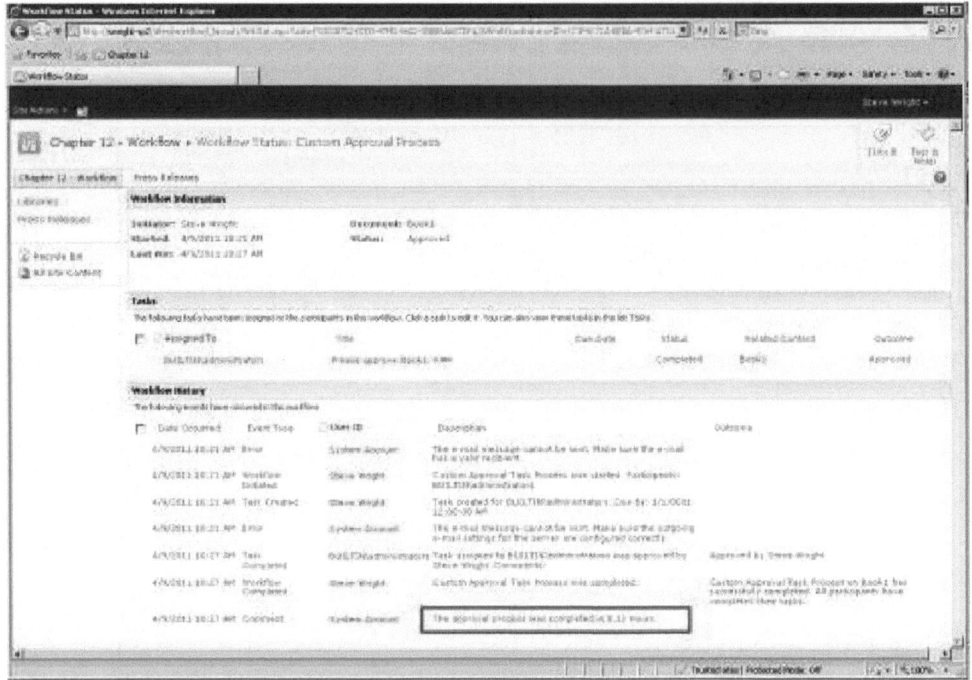

Figure 12-26. *The completed workflow status page*

EXERCISE 12-2. CUSTOMIZE A GENERATED INFOPATH FORM

In this exercise, company design standards require that the forms associated with your workflows use a particular color scheme. You need to update the association, initiation, and task forms for the Custom Approval Process workflow to meet this requirement.

Unlike in previous versions of SharePoint Designer, using and customizing InfoPath forms in workflows is quite easy in SharePoint 2010. This is because SharePoint Designer 2010 automatically generates the forms necessary and adds them to the workflow definition. All you need to do is open the forms and customize them:

1. Open the site in SharePoint Designer 2010.

2. From the Navigation pane, select Workflows.

3. Click the Custom Approval Process link in the gallery list.

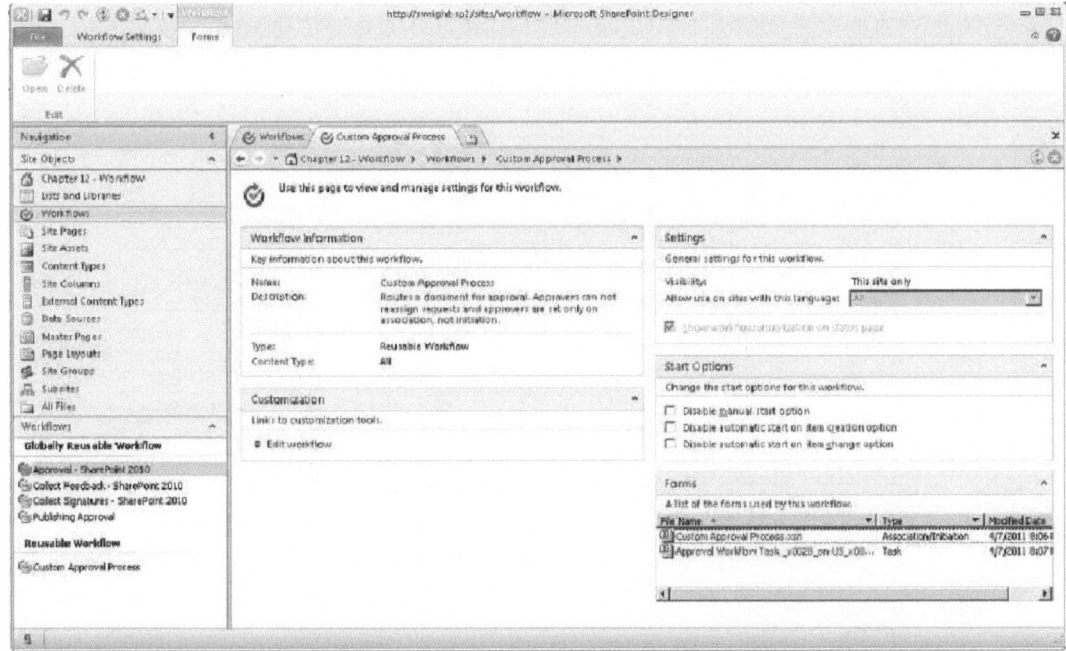

Figure 12-27. *Workflow Settings page*

On the Workflow Settings page, the generated InfoPath forms appear in the Forms panel in the lower-right corner of the screen. The first form contains both the association and initiation forms for the workflow. Each task form is listed as well. In our case, there is only one task form. It is used for the approval task in the workflow.

4. In the Views group, on the Page Design tab of the menu, select Associate from the View drop-down list. This switches to the initiation form view.

5. Click Custom Approval Process.xsn in the Form panel. InfoPath Designer 2010 is launched and it displays the association form template, as shown in Figure 12-28.

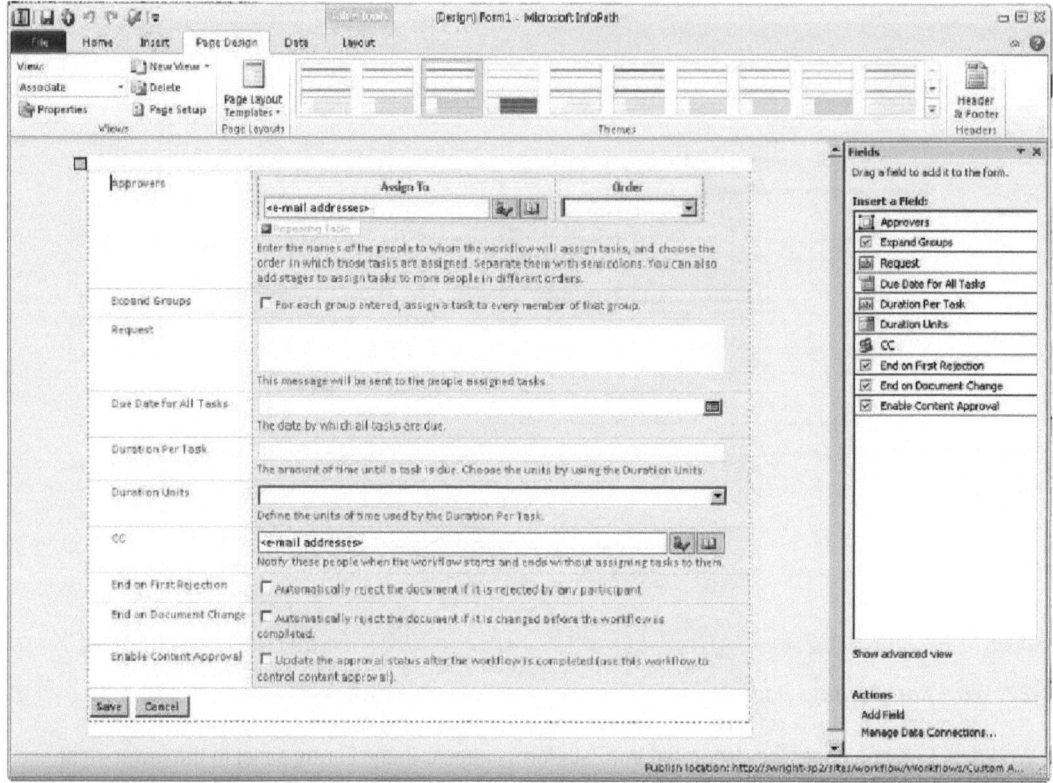

Figure 12-28. *Association form in InfoPath Designer*

6. Click the Page Design tab in the menu.

7. Select one of the themes from the Theme list in the menu. (Personally, I like yellow.)

8. In the Views group, on the Page Design tab of the menu, select Start (Default) from the View drop-down list, as shown in Figure 12-29. This switches to the initiation form view.

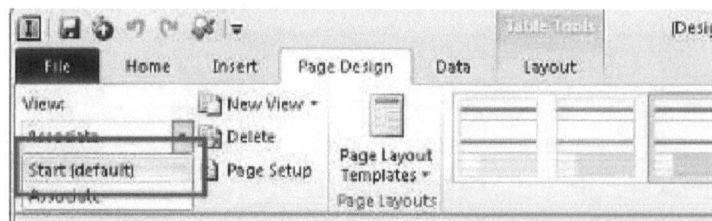

Figure 12-29. *Switching views in InfoPath Designer*

9. Select the same theme you used for the association view.

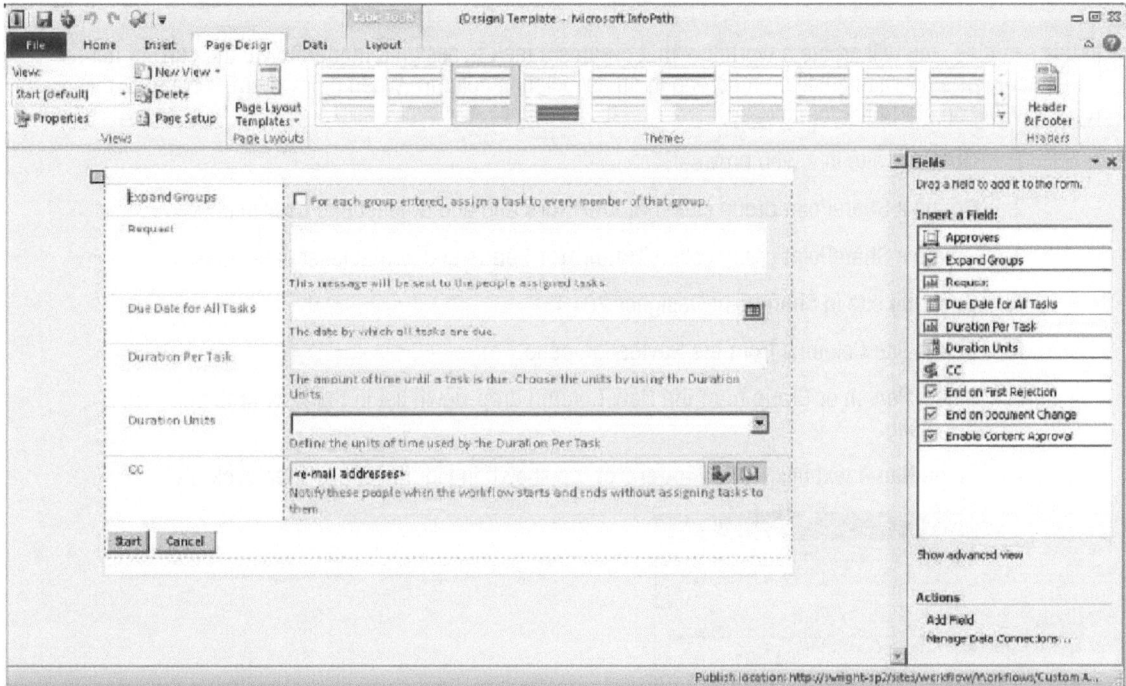

Figure 12-30. Initiation form in InfoPath Designer

10. Click the File menu tab.

11. Click the Quick Publish button.

12. Save the template file somewhere on your hard drive. This is the unpublished version, which you won't be using.

13. When InfoPath indicates that your form template was published successfully, click OK to dismiss the dialog box and close InfoPath Designer.

14. Repeat steps 4–12 to customize the task form for the workflow in the same way.

15. In the web browser, start a new instance of the workflow as you did in the previous exercise. Note the new colors that appear in the various forms.

Obviously, changing the color scheme is not the extent of what you can do to customize these forms. These templates are fully functional forms that can use any of InfoPath's features, as described in Chapter 11. The value of having these forms initially generated by SharePoint Designer is that the workflow author doesn't have to create the forms, configure the data fields, or attach the forms to the workflow. All of this is done for you in SharePoint Designer 2010.

EXERCISE 12-3. CREATE A REUSABLE WORKFLOW

In this exercise, you will create a workflow that creates a task to assign a moderator to the current item. The moderator's username will be recorded in an association column. When a new item is created, this workflow will be started automatically.

1. Open the site in a web browser.

2. Create a SharePoint group called **Moderators** and add at least one user to it.

3. Create a SharePoint group called **Moderator Leads** and add at least one user to it.

4. Open the site in SharePoint Designer 2010.

5. Select Site Columns from the Navigation pane.

6. Select Person or Group from the New Column drop-down list in the New group on the menu.

7. In the Name text box, enter **Moderator**, as shown in Figure 12-31. Then click OK.

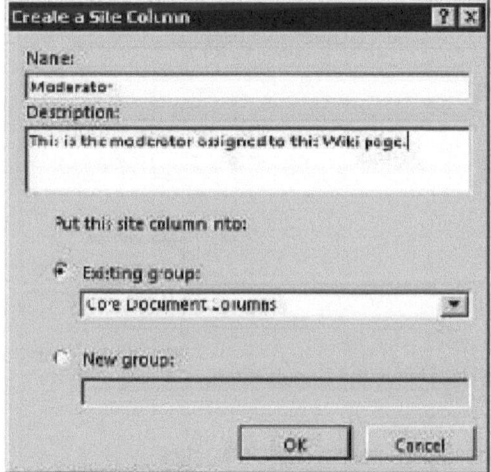

Figure 12-31. Creating a Moderator site clumn

8. Double-click Moderator in the Site Columns Gallery to open the Column Editor dialog box, shown in Figure 12-32.

9. Set the Allow Selection Of radio button to People Only.

10. In the Choose From section, ensure that the SharePoint group radio button is selected and choose Moderators from the drop-down list.

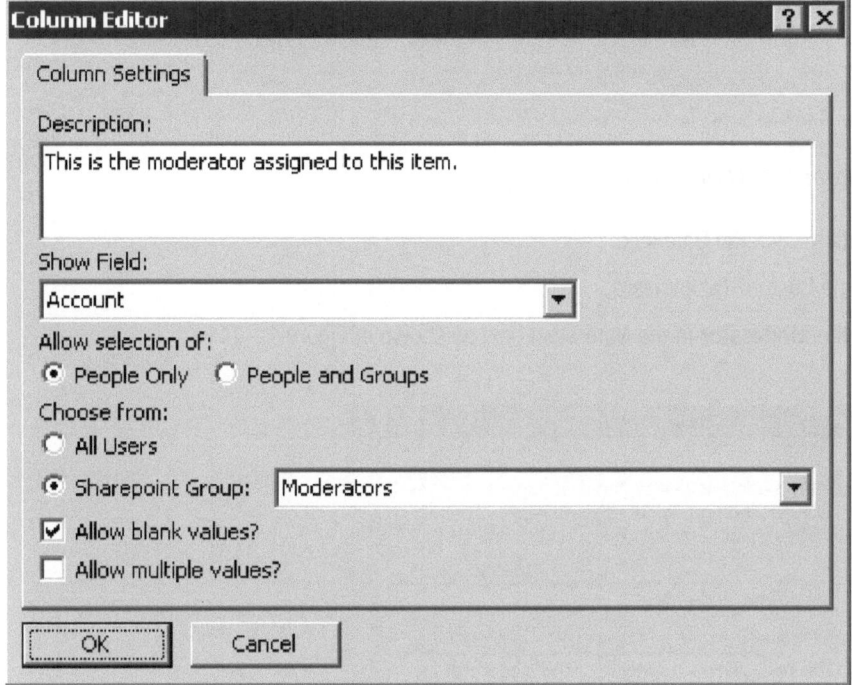

Figure 12-32. Editing the Moderator site column

11. Accept the other defaults and click OK.

12. Save the changes to the site column.

The site column you have created will be used as an association column in the workflow and will be present in any lists with which you associate the workflow.

1. Select Workflows from the Navigation pane.

2. Select Reusable Workflow from the New group in the menu.

3. Enter **Assign Moderator Process** for the workflow name.

4. Select All as the content type. Then click OK.

5. Select Association Columns from the Variables group in the menu.

6. Click Select Site Column.

7. Find and select the Moderator column. Click OK.

8. Click OK again to close the association columns dialog box.

9. From the Action drop-down list in the menu, select the Collect Data from a User action under the Task Actions category.

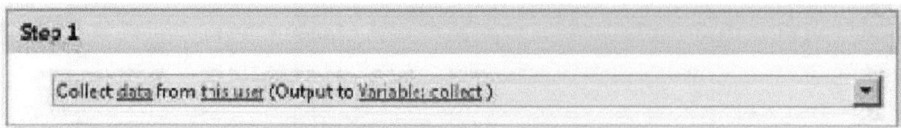

Figure 12-33. *Collect Data from This User action*

10. In the new action, click the Data link.

11. Click Next in the Custom Task Wizard.

12. Type **Assign the Moderator** in the Name text box, as shown in Figure 12-34. Click Next.

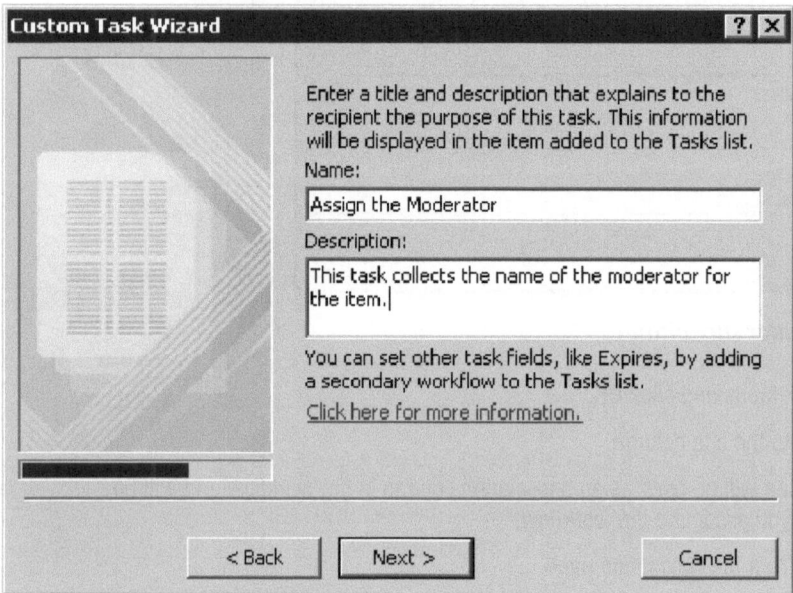

Figure 12-34. *Custom Task Wizard—assigning a task name*

13. Click the Add button.

14. In the Add Field dialog box, type **Moderator** for the field name, as shown in Figure 12-35. In the Information Type drop-down list, select Person or Group. Then click Next.

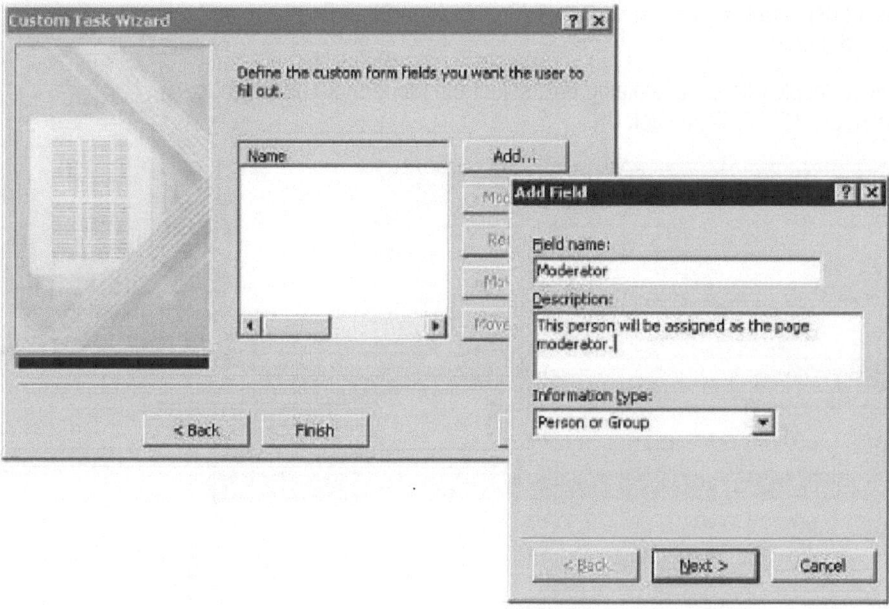

Figure 12-35. Custom Task Wizard—adding a task field

15. In the Column Settings dialog box, select the People Only radio button, as shown in Figure 12-36. Select the Moderators SharePoint Group and deselect the Allow Blank Values check box. Then click Finish.

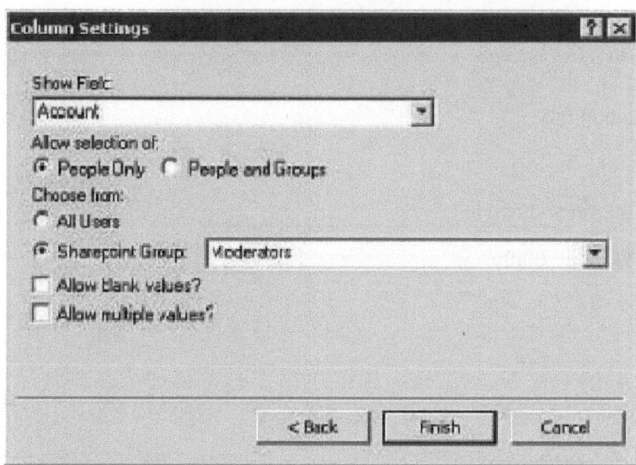

Figure 12-36. Custom Task Wizard—task field settings

16. Click the This User link on the action.

17. In the Select Users dialog box, select People/Groups from SharePoint site and then click the Add button.

18. In the Select People and Groups dialog box, select the Moderator Leads group, as shown in Figure 12-37. Then click OK.

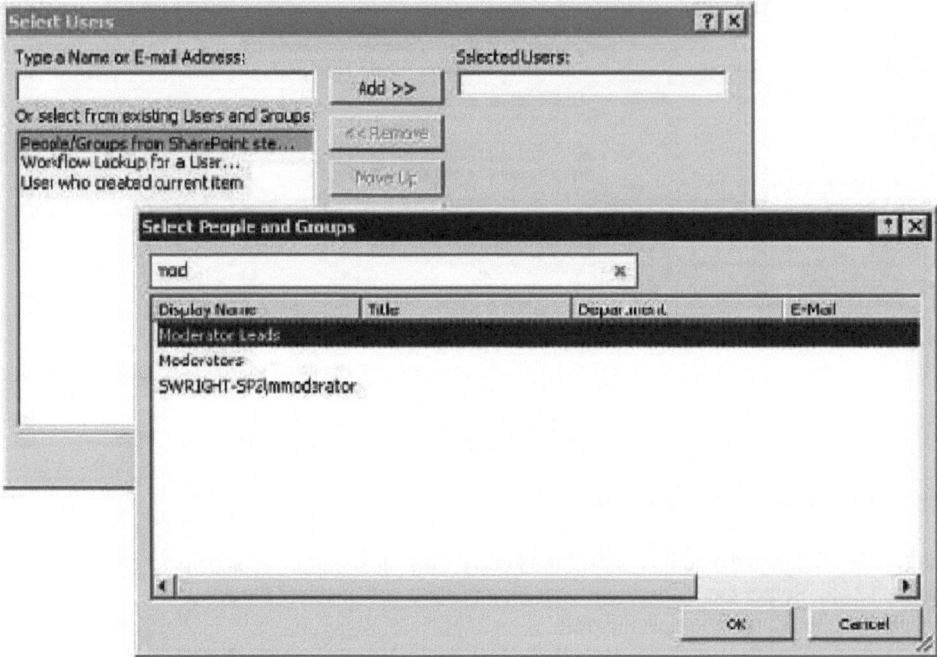

Figure 12-37. Setting the task user/group assignment

19. Click OK to close the Select Users dialog box.

20. Click the Variable: collect link.

21. Select Create a New Variable from the drop-down list.

22. Enter **Assignment Task ID** for the variable name.

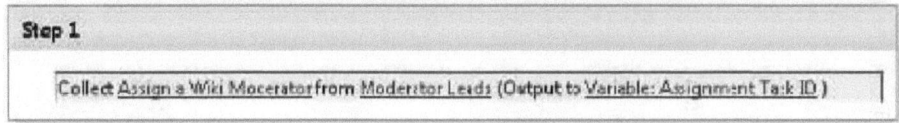

Figure 12-38. Collecting data from the user action (configured)

At this point, you have assigned a task to the Moderator Leads group to collect the name of the new moderator. The action will pause the workflow until one of the members of the group completes the task. The workflow should look like this:

1. From the Action drop-down on the menu, select the Set Field in Current Item action.

2. Click the Field link.

3. Select the Moderator field from the drop-down list, as shown in Figure 12-39.

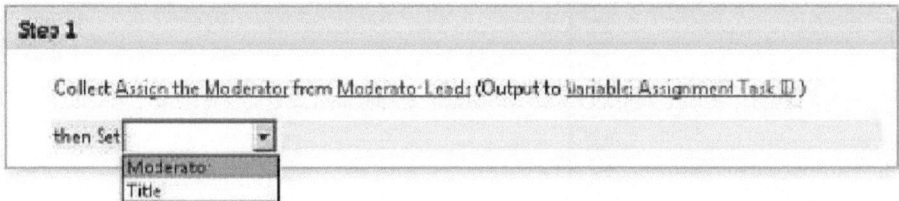

Figure 12-39. Setting the Moderator field in the current item

4. Click the Value link in the action.

5. Select Workflow Lookup for a User.

6. Click the Add button.

7. In the Lookup for Person or Group dialog box, click the Data Source drop-down list and select Association: Task List, as shown in Figure 12-40.

8. From the Field from Source drop-down list, select Moderator.

9. From the Return Field As drop-down list, select Login Name.

10. In the Find the List Item section, select ID from the Field options.

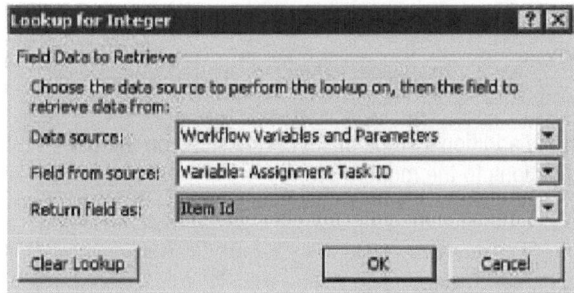

Figure 12-40 Moderator lookup from the data collection task

11. Click the function button next to Value.

12. In the Lookup for Integer dialog box, click the Data Source drop-down list and select Workflow Variables and Parameters, as shown in Figure 12-41.

13. In the Field from Source drop-down, select Variable: Assignment Task ID.

14. From the Return Field As drop-down list, select Item Id. Click OK.

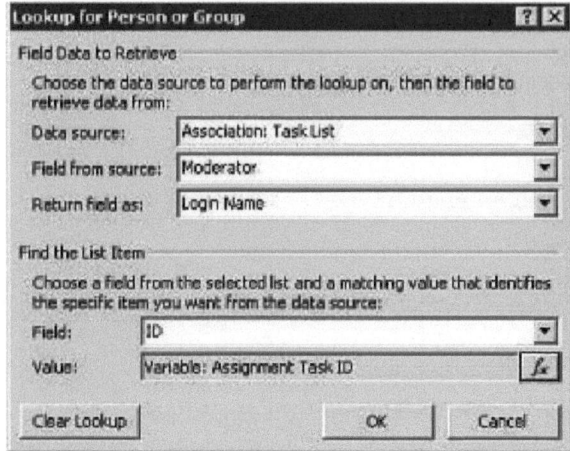

Figure 12-41. Lookup ID of the data collection task

15. Click OK to close the Lookup for Person or Group dialog box.

16. Click OK to close the Select Users dialog box.

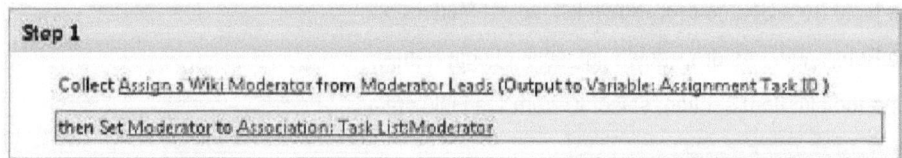

Figure 12-42. Completed workflow

Now your workflow should look like this. You could include additional steps to set permissions on the page by using the impersonation step or to send e-mail notifications to the moderators.

1. Click Save in the menu bar.

2. Click Publish in the menu bar.

3. From the Navigation pane, select Workflows.

4. Select the Assign Moderator Process workflow from the gallery list.

5. Select any list from the Associate to List drop-down in the Manage group on the menu. The Add a Workflow page comes up in your browser.

6. Select the check box labeled "Start this workflow when a new item is created."
    Then click OK.

The workflow is now ready to use. Try adding an item to the list, and the workflow will be started automatically. Also, notice that the list now has a Moderator column because of the association column in the workflow.

EXERCISE 12-4. CREATE A SITE WORKFLOW

In this exercise, you will create a form that allows site users to submit feedback to the site owners. When feedback is submitted, it will be placed into a list on the site, and an e-mail will be sent to the site owners.

This type of feature is fairly common on many sites. It is well suited to using a workflow because the process runs behind the scenes and may change frequently as business needs change. This could be implemented by using a reusable workflow, but that would require creating a visible list and asking users to create a list item for their feedback.

In this exercise, you will create a simple site workflow that collects the required information, stores it on the site, and sends an e-mail to the site owners. The workflow will then immediately terminate without generating any tasks.

1. Open the site in SharePoint Designer 2010.

2. Select the Lists and Libraries gallery from the Navigation pane.

3. Create a new Custom List called **Site Feedback**.

4. Rename the Title field to **Subject**.

5. Add a new column called **Category**, which is a choice field containing options for Design, Functionality, and Content. Make the field required.

6. Add the existing site column Append-Only Comments to the list.

7. Save the changes to the list.

8. Select the Workflows Gallery from the Navigation pane.

9. Select Site Workflow from the New group on the menu.

10. Enter **Provide Site Feedback** for the name of the workflow, as shown in Figure 12-43. Then click OK.

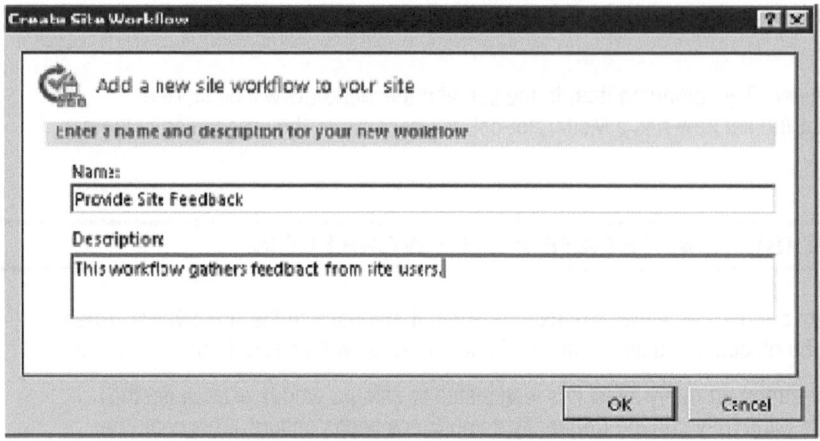

Figure 12-43. Creating a site workflow

11. Select Initiation Form Parameters from the Variables group in the menu.

12. Add the following initiation parameters:

   a. Subject—Single line of text

   b. Category—Choice field with Design, Functionality, and Content

   c. Comment—Multiple lines of text

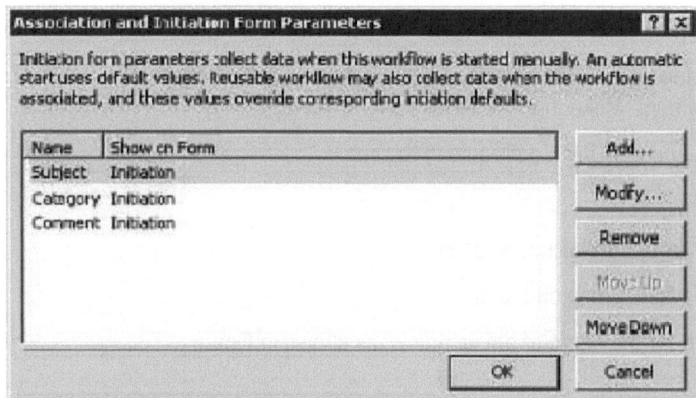

Figure 12-44. Initiation form parameters

13. Click OK.

14. Click within Step 1.

15. Type **cre**. This is another way to select actions. In this case, the first three letters are enough to find the action we want: Create List Item. Press Enter.

16. Click the This List link.

17. Select Site Feedback from the drop-down list at the top of the dialog box. The required fields appear immediately.

18. Double-click Subject (*).

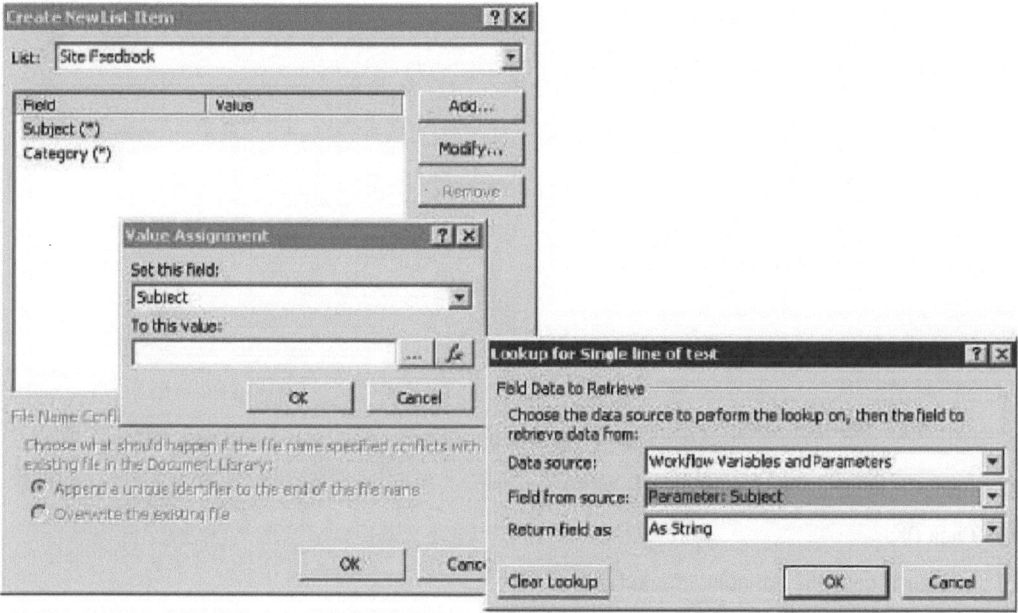

Figure 12-45. Mapping values to a new list item

19. Click the function button next to the value field.

20. Select the Subject workflow parameter.

21. Click OK.

22. Click OK.

23. Use the same procedure to set the Category field using the Category workflow parameter.

24. Click the Add button.

25. Select the Append-Only Comments field from the drop-down list.

26. Map that field to the value of the Comment workflow parameter.

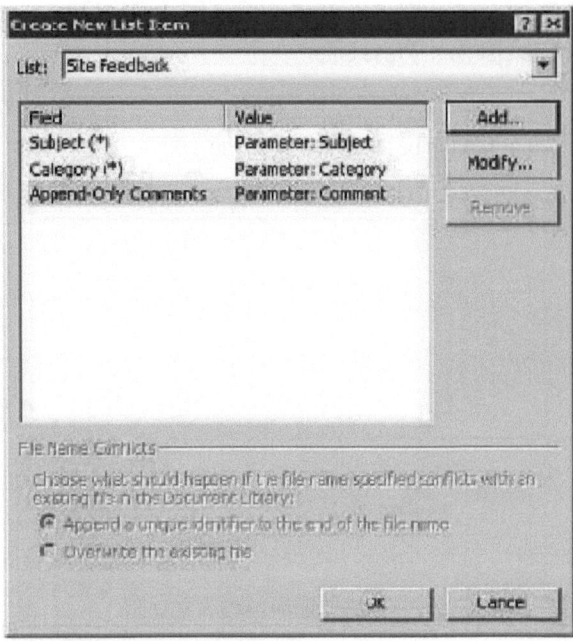

Figure 12-46. Creating a new list item

27. Click OK.

28. Click OK.

29. In Step 1, click the Variable: create link.

30. Select Create a New Variable from the drop-down list.

31. Name the variable **Feedback Item ID**.

32. Select List Item ID for the variable type.

33. Click OK.

34. Insert a Send an Email action into the step.

35. Click the These Users link.

36. Select the site owners group in the To field.

37. Click the function button to the right of the Subject field.

38. Select the Subject workflow parameter.

39. Click OK.

40. Type **URL:**.

41. Click the Add or Change Lookup button.

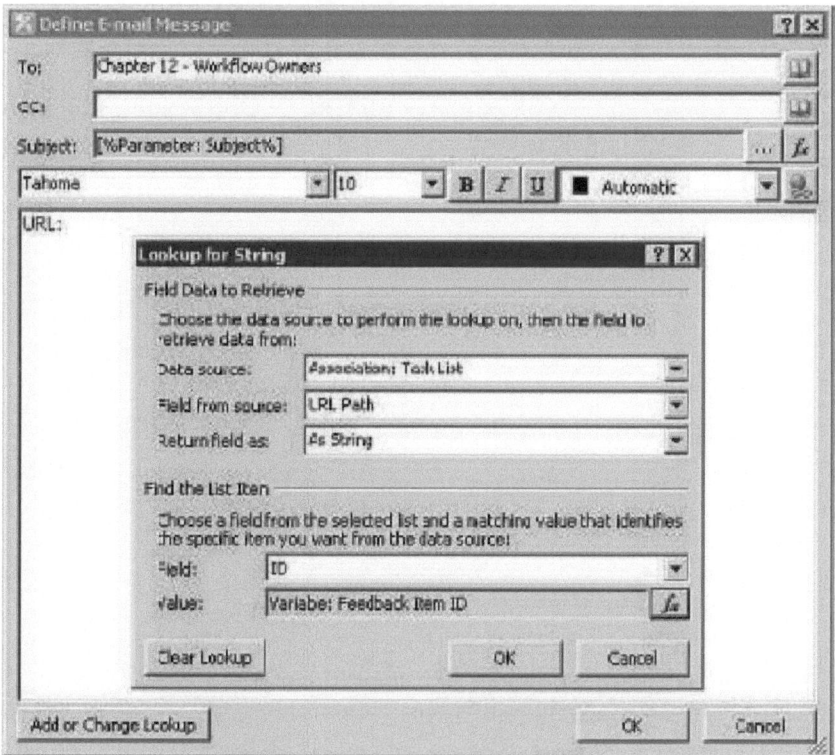

Figure 12-47. Configuring an e-mail message

42. Using the Feedback Item ID variable, look up the URL Path value on the Site Feedback list, as shown here. Then click OK.

43. On the next line of the e-mail, type **Category:**.

44. Press the Add or Change Lookup button.

45. Add the value of the Category workflow parameter.

46. On the next line of the e-mail, type **Feedback:**.

47. Click the Add or Change Lookup button.

48. Add the value of the Comment workflow parameter.

Figure 12-48. *The configured e-mail message, completed*

49. Click OK to close the Define E-mail Message dialog box.

50. Save the workflow.

51. Publish the workflow.

The workflow is now active on the web site. Next, you will open the site and use the workflow to give yourself some feedback. This is known as *positive self-talk*, and it's supposed to be good for you.

1. Open the site in a web browser.

2. Select View All Site Content from Site Actions or the menu if it is there.

3. Click Site Workflows at the top of the All Site Content page, as shown in Figure 12-49.

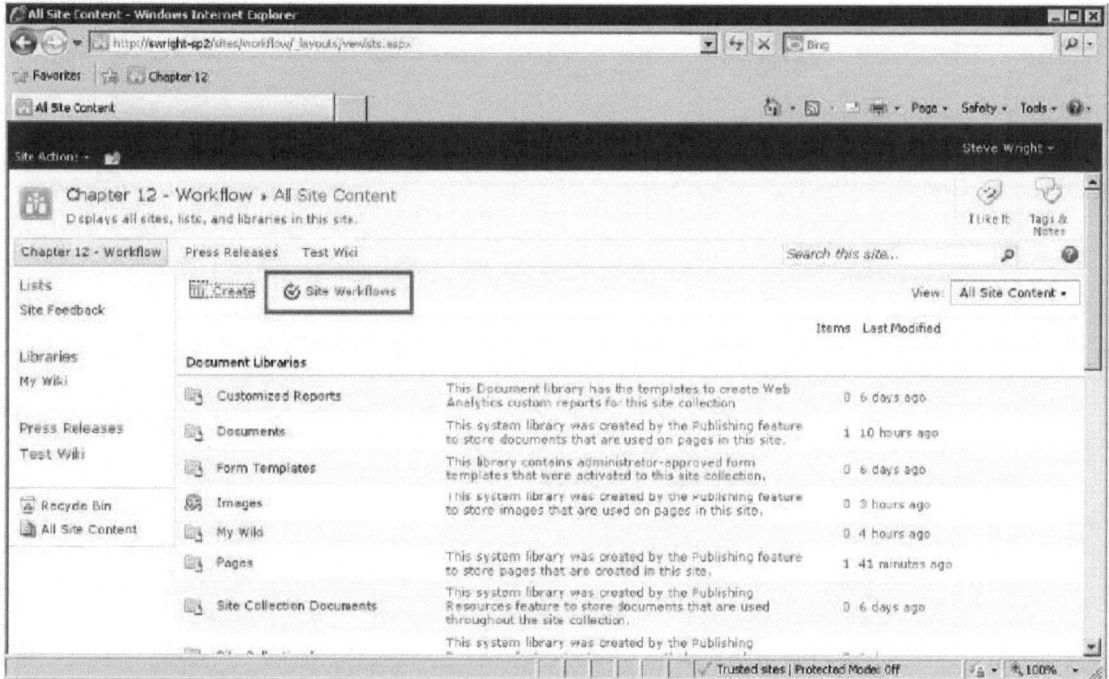

Figure 12-49. Starting a site workflow

4. Click Provide Site Feedback.

5. On the initiation form, enter a subject, category, and comment.

6. Click Start.

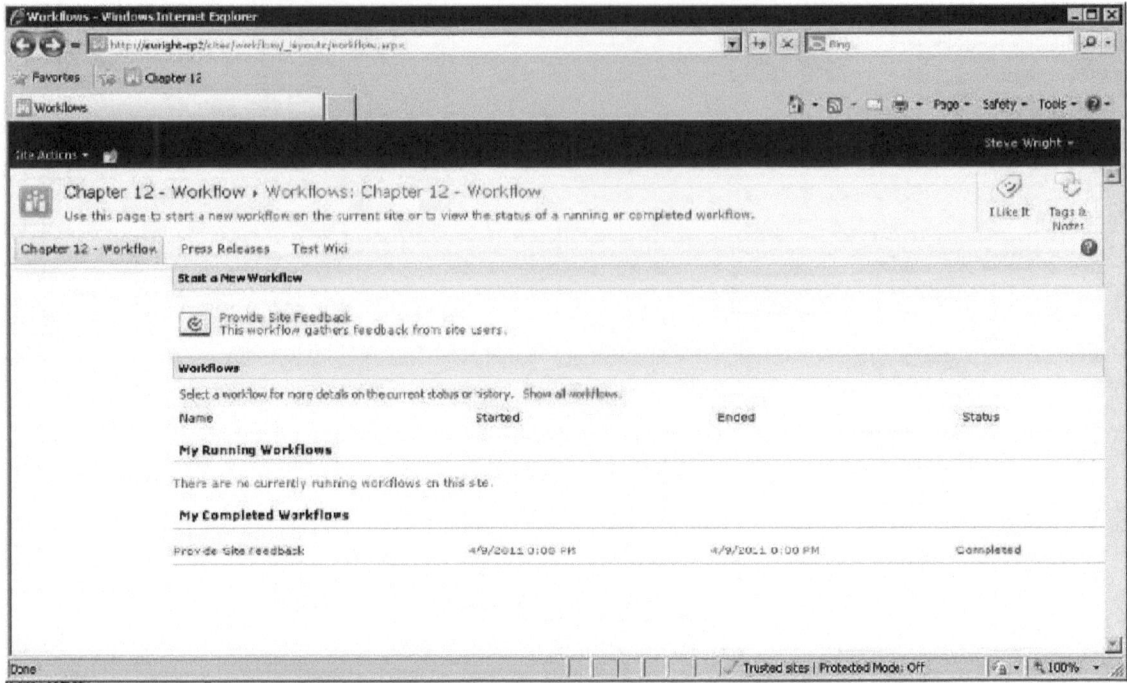

Figure 12-50. Site workflow status page

7. By the time the workflow status page appears again, the workflow has been completed.

8. Go to the Site Feedback list and view the item that was created by the workflow.

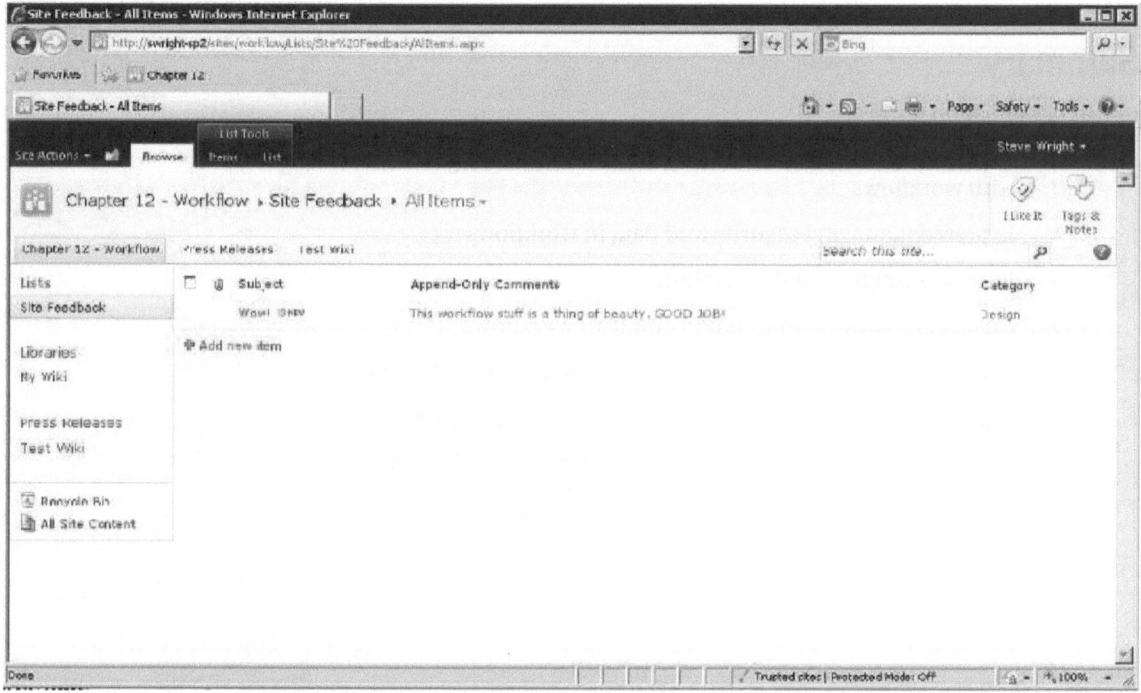

Figure 12-51. *Site Feedback list*

■ **Tip** It is sometimes cumbersome to start a site workflow by opening the View All Site Content page. Many sites do not even surface that page for security reasons. An easy way to let your users start a site workflow is to copy the URL associated with the link for the workflow on the Workflows page. That URL typically looks like this: `<SiteURL>/_layouts/IniWrkflIP.aspx?TemplateID=<FormTemplateGUID>`. Placing a link to this URL somewhere on your site will allow users to start the workflow without having to know how to navigate to it.

Site workflows can be used in any situation where a workflow needs to run outside of the context of a list or a specific list item. They can perform all of the same actions as other workflows except for those that manipulate the current item. This makes them useful in many situations that are not elegantly handled with list or reusable workflows.

Summary

In this chapter, you have:

- Explored the tools available within SharePoint Designer for automating processes with workflows
- Explored managing security and data in workflows
- Built a reusable workflow definition
- Customized one of SharePoint's built-in workflows
- Created a new workflow from scratch in SharePoint Designer
- Customized workflow forms by using InfoPath Designer
- Created a site workflow to run outside of any list or library

Index

■ P, Q

■ R

■ S

■ W

■ X, Y, Z